A SOCIAL HISTORY OF RACIAL VIOLENCE

ALLEN D. GRIMSHAW

EDITOR

AldineTransaction
A Division of Transaction Publishers
New Brunswick (U.S.A.) and London (U.K.)

A SOCIAL HISTORY

E

First paperback printing 2009
Originally published in © 1969 by Transaction Publishers, New Brunswick, New Jersey.

This book is printed on acid-free paper that meets the American National Standard for Permanence of Paper for Printed Library Materials.

Library of Congress Catalog Number: 2009013668
ISBN: 978-0-202-36263-2
Printed in the United States of America

Library of Congress Cataloging-in-Publication Data

Grimshaw, Allen Day.
    [Racial violence in the United States]
    A social history of racial violence / Allen D. Grimshaw.
        p. cm.
    Originally published under title: Racial violence in the United States.
    Includes bibliographical references and index.
    ISBN 978-0-202-36263-2 (alk. paper)
    1. Riots--United States. 2. African Americans--History. 3. United States--Race relations. I. Title.

E185.61.G89 2009
305.800973--dc22

                                                    2009013668

ACKNOWLEDGMENTS

"Lawlessness and Violence in America; An Overview and Some Cases" by Allen D. Grimshaw is reprinted by permission of the publisher from *The Journal of Negro History* 44 (l):52-72, January 1959. Copyright 1959 by The Association for the Study of Negro Life and History, Inc.

Excerpts from *American Negro Slave Revolts* by Herbert Aptheker are reprinted by permission of the author and the publisher, International Publishers Co. Inc. Copyright © 1963.

"New York's Bloodiest Week" by Lawrence Lader is reprinted by permission of the author and the publisher from *American Heritage* 10 (4):48-49, June 1959. Copyright 1959 by the American Heritage Publishing Co., Inc.

"Labor Competition and the New York Draft Riots of 1863" by Albon P. Man, Jr., is reprinted by permission of the author and the publisher from *The Journal of Negro History* 36(4):375, October 1951. Copyright 1951 by The Association for the Study of Negro Life and History, Inc.

"Northern Labor and the Negro During the Civil War" by Williston H. Lofton is reprinted by permission of the author and the publisher from *The Journal of Negro History* 34 (3):265-267, July 1949. Copyright 1949 by The Association for the Study of Negro Life and History, Inc.

"The Atlanta Massacre" is reprinted from *The Independent*, 71:3018:799-800, October 4, 1905.

"The Race War in the North" by William E, Walling is reprinted from *The Independent*, 65:529-534, 1908.

"The So-Called Race Riot at Springfield, Illinois" is reprinted from *Charities and the Commons*, September 19, 1908, pp. 709-711.

"Lynching" is reprinted by permission of the editor, Jessie Parkhurst Guzman, and the publisher, William H. Wise & Co. from the *1952 Negro Yearbook: A Review of Events Affecting Negro Life*, pp. 277-279. Copyright 1952 by the Tuskegee Institute.

"East St. Louis Riots: Report of the Special Committee Authorized by Congress To Investigate the East St. Louis Riots" (65th Congress, 2nd Session, House of Representatives Document No. 1231} is abstracted by permission of the authors, Ben Johnson, John E. Raker, M. D. Foster, and Henry Allen Cooper.

"The Houston Race Riot, 1917" by Edgar A. Schuler is reprinted by permission of the author and the publisher from *The Journal of Negro History* 29:300-338, 1944. Copyright 1944 by The Association for the Study of Negro Life and History, Inc.

"Order in Chicago," Editorial, *The New York Times*, July 31, 1919, is reprinted by permission of the publisher. Copyright 1944 by The New York Times Company.

"Vice and Politics in Chicago Riots" by E. Frank Gardiner is reprinted by permission of the publisher from *The New York Times*, August 3, 1919. Copyright 1919 by The New York Times Company.

"700 Federal Troops Quiet Omaha" is reprinted by permission of the publisher from *The New York Times*, September 30, 1919. Copyright 1919 by The New York Times Company.

Los Angeles: Institute of Government and Public Affairs, University of California, June 1, 1967. Used by permission of the authors.

"Factors Contributing to Color Violence in the United States and Great Britain" by Allen D. Grimshaw is reprinted by permission of the publisher from *Race,* V(l):3-19, 1962. Published by Oxford University Press and copyright © 1962 by the Institute of Race Relations.

"Actions of the Police and the Military in American Race Riots" by Allen D. Grimshaw is reprinted by permission of the publisher from *Phylon,* Fall 1963, pages 271-289. Copyright 1963 by Atlanta University.

"Urban Racial Violence in the United States: Changing Ecological Considerations" by Allen D. Grimshaw is reprinted from the *American Journal of Sociology,* 64 (2):109-119, September 1960, by permission of The University of Chicago Press. Copyright © 1960 by The University of Chicago Press.

"The Detroit Rioters and Looters Committed to Prison" by Elmer R. Akers and Vernon Fox is reprinted by permission of the authors and the publisher from *Journal of Criminal Law and Criminology* 35 (2):105-111, 1944. Copyright 1944 by Northwestern University.

"The Riot Participant" is reprinted from the *Report of the National Advisory Commission on Civil Disorders: Part 111, The Riot Participant* (pages 73-77). United States Government Printing Office, March 1, 1968.

"Who Riots? A Study of Participation in the 1967 Riots" by Robert M. Fogelson and Robert B. Hill is reprinted by permission of the authors from the National Advisory Commission on Civil Disorders, *Supplemental Studies* (pages 221-248). United States Government Printing Office, March 1, 1968.

"Racial Violence and Civil Rights Law Enforcement" by Bernard Weisberg is reprinted by permission of the author and the publisher from *The University of Chicago Law Review* 18 (4):769-783, Summer 1951. Copyright 1951 by *The University of Chicago Law Review.*

"Patterns of Disorder" is reprinted from the *Report of the National Advisory Commission on Civil Disorders: Patterns of Disorder* (pages 64-65). U.S. Government Printing Office, March 1, 1968.

"Hostility, Aggression, and Violence" is used by permission of the author, John Spiegel.

"Minor Studies of Aggression: Correlations of Economic Indices with Lynchings" by Carl Iver Hovland and Robert R. Sears is reprinted by permission of Robert R. Sears and the publisher from *Journal of Psychology* 9:301-310, 1940. Copyright 1940 by The Journal Press.

"A Re-Examination of Correlations between Lynchings and Economic Indices" by Alexander Mintz is reprinted by permission of the author and the publisher from *Journal of Abnormal and Social Psychology* 41:154-160, 1946. Copyright 1946 by the *Journal of Abnormal and Social Psychology.*

"The Precipitants and Underlying Conditions of Race Riots" by Stanley Lieberson and Arnold J. Silverman is reprinted by permission of the authors and the publisher from *American Sociological Review* 30(6):887-898, December 1965. Copyright 1965 by the *American Sociological Review.*

"Urban Disorder: Perspectives from the Comparative Study of Civil Strife" by Ted Gurr is reprinted from *Riots and Rebellion: Civil Violence in the Urban Community* (1968), edited by Louis Masotti and Don R. Bowen, by permission of the author and the publisher, Sage Publications, Inc.

"Civil Disturbance, Racial Revolt, Class Assault: Three Views of Urban Violence" by Allen D. Grimshaw is reprinted by permission of the publisher from *American Behavioral Scientist* 2 (4):2-7, March-April 1968.

PREFACE

One of the contributors to this volume commented, when I asked permission to reprint his article, that I was adding to the "spate" of books
on racial violence. This is true,[1] and I suppose that like all anthologists
I also feel a need to justify time spent in collecting the reports and
thoughts of others rather than in original research and writing. There
are several answers to the question of self-justification which I have
posed for myself. I should like to remark briefly on each of them before
I go on to say something about the organization of this volume and the
criteria for selection.

Kenneth B. Clark, the distinguished (and, incidentally, black) social
psychologist, is another of the authors whose work is included in this
book. Dr. Clark long ago established his *bona fides* as an expert on
race relations (and racial violence); it was natural that when the Report
of the (President's) National Advisory Commission on Civil Disorders
was released in the spring of 1968 his opinion of the document would
be solicited. He has been quoted as remarking that it was generally an
excellent document, but that he had a sense of great familiarity in going
through it, a familiarity based on the fact that he had read several earlier
reports which were equally perceptive, equally rigorous and, he implied,
probably equally effective in precipitating social change. Clark, and some
few other students of relations between blacks and whites in American
society, have seen events of the last several years as following naturally
from a long history, a history which includes a variety of expressions of
social violence in intergroup relations in the United States. Most Americans, however, for a variety of reasons, have chosen to view the violence
of the Sixties as an unexpected and, in some ways, unexplainable phenomenon which somehow has suddenly appeared in a full-blown and

---

1. Recently, while waiting in the office of a sociologist who has been working on
racial violence, I counted more than forty titles on the subject on his library shelves,
all published within the last five years. I am sure that his collection is not inclusive.

extremely threatening form. Among the more obvious reasons has been a preoccupation with other revolutionary changes in American life in the last twenty years. This preoccupation seems to have been accompanied by a pattern of wishful thinking that has somehow assumed that while there have been people in American society who are underprivileged, perhaps even systematically exploited and discriminated against, they have experienced a steadily improving situation both through their own hard work and through legal action by the government. An important stimulus for working on this book has been my concern that current events be put into a proper historical perspective.

Some historians, at least, have long acted on sociological assumptions —that is, they have hypothesized (and demonstrated) that where patterns of social relationships, most particularly of relations of power, are similar, the course of events is likely also to be similar. Sociologists operate on the fundamental axiom that social behavior is not random but ordered, that given similar structural situations history will indeed repeat itself. In spite of this, there has not emerged from all the literature on social violence a systematic theory on this ultimate and most destructive form of social conflict. The literature on racial conflict or on social violence is not atheoretical—it is, rather, eclectic.

Social scientists of every persuasion have attempted to isolate the causes of prejudice and discrimination, social phenomena intimately related to expressions of conflict and violence. Simpson and Yinger (1953), in one of the more sophisticated texts on race relations in the United States, present a classification of types of explanations of prejudice which exemplifies the variety of explanatory theories. They speak of the personality functions of prejudice, prejudice as a weapon in group conflict, and the cultural factor in prejudice. Each of the many causal explanations of prejudice purports to isolate the major etiological factor in prejudice, therefore in discrimination and, presumably, in racial tension and conflict. In any given instance of racial conflict or of prejudice, however, more than one of these causal clusters has served equally well in explanation. In practice, those elements of the varying theories that best fit immediate problems have been selected eclectically. There is an evident need for a presentation of explanations of social violence representing several of the many perspectives now current, so that readers can make their own synthesis, or, even better, see cogent reasons for assigning priority to explanations based on the explication of social structure. (I will return to this topic in the Introduction when I talk about my own bias). This need was a second stimulus for this volume.

I had two additional, personal, reasons for agreeing to do this book. The first is professional-personal. I was no more prescient than any other social scientist in anticipating the new forms that the struggle for full equality would assume in the decade of the Sixties. I did, however, begin studying racial violence in the United States some ten years ago— doing my doctoral dissertation on urban racial violence in the United

States. That dissertation constituted an attempt to learn whether or not patterns in such violence, which had been isolated by Richard D. Lambert in his study of Hindu-Muslim violence in the Indian subcontinent (Lambert, 1952), could also be discerned in Negro-white violence in the United States. Many of the patterns were repeated, and in the years since I have continued to follow up interests in conflict and violence as social processes. Given the relative paucity of research interest in social violence, it was not surprising then, that when the "new" violence began in 1964 people asked me for opinions. It seemed to me that there had had been shifts in the meaning of the violence. I found that some of my observations were questioned by others, and in response I found myself wanting to review again both past history and the various interpretations of contemporary events. Hence, again, a reason for this book.

The second personal reason is non-professional, and related to my concerns as a citizen of this troubled country. On Wednesday night, September 1, 1965, sociologists attending their annual professional meetings at a Chicago hotel encountered the then "Negro" revolution, many of them for the first time. Undoubtedly some had never before personally witnessed a demonstration, though probably all had seen on television the events of Selma and Montgomery, of the March on Washington and, only days before, of the Watts disturbances. As sociologists poured out of the hotel after a day of listening to papers, of talking in the hotel's bars, of committee meetings, job negotiations and just plain socializing— they found several dozen blacks and whites marching in a picket line in front of the main door of the hotel. The pickets were protesting the continuation in office of Chicago Superintendent of Schools Benjamin Willis and the alleged inactivities of Mayor Richard J. Daley in correcting problems related to *de facto* school segregation. While it was true that Willis himself lived only a block away and that the demonstrators visited both Willis and Daley, it was no accident that they also picketed in front of the hotel. Of the approximately 260 papers listed in the program for the meetings, about ten per cent dealt directly with problems of group relations, largely in the United States, and many others had implications for understanding of problems related to racial and ethnic relations. The fact that the pickets came to the hotel was an indication of the growing sophistication of cadres of the civil rights movement. The response of many of the sociologists was an indication of their need to segregate their scholarly activity from the "action" of the real world.

I believe that sociologists and other students of society have an obligation, as citizens, to present scholarly findings in a format which will help the decision-makers of our society to make wise decisions. In this I admit to an unscientific ameliorative bias. This book has been prepared for policy-makers as well as for scholars and interested citizens. My second personal reason for editing this volume is my hope that by underlining the historical continuities in patterns of racial violence and has been a good editor and a good friend. In working at Indiana University I profited immensely from the encouragement and suggestions of John T. Liell, Austin T. Turk and James Watson. Professor Owen Thomas of the Department of English at Indiana University has been a good friend and a friendly editor. Much of what clarity there is in my own writing is his; the shortcomings in sociological interpretation are, of course, my own.

Thanks are due to anonymous black interviewees and to obscure librarians—as well as to numerous professional associates who have encouraged me to think and to rethink about the problem about which this book is organized. Miss Katherine Haack helped on the manuscript; Mrs. Kay Radecki worked long hours in obtaining permissions, in organizing the manuscript, in preparing the master bibliography, in catching at least some of my many editorial blunders. She also protected me from routine problems during the long period in which most of the work was done. Miss Kathleen George picked up, when I moved from Indiana University to Berkeley for a year's visit, the onerous task of completing a number of unfinished and important chores. My wife Polly provided continuing encouragement in a task that seemed to grow more difficult as time passed.

Authors sometimes have tense and conflictful relationships with editors and publishers. I count myself fortunate indeed to have worked with a publisher, Alexander J. Morin, who knew what I was doing and offered both useful criticism and continuing support. Sheila Welch, "my" Aldine editor, showed both critical acumen and a supportive enthusiasm that helped make a difficult task easier and occasionally even enjoyable.

I never agreed with all of the tactics of Malcolm X or of Dr. Martin Luther King, nor did I share their very different ideological perspectives in all details. The full magnitude of their selfless contributions to the solution of the problem of the removal of causes of social violence in America cannot yet, and probably will not ever, be measured. Their contributions were great. This book is dedicated to the memory and to the hopes for freedom of these two men and to other, more anonymous martyrs.

CONTENTS

Racial Violence in the United States

INTRODUCTION

Violence: A Sociological Perspective [1]

My purpose in this introduction, which is not directed to an audience of professional sociologists, is to try to indicate some of the questions about social violence which have seemed important to sociologists and some of the ways in which sociological answers to these questions differ from those of other interested students. The sociologist is interested both in an understanding of the phenomena of violence themselves and, as an exercise in the sociology of knowledge, in the ways in which different varieties of explanations for these phenomena have emerged from the perspectives of the several disciplines which have studied them. Principally, I wish to distinguish social violence as a social process which occurs predictably and understandably from the social structural arrangements of the societies in which it appears; contrasting this view to one that sees it as the sum of a collection of instances of individual behavior. In doing this I am showing my sociological bias and training—just as psychologists reveal their professional predispositions by their emphasis on the importance of the individual and of individual characteristics in the generation of collective violent disturbances.

After defining social violence I turn to a classification of principal theoretical perspectives (commenting in passing on some of the theoretical and practical defects of the National Advisory Commission on Civil Disorders' [Kerner, 1968] criticizing "white racism" as the "root source" of violence involving black citizens). In the second section of the Introduction is a brief sketch of the organization of this book.

---

1. The first section of this Introduction draws heavily on Grimshaw, 1969.

SOCIAL VIOLENCE DEFINED

Social violence is assault upon an individual or his property solely or primarily because of his membership in a social category. Some students would include racial slurs and discrimination in such a definition, but for purposes of this Introduction I mean physical assault resulting in personal injury or in damage to property. Thus, a fight between a Protestant and a Catholic schoolboy would not ordinarily be an instance of social violence in this country. If, however, the fight started because of religious insults it would be, as it would become if other boys joined in on the basis of religious affiliation. Similarly if a black robber always chose white victims (and because of their color rather than their greater likelihood to be good victims [two not unrelated characteristics]), then he would be committing social violence. Violent events which begin as non-social violence not infrequently change during their course into social violence, as in instances where servicemen's brawls become battles between the services or where post-football-game battles become race riots.

SOME THEORIES OF SOCIAL VIOLENCE

There seem to be as many explanations and interpretations of social violence as there are scholarly and applied professions with interest in this variety of behavior. (An excellent and more detailed account of some sociological perspectives can be found in Paige, 1968.) Historians speak of a tradition of lawlessness and violence; anthropologists (and some sociologists) speak of cultures or sub-cultures of violence; social reformers and revolutionaries speak of unjust laws; and pacifists look with horror on violence in any form and see its source in man's unfortunate but perhaps perfectible "nature." This book, however, is limited primarily to inclusion of two sets of theoretical perspectives, the first of which includes the interpretations of violence made by psychoanalysts (and psychiatrists), by psychologists and by social psychologists—the second of which is dominated by sociological interpretations.

The three varieties of interpretation which characterize the first perspective generally look for explanations of social violence by focusing attention on the individual. The psychoanalyst looks for violence proneness as a characteristic of the individual personality, rooted perhaps in traumatic experiences of very early life, but clearly the consequence of the interaction of uniquely personal experiences in molding an individual psyche. To the psychoanalyst, the most important traumas are usually sexual. Sexual fears and sexual competition have characterized relations between black and white people in this country since contact first occurred; it is not surprising then that psychoanalysts have seen sex as crucial in determining the patterns of intergroup relations—including those of violence.[2] Hersey (1968), in his book on the Algiers Motel incident which took place during the course of the 1967 riots in Detroit, criticizes the National Advisory Commission for failing to acknowledge the sexual aspects of race-linked social violence in that incident. The Freudian analyst, however, is likely to see social violence more generally as the acting out of sexual traumas suffered in infancy, or as the sublimation of sexual impulses of adults rather than as direct competition over sex as a commodity. Thus, Sterba (1947), in his commentary on the Detroit race riot of 1943, interprets assaults by whites on black owned automobiles and their occupants as being the acting out of white penis envy. Such an interpretation lies at the fairly extreme end of the individual versus social explanations continuum but continues to be subscribed to by a small but extremely hardy group of professional psychiatric and, particularly, psychoanalytic interpreters.

The psychologist, in contrast, focuses less on the characteristics of the individual personality (either as molded by experiences of infancy and childhood or as givens in the adult personality) than on the dynamics of an individual's interaction with his environment. The frustration-aggression hypothesis has informed much of the theorizing on violence by psychologists; in one pioneering study Hovland and Sears attempted to demonstrate that the number of lynchings was directly related to economic activity, with lynchings increasing in periods of economic depression and declining in periods of prosperity.[3] Some psychologists, of course, have directed themselves to the examination of personality development and particular personality syndromes, e.g., the "authoritarian personality," but have extended the formative period beyond that usually emphasized by psychoanalysts and psychiatrists into the adult years. Their position would seem to be intermediate between that of the more analytically oriented student with his view of the essential rigidity of personality and that of the social psychologist who has a substantially more situational interpretation of individual behavior.

Social psychologists have looked for an explanation of social violence

2. It is true, of course, that sexual fears and sexual competition have characterized relationships between imperial groups and subordinated native groups in a variety of colonial settings. It is also true that in cases where the sexual values of the more powerful groups have been more relaxed (e.g., in Portuguese-controlled as contrasted to British-controlled areas) this area of behavior has been less important in defining intergroup relationships.

3. Carl I. Hovland and R. R. Sears (1940). In a restudy of the Hovland-Sears data, Alexander Mintz concluded that while increases in crimes against the person may have been associated with frustration-linked aggressiveness, property crimes with violence "during depression may be due to inexperience of people driven into property crimes by bad economic conditions rather than to an increase of aggressive tendencies due to frustration." He concluded, moreover, that the high correlations reported by Hovland and Sears were essentially statistical artifacts (Mintz, 1946).

in the acting out of prejudice (as an attitude located in the individual); they have differed from psychoanalysts and from many psychologists in their emphasis on the structural features of society that support socialization into prejudice. In the case of black rioters, they have looked for such socially generated experiences as "relative deprivation" or "a search for identity" as they may relate to individual attempts to find more congenial modes of organization of the personal field. Thus, Clark (1944) and Clark and Barker (1945) have attempted to describe the attitudinal structure of individuals who participate in social violence or who reject it, linking this attitudinal structure to the interaction of a variety of personal experiences, an interaction that is unique in the case of each individual person.[4] Ransford, a sociological social psychologist, has attempted to isolate a number of specific attitudes, and to link the specific attitudes (e.g., isolation and powerlessness) to participation in group violence (1968). In this case, the sets of attitudes are seen as being characteristics of members of categories rather than as individual attributes. In so doing a bridge is suggested between the social psychological position, which emphasizes the importance of individual psychological attributes and attitudes in generating social tensions and violence, and the sociological perspective, which attempts to de-individualize violence phenomena by attending to features of social structure and of the location of power in the larger society. While the need for some kind of bridge is obvious, it should be noted that few contemporary scholars of any of the three individual-oriented disciplines would argue that personality or attitudes alone can serve as an explanation for violence and that few sociologists would argue that personality factors and attitudes are irrelevant.

THE POSITION OF THE NATIONAL ADVISORY COMMISSION ON CIVIL DISORDERS

The Report of the Advisory Commission on Civil Disorders has erred, it seems to me, in attempting (perhaps for programmatic, perhaps for tactical or strategic, purposes) to isolate *a* single most important cause of the events of the Sixties. The Report, in a section "Causes of Disorders," concludes that *the* most fundamental factor in causation is "the racial attitude of white Americans, and the impact of that attitude on their behavior toward black Americans." They have not confronted the

---

4. Jeffrey Paige (in a personal communication) asks, "Why the emphasis on the uniqueness of the individual? Can't psychological mechanisms function in the same manner in large groups of individuals?" It seems to me that psychologists see collective behavior as the outcome of the summing of and interaction of characteristics of individuals—with the social roots of those characteristics being quite remote. Sociologists are interested much more directly in the ways in which social structural arrangements contribute to social conflict and violence.

meaning of structural sources of violence, although they have identified them—they have not attempted to cross the bridge linking psychological and sociological perspectives.

White racism is a salient feature of American society. It is, however, I suspect, as much an effect as it is a cause, and to identify it as the principal cause of the disturbances of recent years (or for that matter of earlier years) is to single out as the single most important factor one that is least immediately amenable to planned social change. A sociological bias is clear in this observation, namely, sociologists see structural features of societies themselves as determining both the attitudes and values of individuals *and* the collective behavior that is sometimes engendered by these values and attitudes. Numerous studies have shown that neither exhortation nor reasoned attempts at persuasion are particularly effective in changing people's attitudes; this seems to have been especially true in the case of prejudiced attitudes about categories of people (see, *inter alia*, Williams, 1947). To suggest that racism is the primary cause of the violence we have witnessed in the United States may be to suggest that the problem is essentially insoluble. This leads me to conclude that the Commission, in emphasizing racism, has made a tactical error.

I believe that emphasis should be placed on the structural characteristics of our society which initiated and now support the continuing subordination of certain groups. Such subordination requires the development or maintenance of "racist" attitudes so that more privileged people can legitimate what is clearly an inequitable situation. It is in this sense that William Graham Sumner was wrong when he stated that "stateways don't make folkways." Quite the contrary. We have learned that if people are required to behave in certain ways, ultimately their attitudes will become consistent with their behavior. It is much easier to attack problems of police behavior by making it clear to officers that if they are guilty of violations of civil rights or civil liberties, sanctions will be applied, than it is to convince them that there is something wrong with their attitudes about members of minority groups (whether these groups are black people, the urban poor, or homosexuals).[5] I am suggesting, here, that the Commission, in emphasizing racism and failing to note the explanatory priority of structural variables as contrasted to attitudes, has made a logical error.

It is my conclusion, based on the discussion immediately above, that the three characteristics of society, which are labelled in the Report as "racism's most bitter fruits," are not fruits of racism but sources of racism. Discrimination and segregation, black migration and the white exodus, and the black ghetto are clearly important in the generation of situations productive of social violence (Hersey, *op. cit.*, starting from a slightly different perspective, lists unequal justice, unequal housing, unequal education, and unequal employment). They are less a conse-

5. See, e.g., Lohman (1947) and Weisberg (1951).

quence of white racism, however, than of the very organization of society itself. Fortunately, racist attitudes are not inherited but are a consequence of social learning within a context of social structural supports. Genetic programming of inherited attributes cannot be changed; social contexts which encourage one or another pattern of learning can be.

A SOCIOLOGICAL PERSPECTIVE ON GROUP VIOLENCE

There is no place in this brief introduction for a systematic review of the major sociological writings on social violence. The principal sociologists who have informed my own thinking about social conflict as a process, and social violence as the extreme mode of conflict resolution, have been Marx, Weber, Simmel (and his contemporary follower and interpreter, Coser) and Dahrendorf. None of these men have ignored the individual and his personality in their writing. Indeed, Marx coined the now multi-faceted term "alienation" that appears so frequently in psychological and social psychological interpretations of black ghetto violence. Yet each of them in their discussions of social conflict emphasized the structural features of society, particularly insofar as that structure is related to the distribution of power and its exercise.

Without going into detail let me suggest the perspective from which Simmel viewed social conflict. Simmel asserted that it is possible to make an analytical distinction between the forms which interaction takes and the actual content of any given interaction. The forms can be discussed and understood in the abstract, without regard to the personalities or other characteristics of the particular incumbents in the particular roles involved. He identified four such "forms," all of which ultimately refer back to the inevitability (about which more later) of conflict. People are continuously attempting to maximize their share of scarce resources; when they do not know one another (e.g., a national scholarship competition) the "form" (or process) is labelled by Simmel as competition. When the person or group with whom one is competing is identified (as in an instance when only one of several "star" law students can become editor of a law journal, or when only one man can be elected president, or when there is only enough water in the boat for one person to survive), the competition becomes personalized and the "form" becomes conflict (this does not, of course, exclude the possibilities of sacrifice, abnegation, cooperation or collusion). When conflict is resolved, either by the defeat of one party or through stalemate, the form which results is accommodation. Accommodation is always unstable, since one party (or in the case of truce or stalemate, both) is forced to settle for less than he (they) wants. Only when assimilation occurs, a form of interaction in which the differences between those interacting have disappeared (a goal variously of Americanization programs for immigrants and of "integrationist" policies in race relations), is an ultimate resolution of conflict possible. Even here, of course, differences are likely to emerge as different persons or groups begin to accumulate power and to invest that power in attempts to maximize their share of scarce commodities.[6]

Accommodation, which is the characteristic form of interaction between dominant and dominated groups in all societies in periods when there is no open conflict, can be discussed and analyzed without reference to the characteristics of the parties involved. Thus, in the accommodative relationship of superordination-subordination, which can be exemplified by the relationships of master-slave, employer-employee, officer-enlisted man, doctor-patient, priest-parishioner, in earlier days in this country that of parent-child, and so on, it is expected that demands and directives flow in one direction and deference and compliance flow in the other.[7] In instances of personal interaction there are, of course, individual cases in which incumbents of institutionally subordinated roles may, because of dominant personalities or resources external to the particular role relationship, exercise particularistic power. The American military folk literature is filled with variations of the story of the millionaire private who expects to hire his commanding officer after the war is over; secretaries have been known to dominate over their employers because of non-office skills. In the case of group relationships, however, sharp disparities in power are likely to be translated into attempts to reverse the relationship or, at the very least, to establish parity.

Seen from this perspective a number of apparently quite different cases of large-scale conflict and social violence turn out to be, analytically, quite similar. Historically, relations between blacks and whites in American society have represented almost a type case of the superordinate-subordinate variety of accommodative relationship.[8] This book is about black and white violence in American society, but it should be emphasized that there are other cases which exemplify the pattern. There have been, in American society, other groups than blacks which have been subordinated to the majority community and to the holders of power in the establishment. Among them have been a variety of ethnic groups, including, at various times, religious minorities (Catholics and Mormons) and racially or culturally distinguishable groups (Southeastern European immigrants, Orientals, American Indians and Spanish Americans). At one time or another each of these categories of Americans has been subjected to attack ranging from economic and legal

6. Commodities as used here include prestige and status as well as Cadillacs and caviar.
7. This may possibly be a cross-cultural universal, although the anthropological literature provides us with some questionable cases (e.g., the Zuni). There are substantial definitional difficulties in attempting to determine exactly how superordination and subordination can be measured in different societies.
8. Paige (personal communication) has suggested that a more precise description of these relations would be that of "unstable accommodation alternating with periods of open conflict (1917–1919; 1943)."

discrimination to occasional violence to full-scale mob violence and even military activity.[9]

Readers from the several scholarly disciplines represented in this book will doubtless bring to their own reading predispositions to favor one or another theoretical perspective. I, personally, have found the social structural perspective of sociology most useful. Unbiased readers, particularly beginning students and practicing decision-makers, should realize that the fact that so many of the views presented will seem cogent underlines the danger of unicausal interpretations of social phenomena and the necessity of synthesizing the best of a number of perspectives into some larger theory. This book will not provide such a synthesis. It does provide evidence that there are, in addition to polemic positions, scientific attempts to isolate regularities in racial violence and to identify patterns that are found. It does juxtapose previous scattered positions in a way that may suggest to some reader new ways of thinking about violence. Readers should keep in mind that it is in the search for patterns and their causes that solutions will ultimately be found, and I hope that in reading the historically descriptive materials which appear early in the book they will themselves discern such patterns which they can then use to test the validity and usefulness of the theoretical interpretations presented in later parts of the book.

The organization of the book is, it seems to me, fairly straightforward, and it should be possible for readers who have special interests to read only those sections which are most immediately relevant to those interests without a sense of incompleteness. Following this brief introductory statement there is a long section devoted to description of actual cases of violence, ranging from brief selections on slave insurrections and the violence of the Civil War and Reconstruction periods to more extensive materials from the First and Second World Wars and the contemporary disorders of the Sixties. Included in this nonanalytic section are materials on the Detroit riot of 1943 intended as "a short lesson in historiography," one of many possible ways of indicating that the same set of events can be seen very differently by observers with different initial attitudes and with motivations which permit sharply different interpretations—a lesson which is subsequently formally stated in an article on different perspectives on the current disorders. At the end of this historical and descriptive section there are papers by Tomlinson and by Murphy and Watson that begin a transition to a set of explicitly analytic and theoretical papers. Earlier selections, for example those

9. See Allen D. Grimshaw, Chapter 1 in this volume. Some observers have suggested that students are coming to be defined as such a group in our society. See, *inter alia*, Walker, 1968, and the several reports of the Task Force on Violent Aspects of Protest and Confrontation (headed by Jerome H. Skolnick) of that Commission. See especially Skolnick, 1969.

from the Chicago Commission on Race Relations report, *The Negro in Chicago,* attempt to isolate causal patterns. Only in the more contemporary studies, however, such as those at the end of the section, are there attempts to marshal evidence to explicitly test for repeated patterns.

Section III is devoted to papers which seek the delineation of patterns in racial violence in the United States which have been trans-temporal and trans-urban (and in my paper on the United States and Great Britain, trans-societal). Other papers in this section are on the actions of agencies of formal control, on the ecology of urban racial violence, on the characteristics of offenders, on the interpretation of attitudinal material, on the consequences of different patterns of law enforcement in the civil rights area, and on the patterns in the disorders of the Sixties.

There are two chapters in Section IV. While they are labeled as empirical generalizations and theory, respectively, the overlap between the treatments in the two chapters is considerable. The selections in Chapter 11 on empirical generalizations are, in each instance, informed by some general theoretical notion (for example the frustration-aggression hypothesis in the papers on correlations of economic indices with lynching) but direct their attention primarily to co-occurrence and co-variation of different varieties of social behavior and less to the inter-implications of these behaviors. The other two papers, by Lieberson and Silverman and by Gurr, represent attempts to bring increasingly sophisticated data handling technologies to the effort of sorting out the complexities of causation in what President Johnson, in his charge to the Advisory Commission, labelled as the "thicket of tension, conflicting evidence, and extreme opinions."

Chapter 12 includes selections representing most of the spectrum of theoretical interpretation. In the initial paper I have attempted to suggest some of the structural sources for varying interpretations of urban violence. The paper by Dahlke represents an early taxonomic attempt to find cross-culturally consistent patterns in causes of and actual events of ethnic violence. That by Sterba represents a position at the fairly extreme end of the individual versus social explanations continuum which will seem exotic to many readers but is included because the position outlined is, as was suggested above, subscribed to by a small but extremely hardy group of professional psychoanalytic and psychiatric interpreters. The two papers by Clark (in one instance with Barker) and by Ransford serve as a social psychological bridge to several more sociological interpretations that follow in the papers by Waskow and by Williams as well as in one of my own. The social phychologists, as noted above, present an interpretation that emphasizes the importance of individual psychological attributes and attitudes in generating social tensions and violence. The sociological perspectives represent an attempt to de-individualize violence phenomena by attending to features of social structure and of the location of power in the larger society.

Finally, in a short concluding section, there are three papers on possible shifts in the meaning of urban violence in this country. My first paper, which was partially obsolete even before it was published, suggested that massive shifts in the location of power in American society could be expected to bring shifting alliances among underprivileged groups and possibilities for new modes of attack upon the accommodative structure. Janowitz, in a paper with strong programmatic overtones, emphasizes the need for innovation in practices by formal control agencies and for changes in the practices of major socializing agencies in American society. Finally, in a very nonprofessional paper (from the austere sociologist's point of view), I attempt to raise some questions about moral responsibility and the complexities involved in the assignment of guilt to governments and to citizens. I am not sure that the questions are resolved, but I think that it is as important that they be raised as it is to attempt to produce reliable statements on patterns of violence and "valid" assessments of cause.

PART I

The History of Negro-White Violence in America

1

LAWLESSNESS AND VIOLENCE

Popular fears of the "black rebellion" and a sometimes politically nourished public concern with "crime in the streets" were important motives for President Johnson's establishment of National Advisory Commissions on Civil Disorders (1967) and on Violence (1968). Exploitation of these same concerns made them a major issue of the 1968 presidential campaign. Much of this concern and fear reflects the lack of historical perspective of American citizens.

Neither individual crime nor collective violence are new phenomena in our society. In this chapter I have attempted to bring some historical perspective to the discussion of violence by briefly reviewing instances of collective violence in the United States. While the emphasis is on the continuing struggle between whites and blacks, historical evidence is given to demonstrate that violence and lawlessness have always been a part of American life and have involved many of the groups that constitute American society.

Allen D. Grimshaw

Lawlessness and Violence in America and Their Special Manifestations in Changing Negro-White Relationships

Ours has been a lawless and violent nation. Indeed, race riots and bombings, although they are particularly dramatic manifestations of conflict, have claimed fewer lives than many other varieties of violence, individual or social. There are more criminal homicides in some American metropolises every year than there have been deaths from all the urban race riots of the twentieth century combined. A few famous feuds and some important labor disputes have rolled up casualty lists which compare in length with the most spectacular interracial disorders. Social violence (assault upon individuals or their property solely or primarily because of their group [ethnic, religious, or racial] affiliations), and lawlessness generally, have not been phenomena expressed only in interracial relations in this country. This article reviews briefly two sets of historical data relevant to an understanding of those patterns of race relations in urban areas which have culminated in violence. An introductory section consists of a simple listing of some other varieties of social violence which have characterized intergroup relations in the United States and notes a widespread tradition of lawlessness, a tradition which has been manifested in every area of civic life. The remainder of the article reviews the changing character of interracial relations and their more specific manifestations in social, interracial violence.

OUR LAWLESS HERITAGE [1]

It is possible to make a rough classification of types of lawlessness and violence by reference to the areas of social interaction in which such lawlessness and violence occur. The two categories which emerge from such simple classification overlap, but are nonetheless distinguishable. The first category, that of ethnic violence includes, in addition to Negro-white social violence, conflict and violence focussed on religion and nativity. While the motivation behind much of this violence falls more accurately into the secular area of economic and political violence, the manifest reasons for "punishing" religious and nationality and racial groups have usually referred to religious, cultural and "racial" differences distinguishing these groups from "real Americans."

1. The title of this section is taken from Adams, 1928.

14

An anti-Catholic tradition, which has been expressed even in the twentieth century, was responsible for frequent eruptions in the last century, particularly in the period before the Civil War. In the three decades immediately preceding that war, street fights were frequent; sometimes taking on the proportions of major riots, convents and other religious edifices were attacked and sometimes destroyed, and Catholics both within and without the Church hierarchy were subject to constant vilification and occasional physical assault. This anti-Catholicism, particularly as related to an expression of Native-Americanism and the "Know-Nothing" movement, was most frequently directed against Irish Catholics, perhaps because they were resistant to accepting a subservient accommodative status, and had significant economic and political overtones. Jews and Mormons, to mention only two other religious communities, have also been the focus of hostility and violence.

While the Irish Catholics may have received the brunt of the animus and overt violence in native American riots, they were by no means the only ethnic group attacked. Almost all immigrant groups went through a period of unpopularity, an unpopularity inextricably tied up with their status as perceived economic and political threats to the "older" immigrant groups. Groups distinguishable from the larger population by virtue of physical characteristics were a particular focus of hostility. Assaults upon the indigenous Indian population, commonplace throughout the historical period, were certainly not always necessary for the protection of the white population. A growing resentment toward the Chinese, originally imported as laborers on the transcontinental railroads, culminated in anti-Chinese riots in the closing decades of the nineteenth century. Treatment of Mexican-Americans in the American Southwest has been similar to treatment of Negro-Americans in the American South. And the 1940's saw attacks not only on the civil rights of, but also against the persons and property of Japanese-Americans and Mexican-Americans as well as against Negroes.

The second general category includes a variety of secular types of violence. Most important here are lawlessness and violence growing out of politics and the relations of the populace to the government and out of economic competition. The Republic itself originated in an armed rebellion against the then established government. Like all civil wars and internecine strife, the Revolutionary War was a particularly vicious one, and the treatment accorded Loyalists by "Patriots" was no more gentle than that accorded the central figure in any lynching. The new government hardly found its constituents more tractable. Revolt against the new Republic was manifested in Shays' Rebellion in Massachusetts in 1787, in Pennsylvania's Whiskey Rebellion in 1794, in smuggling and trading with the enemy in the War of 1812 and in the Draft Riots of the Civil War. In the Depression of the 1930's the agrarian population manifested its hostility to the government in the "Penny Bankrupt Sales" and in other rural disturbances. Political hostility has not been limited to direct action against the government. The last century saw spectacular election riots, and even today elections are often characterized by sharp violations of the law.[2]

Economic strife has erupted into violence countless times in the last one hundred years. No major industry accepted unionization without a struggle, but in some, such as the railroads and the mines, the struggle assumed the character of wars. "Bloody Harlan" and the "Herrin Massacre," the Haymarket riot and the Homestead strike, these names conjure up a pageant of lawlessness and violence continuing well into the present century. Assassination and terrorism have been used by both labor and management, and in the "Big Steel" strikes of the 1930's the steel companies spent thousands upon thousands of dollars on machine guns and tear gas. Indeed, organizing strikes of today, such as that at Koehler, and similar protracted work stoppages, are still occasionally productive of violence.

America has been, then, a land of lawlessness and violence, ranging from spontaneous brawls between servicemen of different branches and schoolboys from different schools, through the "blood feud" and gangster warfare, to the full-fledged military campaigns which have occurred in struggles between class and class and between adherents of different religious faiths. The tradition of lawlessness includes both a contempt of parking regulations and an admiration of gangster heroes and, on the other hand, an excess zeal in the administration of "vigilante justice," "lynch law," and "six-shooter law" on the frontier. Some areas, such as Harlan County in Kentucky and "Bloody Williamson" in Illinois, have run practically the full gamut of types of social violence suggested above. (For a journalistic but suggestive account of violence in one such area, see Angle, 1952.) But there is practically no section of the United States which has not, at one time or another, been a center of lawlessness and violence. If there is less actual participation in violence today, and if Americans must sublimate their propensities to violence by watching television, the potentiality still remains.

The violence and bloodshed which have accompanied adjustments in the accommodative pattern between whites and Negroes in the United States are not unique to interracial relations. It is a thesis of the research on which this article is based that the violence which occurs in interracial relations is an inevitable product of assaults upon the accommodative pattern. Further research on the forms of violence which have been listed in this brief outline will, the writer believes, demonstrate that all social violence results from the interaction of conceptually similar forces in defining patterns of accommodation.

2. E.g., illegal disfranchisement of the Negro electorate in some Southern States.

THE CHANGING CHARACTER
OF NEGRO-WHITE RELATIONS AND NEGRO-WHITE
VIOLENCE IN THE UNITED STATES

In this section a rough classification has been made of periods in race relations in this country, the social forces which defined them, and the types of social violence which characterized them. The periods covered are roughly as follows: the period of slave insurrections and resistance (1640–1861); Civil War and Reconstruction (1861–1877); the Second Reconstruction and the beginnings of the Great Migration (1878–1914); World War I and postwar boom and racial readjustment (1915–1929); interwar and Depression (1930–1941); World War II (1942–1945); and the period from World War II to 1963. The suggestion is made that in each of these periods the patterns of race relations and social racial violence were determined more by reaction of the dominant white community to attacks on the accommodative patterns by Negroes than by any conscious determination of policy by the white group. Some major areas in which conflict develops are noted and parallels to other group conflicts pointed out. Thus, it is shown that the Draft Riots of the Civil War were, at least in part, an expression of the hostility of laboring groups to "cheap labor," as had been the case with other immigrant groups, rather than an expression of specifically anti-Negro animus.

THE PERIOD OF SLAVE INSURRECTIONS AND RESISTANCE (1640–1861)

While the importation of Negro labor into this country began in 1619, the Negro's status as a member of a racial group was only gradually defined. Frazier has pointed out that the distinction between slavery and servitude was not clear, and that during early years the status of the Negro was similar to that of the white indentured servant (Frazier, 1957). It is only with a clarification of the Negro's status as being a racial one, rather than one of social class, that it becomes legitimate to speak of Negro-white relationships. This clarification was under way by the middle decades of the seventeenth century. Even before the beginnings of what has been called the classic period of "antebellum slavery" race relations in this country had begun to emerge as a unique pattern of intergroup relations.

However, while there were slave insurrections and abortive rebellions in the eighteenth century, interracial violence was interpreted less in racial terms than in class or social terms, particularly in terms of the master-servant relationship. The racial "threat" concerning white Americans was the American Indian. There are reports of individual interracial assaults and homicides. There were slave plots of considerable scope, interestingly enough in New York, in 1712 and 1741 (note eighteenth-century reports from *Gentleman's Magazine* cited in Wish, 1937). But while whites were killed in these plots and Negroes slain or transported in retaliation, they were interpreted as uprisings of a servant class or as political plots inspired by "foreign agents" rather than as uprisings of Negroes. Indeed, in the second of these plots, whites were implicated and a white man and his family and a Catholic priest were executed.

With the firm establishment of capitalistic slavery as an American institution, a process catalyzed by well-known developments in agriculture, the black man and his activities, and his racial status, took on a new character and significance. It was after 1800 that apologies for the treatment of the Negro, since that time one of the South's leading literary exports, first began to appear. Approximately the same date marks a burgeoning concern by white Southerners over the control of their Negro slaves in ever broader aspects of their lives ranging from reproduction to religion, but particularly in those areas in which possible crisis lay. A number of authors have shown the near obsession of many southern whites over the possibilities of slave revolts and have further demonstrated that in many cases this concern and anxiety were well founded. A number of factors contributed to the failure of slave rebellions. But the plans of Vesey, Gabriel and Turner, to mention only the most well-known insurrectionaries, came alarmingly close to fruition. And, these planned rebellions were not the protest merely of an economically downtrodden and subservient class. That they were racial in character is demonstrated by the fact that whites of all classes were to be exterminated, with the exception of those who had shown good will toward Negroes. The characteristics of the rebels varied. Some were relatively new arrivals still imbued with the militance of their African tribal heritage, others were longer sojourners in this country who had become literate, acculturated and too familiar with ideas of equality which were meant only for their white masters. But all of them shared, in common with the white group, a conception of a society divided along racial, rather than simply social, lines. They differed from the whites in their refusal to accept the sanctity of the established accommodative pattern.

Other patterns of resistance to slave status are less clearly racial and more frequently individual in nature. There is documentation that suicide, infanticide and self-mutilation were widespread, not only in this country, but also on the boats which brought the slaves and even before that in the slave coffles of Africa itself. Other slaves took an easier pattern of resistance through what we now call the "slowdown" and various forms of "goldbricking." Correspondence of owners and their overseers is replete with complaints about the abuse of working equipment by field hands, the widespread and undiagnosable "miseries," and the unauthorized vacations in the swamps or actual runaways. Rejection of slave status was shown by continual destruction of property; the burnings of barns and hayricks, the failure to cinch the master's saddle up tight enough to prevent his being thrown; by the studied insult which is not an insult. In a large number of ways short of physical violence the Negro slave protested his subservient status.[3] It is true that much of this protest was not channeled into social racial protest. But the underlying substratum was one of protest against an accommodative pattern in which the Negro was in a permanently subordinate position.

Many of the activities of whites in the owning class during this period can be viewed as reactions to the various forms of resistance offered by their Negro slaves. It is true that as slavery became an entrenched institution the master had increasing control over the lives of his slaves until ultimately, control over the very life and death of the slave came into the hands of the master. Yet, in spite of the Simon Legree tradition, most Southerners engaged in latifundiary activities had a purely capitalistic orientation. Slaves as instruments of production should have a certain minimum of decent treatment in order to ensure their survival and relative productivity as plantation labor.[4] While there were doubtless many cruel men and women who maltreated their slaves, or, in the case of overseers, the slaves of their employers, it seems highly probable that much of the brutal treatment was meted out to slaves in an attempt to force non-cooperative workers to produce, to discourage malingering, or to cow potential rebels and insurrectionaries. It is doubtful that many white Southerners enjoyed giving up their evenings to riding on "patrol" enforcing "Black Codes." More likely such activity was interpreted as being necessary for survival. The same may be said of patterns of slave punishment which in retrospect may seem unnecessarily brutal. In this period, as in others, given an initial pattern of superordination-subordination, the attitude and behavior of the Negro determined the pattern of interracial relations.

CIVIL WAR AND RECONSTRUCTION (1861–1877)

The period immediately prior to the Civil War was one in which the status of the Negro, and of his relationships to the dominant white group, became increasingly a matter of national concern. While almost all white Americans, from North or South, of Abolitionist or Slavery politics, were agreed on the innate inferiority of the Negro to the white man, there were those who felt that this inferiority did not justify holding the black man in slavery. The War of the Rebellion was an attempt to decide issues in the area of "State's Rights." But lying behind and

3. The ambivalent status of the free Negro produced a wide variety of reactions within that group ranging from militant support of slave resistance, through flight, to complete acceptance and support of white dominance.

4. This may not have been the case with entrepreneurs who contracted for slave labor.

around all other issues was that of slavery and, more broadly, the relationships between whites and Negroes in all parts of the country.

Even before the War had begun it was apparent that not all Northerners felt toward the Negro as did the abolitionists. Nor was this lack of unanimity confined to areas of Copperhead strength. The domestic situation in the North during the War was marked by numerous civil disturbances (see Lofton, 1949). There was violent rioting in Cincinnati in 1862, apparently growing out of competition between Negro and Irish hands on the riverboats. There were lesser riots in Newark, New Jersey, and in Buffalo and Troy, New York. These latter riots, like other riots of the War period, combined as their basic causes hostility to the wartime draft and its inequities and a concomitant fear that Negroes would take over the jobs of white labor. The most spectacular of the so-called Draft Riots, however, was that which took place in New York City in July of 1863 (a dramatic journalistic account of these riots can be found in Werstein, 1957).

The draft disturbances in New York remain the most sanguinary case of interracial violence in American history. Estimates of deaths of white rioters alone range as high as 1,500, and while the total number of Negroes slain is unknown, the population of Negroes in the city dropped by 20 per cent, from 12,472 to 9,945, between 1860 and 1865 (Man, 1951). A major factor in the origin of these riots was a fear of black labor competition which flourished among the contingent of unskilled Irish labor in the city's labor force, a fear nourished and encouraged by anti-Administration politicians and the Democratic press. The Draft Riots in New York had at least two interacting causes, one direct and one indirect, which were related to the status of the Negro. The discriminatory nature of the draft legislation was felt particularly by working-class people who were unable to pay for substitutes. They were being forced to fight in a war about which they had no enthusiasm. In addition, they felt that they were being forced to fight to "free the niggers," whom they perceived as a threat as a source of cheap labor. In some of its aspects the New York riot was similar to earlier riots directed against various foreign-born groups, particularly the Irish themselves, who were considered as undermining the position of native-born white labor.

The Civil War also saw the first large-scale participation of Negroes in military activities in an American war. Negroes were utilized by both Union and Confederate forces, though in the South their participation was largely limited to work in labor battalions. In the Northern armies they fought in several major campaigns, occasionally distinguishing themselves to a minor degree. When captured by Southern troops they could expect no quarter and in at least one case were slaughtered wholesale. Relations with Northern white officers were frequently not much better; a unit of the Corps d'Afrique mutinied against its white officers, and other incidents are recorded (Harrington, 1942).

The situation of Negroes in the South during the War period was not uniform. In some cases white owners and other representatives of the dominant racial group thought it expedient to introduce even more rigid controls over their slaves. In other areas Negroes were given added responsibilities and loyal servants stayed at home and protected the "women folk." Even in areas characterized by the latter situation, however, there was a general air of tenseness and the number of slaves who attempted to gain their freedom in the confusion swelled to the point where they hindered the movements of the Northern military forces. The latter, at least in some cases, showed their attitude by returning the runaway slaves to their masters. Some areas were swept with panic as rumors circulated of impending insurrection. The accommodative structure was disintegrating, but no new structure of social relationships was as yet appearing to take its place.

The bitterness of white Southerners at losing the war was hardly assuaged by events of the immediate post-War years. To the injury of shattered pride and economic ruination was added the insult of disfranchisement and "Black Republicanism." The oft-told activities and exploits of "carpetbaggers," "scalawags" and the members of the various "black governments" need no re-telling. While not all of those who governed the South in the post-War years were scoundrels, and while there was doubtless progressive and intelligent legislation passed in states dominated temporarily by Negroes, the fact remains that there were scoundrels and that illiterate Negroes, unprepared for political responsibility, did put their votes up for sale. There was enough misuse of political power to convince many white Southerners of the venality and incompetence of all Negroes. Motives of revenge did dominate some Negroes, and many white Southerners underwent harrowing experiences during this period of continued disorganization. It was in desperation that respectable elements of the white community organized the "Bald Knobbers" of Missouri and other "pre-Klan night-riding" organizations. Only later did these organizations fall into the hands of criminals and outlaws. Repressive activity against Negroes (and some whites) in this period was, again, an attempt to bring some coherence into a disrupted accommodative structure.

By the end of this period the relationship between whites and Negroes had been clearly defined as an interracial relationship, and any interclass aspects were clearly secondary.[5] Henceforward, particularly in the South but with increasing frequency in the North, disputes between whites and Negroes were interpreted as interracial disputes no matter what may have been the initiating incident. Historians may interpret the War as a struggle over "State's Rights." White persons in both the North and the South have come to regard it as the war to "free the

5. This is not to deny the continued importance of economic factors in defining race relations. Perhaps the strongest statement of the economic interpretation of race relations is found in Cox, 1948. In the decade following the original publication of this article a strong class element reappeared in racial violence. See pp. 385-396; 488-501.

niggers." Any attempt after this time to resolve differences between the two sections has led to recriminations by Southerners concerning the crime of the North in unloosing the Negro.

THE SECOND RECONSTRUCTION AND THE BEGINNINGS OF THE GREAT MIGRATION (1878–1914)

Although considerable hostility had been generated by events of the post-War period, the withdrawal of Federal troops from the South after the Compromise of 1877 was not followed by an immediate wave of savage repression against the Negro in the South. Indeed, for a decade it seemed that the lines of struggle in the new South might be defined along class lines rather than along racial lines (see Frazier, 1953, and Woodward, 1957). For a brief period, that of the acme of Populist power, a tenuous alliance existed between the poor whites and the Negro populace. White and Negro alike united in a temporary and doomed attempt to overthrow the "Bourbon aristocracy." It was after the breakdown of this alliance with the creation of another coalition including the Bourbons, Northern business interests and the demagogic leaders of the lower-class whites that the classic period of repression and lynching began.

During this period of interracial violence the attitude of the white Southern governments was a "hands off" expression of tacit approval. Northern liberals were suddenly disinterested; they were tired of breast-beating about an admittedly inferior race in a remote section and allowed themselves to be convinced that the South did, indeed, know the best way to handle its own problem. It was between the middle 1880's and the early 1900's that most of the increasingly discriminative and repressive legislation, the "Jim Crow" laws, was passed. During the same period these laws received support through the courts to the supreme judicial bench. The Negro was deprived effectively of the franchise, of equality in compulsory public education [6] and of protection against discrimination in the use of public facilities. The Negro did not succumb to this attack on his rights without a struggle. The use of widespread repression and the high incidence of violence against the Negro populace was, at least in part, the manifest expression of white reaction to Negro resistance. If Negroes had "known their place" it would not have been necessary to lynch Negroes in order to remind them of that "place." There was considerable resistance, though usually unorganized, on the part of the Negro population. When that resistance failed, a trickle of northward migration began, a trickle which was to swell into a flood by the end of the First World War.[7]

6. Compulsory education made law by Negro legislators in some Southern states.
7. "Pull" factors based on the glowing pictures of the North and on recruitment of Southern Negro labor were also important in this migration.

The manifest reason for much of the savage repression of this period was the protection of Southern white womanhood, still a major plank in the foundation of programs for maintaining white supremacy. However, while this may have been the public explanation for lynching, rape was not the most frequent alleged cause for the necessity of the primeval justice of lynching, even during the two big lynching decades, the last of the nineteenth and the first of the twentieth centuries.[8] Failure to show the proper respect to a white man was equally important, and a cause which included a variety of offenses ranging from a demand for an explanation of financial transactions to the more heinous crime of engaging in political activity. Political activity was the underlying cause of the two most savage outbreaks of this period, riots in Wilmington, North Carolina, in 1896 and in Atlanta, Georgia, in 1906. In the latter case the alleged reason for the outbreak was a series of assaults on white women, but it is clear that the disturbance had as a latent function the exclusion of Negroes from political participation.

Emancipation and military defeat, "Black Republicanism" and the Freedmen's Bureau, the First Reconstruction with its schoolmarms and scalawags, had completely disrupted the antebellum pattern of accommodation between the two races in the South. The Second Reconstruction, with its Jim Crow legislation, its nightriders and lynching "bees" to enforce racial "etiquette," was an attempt to re-establish that accommodative pattern.

WORLD WAR I AND THE POST-WAR BOOM AND RACIAL READJUSTMENT (1915–1929)

Events of this period made clear the fact that the Negro problem was no longer a regional one, but one shared by North and South alike. Indeed, while lynching continued in the South, major outbreaks of interracial violence increasingly occurred in Northern urban areas with their growing concentrations of Negro population.

There are five patterns of interracial social violence in this period different enough in characteristics to be identifiable. They are (a) lynching, (b) mutiny and insurrection, (c) individual interracial assaults and homicides, racial arson and bombings, (d) "Southern style" race riots (The Chicago Commission on Race Relations, 1922), and (e) "Northern style" race riots.

Lynching. The first decade of the twentieth century was a peak period for lynching in the South. During the same decade this pattern of interracial violence spread into Northern States. The most spectacular lynching of this century occurred immediately after World War I in Omaha, Nebraska. The immediate alleged cause was the assault of a

8. See Jessie P. Guzman, pp. 56-59.

Negro upon a white woman. The real cause, however, was at least in part a reflection of the nationwide reaction of whites to the new militance of the Negro's assault upon the accommodative structure. This new militance was a result partly of the not unsubstantial gains of the Negro in moving North during the war and partly a result of the much publicized treatment of Negro soldiers overseas, particularly in France. Large numbers of whites shared in a determination to "put these uppity niggers back in their place," and violence occurred in widely scattered points throughout the country.

Lynchings continued to occur until the time of World War II and it is only since the war that the Bureau of Records and Research of Tuskegee has stopped publication of data on lynchings on the ground that their occurrence is no longer of major consequence. A common cause continued to be alleged Negro assaults upon white women, but the actual pattern of precipitating causes remained as varied as it had been in earlier periods. It is probable that here, as in the case of other types of violence, there have been changes in etiology. Attempts, none very successful, have been made to demonstrate that lynchings, particularly during the Depression, were closely related to the fluctuation of various economic indices (see Hovland and Sears, 1940, and Mintz, 1946. These two articles are included in this volume, pp. 344-348 and 349-353). While documentation for such relationships has proved insufficient, it is probably true that in later years lynching was founded less frequently on the myth of sexuality and more frequently was a direct expression of reaction against "felt" Negro aggression in the economic sphere.

Mutiny and insurrection. Such aggression, in at least one instance, found expression in the renewal of a pattern which had not occurred since before the Civil War. In October, 1919, there occurred an insurrection of the Negro populace near Elaine, Arkansas. It was claimed that the inspiration for this rebellion came from "Bolshevik" agitation and there is some evidence that the "Progressive Farmer's Household Union" was active in promoting the notion that Negroes were entitled to economic and social equality. Negroes of the area were well organized and were prepared, according to confessions made by several of their number, to follow up demands for fair payment for their cotton with an armed uprising. After a series of brief battles the Negroes were subdued and hunted down, given quick trials and several sentenced to death.

In addition to this uprising there were a number of mutinies in the military, the most famous of which developed into the Houston race riot of 1917. Schuler (1944, included *infra.*) remains the best treatment of this uprising of Negro troops. In this affair, Negro soldiers, enraged by the shooting of one of their comrades in an affray with the white police over alleged mistreatment of a Negro woman, mutinied against their officers, took weapons and proceeded to storm downtown Houston.

Several people were killed, and as a result of the disturbance 65 Negro soldiers received sentences, several of them for life imprisonment.[9]

It is interesting to note that the soldiers involved in the Houston race riot were largely from Northern States. The Elaine uprising and the several mutinies which occurred during the War make up the bulk of cases of direct assaults by Negroes upon the accommodative structure.

Individual interracial assaults and homicides, arson and bombings. A third pattern of social violence consisted of individual interracial assaults and homicides and other attacks such as arson and bombing. Not all interracial homicides and assaults can be considered to be social violence. In any case where racial membership was important in the interactive pattern and the violence based ultimately on that membership, social violence may be said to have occurred. These manifestations of violence are a part of the riot cycle itself. During the period of increasing tension prior to major riots, during lulls within the riot and in decreasing tempo after the riot has played itself out or has been quelled, such acts are indicators of the character of interracial relations. In those situations where adequate policing or firm governmental action prevent the actual eruption of hostility into full-fledged riots such behavior patterns may be the sole indication of the high degree of tension.

"Southern style" race riots.[10] The Atlanta riot of 1906 and the Springfield, Illinois, riot of 1908 are examples of Southern style race riots. During the period under discussion, the Washington, D. C., riot of 1919 and the Tulsa, Oklahoma, riot of 1921 can be taken as typical examples. In every such riot violence is largely one-sided and consists of attacks, of varying degrees of organization, by whites on Negroes and on the Negro community. In all such riots, whatever may have been the actual background of the riot, there are charges of Negro assaults upon white women.

"Northern style" race riots. The Chicago riot of 1919 may be taken as the type-case of the Northern style urban race riot. Here the causation, both in background and in actual precipitating incident, is secular in nature and there is no focusing on the alleged violation of the sanctity of white womanhood. Rather there was a long period of constantly increasing tension in other areas, and a series of assaults upon the accommodative pattern by Negroes, indeed, a challenge to the very continued existence of that pattern. The assault was felt particularly in the areas of housing, labor competition and the use of public facilities, espe-

9. Many of these sentences were later reduced.
10. Fuller accounts of "Southern" and "Northern" style riots, along with a description of a mixed-type outbreak, are included in this volume.

cially transportation. The actual precipitating incident was the death, perhaps accidental, of a Negro youth during a dispute over segregated swimming. The riot found organized and unorganized groups of both races engaged in occasional pitched battles and a widespred occurrence of attacks upon isolated individuals of one race by roaming gangs of the other race. While there were claims of police partiality and governmental inefficiency the role of the government was far more neutral than was the case in disturbances in the South, urban or rural.

INTER-WAR AND DEPRESSION (1930–1941)

In many ways this period is an extension of the immediate preceding one. It has been accorded separate treatment because of the sharp decline of reported violence of an interracial nature during the 1930's. While lynchings continued, particularly in the South, they decreased in number if not in barbarity. Only one major urban disturbance is recorded for the decade, the Harlem riot of 1935. The end of the period was characterized by an increasing incidence of individual interracial violence, presaging the major outbreaks of urban social violence which were to occur in the following period. The period was one in which there was a gradual building up of the strength of organizations on the extreme political left and the extreme political right. These organizations played an as yet incompletely assessed role in the struggles which were coming.

WORLD WAR II (1942–1945)

The most dramatic racial outbreaks of the Second World War were the Detroit and Harlem disturbances of 1943. While there are some similarities between these two outbreaks, there are sharp differences both in background and in the actual course of events in the two cities. The Detroit race riot was, in background, in precipitating incident, and in chronology of violence a "Northern style" riot much like the 1919 Chicago riot. There was little actual interracial violence in the Harlem outbreak, but this lack of overt interracial conflict resulted from differences in ecology and in the application of police controls rather than from differences in general background factors in Detroit and Harlem or from any lower degree of strain in the accommodative relationship in Harlem.

The Harlem and Detroit riots of 1943 were only two of the more spectacular expressions of the resurgence of interracial conflict during World War II. There were riots in other urban centers, both North and South. Nor were riots the only form of conflict and violence occurring

during the war. There were difficulties involving Negro service personnel which in at least a few cases came close to ending in old-fashioned
lynchings. There was a continuation of the pattern of individual assaults
and homicides. Intimately related to all these patterns of actual violence
was a much increased militance shown by the Negro press and by a
number of Negro organizations. Perhaps most important in terms of
long-range consequences was the burgeoning utilization of political,
economic and legal coercion in the assault upon the pattern of interracial accommodation. Results of the interaction of all these factors have
become obvious in the post-War period.

POST WORLD WAR II (1946–1963)

In this period of nearly twenty years following the ending of World
War II there were large-scale urban disturbances but no real race riots.[11]
There were, however, a number of incidents which might easily have
erupted into major urban riots had it not been for the presence of better
police controls than had existed in the past. In the North, these incidents tended to cluster into two categories; incidents concerning Negro
invasion of white residential areas and incidents over the use of public
facilities, particularly recreational facilities. In the latter area, St. Louis
and Youngstown experienced near-riots over the use of swimming facilities by Negroes. (George Schermer's report [pp. 162-169] on the Fairgrounds Park incident in St. Louis provides a careful analysis of one
such disturbance.) Housing incidents have caused near-riots in a number
of Northern cities. Two which attracted wide attention were those in
Cicero (see pp. 170-183) and Chicago, Illinois (pp. 170-183). In some
cases, as in Cicero, police partiality toward the white aggressors seems
to have been partly responsible for the growth of an initially small disturbance. In Chicago, on the other hand, where a struggle over Negro
entrance into Trumbull Park, a formerly all-white public housing project, tied up police for four years the Negroes remained, and were
protected by a well-organized police force that had had special training in interracial problems. In addition to these disturbances there were
bombings in Kansas City, Missouri, and Chicago and demonstrations
against the movement of a Negro family into all-white Levittown,
Pennsylvania, and scattered incidents in other Northern urban areas.

The sharpest changes in the pattern of interracial relations until
1963, however, were brought about by the renewed and increased vigor
of the use of the courts by Negroes (activity in this area is covered in
detail in the periodical *Race Relations Law Reporter*). This was true in
the areas already mentioned, housing and access to public facilities and

11. The labeling of the events of the summers of the 1960's is discussed on pp.
385-396.

also, more importantly, in the crucial area of school desegregation (events in this area were covered in detail in the *Southern School News*). Eruptions of violence occurred in Southern communities where court orders to integrate schools were greeted by organized resistance of the white community. There were riots in Kentucky, Tennessee and Arkansas and disturbances in other states. Schools were closed by the governors of Virginia and Arkansas, ostensibly to prevent further outbreaks of violence.

Reflecting the new militance of the Negro population in the area of school desegregation, in attempts to gain the franchise, in bus boycotts, and in other breaches of the accommodative pattern, there were sporadic outbreaks of violence in the South. The pattern, however, was not that of the mass lynching or the rural pogrom, but rather one of kidnapping and summary "execution" or of sudden assault in a fashion more reminiscent of Northern gang warfare of the 1930's or of post-Civil War Klan activities.

With the exception of a brief period after the Civil War, the pattern of American Negro-white relationships, especially in the American South, closely approximated the classic accommodative pattern of superordination-subordination, with the whites a continually dominant group. The most savage oppression, whether expressed in rural lynchings and pogroms or in urban race riots, has taken place when the Negro refused to accept a subordinate status. The most intense conflict has resulted when the subordinate minority attempted to disrupt the accommodative pattern or when the superordinate group defined the situation as one in which such an attempt was being made. Conflict in Negro-white relationships in the United States has been conflict generated by the breakdown of an essentially unstable accommodative pattern, essentially unstable because the subordinated group has refused to accept its status and has had sufficient power to challenge it.[12]

12. As I prepare this article for republication (Spring, 1968), I see no reason for any major changes in assessment of the historical patterns and meaning of interracial violence in America. When a historical perspective becomes possible, "Black power" and the "long, hot summers" will be, I believe, most clearly interpretable through a conflict-accommodation framework.

2

THE PERIOD OF SLAVE INSURRECTIONS
AND RESISTANCE
1640–1861

The publication of William Styron's *The Confessions of Nat Turner* in early 1968, and the subsequent negative response to it by ten black writers (Clarke, 1968),[1] created a minor literary stir. There was sharp disagreement over Styron's characterization both of Turner and of the rebellion, the blacks believing that Styron had caricatured Turner and misleadingly pictured the rebellion itself as a total debacle.

Relatively few Americans knew what the stir was all about, although by 1968 many more black people were aware of their own history in this country than had been the case even a decade earlier. There had, however, been earlier attention to slave rebellions in America and to other varieties of black resistance to slavery. The earliest full-scale examination of such rebellions was that by Herbert Aptheker (1943). Aptheker's study clearly reflected his own political orientation, and it has been claimed that he made errors in scholarship. For some years, however, his was the only study, and this chapter is intended to indicate the kinds of events that he reported and the kind of perspective that informed his analysis.

In the years following the publication of Aptheker's book the *Journal of Negro History* published numerous studies of slave insurrections and other varieties of slave resistance, several of which are cited in the bibliography.

1. The nine writers, in addition to Clarke, who contributed to the volume were Lerone Bennett, Jr., Alvin F. Poussaint, Vincent Harding, John Oliver Killens, John A. Williams, Ernest Kaiser, Loyle Hairston, Charles V. Hamilton, and Mike Thelwell.

Herbert Aptheker

American Negro Slave Revolts *

EARLY PLOTS AND REBELLIONS

A slave state offered the following definition of the term *slave insurrection:* "By 'insurrection of slaves' is meant an assemblage of three or more, with arms, with intent to obtain their liberty by force." Were one to follow this definition literally the number of slave insurrections and conspiracies within the present borders of the United States would be huge, certainly reaching several hundreds.

In this study, however, the tests for insurrection or conspiracy are more severe. The elements of the definition herein subscribed to are: a minimum of ten slaves involved; freedom as the apparent aim of the disaffected slaves; contemporary references labelling the event as an uprising, plot, insurrection, or the equivalent of these terms. The study, moreover, excludes, with a few exceptions, the scores of outbreaks and plots that occurred upon domestic or foreign slave-traders.

Observing such restrictions, the author has found records of approximately two hundred and fifty revolts and conspiracies in the history of American Negro slavery. Two additional facts of particular interest appear from the study. These are, first, that occasionally the plans or aspirations of the rebels were actually reported as going beyond a desire for personal freedom and envisioning, in addition, a property redistribution; and, second, that white people were frequently implicated—or believed to be implicated—with the slaves in the plans or efforts to overthrow the master class by force.

. . . .

THE TURNER CATACLYSM

The decade preceding the Southampton Insurrection was one of economic depression throughout the South, and in the old South, especially eastern Virginia and eastern North Carolina, it was marked by a dangerously disproportionate rate of population growth, that of the Negroes distinctly outstripping that of the whites. To complete the picture of environmental conditions one should examine the specific locale of Turner's uprising.

* In the original, Aptheker's study is heavily documented with references to articles in contemporary journals and to primary sources including papers and letters of contemporary figures and legal codes, decisions, and so on.

Southampton is a tidewater county, located in the southeastern part of Virginia, bordering the state of North Carolina. Covering six hundred square miles, it was an important economic unit in the tidewater area. In 1830 it was second in the State in its production of potatoes and rice, and, in 1840, was the leading county in cotton production, in the value of its orchard produce, and in the number of its swine. Its population trend was that of the section, i.e., a more rapid growth of the Negro than of the white element. Thus, one finds that while, in 1820, there were 6127 whites and 8043 Negroes in Southampton County, in 1830 the figures read 6574 whites and 9501 Negroes. In 1830 out of a total of thirty-nine tidewater counties only three surpassed Southampton in the number of free Negroes, and only four in the number of slaves and in the number of whites.

In its economic decline Southampton is also typical of the condition in eastern Virginia during the period. Thus, for example, it ranked fifth in the State in 1810 in the amount of taxes it paid on the assessed valuation of its land and lots, but dropped to forty-fourth in 1820 and to forty-sixth in 1830.

The situation, then, in the decade prior to the Southampton revolt is one of extraordinary *malaise* in the slaveholding area. It is marked by a considerable expansion and development of antislavery feeling, national and internationally (as part of an all-embracing upsurge of progressive and radical thought and action throughout the western world), by great and serious unrest among the slave populations, in the West Indies as well as on the Continent, by severe economic depression, and by the more rapid growth of the Negro population than the white throughout the old South. Testifying to the uneasiness of the master class there appear numerous precautionary measures for the purpose of overawing, or further restricting the activities of the slave population (which, in turn, very likely stimulated discontent), and, as a last resort, in order to assure the speedy suppression of all evidences of slave insubordination.

It was into such a situation (one is tempted to assert, though proof is, of course, not at hand, that it was *because* of such a situation) that the upraised dark arms of vengeance of Turner and his followers crashed in the summer of 1831.

Nat Turner was born October 2, 1800, and apparently lived all his life in Southhampton County. At the time of the rebellion he was:

5 feet 6 or 8 inches high, weighs between 150 and 160 pounds, rather bright complexion, but not a mulatto, broad shoulders, large flat nose, large eyes, broad flat feet, rather knock-kneed, walks brisk and active, hair on the top of the head very thin, no beard, except on the upper lip and the top of the chin, a scar on one of his temples, also one on the back of his neck, a large knot on one of the bones of his right arm, near the wrist, produced by a blow.

Very naturally, William Lloyd Garrison, in commenting upon this description, pointed to these scars as important explanations for Turner's actions. But the Richmond *Enquirer* assured its readers that Turner got two of his bruises in fights with fellow slaves and one of them, that on his temple, through a mule's kick. Drewry, notwithstanding the fact that his description of Turner hardly indicates a pugnacious individual, accepts the explanation of the southern newspaper, and points out, correctly, that Turner himself stated that his last master, Joseph Travis, had not been severe. But he had had other masters—Benjamin Turner and Putnam Moore—and he had, in 1826 or 1827, run away from one of these after a change in overseers.

However that may be, mere personal vengeance was not Nat Turner's motive. He had learned how to read—precisely when, he did not know—and, when his labors permitted, he had immersed himself in the stories of the Bible. He was a keen, mechanically gifted man whose religion offered him a rationalization for his opposition to the status quo. Later writers have described him as an overseer or foreman, and while no convincing support for this has been found, it is certain that his considerable mental abilities were recognized and appreciated by his contemporaries. He was a religious leader, often conducting services of a Baptist nature and exhorting his fellow workers. It appears that even white people were influenced, if not controlled, by him, so that, as he said, he immersed one Ethelred T. Brantley and prevailed upon him to "cease from his wickedness."

Turner became convinced that he "was ordained for some great purpose in the hands of the Almighty." In the spring of 1828, while working in the fields, he "heard a loud noise in the heavens, and the Spirit instantly appeared to me and said the Serpent was loosened, and Christ had laid down the yoke he had borne for the sins of men, and that I should take it on and fight against the Serpent, for the time was fast approaching when the first should be last and the last should be first."

The slave waited for a sign from his God. This came to him in the form of the solar eclipse of February 12, 1831. Then apparently for the first time, he told four other slaves of his plans for rebellion. All joined him, and these American Negroes selected the Fourth of July as the day on which to strike for liberty, a choice which led a later commentator to curse them because they had "perverted that sacred day."

Turner was ill on the "sacred day," and the conspirators waited for another sign. This appeared to them on Saturday, August 13, in the "greenish blue color" of the sun. According to Drewry, Turner the next day exhorted at a religious meeting of Negroes in the southern part of Southampton County (not in North Carolina, as has been said) where some of the slaves "signified their willingness to co-operate with him by wearing around their necks red bandana handkerchiefs." There was certainly, a meeting of plotters in the afternoon of Sunday, August 21, and it was then decided to start the revolt that evening.

Appreciating the value of a dramatic entrance, Turner was the last to join this gathering. He noticed a newcomer in the group, and declared:

I saluted them on coming up, and asked Will how came he there, he answered, his life was worth no more than others, and his liberty as dear to him. I asked him if he meant to obtain it? He said he would, or lose his life. This was enough to put him in full confidence.

These six slaves, then, started out, in the evening of August 21, 1831, on their crusade against bondage. Their first blow—delivered by Turner himself—struck against the person and family of Turner's master, Joseph Travis, who were killed. Some arms and horses were taken, the rebels pushed on, and everywhere slaves flocked to their standard; a result which Turner, starting out with but a handful of followers, must have had excellent reasons to anticipate. Within twenty-four hours approximately seventy slaves were actively aiding in the rebellion. By the morning of August 23rd, at least fifty-seven whites—men, women, and children—had been killed, and the rebels had covered about twenty miles.

Turner declared that "indiscriminate slaughter was not their intention after they obtained a foothold, and was resorted to in the first instance to strike terror and alarm. Women and children would afterwards have been spared, and men too who ceased to resist." According to Governor John Floyd the slaves "spared but one family and that was one so wretched as to be in all respects upon a par with them."

In the morning of the twenty-third Turner and his followers set out for the county seat, Jerusalem, where there was a considerable store of arms. When about three miles from this town several of the slaves, notwithstanding Turner's objections, insisted upon trying to recruit the slaves of a wealthy planter named Parker. Turner, with a handful of followers, remained at the Parker gate while the rest went to the home itself, about half a mile away. Once at the Parker home many of the slaves appear to have slaked their thirst from its well-stocked cellar and to have rested. Turner became impatient and set out to get his tardy companions. The eight or nine slaves remaining at the gate were then attacked by a volunteer corps of whites of about twice their number. The slaves retreated, but upon being reinforced by the returning Turner and his men, the rebels pressed on and forced the whites to give ground. The latter, however, were in turn reinforced by a company of militia and the Negroes, whose guns, according to the Richmond *Compiler* of August 29, were not "fit for use," fled.

Though Turner later tried to round up sufficient followers to continue the struggle, his efforts were futile and this battle at Parker's field was the crucial one. Late in the day of this encounter the commander at Fort Monroe, Colonel Eustis, was requested by the Mayor of Norfolk to send aid. By the morning of the twenty-fourth, three companies of artillery with a field piece and one hundred stands of spare arms, together with detachments of men from the warships *Warren* and *Natchez* were on their way to the scene of the trouble. They made the sixty miles in one day, and met hundreds of other soldiers from volunteer and militia companies of the counties, in Virginia and in North Carolina, surrounding Southampton.

Massacre followed. Phillips simply notes, "a certain number of innocent blacks shot down," and Ballagh asserts, "A most impartial trial was given to all, except a few decapitated" in Southampton, while Drewry thought "there was far less of this indiscriminate murder than might have been expected." Just how much "indiscriminate murder" one ought to "expect" is not clear, but this statement by General Eppes, the officer in command of the affected county, leads one to believe that these historians were rather uncritical in dealing with this phase of the event:

He [the General] will not specify all the instances that he is bound to believe have occurred, but pass in silence what has happened, with the expression of his deepest sorrow, that any necessity should be supposed to have existed, to justify a single act of atrocity. But he feels himself bound to declare, and hereby announces to the troops and citizens, that no excuse will be allowed for any similar acts of violence, after the promulgation of this order, and further to declare, in the most explicit terms, that any who may attempt the repetition of such acts, shall be punished, if necessary, by the rigors of the articles of war. The course that has pursued, he fears, will in some instances be the means of rendering doubtful the guilt of those who may have participated in the carnage . . . . This course of proceeding dignified the rebel and the assassin with the sanctity of martyrdom, and confounds the difference that morality and religion makes between the ruffian and the brave and the honorable.

The editor of the Richmond *Whig* also referred "with pain" to this "feature of the Southampton Rebellion. . . . We allude to the slaughter of many blacks without trial and under circumstances of great barbarity." He thought that about forty had thus been killed. A Reverend G. W. Powell, writing August 27, when the reign of terror was by no means over, reported, "Many negroes are killed every day. The exact number will never be known." The reverend gentleman was correct, but it appears certain that more, many more, than forty were massacred. The Huntsville, Alabama, *Southern Advocate* of October 15, 1831, declared that over one hundred Negroes had been killed in Southampton. It seems accurate to say that at least twice as many Negroes were indiscriminately slaughtered in that county, as the number of white people who had fallen victim to the vengeance and bondage-hating spirit of the slave.

That some considered themselves martyrs, as General Eppes suggested, is indicated by Governor Floyd's comment that "All died bravely indicating no reluctance to lose their lives in such a cause;" and a letter to Judge Thomas Ruffin of North Carolina declared, "some of them that were wounded and in the aggonies [sic] of Death declared that they was going happy fore that God had a hand in what they had been doing."

Nat Turner eluded his pursuers from the end of August until October 30, when he was caught, armed only with an old sword, by Benjamin Phipps. During those weeks there had been rumors that he was drowned, but as a matter of fact he never left his native county. He forsook his hiding place only at night for water, having supplied himself with food.

Turner was tried and, though pleading not guilty, since, as he said, he did not feel *guilty,* he was condemned to hang. The honorable Jeremiah Cobb pronounced sentence on November 5, in these words: "The judgment of the Court, is that you be taken hence to the jail from whence you came, thence to the place of execution, and on Friday next, between the hours of ten A. M and 2 P. M. be hung by the neck until you are dead! dead! dead! and may the Lord have mercy upon your soul." About sixteen other slaves and three free Negroes had previously been executed, and on November 11, 1831, their leader, the Prophet, he who had inspired them to value liberty above life, went calmly to his death.

Some of the first contemporary accounts of the revolt stated that it was led by about three whites, but this was later denied, and no good evidence has been seen to demonstrate that any but Negroes were implicated in the uprising itself. There is, however, evidence of joint activity in the troubles and plots immediately following the outbreak. Governor Floyd of Virginia in his legislative message of December 6, 1831, darkly hinted that the unrest was "not confined to the slaves." The best evidence observed concerning this, in Virginia, is a semiliterate letter from a white person, Williamson Mann, dated Chesterfield County, August 29, 1831, to a slave, Ben Lee, reading:

My old fellow
Ben—
You will tell or acquaint every servant in Richmond and adjoining countys they all must be in strict readiness, that this occurrence will go throug Virginia with the slaves and whites if there had never been an association—a visiting with free and slaves this would never of been. They are put up by the free about their liberation. I've wrote to Norfolk, Amelia, Nottoway and sevel other countys to different slaves bob and bill Miller Bowler john ferguson— and sevel other free fellows been at Dr. Crumps—and a great many gentlemens servents how they must act in getting their liberation they must set afire to the city [Richmond] beginning at Shokoe Hill then going through east west north south Set fire to the bridges they are about to break out in Goochland and in Mecklenburg and several other countys very shortly. now their is a barber here in this place—tells that a methodist of the name edmonds has put a great many servants up to how they should do and act by setting fire to this town. I do wish they may succeed by so doing we poor whites can get work as well as slaves or collord. this fellow edmonds the methodist says that judge T. F.—is no friend to the free and your Richmond free associates that your master Watkins Lee brokenberry Johnson Taylor of Norfolk and several other noble delegates is betterly against them all—servants says that billy hickman has just put him up how to do to revenge the whites—edmonds says so you all ought to get

revenge—every white in this place is sceared except myself and a few others this methodist has put up a great many slaves in this place what to do I can tell you so push on boys puch on

Your friend Williamson Mann

With the news of this outbreak panic flashed through Virginia. The uprising was infectious and slaves everywhere became restless (or, at least, it was believed that they had become restless) so that the terror, momentarily localized in Virginia, spread up to Delaware and through Georgia, across to Louisiana and into Kentucky. This naturally led some to believe that Turner had concerted measures for rebellion over a wider area than his own county. Thus, Governor Floyd wrote: "From all that has come to my knowledge during and since this affair—I am fully convinced that every black preacher in the whole country east of the Blue Ridge, was in the secret," and again, "In relation to the extent of the insurrection I think it greater than will ever appear." A few other contemporary statements of similar purport appeared, and some later writers have adopted the same viewpoint.

The final authority on this question, however, is Nat Turner himself, and he affirmed that the revolt he led was local, and that his activities had been confined to his own neighborhood. He added: "I see, sir, you doubt my word but can you not think the same ideas and strange appearances about this time in the heavens might prompt others, as well as myself, to this undertaking?" In the absence of any evidence of equal weight to the contrary, one must conclude that Turner possessed the characteristic of great leaders in that he sensed the mood and feelings of the masses of his fellow beings, not only in his immediate environment, but generally. The years immediately preceding his effort had been marked by a great rumbling of discontent and protest. Turner's act, itself carrying that rumbling to a high point, caused an eruption throughout the length and breadth of the slave South—which always rested on a volcano of outraged humanity.

3

CIVIL WAR AND RECONSTRUCTION
1861–1877

During the Civil War and the decade that followed it, three new varieties of collective violence reflecting membership in racial categories emerged. Toward the end of the War, black troops (with white officers) were increasingly used by the Federal forces; not all of these troops were used solely in support, though such was generally the case until almost the end of World War II. During the Civil War, also, large-scale racial violence occurred for the first time in the North. After the War there emerged a variety of vigilante groups, "Bald Knobbers" and similar quasi-bandit, quasi-legitimate, organizations that operated to keep the lid on social change and to attempt reinstatement of the "proper" superordinate-subordinate relationship that had obtained between whites and blacks in the antebellum South.

There is not sufficient space to enable treatment in this volume of the legitimate involvement of blacks in the military establishment of the United States. There are accounts elsewhere of vigilante terrorism (see, for example, the selection in this volume on lynching in Omaha, Nebraska, or, for another view, Griffith's film, *Birth of a Nation*). In the following selections an attempt is made to convey some of the flavor of major disorders in the North that included antiblack violence and to indicate some of the social causes of these disturbances.

New York's Bloodiest Week

The Negro population, numbering less than 15,000, suffered most of all. No Negro dared appear on the street. "Small mobs are chasing isolated Negroes as hounds would chase a fox," Major Edward S. Sanford of the U.S. Military Telegraph Service wired Secretary of War Stanton. Many hotels, fearful of being attacked, displayed large signs: "No Niggers in back!" Abraham Franklin, who supported himself and his mother as a coachman, managed to get to his mother's house on Seventh Avenue to make sure she was safe. They talked a few minutes, then decided to pray together. A group of rioters burst open the door, beat Franklin, and hanged him before his mother's eyes.

Peter Heuston, a 63-year-old Mohawk Indian and army veteran of the Mexican War, was mistaken for a Negro and beaten to death near his home on Roosevelt Street, leaving an orphaned daughter of eight.

The mob's savagery to the Negro sprang from complex motivations— economic, social, and religious. Most of its members were Irish. Comprising over half the city's foreign-born population of 400,000, out of a total of about 814,000, the Irish were the main source of cheap labor, virtually its peon class. Desperately poor and lacking real roots in the community, they had the most to lose from the draft. Further, they were bitterly afraid that even cheaper Negro labor would flood the North if slavery ceased to exist.

All the frustrations and prejudices the Irish had suffered were brought to a boiling point by the draft. At pitiful wages they had slaved on the railroads and canals, had been herded into the most menial jobs as carters and stevedores. Many newspaper ads repeated the popular prejudice: "No Irish need apply." An Irish domestic worker was lucky to earn seven dollars a month. Their crumbling frame tenements in areas like the Five Points were the worst slums in the city. Already pressed to the wall, the Irish could logically view the draft as the final instrument of oppression by the rich. One worker wrote the *Times:* "We love our wives and children more than the rich because we got not much besides them; and we will not go to leave them at home for to starve. . . ."

In an objective assessment of the Irish role in the riots, *Harper's Weekly* later pleaded that it "be remembered . . . that in many wards of the city the Irish were during the late riot staunch friends of law and order. . . ." Many loyal fire companies were made up of Irishmen. Irish priests opposed the rioters at every step, one risking his life to succor Colonel Henry O'Brien as he was being beaten to death, another persuading a mob not to burn Columbia College at 49th Street and Madison Avenue. Most important of all, a large segment of the Metropolitan Police were Irishmen who fought the mob with a bravery and devotion probably unequaled in police history.

In the war itself, four New York Irish regiments made impressive records. A former Irish editor, Brigadier General Francis Thomas Meagher, commanded the Irish Brigade. The Irish distinguished themselves at Antietam and Fredericksburg, losing 471 wounded and dead in the latter battle. Of 144,000 Irishmen in the Union Army, over 51,000 were from New York.

But on that Monday afternoon, unfortunately, their pent-up hatred of the Negro exploded in its most savage form. Its object was the Orphan Asylum for Colored Children, a four-story building on Fifth Avenue and 43rd Street, where 233 children were housed.

"Clamoring around the house like demons," as the *Tribune* described it, the mob burst the door with axes. The children knelt with Superintendent William E. Davis to pray. Then a long line of frightened boys and girls, two of them infants carried in teachers' arms, followed Davis out the rear door.

The mob surged through the building, stripping it bare. Hundreds of beds were carried from the dormitory wing. Women and boys grabbed them and carted them down the avenue—a strange procession that one reporter estimated ran for ten blocks. Carpets, desks, chairs, pictures, books, even the orphans' clothes, were tossed out the windows to the waiting plunderers. Then the handsome building was set on fire.

Fire Chief Decker and two engine companies responded to the call, Decker racing alone into the building, struggling to extinguish the brands tossed by the mob. But rioters followed him, setting new fires. Decker went back, accompanied by six of his men, and put them out again.

This time two dozen rioters grabbed him and would have beaten him to death had not ten firemen rushed to his rescue and warned that their chief would be taken only over their dead bodies. Frustrated, the mob turned suddenly on the Negro children, who huddled in a circle on the corner watching their home go up in flames.

Twenty children were cut off from the main group. "There is little doubt that many and perhaps all of these helpless children would have been murdered in cold blood," reported the *Times*. But a young Irishman on the edge of the crowd, Paddy McCaffrey, aided by two drivers from the 42nd Street cross-town bus line and members of Engine Company No. 18, surrounded the children and fought off the mob. While rioters pelted them with stones, they managed to get the children to the thirty-fifth precinct station house. An hour later the orphan asylum was a mess of charred rubble.

Paddy McCaffrey's heroism was one more contradiction of the assumption that all Irishmen supported the rioters.

Albon P. Man, Jr.

Labor Competition and the New York Draft Riots of 1863

The New York draft riots of July, 1863, had their origin largely in a fear of black labor competition which possessed the city's Irish unskilled workers. Upon emancipation, they believed, great numbers of Negroes would cross the Mason-Dixon line, underbid them in the Northern labor market, and deprive them of jobs. Similar fears helped produce mass anti-Negro violence in World Wars I and II and also in periods of acute labor shortage. The movement of Negro strikebreakers into the East St. Louis, Illinois, area, for example, touched off the demonstrations which occurred there in July, 1917, while the upgrading of a few Negro employees signaled the start of the ugly Philadelphia transit strike of August, 1944.

But the New York draft disturbances remain the bloodiest race riots of American history. Police figures on deaths among the white rioters ranged from 1,200 to 1,500, and it is impossible to know how many bodies of Negro victims of the lynch mobs were borne away by the waters on either side of Manhattan Island. Significantly, the Negro population of the metropolis dropped 20 per cent between 1860 and 1865, declining from 12,472 to 9,945.

Williston H. Lofton

Northern Labor and the Negro During the Civil War

When the registration of men for the draft began in the city on July 12, there was little evidence of opposition, but on the following morning "organized parties of men went from yard to yard, from shop to shop, to compel the workmen to leave their labor, and join the several processions which were wending their way toward the corner of Third Avenue and Forty-sixth Street." Another report warned that the laborers of the city were preparing to resist the draft.

On the next day rioting began with attacks upon the military and upon the colored residents of the city. One observer felt that "the fact that nearly all the men drafted were laborers and mechanics added fuel to the flame." It seemed that the outbreak had some organization and planning and was not chance attacks by inflamed workers. It was reported that on the morning of July 14, a large number of "respectable workmen and others were seen to assemble at certain specified spots, and between eight and nine o'clock began moving along various avenues west of Fifth Avenue towards their appointed place of general meeting." From the beginning the rioters were chiefly workingmen. As the mobs formed, those composing them entered shops and forced the employers to release their workers under threat of destroying the shop if the demands were resisted.

The rioters of the first day were described as being composed of "the employees of the several railroad companies; also the employees of Brown's iron factory in 41st Street; Cummin's street contractor, and numerous manufactories in the upper part of the city."

The rioters turned with great intensity against the colored people, even more than against the military officers and soldiers in the city, who were aiding the metropolitan police in enforcing the Draft Law. As soon as the disturbance began, mobs threatened to burn factories and foundries, giving as the reason that "negroes were employed in them." Some employers sought to forestall the rioters by discharging their colored workers.

By the second day of the rioting, the anger of the mob seemed to be turned more and more against the Negro population of the city. The draft seemed to be forgotten. The police and the few soldiers aiding them were attacked as a rule only when they went to the aid of the helpless people of color. The charge was made that the outbreak could not be attributed to "anything else than sympathy with the Rebels." The cry of the rioters was raised against "nigger, Abolition, Black Republican," along with denunciations of prominent members of the Republican party.

The Negroes of the city were hunted down, beaten, and killed with unbelievable ferocity. One of the city's newspapers reported that

A perfect reign of terror exists in the quarters of this helpless people, and if the troubles which now agitate our city continue during the week it is believed that not a single negro will remain within the metropolitan limits.

Other evidence indicated that when Negroes were caught by the rioters "they were hung up to lampposts, or beaten, jumped on, kicked and struck with iron bars and heavy wooden clubs." Not only were men attacked but women and children felt the hands of the rioters. Homes were sacked and the inmates driven to the streets.

The sacking of the homes of Negroes was not only evidence of the anti-Negro spirit of the mobs, but was also a display of the desire for loot. As it happened, the riot once under way took curious turns. Grogshops, stores, and the homes of the wealthy were looted.

The vicious attacks upon the Negroes drove them from the city by the thousands. By the time that thousands of soldiers had been brought into the city to restore order, over 3,000 colored people had been made homeless, and hundreds of others were lurking about the suburbs on Long Island and in the woods along the Harlem River. It seemed that they sought especially to escape their Irish persecutors. It was reported that many Negroes had fled to Hoboken because that place "has been a pretty safe refuge for them, as there are but few Irish living in that city." If the desire of the Irish was to intimidate the Negro workers of New York, they succeeded. By the third day of the riot one observer stated that "the negroes have entirely disappeared from the docks. Many of them, it is said, have been killed and thrown into the river."

4

THE SECOND RECONSTRUCTION AND THE
BEGINNINGS OF THE GREAT MIGRATION
1878–1914

In the last decades of the nineteenth century lynching became an institutionalized mode of social control, used against both whites and blacks in both the North and the South. Between 1882 (the first year for which records are available) and the turn of the century there was only one year in which fewer than one hundred lynchings were recorded—within most years, there were more Negro victims than white. The selection by Guzman details instances of collective violence against individuals by year, race, state, and alleged cause, for the period 1882–1951.

In the decade immediately preceding World War I a pattern began to emerge in which white assault was no longer directed against individual victims but against the black community as a whole. These assaults, in which no distinction of the guilt or innocence of the victims were made, occurred in both the South and the North. In some instances alleged crimes of individual Negroes were generalized to a characterization of a criminal black community; in others, causation was considerably more complex and reflected political disputes among whites as well as resentment against a growing Negro middle class. Two such riots, one in Atlanta and one in Springfield, Illinois, are described in the other selections in the chapter.

The Atlanta Massacre

[The following article is from an educated negro, a life-long resident of Georgia, in whom, were it safe to print his name, our readers would have every confidence. —Editor.]

Atlanta, Ga., has again demonstrated that it is not a civilized community. Last Saturday the Atlanta *News,* hard pressed for existence in competition with two other afternoon papers, felt called upon to print sensational charges of assault upon white women by negroes. Not one of these charges has yet been proved, but the mere report was enough to call together all the white "toughs" in the city as soon as they had drawn their week's wages, and to give them license to set upon innocent and unsuspecting blacks wherever found and butcher them upon the spot.

The cause of all this violence, by careful inquiry, I have traced to four sources—one remote and three immediate.

The remote cause is the contest between Hoke Smith and Clark Howell for Governor, in which both men openly declared that negroes have no rights save those granted thru sufferance by the white people. The three immediate causes are: (1) There was circulated by the Atlanta newspapers—*The News* and *The Georgian* especially—the report that five assaults had occurred in one week and an additional one on Saturday—*not one of which charges has been proved.* (2) There is a sharp struggle for existence among three evening papers, which feel called upon to use any measures whatsoever to attract readers among a population that can be best attracted by abuse of the negro. (3) There is an increasing number of educated and prosperous negroes, whose business and whose success are an eyesore to some of the whites, who can in no peaceable way prevent that progress, as the facts here will show.

The facts about the most aggravating case of assault I have found to be as follows: A negro whose purpose was unknown was seen in the yard of a white woman; she drove him away with abusive language without asking him about his mission; the negro again returned and the woman again began to call him vile names and to scream and to cry that the negro was attempting to assault her. A mob at once assembled, and before they had well got together all the evening papers— *The News* and *The Georgian* especially—were circulating "extras" under the glaring headlines, "Another Assault." Then separate and extra editions of *The News* appeared hourly until dark, saying, "Another Assault." It seemed only necessary for a white woman to see a negro meeting her in the same street or looking at her on her front porch to make her cry out, "Assault!"

That is the evidence that drove the editors mad and made them advocate the gathering of a mob to murder peaceable negroes. It is coming out little by little that the whole affair was planned. A negro lad, the driver of a laundry wagon, told me that his employer said to him Saturday morning, "Well, Sammie, we are going to kill all the niggers tonight." The most horrible exhibition of savagery was in the treatment of negro passengers on the street cars as often as they came into the public square—negro men, women and children were beaten unmercifully. Even the negro barbers were dragged out of their shops while they were shaving white men, beaten and their shops demolished. One of the finest shops in the whole country had the glass front smashed because the owner was colored. It is believed that this violence upon the barbers was done by white barbers who were members of the mob and who have been unable to cope successfully in Atlanta in competition with negro barbers. They used the mob as a cover to destroy their competitors.

A hardware store and a pawnshop were broken into by the mob, and all revolvers and ammunition taken, but none of the stores would sell weapons to negroes. A negro fled thru a fruit house kept by Greeks, and when the Greeks attempted to defend their store against the mob, it was straightway demolished and the fruit taken. A stable owner, with revolver in hand, defied the mob to break open his door to take his horses to chase negroes to the suburbs. This only shows what one policeman might have done.

Where were the policemen? That is what all negroes asked at first, but when the bluecoats began to halt them on back streets, arrest them upon State charges for carrying concealed weapons, it became plain that the policemen were not interested in quelling the mob. When one was seen in a crowd he made no effort to use his club or his gun to rescue a prisoner. One of the newspapers confesses that on Peachtree street, in the heart of the city, where the mob gathered, "only one policeman could be seen, and, of course, he could do nothing with such a mob."

Where were the conservative, good white people? That is not a question any one will ask when he knows that *ten* of the leading white pulpits in Atlanta are vacant because the pastors of moral courage have either been driven away or will not come to stifle their conscience in such service. On Sunday morning only one pastor stood up *positively* for law and order, according to statements published in the Atlanta *Constitution,* and that one was a Catholic bishop. All the others said it was what you might expect.

What will be the outcome of all this? That is more a question for the white people North and South than it is for negroes. It certainly is not going to make the lawless element of whites, who are very much in the majority in Georgia, disposed to hate the negro less when he beats them in competition, as in the case of the barbers; it certainly is not going to frighten the negroes who are actually bad, and it certainly is not going to make the great majority of negroes, who are honest, law-abiding folk, assume the responsibility of chasing down every one of their number who is merely accused by some malicious, frightened white woman, any more than a report of theft is going to make the honest bankers of New York close their doors to hunt down absconding cashiers because they happen to be of the same race. All that Christian piety in humble homes, all that honest labor and forbearance, and all that teaching and preaching can do has been done by the better element of negroes to help their fellows; and if the white people of the South are going to expect negroes to co-operate in catching negroes accused of crime, or actual criminals, when experience proves every day that such persons have no hope in the world of a fair trial, then the white people are doomed to disappointment.

William English Walling

The Race War in the North

"Lincoln freed you, we'll show you where you belong," was one of the cries with which the Springfield mob set about to drive the negroes from town. The mob was composed of several thousand of Springfield's white citizens, while other thousands, including many women and children, and even prosperous business men in automobiles, calmly looked on, and the rioters proceeded hour after hour and on two days in succession to make deadly assaults on every negro they could lay their hands on, to sack and plunder their houses and stores, and to burn and murder on favorable occasion.

The American people have been fairly well informed by their newspapers of the action of that mob; they have also been told of certain alleged political and criminal conditions in Springfield and of the two crimes in particular which are offered by the mob itself as sufficient explanation why six thousand peaceful and innocent negroes should be driven by the fear of their lives from a town where some of them have lived honorably for half a hundred years. We have been assured by more cautious and indirect defenders of Springfield's populace that there *was* an exceptionally criminal element among the negroes encouraged by the bosses of both political parties. And now, after a few days of discussion, we are satisfied with these explanations, and demand only the punishment of those who took the most active part in the destruction of life and property. Assuming that there were exceptionally provocative causes for complaint against the negroes, we have closed our eyes to the whole awful and menacing truth—that a large part of the white population of Lincoln's home, supported largely by the farmers and miners of the neighboring towns, have initiated a permanent warfare with the negro race.

We do not need to be informed at great length of the character of this warfare. It is in all respects like that of the South, on which it is modeled. Its significance is threefold. First, that it has occurred in an important and historical Northern town; then, that the negroes, constituting scarcely more than a tenth of the population, in this case could not possibly endanger the "supremacy" of the whites, and, finally, that the public opinion of the North, notwithstanding the fanatical, blind and almost insane hatred of the negro so clearly shown by the mob, is satisfied that there were "mitigating circumstances," not for the mob violence, which, it is agreed, should be punished to the full extent of the law, but for the race hatred, which is really the cause of it all. If these outrages had happened thirty years ago, when the memories of Lincoln, Garrison and Wendell Phillips were still fresh, what would not have happened in the North? Is there any doubt that the whole country would have been aflame, that all flimsy explanations and "mitigating circumstances" would have been thrown aside, and that the people of Springfield would have had to prove to the nation why they proposed to drive the negroes out, to hold a whole race responsible for a handful of criminals, and to force it to inferior place on the social scale?

For the underlying motive of the mob and of that large portion of Springfield's population that has long said that "something was bound to happen," and now approves of the riot and proposes to complete its purpose by using other means to drive as many as possible of the remaining two-thirds of the negroes out of town, was confessedly to teach the negroes their place and to warn them that too many could not obtain shelter under the favorable traditions of Lincoln's home town. I talked to many of them the day after the massacre and found no difference of opinion on the question. "Why, the niggers came to think they were as good as we are!" was the final justification offered, not once, but a dozen times.

. . . Springfield had no shame. She stood for the action of the mob. She hoped the rest of the negroes might flee. She threatened that the movement to drive them out would continue. I do not speak of the leading citizens, but of the masses of the people, of workingmen in the shops, the storekeepers in the stores, the drivers, the men on the street, the wounded in the hospitals and even the notorious "Joan of Arc" of the mob, Kate Howard, who had just been released from arrest on $4,000 bail. [She has since committed suicide.—*Editor.*] The *Illinois*

State Journal of Springfield expressed the prevailing feeling even on its editorial page:

While all good citizens deplore the consequences of this outburst of the mob spirit, many even of these consider the outburst was *inevitable,* at some time, from existing conditions, needing only an overt act, such as that of Thursday night, to bring it from latent existence into active operation. The implication is clear that conditions, not the populace, were to blame and that many good citizens could find no other remedy than that applied by the mob. It was not the fact of the whites' hatred toward the negroes, but of the negroes' own misconduct, general inferiority or unfitness for free institutions that were at fault.

On Sunday, August 16th, the day after the second lynching, a leading white minister recommended the Southern disfranchisement scheme as a remedy for *negro* (!) lawlessness, while all four ministers who were quoted in the press proposed swift "justice" for *the negroes,* rather than recommending true Christianity, democracy and brotherhood to the whites. Even the Governor's statement of the situation, strong as it was on the whole, was tainted in one place with a concession to Springfield opinion. He said that Burton, the first negro lynched, was killed after he had incensed the crowd by firing into it to protect his home from incendiaries. But when Burton's home was attacked there had already been considerable shooting between the blacks and the whites. Moreover, according to his daughters, men had entered the house and threatened him with an axe and other weapons, while his firing of buckshot at random into a mob is by no means necessarily a murderous procedure. The Governor made, then, an understatement of the character of the mob, suggesting that the negroes had lost their heads and were accepting the mob's challenge to war. It is probable that Burton was defending not his home, but his life.

Besides suggestions in high places of the negro's brutality, criminality and unfitness for the ballot we heard in lower ranks all the opinions that pervade the South—that the negro does not need much education, that his present education even has been a mistake, that whites cannot live in the same community with negroes except where the latter have been taught their inferiority, that lynching is the only way to teach them, etc. In fact, this went so far that we were led to suspect the existence of a Southern element in the town, and this is indeed the case. Many of the older citizens are from Kentucky or the southern part of Illinois. Moreover, many of the street railway employees are from the South. It was a street railway man's wife that was assaulted the night before the riots, and they were street railway employees, among others, that led the mob to the jail. Even the famous Kate Howard had received her inspiration she told us, from the South. While traveling with her brother in Texas and Arkansas she had observed enviously that enforced separation of the races in cars and public places helped to teach the negro where he belonged. Returning home she had noticed the growing boycott of negroes in Springfield stores and restaurants, participated in

the alarm that "no white woman was safe," etc., and in the demand for
negro blood. A woman of evident physical courage, she held that it was
time for the population to act up to their professions, and by the cry
of "cowards" is said to have goaded the mob into some of the worst of
its deeds. She exhibited to us proudly the buckshot wounds in her fleshy
arms (probably Burton's), and said she relied confidently on her fellow
citizens to keep her from punishment.

This was the feeling also of the half hundred whites in the hospital.
It was, in fact, only three days after the first disturbance when they fully
realized that the lenient public opinion of Springfield was not the public
opinion of Illinois or the North, that the rioters began to tremble. Still
this did not prevent them later from insulting the militia, repeatedly
firing at their outposts and almost openly organizing a political and
business boycott to drive the remaining negroes out. Negro employers
continue to receive threatening letters and are dismissing employees
every day, while the stores, even the groceries, so fear to sell the negroes
goods that the State has been compelled to intervene and purchase
$10,000 worth in their behalf.

The menace is that if this thing continues it will offer *automatic
rewards* to the riotous elements and negro haters in Springfield, make
the reign of terror permanent there, and offer every temptation to similar white elements in other towns to imitate Springfield's example.

If the new Political League succeeds in permanently driving every
negro from office; if the white laborers get the negro laborers' jobs; if
masters of negro servants are able to keep them under the discipline of
terror as I saw them doing at Springfield; if white shopkeepers and sa-
loonkeepers get their colored rivals' trade; if the farmers of neighboring
towns establish permanently their right to drive poor people out of their
community, instead of offering them reasonable alms; if white miners
can force their negro fellow-workers out and get their positions by closing the mines, then every community indulging in an outburst of race
hatred will be assured of a great and certain financial reward, and all
the lies, ignorance and brutality on which race hatred is based will
spread over the land. For the action of these dozen farming and four
coal mining communities near Springfield shows how rapidly the thing
can spread. In the little town of Buffalo, fifteen miles away, for instance,
they have just posted this sign in front of the interurban station:

All niggers are warned out of town by Monday, 12 m. sharp.
                                        BUFFALO SHARP SHOOTERS

Part of the Springfield press, far from discouraging this new effort to
drive the negroes out, a far more serious attack on our colored brothers
than the mob violence, either fails to condemn it in the only possible
way, a complete denial of the whole hypocritical case against the negro,
or indirectly approves it. An evening paper printed this on the third
day after the outbreak:

NEGRO FAMILY
      LEAVES CITY
         WHEN ORDERED

The first negro family routed from Springfield by a mob was the Harvey family residing at 1144 North Seventh street, who were told Sunday morning to 'hike,' and carried out the orders yesterday afternoon. The family proved themselves obnoxious in many ways. They were the one negro family in the block and their presence was distasteful to all other citizens in that vicinity.

The tone of this notice is that of a jubilant threat. As the family left town only the day after, not on account of the mob, but the standing menace, the use of the word "first" is significant.

We have not mentioned the negro crimes which are alleged to have caused the disorders, as we are of the opinion that they could scarcely in any case have had much real connection either with the mob violence or the far more important race conflict that is still spreading geographically and growing in intensity from day to day.

The first crime is called a murder, resulting from an assault on a woman. An unknown negro was discovered at night in the room of two young white girls. The father and mother and two sons were also at home, however, and there is every probability that it was no assault but a common burglary. The father attacked the negro, was terribly cut up, and died. A few hours later a negro was found sleeping not very far away, and the press claimed that there was every evidence that he was the criminal. However, Judge Creighton, a man respected by the whole community, saw cause to postpone the case, and it was this short delay of six weeks that was used by the enemies of the negro in Springfield to suggest that the negroes' political influence was thwarting the "swift justice" of the law.

The *State Journal*, ignoring the common sense of the situation, stated editorially that Ballard, the victim, "had given his life in defense of his child," and added significantly: "This tragedy was not enacted in the black belt of Mississippi or of Georgia," and further, twelve lines below,

Concerning him (the negro) and the questions which arise from his presence in the community, it is well to preserve silence at the present time. The state of the public mind is such that comment can only add fuel to the feeling that has burst forth with general knowledge of the crime.

The writer has been rather cautious, but has he not succeeded in suggesting clearly enough to readers of the character we have mentioned (1) that the deed was to be connected in some way with the race question; (2) that the public mind as it was, and events have since shown the world clearly what the writer must have known at that time, was justified; and (3) in directing their attention to the South as a basis of comparison?

Then what was the second crime, which occurred six weeks later, early in the morning of August 15th? This was an assault by a negro on a white woman in her home. There is little doubt of the nature of the crime intended. But in this case there was far more doubt of the identity of the negro arrested for the crime, who was of a relatively good character. However, the victim's portrait was printed and circulated among the crowd, first as an incentive to lynch the suspected negro, then as a pretext for driving the negroes out.

As we do not lay much emphasis on these or the previous crimes of Springfield negroes, which were in no way in excess of those of the corresponding social elements of the white population, so we do not lay much stress on the frenzied, morbid violence of the mob. Mob psychology is the same everywhere. It can begin on a little thing. But Springfield had many mobs; they lasted two days and they initiated a state of affairs far worse than any of the immediate effects of their violence.

Either the spirit of the abolitionists, of Lincoln and of Lovejoy must be revived and we must come to treat the negro on a plane of absolute political and social equality, or Vardaman and Tillman will soon have transferred the race war to the North.

Already Vardaman boasts "that such sad experiences as Springfield is undergoing will doubtless cause the people of the North to look with more toleration upon the methods employed by the Southern people."

The day these methods become general in the North every hope of political democracy will be dead, other weaker races and classes will be persecuted in the North as in the South, public education will undergo an eclipse, and American civilization will await either a rapid degeneration or another profounder and more revolutionary civil war, which shall obliterate not only the remains of slavery but all the other obstacles to a free democratic evolution that have grown up in its wake.

Yet who realizes the seriousness of the situation, and what large and powerful body of citizens is ready to come to their aid?

Anonymous

The So-Called Race Riot at Springfield, Illinois

No mob, or mob violence can disturb a community unless there exists behind the immediate cause of the outbreak a wrong state of affairs, vicious conditions, as complex as society itself, of which it is the inevitable outcome.

The conditions which led up to the rioting in Springfield grew out of bad politics. The seeds of mob violence were sown, not when the first Negroes came to Springfield, but when municipal rottenness fertilized the lower strata of society.

The buying and selling of votes in Springfield began about twenty years ago when the infamous Indiana "blocks of five" system of delivery of votes was introduced into this community. About the same time the gamblers' ring began to dominate municipal affairs. This it did by securing, previous to an election, pledges of immunity from the candidates of both parties, if possible. If a candidate failed to give such a pledge, its money and energy were used to defeat him. The Negro vote is large enough to be of importance in the elections and the Negro vote can be bought. While money is a consideration, the real price is immunity for the notorious law-breakers who are understood to be in a position to deliver the votes.

This failure on the part of officials to enforce the law, either for political preferment or for graft, has fostered for years a lawless class among both Negroes and whites, until it violated every law with impunity. The mob which almost took possession of Springfield, and came very near burning the whole city, was made up almost entirely of flagrant law-breakers. The vile criminal whose punishment served as a pretext for the riot was but little, if any, worse than the men who made up the mob. That murder, arson and loot, and not outraged justice prompted them was evident to any observer, and was proven by the fact that stolen property was found in the possession of nearly everyone indicted.

I was an eye witness of the affair, and have gained many facts from conversation with the governor, the sheriff, and the firemen who fought the flames while shots were being fired about them, and I am positive that the mob proper numbered, at no time, more than four hundred lawless men and women. The crowd, at one time numbering ten thousand people, was composed of mere onlookers, attracted by curiosity. A determined show of authority on the part of the police at the beginning would have prevented the whole trouble. Fifteen men who meant business could have handled the situation.

A few weeks before the riot, the city was aroused by the murder of a Mr. Ballard, a thoroughly reputable citizen, by a Negro named James, who had been discovered by Mr. Ballard's nineteen year old daughter in her room in the night. Ballard grappled with the Negro, and was stabbed to death with a knife. The Negro was discovered later by a searching party, stupefied with drink, and asleep on the ground. The men who found him kicked and beat him, but no attempt was made to lynch him. He was confined in the jail awaiting trial.

On August 13 Mrs. Hallam, the young wife of a street car conductor, alleged that she was attacked while in her home, in bed, dragged into the yard and outraged. She accused George Richardson, a Negro who had been working on a house near her home. The Negro was taken into custody by the sheriff about noon. At two o'clock he was identified by Mrs. Hallam. Before the sheriff was satisfied with the identification he was compelled to take the Negro to the jail because of threats of violence to his prisoner. The mob began to assemble about the jail, and at four o'clock the crowd numbered about three thousand people. At five o'clock, after an alarm of fire was turned in, the two Negroes, James and Richardson, in view of part of the crowd, were placed in an automobile owned and driven by Mr. Loper who had frequently done automobile service for the sheriff or his deputies, and taken a few miles north of the city, where a train was flagged, and thence carried to Bloomington, sixty miles north. A large number of persons in the crowd, not believing the Negroes had been taken away, demanded to go through the jail. The sheriff permitted them to select a committee of three, though they wanted seven, who about seven o'clock went through the jail. The mob was still unsatisfied and a half hour later three others were allowed to make the search. Those outside were still not satisfied but the sheriff then told them emphatically that he would not permit any more foolishness and he began clearing the streets about the jail. The members of Company C and Troop D, I. N. G., who had begun assembling at the jail about 6:30 P.M. assisted the sheriff in dispersing the mob, firing two volleys over the heads of the crowd. The officers and soldiers were stoned by the rioters. Some of the crowd, among them the woman, Mrs. Kate Howard, who was later arrested, indicted for murder for participation in the lynching of Scott Burton, and who committed suicide on the way to the jail,—started the cry, "To Loper's"—Loper's being the restaurant owned by the man who had taken the Negroes away in his automobile.

About eight o'clock the mob reached Loper's restaurant. The obnoxious automobile was standing in front. The rioters demanded of Mr. Loper that he tell them where the Negroes were. This he refused to do, in spite of their threats. Then they broke in the front of the building with bricks and stones, upturned the automobile and set fire to it, and looted the place. The basement was used as a saloon, and they drank the liquors. I saw one group carrying off a tub of bottles of champagne; all were drinking from bottles. The money was stolen from the cash register, and even the silver and table linen were carried off, many of those arrested being found with the loot in their possession.

It took about three hours to wreck Loper's place. From there the now drunken mob went to East Washington street, the "Levee," where it demolished and looted the Negro saloons and stores. One pawn shop was looted, on the pretext—purely fabricated—that the owner had furnished firearms to the Negroes, and here a number of revolvers were secured by the rioters who then went to the "bad lands" and began burning the houses of the Negroes. All the houses occupied by Negroes were burned from Ninth eastward to Twelfth street where Burton was hanged to a tree, after being shot, he having fired three shots at the mob from his door.

It was here that the first troops to arrive encountered the mob. After warning the rioters and firing two volleys in the air, they fired low and the rioting immediately ceased.

The personnel of the mob changed materially in its course from the time it left the jail until the troops dispersed it. At the jail the mob was made up of determined men, bent upon lynching the Negroes. The rioters at Loper's were largely very young men, lawless and bent on any kind of mischief, and a gang of thieves and anarchists. Later, on the Levee, still more of the worst class joined them and all of them, drunk with liquor from the wrecked saloons, were ready for murder and arson. One of the leaders carried a red flag. By the time the troops arrived on the scene the better element had almost entirely disappeared from the ranks of the mob.

Enough cannot be said in praise of Governor Deneen and his firm and efficient handling of the situation. He was in his office at the state house all night directing the movements. As soon as the troops arrived he ordered that the refugees should be quartered in the state arsenal located across the street from the state house, and also opened up Camp Lincoln for their protection.

The police force of the city was flagrantly unequal to its task of restoring order; some of the policemen were even criminally indifferent. Four in uniform were stationed in front of Loper's restaurant while the mob was slowly breaking in the glass front by throwing bricks. These policemen stood in the front rank of the mob, calmly watching the destruction, with no more attempt at interference than there would have been if the destruction had been ordered by their chief.

The flying bricks and stones kept a space cleared in front of the restaurant. I saw one young man jostle a policeman, step out into the clear space directly in front of him, hurl a brick through the plate glass, turn about as the mob cheered, look the policeman squarely in the face, and swagger back into the mob, the policeman seeming to say by his manner, "That was well done."

A dozen determined policemen could have stopped the rioting in front of Loper's—probably not without some bruises, but wounds would be glorious compared with the ignominy of being indicted for cowardice and neglect of duty as four of them were, and denounced as they all were by the grand jury in its special report. . . .

The conviction of the policemen will do more to atone for the great outrage against this community than the conviction of the rioters.

The killing of the Negro, Donnegan, was a cold-blooded murder, perpetrated by a handful of young desperadoes on the flimsy pretext that he had a white wife, and that he refused to sell his property or move away from the neighborhood of white people. The act was in no way representative of any but the worst criminal class who, emboldened by the acts of defiance of the mob, determined to satisfy a lust for murder.

On August 31 the community was horrified to learn that Mrs. Hallam had made affidavit that the Negro, George Richardson, was not the one that had assaulted her.

Here is what followed the arrest of the wrong man:

Two Negroes killed by mob.

Five white men killed by rioters.

One woman ended her life, following her indictment for murder.

One Negro child died of exposure when parents were fleeing from the city.

One hundred persons were more or less seriously injured; many of them maimed for life.

Property estimated at $120,000 destroyed.

Forty Negro families rendered homeless through the burning of their residences.

Fifteen business houses wrecked.

Two thousand black men, women and children driven from the city.

Four thousand militiamen brought to the city to re-establish order; cost to state $200,000.

Business paralyzed for period of ten days.

One hundred and seven indictments returned by a special grand jury, charging men and women with the various crimes of murder, arson, burglary and larceny, rioting and malicious mischief.

Suits and claims aggregating $120,000 filed against the city for damages resulting from deaths, personal injuries and destruction of property.

There are about 4,500 Negroes in Springfield, with a total population of sixty thousand. The Negro of Springfield is not the Negro of the South. He is usually ready to open up an argument that he is just as good as a white man. Whether he is or not matters little. A Jap [sic!] would create just as much hatred and opposition if he should take this aggressive attitude.

The politicians who have truckled for their votes have told the Negroes again and again that they are the white man's equal, and have given them places on the police force and other city jobs. This, with their arrogant bearing toward those of our people who resent their pretensions; their laziness, dishonesty and vicious tendencies, have created a strong feeling against them among our citizens, and a mutual distrust and dislike unknown to the South. There is a saving element of the thrifty and law-abiding class, who are respectable and respected, but the majority are worthless or genuinely bad, and have brought the whole race under condemnation in the community.

The city has been, through a trial by fire and blood, brought to a sudden and solemn realization of these evil conditions and their results.

If the good citizens are aroused and inspired to act wisely and firmly the city will be purified, and a wiser and better Springfield will result from this chastisement.

Jessie Parkhurst Guzman, Editor

Lynching

LYNCHINGS BY STATES AND RACE

Table 1 presents the number of lynchings that have occurred in the United States, 1882–1951, for each state for Negroes and whites. During this period more than two and one-half times as many Negroes as whites were put to death by lynching. The State of Mississippi has the highest incidence of lynchings for the South as well as the highest for the United States, with Georgia and Texas taking second and third places, respectively.

LYNCHINGS BY YEAR AND RACE

Table 2 gives the number of whites and Negroes lynched yearly from 1882 through 1951. The largest number of lynchings occurred in 1892. Of the 230 persons lynched during that year, 161 were Negroes and 69 whites. But during 1884, the next highest year, with 211 lynchings, 160 were white and 51 Negroes. Each year since 1882 at least 1 Negro has been lynched.

CAUSES OF LYNCHINGS CLASSIFIED

Being charged with a crime does not necessarily mean that the person lynched was guilty of the crime. Mob victims have been known to be innocent of misdeeds. Sometimes mobs have been mistaken in the identity of their victims. Lynchings have occurred for such trivial matters as "peeping in a window," "disputing with a white man," or

Table 1. *Lynchings, by States and Race, 1882-1951*

State	Whites	Negroes	Total
Alabama	48	299	347
Arizona	31	0	31
Arkansas	58	226	284
California	41	2	43
Colorado	66	2	68
Delaware	0	1	1
Florida	25	257	282
Georgia	39	491	530
Idaho	20	0	20
Illinois	15	19	34
Indiana	33	14	47
Iowa	17	2	19
Kansas	35	19	54
Kentucky	63	142	205
Louisiana	56	335	391
Maryland	2	27	29
Michigan	7	1	8
Minnesota	5	4	9
Mississippi	40	534	574
Missouri	53	69	122
Montana	82	2	84
Nebraska	52	5	57
Nevada	6	0	6
New Jersey	0	1	1
New Mexico	33	3	36
New York	1	1	2
N. Carolina	15	84	99
N. Dakota	13	3	16
Ohio	10	16	26
Oklahoma	82	40	122
Oregon	20	1	21
Pennsylvania	2	6	8
S. Carolina	4	156	160
S. Dakota	27	0	27
Tennessee	47	204	251
Texas	141	352	493
Utah	6	2	8
Virginia	17	83	100
Washington	25	1	26
W. Virginia	20	28	48
Wisconsin	6	0	6
Wyoming	30	5	35
TOTAL	1,293	3,437	4,730

"attempting to qualify to vote." Such causes are classified under "All Other Causes." Homicides lead all causes of lynchings. See Table 3.

LYNCHINGS PREVENTED

The wide publicity given to lynchings has created sentiment against the practice to the extent that communities do not desire the criticism they receive when a lynching occurs within their borders. Officers of the law are condemned when they are suspected of making no attempt to prevent

Table 2. Lynchings, by Years and Race, 1882–1951

Year	Whites	Negroes	Total
1882	64	49	113
1883	77	53	130
1884	160	51	211
1885	110	74	184
1886	64	74	138
1887	50	70	120
1888	68	69	137
1889	76	94	170
1890	11	85	96
1891	71	113	184
1892	69	161	230
1893	34	118	152
1894	58	134	192
1895	66	113	179
1896	45	78	123
1897	35	123	158
1898	19	101	120
1899	21	85	106
1900	9	106	115
1901	25	105	130
1902	7	85	92
1903	15	84	99
1904	7	76	83
1905	5	57	62
1906	3	62	65
1907	2	58	60
1908	8	89	97
1909	13	69	82
1910	9	67	76
1911	7	60	67
1912	2	61	63
1913	1	51	52
1914	4	51	55
1915	13	56	69
1916	4	50	54
1917	2	36	38
1918	4	60	64
1919	7	76	83
1920	8	53	61
1921	5	59	64
1922	6	51	57
1923	4	29	33
1924	0	16	16
1925	0	17	17
1926	7	23	30
1927	0	16	16
1928	1	10	11
1929	3	7	10
1930	1	20	21
1931	1	12	13
1932	2	6	8
1933	4	24	28
1934	0	15	15
1935	2	18	20
1936	0	8	8
1937	0	8	8
1938	0	6	6
1939	1	2	3

Year	Whites	Negroes	Total
1940	1	4	5
1941	0	4	4
1942	0	6	6
1943	0	3	3
1944	0	2	2
1945	0	1	1
1946	0	6	6
1947	0	1	1
1948	1	1	2
1949	0	3	3
1950	1	1	2
1951	0	1	1

Table 3. Causes of Lynchings Classified, 1882-1951

	Number	Per Cent
Homicides	1,937	41.0
Felonious assault	204	4.3
Rape	910	19.2
Attempted rape	288	6.1
Robbery and theft	232	4.9
Insult to white person	84	1.8
All other causes	1,075	22.7
TOTALS	4,730	100.0

lynchings, when they are a party to a lynching, or when they connive with those bent on lynching. However, throughout the history of lynching in the United States, some officers have "out-thought and out-maneuvered mobs." The vigilance of law enforcement officials and the intelligent action of numbers of private citizens have kept many intended victims from being put to death. Were precautions not taken to save accused persons from mob law, such as augmenting guards, removing the prisoner to a place of safekeeping, using force to disperse the mob, or some other stratagem, the annual lynching record would contain more names than are now listed.

5

WORLD WAR I AND POSTWAR BOOM AND RACIAL READJUSTMENT 1915–1929

Large-scale interracial violence became almost endemic in the United States toward the end of the first World War and during the months immediately following it. In extent and distribution of violence the period can be compared only with that of the past five years. Two of the more dramatic and costly disturbances occurred in East St. Louis in 1917 and in Chicago in 1919. There are selections in the chapter following from the formal investigations of those disturbances, a select congressional committee investigation of East St. Louis and a "blue-ribbon" committee report on race relations in Chicago. Although some recent scholars have begun to be critical of the Chicago Commission report (Waskow, 1966), it probably is still the best single case study.

In 1917 Negro troops stationed in Houston mutinied and actually seized arms and marched on the city. Schuler's article reviews the chronology of this unusual event and comments on the causes. Another unusual manifestation of racial violence, one with strong class overtones, occurred in Arkansas in 1919 when black tenant farmers assaulted whites in what some observers felt was an IWW-inspired insurrection. Two brief selections from *The New York Times* detail both the events and speculations about their cause. Other selections from the *Times* include a fragment of the coverage of a lynching in Omaha that developed into a more general assault and editorial comment on the Chicago riot. Readers will observe that the *Times* itself has changed its perspective.

In the final selection I have examined in some detail the riots of East St. Louis, Chicago, and Tulsa, and have attempted to distinguish among "Southern style," "Northern style," and "mixed type" riots, with reference to differences both in modes of assault on the accommodative structure and in the actual chronologies of the several disturbances.

Ben Johnson, John E. Raker, M. D. Foster and Henry Allen Cooper

East St. Louis Riots: Report of the Special Committee Authorized by Congress to Investigate the East St. Louis Riots

Your committee, appointed under House resolution No. 128 for the purpose of making investigation of the East St. Louis riots which occurred on May 28 and July 2, 1917, reports that as a result of unlawful conditions existing at that place, interstate commerce was not only openly and violently interrupted but was virtually suspended for a week or 10 days during and following the riot of last July. For months after the July riot, interstate commerce was interfered with and hindered, not, however, by open acts of violence, but by a subtle and effective intimidation of colored men who had been employed by the railroads to handle freight consigned from one State to another. So many of these men were driven out of East St. Louis as the result of the July riot that the railroads could not secure necessary help. After the worst effects of the riot had passed, this class of labor remained so frightened and intimidated that it would not live in East St. Louis. Some of them took up their residences across the river in St. Louis, and would go over to East St. Louis in the morning to work and would return to that place before nightfall. In order to get out of East St. Louis and back to St. Louis before night came on the length of the day's work was reduced. The fright of these laborers went to such an extent—and it was fully justified by existing conditions—that special means of transportation had to be provided for them back and forth between St. Louis and East St. Louis in order to get them to work at all. Besides the killing of a number of these negro laborers, a very large number, indeed, fled from the work and never returned to it. In addition to this, 44 freight cars were burned and serious damage done to the railroad tracks, all of which will be referred to further along in this report.

Your committee made an earnest, nonpartisan effort to determine the basic cause of the riot. We endeavored to pursue every avenue of information to its source, searched the hearts and consciences of all witnesses, and sought the opinions of men in every walk of life. The officers of the mills and factories placed the blame at the door of organized labor; but the overwhelming weight of testimony, to which is added the convictions of the committee, ascribes the mob spirit and its murderous manifestations to the bitter race feeling that had grown up between the whites and the blacks.

The natural racial aversion, which finds expression in mob violence in the North as in the South, was augmented in East St. Louis by hundreds of petty conflicts between the whites and the blacks. During the year 1917, between 10,000 and 12,000 negroes came from the Southern States to seek work at promised high wages in the industries of St. Clair County. They swarmed into the railroad stations on every train, to be met by their friends who formed reception committees and welcomed them to the financial, political and social liberty which they had been led to believe Illinois guaranteed. They seldom had more than enough money to exactly defray their transportation, and they arrived dirty and hungry. They stood around the street corners in homesick huddles, seeking shelter and hunting work.

How to deal with them soon became a municipal problem. Morning found them gathered at the gates of the manufactories, where often they were chosen in preference to the white men who also sought employment. But as rapidly as employment was found for those already there, fresh swarms arrived from the South, until the great number without employment menaced the prosperity and safety of the community.

The Aluminum Ore Co. brought hundreds and hundreds of them to the city as strike breakers, to defeat organized labor, a precedent which aroused intense hatred and antagonism and caused countless tragedies as its aftermath. The feeling of resentment grew with each succeeding day. White men walked the streets in idleness, their families suffering for food and warmth and clothes, while their places as laborers were taken by strange negroes who were compelled to live in hovels and who were used to keep down wages.

It was proven conclusively that the various industries in St. Clair County were directly responsible for the importation of these negroes from the South. Advertisements were printed in various Southern newspapers urging the negroes to come to East St. Louis and promising them big wages. In many instances agents were sent through the South to urge the negroes to abandon profitable employment there and come to East St. Louis, where work was said to be plentiful and wages high.

One of the local railroads sent an agent to the Southern states, and on some trips he brought back with him as many as 30 or 40 negro men, all of them employed at their southern homes, making from $2 to $2.50 a day. A number of these men testified before the committee that they were promised $2.40 a day "and board" if they would come to East St. Louis; but when they did come they were paid only $1.40 a day, with an allowance of 60 cents a day for board, and were fed on coffee, bread and "lasses" and made to sleep on sacks in box cars, where they suffered keenly from the cold.

Responsibility for this influx of 10,000 or more negroes into East St. Louis rests on the railroads and the manufacturing establishments, and they must bear their share of the responsibility for the ensuing arson and murder that followed this unfortunate invasion.

It is a lamentable fact that the employers of labor paid too little heed to the comfort or welfare of their men. They saw them crowded into wretched cabins, without water or any of the conveniences of life, their wives and children condemned to live in the disreputable quarters of the town, and made no effort to lift them out of the mire.

The negroes gravitated to the unsanitary sections, existed in the squalor of filthy cabins, and made no complaint; but the white workmen had a higher outlook, and the failure to provide them with better homes added to their bitter dissatisfaction with the burdens placed upon them by having to compete with black labor. This resentment spread until it included thousands who did not have to work with their hands.

Ten thousand and more strange negroes added to the already large colored population soon made East St. Louis a center of lawlessness. Within less than a year before the riot over 800 "holdups" were committed in the city. More than 80 per cent of the murders were committed by negroes. Highway robberies were nightly occurrences; rape was frequent; while a host of petty offenses kept the law-abiding citizens in a state of terror.

White women were afraid to walk the streets at night; negroes sat in their laps on street cars; black women crowded them from their seats; they were openly insulted by drunken negroes. The low saloons and gambling houses were crowded with idle vagabonds; the dance halls in the negro sections were filled with prostitues, half clad, in some instances naked, performing lewd dances.

Negroes were induced to buy homes in white districts by unscrupulous real estate agents; and, as a consequence, the white people sold their homes at a sacrifice and moved elsewhere.

Owners of cheap property preferred negroes as tenants, charging them $15 a month rent for houses for which white workmen had paid only $10.

Corrupt politicians found the negro vote fitted to their foul purposes and not only bought them on election day, but in the interval protected them in their dens of vice, their low saloons and barrel houses. They had immunity in the courts; crooked lawyers kept them out of jail; and a disorganized, grafting police force saw to it that they were not molested.

East St. Louis wallowed in a mire of lawlessness and unshamed corruption. Criminals from every quarter of the country gathered there, unmolested and safe from detection.

This was the condition of affairs on the night of July 1, 1917, when an automobile—some witnesses say there were two—went through a negro section of the city and fired promiscuously into their homes. No one was injured, but the act aroused a fierce spirit in the breasts of the negroes.

The ringing of a church bell at midnight, which was a prearranged signal, drew a crowd of negroes from that immediate section armed with guns and pistols. They marched through the streets ready to avenge the attack on their homes. They had not gone far until an automobile containing several policemen and a newspaper reporter crossed their path, having been notified by telephone that there was danger of an outbreak. The negroes cursed them and told them to drive on, although one of the detectives flashed his police badge and assured them that they had come to protect them.

For answer the negro mob fired a volley into the machine which, at the first shot, drove rapidly away. The negroes continued to empty their guns and pistols, with the result that one of the officers was instantly killed and another so badly wounded that he died later.

The police automobile, riddled with bullets, stood in front of police headquarters next morning and thousands viewed it. The early editions of the papers gave full details of the tragedy of the night before. And, on July 2, East St. Louis awoke to a realization of the awful fact that the dread which had knocked at every heart for months could no longer be denied. Years of lawlessness had at last borne bloody fruit. As the day wore on negro mobs killed other white men, and shot at men and women who were offering them no wrong.

Dr. McQuillan, a well-known physician, and his wife were dragged from their machine and shamefully abused. The doctor was shot, his ribs were broken, and both he and his wife were badly beaten. One of his assailants remarked, "Boys, this is Dr. McQuillan, the Aluminum Ore Co. doctor," and pleaded for his life. The would-be murderers, some of whom must have been employed by the Ore Co., helped the doctor and his wife into their machine and, cranking it for them, sent them on their way.

The news of these attacks and fresh outrages spread rapidly, and the streets soon filled with excited people. Men and boys, girls and women of the town began to attack every negro in sight. All fared alike, young and old, women and children; no one was spared. The crowd soon grew to riotous proportions, and for hours the manhunt continued, stabbing, clubbing and shooting, not the guilty, but unoffending negroes. One was hanged from a telephone pole and another had a rope tied around his neck and was dragged through the streets, the maddened crowd kicking and beating him as he lay prostrate and helpless.

The negroes were pursued into their homes, and the torch completed the work of destruction. As they fled from the flames they were shot down, although many of them came out with uplifted hands, pleading to be spared.

It was a day and night given over to arson and murder. Scenes of horror that would have shocked a savage were viewed with placid unconcern by hundreds, whose hearts knew no pity, and who seemed to revel in the feast of blood and cruelty.

It is not possible to give accurately the number of dead. At least 39 negroes and 8 white people were killed outright, and hundreds of negroes were wounded and maimed. "The bodies of the dead negroes," testified an eyewitness, "were thrown into a morgue like so many dead hogs."

There were 312 buildings and 44 railroad cars and their contents destroyed by fire; a total loss of $393,600. Your committee can not go into all the harrowing details of how the negroes—men, women and children—were killed and burned during the riot, but there were so many flagrantly cruel cases that a bare recital of the facts concerning some of them will be given.

At Collinsville and Illinois avenues a negro man and his wife and 14-year-old boy were assaulted. The man was beaten to death; his head was crushed in as if by a blow from a stone, and the boy was shot and killed. The woman was very badly injured; her hair was torn out by the roots and her scalp was partly torn off by someone who took hold of the ragged edges of a wound and scalped her. After a time an ambulance drove up and the bodies of these three negroes were loaded into it. The father and the son were dead, and when the woman regained consciousness she found herself lying on the dead bodies of her husband and child. This family lived across the Mississippi River in St. Louis and were on their way home after having been on a fishing trip north of East St. Louis. They were innocent of any connection with the race feeling that brought about the riot and were victims of the savage brutality of the mob, who spared neither age nor sex in their blind lust for blood.

Another negro who was trying to escape from a mob of 30 or 40 men was knocked down, kicked in the face, beaten into insensibility; and then a man stood over him and shot him five times as he lay helpless in the street.

A white man shot at a negro and killed another white man, his bad aim infuriating the mob that pursued the unoffending negro.

Two negroes were taken from a streetcar at Illinois and Collinsville avenues. They were on their way to St. Louis to escape the fury of the mob. Both were killed.

Near the stock yards a white man knocked a negro senseless from a wagon, and when two reporters offered to take the wounded man to the hospital another white man threatened their lives and forced them to drive away and leave him.

At Collinsville and Division avenues a mob of about 100 men drove a negro into the street, knocked him down, stamped on his face, and one of the crowd drew a pistol and shot him through the head, the bullet coming out between his eyes.

An old negro, about 70 years old, stepped off a streetcar, having come from St. Louis on his way home. The mob immediately attacked him with such fury that he was left senseless after being stoned and beaten. A witness who described this particular case to your committee said: "This old man, his dinner bucket lying on the ground beside him, apparently was dead, although he had his arm arched up over his face as if to protect himself from blows. About that time an ambulance driver came up and started to pick him up to put him into the ambulance. A white man standing over him said, "If you pick up this negro, you'll get what he got." I saw that same negro in the undertaking establishment the next day, dead, with his arm still arched over his face."

Around Third Street and Brady Avenue the mob was firing promiscuously into houses and sheds where the negroes had taken shelter. Every time one of them ran from these houses he was shot and killed.

The rioting continued all along Broadway, between Collinsville Avenue and Eighth Street; houses were burned and the poor wretches were driven from their homes or shot as they were trying to escape the flames. Two of them, with hands above their heads, were shot and killed.

A negro child 2 years old was shot and thrown into the doorway of a burning building, and nothing ever was found of the remains.

There was a crippled negro who took care of the horses and mules for the Hill-Thomas Lime & Cement Co. He was a faithful, hardworking, loyal fellow. The day of the riot his employer's stable was in the path of the flames. He called up Mr. Thomas, his boss, on the telephone, and said: "I just called you up to tell you good-bye. I'm here in the barn, and I ain't goin' to leave; I've turned all the stock out; I'm going to stay here; I'm not going outside to be shot."

This faithful negro must have been consumed in the flames as no trace of him ever was found.

It is impossible to say how many people perished in the 312 houses that were burned by the mob, but many negroes who lived in those houses still are missing, and it is not possible to get an accurate report as to just how many found death in the flames.

East St. Louis for many years has been a plague spot; within its borders and throughout its environs every offense in the calendar of crime and every lapse in morals and public decency has been openly committed, each day increasing the terrors of the law abiding. No terms of condemnation, applied to the men who were responsible for the appalling conditions revealed before your committee, can be too severe. No punishment that outraged justice may visit upon them will be adequate. In many cases they deserve the extreme penalty; in every case they merit the execration of a despoiled and disgraced community.

The purpose of the politicians of both political parties, who found East St. Louis respected and prosperous and who, in a few years, robbed its treasury, gave away valuable franchises, sank it in the mire of pollution, and brought upon it national censure and disgrace, was deliberate. They united to elect men to high office who would further their schemes of spoliation even when they feared to share their plunder. It was a conspiracy as shameless as it was confident. They left nothing to chance. It took account of the executive; it provided for an unscrupulous legislative board; it made certain of police commissioners who would take orders and deliver the goods; it embraced the courts high and low; it went into partnership with every vile business; it protected every lawless saloon; it encouraged houses of prostitution in the very shadow of the city hall; it gave protection to gamblers, immunity to thieves and murderers.

The gang that took possession of East St. Louis harbored the off-scourings of the earth. The vag, the safe blower and the "stick-up man" flocked to its sheltering arms, safe from arrest or disturbance.

The good people of this sorely afflicted community were powerless. The chamber of commerce, which should have had the courage to rally the law-abiding and drive out the lawless, was ineffective. They actually "laid upon the table" a resolution of inquiry to investigate the conditions that made property unsafe and life perilous.

The owners of the great corporations whose plants were in and about East St. Louis lived in other cities. They pocketed their dividends without concern for the municipal dishonesty that wasted the taxes, and without a thought for the thousands of their own workmen, black and white, who lived in hovels, the victims of poverty and disease, of long hours and incessant labor.

The greed that made crooks of the politicians made money grabbers of the manufacturers, who pitted white labor against black, drove organized labor from their plants, brought thousands of inefficient Negroes from the South, crowding the white men from their positions. All this stirred the fires of race hatred until it finally culminated in bloody, pitiless riot, arson and wanton murder.

Mayor Mollman surrounded himself with advisers who were familiar with the game of politics. They were not interested in securing an honest and economical administration. Their business first was to elect a man who would be subservient; one who possibly might not put his own hand into the public treasury, but would look the other way if a friend were so engaged. They needed a man who would stand between them and the indignant taxpayer; a fair promiser but a poor performer; personally honest, maybe, but so weak, so feeble, and so easily influenced that the conspirators were able to dictate his policies, and in the shadow of his stupidity, loot the municipality. This was not the result of corruption in only one political party. It was brought about by a combination between the leaders of the worst elements in both parties. They pooled issues in the city election and declared regular dividends on their investment at the expense of honest people.

In the history of corrupt politics in this country there never has been a more shameless debauchery of the electorate nor a more vicious alliance between the agencies and beneficiaries of crime than for years existed in East St. Louis. It is a disgraceful chapter. It puts an ineffaceable brand on every man engaged in the conspiracy. Its contamination, spreading from a reservoir of corruption in the city hall, filtered through carefully laid conduits into every street and alley; into the hotels where girls, mere children of 15 years of age, were violated; into the low dance halls where schoolgirls listened to lewd songs and engaged in lascivious dances, and in the interval retired to assignation rooms with the drunken brutes who frequented these resorts; into the gambling houses where poorly paid workmen were robbed of their daily earnings; into the 350 saloons which kept open on Sunday, many of them running without license; into the barrel houses, where the vilest of whisky was sold in bottles, the resort of vagrants and drunkards, rendezvous of criminals and schools of crime.

This corruption palsied the hands of prominent officials whose duty it was to enforce the law. Lawyers became protectors of criminals; the courts were shields for the highwayman, the prostitute, the gambler, the sneak thief and the murderer. The higher courts were not free from this baneful influence, which invaded all ranks and brought them to its low level.

Local judges were found who would take straw bonds that the worst criminals might escape; exacting only costs, two-thirds going into the pockets of the judge and one-third into the waiting palm of the chief of police.

A police force is never better than the police commissioners; and the police commissioners, in turn, reflect the character and wishes of the mayor. If a city has a mayor of courage and ability, who is not the weak and willing prey of political crooks and grafters, he is certain to appoint a board of police commissioners who will name policemen intelligent enough to know the law and brave and honest enough to enforce it.

East St. Louis was doubly unfortunate. In the person of Mayor Mollman it had an executive who obeyed orders from a gang of conscienceless politicians of both political parties, who were exploiting the city for their own aggrandizement, careless alike of its good name, its security or its prosperity. They were harpies who closed their eyes to the corruption that saturated every department of the public service and fattened on its festering carcass. Without conscience and without shame they led the mayor into devious paths, tempted him with assurances of political support for his future ambitions, packed the police force with men whose incompetency was only surpassed by their venality, and so circumscribed him with flattery and encouraged his cupidity that they were able to take the reins of the government from his feeble hands and guide it to suit their own foul and selfish purposes.

The great majority of the police force appointed by Mayor Mollman's board of police commissioners had served an apprenticeship as connivers at corrupt elections; as protectors of lawless saloons and hotels run openly as assignation houses. They turned criminals loose at the dictation of politicians and divided with grafting justices of the peace the fines that should have gone into the treasury.

This was the general character of the police force of the city of East

St. Louis on July 1, 1917, when the spirit of lawlessness, long smoldering, burst into flame.

When acts of violence were frequent on the night of May 28, after a largely attended public meeting in the city hall, at which Attorney Alexander Flannigan, by unmistakable implication, suggested mob violence, the police department failed to cope with the incipient mob.

When the lawlessness began to assume serious proportions on July 2, the police instantly could have quelled and dispersed the crowds, then made up of small groups; but they either fled into the safety of a cowardly seclusion, or listlessly watched the depredations of the mob, passively, in many instances actively sharing in its work.

The testimony of every witness who was free to tell the truth agreed in condemnation of the police for failure to even halfway do their duty. They fled the scene where murder and arson held full sway. They deserted the station house and could not be found when calls for help came from every quarter of the city. The organization broke down completely; and so great was the indifference of the few policemen who remained on duty that the conclusion is inevitable that they shared the lust of the mob for negro blood, and encouraged the rioters by their conduct, which was sympathetic when it was not cowardly.

Some specific instances will be given in proof of the above conclusions:

After a number of rioters had been taken to the jail by the soldiers under Col. Clayton, the police deliberately turned hundreds of them loose without bond, failing to secure their names or to make any effort to identify them.

In one instance the mob jammed policemen against a building and held them there while other members of the gang were assaulting unoffending negroes. The police made no effort to free themselves and seemed to regard the performance as highly humorous.

The police shot into a crowd of negroes who were huddled together, making no resistance. It was a particularly cowardly exhibition of savagery.

When the newspaper reporters were taking pictures of the mob, policemen charged them with their billies, broke their machines, destroyed the negatives, and threatened them with arrest if any further attempt was made to photograph the rioters who were making the streets run red with innocent blood, applying the torch to reach their victims who were cowering in their wretched homes.

A negro was brutally clubbed by a policeman who found him guilty of the heinous offense of hiding in an ice box to save his life.

Two policemen and three soldiers were involved in the shooting of Minneola McGee under circumstances of extreme brutality. This occurred, not at the scene of the riots, but as she was going from an outhouse to the kitchen of the residence where she was employed, when the police and the soldiers who accompanied them fired at her deliberately, without even the slightest provocation, and shot off her arm near the shoulder.

Minneola McGee is a negro girl about 20 years old. She was induced to leave one of the Southern states and go to East St. Louis by the many enticing but misleading advertisements scattered among southern negroes. It is apparent that even before her injury she was a frail and rather delicate girl. When she appeared before your committee, with one arm off just below the shoulder, she was a physical wreck. She has no education whatever. It is not possible for her to earn a living in any other way than by manual labor. Now, as the result of as fiendish a piece of work as was ever perpetrated, she must, at least to some extent, be an object of charity. Because of her youth this sort of a life is before her. She was interrogated by your committee to ascertain whether it was possible for her to have been shot by accident. Her simple story removed all doubt upon that score, as she satisfied everyone who heard her that she was purposely and deliberately shot. In answer to questions put to her by your committee she said:

I wuz in a outhouse in de garden. I hea'd de shootin' an' started fo' de house. When I got put'y nigh de house a soljer histed his gun and pinted it right at me and shot my arm off. Dar wuzn't nobody twixt me and de soljer fo' him to be shootin' at, an' dar wuzn't nobody on de udder side of me for him to be shootin' at. He jist histed his gun and pinted it at me an' shot my arm off when I hadn't done nothin'. When he shot me I fell on de ground an' didn't know nothin'.

Her pitiful recital of this piece of brutality toward her had the effect of stirring the indignation of everybody in the room where the hearing was being conducted, and at the same time to arouse the utmost sympathy for her.

. . . The offenses committed against law, order and decency in East St. Louis and St. Clair County include every known act in the catalogue of crime. We have selected some of the high lights that luridly illumine the landscape of crime.

One-third of all the stealing from freight cars engaged in inter-state commerce, as reported from 27 states, was done in East St. Louis and St. Clair County. It was not only a fertile field for the car thief, but he found a ready sale for his plunder through agencies that were protected by the police and other officials.

. . . The politicians and the police force of East St. Louis and St. Clair County divided among themselves at least $60,000 a year in graft which they exacted from the gamblers and prostitutes for protection.

Constables and deputy sheriffs picked up some easy money in the vile dance halls that were open on Sunday in the various saloons in St. Clair County. They were each paid $5 a day by proprietors of these places under the pretense of maintaining order, but under their oaths they should have arrested and prosecuted the keepers and all those present for violating the law.

Records show that more than 300 girls between the ages of 13 and 16 years visited the dance halls run in connection with saloons and so-called hotels, which were in reality assignation houses. These children, their hair hanging down their backs, and in short dresses, publicly engaged in lascivious dances with a motley crew of drunken toughs. The police took no notice of these offenses, nor did the mayor make any effort to close these joints notoriously violating the law.

Many other cases of police complicity in the riots could be cited. Instead of being guardians of the peace they became a part of the mob by countenancing the assaulting and shooting down of defenseless negroes and adding to the terrifying scenes of rapine and slaughter.

Their disgraceful conduct was the logical fruit of the notorious alliance between City Hall and criminal elements, aided by saloons, gambling houses and houses of prostitution. The city administration owed its election to their support and rewarded them for their fealty by permitting them to debauch the innocent, rob drunken victims, make assignation houses of the hotels, protect the gambler and the thief, and commit any act by which they might profit.

Mayor Mollman appointed the police commissioners. He was responsible for their failure to divorce the police from its partnership with crooked lawyers, corrupt justices of the peace and notorious criminals. He knew full well what the conditions in the police department were. Prominent citizens had warned him repeatedly and had supplied convincing proof of their charges against the department. He paid no attention to their warnings and appeals. By his failure to remove the police commissioners he acquiesced in their misfeasance, and is equally responsible with them for the heartless crimes committed by an unrestrained mob, and for the lawlessness that was encouraged and fostered by his failure to enforce the law and to hold his subordinates responsible for the proper conduct of the police department.

. . . Between the first of September, 1916, and July 2, 1917, the day of the riot, there were eight hundred crimes of various characters, ranging from larceny to rape and murder committed in East St. Louis. In hundreds of these cases, straw bonds were taken; and when the criminals failed to answer, a small fine was entered, of which the justice of the peace received two-thirds and the chief of police one-third. It was a profitable business for the justices, one of whom, now dead, is said to have made $25,000 in one year.

Women of the street in kimonas, with frowsy heads and painted faces, took part in the riots and were, if possible, more brutal than the men. They attacked negro women and children and beat them unmercifully.

. . . One of the unique features of official life in East St. Louis was that permitting constables to summon juries from the barrel houses and saloons. They were known as "irrigation juries." These juries always returned a verdict in favor of the clients of Alexander Flannigan, a friend of the court, or of any other lawyer or gang leader with "pull"; and it was the invariable custom for the court to impose a sufficient additional fine to pay for a "treat" all around for the jurymen and officers. These lawyers with a "pull" proudly took them to a nearby saloon on which was the large sign, "Court Bar," where they were "irrigated."

. . . During the riot a negro was arrested and taken to jail, that the mob might not get him. He had not committed any offense; and, presumably, was in the safe custody of the jailer. One of the police officers, learning that he had some money in his pocket, constituted himself judge, jury and witness, and fined him $11.50 and also made him contribute $5 additional to raise the assessment of one of his fellow prisoners to the proper amount. This petty crook, in learning afterward that the negro had some change left, no doubt was surprised at his own moderation.

. . . The looting of the city and county treasury has grown into a habit in East St. Louis. More than $250,000 has been stolen by various defaulting officials in the last five years. In one instance, the school fund was robbed of $45,000, but the prosecution of the thief has gone on listlessly for several years without any real effort to convict him. He was not arraigned for trial until after your committee had left East St. Louis. He then pleaded guilty. Everybody knows who was protecting him, but so many similar thefts have been overlooked that there is but little public sentiment against him.

After one of the defalcations the thieves took everything in the vault but the metal hinges of a loose-leaf ledger, and the fire they started to destroy the evidence of their guilt left that as the only souvenir for the taxpayers.

. . . On the night of July 1 Mayor Mollman telephoned the acting adjutant general of Illinois that the mob spirit was rampant; that the police were unable to cope with the situation; and that it would take the strong hand of the militia to preserve order.

. . . The conduct of the soldiers who were sent to East St. Louis to protect life and property puts a blot on that part of the Illinois militia that served under Col. Tripp. They were scattered over the city, many of them being without officers to direct or control them. In only a few cases did they do their duty. They seemed moved by the same spirit of indifference or cowardice that marked the conduct of the police force. As a rule they fraternized with the mob, joked with them and made no serious effort to restrain them.[1]

. . . Special commendation is due Attorney General Brundage and

1. For the details on actions of police and the military in this and in other disturbances see Allen D. Grimshaw, "Actions of Police and the Military in American Race Riots," pp. 269-286 in this volume.

Assistant Attorney General Middlekauf. The attorney general answered every appeal made to him by the good people of East St. Louis and St. Clair County and, virtually without assistance from the local authorities, remedied many evils. It was due entirely to his efforts that lawless resorts were closed, and wherever there had been a violation of the State law he was quick to order the arrest and prosecution of the offender.

Assistant Attorney General Middlekauf had active charge of the prosecutions growing out of the riot, and he showed neither fear nor favor. Capable, determined and courageous, he allowed neither political influence nor personal appeals to swerve him from the strict line of duty.

As a result of these prosecutions by the attorney general's office 11 negroes and 8 white men are in the State penitentiary; 2 additional white men have been sentenced to prison terms; 14 white men have been given jail sentences: 27 white men, including the former night chief of police and three policemen, have pleaded guilty to rioting and have been punished.

These convictions were obtained in the face of organized, determined effort, backed with abundant funds, to head off the prosecutions and convictions. In the case of Mayor Mollman there seems to have been an open, paid advertising campaign to slander and intimidate the attorney general.

Edgar A. Schuler

The Houston Race Riot, 1917 *

The most serious riot involving Negro soldiers which occurred in the United States during the first World War took place in Houston, Texas, on the night of Thursday, August 23, 1917. At that time over a hundred Negro United States Army regulars seized rifles and ammunition by force, and marched upon the city. This outbreak followed a period of rising racial tension climaxed by an altercation between white police officers and Negro "military police." The following morning it was announced that there were thirteen known dead, of whom only one was a Negro, and nineteen wounded, including five Negro soldiers, as a result of the riot.

A few days later the mayor of Houston appointed a special investi-

* This article has been abridged and edited by Edgar A. Schuler for inclusion in this volume.

gating commission which sat in open session for several days. Much of the testimony there presented is quoted in subsequent issues of *The Houston Daily Post;* upon these reports the following analysis is based.[1]

THE SOCIAL AND PSYCHOLOGICAL SETTING

The several companies of Negro troops of the 24th United States Infantry who later took part in the riot had been sent from a western army post to Houston to guard government property during the construction of Camp Logan (July 28). This detachment, totaling about 600 men, included both men who had been in service for some time and were more or less seasoned troops, and more recent enlistees who came from various parts of the country, particularly from the North (Editorial, August 27).

Houstonians were expecting the early arrival of a considerably larger number (about 3,000) of Negro troops along with the white National Guardsmen from Illinois who were to be housed at Camp Logan upon its completion. In addition to some of the white Guardsmen, one company of Negroes had arrived on Monday, August 20 (August 21). The anticipated arrival of further substantial contingents of Northern Negro troops, alarming in itself to some Houstonians, gained special significance in its relation to the hotly debated issue of local prohibition.

Another point which needs to be mentioned is the fact that Houston was currently being considered by military authorities as the site of a new aviation center. Probably this circumstance had something to do with the lack of public admission of the race tension which was mounting prior to the outbreak itself. A final element in the situation, which may or may not have been of importance, was the fact that early in the week during which the riot occurred there was a change in commanding officers at the Camp. The new commander, possibly less experienced than his predecessor, apparently had not fully gained the respect of the Negro troopers.[2]

This brief résumé of the objective social factors in the situation leads to a consideration of what various segments of the population of Hous-

1. To keep the length of the citations to a minimum, all references unless otherwise noted will be to *The Houston Daily Post* for 1917, the editions being those on file in the Library of Congress.

2. It is reported that "The life of the major [Major K. S. Snow in charge of the Negro troops following the departure of Colonel Newman, on the Tuesday preceding the riot] was threatened as he tried to quell the rioting troops." (August 24.) Elsewhere it is stated that after the trouble had begun, and Major Snow had talked to the men, ". . . trying to get them to return to the camp . . . they turned upon him and said, 'You white ――, get back into camp.' . . ." (August 30.) It should be pointed out that Major Snow was sometimes referred to as "Captain Snow" in the published testimony. The fact that he had been promoted to the rank of Major and made commanding officer at Camp Washington only two days prior to the riot helps to account both for the inconsistencies in the rank by which he was designated and for his inexperience as a commander. (August 21.)

ton were thinking and doing, and particularly what types of interracial interaction patterns were developing prior to the riot. . . .

[The following elements in the psycho-social situation which spawned the Houston riot are then identified and documented by press clippings: (1) the local press; (2) law enforcement officials; (3) white officers in command of Negro troops; (4) prohibitionists; (5) white workmen, members of the construction crews working at Camp Logan; and (6) street car motormen and conductors.]

Buried on the 14th page of the issue for Sunday, August 19, is the only item the writer found published prior to the time of the riot which indicated the existence of local racial friction:

While standing in the pay line at Camp Logan Saturday noon, Sam Blair, a negro employed at the camp, was stabbed and slightly wounded in the back by an unknown white man. The negro is said to have pushed his way into the pay line ahead of the white man, who resented it.

Blair, it is said, grabbed the white man by the shoulder while someone else hit him with a shovel, when the white man, with a free arm, pulled a knife and stabbed Blair in the back. The latter was taken to the infirmary in the ambulance of the Houston Undertaking Company.

It would seem that most middle and upper class white Houstonians knew little about the developing racial friction, for they were too far removed to learn about it at first hand, and the press did not inform them. Those who were in a position to know the facts thought it better not to publicize them. It is impossible to determine on the basis of available evidence the extent or importance of rumor and gossip in this connection. . . .

THE PRECIPITATING INCIDENT: MORNING

On the day after the riot there appeared on an inside page of the *Post* a brief item which evidently was written and prepared for publication prior to the outbreak of the riot. Inconspicuous in comparison with the blaring headlines of the riot itself, it gives the first account of the incident which precipitated the riot.

Two negro soldiers, one of them a member of the military police, were arrested by Officers Daniels and Sparks on Thursday afternoon and claim to have been beaten up to some extent by the officers. Later two other negro soldiers from Camp Logan approached the officers to ascertain what had become of their comrades, and on receiving the information reported to their superior officers at the camp.

Afterward the officers in command of the negro soldiers had a conference with Superintendent of Police Brock, which resulted in the issuance of an order by the chief that hereafter negro soldiers are not to be referred to by members of the department as negroes, but as "colored" soldiers. It is said that the order has stirred up a good deal of feeling.

Officers Daniels and Sparks gave their version of the trouble as follows: they had arrested a negress on San Filipe Street Thursday afternoon, when a negro soldier came up to them and asked them to turn the negress over to him. They refused and finally the soldier became so insistent that the officers were obliged to subdue him and send him to the station. Shortly afterward another negro soldier, one of the military police, asked the same officers what had become of his comrade and one word led to another and this soldier also was sent to the station *a little the worse for wear.* [Italics by the writer.]

In speaking of the occurrence Thursday evening, Superintendent Brock said one of the soldiers had been returned to the camp, while the other was still detained at police station. He could not say what action would be taken by the government against the two officers who are alleged to have hit the soldiers, but he had put the whole thing up to the government. The chief said he was doing all in his power to preserve order between the two elements and would continue to do so. (August 24.)

It is worth pointing out that the central importance of this incident is admitted in the front-page major story of the riot following a brief version of the same incident: "From every source Thursday night, reports came that this treatment of the troops led to the riot." To avoid confusion in the material about to be presented it should be noted that the "trouble" referred to occurred Thursday morning rather than Thursday afternoon, as the above account has it. It seems hardly necessary to state that the order issued by Superintendent of Police Brock regarding the mode of address to be employed by police officers in dealing with Negro soldiers was later stricken from the police records.

At two points in the investigation testimony was taken regarding the incident which precipitated the riot, and certain basic inconsistencies between the versions of the white policeman who participated and of other informants were clearly developed.[3] The crux of the matter seems to be whether the treatment of the Negro soldiers by the white civil policemen was justified. The following is that of the white policeman:

Mr. Sparks said that he and his partner arrested a negro woman on Bailey and San Felipe streets Thursday morning on a charge of abusive language. They took her to the police box at San Felipe and Wilson streets and sent in a call for the patrol wagon. While waiting there they saw a negro soldier running toward the negro woman, and when told that he could not have her he said that he would take her anyway.

Sparks said that he told the negro Edwards three different times to get back, but that when he kept coming in he struck him four times with his revolver. He then made him sit down and wait for the patrol wagon, and he and the negro woman were put in it together and sent to the police station. Edwards was drunk, he said. (August 30.)

Officer Sparks was called to the witness stand a second time in the course of the next day of the investigation. This time he was quoted as follows:

3. Only one of the two police officers involved survived the riot.

I arrested the negro woman for abusive language. While I was waiting for the wagon Edwards came up with about 20 negroes following him and said he wanted the woman. I said he couldn't have her. He said he was going to have her and reached over. I hit him over the head three or four times till his heart got right and he sat down. (September 1.) . . .

Here is the pivotal question in the entire affair: what was the nature of the interaction between Sergeant Baltimore, a colored soldier playing the role, but not clothed with the authority of, a military policeman, and the two white civil policemen, Sparks and Daniels, resentful of being questioned by the Negro, and possibly covering up an inward fear by an outward show of violence?

Superintendent of Police Brock was recalled to the witness stand and was questioned by Judge Henry J. Dannenbaum regarding the encounter between Sparks and Sergeant Baltimore and the latter's arrest. He said that the negro soldier made a statement at the station which was produced and read. He said Captain Haig Shekerjian, Detectives Daugherty and Fife and he were present at the time.

According to the statement, Sparks struck Baltimore over the head with his pistol, then fired at him, and Baltimore ran into a house and got under a bed. Sparks followed him, according to the statement, and made him get up, and then struck him twice. Baltimore said he was just inquiring what had become of his brother officer and that it was his duty to investigate the matter. . . .

Sparks said he only struck Baltimore once, that he did not strike him after he had run into the house. He said Baltimore had no arms or police club with him. . . . Asked why he hit the negro more than once he said he wasn't going to wrestle with the big negro.

He admitted that in making arrests in the thickly populated negro sections where the more vicious elements of the negroes congregate, he thought it necessary to use more force than was legally or morally necessary in order to keep the other negroes from running away with him.

In answer to General Chamberlain, he said he had received no instructions as to the relations to be maintained between the police officer and the military police and General Chamberlain observed, "I thought so." . . .

Sparks and Daniels made a verbal statement, said Mr. Brock, and he told Sparks he would be suspended in the morning. Sparks said he could not afford to be suspended, that he had been suspended before and Brock told him he would wait until he investigated the matter. . . . (September 1.)

. . . Sparks said that he told the chief and the officer that nothing more was said except that Chief Brock told him to go home and stay away until he was called for. Baltimore seemed to have been drinking, he said. (August 30.)

Detective E. F. Daugherty, who took the negro Baltimore's statement on the typewriter, explained the conversation in Superintendent Brock's office. He said that besides himself, Officers Fife and McPhail, Superintendent Brock, Captain Shekerjian of the Twenty-fourth Infantry and Baltimore were in the office. He said that Baltimore stated that he was coming down San Felipe Street when he met another negro soldier of whom he inquired where the police officers could be found. He said he went to them and asked them why they had arrested another negro soldier that morning, telling them that he wanted the information in order to be able to report to his commanding officer.

Baltimore, according to Detective Daugherty, said that Officer Sparks then hit him with his pistol, and that when he turned and ran three shots were fired at him. He said he was arrested in a house about a block down the street.

Daugherty said that later Superintendent Brock and Sparks were in the former's office alone, and that when Sparks came out he said something to the effect that he wasn't getting a square deal. He also said that any man who would stick up for a negro was no better than a negro himself, Daugherty testified, and as he went out of the door he continued that if that wasn't enough he would give him (Brock) the rest of it. Later Daugherty said that Sparks sent an apology to Superintendent Brock by Captain Anderson.

When asked whether he knew if Sparks had been suspended by Superintendent Brock, Daugherty said that Brock and Captain Sherkerjian were to have had a conference Friday morning, and that he understood Sparks was to be suspended until the matter had been settled. He said that Sparks said after his interview with the Superintendent that "if Chief Davidson had been in the office he would have told Captain Shekerjian to get out and take his negroes with him. . . ." (September 1.)

About a month after the riot, the following was reported from El Paso, Texas. It was based on testimony taken before the special board of inquiry at the Fort Bliss stockade, where the Negro troopers were being tried for their role in the riot.

The evidence taken before the board of inquiry develops that the meeting was carefully planned, and that it was the result of the beating up of a negro provost guard by a Houston policeman. This negro, with his face still showing the scars of combat, was before the board of inquiry Wednesday and told his story.

According to this story the man returned to the camp at 11 in the morning of the day of the mutiny. He told of his experiences at the hands of the police and two hours later it had spread throughout the entire battalion. (September 20.)

THE ROLE OF RUMOR: EARLY AFTERNOON

We are now in a position to give a brief synthetic account of the *supposed* sequence of events up to mid-afternoon. It began with the arrest of a Negro woman, drunk and therefore using abusive language, by the white policemen Sparks and Daniels. In this process they treated her with considerable severity if not actual brutality as a result of which Edwards, a Negro soldier (a private, but also a provost guard, and therefore Baltimore's "brother officer"), attempted to intervene. This led to his beating, arrest, and incarceration; but as he was not kept long at the station he was able to be back at the camp in the late morning.

Early in the afternoon Corporal Baltimore, another provost guard, attempted to locate the police officers stationed in the San Felipe district to find out what had happened to Edwards and why. Directed by another Negro soldier, he soon located Officers Sparks and Daniels.[4] Being refused the information he sought he attempted to escape from the policemen, was chased, shot at, captured, beaten, arrested, taken to the station and locked up in the early afternoon. Sparks and Daniels, meanwhile, returned to their beat, where they were subsequently approached and questioned by a pair of Negro soldiers whose demeanor was such that they saw fit to reward them with the desired information Meanwhile, also, the story of Baltimore's ill treatment at the hands of the same policemen who had that morning beaten up Edwards had been carried back to the camp by the soldier who had directed Baltimore to the policemen, and who had hung around awaiting developments. Broadcast throughout the camp by the grapevine, and at the same time exaggerated, this news proved to be the straw that broke the camel's back. For it tended to confirm the already current notion that the only way to release the cumulative pressure of resentment and rage was to retaliate directly against the offending San Felipe policemen.

It seems clear that the resentment aroused by the returned Edwards was terrifically intensified when the report that Baltimore had been "shot at" became transformed into the rumor that he had been shot and killed. . . .

PLANNING, PREPARATION FOR, AND EXECUTION OF THE RIOT: MID-AFTERNOON AND LATER

James Divins, member of Company I of the Negro regiment, in an affidavit obtained by the District Attorney's department, stated that he

. . . came off guard duty at about 2:30 and heard some of the men of [his] company talking about Corporal Baltimore having been shot downtown by a police officer, and they were all talking among themselves as to who would go down town and raid. They all agreed to wait until night, so they could see about the ammunition. . . . (August 25.)

According to the news dispatch from El Paso at the time of the soldiers' trial,

About three in the afternoon the men commenced stealing their rifles and ammunition and planning the descent on the town. The real leader of the

4. From the conflicting testimony and news accounts it is not clear, however, whether Baltimore had previously had direct or indirect contact with Edwards; whether he had been ordered by his superior officers to make the inquiry; whether he was supposed to relieve Edwards on provost guard duty, and made inquiry when he could not be located; whether the Negro soldier who directed him to the policemen's station also accompanied him there; whether Baltimore had been informed that the policemen had been beating the Negro woman whom they had arrested that morning; and whether he asked them only about the reason for the arrest of Edwards, of the woman, or both.

mutiny, Sergeant Henry, committed suicide with his own pistol rather than surrender. (September 20.)

The news of the imminent riot spread quickly from soldiers to civilians. . . .

Said E. Hartwell, captain of the temporary fire station at the government warehouse, in response to the question, "Did those men [the Negro guards at the warehouse] tell you anything of the trouble?":

They said when the wagon came that night bringing provisions the men had been told that the police in town had shot one of their number. When they left the camp they said they were going to the police station to get revenge. . . . (August 30.)

Leroy Pinkett, a Negro soldier previously quoted, asserted in his affidavit:

. . . It was getting late then, and we stood retreat at 6 o'clock and then our men began changing by talking. I heard Sergeant Henry of our company say: "Well, don't stand around like that. If you are going to do anything go ahead and do it."

After that I saw some of the boys slip over to Company K and I heard them say they had stolen the ammunition. Then Captain Snow called the men out in line. He asked what we were doing and ordered a search made for the ammunition and also ordered that our rifles be taken up. Another sergeant (I forget his name) took up our rifles from our tent. In this same talk Captain Snow told us that Baltimore was not in the wrong. I heard him say that. . . . (August 25.)

A white grocery salesman, B. A. Calhoun, testified as follows:

. . . I took Captain Snow to the police station. We went to the station at 4:30 and returned at 6:00 o'clock.

Q. What was the temper of the negroes?

A. They were surly at 6 o'clock. Captain Snow talked to them about the trouble Sergeant Baltimore had with police officers and told them that Chief Brock had said his police officers were wrong in his case and they would be suspended and would be punished. . . . The men seemed ugly and congregated in groups. . . . About 8 p.m. Sergeant Henry came to Captain Snow and told him he could not make the men obey. Five men of Company K were put in the guard house. The bugle was sounded for the officers' call. All officers came out and reported to their companies, and they were assembled. They all lined up and were without arms. This was about 8:10 o'clock. Captain Snow said to me, he had collected all arms, and ordered all negro civilians out of camp. Just at that time someone cried out "break ranks, and get your guns." Firing began. I don't know who fired. It may have been the men designated to do police duty downtown. [It will be recalled that Supt. Brock stated the military police were armed with night sticks only.] But all seemed to have ammunition. . . . I ran into Captain Snow's tent and his negro attendant told me to lay down. He told me if the troops knew he had not joined them they would kill him. A part of them marched right by the tent I was in. Others refused to join them and were threatened with death. Some officers ordered them to halt. They kept on, about 150 in line, I guess. Some one said, "Stop firing, save our ammunition, for we will need it later." I heard one say, "We are headed for the police station!" . . . (August 29.)

The soldier who gave the signal for the break is identified in the statement of Leroy Pinkett:

A big fellow in our company named Frank Johnson then came running down the company street hollering, "Get your rifles, boys." We all made a rush then for the supply camp and got our rifles and we went to a large ammunition box and got our ammunition. Sergeant Henry was the leader. . . . (August 25.)

The following statement of James Divins takes up immediately after the company had been checked for ammunition, and the rifles had been collected and turned in to the supply tent:

About half the company then gathered around the stump and they were talking about someone getting the box of ammunition. Captain Scurgion walked up and said he wanted to speak to the company. About that time some member of the company said, "There is a mob coming, get your gun," and everyone commenced hollering, "Get your gun" and we all rushed to the supply tent and got our guns. Someone then was pitching ammunition out of the box and Sergeant Henry asked, "Has everybody got their ammunition?" and some hollered "I have not got enough." Sergeant Henry formed the company in front of the officers' line and Sergeant Henry made a little talk and said this is serious business and everyone was asked to stay with him.

As we all went off towards town I heard a demand to halt but it was not given by anyone in our company and no one obeyed the command. Sergeant Henry after going a short distance halted the company and said, "We will go back and make L company go with us," and we marched down to L company's street and some said that L company would not go. We came back and Sergeant Henry stopped the company again and said his father was a soldier and had gone down, but we men would have to follow him and he would carry us down. Sergeant Henry then ordered a flank guard put out in the rear and he also put one out in front and we marched down the shell road. . . . I think there were about 150 men in this company and a little over half of them were from my company and the others were made up from other companies. . . .

None of the men were drunk that I know of; they didn't seem like they were drunk to me. We did not have any beer at the camp and I never heard of any men getting any beer that day. . . . (August 25.)

Meanwhile what was happening in Houston? We can get some idea from the story of P. F. Lowder, a reporter representing the Chicago *Herald,* which was reproduced in the *Post:*

The first Houston knew of the trouble was at 8 o'clock. A few scattering shots were heard. Everybody began to ask everybody else what the trouble was. Then the telephone began to ring.

"Send help! Send help! The niggers are shooting up the town."

Three automobiles loaded with police officers started for Camp Logan. They halted at the city limits and confined their activities to warning people not to go near the camp. An ambulance that ventured near to pick up the wounded girl [hit by a stray shot while she was within her home] was stopped by the colored troops.

The tires were shot full of holes, the driver told to turn around, a few shots were fired in the air and the machine came tearing back the road on flat tires. (August 24.)

Other reporters, out to see what was happening, had the following to say:

Eighty of the negroes, marching in military formation, in column of twos, led by a tall private, marched south . . . This was at 9:20 o'clock. The men were in perfect order, though they were marching along out of step. When two other newspaper men, bound for the camp to find out the cause of the trouble, ran into the column, they made no threatening move, except that the tall leader shoved one of the reporters in the ditch. . . . The two civilians were allowed to go on toward the army camp unmolested. As they were abreast of the middle of the column, one negro called out: "See here, boys, what you let them two go by for? You goin' to pass up them two? Let's get 'em."

There was no answer and no move was made to "get 'em." . . . It is thought that these soldiers marched down the Shepherd's Dam road, across the bridge, and entered the city in the San Felipe Street section where the fighting kept up long after it had ceased everywhere else. . . . (August 24.)

Testified Mrs. Maude Potts, a jitney operator, in response to the question, "What do you know about the riot?":

I was in the center of it. . . . I heard a negro soldier tell me, "get away from here, white lady, we don't want to kill you, but we are after the white police-men who have called us names and have been beating our men up." . . . I saw many civilian negroes go along with the negro soldiers and they were armed and some of them were shooting wild. . . . (August 29.)

James Divins further testified:

We crossed the bridge and we met two United States officers in a car on San Felipe Street and halted them and returned their guns to them and let them go. . . . I saw two officers (police officers) in uniform. One lying in the street on his back had been shot but he was not dead and the other one was lying on his side in the bend of the road. I don't know if he was dead or not. . . . (August 25.)

From the last four items it seems clear that the Negro troops were not out to mow down Houston whites indiscriminately. That some of the Negroes, both soldiers and civilians, may have had an inclination to be less discriminating in their violence is entirely possible. But the disciplined and relatively orderly way in which the departure from the camp was organized and carried out strongly suggests that the leaders, while inflexibly determined to punish the San Felipe policemen, had no intention of generally "shooting up the town." This interpretation is corroborated by the statement of Captain Tuggle:

"Of course everyone knows . . . Captain Mattes and the [police] officer (Meineke) . . . had gone on ahead of the troops, had met the crowd of negroes advancing up San Felipe, and had been killed. . . . I am fully convinced that Captain Mattes would never have been shot if he had not been in the car with a police officer. I believe that the negroes thought he was another policeman."

After Captain Tuggle had made this statement a negro prisoner, in a signed confession, made a similar statement that bore out Captain Tuggle's theory. The negro said that if they had known that Captain Mattes was an army officer they would never have harmed him. They had shot out the street lights. They saw, in the front seat, a man whom they knew to be a police officer. In the dark they thought Captain Mattes was another and killed both. Then they plunged bayonets into them. (August 26.)

More light is thrown on the general turmoil and alarm among the civilians of Houston by the following quotations:

Houston policemen, armed civilians, and members of the Texas National Guard, as well as Illinois guardsmen who were in town when the trouble started quickly went to the scene of the shooting . . . where Captain W. P. Rothrock, constructing quartermaster of Camp Logan, assumed command.

Angry cries of "lynch them" and "come, let's go kill 'em," were heard on all sides. Captain Rothrock placed an armed guard across Washington Avenue with instructions not to let anyone pass, then climbed upon the hood of an automobile and appealed to the men to listen to reason. . . .

About the undertaking establishments great throngs gathered and there was muttering and denunciation of the most rabid sort.

At the police station probably a thousand men, many of them armed, gathered and there was a seething mass which circulated wild rumors and offered their services to the chief of police and his lieutenants. This crowd stayed around most of the evening, though there was a gradual thinning out and at midnight there were only a score or so.

At 10 o'clock every available member of the police department was being rushed to the scene of the trouble in autos, armed with repeating rifles and pistols.

A report reached police station that one-third of the riotous negro soldiers were under restraint and that the balance had divided up into small groups and were rushing their way into other parts of the city. . . .

Someone broke in the front window of Bering's Main Street [hardware] store, but Lieutenant G. G. Howard stationed himself in front of the door and refused to let anyone in.

A large crowd gathered in front of Bering-Cortes wholesale [hardware] store in Prairie Avenue upon the report that negroes had broken into the store to get arms, and in some way a number of them gained admittance to the store and obtained guns. (August 26.)

The importance of the rumors which accompanied the beginning of the outbreak is indicated in the following report:

. . . The vaguenes and uncertainty of early reports of the trouble of Thursday night caused much uneasiness and fear. . . .

Added to the more or less authentic reports as to what was actually taking place were rumors—wild imaginings of disordered brains. One was to the effect that the negro troopers were moving upon the city, 600 strong, sweeping everything in their path. Another was that local negroes had joined the soldiers in a general uprising; that they were forming in various parts of the city and awaiting a general. signal to start their work of destruction. As a result of these rumors many spent an anxious and sleepless night. . . . (August 25.)

A brief account of the role of the Illinois National Guardsmen concludes the section on the riot proper.

Companies were marched to the camp site of the negro companies. Other companies went to the San Felipe district where the army negroes had gone.

The camp site was surrounded and not a man, white or black, was allowed to leave.

Word was received late at night that the San Felipe quarter was surrounded by Illinois troops and that they were waiting for daylight to capture the negro company. . . . (August 24.)

AFTERMATH

Peace and quiet failed to settle upon troubled Houston with the capture of the last of the riotous Negro soldiers. . . . Hysterical fear and the rumors engendered thereby continued to agitate the people of Houston. Almost two weeks after the riot the following notices were published conspicuously on the front page of the *Post:*

By Maj. Gen. Geo. Bell, Jr.
To the Public:

The frenzied appeals made to me personally and to the officers of the staff of the 33rd division during the last 24 hours, coupled with the rumors which have come to us, demonstrated that a condition of apprehension exists in the minds of the people of Houston which demands a statement from me.

The only colored troops in Camp Logan are in Company G of the Eighth Ill. infantry, which numbers three officers, 134 men, 10 men attached, 3 men sick, and 4 men absent on leave, a total of 154.

. . . they have no service ammunition in their possession and no organiaztion is quieter or better behaved. . . .

There is abundant evidence to show that many people in Houston have worked themselves up into a state of frenzy bordering on hysteria on the subject of these colored troops.

A certain newspaper in Houston has under large headlines given circulation to a rumor that "negro soldiers and civilians are preparing for a raid," and that "the time of the attack has been set for 11:15 o'clock Wednesday night." [That very night.]

It is impossible for me to find terms sufficiently strong to condemn such statements as these. They, and every one of the rumors which have come to my ears in the last 24 hours, are absolutely and unqualifiedly false and without the slightest justification in fact. . . . I therefore appeal to the sensible people of the city to put an end to all the unfounded reports and resultant hysteria created thereby for the good, not only of Camp Logan, but for your city as well.

GEORGE BELL, JR.
Major General, U. S. Army. (September 12.)

By Mayor J. C. Hutcheson, Jr.
To the Public:

So many hysterical and unfounded rumors calculated to disturb the peace of the city of Houston and to bring discredit upon our city if persisted in have reached me and there seems to be such a feeling of uncertainty and unrest generally prevalent that I feel it necessary to personally state that I have been assured by Gen. Bell that every precaution has been taken against disorder arising out of or connected with Camp Logan, and that I have arranged with Gen. Bell for placing in the city, beginning Wednesday, a sufficient number of white military police, composed of picked men, to thoroughly police all quarters where the soldiers from Camp Logan may be. . . . *Certainly it is utterly inexcusable for any of our citizens when thus reassured on the matters of original apprehension, to circulate or give credence to wild and disturbed rumors,* wholly without foundation such as have been recently current. . . .

J. C. HUTCHESON, JR.
Mayor. (September 12.)

These statements speak for themselves. But along with the general hysteria the conception of the riot held by the people of Houston was undergoing a transformation; a legend was being born.

At the time of the riot it was generally admitted that the Negro troops were bent on wreaking vengeance on the civilian policemen who they felt had treated them very badly. The first attempt to re-define the event seems to be that of a minister preaching a funeral sermon:

Dr. W. S. Lockhart, pastor of the South End Christian Church, who delivered the funeral sermon over the remains of Officer Ira D. Raney, who was killed by negro soldiers in the mutiny Thursday night, declared in the sermon that, while there appeared to be an attempt on the part of many to attribute this mutiny to race troubles, the real facts were that the mutiny was due to just two causes—"vice and booze". . . It was simply a case of a bunch of "bad niggers" dressed up in a uniform, given a little authority and put under very lax discipline, who, under the influence of women and booze, perpetrated this murderous crime against the army and the city of Houston.

The blame ought to be placed where it belongs, he said, and a great mistake will be made if Houston allows the impression to grow abroad that it was race prejudice that caused the trouble, and it is a slander on the Houston people, white and black, to make it appear so . . . He praised the police force for the brave fight it put up against the armed desperadoes. . . . (August 28.)

A week later the sermon of another Houston minister was reported as follows:

A beautiful tribute to the men who gave up their lives for the defense of the people of Houston on the night of the mutiny of the negro soldiers, was paid by Dr. H. D. Knickerbocker, at the First Methodist Church, Sunday morning.

The minister was preaching on "The Atonement" and he used this incident to illustrate his sermon. Those soldiers and policemen who died that night to stem the black tide of death sweeping toward the homes of Houston, they entered into the glory of God himself, who gave the fullest exhibition of vicarious suffering in the death of his Son. . . . (September 3.)

Thus we see the role of the Houston policemen identified with that of Jesus Christ himself, beyond which it would seem difficult for any apologist to go.

Four weeks after the riot from a special Camp Logan section of the *Post* we learn how complete the transformation has already become: the conception of the event has shifted from one in which direct retaliation is central into one featuring incipient mass slaughter. Say the headlines: "How Illinois Guardsmen Saved City of Houston—Nothing Stopped Mutineers on the Night of August 23 Until They Faced the Unflinching White Soldiers from Camp Logan."

Illinois guardsmen on the night of August 23 saved Houston. There is not a Houstonian who will contest this statement. . . .

[The Negro soldiers] with their rifles and belts and bandoliers filled with ball ammunition . . . marched into Houston, then down Felipe street shooting at every white face they saw. . . .

What broke up the organization? What was it that crumpled the will of these angry soldiers, that scared them into slinking away up side streets, each man by himself? What was it that checked their march on Houston, saved dozens, perhaps hundreds of lives?

It was the men in khaki, from the State of Illinois. . . . (September 20.)

One more item must be presented to round out this account:

Thirteen negro soldiers of the 24th United States Infantry were hanged at dawn today for murders committed at Houston last August, when members of that regiment engaged in mutinous rioting in the city's streets. Forty-one other negroes were sentenced to life imprisonment, four others for short terms, and five were acquitted. . . . (*New York Times,* Dec. 12, 1917.)

But this is not the final scene, for that lives on with the people who experienced directly or indirectly the terror and hatred of the riot and its aftermath.

CONCLUSION

The data presented in the course of the municipal investigation demonstrate that the stage was all set for a serious disturbance growing out of race ill feeling.

The data also indicate that although there were other situations in which tension was aroused, it was the members of the Houston police force, and particularly those stationed in the Negro district around San Felipe Street, against whom the colored troopers' hostility was directed.

As a case study of racial conflict involving Negro soldiers, this particular event yields a number of hypotheses which should be tested for validity as principles of general significance in the phenomena of race conflict, particularly of riots.[5]

1. Transportation difficulties growing out of resentment due to segregation are significantly symptomatic of growing tension.

2. Mistreatment of Negro women being arrested by white police officers is keenly resented by Negro men; this resentment is likely to cause Negro men, particularly military personnel, to say or do something which is unacceptable to white policemen.

3. The pattern of relationships and interaction between Negro military police and white civilian police is perhaps of crucial importance in understanding and controlling racial relationships in which Negro military personnel are involved.

4. Whether on the basis of factual or rumored incidents of mistreatment, when the feeling of tension or resentment becomes sufficiently oppressive a nucleus of Negro military leadership is likely to appear, organized about the attempt to secure arms and ammunition, with the objective of taking direct retaliatory action.

Editorial, New York Times, July 31, 1919

Order in Chicago

Governor Lowden said yesterday that the crisis in Chicago seemed to have been passed—an optimistic opinion which we all hope was justified. It was not passed, however, till thirty-one persons had been killed and several hundred wounded. Night before last it was reported that four thousand troops were on duty in the armories "awaiting developments." The developments going on at that moment included shooting and stabbings at scores of street corners and the procession of armed mobs through various streets of the city. It is hard to see what more serious developments could have been awaited by officials who were charged with the responsibility of maintaining order.

5. See Schuler and Gomillion: n.d.

The Governor approves the reluctance of Mayor Thompson and Chief of Police to call for the troops on the ground that "sending the troops into the trouble districts might arouse some antagonism, and then when the regiments were withdrawn fresh trouble might break out." This would be an excellent theory if the trouble so far had been only a little sporadic stone-throwing, but with fusillades over a large part of the city and a death roll of two dozen or so, it would seem as if some antagonism had already been aroused. The families of the several hundred wounded will hardly be impressed by the fear of the authorities that use of troops would provoke the peaceful population to something really violent.

Political intrigues, as well as economic conflicts, may have had something to do with preparing the ground for the riots, and in the riots themselves the evidence at hand indicated that the blame is to be pretty evenly divided between the two races. The people of Chicago, however, had known in advance that these conditions existed; if they did not foresee such a dreadful consequence it was quite possibly because they supposed that their City Government was able to keep order. Riots extending over four days and running up a casualty list of somewhere between three and six hundred are evident indication that the police are either insufficient or incompetent. Four thousand soldiers might have stopped the rioting much sooner if they had not awaited developments in the armory. To remove the causes of race riots is a matter that will require a good deal of thought and a good deal of time, if it can ever be done at all, but to repress the outbreaks of rioting nothing seems to be needed but officials with courage to use the force that they have in hand.

E. Frank Gardiner

Vice and Politics as Factors in Chicago Riots

Negroes and Whites Drank and Danced Together in All Night Cabarets of the Black Belt—How the Pro-German Thompson Got Nomination as Mayor

Exploitation of the negro in Chicago by politicians is regarded by many as the chief underlying cause of the race riots in that city. The bestowal of political preferment, and the license under which "everything went" in the Black Belt of the second largest American city was the inflammable part of the tinder which finally set the city ablaze.

The influx of thousands of negroes from the South in the last three years was a contributing factor. Their arrival in an already congested district made expansion necessary. Steadily the Black Belt, which stretches for five miles through the heart of the densely populated South Side of Chicago, bulged out into what a few years ago was a choice residential district. This continuous encroachment aroused protests and bitter feeling.

The advance guard of the colored race which moved into white neighborhoods was the better class of negro families, who sought to escape the steady encroachment of the undesirable element of their own race. They had no desire to antagonize their white neighbors. Their relations had always been friendly. But they were between two fires. Pressing always behind them was the influx of a lawless element of their own race. Few of the newcomers brought negro women with them, and some Chicago observers hold the absence of home life among them partly accountable for the present trouble.

POLITICAL POWER

The Second Ward in Chicago is the heart of the Black Belt. Eighty per cent of the voters in this ward are black. White men represented this ward in the City Council until 1915, but now both Aldermen are negroes.

Two men control most of the negro vote in Chicago. They are Congressman Martin B. Maulden of the First Illinois District and George F. Harding, former Alderman, later State Senator, and now City Controller.

It was the balance of power held by the negroes and swung by Harding that gave William Hale Thompson, more widely known as a pro-German than for his kindnesses to negroes, the nomination for Mayor of Chicago in the Spring of 1915. Harding had represented the Second Ward to Chicago for several years. He retired and permitted Oscar De Priest, a negro, to be elected. In return for this favor the negroes swept the Mayoralty nomination into Thompson's lap. Thompson won the nomination by a margin of a few hundred votes.

De Priest became one of the chief floor leaders in the City Council for the Thompson administration. His public career was cut short by his indictment in connection with the alleged collection of tribute in the Black Belt, but he was later acquitted. Another negro succeeded him. Then the Second Ward negroes grew bolder, demanded both seats in the City Council, and got them.

In his campaign for the nomination and election in 1915 Thompson catered to the negro voters. After his election he rewarded many of their leaders with jobs.

So openly did the Thompson crowd treat with the negroes, that somebody dubbed the City Hall "Uncle Tom's Cabin." One man caused handbills to be printed setting forth a complete cast of characters, which included Mayor Thompson and other City Hall jobholders, white and black. It got a big laugh, which is Chicago's usual good-natured way of disposing of her problems.

LID OFF THE BLACK BELT

Thompson had been Mayor only a short time when evidence was apparent that there was no lid as far as the Black Belt was concerned. From other sections of the city white men and women of the old underworld, who had experienced some long, lean years, flocked to the neighborhood. White men bought saloons and cabarets, and pushed negroes to the front as their ostensible owners. Soon the Black Belt became known as the district where "everything went."

At night cabarets were jammed with whites and blacks until the morning sun streaked the sky over Lake Michigan. In other parts of the city saloons and cabarets closed at 1 A.M. But automobiles lined the curbs for blocks all night in the Black Belt, and latecomers stood in line for hours outside some of the more notorious "black and tan" cabarets waiting for a chance to get inside. Jazz bands filled the air with syncopated sound, while in the cabarets whites and blacks mingled in carousel. It was here that the "shimmy" dance is said to have originated.

The rattle of dice and the click of poker chips were seldom stilled in the heart of the district. Gambling was conducted on a business scale. A "syndicate" was formed and no independent could operate successfully in that district without its approval. These gambling games were run under the name of clubs, but a fat bankroll gained easy admission to them.

"Bill" Lewis, noted for years as a gambler, conducted a game in Thirty-fifth Street near State Street. So brazen was the conduct of this gambling house that for a long time Lewis did not bother to pull the curtains down, and the games could be watched from the platform of the elevated railroad station near by. Finally, out of seeming consideration for the feelings of the police, the shades were drawn.

CONDITIONS GENERALLY KNOWN

The newspapers of Chicago repeatedly exposed conditions in the Black Belt. Members of the City Council sometimes denounced it. Reformers visited the all-night cabarets and wrote long reports about them.

Numerous complaints were made to the police. Conditions finally became so notorious that the all-night cabarets were closed. For a few weeks the Black Belt was comparatively quiet, except for the gambling games, which were seldom molested.

Then came vice in a new form; in the shape of clubs which were in reality dance halls. These new places had no liquor licenses, although most of them sold intoxicants and they didn't open their doors until midnight or 1 A.M. They caught the crowds which surged out of the cabarets at the closing hour and held them until sunrise.

The old Pekin Theatre at 2700 State Street, for years one of the leading negro amusement houses in the country, became one of these dance halls. [The establishments] were openly condemned for a long time without being molested, but early in 1918 the City Council passed an anti-cabaret ordinance which put a damper for a time on the night life of the city.

Last Spring, however, the Mayoralty election came around again. Mayor Thompson was a candidate for re-election and was re-elected. The Black Belt did its duty.

When the primary campaign opened the lid was tossed overboard. Resorts which had been closed reopened. The Black Belt became again the centre of night activities.

With the elections over in April and prohibition looming up in the near future, the hearts of the city officials were softened, and the lid stayed off. In the last few months conditions in the Black Belt have been almost unprecedented. Men who have traveled the country over say that nowhere in the United States have they witnessed such scenes as they saw in the notorious "black and tan" resorts in the South Side in Chicago.

State's Attorney Maclay Hoyne of Chicago a few days ago laid the blame for the race riots at the door of the politicians, who, he said, taught the negroes disrespect for the law.

"The Police Department," said Mr. Hoyne, "has been demoralized to such an extent by the politicians, black and white, on the South Side that they are afraid to arrest and prosecute men with political backing or who claim to have political influence."

Others have issued similar warnings from time to time in the last two or three years.

Municipal Judge Harry M. Fisher, after sitting for a time in the Morals Court, where the larger per cent of the offenders were negro men and women said:

"My opinion, based on observation in this court, is that crime conditions among colored people are being deliberately fostered by the present City Administration. Disorderly cabarets, thieves and depraved women are allowed in the section of the city where colored people live. They have an expression, 'the law is around tonight,' as a warning to behave, so seldom is the law enforced."

New York Times, September 30, 1919

Lynching in Omaha

700 Federal Troops Quiet Omaha; Mayor Recovering; Omaha Mob Rule Defined by Most of the Population

SPECIAL TO THE NEW YORK TIMES: *Lynching of Negro Openly Rejoiced in, Although Business Men Condemn It. TROOPS PATROL STREETS. Balloon Watches Over Negro Section—Gen. Wood Arrives Today to Take Command. WILL PROSECUTE RIOTERS. Grand Jury to be Summoned Today—Hundreds of Arrests Threatened.*

OMAHA, Neb. September 29—With 700 Federal soldiers on guard in the streets, the city is calm tonight, and there has been no renewal of the violent outbreaks of yesterday and early this morning, which resulted in the lynching of a negro and an attempt to lynch Mayor E. P. Smith, the fatal shooting of a rioter and injuring of several score of others, and the partial destruction of the County Court House by bombs thrown by members of the mob.

Meanwhile, the condition of Mayor Smith, who was in a critical state early this morning, is reported better tonight.

The Federal troops arrived during the early morning and daytime from Forts Omaha and Brooks, Neb., and Camp Dodge, Iowa, for riot duty. More troops are on the way, and when all arrive there will be nearly 2,000 regulars on duty in the city.

The troops are distributed at strategic points throughout the city, and have machine guns ready for use if necessary.

Military headquarters has been established at Central Police Station, by Colonel J. E. Morris of the 20th Infantry. Members of the Police Department were put under his orders. General Leonard Wood, Commander of the Central Department of the Army, who was ordered here by Secretary Baker to take charge of the situation, is expected tomorrow morning.

Governor McKelvie, who has been in the western part of the State, telegraphed the authorities today that he would be in Omaha late tonight.

The calm in the city is due partially, the police think, to the fact that at dark tonight a heavy electrical storm and rainstorm broke over the city, driving everybody to cover. For more than an hour the downpour continued, flooding the streets and rendering traffic almost impossible. Street cars were impeded and were forced to stop half an hour.

During the storm the 700 regulars continued to patrol their beats around the riot district, in the business section of the city and in the negro districts.

OBSERVATION BALLOON ON DUTY

At Twenty-fourth and Lake streets, in the heart of the negro district, 300 soldiers are stationed. Eighteen machine guns are trained down the adjacent streets.

Up aloft an observation balloon from Fort Omaha swings to and fro, while observers in the basket watch for fires that might be started in the negro district.

The negroes are well armed. Negro leaders today told the City Commissioners that practically every one of the 10,000 negroes in Omaha was armed and is ready to fight for his life and home. Last night the negroes looted several hardware stores in the north end of the city and obtained additional weapons.

. . . A meeting attended by several hundred of the prominent business and professional men in the city was held today. At its close a statement was issued, stating in part:

In response to a call from the civil authorities in Omaha and in the State of Nebraska, General Leonard Wood has instructed Colonel Weiss to have the streets of Omaha patrolled by regular soldiers of the United States Army.

Full protection will be afforded to all persons threatened with disorder and no further attacks or outbreaks of any kind will be permitted. Arms carried by private citizens must be surrendered. No crowds will be permitted to congregate where disorders may arise.

Those persons who took part in the mob violence last night are in the eyes of the law guilty of murder. Civil government will be immediately restored in the City of Omaha, and all criminal participants in the mob will be promptly prosecuted.

But while the mob does not meet with the approval of business and professional men of the city, it undoubtedly met with the approval of the average workingman as well as clerks, stenographers and people of those classes.

These constituting by far the majority, are not only not ashamed but are actually pleased at the work of the mob last night. They are proud that Omaha lynched a negro, burned the body, wrecked a million-dollar courthouse and jail, burned thousands of invaluable records and strung the Mayor of the city up to a trolley pole because he refused to order the police to throw the negro Brown into the hands of thousands who were clamoring for his blood.

That sentiment is not confined to the men. Many Omaha women glory in the fact that Brown, who assaulted a 19-year-old white girl and who was living with another white woman, had been burned and hanged.

Many women, of course, are ashamed of the action of the mob, but in the main the women are pleased.

Today scores of young girls in stores and offices were bragging about their part in the mob last night. Many told of being in the mob from its inception in the early afternoon until the closing scene when Brown's body was burned just across the street from the Federal Courthouse and Post Office.

A vigorous prosecution of the men responsible for the lynching of Brown is being prepared by County Attorney Shotwell. Several arrests were made this afternoon of small boys who threw bricks through the windows of the Court House, but these were released on the promise of their parents that they would be in Juvenile Court when called. The Sheriff had been afraid to put the boys in jail for fear the mob would return tonight and destroy the building.

A Grand Jury will be called tomorrow by the District Court to inquire into the rioting. A list of hundreds of those who were in the mob is being prepared and these will be summoned to testify. Photographs made by newspaper photographers, which plainly show the faces of men and women, are being obtained by the authorities, and will be used as proof in the trials which the County Attorney says will follow swiftly.

Lieut. Col. Wuest today issued this proclamation:

To the Citizens of Omaha:

Rioting in the streets of Omaha has been suppressed and the situation is well in hand. All law-abiding citizens of whatever race or color will be given full protection of person and property. It is requested of all good citizens that all firearms and ammunition be surrendered without delay to Chief of Police or to the nearest military headquarters. This will be expected of all irrespective of race or color. Property so surrendered will be receipted and later returned. All persons are warned that looting will be summarily dealt with. The carrying of arms wil be looked upon as an intention to disregard the law.

Have confidence in the military forces that are protecting you and assist them in restoring order by obeying their instruction.

JACOB S. WUEST
Lieutenant Colonel, U.S.A., Commanding First Omaha

The American Legion this afternoon decided to assist in maintaining law and order, although returning soldiers and sailors cut a sorry picture last night. Many leading spirits of the mob wore uniforms and soldiers with guns were scattered through the mob everywhere. The only man killed besides the negro Brown was a returned soldier.

But this afternoon 300 members of the Legion have been shipped from the State arsenal at Lincoln and will arrive tomorrow morning.

New York Times, October 2, 1919

Nine Killed in Fight with Arkansas Posse

HELENA, Ark. Oct. 2——Clinton Leonard, J. A. Tappen of Helena, whites, and seven negroes are known to be dead at Elaine, near Helena, as a result of clashes today, with a posse searching for the persons who last night from ambush fired upon and killed W. D. Adkins, railroad special agent, according to reports reaching here tonight.

A third white man, Ira Proctor, and a number of negroes are known to have been wounded.

Tappen, who was prominent in business in Helena, died at a hospital here from wounds received in the fighting in the streets of Elaine. Proctor, who was also brought here, is not expected to live. The body of Lee, who died from wounds at Elaine, was brought to his home here.

Women and children of Elaine and vicinity are being brought to Helena on a special train for safety. Armed men are patroling the streets of Helena.

An engineer of the Missouri Pacific Railroad, who arrived in Helena tonight, said that he pulled a steel gondola loaded with women and children out of Elaine late today and that his train was fired upon by negroes from trees along the track.

A white prisoner was brought to this city late tonight with a group of fifteen negroes who were placed in the County Jail. The white man is alleged to have been the leader of the negroes who fought the Sheriff's posse throughout the day. The jail is under strong guard.

The trouble began last night when Deputies Pratt and Adkins and a negro "trusty" were ambushed opposite a negro church at Hoop Spur, ten miles north of Elaine, while on their way to arrest members of the Clem family, who are said to be involved in a row among themselves.

The accounts of the surviving deputy and the negro trusty indicating that the attack on the three men had been made by an organized band of negroes, posses were hastily organized by the Sheriff and rushed to Elaine. The first posse to arrive was met by a force of armed negroes and immediately sent back urgent calls for reinforcements, declaring the negroes were assembling in large numbers and had begun promiscuously firing on white persons. Within an hour reports came of a pitched battle in the streets of Elaine between the posse and negroes.

Later it was reported that the negroes had been driven from Elaine, but that fighting was still in progress a mile to the north, where the band was said to have received reinforcements. Fighting in this vicinity continued late in the afternoon, but died down toward dark.

Returning members of the posse brought numerous stories and

rumors, through all of which ran the belief that the rioting was due to propaganda distributed among the negroes by white men. It was clearly indicated they said, that there was an organization of negroes antagonistic to the white residents in the southern part of the county. Negroes in that section, it was said, had asserted that they would not pick the present cotton crop unless paid their own price, and numbers of them are reported to have refused to work for the white farmers for day wages.

It is stated on good authority that negroes in the vicinity of Elaine have been holding secret meetings at night and that unidentified white men have been circulating literature among them.

Editorial, New York Times, October 8, 1919

Plotters Behind the Plots

Two facts, or perhaps it is safer to say two natural conclusions from available knowledge give a high degree of plausibility to the charge made by several responsible officials in the State of Arkansas that the I.W.W. have been inciting the negroes there to rise in armed revolt and massacre their white neighbors.

The first of these facts or conclusions is that no other group of people living in this country would do such a thing, and the other is that the record of the I.W.W. shows that among its members are men quite capable of it.

That, of course, is not evidence of the sort that would lead to conviction in court, or that even would justify arrests. There is more than a chance, however, that the investigation which the Attorney General and the Postmaster General have been asked to make, and which presumably they will undertake at once, will reveal just who have been working on the ignorance and animosities of the negroes and deluding them into the belief that such wrongs as they have and such ambitions as they nourish can be attained by a "revolution."

None knows better than the I.W.W. leaders the utter hopelessness of accomplishing in that way more than a few murders, at frightful ultimate cost to the negroes themselves, but such considerations would not cause either hesitation or compunction in minds aiming to bring about any and every disturbance of the peace that can be devised. So the promoters of the abhorrent enterprise have been spending not a little money in organizing and arming the victims of their plot, and they have secured, by means easily imaginable, the support of certain papers in the North, not openly to preach a race war, indeed, but to exaggerate real grievances and to create unreal ones, and by clear implication to convey the thought that for such a situation only one remedy—the most desperate—exists.

The Chicago Commission on Race Relations

The Negro in Chicago: A Study of Race Relations and a Race Riot

BACKGROUND

In July, 1919, a race riot involving whites and Negroes occurred in Chicago. For some time thoughtful citizens, white and Negro, had sensed increasing tension, but, having no local precedent of riot and wholesale bloodshed, had neither prepared themselves for it nor taken steps to prevent it. The collecting of arms by members of both races was known to the authorities, and it was evident that this was in preparation for aggression as well as for self-defense.

Several minor clashes preceded the riot. On July 3, 1917, a white saloon-keeper who, according to the coroner's physician, died of heart trouble, was incorrectly reported in the press to have been killed by a Negro. That evening a party of young white men riding in an automobile fired upon a group of Negroes at Fifty-third and Federal streets. In July and August of the same year recruits from the Great Lakes Naval Training Station clashed frequently with Negroes, each side accusing the other of being the aggressor.

Gangs of white "toughs," made up largely of the membership of so-called athletic clubs from the neighborhood between Roosevelt Road and Sixty-third Street, Wentworth Avenue and the city limits—a district contiguous to the neighborhood of the largest Negro settlement—were a constant menace to Negroes who traversed sections of the territory going to and returning from work. The activities of these gangs and athletic clubs became bolder in the spring of 1919, and on the night of

June 21, five weeks before the riot, two wanton murders of Negroes occurred, those of Sanford Harris and Joseph Robinson. Harris, returning to his home on Dearborn Street at about 11:30 at night, passed a group of young white men. They threatened him and he ran. He had gone but a short distance when one of the group shot him. He died soon afterward. Policemen who came on the scene made no arrests, even when the assailant was pointed out by a white woman witness of the murder. On the same evening Robinson, a Negro laborer, forty-seven years of age, was attacked while returning from work by a gang of white "toughs" at Fifty-fifth Street and Princeton Avenue, apparently without provocation, and stabbed to death.

Negroes were greatly incensed over these murders, but their leaders, joined by many friendly whites, tried to allay their fears and counseled patience.

After the killing of Harris and Robinson, notices were conspicuously posted on the South Side that an effort would be made to "get all the niggers on July 4th" The notices called for help from sympathizers. Negroes, in turn, whispered around the warning to prepare for a riot; and they did prepare.

Since the riot in East St. Louis, July 4, 1917, there had been others in different parts of the country which evidenced a widespread lack of restraint in mutual antipathies and suggested further resorts to lawlessness. Riots and race clashes occurred in Chester, Pennsylvania; Longview, Texas; Coatesville, Pennsylvania; Washington, D. C.; and Norfolk, Virginia, before the Chicago riot.

Aside from general lawlessness and disastrous riots that preceded the riot here discussed, there were other factors which may be mentioned briefly here. In Chicago considerable unrest had been occasioned in industry by increasing competition between white and Negro laborers following a sudden increase in the Negro population due to the migration of Negroes from the South. This increase developed a housing crisis. The Negroes overran the hitherto recognized area of Negro residence, and when they took houses in adjoining neighborhoods friction ensued. In the two years just preceding the riot, twenty-seven Negro dwellings were wrecked by bombs thrown by unidentified persons.

STORY OF THE RIOT

Sunday afternoon, July 27, 1919, hundreds of white and Negro bathers crowded the lake-front beaches at Twenty-sixth and Twenty-ninth streets. This is the eastern boundary of the thickest Negro residence area. At Twenty-sixth Street Negroes were in great majority; at Twenty-ninth Street there were more whites. An imaginary line in the water separating the two beaches had been generally observed by the two races. Under the prevailing relations, aided by wild rumors and reports, this line served virtually as a challenge to either side to cross it. Four Negroes who attempted to enter the water from the "white" side were driven away by the whites. They returned with more Negroes, and there followed a series of attacks with stones, first one side gaining the advantage, then the other.

Eugene Williams, a Negro boy of seventeen, entered the water from the side used by Negroes and drifted across the line supported by a railroad tie. He was observed by the crowd on the beach and promptly became a target for stones. He suddenly released the tie, went down and was drowned. Guilt was immediately placed on Stauber, a young white man, by Negro witnesses who declared that he threw the fatal stone.[1]

White and Negro men dived for the boy without result. Negroes demanded that the policeman present arrest Stauber. He refused; and at this crucial moment arrested a Negro on a white man's complaint. Negroes then attacked the officer. These two facts, the drowning and the refusal of the policeman to arrest Stauber, together marked the beginning of the riot.

Two hours after the drowning, a Negro, James Crawford, fired into a group of officers summoned by the policeman at the beach and was killed by a Negro policeman. Reports and rumors circulated rapidly, and new crowds began to gather. Five white men were injured in clashes near the beach. As darkness came, Negroes in white districts to the west suffered severely. Between 9:00 P.M. and 3:00 A.M. twenty-seven Negroes were beaten, seven stabbed, and four shot. Monday morning was quiet, and Negroes went to work as usual.

Returning from work in the afternoon, many Negroes were attacked by white ruffians. Streetcar routes, especially at transfer points, were the centers of lawlessness. Trolleys were pulled from the wires, and Negro passengers were dragged into the street, beaten, stabbed, and shot. The police were powerless to cope with these numerous assaults. During Monday, four Negro men and one white assailant were killed, and thirty Negroes were severely beaten in streetcar clashes. Four white men were killed, six stabbed, five shot, and nine severely beaten. It was rumored that the white occupants of the Angelus Building at Thirty-fifth Street and Wabash Avenue had shot a Negro. Negroes gathered about the building. The white tenants sought police protection, and one hundred policemen, mounted and on foot, responded. In a clash with the mob, the police killed four Negroes and injured many.

Raids into the Negro residence area then began. Automobiles sped through the streets, the occupants shooting at random. Negroes retaliated by "sniping" from ambush. At midnight surface and elevated car service was discontinued because of a strike for wage increases, and thousands of employees were cut off from work.

On Tuesday, July 29, Negro men en route on foot to their jobs

1. The coroner's jury found that Williams had drowned from fear of stone-throwing which kept him from the shore.

through hostile territory were killed. White soldiers and sailors in uniform, aided by civilians, raided the "Loop" business section, killing two Negroes and beating and robbing several others. Negroes living among white neighbors in Englewood, far to the south, were driven from their homes, their household goods were stolen, and their houses were burned or wrecked. On the West Side an Italian mob, excited by a false rumor that an Italian girl had been shot by a Negro, killed Joseph Lovings, a Negro.

Wednesday night at 10:30 Mayor Thompson yielded to pressure and asked the help of the three regiments of militia which had been stationed in nearby armories during the most severe rioting, awaiting the call. They immediately took up positions throughout the South Side. A rainfall Wednesday night and Thursday kept many people in their homes, and by Friday the rioting had abated. On Saturday incendiary fires burned forty-nine houses in the immigrant neighborhood west of the Stock Yards. Nine hundred and forty-eight people, mostly Lithuanians, were made homeless, and the property loss was about $250,000. Responsibility for the fires was never fixed.

The total casualties of this reign of terror were thirty-eight deaths— fifteen white, twenty-three Negro—and 537 people injured. Forty-one per cent of the reported clashes occurred in the white neighborhood near the Stock Yards between the south branch of the Chicago River and Fifty-fifth Street, Wentworth Avenue and the city limits, and 34 per cent in the "Black Belt" between Twenty-second and Thirty-ninth streets, Wentworth Avenue and Lake Michigan. Others were scattered.

Responsibility for many attacks was definitely placed by many witnesses upon the "athletic clubs," including "Ragen's Colts," the "Hamburgers," "Aylwards," "Our Flag," the "Standard," the "Sparklers," and several others. The mobs were made up for the most part of boys between fifteen and twenty-two. Older persons participated but the youth of the rioters was conspicuous in every clash. Little children witnessed the brutalities and frequently pointed out the injured when the police arrived.

RUMORS AND THE RIOT

Wild rumors were in circulation by word of mouth and in the press throughout the riot and provoked many clashes. These included stories of atrocities committed by one race against the other. Reports of the numbers of white and Negro dead tended to produce a feeling that the score must be kept even. Newspaper reports, for example, showed 6 per cent more whites injured than Negroes. As a matter of fact, there were 28 per cent more Negroes injured than whites. The *Chicago Tribune* on July 29 reported twenty persons killed, of whom thirteen were white and seven colored. The true figures were exactly the opposite.

Among the rumors provoking fear were numerous references to the arming of Negroes. In the *Daily News* of July 30, for example, appeared the subheadline: "Alderman Jos. McDonough tells how he was shot at on South Side visit. Says enough ammunition in section to last for years of guerrilla warfare." In the article following, the reference to ammunition was repeated but not elaborated or explained.

The alderman was quoted as saying that the mayor contemplated opening up Thirty-fifth and Forty-seventh streets in order that colored people might get to their work. He thought this would be most unwise for, he stated, "They are armed and white people are not. We must defend ourselves if the city authorities won't protect us." Continuing his story, he described bombs going off: "I saw white men and women running through the streets dragging children by the hands and carrying babies in their arms. Frightened white men told me the police captains had just rushed through the district crying, 'For God's sake, arm; they are coming; we cannot hold them.' "

Whether or not the alderman was correctly quoted, the effect of such statements on the public was the same. There is no record in any of the riot testimony in the coroner's office or state's attorney's office of any bombs going off during the riot, nor of police captains warning the white people to arm, nor of any fear by whites of a Negro invasion. In the Berger Odman case before a coroner's jury, there was a statement to the effect that a sergeant of police warned the Negroes of Ogden Park to arm and to shoot at the feet of rioters if they attempted to invade the few blocks marked off for Negroes by the police. Negroes were warned, not whites.

CONDUCT OF THE POLICE

Chief of Police John J. Garrity, in explaining the inability of the police to curb the rioters, said that there was not a sufficient force to police one-third of the city. Aside from this, Negroes distrusted the white police officers, and it was implied by the chief and stated by State's Attorney Hoyne, that many of the police were "grossly unfair in making arrests." There were instances of actual police participation in the rioting as well as neglect of duty. Of 229 persons arrested and accused of various criminal activities during the riot, 154 were Negroes and seventy-five were whites. Of those indicted, eighty-one were Negroes and forty-seven were whites. Although this, on its face, would indicate great riot activity on the part of Negroes, further reports of clashes show that of 520 persons injured, 342 were Negroes and 178 were whites. The fact that twice as many Negroes appeared as defendants and twice as many Negroes as whites were injured, leads to the conclusion that whites were not apprehended as readily as Negroes.

Many of the depredations outside the "Black Belt" were encouraged by the absence of policemen. Out of a force of 3,000 police, 2,800 were massed in the "Black Belt" during the height of the rioting. In the "Loop" district, where two Negroes were killed and several others wounded, there were only three policemen and one sergeant. The Stock Yards district, where the greatest number of injuries occurred, was also weakly protected.

THE MILITIA

Although Governor Lowden had ordered the militia into the city promptly and they were on hand on the second day of the rioting, their services were not requested by the mayor and chief of police until the evening of the fourth day. The reason expressed by the chief for this delay was a belief that inexperienced militiamen would add to the deaths and disorder. But the troops, when called, proved to be clearly of high character, and their discipline was good, not a case of breach of discipline being reported during their occupation. They were distributed more proportionately through all the riotous areas than the police and, although they reported some hostility from members of "athletic clubs," the rioting soon ceased.

RESTORATION OF ORDER

Throughout the rioting, various social organizations and many citizens were at work trying to hold hostilities in check and to restore order. The Chicago Urban League, Wabash Avenue Y.M.C.A., American Red Cross, and various other social organizations and the churches of the Negro community gave attention to caring for stranded Negroes, advising them of dangers, keeping them off the streets and, in such ways as were possible, co-operating with the police. The packing companies took their pay to Negro employees, and various banks made loans. Local newspapers in their editorial columns insistently condemned the disorder and counseled calmness.

THE AFTERMATH

Of the thirty-eight persons killed in the riot:

Fifteen met death at the hands of mobs. Coroner's juries recommended that the members of the unknown mobs be apprehended. They were never found.

Six were killed in circumstances fixing no criminal responsibility: three white men were killed by Negroes in self-defense, and three Negroes were shot by policemen in the discharge of their duty.

Four Negroes were killed in the Angelus riot. The coroner made no recommendations, and the cases were not carried farther.

Four cases, two Negro and two white, resulted in recommendations from coroner's juries for further investigation of certain persons. Sufficient evidence was lacking for indictments against them.

Nine cases led to indictments. Of this number four cases resulted in convictions.

Thus in only four cases of death was criminal responsibility fixed and punishment meted out.

Indictments and convictions, divided according to the race of the persons criminally involved, were as follows:

	NEGRO		WHITE	
	Cases	*Persons*	*Cases*	*Persons*
Indictments	6	17	3	4
Convictions	2	3	2	2

Despite the community's failure to deal firmly with those who disturbed its peace and contributed to the reign of lawlessness that shamed Chicago before the world, there is evidence that the riot aroused many citizens of both races to a quickened sense of the suffering and disgrace which had come and might again come to the city, and developed a determination to prevent a recurrence of so disastrous an outbreak of race hatred. This was manifest on at least three occasions in 1920 when, confronted suddenly with events out of which serious riots might easily have grown, people of both races acted with such courage and promptness as to end the trouble early. One of these was the murder of two innocent white men and the wounding of a Negro policeman by a band of Negro fanatics who styled themselves "Abyssinians"; another was the killing of a white man by a Negro whom he had attacked while returning from work; and still another was the riotous attacks of sailors from the Great Lakes Naval Training Station on Negroes in Waukegan, Illinois.

OUTSTANDING FEATURES OF THE RIOT

This study of the facts of the riot of 1919, the events as they happened hour by hour, the neighborhoods involved, the movements of mobs, the part played by rumors, and the handling of the emergency by the various authorities, shows certain outstanding features which may be listed as follows:

a. The riot violence was not continuous hour by hour, but was intermittent.

b. The greatest number of injuries occurred in the district west and inclusive of Wentworth Avenue, and south of the south branch of the Chicago River to Fifty-fifth Street, or in the Stock Yards district. The next greatest number occurred in the so-called Black Belt: Twenty-second to Thirty-ninth streets, inclusive, and Wentworth Avenue to the lake, exclusive of Wentworth Avenue; Thirty-ninth to Fifty-fifth streets, inclusive, and Clark Street to Michigan Avenue, exclusive of Michigan Avenue.

c. Organized raids occurred only after a period of sporadic clashes and spontaneous mob outbreaks.

d. Main thoroughfares witnessed 76 per cent of the injuries on the South Side. The streets which suffered most severely were State, Halsted, Thirty-first, Thirty-fifth, and Forty-seventh. Transfer corners were always centers of disturbances.

e. Most of the rioting occurred after work hours among idle crowds on the streets. This was particularly true after the streetcar strike began.

f. Gangs, particularly of young whites, formed definite nuclei for crowd and mob formation. "Athletic clubs" supplied the leaders of many gangs.

g. Crowds and mobs engaged in rioting were generally composed of a small nucleus of leaders and an acquiescing mass of spectators. The leaders were mostly young men, usually between the ages of sixteen and twenty-one. Dispersal was most effectively accomplished by sudden, unexpected gun fire.

h. Rumor kept the crowds in an excited, potential mob state. The press was responsible for giving wide dissemination to much of the inflammatory matter in spoken rumors, though editorials calculated to allay race hatred and help the forces of order were factors in the restoration of peace.

i. The police lacked sufficient forces for handling the riot; they were hampered by the Negroes' distrust of them; routing orders and records were not handled with proper care; certain officers were undoubtedly unsuited to police or riot duty.

j. The militiamen employed in this riot were of an unusually high type. This unquestionably accounts for the confidence placed in them by both races. Riot training, definite orders, and good staff work contributed to their efficiency.

k. There was a lack of energetic co-operation between the police department and the state's attorney's office in the discovery and conviction of rioters.

The riot was merely a symptom of serious and profound disorders lying beneath the surface of race relations in Chicago. The study of the riot, therefore, as to its interlocking provocations and causes, required a study of general race relations that made possible so serious and sudden an outbreak. Thus to understand the riot and guard against another, the Commission probed systematically into the principal phases of race contact and sought accurate information on matters which in the past have been influenced by dangerous speculation; and on the basis of its discoveries certain suggestions to the community are made.

Allen D. Grimshaw

Three Cases of Racial Violence in the United States

Racial violence is a consequence not of conscious policy decisions but results rather from reactions by the dominant group to real or perceived assaults upon the *status quo* within a context of variations of attitude and action in agencies of external control. The understanding of cases of color violence necessitates a prior understanding of the nature of the accommodative structure, and of different kinds of assault upon that structure.

Color violence has occurred in every region of the United States and in both rural and urban areas. The purpose of this paper is to distinguish between two major types of racial disturbances in the United States, the "Southern-style" race riot and the "Northern-style" race riot, and to attempt to delineate some of the differences both in the modes of assault on the accommodative structures and in the actual chronologies of these disturbances.[1] Discussions of the Tulsa (Oklahoma) riot of 1921, essentially a Southern-style race riot; the Chicago (Illinois) riot of 1919, an almost "ideal-typical" Northern-style riot; and the East St. Louis (Illinois) riot of 1917, a riot which in background and in actual pattern of violence could be classified as a "mixed-type" riot, will be followed by an attempt to sort out some of these differences.

TULSA[2]

In 1920 Tulsa had a total population of 72,075, including 8,878 Negroes.[3] Although the Negro population was concentrated in one segre-

1. Myrdal, 1944, distinguished between riots where "Negroes fight as unreservedly as whites" and what he called "One way terrorization." The similarities and differences between the distinction and that of "Northern" and "Southern-style" riots will be seen below.

2. This account of the rioting in Tulsa draws heavily on the reports in the *New York Times* (hereinafter cited as *Times*), 70:23,140; 23,143; 23,146; 23,158; 23,164; and 23,167, June 1921. A shorter account drawing on a number of newspapers for details and editorial comment is *The Literary Digest*: 1921.

3. United States Department of Commerce, Bureau of the Census: 1920.

gated area, Tulsa was in other respects a Southern city in so far as race relations were concerned.[4] While a few Negroes identified as "lackeys" of the white community had achieved a certain amount of economic security, the majority of Negroes in the labor force were engaged in menial occupations.

For some months prior to the outbreak of large-scale color violence in Tulsa, that city, along with the entire state, had been experiencing a steady deterioration in patterns of race relations. White Oklahomans, along with those elsewhere in the South and for that matter throughout the United States, had observed with dismay the new attitudes brought back by Negro veterans of the First World War. Within the country the war had been accompanied by a new militance in the Negro population's demands for rights and opportunities due to Negroes as citizens. Oklahoma was in early 1921 experiencing a minor agricultural recession, particularly manifested in the fall of cotton prices (*Times*, 70:23,141, 3 June 1921). Rural Negroes moving into urban centers added to the increase of social tensions. Finally, it was alleged that agitators, particularly "I.W.W." and "Bolshevik" organizers, but some also from growing American nationalist groups of the period, were contributing to disaffection of the Negro community (*Times*, 70:23,142, 4 June 1921).

On the last day of May 1921, a Negro named Rowland was arrested, accused of attacking a white elevator girl (who in addition to being white was also an orphan, making his alleged offence even more heinous). He was taken to the County Court House and rumors circulated in the Negro community that he was to be lynched. Early in the evening a crowd of "heavily armed blacks" assembled before the Court House with the ostensible purpose of preventing a lynching. A police attempt to disperse the Negro crowd and to throw a protective cordon around the building was met by a volley of shots from the Negroes.

News of this incident quickly spread and armed whites soon began to converge on the area. Some broke into hardware and sporting-goods stores and armed themselves. Automobiles loaded with armed whites sped through the city in all directions. The police were unable to gain control of the situation. According to reports in the *New York Times*, the first actual shooting occurred when a Negro was stopped by a police officer and disarmed. When, as reported by the officer, he resisted, the officer shot him dead.

The crowd of whites near the Court House increased in size and belligerency. When a white detective was unable to stop a verbal dispute between Negro and white factions firing broke out and soon became general. The Negroes gradually fell back on the Negro area where they "entrenched" themselves and held the white mob at bay until daybreak. Convinced by the firing at the Court House that the local police had

---

4. Racial segregation in housing is a relatively recent phenomenon in Southern cities. Until a few years ago Negro residence was scattered throughout urban areas, at least in part to facilitate the use of Negroes as domestic servants.

lost control, the municipal authorities appealed to the Governor for armed assistance. He, in turn, promptly directed the Attorney General to take steps necessary to establish control. Three companies of guardsmen were rushed to Tulsa and surrounded the Court House. Other guard units were alerted. The Court House mob was dispersed by morning, and in the confusion Rowland was spirited away.

It was on the following day, when the alleged culprit had already been removed from the city, that major violence occurred. Armed whites participated in a mass assault upon the Negro section, most of which was burned during the rioting. Although heavy armed resistance occasionally met the white attack, Negro activity was primarily defensive. Many fled the area and gave themselves up to white authorities. A Negro deputy sheriff was active in disarming many Negroes. What seems to have started as a result of the intention of some Negroes to prevent a possible lynching became, before its bloody conclusion, a massacre of Negroes reminiscent in character, if not in scale, of pogrom. Many people were killed, more Negroes than whites,[5] and property damage in the Negro area amounted to almost total devastation of an area a mile square.

If the demands for completeness of explanation are not too rigorous, a distinction between "sacred" and "secular" precipitating incidents in color violence can prove suggestive. A major foundation of the "sacred" doctrines of white supremacy is the need for protection of white Southern womanhood. Northern urban race riots have usually resulted from assaults upon the accommodative pattern related to secular spheres: housing, recreation, transportation and employment (though precipitating incidents may still be more "sacred" in content). Violation of "sacred" spheres of the accommodative pattern has been the immediate cause of Southern-style riots. The Tulsa riot, with its case of alleged Negro assault upon a white woman, provides therefore a classic example of a Southern-style riot in precipitating incident.[6]

A second characteristic of Southern riots is a pattern of non-resistance on the part of the minority population. This pattern did not characterize the Tulsa disorders in its early stages, as can be seen from the account above. Once the riot was underway, however, the colored population retreated to the Negro section and in subsequent violence acted defensively. Most Negroes did not resist but fled to the protection of whites. Had there been no resistance, property destruction would have been much smaller and the number of dead much reduced.

The Tulsa riot served to re-establish patterns of race relations in their traditional form. Negroes fled the city and some the state. For at least a time the colored population became cowed and submissive.

5. First reports were of 25 white and 60 Negro dead. Later this figure dropped to 9 whites and 15 Negroes; still later the total figure was raised again.

6. It would be sophistical to attempt to press this sacred-secular dichotomy too far. It is obvious that there are economic bases involved in the doctrine of white supremacy. But, it may be argued, the economic factors themselves reflect status concerns.

White business leaders prepared, in the post-riot period, to rebuild the Negro community though there is no evidence that this paternalistic project was ever carried through (*Times,* 70:23,143, 5 June 1921).

CHICAGO

The Negro population of Chicago in 1920 was a little over 109,000, slightly less than five per cent of a total population of over two million (Duncan and Duncan, 1957, is probably the best study available of the growth and changes in a Negro population of any major American city). While white Chicagoans shared the generalized discomfort of the white reaction to Negro gains during the war period and to new Negro "arrogance," there were in Chicago additional conflicts between whites and Negroes in a large number of secular areas.

The summer of 1919 found Chicagoans, like other Americans, trying to forget the war, to relax and to "return to normalcy." The Chicago of 1919, however, was a city vastly different not only from the Windy City of 1900, but even from the Chicago of immediately prewar years. Along with other Northern industrial communities the city had experienced sharp changes in its demographic structure during the war years. Not only had growth created great pressures on facilities; but it had also been accompanied by noticeable changes in population composition. Large numbers of migrant Negroes, largely from the rural South, had been drawn to the city by the attraction of high wages in war production.

It is a truism that outside conflict increases internal solidarity. It is equally true that when outside struggle terminates, suppressed internal frictions re-emerge, perhaps with an increment built up through the period of temporary truce. Even during the war there had been housing disputes and struggles over recreational facilities and public transport and occasional clashes over "racial insults" and breaches of "racial etiquette." With the disappearance of the unifying pressures of war these disputes took on deeper significance.

It has been observed that large numbers of Negroes entered the Chicago labor market during the war. They entered as non-union workers. The war over union versus non-union employment re-emerged as an issue. The antagonism of white union men against "scabs" and "strikebreakers" was augmented by anti-Negro prejudice. Veterans in the labor market made the problem even more complex. Chicago had been the scene of some of the most bitter struggles for union recognition. White workers had no intention of having this fight negated by employment of non-union labor, particularly Negroes. The latter were understandably reluctant to give up advances made during the war years (Grimshaw, 1962b). Whites and colored alike perceived threats to their means of livelihood.

Another problem area involved both the distribution of power and authority in specific areas and a number of underlying ideological values of American society was of more than local interest in 1919.[7] During the war, Negro citizens had raised questions as to why they should participate in a "white man's war." (Note parallel to complaints of white labor at the time of the Civil War "Draft" riots. See Grimshaw 1962b.) They were loyal and contributed heavily to the war effort, but the Negro press maintained adamantly that the full benefits of democracy should be extended to all citizens. Returning Negro veterans felt they had earned these rights, and some said that if they were not freely extended they would take them. More militant expressions of this attitude became widespread with the war's conclusion. The dominant white population, particularly in the South but in the North as well, expressed its concern over apparent breaches of the accommodative structure. With the disappearance of external threat expressions of anxiety about the Negro "forgetting his place" came from spokesmen of the white community who said he would be kept in that "place," by force if necessary. There had been scattered cases of violence even during the war. The war over, whites and Negroes confronted one another in sharp disagreement over the distribution of power and authority and over interpretations of basic ideological values—those of white supremacy and those of equality.

At the same time, a climate of fear and suspicion concerning the "Red Menace" further confused the national scene. The revolution in Russia seemed frightening, and the Government and policies of the new nation were unknown quantities. Predictions of "world revolution" did not relieve anxieties. Alarms of "Bolshevik" propaganda were abroad and the nonracial policy of the I.W.W. was widely interpreted as evidence of a "red and black conspiracy" (see, e.g., *Times* 68:22,465; 22,471; 22,472 22,494; and 22,495 [all during the summer of 1918]). Activities of the Negro press during the war had raised questions of Negro loyalty and, although Attorney General Mitchell had given the Negro press a clean bill of health, a more radical press was appearing in the North.

Between 1 July 1919 and 1 March 1921, there were fifty-eight bomb explosions in Chicago, almost all of them obviously related to the Negro housing problem. Only two suspects were apprehended and there were no convictions (Chicago Commission on Race Relations, 1922). Every expansion of the area of Negro residence was met with resistance, frequently violent. Disputes over recreational facilities were heightened by unofficial discrimination, the activities of gangs of white hoodlums, and by the inefficiency of the police. Difficulties in transport, an area in which many whites had their only contacts with Negroes, centered around the blundering efforts of Negro migrants to adjust themselves to the complexities of Northern city life and were aggravated by excite-

7. J. S. Coleman, 1957, suggests a classification of the general areas of conflict: the economic, that of power or authority, and that of cultural values or beliefs. Each can be seen to be involved in the background of the Chicago disturbances.

ment at the novelty of non-"Jim Crow" transport. In schools there were cases of encouragement of white children in aggressive behavior towards Negroes and some school rivalries took on aspects of interracial conflict. Finally, because of concentration of Negroes in the ghetto areas there was contact with criminal elements of the larger community and although whites and Negroes alike protested, vice flourished in the "Black Belt." There is evidence of ties between certain Negro leaders and politicians, the Chicago underworld and the municipal administration (Chicago Commission on Race Relations, 1922, and Gardiner, 1919, reprinted in this volume on pages 97 and 88, respectively).

Chicago in 1919 was a city characterized by high social tensions. Like other urban industrial areas it shared a concern over postwar economic adjustments and, more particularly, over the role of unions and of Negroes in the post-war labor force. Negroes and whites alike were disturbed by the disruption of the accommodative patterns of political power and social inequality of the pre-war period. Superimposed on these problems was a vague and not very well defined fear of "Bolshevik subversion."

The local atmosphere reflected national tensions. Specifically there were labor disputes and concern about corruption in municipal government. There was anxiety about a series of quarrels and eruptions of minor violence in housing, recreation and transport. There had been bombings. There had been interracial assaults, including two murders of Negroes. During the previous spring signs had appeared warning, "We're going to get the niggers on 4 July." Police efforts redoubled; there was no violence on that date. But Chicago was ripe for social violence.

July 27, 1919, in Chicago, was a hot Sunday following a hot and sultry summer week. Crowds of Negroes and whites bathed on the beach at Twenty-ninth Street and Lake Michigan. As was usual, an unseen line divided the two groups—but on this particular afternoon a Negro youth slipped across the line and climbed onto a raft in the "white" section. Rocks were thrown, and whatever the sequence of events may actually have been, the Negro youth was drowned (a coroner's jury ruled that he died of drowning beause he feared to swim in to shore; see Chicago Commission on Race Relations [1921], p. 97 in this volume). Negroes and whites joined in attempting to recover the body.

As the crowd increased, demands were made that the boys who had thrown the stones be arrested. The policeman on duty refused. At this juncture the first violence occurred as Negroes and whites jostled one another and insults were exchanged. In this already rumor-rife situation a Negro was arrested—by the same policeman, on the complaint of a white person. Negroes attacked the policeman. The riot had begun.

Color violence spread inland from the lake and by that evening large mobs of whites and Negroes were attacking members of the other racial group in areas near the beach. During the night violence spread through the city, remaining concentrated on the South Side. Rumors spread and the tempo of violence increased. Typical patterns of Northern urban color violence were manifested. Streetcars were stopped and Negroes hauled from them, beaten, sometimes killed. Mobs of both races operated along the peripheries of Negro neighborhoods, attacking isolated members of the other race. Negroes returning to the "Black Belt" from employment in the stockyards district were attacked by young hoodlums. Occasionally pitched battles occurred between mobs of one or the other race and policemen. Police control was ineffective and, after considerable vacillation, the Governor was petitioned for support—which he promptly provided. The Negro area was then quarantined. After a week the fighting stopped—with thirty-eight known dead, twenty-three of them Negroes. Many of both races were seriously injured and property damage was substantial. Rumors circulated of "hundreds of Negro dead," many allegedly thrown into a creek running through the area. Tenements had been razed in the district "back of the yards," apparently in an attempt by provocateurs further to inflame anti-Negro sentiment.

EAST ST. LOUIS [8]

The East St. Louis riot of 1917 shares patterns, both in background characteristics and in actual violence, with both Southern and Northern-style race riots. There is a mixture of "secular" and "sacred" patterns in causation, the actual precipitating incident being one which could be considered as mixed in meaning. In 1917 East St. Louis was already notorious as a vice center and was equally well-known as a city with a corrupt municipal administration and a weak and ineffective police force. Primarily an industrial community, it was also a railroad center.

The city had suffered a general shortage of labor, a situation aggravated by a series of strikes in the packing industry and in the plants of the Aluminum Company of America. In attempting to "break" these strikes the companies involved had sent recruiters through the South to persuade rural Negroes to come to East St. Louis. Arriving in the city, these new laborers found the claims of the recruiting agents to be at best somewhat exaggerated. Many found that they were paid considerably less than they had been promised, that there was no housing available (some were crowded into freight cars) and that the employment was not permanent as they had been promised. In addition they found considerable hostility on the part of the white laboring classes of the community who saw them not only as Negroes but, which in that situation was even worse, as "strikebreakers." At the end of one strike

---

8. This account is based in large part on United States Congress, House of Representatives, 1918. A condensed version is reprinted in this volume, pp. 61-72.

Negroes were kept in their new jobs (it was claimed at lower wages) thereby displacing white workers. When a second strike occurred the Negroes stayed, thus becoming "scabs."

Some Negroes were unable to find or retain any employment. Jobless, and without the resources upon which they could have called in the rural Southern setting, they found themselves trapped in crowded Negro slums. In early 1917 the city experienced sharp increases in crime. Freight cars were burgled, "hold-ups" were frequent, and stories began to circulate of crimes of assault and violence upon white women.

In May the trade-union leaders demanded that the local government find a way to stop the flow of "cheap Negro labor" into East St. Louis— and a way to return to their homes in the South the Negroes who had already come (*Times,* 66:21,675, 29 May 1917). At the end of the month a mob of some 3,000 whites swept through the city after a protest delegation of trade-union members had visited the City Council. Negroes were beaten, streetcars stopped and guardsmen stationed in the city were called upon to help quell the disturbances. Many Negroes left the city (*Times,* 66:21,677, 31 May 1917).

On the night of Saturday, June 30, 1917, there were minor disturbances throughout the city, as there had been all through the spring. The incident which precipitated the major eruption is obscure.[9] The Negro population apparently had organized for defence in event of a major attack, assembly to be signalled by the ringing of a church bell. It was claimed that "joy riders" rode through the Negro section, firing into residences. The church bell was rung and a large body of armed Negroes gathered. Someone telephoned the police that a mob of armed Negroes was gathering in response to the "call to arms." An automobile filled with police officers in plain clothes drove to the scene to disperse the crowd. The car was fired on, supposedly in the belief that it was the "joy riders" returning. The police retired, one of them dead and three wounded. Whatever may have been the intent of those involved in this initial incident, large mobs quickly formed to "avenge" the death of the slain policeman.

There was no major attempt to "invade" the Negro section, as had happened in Tulsa. Nor was there any large-scale aggressive activity on the part of the Negro populace as there had been in Chicago. Small mobs of from 50 to 100 whites, largely males but with a sprinkling of female leaders, pursued and assaulted individual Negroes. Fires were started on the edges of the Negro district and Negroes were shot down as they fled burning buildings. The entire area was soon in flames, but white activities seldom penetrated beyond the borders of the district. Whenever such an attempt was contemplated the appearance of sizeable bodies of armed Negroes drove the white mobs away to seek isolated victims. Streetcars were stopped and Negroes pulled from them, beaten,

9. The chronology of the riot in the *Times,* especially in 66:21,710–721, 723, is somewhat more complete than that found in the Congressional report.

and sometimes killed. Negroes found in white areas, whatever their business, were caught and beaten.

The city administration was either unable or unwilling to take effective action to halt the rioting and state troops were called in. Neither the local police nor the state troops were effective and a Congressional Committee which investigated the riots held the commander of the troops responsible. Beatings and even lynchings occurred in full view of armed soldiers who took no steps to halt the carnage. The investigating committee found that nine whites and twenty-five Negroes were known to have died but noted that other Negro dead had probably been consumed in the flames. Damage estimates of over three million dollars were later somewhat reduced. Negroes left the community in large numbers (estimates ranged as high as half the Negro population of East St. Louis), some fleeing across the river to St. Louis, others returning South (*Times,* 66:21,712 5 July 1917).

COMMENT

Southern-style race riots had three major differentiating characteristics. The immediate precipitating incident was always an alleged violation of "sacred" aspects of the accommodative pattern, though broader analysis of background factors in social tension would certainly reveal more "secular" sources of economic competition and other more mundane facts. Resistance of the Negro population, with a few sharp exceptions, was minimal—and quickly disappeared. A net result of disorders and their aftermath was a re-establishment of earlier accommodative patterns with the white community firmly in a superordinate position. This pattern—a gradual build-up of tension through assault, however moderate, on the *status quo,* followed by a real or imagined incident in which the very tenets of white supremacy were questioned and sharp reprisals in force against the Negro populace culminated in re-assertion of white dominance—occurred in all major color violence in the American South in the nineteenth and early twentieth centuries. The past tense is used advisedly, it is unlikely that such a pattern would now occur.

Causation in Northern-style riots has been more clearly "secular," even though in some instances the immediately precipitating incident may have "sacred" overtones. As has been remarked, given a sufficiently high level of social tension and a sufficiently low level of police efficiency or determination to prevent violence, almost any incident can serve to precipitate violence. And almost any incident may be so defined or re-defined as to become a "sacred" one.

In the Northern riot, however, resistance of the Negro community is typical, and white aggression and violence is met with Negro aggression and violence. Further, the social tensions which have been expressed in color violence do not disappear through the re-establishment of an earlier accommodative pattern. After the Tulsa riot there were no major interracial disturbances in that city. The Chicago riot, however, was followed by other disturbances of lesser magnitude, and Chicago has continued to be characterized by social tensions between the two racial groups and by continued assaults by Negroes upon the accommodative structure. Minor violence continued to occur in Chicago through the forties and fifties following the Second World War, and only major changes in the policing of the city prevented the occurrence of a major interracial disaster (cf. Grimshaw, 1963b).

Color violence expressed in the patterns of the Southern-style race riots is unlikely to occur again in the United States. This is not because all urban police forces have attained levels of efficiency and objectivity which permit them to exercise effective control over expressions of social tensions. Nor is it because appeals are no longer made to whites to defend the tenets of white supremacy doctrines. There are many individuals, both in the South and in the North, who are either fanatically committed to those doctrines or sufficiently cynical to use appeals to them to screen more secular motives. Southern-style riots cannot occur again because of changes in the basic temper of the Negro population. There are still many "Uncle Toms." Many members of the older generation of Negroes have been opposed to the militance with which the struggle for equal rights has been pushed by Negro youth in the South, whether in the attempt to go to schools or in attempts to eat at lunch counters. But it is doubtful that even these older Negroes would now fail to provide some resistance to large-scale attempts by whites physically to punish the Negro population as a collectivity.

Interestingly enough, the new Negro militance is most frequently expressed within a frame of Gandhian non-resistance, particularly in those groups under the leadership of the Rev. Martin Luther King and his colleagues. World-wide attention has been focussed on the nonviolent but insistent attempts by these groups to conquer "their white brothers" with love—with the help of an occasional boycott if necessary. The appeal of the picture of a church filled with praying Negroes and protected from angry whites by sullen white policemen is great, as is that of Negro young people unflinchingly permitting white hoodlums to burn them with lighted cigarettes—but refusing to respond with violence. But refusal to act with violence reaches its limits—as Gandhi himself came to know. And just as there are prayerful young Negroes courting arrest in "sit-ins," there are Negroes of many ages who sit in darkened homes with shotguns on their knees, prepared to defend themselves if the necessity arises. And, particularly in Northern cities, there are some young Negroes who do not wait for violence to come to them but are prepared to carry it into the enemy camp.

The occurrence or non-occurrence of large-scale color violence in cities in the United States continues at this juncture to depend upon the police—and other agencies of external constraint. Police forces in several Southern cities have shown in recent years that they are capable of controlling social tensions and preventing the eruption of violence. It is not clear that either the leaders or the rank and file of police forces in some other Southern cities, however, share a determination to prevent violence at the possible cost of violations of white supremacy doctrines.

If and when major color violence does erupt, it will follow the form of the Northern race riot, whether in a Northern or a Southern city. Whatever the precipitating incident may be, it can be expected that in the absence of quickly introduced police controls from outside the affected community, violence will become endemic and directed against both racial groups by members of the other race. And, when peaceful relations are finàlly re-established, it will not be with the accompaniment of restoration of an apparently harmonious accommodative structure, with whites in the dominant position. There will be no easing of the assaults by Negroes upon the *status quo,* however peaceful the actual modes of attack may be. Social tension will continue at a high level until some of the underlying "secular" causes of that tension are changed, and until members of the dominant group adopt new attitudes which will allow them to accept a new *status quo.*

6

INTERWAR AND DEPRESSION 1930–1941

Racial violence declined sharply during the interwar years, particularly as the nation became mired in the Great Depression. There was social violence, but it occurred primarily among labor groups as working men made their assault on the accommodative structure. There were fewer lynchings than had been the case in earlier decades; by the the end of the Thirties fewer than ten a year were occurring. There was only one major urban disturbance during the Thirties, the Harlem riot of 1935.

This riot, like that of 1943, differed from other so-called race riots that had occurred in earlier years (and occurred in Detroit in 1943) and was more like the disorders of the Sixties. In many ways it seemed more a class than a racial disturbance—attacks were generally directed against property or the police and there were no direct confrontations between whites and blacks. The first selection in this chapter is an early attempt I made to delineate some of these differences. This is followed by a fragment of Ralph Ellison's fictional treatment of the riot from his superb novel, *The Invisible Man*. Finally, I have included selections from the Report of the Mayor's Commission on Conditions in Harlem, a report which was suppressed by LaGuardia and published in full only in *The New York Amsterdam News*.

Allen D. Grimshaw

The Harlem Disturbances of 1935 and 1943: Deviant Cases?

There has been no attempt in the pages above to define a "race riot." Legally, the term "riot" itself has a number of variant definitions, applying to large categories of collective behavior which have not been discussed in this paper. Under English common law, "A riot is a misdemeanor which consists of a tumultuous disturbance of the peace by an assembly of three or more persons. It must employ such a show of violence that at least one person of reasonable firmness is put in fear." (See Seagle, 1934, p. 389.) Under this common law definition every variety of interracial conflict from slave rebellion and insurrection to lynching and inclusive of all the disturbances noted in this paper would be labelled riot. The disturbances in Harlem in 1935 and 1943 *were* riots.

Both of the Harlem riots had roots in social tensions arising in part from discrimination against Negroes as members of a social, and racial, category. At the same time, however, membership of the citizens of Harlem in a larger social category of a depressed socio-economic group was of central importance. It has been suggested (by Kenneth B. Clark, among others) that the membership of Harlem Negroes in the socio-economic category was of greater importance than their racial membership in the two disturbances here noted.

Two dissenting points of view on the rioting in Harlem in August, 1943, can be seen in the following quotations. The *New York Times,* in a news article dated August 3, 1943, commented:

Prompt and courageous action by Mayor LaGuardia and the police, plus the calm maintained by the white population and most of the Negroes of New York, kept the trouble from developing into a race riot as did the recent disorders in Detroit.

Both riots had similar powder-keg backgrounds in the rapid growth and over-crowding of Negro districts in recent years, charges of discrimination in the Army, Navy and war industry, demands for social and economic equality, and the rise of Negro and radical agitators preying on these conditions. Both were marked by the spread of false rumors magnifying relatively minor incidents that served as sparks for the tinderbox.

There the similarity ended, however. Whereas gangs of white hoodlums organized in Detroit to hunt down individual Negroes who ventured out of the Negro district, thus emulating Negro gangs in Negro districts, nothing like this occurred in New York.

Negroes from Harlem and other districts traveled to and from their work in other areas of the city yesterday, and carried on their duties without molestation. (*New York Times*, 92:31,237, 3 August 1943.)

Orlansky (1943), in a sharply divergent opinion, wrote:

City officials and the press were far off the truth in claiming that the riot was not racial. Although white citizens were not widely assaulted, the riot was obviously a racial manifestation. Looting was restricted almost exclusively to white property, and attacks and insults were centered on white policemen, though some Negro policemen and 1,000 Negro wardens were later on the scene; no rioter dared to spit into the face of a Negro officer. Attempts were made by the wilder elements to attack whites on the streets, buses and trolleys, but no such attempts were made against Negroes. "Hoodlumism is not racial," argued the *Times*, but at no point did white "hoodlums" from neighboring districts engage in the looting. The precipitating incident is also indicative of this racial basis: crowds were aroused by a *white* policeman attacking a colored soldier. It can scarcely be questioned that had a *Negro* policeman shot Bandy, or had a white policeman shot a white soldier, the riot would not have occurred.

There is little to be gained from argument over whether or not the 1943 disturbance would or would not have occurred had individuals of different racial membership been involved in the precipitating incident. There is evidence, however, from both the 1935 and the 1943 riots, that Negro hostility toward the police was generalized to include Negro policemen; indeed, among the lower class Negroes involved there was a generalized animus directed against *all* authority (see, e.g., Clark and Barker, 1945).

The three major differences may be noted which distinguish the Harlem disturbances from others which have been discussed in this paper:

1. The social violence which occurred in the Harlem disorders was directed almost completely against property. If this violence was directed primarily against white property it was because whites owned most such property in the Harlem area. Negro owners were not spared, and distinctions were made on other than racial bases. (See also, pp. 119–127 in this volume, the *Mayor's Commission on Conditions in Harlem: the Complete Harlem Riot Report*, the section entitled "Communists Not Cause of Riot.")

2. There were no clashes between racial groups. This was true both within Harlem itself and in other New York areas.

3. The struggles in Harlem were almost solely struggles between the lower-class Negro population and the police forces. There was occasional and transitory participation of more substantial Negro citizens, but it soon stopped and middle-class Negroes were active in anti-riot activities. Negro police were not, as suggested by Orlansky, treated any differently than were white policemen. Indeed, the findings of the Mayor's Commission on Conditions in Harlem suggest that Negro police may have been a particular focus of hostility.

It is clear that these disturbances differ markedly from others discussed in the pages above. No major clashes occurred between whites and Negroes, except in the case of the police. This may be partly a result of the ecology of New York and of the size of the Negro concentration in that city. Yet, in other major disturbances, such as those of Chicago in 1919 and Detroit in 1943, Negroes were not safe in downtown districts, as was the case in New York. The complete absence of any recorded activity of young gangs of whites against Negro stragglers lends some credence, at least, to the claim that the Harlem disorders were manifestations more of economic status deprivation which, because of the generally low status of the Negro in American society, took on many of the external characteristics of race rioting. At least one observer has claimed that a similar disturbance could easily occur in similarly depressed areas of Manhattan occupied entirely by whites.

Mayor's Commission on Conditions in Harlem

Excerpts from
The Complete Harlem Riot Report, March 19, 1935

On March 19, 1935, several thousands of Harlem's citizens, after five years of the depression which had made them feel more keenly than ever the injustices of discrimination in employment, the aggressions of the police, and the racial segregation, rioted against these intolerable conditions. This spontaneous outbreak, the immediate cause of which was a mere rumor concerning the mistreatment of a Negro boy, was symptomatic of pent-up feelings of resentment and insecurity.

Today, extra police stand guard on the corners, and mounted patrolmen ride through the streets of Harlem. To the citizens of Harlem they symbolize the answer of the city authorities to their protest of March 19th. To Harlem this show of force simply signifies that property will be protected at any cost, but it offers no assurance that the legitimate demands of the citizens of the community for work and decent living conditions will be heeded. Hence, this show of force only tends to make the conditions which were responsible for the occurrence last March 19th more irritating. And so long as these conditions persist, no one knows when they will lead to a recurrence, with possibly greater violence, of the happenings of that night.

The commission wishes therefore to present its conclusions relative to the data on these conditions presented in the preceding chapters and to offer such recommendations as seem proper to deal with them in order to allay much of the present unrest in Harlem.

The first and most fundamental problem of the Negro citizens of Harlem is the economic problem. While it is true that the present economic crisis has been responsible for the appalling amount of unemployment and dependency in Harlem, the great mass of the workers in the community live even during normal times close to the subsistence level and many of them are forced to be supported by charitable agencies. The majority of Negro men are employed as unskilled workers and in domestic and personal service, while 85 per cent of the women are engaged exclusively in the latter type of occupation. The generally low economic status of Negro workers is, of course, due fundamentally to the operation of our competitive capitalistic system. Negro workers, being newcomers to the city and the most recent entrants into industry, are, on the whole, marginal workers.

But, in addition to the operation of the factors which are inherent in our economic system, there are certain social factors which keep the Negro worker in the ranks of unskilled laborers and in a state of perpetual dependency. The main social factor which is responsible for this condition is racial discrimination in employment. It is this factor more than any other that arouses so much resentment in the Negro worker. If the economic system through competition, he reasons, inevitably condemns many workers to a starvation level, then he demands the right to compete on equal terms with other workers for a decent standard of living. This he is not permitted to do.

Racial discrimination as a factor in limiting the employment of Negroes is especially characteristic of the public utilities. These corporations upon which the community must depend for such necessities as heat, light, and the means of communication and transportation have maintained a strict color caste in regard to employment. Thus the Negro is forced by necessity to give up a relatively large part of his meager earnings while these corporations remain adamant in the policy of excluding Negroes from employment.

However, they are teaching the Negro slowly but surely the lesson that only through collective or public ownership of the public utilities can he enforce his right to employment on the same basis as other races. While the Independent Subway System attempted in the beginning to apply the caste principle to the employment of Negroes and allowed them to work only as porters, when this system was placed under civil service, Negroes were able to assert their legal right to compete on the same basis as other people. While the Negro worker has only won a more or less paper victory, he has placed the City of New York in a position where it must either uphold the laws or follow the example of private employers in keeping the Negro in menial positions at starvation wages.

Our analysis of the policy of discrimination in the employment of

Negroes as practiced by private employers has been set forth above. Here we need only emphasize the fact that when employers exclude Negroes from employment or place the badge of inferior status upon them by keeping them in menial positions, they are only helping to make more acute the conflict between the employers and a large section of an urban proletariat which is coming to look more and more upon employers as mere exploiters. When the outbreak occurred last March, the black proletariat attacked property, which had become a symbol of racial discrimination and exploitation without even the compensating virtue of offering means of employment.

However, we are fully aware that private employers count upon competition between white and black workers as a means of holding the unemployed and dependent black masses in check. The attitudes of many unions confirm this faith, since, as we have shown above, they are among the chief obstacles to the employment of Negro workers. Yet these very craft unions, by their exclusion of Negro workers, are driving them into the camp of labor leaders, who see that the craft organizations are ineffective as a means of securing the rights of labor. More specifically, labor unions that discriminate against black labor cannot expect to be recognized as the representatives of labor.

The Negro worker gets a certain revenge against a community that discriminates against him through the money which the community must spend upon him in the form of relief. Discrimination against the Negro in employment is responsible at all times for a large number of Negroes who are supported by the relief agencies. The present economic crisis has simply accentuated the dependency of the Negro. But in the relief setup, as in other institutions in the community, Negro personnel was not employed upon the basis of individual merit but according to the prevailing conceptions concerning the Negro's proper place or status in relation to whites. For anyone to argue that Negroes were given positions in the personnel of the Home Relief Bureau solely on the basis of individual merit exposes him to the charge of being unbelievably naive or dishonest. To be sure, racial discrimination was not as open and brutal as in private employment, but it accomplished the same end.

For example, Negroes were not put in such strategic positions as to see that work relief was given on equitable basis. While naturally many mistakes were made in the classification of relief clients, mistakes do not explain the fact that most Negroes, no matter what their skill, were given the classification of laborers. It was only the standardization of relief budgets that prevented many Southern-born white relief workers from giving Negro families a smaller allowance which would have conformed to their ideas of the needs of Negroes. At any rate, it appears that only in the giving of home relief was the Negro treated on the whole as other citizens.

In view of the Negro's impoverished condition, it is not surprising to find him living in the often dilapidated and dangerous living quarters which whites have abandoned. Innumerable housing conferences, after having discussed the deplorable housing conditions of the Negro, have either passed resolutions or made known their desire that the Negro should have more wholesome housing. But nothing has resulted from these pious and sentimental expressions of humanitarian feelings. No doubt it is true, that, to give a new context to an old saw, if wishes were houses Negroes would live in palaces.

But houses are built for people who can pay a price that assures a profit to the contractor. Since building contractors do not find it profitable to construct homes for the low income groups among the whites, it is not surprising that Negro wage earners who live on the margin of subsistence cannot find decent homes. But here again color caste places an additional burden upon the Negro tenant. Crowded in a black ghetto, the Negro tenant is forced to pay exorbitant rentals because he cannot escape. He is the veritable slave of the landlord, and because of the helplessness which his poverty and ignorance imposes upon him, he cannot force municipal authorities to see that he gets the minimum protection which the housing laws provide.

We must turn again to the economic factor for an explanation of the ravages of tuberculosis and infant mortality in the Harlem community.

Ignorant and unsophisticated peasant people without experience with urban living would naturally find survival difficult in the city; but when poverty and inadequate health agencies are added to their burdens, they are doomed to extinction! Thus we find in Harlem that the Negro's battle against tuberculosis seemingly was bringing victory until, following the migration from the South, the death rate ceased its downward trend about fifteen years ago. The health agencies, as in the case of housing, were designed for a community with a different pattern of life and a different set of problems. There has been no systematic and comprehensive effort to modify these agencies to serve the needs of the present community.

Harlem Hospital, the chief health agency in the community, has taken on Negro physicians and offered training to Negro interns and nurses; but this has really been done with the apparent intention of transforming the hospital into a Jim Crow institution. The lack of morale among the medical staff, the treatment accorded the patients, and the general management of the hospital have all indicated that standards are being set up to harmonize with the generally inferior status of the Negro as a distinct racial group.

As with the health agencies, so with the educational institutions which the Negro inherited when he took over a community which the whites had abandoned. The disgraceful physical condition of the schools of Harlem as well as the lack of recreational facilities and the vicious environments that surround the schools, all indicate the presence of a poverty-stricken and therefore helpless group of people in the commu-

nity. One can almost trace the limits of the Negro community through the character of the school buildings.

That these conditions are due primarily to the fact that the Negro community is powerless to force the indifferent city authorities to afford adequate educational and recreational facilities was forcibly demonstrated by the fact that a recently proposed building program involving the expenditure of $120,747,000 included only $400,000 for an annex in Harlem, although most of the schools in this area were built before 1900.

Such an environment as Harlem is naturally a breeding place of juvenile and adult delinquency. What has been found in Harlem concerning juvenile delinquency only confirms the studies that have shown the decisive influence of community disorganization as a ccmplex of causative factors no matter what racial group inhabits such a community. Yet in the case of Harlem we find few of the agencies that have an ameliorative influence upon juvenile delinquency. In regard to adult delinquency, we find no organized criminal gangs, but a preponderance of such crimes as flourish among poverty-stricken and disorganized people. Moreover, the fact should be stressed that the very economic impotence of the community and its subjection to exploitation by outside interests, such as the policy racket and the location of institutions in the community for the pleasures and vices of whites who seek this means of escape from the censure of their own groups, encourages antisocial behavior and nullifies the efforts of responsible citizens to maintain social control.

While one would not expect the policemen in Harlem to show any appreciation or understanding of the sociological factors responsible for crime in the community, the discipline of the Police Department should see to it that they do not become the persecutors and oppressors of the citizens of the community. Nevertheless, it is true that the police practice aggressions and brutalities upon the Harlem citizens not only because they are Negroes but because they are poor and therefore defenseless. But these attacks by the police upon the security of the homes and the persons of the citizens are doing more than anything else to create a disrespect for authority and to bring about mass resistance to the injustices suffered by the community.

The commission fully realizes that the economic and social ills of Harlem, which are deeply rooted in the very nature of our economic and social system, cannot be cured by any administration under our present political and civic institutions. Yet the commission is convinced that, if the administrative machinery set itself to prevent racial discrimination in such municipal institutions as the schools and the city's subway system and penalized, as far as possible, private concerns and individuals that practiced racial discrimination, the people of Harlem would at least not feel that their economic and social ills were forms of racial persecution.

At about 2:30 on the afternoon of March 19, 1935, Lino Rivera, a 16-year-old colored boy, stole a knife from a counter in the rear of E. H. Kress and Company on 125th Street. He was seen by the manager of the store, Jackson Smith, and an assistant, Charles Hurley, who were on the balcony at the time. Mr. Hurley and another employee overtook the boy before he was able to make his escape through the front door. When the two men took the knife from Rivera's pocket and threatened him with punishment, the boy in his fright tried to cling to a pillar and bit the hands of his captors. Rivera was finally taken to the front entrance, where Mounted Patrolman Donahue was called. The boy was then taken back into the store by the officer, who asked the manager if an arrest was desired. While Mr. Smith, the manager, instructed the officer to let the culprit go free—as he had done in many cases before— an officer from the Crime Prevention Bureau was sent to the store.

This relatively unimportant case of juvenile pilfering would never have acquired the significance which it later took on had not a fortuitous combination of subsequent events made it the spark that set aflame the smouldering resentments of the people of Harlem against racial discrimination and poverty in the midst of plenty. Patrolman Donahue, in order to avoid the curious and excited spectators, took the boy through the basement to the rear entrance on 124th street. But his act only confirmed the outcry of a hysterical Negro woman that they had taken "the boy to the basement to beat him up." Likewise, the appearance of the ambulance which had been summoned to dress the wounded hands of the boy's captors not only seemed to substantiate her charge, but, when it left empty, gave color to another rumor that the boy was dead. By an odd trick of fate, still another incident furnished the final confirmation of the rumor of the boy's death to the excited throng of shoppers. A hearse which was usually kept in a garage opposite the store on 124th street was parked in front of the store entrance while the driver entered the store to see his brother-in-law. The rumor of the death of the boy, which became now to the aroused Negro shoppers an established fact, awakened the deep-seated sense of wrongs and denials and even memories of injustices in the South. One woman was heard to cry out that the treatment was "just like down South where they lynch us." The deep sense of wrong expressed in this remark was echoed in the rising resentment which turned the hundred or more shoppers into an indignant crowd.

POLICEMAN'S ATTITUDE AROUSES CROWD

The sporadic attempts on the part of the police to assure the crowd within the store that no harm had been done the boy fell upon unbelieving ears, partly because no systematic attempt was made to let representatives of the crowd determine the truth for themselves, and partly because of the attitude of the policeman. According to the testimony of one policeman, a committee of women from among the shoppers was permitted to search the basement, but these women have never been located. On the other hand, when the crowd became too insistent about learning the fate of the boy, the police told them that it was none of their business and attempted to shove them towards the door. This only tended to infuriate the crowd and was interpreted by them as further evidence of the suppression of a wronged race. At 5:30 it became necessary to close the store.

The closing of the store did not stay the rumors that were current inside. With incredible swiftness the feelings and attitude of the outraged crowd of shoppers was communicated to those on 125th street and soon all of Harlem was repeating the rumor that a Negro boy had been murdered in the basement of Kress' store. The first sign of the reaction of the community appeared when a group of men attempted to start a public meeting at a nearby corner. When the police ordered the group to move from the corner, they set up a stand in front of Kress' store. A Negro who acted as chairman introduced a white speaker. Scarcely had the speaker uttered the first words of his address to the crowd when someone threw a missile through the window of Kress' store. This was the signal for the police to drag the speaker from the stand and disperse the crowd. Immediately, the crowd reassembled across the street and another speaker attempted to address the crowd from a perch on a lamppost. He was pulled down from his post and arrested along with the other speaker on a charge of "unlawful assemblage." These actions on the part of the police only tended to arouse resentment in the crowd which was increasing all the time along 125th Street. From 125th Street the crowds spread to Seventh Avenue and Lenox Avenue and the smashing of windows and looting of shops gathered momentum as the evening and the night came on.

LIBERATORS' LEAFLET DISCUSSED

During the late afternoon the rumor that a Negro boy had been beaten and killed in Kress' store reached the headquarters of a group comprised mainly of Negroes and known as the "Young Liberators." The purpose of this organization is the protection of the rights of Negroes. Although it is not a Communist group, as been rumored, it has Communists among its members, one being a member of its executive committee. According to Joseph Taylor, the president of the organization, upon hearing the story of the death of the Negro boy, he went to Kress' store in order to verify the rumor and when he was refused entrance to the store he went to the nearby police station from which he was also ordered away.

Accepting the rumor as true (although Mr. Taylor denies that he was personally responsible) the Young Liberators printed and circulated an exciting leaflet.

CHILD BRUTALLY BEATEN
WOMAN ATTACKED BY BOSS AND COPS.
CHILD NEAR DEATH.
   One hour ago a 12-year-old Negro boy was brutally beaten by the management of Kress' Five and Ten Cent Store.
   The boy is near death, mercilessly beaten because they thought he had stolen a five-cent knife. A Negro woman, who sprang to the defense of the boy, had her arm broken by the thug and was then arrested.

———

WORKERS: NEGRO AND WHITE.
   Protest against this Lynch Attack of Innocent Negro People.
   Demand Release of Boy and Woman.
   Demand the immediate arrest of the management responsible for this lynch attack.
   Don't Buy at Kress'.
   Stop Police Brutality in Negro Harlem.
   JOIN THE PICKET LINE.

   About the same time, the Young Communist League, without attempting to verify the rumor, issued a similar leaflet. Since neither of these leaflets, according to the testimony given to the commission, appeared on the streets before 7:30 P.M., the actions of these two groups, though exhibiting a lack of due regard for the possible serious consequences of acting on mere rumors, were not responsible for the disorder and attacks on property which were already in full swing. Already a tabloid in screaming headlines was telling the city that a race riot was going on in Harlem.
   In fact, the Communists defend their part in the riot on the grounds that they prevented the riot from becoming a clash between whites and Negroes. While one, in view of the available facts, would hesitate to give the Communists full credit for preventing the outbreak from becoming a race riot, they deserve more credit than any other element in Harlem for preventing a physical conflict between whites and blacks. The young white men who mounted the ladder and lamppost on 125th Street and were beaten and arrested because they took the part of the indignant Negro crowds certainly changed the complexion of the outbreak. It was probably due in some measure to the activities of these racial leaders, both white and black, that the crowds attacked property rather than persons.

COMMUNISTS NOT CAUSE OF RIOT

In fact, the distinguishing feature of this outbreak was that it was an attack upon property and not upon persons. In the beginning, to be sure, the resentment was expressed against whites—but whites who owned stores and who, while exploiting Negroes, denied them an opportunity to work. Although the Jewish merchants in the Harlem community naturally came in for their share of the attacks upon the stores, there does not seem to be any foundation for the report circulated at first that these attacks were directed mainly at them. While, of course, tiny motives were responsible for the actions of these crowds, it seems that as they grew more numerous and more active, the personality or racial identity of the owners of the stores faded out and the property itself became the object of their fury. Stores owned by Negroes were not always spared if they happened to be in the path of those roving crowds, bent upon the destruction and the confiscation of property.

OUTBREAK SEEN AS SPONTANEOUS

From its inception, as we have pointed out, the outbreak was a spontaneous and unpremeditated action on the part, first, of women shoppers in Kress' store and, later, of the crowds on 125th Street that had been formed as the result of the rumor of a boy's death in the store. As the fever of excitement based upon this rumor spread to other sections of the community, other crowds, formed by many unemployed standing about the streets and other onlookers, sprang up spontaneously. At no time does it seem that these crowds were under the direction of any single individual or that they acted as a part of a conspiracy against law and order. The very susceptibility which the people in the community showed toward this rumor—which was more or less vague, depending upon the circumstances under which it was communicated— was due to the feeling of insecurity produced by years of unemployment and deep-seated resentment against the many forms of discrimination which they had suffered as a racial minority.

While it is difficult to estimate the actual number of persons who participated in the outburst, it does not seem, from available sources of information, that more than a few thousand were involved. These were not concentrated at any time in one place. Crowds formed here and there as the rumors spread. When a crowd was dispersed by the police, it often re-formed again. These crowds constantly changed their make-up. When bricks thrown through store windows brought the police, the crowds would often dissolve, only to gather again and continue their assaults upon property. Looting often followed the smashing of store windows. The screaming of sirens, the sound of pistol shots and the cracking of glass created in many a need for destruction and excitement. Rubbish, flower pots, or any object at hand were tossed from windows into the street. People seized property when there was no possible use which it would serve. They acted as if there were a chance to seize what rightfully belonged to them, but had long been withheld. The crowds showed various needs and changed their mood from time to time. Some of the destruction was carried on in a playful spirit. Even the looting, which has furnished many an amusing tale, was sometimes done in the spirit of children taking preserves from a closet to which they have accidentally found the key. The mood of these crowds was determined in many cases by the attitude of the police toward their unruly conduct. But, in the end, neither the threats nor the reassurances of the police could restrain these spontaneous outbursts until the crowds had spent themselves in giving release to their pent-up emotions. The final dramatic attempt on the part of the police to placate the populace by having the unharmed Lino Rivera photographed with the Negro police lieutenant, Samuel Battle, only furnished the basis for the rumor that Rivera, who was on probation for having placed a slug in a subway turnstile, was being used as a substitute to deceive the people.

Ralph Ellison

Invisible Man

[*No other fictional treatment of violence is included in this volume. Many authors have attempted to capture the subjective flavor of rioting—the sense of suspended animation. of fear and exhilaration—that sweeps contagiously through the streets; none has done it with the skill of Mr. Ellison. Mr. Ellison covered the 1943 Harlem riot for the New York* Post; *he properly insists, however, that the selection reprinted here is not journalism—neither is it history or sociology. As is not infrequently the case, the fictional treatment seems to illuminate the objective event far more clearly and meaningfully than does objective social science research.—A.D.G.*]

When I reached Morningside the shooting sounded like a distant celebration of the Fourth of July, and I hurried forward. At St. Nicholas the street lights were out. A thunderous sound arose and I saw four men running toward me pushing something that jarred the walk. It was a safe.

"Say," I began.

"Get the hell out the way!"

I leaped aside, into the street, and there was a sudden and brilliant suspension of time, like the interval between the last ax stroke and the felling of a tall tree, in which there had been a loud noise followed by a loud silence. Then I was aware of figures crouching in doorways and along the curb; then time burst and I was down in the street, conscious but unable to rise, struggling against the street and seeing the flashes as the guns went off back at the corner of the avenue, aware to my left of the men still speeding the rumbling safe along the walk as back up the street, behind me, two policemen, almost invisible in black shirts, thrust flaming pistols before them. One of the safe rollers pitched forward, and farther away, past the corner, a bullet struck an auto tire, the released air shrieking like a huge animal in agony. I rolled, flopping around, willing myself to crawl closer to the curb but unable, feeling a sudden wet warmth upon my face and seeing the safe shooting wildly into the intersection and the men rounding the corner into the dark, pounding, gone; gone now, as the skittering safe bounded off at a tangent, shot into the intersection and lodged in the third rail and sent up a curtain of sparks that lit up the block like a blue dream; a dream I was dreaming and through which I could see the cops braced as on a target range, feet forward, free arms akimbo, firing with deliberate aim.

"Get hold of Emergency!" one of them called, and I saw them turn and disappear where the dull glint of trolley rails faded off into the dark.

Suddenly the block leaped alive. Men who seemed to rise up out of the sidewalks were rushing into the store fronts above me, their voices rising excitedly. And now the blood was in my face and I could move, getting to my knees as someone out of the crowd was helping me to stand.

"You hurt, daddy?"

"Some—I don't know—" I couldn't quite see them.

"Damn! He's got a hole in his head!" a voice said.

A light flashed in my face, came close. I felt a hard hand upon my skull and moved away.

"Hell, it's just a nick," a voice said. "One them forty-fives hit your little finger you got to go down!"

"Well, this one over here is gone down for the last time," someone called from the walk. "They got him clean."

I wiped my face, my head ringing. Something was missing.

"Here, buddy, this yours?"

It was my brief case, extended to me by its handles. I seized it with sudden panic, as though something infinitely precious had almost been lost to me.

"Thanks," I said, peering into their dim, blue-tinted features. I looked at the dead man. He lay face forward, the crowd working around him. I realized suddenly that it might have been me huddled there, feeling too that I had seen him there before, in the bright light of noon, long ago . . . how long? Knew his name, I thought, and suddenly my knees flowed forward. I sat there, my fist that gripped the brief case bruising against the street, my head slumped forward. They were going around me.

"Get off my foot, man," I heard. "Quit shoving. There's plenty for everybody."

There was something I had to do and I knew that my forgetfulness wasn't real, as one knows that the forgotten details of certain dreams are not truly forgotten but evaded. I knew, and in my mind I was trying to reach through the gray veil that now seemed to hang behind my eyes as opaquely as the blue curtain that screened the street beyond the safe. The dizziness left and I managed to stand, holding onto my brief case, pressing a handkerchief to my head. Up the street there sounded the crashing of huge sheets of glass and through the blue mysteriousness of the dark the walks shimmered like shattered mirrors. All the street's signs were dead, all the day sounds had lost their stable meaning. Somewhere a burglar alarm went off, a meaningless blangy sound, followed by the joyful shouts of looters.

"Come on," someone called nearby.

"Let's go, buddy," the man who had helped me said. He took my arm, a thin man who carried a large cloth bag slung over his shoulder.

"The shape you in wouldn't do to leave you round here," he said. "You act like you drunk."

"Go where?" I said.

"Where? Hell man. Everywhere. We git to moving, no telling where we might go— Hey, Dupre!" he called.

"Say, man—Goddam! Don't be calling my name so loud," a voice answered. "Here, I am over here, gitting me some work shirts."

"Git some for me, Du," he said.

"All right, but don't think I'm your papa," the answer came.

I looked at the thin man, feeling a surge of friendship. He didn't know me, his help was disinterested . . .

"Hey, Du," he called, "we go'n do it?"

"Hell yes, soon as I git me these shirts."

The crowd was working in and out of the stores like ants around spilled sugar. From time to time there came the crash of glass, shots; fire trucks in distant streets.

"How you feel?" the man said.

"Still fuzzy," I said, "and weak."

"Le's see if it's stopped bleeding. Yeah, you'll be all right."

I saw him vaguely though his voice came clear.

"Sure," I said.

"Man, you lucky you ain't dead. These sonsabitches is really shooting now," he said. "Over on Lenox they was aiming up in the air. If I could find me a rifle, I'd show 'em! Here, take you a drink of this good Scotch," he said, taking a quart bottle from a hip pocket. "I got me a whole case stashed what I got from a liquor store over there. Over there all you got to do is breathe, and you drunk, man. Drunk! Hundred proof bonded whiskey flowing all in the gutters."

I took a drink, shuddering as the whiskey went down but thankful for the shock it gave me. There was a bursting, tearing movement of people around me, dark figures in a blue glow.

"Look at them take it away," he said, looking into the dark action of the crowd. "Me, I'm tired. Was you over on Lenox?"

"No," I said, seeing a woman moving slowly past with a row of about a dozen dressed chickens suspended by their necks from the handle of a new straw broom . . .

"Hell, you ought to see it, man. Everything is tore up. By now the womens is picking it clean. I saw one ole woman with a whole side of a cow on her back. Man, she was 'bout bent bowlegged trying to make it home— Here come Dupre now," he said, breaking off.

I saw a little hard man come out of the crowd carrying several boxes. He wore three hats upon his head, and several pairs of suspenders flopped about his shoulders, and now as he came toward us I saw that he wore a pair of gleaming new rubber hip boots. His pockets bulged and over his shoulder he carried a cloth sack that swung heavily behind him.

"Damn, Dupre," my friend said, pointing to his head, "you got one of them for me? What kind is they?"

Dupre stopped and looked at him. "With all them hats in there and I'm going to come out with anything but a *Dobbs?* Man, are you *mad?* All them new, pretty-colored *Dobbs?* Come on, let's get going before the cops git back. Damn, look at that thing blaze!"

I looked toward the curtain of blue fire, through which vague figures toiled. Dupre called out and several men left the crowd and joined us in the street. We moved off, my friend (Scofield, the others called him) leading me along. My head throbbed, still bled.

"Look like you got you some loot too," he said, pointing to my briefcase.

"Not much," I said, thinking, loot? *Loot?* And suddenly I knew why it was heavy, remembering Mary's broken bank and the coins; and now I found myself opening the brief case and dropping all my papers— my Brotherhood identification, the anonymous letter, along with Clifton's doll—into it.

"Fill it up, man. Don't you be bashful. You wait till we tackle one of these pawnshops. That Du's got him a cotton-picking sack fulla stuff. *He* could go into business."

"Well, I'll be damn," a man on the other side of me said. "I *thought* that was a cotton sack. Where'd he get that thing?"

"He brought it with him when he come North," Scofield said. "Du swears that when he goes back he'll have it full of ten-dollar bills. Hell after tonight he'll need him a warehouse for all the stuff he's got. You fill that brief case, buddy. Get yourself something!"

"No," I said, "I've enough in it already." And now I remembered very clearly where I'd started out for but could not leave them.

"Maybe you right," Scofield said, "How I know, you might have it full of diamonds or something. A man oughtn't to be greedy. Though it's time something like this happened."

We moved along. Should I leave, get on to the district? Where were they, at the birthday celebration?

"How did all this get started?" I said.

Scofield seemed surprised. "Damn if I know, man. A cop shot a woman or something."

Another man moved close to us as somewhere a piece of heavy steel rang down.

"Hell, that wasn't what started it," he said. "It was that fellow, what's his name . . . ?"

"Who?" I said. "What's his name?"

"That young guy!"

"You know, everybody's mad about it . . ."

Clifton, I thought. It's for Clifton. A night for Clifton.

"Aw man, don't tell me," Scofield said. "Didn't I see it with my own eyes? About eight o'clock down on Lenox and 123rd this paddy slapped a kid for grabbing a Baby Ruth and the kid's mama took it up and then the paddy slapped her and that's when hell broke loose."

"You were there?" I said.

"Same's I'm here. Some fellow said the kid made the paddy mad by grabbing a candy named after a white woman."

"Damn if that's the way I heard it," another man said. "When I come up they said a white woman set it off by trying to take a black gal's man."

"Damn *who* started it," Dupre said. "All I want is for it to last a while."

"It was a white gal, all right, but that wasn't the way it was. She was drunk—" another voice said.

But it couldn't have been Sybil, I thought; it had already started.

"You wahn know who started it?" a man holding a pair of binoculars called from the window of a pawnshop. "You wahn really to know?"

"Sure," I said.

"Well, you don't need to go no further. It was started by that great leader, Ras the Destroyer!"

"That monkey-chaser?" someone said.

"Listen, bahstard!"

"Don't nobody know how it started," Dupre said.

"Somebody has to know," I said.

Scofield held his whiskey toward me. I refused it.

"Hell, man, it just exploded. These is dog days," he said.

"*Dog* days?"

"Sho, this hot weather."

"I tell you they mad over what happen to that young fellow, what's-his-name . . ."

We were passing a building now and I heard a voice calling frantically, "Colored store! Colored store!"

"Then put up a sign, motherfouler," a voice said. "You probably rotten as the others."

"Listen at the bastard. For one time in his life he's glad to be colored," Scofield said.

"Colored store," the voice went on automatically.

"Hey! You sho you ain't got some white blood?"

"No, *sir!*" the voice said.

"Should I bust him, man?"

"For what? He ain't got a damn thing. Let the motherfouler alone."

A few doors away we came to a hardware store. "This is the first stop, men." Dupre said.

"What happens now?" I said.

"Who you?" he said, cocking his thrice-hatted head.

"Nobody, just one of the boys—" I began.

"You sho you ain't somebody I know?"

"I'm pretty sure," I said.

"He's all right, Du," said Scofield. "Them cops shot him."

Dupre looked at me and kicked something—a pound of butter, sending it smearing across the hot street. "We fixing to do something what needs to be done," he said. "First we gets a flashlight for everybody . . . And let's have some organization, y'all. Don't everybody be running over everybody else. Come on!"

"Come on in, buddy," Scofield said.

I felt no need to lead or leave them; was glad to follow; was gripped by a need to see where and to what they would lead. And all the time the thought that I should go to the district was with me. We went inside the store, into the dark glinting with metal. They moved carefully, and I could hear them searching, sweeping objects to the floor. The cash register rang.

"Here some flashlights over here," someone called.

"How many?" Dupre said.

"Plenty, man."

"Okay, pass out one to everybody. They got batteries?"

"Naw, but there's plenty them too, 'bout a dozen boxes."

"Okay, give me one with batteries so I can find the buckets. Then every man get him a light."

"Here some buckets over here," Scofield said.

"Then all we got to find is where he keeps the oil."

"Oil?" I said.

"*Coal* oil, man. And hey, y'all," he called, "don't nobody be smoking in here."

I stood beside Scofield listening to the noise as he took a stack of zinc buckets and passed them out. Now the store leaped alive with flashing lights and flickering shadows.

"Keep them lights down on the floor," Dupre called. "No use letting folks see who we are. Now when you get your buckets line up and let me fill 'em."

"Listen to ole Du lay it down—he's a bitch, ain't he, buddy? He always liked to lead things. And always leading me into trouble."

"What are we getting ready to do?" I said.

"You'll see," Dupre said. "Hey, you over there. Come on from behind that counter and take this bucket. Don't you see ain't nothing in that cash register, that if it was I'd have it myself?"

Suddenly the banging of buckets ceased. We moved into the back room. By the light of a flash I could see a row of fuel drums mounted on racks. Dupre stood before them in his new hip boots and filled each bucket with oil. We moved in slow order. Our buckets filled, we filed out into the street. I stood there in the dark feeling a rising excitement as their voices played around me. What was the meaning of it all? What should I think of, *do* about it?

"With this stuff," Dupre said, "we better walk in the middle of the street. It's just down around the corner."

Then as we moved off a group of boys ran among us and the men started using their lights, revealing darting figures in blonde wigs, the tails of their stolen dress coats flying. Behind them in hot pursuit came a gang armed with dummy rifles taken from an Army & Navy Store. I laughed with the others, thinking: A holy holiday for Clifton.

"Put out them lights!" Dupre commanded.

Behind us came the sound of screams, laughter; ahead the footfalls of the running boys, distant fire trucks, shooting, and in the quiet intervals, the steady filtering of shattered glass. I could smell the kerosene as it sloshed from the buckets and slapped against the street.

Suddenly Scofield grabbed my arm. "Good God, look-a-yonder!"

And I saw a crowd of men running up pulling a Borden's milk wagon, on top of which, surrounded by a row of railroad flares, a huge woman in a gingham pinafore sat drinking beer from a barrel which sat before her. The men would run furiously a few paces and stop, resting between the shafts, run a few paces and rest, shouting and laughing and drinking from a jug, as she on top threw back her head and shouted passionately in a full-throated voice of blues singer's timbre:

> *If it hadn't been for the referee,*
> *Joe Louis woulda killed*
> *Jim Jefferie*
> *Free beer!!*

—sloshing the dipper of beer around.

We stepped aside, amazed, as she bowed graciously from side to side like a tipsy fat lady in a circus parade, the dipper like a gravy spoon in her enormous hand. Then she laughed and drank deeply while reaching over nonchalantly with her free hand to send quart after quart of milk crashing into the street. And all the time the men running with the wagon over the debris. Around me there were shouts of laughter and disapproval.

"Somebody better stop them fools," Scofield said in outrage. "That's what I call taking things too far. Goddam, how the hell they going to get her down from there after she gits fulla beer? Somebody answer me that. How they going to get her down? 'Round here throwing away all that good milk!"

The big woman left me unnerved. Milk and beer—I felt sad, watching the wagon careen dangerously as they went around a corner. We went on, avoiding the broken bottles as now the spilling kerosene splashed into the pale spilt milk. How much has happened? Why was I torn? We moved around a corner. My head still ached.

Scofield touched my arm. "Here we is," he said.

We had come to a huge tenement building.

"Where are we?" I said.

"This the place where most of us live," he said. "Come on."

So that was it, the meaning of the kerosene. I couldn't believe it, couldn't believe they had the nerve. All the windows seemed empty. They'd blacked it out themselves. I saw now only by flash or flame.

"Where will you live?" I said, looking up, up.

"You call *this* living?" Scofield said. "It's the only way to git rid of it, man . . ."

7

WORLD WAR II AND POSTWAR BOOM AND RACIAL READJUSTMENT 1942–1954

During World War II there were a number of small racial disorders but only one large-scale race riot. This was the Detroit riot of 1943, a disturbance that compared in magnitude both to the violence of the World War I period and to that which has occurred in a number of cities (including Detroit, almost on the 25th annivarsary of the World War II riot) in the last few years.

This chapter is divided into two parts. In the first I have included selections presenting three different perspectives on the Detroit riot, which can be read as an independent lesson in historiography and as a caveat against uncritical acceptance of much of what has been written about the events of the Sixties. The first piece in this part is condensed from the report of an official committee appointed to study the riot, a committee including the police commissioner and charged with a review of police behavior. The second piece was written by Thurgood Marshall, at that time legal counsel of the NAACP, and presents an unofficial viewpoint that is sharply critical of police activities. The third piece is a chapter from Lee and Humphrey's book on the riot (1943), in which they undertook a somewhat more dispassionate analysis of the causal background of the riot.

In the second part of this chapter I have included a sampling of the kinds of events that occurred immediately after the war and of the changes that began to emerge in the second half of the post-war decade. The first two pieces, on minor riotous disturbances growing out of the return of veterans, are reminiscent of the types of disorders which followed the return of World War I black veterans who had "forgotten their place." The last two pieces in the second part deal with events which occurred as a consequence of direct assaults upon the segregated social structure, a swimming pool integration incident in St. Louis and the first major housing dispute, in Cicero, Illinois.

A. THE DETROIT RIOT
A Short Lesson in Historiography

H. J. Rushton, W. E. Dowling, Oscar Olander, and J. H. Witherspoon

Factual Report of the Committee to Investigate the Riot Occurring in Detroit on June 21, 1943

Frequent reference has been made to the racial tension prevalent in certain Negro and white groups prior to the outbreak of June 20 and 21. This report would be incomplete without some reference to factors which have created and inflamed that tension. There never was a time when people were not conscious of certain racial differences. Characteristics of color, stature, and speech have always marked off and distinguished one people from another. This, of course, is neither an argument for, nor a justification of, any feeling of superiority on the part of any race. That certain misinformed people have relied upon their peculiar racial characteristics in asserting an alleged superiority over another race is unfortunate. But it must be recognized that only by education can this unwarranted assumption be dispelled. The animosity arising from this misinformation and want of education can be observed, not only in Detroit, but wherever different races are thrown together. Of present concern to this committee, however, is the increasing tendency among certain hoodlum elements in Detroit, both white and Negro, openly to flaunt established social order in combatting this animosity. Certainly no criticism is to be made of the honest efforts of responsible leaders, both Negro and white, who seek by lawful means the removal of unjust barriers between the races. But it is equally certain that vigorous criticism should be directed to those irresponsible leaders, who by their words and conduct, actively inspire among their followers a disregard for law, order, and judicial process, in seeking the racial equality to which they are entitled.

In studying the factors which created that state of mind which made whites and Negroes willing participants in a tragic riot, an answer has been sought to the questions: What particular factor is responsible for the uncontrolled belligerency prevalent in certain white and Negro groups in Detroit? Where have these young hoodlums been told they have a license to lawlessness in their "struggle to secure racial equality"? Who has told them it is proper themselves to redress actual and presumed grievances? Who has exhorted them violently to overthrow established social order to obtain "racial equality"? Who exaggerates and parades before these same elements sordid stories of sensational crime, giving an antisocial complexion to these incidents readily absorbed by the audience? Who constantly beats the drums of: "racial prejudice, inequality, intolerance, discrimination" and challenges these hoodlum elements "militantly" to rise against this alleged oppression? Who charges by their news stories and their editorials that all law enforcement agencies are anti-Negro, brutal, and vicious in the handling of Negroes, and bent upon their persecution?

Typical of the Negro press is the front page of the July 17, 1943, issue of the *Michigan Chronicle.* "DENIES BOY HANGS SELF, Eleven-Year-Old Boy Found Hanging by Neck from Tree"; "WIFE SLAYER PLEADS GUILTY, Let Her Kiss Baby Boy Before He Fired Fatal Shots"; " 'GOOD-BYE DARLING' MAN TELLS WIFE" (with a detailed description of an attempted suicide following); "JILTED SUITOR STABBED WOMAN" are the headlines and subcaptions of some of the stories appearing on that page. Above the picture of a man wanted in Tennessee for murder appears the headline: "DON'T TAKE ME TO TENNESSEE." Another feature story appearing on the same page is entitled: "SOLDIER BEATEN BY MISSISSIPPI PO-LICE," under which is reported a strike at Flora, Mississippi. The second paragraph of that story reads:

Immediate cause of the strike is said to have been the serious beating of a colored soldier and the abuse of several of the soldiers' wives and women companions by Jackson civilian police.

These stories are not isolated instances of inflammatory news reporting, but are characteristic of the news sheets mentioned.

A second theme, repeatedly emphasized by these papers, is that the struggle for Negro equality at home is an integral part of the present world-wide struggle for Democracy. Editorially and otherwise these papers repeatedly charge that there is no more Democracy here than in Hitler's Europe, or in Japan, and loudly proclaim that a victory over the Axis will be meaningless unless there is a corresponding overthrow in this country of the forces which these papers charge prevent true racial equality.

The topic is developed by numerous references to alleged "Jim-Crowism" practiced in our own Army and Navy. The refusal of certain Negroes to report for induction into the Army is reportorially justified by charging racial discrimination. Frequently recurring through these papers is the statement: "This nation cannot exist half free and half slave," the obvious purpose of which is to drive home to the Negro readers the alleged fact of their servitude and to arouse a belligerent reaction.

The papers discuss a "Civil Disobedience Campaign" and condemn the leaders of the March on Washington Movement for failing to authorize such a program at their convention held in Chicago June 30 to July 4, 1943.

Every instance of actual or presumed discrimination is reported with exaggeration,[1] and statements of charges made by Negro people, for which there is no support in fact, are worded to leave an impression of conviction of truth with the reader.

While these papers consistently charge discrimination and plead for absolute equality between all races, at least some Negro organizations would disclaim all responsibility for the crimes committed by Negroes, and would conceal from the public the racial identity of law violators. A portion of the NAACP Conference Statement, Adopted in Detroit on June 5, 1943, reads:

The Associated Press, United Press and local editors should eliminate the designation of "Negro" in reporting crime news.

This committee feels that the fact that the Negroes in Detroit, who constitute less than 10 per cent of the population, commit more than 71 per cent of the major crimes is one the public should know, that this circumstance may receive the public attention and constructive social measures it deserves.

Perhaps most significant in precipitating the racial tension existing in Detroit is the positive exhortation by many so-called responsible Negro leaders to be "militant" in the struggle for racial equality. A. Philip Randolph's statement appearing in the January 2, 1943, issue of the *Detroit Tribune* charging that:

Justice is never granted, it is exacted. It is written in the stars that the darker races will never be free until they make themselves free. This is the task of the coming year.

clearly constitutes an appeal to extract "justice" by violence.[2]

Such appeals unfortunately have been commonplace in the Negro newspaper. Can it be doubted that they played an important part in

1. Reference is made here to NAACP complaints on the Red Cross policy of segregating plasma of white and black donors (Ed.).

2. In an earlier footnote the Committee published another extract from the M.O.W.M. Constitution. It read as follows:

"To awaken, teach, organize, mobilize, direct and lead the Negro masses to struggle and fight for their own liberation from racial discrimination, segregation, and Jim Crowism, and achievement of complete recognition and enjoyment of Democratic citizenship, rights, freedom, justice, and equality, and to cooperate and collaborate with progressive movements, social, economic, political, and religious; to help build a free world for free men without regard to race, color, religion, or national origin" (Ed.).

exciting the Negro people to the violence which resulted in Detroit on June 21?

Some self-designated responsible Negro leaders must share with the colored newspapers responsibility for the unfortunate attitude of certain Negro elements. Some of these leaders have themselves demonstrated an anti-social and factional outlook, which, if carried to their followers would account for the militantly rebellious attitude of those elements.

Thurgood Marshall

The Gestapo in Detroit

Riots are usually the result of many underlying causes, yet no single factor is more important than the attitude and efficiency of the police. When disorder starts, it is either stopped quickly or permitted to spread into serious proportions, depending upon the actions of the local police.

Much of the blood spilled in the Detroit riot is on the hands of the Detroit police department. In the past the Detroit police have been guilty of both inefficiency and an attitude of prejudice against Negroes. Of course, there are several individual exceptions.

The citizens of Detroit, white and Negro, are familiar with the attitude of the police as demonstrated during the trouble in 1942 surrounding the Sojourner Truth housing project. At that time a mob of white persons armed with rocks, sticks and other weapons attacked Negro tenants who were attempting to move into the project. Police were called to the scene. Instead of dispersing the mob which was unlawfully on property belonging to the federal government and leased to Negroes, they directed their efforts toward dispersing the Negroes who were attempting to get into their own homes. All Negroes approaching the project were searched and their automobiles likewise searched. White people were neither searched nor disarmed by the police. This incident is typical of the one-sided law enforcement practiced by Detroit police. White hoodlums were justified in their belief that the police would act the same way in any further disturbances.

In the June riot of this year, the police ran true to form. The trouble reached riot proportions because the police once again enforced the law with an unequal hand. They used "persuasion" rather than firm action with white rioters, while against Negroes they used the ultimate in force: night sticks, revolvers, riot guns, sub-machine guns, and deer guns. As a result, 25 of the 34 persons killed were Negroes. Of the latter, 17 were killed by police.

The excuse of the police department for the disproportionate number of Negroes killed is that the majority of them were shot while committing felonies: namely, the looting of stores on Hastings Street. On the other hand, the crimes of arson and felonious assaults are also felonies. It is true that some Negroes were looting stores and were shot while committing these crimes. It is equally true that white persons were turning over and burning automobiles on Woodward Avenue. This is arson. Others were beating Negroes with iron pipes, clubs, and rocks. This is felonious assault. Several Negroes were stabbed. This is assault with intent to murder.

All these crimes are matters of record; many were committed in the presence of police officers, several on the pavement around the City Hall. Yet the record remains: Negroes killed by police—17; white persons killed by police—none. The entire record, both of the riot killings and of previous disturbances, reads like the story of the Nazi Gestapo.

Evidence of tension in Detroit has been apparent for months. The *Detroit Free Press* sent a reporter to the police department. When Commissioner Witherspoon was asked how he was handling the situation he told the reporter: "We have given orders to handle it with kid gloves. The policemen have taken insults to keep trouble from breaking out. I doubt if you or I could have put up with it." This weak-kneed policy of the police commissioner coupled with the anti-Negro attitude of many members of the force helped to make a riot inevitable.

.   .   .   .

Throughout Monday the police, instead of placing men in front of the stores to protect them from looting, contented themselves with driving up and down Hastings Street from time to time, stopping in front of the stores. The usual procedure was to jump out of the squad cars with drawn revolvers and riot guns to shoot whoever might be in the store. The policemen would then tell the Negro bystanders to "run and not look back." On several occasions, persons running were shot in the back. In other instances, bystanders were clubbed by police. To the police, all Negroes on Hastings Street were "looters." This included war workers returning from work. There is no question that many Negroes were guilty of looting, just as there is always looting during earthquakes or as there was when English towns were bombed by the Germans.

Woodward Avenue is one of the main thoroughfares of the city of Detroit. Small groups of white people began to rove up and down Woodward beating Negroes, stoning cars containing Negroes, stopping street cars and yanking Negroes from them, and stabbing and shooting Negroes. In no case did the police do more than try to "reason" with these mobs, many of which were, at this stage, quite small. The police did not draw their revolvers or riot guns, and never used any force to disperse these mobs. As a result of this, the mobs got larger and bolder and even attacked Negroes on the pavement of the City Hall in demonstration not only of their contempt for Negroes, but of their contempt for law and order as represented by the municipal government.

·   ·   ·   ·   ·   ·   ·

While investigating the riot, we obtained many affidavits from Negroes concerning police brutality during the riot. It is impossible to include the facts of all of these affidavits. However, typical instances may be cited. A Negro soldier in uniform who had recently been released from the army with a medical discharge was on his way down Brush Street Monday morning, toward a theatre on Woodward Avenue. This soldier was not aware of the fact that the riot was still going on. While in the Negro neighborhood on Brush Street, he reached a corner where a squad car drove up and discharged several policemen with drawn revolvers who announced to a small group on the corner to run and not look back. Several of the Negroes who did not move quite fast enough for the police were struck with night sticks and revolvers. The soldier was yanked from behind by one policeman and struck in the head with a blunt instrument and knocked to the ground, where he remained in a stupor. The police then returned to their squad car and drove off. A Negro woman in the block noticed the entire incident from her window, and she rushed out with a cold, damp towel to bind the soldier's head. She then hailed two Negro postal employees who carried the soldier to a hospital where his life was saved.

There are many additional affidavits of similar occurrences involving obviously innocent civilians throughout many Negro sections in Detroit where there had been no rioting at all. It was characteristic of these cases that the policemen would drive up to a corner, jump out with drawn revolvers, striking at Negroes indiscriminately, ofttimes shooting at them, and in all cases forcing them to run. At the same time on Woodward Avenue, white civilians were seizing Negroes and telling them to "run, nigger, run." At least two Negroes, "shot while looting," were innocent persons who happened to be in the area at that time.

One Negro who had been an employee of a bank in Detroit for the past eighteen years was on his way to work on a Woodward Avenue street car when he was seized by one of the white mobs. In the presence of at least four policemen, he was beaten and stabbed in the side. He also heard several shots fired from the back of the mob. He managed to run to two of the policemen who proceeded to "protect" him from the mob. The two policemen, followed by two mounted policemen, proceeded down Woodward Avenue. While he was being escorted by these policemen, the man was struck in the face by at least eight of the mob, and at no time was any effort made to prevent him from being struck. After a short distance this man noticed a squad car parked on the other side of the street. In sheer desperation, he broke away from the two policemen who claimed to be protecting him and ran to the squad car, begging for protection. The officer in the squad car put him in the back seat and drove off, thereby saving his life.

During all this time, the fact that the man was either shot or stabbed was evident because of the fact that blood was spurting from his side. Despite this obvious felony, committed in the presence of at least four policemen, no effort was made at that time either to protect the victim or to arrest the persons guilty of the felony.

.   .   .   .   .   .

On the night of June 21 at about eight o'clock, a Detroit policeman was shot in the two hundred block of Vernor Highway, and his assailant, who was in a vacant lot, was, in turn, killed by another policeman. State and city policemen then began to attack the apartment building at 290 E. Vernor Highway, which was fully occupied by tenants. Searchlights were thrown on the building and machine guns, revolvers, rifles, and deer guns were fired indiscriminately into all of the occupied apartments facing the outside. Tenants of the building were forced to fall to the floor and remain there in order to save their lives. Later slugs from machine guns, revolvers, rifles, and deer guns were dug from the inside walls of many of the apartments. Tear gas was shot into the building and all the tenants were forced out into the streets with their hands up in the air at the point of drawn guns.

State and city policemen went into the building and forced out all the tenants who were not driven out by tear gas. The tenants were all lined up against the walls, men and women alike, and forced to remain in this position for some time. The men were searched for weapons. During this time these people were called every type of vile name and men and women were cursed and threatened. Many men were struck by policemen.

While the tenants were lined up in the street, the apartments were forcibly entered. Locks and doors were broken. All the apartments were ransacked. Clothing and other articles were thrown around on the floor. All of these acts were committed by policemen. Most of the tenants reported that money, jewelry, whiskey, and other items of personal property were missing when they were permitted to return to their apartments after midnight. State and city police had been in possession of the building in the meantime.

Many of these apartment were visited shortly after these events. They resembled part of a battlefield. Affidavits from most of the tenants and lists of property destroyed and missing are available.

Although a white man was seen on the roof of an apartment house up the street from the Vernor apartments with a rifle in his hand, no effort was made to search either that building or its occupants. After the raid on the Vernor apartments, the police used as their excuse the statement that policeman Lawrence A. Adams had been shot by a sniper from the Vernor apartments, and that for that reason, they attacked the building and its occupants. However, in a story released by the police department on July 2 after the death of Patrolman Lawrence A. Adams, it was reported that "The shot that felled Adams was fired by Homer Edison, 28 years old, of 502 Montcalm, from the shadows of a parking lot. Edison, armed with a shot gun, was shot to death by Adams' partner." This is merely another example of the clumsy and obvious subterfuges used by the police department in an effort to cover up their total disregard for the rights of Negroes.

.   .   .   .

This record by the Detroit police demonstrates once more what all Negroes know only too well: that nearly all police departments limit their conception of checking racial disorders to surrounding, arresting, maltreating, and shooting Negroes. Little attempt is made to check the activities of whites.

The certainty of Negroes that they will not be protected by police, but instead will be attacked by them, is a contributing factor to racial tensions leading to overt acts. The first item on the agenda of any group seeking to prevent rioting would seem to be a critical study of the police department of the community, its record in handling Negroes, something of the background of its personnel, and the plans of its chief officers for meeting possible racial disorders.

Alfred McClung Lee and Norman Daymond Humphrey

Race Riot

Race riots—like wars, depressions, booms—must be caused. And, in the minds of most people, they must be thought of as being caused by one man, one organization, one or at most a small number of people or things. It is difficult to face a social catastrophe and not be able to blame it on someone who can be placed in the prisoner's dock, tried by the virtuous members of society, and then "burned" in an electric chair.

That kind of explanation for human disgrace fits in with our ideas of the victory of virtue over vice, the sending of the sinner to his just rewards. That the Savior professed by most Americans came into this world "to *save* sinners" and not to pillory them escapes the reasoning of those who must have a moral and intellectual scapegoat.

The fact that the Detroit race riots were immediately blamed on almost every possible excuse at hand illustrates this common human failing. One immediately heard or read of how the mobs of whites and blacks went to war against one another because of: the weather, President Roosevelt, Mrs. Roosevelt, the Negroes, the "100% Americans," the unions, the southern whites recently arrived in Detroit, the Poles, the Jews, the Roman Catholics, Mayor Jeffries, Father Coughlin, Pastor J. Frank Norris, Gerald L. K. Smith's "America First Party," the war, strained nerves, bad housing, worse recreational facilities, and so on. Here are some sample reasonings picked up at random from the whites by a competent interviewer:

The riot was, in the last analysis, the result of efforts of the "Association for the Advancement of the Negro" [N.A.A.C.P.]. For years that organization has been working, filling the Negro with false ideas as to race equality. Many Negroes have a stereotyped reply to almost any situation—such as, "Our boys are good enough to fight for America, but not good enough for equal privileges." A small incident like the Belle Isle affair would not have had such far-reaching results had the Association not thoroughly prepared the ground in advance.

It all started long ago because the politicians have been too lenient with them. They're afraid to lose too many votes if they clamp down on them. They should have been segregated long ago. Roosevelt—Jeffries—are mostly to blame.

It looks like an organized effort because of what's been happening all over the country, New York, Los Angeles and other cities.

The colored people are mostly to blame. They can't stand prosperity.

Here are some sample Negro views:

The Ku Klux Klan started it.
Enemy agents started the whole thing.
Youngsters and 4Fs.They didn't know what mob violence was.
Nobody will ever know [why it started]. Well, some one or two people may know but they will never tell. And it doesn't matter particularly what started it. We all knew it was bound to happen.
I don't think anything that happened Sunday started it. I think it has been started from ten months ago when the migration of southern whites and illiterate Negroes started . . . and I think it was just like that in 1917 when they killed the Duke. It was just something that started it, but not that caused it.

This last explanation comes much closer than does any single cause to the explanation that facts force upon social scientists. For that matter, the Detroit race riots furnish an excellent illustration of what scientists label "multiple causes" and "multiple consequences."

Each event in our lives—marriage, war, a football game—results from a vast number of factors, persons, and events that have influenced us, the others involved in the event, and the scene of this event. And, at the same time, each human event of any importance results in a number of consequences, most of which we are not able to *predict*, many of which we are not even able to *trace*.

As the Detroit *Free Press* put it, "Detroit has been building steadily for three years toward a race riot." It might as well have said, "for a generation." As *Life* magazine summed up conclusions of *Free Press* editorialists and other writers, the following factors made large immediate contributions to Detroit Bloody Week of 1943:

(1) Detroit's abominable housing situation, which condemns thousands of white and Negro war workers to living in slums, tents and trailers; (2) the tremendous migration of white and Negro war workers from the South since 1940; (3) "race" strikes and friction in war plants (a month ago [3,000 Packard workers walked out and 17,000 more were affected] because three Negro workers were up-graded to the assembly line); and (4) juvenile rowdyism, which has increased during the war (last month 100 white and Negro youths fought a pitched battle in a Detroit playground).

To this, *Life* added these longer term aspects:

Although the riot was definitely a victory for Adolf Hitler and other enemies of the U. S., there was no evidence that it had been planned by foreign agents, local Fascists or anyone else. It broke out suddenly on a hot Sunday night, and its basic cause was an old, ugly fact in U. S. life: prejudice and misunderstanding between the white and black races.

Let us elaborate this estimate with the aid of some facts and illustrations concerning (1) the Red Cross and the armed forces, (2) in-migration and employment, (3) overcrowding in dwellings, recreation, transportation, (4) delinquency and crime, and (5) prejudiced attitudes.

THE RED CROSS AND THE ARMED FORCES

The Negro race has resented deeply that the blood it has given to Red Cross "blood banks" is segregated from "white blood." Even though physicians, physiologists, and physical anthropologists have assured the Red Cross that the blood plasma of the two races is chemically indistinguishable and may be used interchangeably without any possible damage to patients, the Red Cross has continued to Jim-Crow Negro blood plasma, and Negroes throughout the country have continued to tear up Red Cross pledge cards. Negroes say: "They are treating our blood as though we are not human." "This is one of the greatest insults of all."

In addition to this provocative policy, the newspapers—both white and Negro—have carried accounts of Negro-white clashes in Army camps, the segregation of Negro soldiers in Negro units and in Jim-Crow transportation facilities, and the traditional limitation of Negroes to few jobs other than mess attendants in the Navy. The Negroes are supplying their share of soldiers, and, as the National Urban League (Negro-white) has put it in a pamphlet on *The Negro and National Defense*, "there must be no question as to the Negro's loyalty and willingness to defend his country." But many Negroes still tell public opinion interviewers:

Our boys in camps [are] being treated so bad.
They make Jim Crow of the soldiers.
They're just not being given a fair chance [in the Army].
They're putting up their lives for nothing to fight for.

These statements remind one of the charge by Judge William H. Hastie when he resigned in 1943 as civilian aide to Secretary of War Stimson. Hastie, a Negro who was concerned with the morale of Negro soldiers, said that the War Department has "an anti-Negro bias that made [his] work there a travesty." Opinion pollers also found that, among the Negroes,

One-half feel the *Air Force* is all but closed to them.
One out of three is pessimistic about the *Navy*.
Three in ten feel Negroes have little chance of becoming *officers*.
Only one in ten is similarly discouraged about Negro chances in the *WACS*.

And the Detroit Negroes were found by these reporters to be "consistently more skeptical of colored people's chances in the armed forces" than Negroes elsewhere.

These Red Cross and armed-forces situations are parts of the Detroit picture that must be remembered in thinking of the causes of the 1943 race riots.

IN-MIGRATION AND EMPLOYMENT

"Commentator" W. K. Kelsey analyzed the riots in the Detroit *News* the day after Bloody Monday as follows:

The present fracas is due to the fact that the immensity of the war work here has brought scores of thousands of people to Detroit who have encountered new conditions to which they apply old standards. Southern whites have come here in vast numbers, bringing with them their Jim Crow notions of the Negro. Southern Negroes have come here to take jobs which give them for the first time in the lives of many of them a decent wage, and a sense of freedom they have never known before. Some of them have become, in white opinion, too "uppity." The embers smouldered a long time, and at last a slight incident caused them to burst into flame.

The effort to make Detroit conform to Kentucky "hillbilly" and Georgia "red neck" notions of white domination is reflected in frequent white comments in buses and streetcars and bars, such as: "It wouldn't have

happened down home. We know how to keep niggers in their place."
"Southern niggers aren't like these bold brassy Northern niggers." As
a comment, too, on the headline, "20 NEGROES KILLED IN RACE
RIOT," some whites commented, "Served them right. They were getting
too chesty anyway."

The statistical picture beneath these patterns makes them clearer:
In 1916, Detroit had about 10,000 Negroes; in 1925, about 80,000; in
1940, about 160,000; in 1943, about 220,000. During the past three years,
the entire population of Detroit had increased from 1,600,000 to roughly
2,100,000 or more. The 440,000 whites added during these three years
came from Canada, the Middle West, the East, but by all odds the most
riotous potentially came chiefly from the South: Kentucky, Tennessee,
Oklahoma, Arkansas. They, like the Negroes, were refugees from the
sharecropper system of Negro-white peonage, from blighted land and
stunted opportunities. As Isaac Franck, a social work executive, has
analyzed the situation:

There has been a large influx of southern white[s]. . . . They are ignorant and
hold traditional southern attitudes toward the Negroes. Socially, they are
classed with the "foreign" elements in Detroit. They are in great need for
compensation—to look down upon other groups. The Negroes make a convenient target. . . . [The southern whites] have moved into the best areas and
have no basic community ties. They constitute a thoroughly dislocated element
in the population.

Even though in March, 1943, Negroes constituted roughly 10 percent
of Detroit's population, their industrial gains had only given them 8.4
percent of the jobs and those the poorer ones in 185 major war plants
in the Detroit area; 55 of these plants employed less than 1 percent
Negroes. Of the 107,000 women employed in these same plants at that
time, less than 3,500 were Negroes, and these few were holding largely
custodial positions. Walter White of the N.A.A.C.P. also makes the
statement,

It is significant that so far as I know not one important industrialist or employer or employers' association in Detroit has taken any public position on
the riot. On the contrary, as in the Packard strike, some of the officials of
companies have definitely encouraged rioting against Negroes.

OVERCROWDING IN DWELLINGS, RECREATION,
AND TRANSPORTATION

Add 60,000 new in-migrants to slum areas in which few of 160,000 Negroes living there previously had had more than the most abject slum
conditions. To this add the fact that all the Negroes began making more
money than they had had since the 1920's and much more than the new
Negro in-migrants had ever had. And then you have the beginnings of

a conception of the internal pressures that developed in Detroit's Negro ghettos, especially the one surrounding Paradise Valley. The Negro population was literally "bursting out of its seams." Take an already crowded situation, add half again as many people, give them a great purchasing power, and still attempt to confine them within approximately the old area, and the pressures developed within that increasingly inadequate "container" will burst the walls.

The Detroit *Tribune* (Negro) summed up the situation on July 3, 1943, thus: "During this same period when living standards were gradually rising and Negroes had a little more money to improve their conditions, they were nevertheless forced to remain in restricted areas, huddled together in shelters with leaky roofs, crumbling interiors, unsafe stairways and bad plumbing." Beneath a photograph of such an interior, the *Tribune* commented:

The dwelling . . . is typical. . . . The unsanitary edifice, which was formerly used for a church, housed 18 Negro families, most of the groups occupying one room [each]. Here the couple, their girls and boys must eat, sleep, play, work, seek a new start each morning and comfort each night.

Some 3,500 houses in the Paradise Valley district have only outside toilets in shacks over holes in city sewer mains to provide "sanitary" facilities. A city housing expert points out that any improvement in the slum dwelling short of rebuilding would merely make it all the more difficult to put through slum clearance projects "some day." The *Seventh Annual Report* of the Detroit Housing Commission (covering chiefly 1941) states that "50.2 per cent of all dwellings occupied by Negroes were found to be substandard, while only 14 per cent of the white dwellings were substandard."

This housing situation had one of its crises in the Sojourner Truth Homes race riots of February 28, 1942. The *Tribune* described this event as follows:

On the day that Negroes, who had been accepted as tenants in the project, attempted to move in, hundreds of whites blocked the roads, stoned cars and trucks and brutally beat unsuspecting Negroes. As is shown above [in an accompanying picture], police pointed their horses, guns and tear gas at colored citizens who grouped themselves for protection and allowed the whites to congregate and openly display weapons.

At that time, Negroes and their white sympathizers used as a slogan "WE WANT HOMES NOT RIOTS." They got a few more homes but chiefly they got the riots.

From the standpoint of the relations of the dwellers in the Negro slums with those in the nearby white slums, one's attention is immediately focused upon two dramatically opposing processes: (1) a tremendous accumulation of pressures within the hemmed-in Negro district, expressed in terms of high rents, bad facilities, and insolent landlords; (2) sharp defensive movements by landlords, real estate interests, and "unmixed" white slum dwellers to keep the Negro community from expanding in directions where the landlords and real estate interests fear that Negro occupancy would lower property values.

Recreation facilities in both the white and the black slums match the dwellings in inadequacy. "The kids particularly," said a Detroit newspaperman, "get tired of the bars and juke joints. You go in those places any night and you see them sitting around with perfectly vacant faces. They don't know what to do with themselves. They don't even talk. . . . Aren't they ready for any kind of excitement?" Few playgrounds, almost no swimming pools, the newspaperman's picture is an accurate one. No wonder that Msgr. Francis J. Haas, Chairman of the Federal Fair Employment Practice Committee, stressed "inadequate housing, recreation and public transportation" in discussing factors responsible for the 1943 race riots.

A person said to be a "high official in Detroit's housing projects" is quoted by Philip A. Adler in the Detroit *News* as calling the Negro housing situation "appalling."

Even in normal times, rent in the Negro slums was about two or three times higher than in white districts [he said]. A hovel, worth about $10 a month, rented in the Negro section for about $25. A five-room shack, which would normally rent for about $25 a month, often is rented out to five families, one room to a family, at $10 to $15 per month each.

With housing preference given in the war industries to in-migrant Negroes, the old Negro families in Detroit, even those engaged in war production, have been left with no place to go, even at the exorbitant rents they are paying. Detroit's Negro housing is one of the sorest spots in our economy.

It is little wonder, therefore, that the Negro 10 percent of Detroit is said by Adler to contribute 65 percent of the people the police arrest, called by some 65 percent of the "community's crimes."

DELINQUENCY AND CRIME

The imprisoning walls of the slums breed frustrations,, and these frustrations of overcrowding demand outlets that take the forms of juvenile delinquency and crime as well as diseases and other symptoms of moral and social distintegration. And these social and physical diseases do not confine themselves to their breeding grounds but spread their venom over the rest of the community. The Negro aspect of overcrowding, delinquency, and crime is summed up by Adler thus:

Trouble began with the growth of the Negro community after the [first world] war. To the police this meant that the Negro settlement had become a hotbed of blind pigs, brothels and gambling joints. It was then that the KKK began to grumble about sending Negroes back "where they belonged."

Social workers knew better. They knew the Negroes belonged where they were, since the Detroit industries needed them for the menial jobs which the white men would not do. As for immorality, this, to the social workers, white as well as black, meant simply that the Negroes' social and cultural level was not rising as fast as their financial and economic status. The solution was more education.

During the war days, both before and after Pearl Harbor, juvenile delinquency in particular was vastly on the increase among both whites and Negroes. It could be said of Detroit as J. Edgar Hoover, F.B.I. Chief, said of the nation, that the "arrests of 'teen age boys and girls, all over the country, are staggering. Some of the crimes youngsters are committing are almost unspeakable. Prostitution, murder, rape. These are ugly words. But it is an ugly situation." Little wonder that he said, "This country is in deadly peril. We can win this war, and still lose freedom for America. For a creeping rot of moral disintegration is eating into our nation." The same could be said and was said of the under-war-age youth of Detroit, the youngsters who were numbered among the 100,000 race rioters of Paradise Valley and Woodward Avenue.

PREJUDICED ATTITUDES

Student interviewers found relatively few "impartial" observers of the Detroit race riots, and those few they found were mostly fellow students and their teachers. Interviews with 166 mixed Detroiters on Bloody Monday indicated this rough line-up of sentiments: strongly pro-white, 53%; pro-white, 17%; impartial, 17%; pro-Negro, 10%; and strongly pro-Negro, 3%. A more general poll, more systematically undertaken, would have revealed an even greater polarization of Detroit sentiments, in the estimation of the interviewers and of the authors. The race riots, at least temporarily, drove the races farther apart than before, into two suspicious and fearful "camps."

But these prejudices were not created by the race riots. They were merely rendered more vocal, more sharply defined. Such conversations as the following were overheard:

Such brutality and lawlessness should be stopped! It's horrible the way they have beaten the Negroes.

But, Carrie, they're only *niggers,* and everyone knows that niggers *always* revert to that cannibal blood in them and *always* kill or something!

Such myths are of long standing, like the elements out of which developed these remarks:

Do you know what is going to happen next? There's going to be a battle between Jews and niggers, and the Governor's bringing in 15,000 troops.

And this report by a Wayne University student bears out the same point:

I talked to many who were usually decent, respectable people who thought the treatment of Negroes was all right. A reason given for the approval was that the colored people had killed several people and looted white stores. . . . Incidentally, these same people are also prejudiced against Jews but still they said they were in sympathy with the Jews whose stores were looted.

On the Negro side, the stimulation of intolerance is illustrated by this report by another student:

A colored woman who had worked for years in this home and had become a part of the family, appeared for work the day of the riot. Things went along as usual that day, but the following morning Rosa appeared late and with disheveled hair and demanded her pay. "I ain't goin' ta work for white trash no more," she asserted. "You'll be workin' for *me* soon instead!"

The sources of anti-Negro, anti-White, and similar prejudice are not in the schools, the churches, and like organizations. Sentiments of prejudice begin in the intimate social relationships of home and play-group, and they develop and solidify into deepset habit patterns chiefly through ignorance—ignorant mothers and fathers who try to give their children a feeling of status through "running down" other groups and races—ignorant associates in play and work activities. *All this is ignorance that we have failed to dispel through positive preparations for democratic living.* These prejudices provide emotional satisfactions, which are then fanned by irritations of all kinds, by demagogic orators, by organizations that feed upon hate, and by such subversive groups as the Christian Front, the Black Legion, the Ku Klux Klan, and the many others that proselytize the psychologically conditioned with wonderfully satisfying "panaceas."

B. POSTWAR DEVELOPMENTS

Maurice Weaver and Z. Alexander Looby

What Happened at Columbia

On Monday, February 25, 1946, at or about 10:00 the Stephensons, Mrs. Stephenson and her son, James Stephenson, went into the Castner-Knott Electric Appliance Store in Columbia, Tennessee. Mrs. Stephenson, believing that the faulty repair work done on her radio was not what she had paid for, declared to the radio repair-man that he was taking her money without giving her full value. The radio repairman, being the brother of the sheriff-elect of Maury County, was indignant and slapped and kicked Mrs. Stephenson. Whereupon her son reacted by hitting the man who had assaulted his mother. At that time the Stephensons were assaulted by people on the street and attacked by police officer Frazier, who hit at the young man, James Stephenson, and when Mrs. Stephenson declared that the police officer should investigate the facts, she was struck over the eye by the officer. Various people witnessed the incident from across the street and will testify to the above facts. They are Negro people in part and presently are afraid and in great fear for their lives and ask that they not be named as witnesses in this matter.

The sheriff, being the chief law enforcement agent for Maury County, is hereafter quoted. Due to the fact that he is charged with this responsibility as a most responsible person in the County, the sheriff made the following statement to Maurice Weaver of Chattanooga regarding the developments after the assault on the Stephensons.

THE SHERIFF EXPLAINS

After the incident of the attacks on the Stephensons, the sheriff declared voluntarily that he was in court at the time the incident occurred and that reports reached him in the court that a Negro and white man were involved in an affray but that they had been placed under arrest and were in custody. The sheriff declared that he remained in court and continued about the court business until the court adjoined at or about 2:00 o'clock. During that time, however, he heard rumors and reports of the development of mass public opinion against Negroes in the community. After he was out of court he went back to the jail and thereafter was about town and the ominous threat of mob violence against the Stephensons, so he declared, came so forcibly to his attention that he called Mr. Saul Blair and other Negro citizens and asked them to cooperate with him to the end that they might be able to take the Stephensons out of town to avert possible and probable mob action.

At 6:00 o'clock, according to the sheriff, there was a mob of white men congregating on the public square at the courthouse numbering approximately seventy-five (75). The sheriff declares that he asked the mob of white men to disband and to go to their homes and thereafter went into the Negro section and talked to Mr. James Morton, giving him assurance that he and all of the Negro people would be protected against the mob that was congregated on the public square. The sheriff declares that after he talked to Mr. Morton he came back by the public square; the mob was still formed and assembled, and after the sheriff returned to the jail a mob of white men came down to the jail at about 6:30 or 7:00 o'clock at night on Monday, February 25, and kicked on the door of the jail. The sheriff reports that he responded by throwing open the door and levelling a tommy-gun on them; whereupon they demanded the release of the Stephensons to them. The sheriff told them, he declares, that he would not permit mob violence to be committed against the Stephensons if they were in jail, but that they had already been released (mother and son are now reported to be in Chicago) and thereupon told the mob to disband. Two white men were so drunk that they were unable to get away and were placed under arrest for being drunk. No charges as far as we were able to determine were placed against them for inciting to riot or mob action.

LYNCH ACTION THREATENED

After the arrest and after the mob action for the declared lynch purposes, there continued to be mob and lynch action on the public square less than one block from the Negro section. There is definite and concrete evidence that members of the mob had purchased rope and declared they were doing so for the purpose of hanging the two Negroes.

The Negroes were so afraid lest their section be invaded they turned out all the lights in the principal Negro business sections of town. The only illumination was at the center of the block on East Eighth Street and Chaffin Alley. During this time the city police went into a dark street with no illumination to show that they were policemen. The Negroes were afraid lest the mob was moving in on them. A cry was set up that "Here they come," and then there was firing. No one knows who fired the shots but the policemen were shot.

Thereafter the police retired from the business section and following it the sheriff reports a cordon of State Patrolmen and Guards were thrown around one block of the Negro section so that no one would be permitted to enter that section. After the official control of the Negro business section had been established, and at about dawn on Tuesday morning, members of the State Patrol and the State Guard entered the section, firing into various buildings and invading these business establishments, committing officially the following vandalism.

GESTAPO-LIKE VANDALISM

They shot out windows, broke up the show-cases, tore up the cash register taking about $60.00 in money, broke and robbed the piccolo, tore up the radio, threw the pool table balls away, cut the cloth off, broke up all tables, chairs, tore the top off the frigidaire, knocked the clock off the wall.

In Dr. Hawthorne's place they threw out all the instruments and generally destroyed his office. In the Atlanta Life Insurance Company office they destroyed all files and records and at the Morton Funeral Home they likewise destroyed all records, broke chandeliers, lights, venetian blinds, cut up draperies, broke floor lamps, file cabinets and sprinkled white powder on a navy blue casket and marked on the casket "K.K.K." They soiled all caskets. The barber shop was shot into and completely wrecked after the State Patrol had entered and had the situation under control. The four barber chairs were completely cut up and destroyed, the big mirror shot up, all electric clippers were taken out, and the premises completely destroyed.

It is significant that the entire section, after it was under control and in the hands of the State Guard and the State Highway Patrol, was invaded and wanton destruction of property occurred. Thereafter the State Highway Patrol and State Guard, supposedly acting under the sheriff's orders, went to all the Negro homes, removing from them all arms. In the jail were many shotguns and rifles people would normally have for hunting purposes. The sheriff declared that they had been taken uniformly from Negroes and whites for the purpose of completely and totally disarming the town. He also declared that they had been taken without search warrants.

POLICE TERROR

All of the Negroes had retired to their homes for their own protection. The State Guard and State Highway Patrol terrorized the entire Negro residential as well as the business section. They fired into the homes, searched them and lined up all the Negroes, men, women and children, with their hands in the air, and arrested most of the Negroes in the area. All were held in jail and not permitted to get in touch with their families, friends or lawyers. All were held without bail and without formal charges.

One of the leaders arrested who was said to be a leader of the armed rebellion of Negroes for the past three years has been assistant chairman of the Red Cross drive. His business was the center for the meeting of the Red Cross drive—all monies were collected and turned over to the white chairman by him. He was chairman of the Sixth War Loan Drive and Seventh War Loan Drive. His wife is co-chairman. He represents the third generation of colored undertakers in Columbia and has been in business himself for the past twenty-three years.

Two men were killed at the jail waiting to appear before the Board of Investigation. The declared official position is that one of these men endeavored to take a rifle or gun that had been confiscated from some citizens in the town, which was in the sheriff's office, and endeavored to load this gun with ammunition from the confiscated ammunition in the sheriff's office. It is charged officially that this Negro man shot a white officer in the arm with a Japanese rifle or gun.

The entire pattern in Maury county appears to be an attempt to develop and support the idea that there has been an endeavor on the part of the Negro citizens to establish and bring about an armed insurrection; that some six or more Negroes in Maury county were endeavoring to set up a dictatorship of Negro citizens. It is further declared that there would be no peace until whites and "good" Negro citizens organize to surmount the bad relations existing.

The entire investigation has been carried on by the State with the greatest intimidation and coercion with milling mobs of authority, so that Negro citizens held in jail have been alarmed and disturbed for their future safety and have been forced to make completely involuntary statements that may probably in the future be held or used against them.

At the request of the victims of the unlawful action of the officials in Columbia, Tennessee, the NAACP has agreed to defend the Negroes wrongfully charged with crimes and to take all necessary action to punish the local and state peace officers guilty of disregarding the constitutional rights of these people. The entire resources of the NAACP are pledged to this end, and a series of nationwide mass meetings to collect defense funds and to publicize the facts will be held.

R. W.

Tennessee Trial

Although 23 of the 25 Negro defendants accused of attempted murder were acquitted October 4, by an all-white jury in Lawrenceburg, Tenn., the shouts of rejoicing were premature.

The sobering facts are: (a) two more defendants, separated from the 25 on a technicality, are still to be tried on the same charge of attempted murder; (b) they are also under indictment on a charge of assault with intent to kill; (c) all defendants are also under indictment on lesser charges; (d) the two men convicted and sentenced to not more than 21 years in prison must have their cases appealed to higher courts.

Thus the only rejoicing must be over the fact that the *first* hurdle has been taken. There is still a long, weary way to go.

Said Dr. Leon A. Ransom, one of the three NAACP attorneys in the case: "I am a bit concerned over expressions of jubilation over the Lawrenceburg verdict. I am afraid that many people are of the opinion that this case is finished. Nothing could be farther from the truth."

DEFENDANTS PARTIALLY FREE

For the defendants acquitted it was a great day, but outwardly no different from the other days. Each day of the long trial they had been coming to the courtroom from their homes in Columbia, 34 miles distant. Each night they returned to their homes, being free on bail. On the day of acquittal they followed their same routine. They now go about their business in Columbia awaiting the next legal moves in the case.

Columbia is quiet. There is no more racial tension than usual. The trial is not discussed. The colored people of Columbia are confident that in the long pull they will win. They have this confidence in spite of (or, perhaps, because of) the fact that the trial just completed in Lawrenceburg was one of the most fantastic ever held in an American courtroom.

TRIAL UNWELCOME

The town of Lawrenceburg did not want the trial in the first place. It was thrust upon the community by a change of venue granted in Columbia where the trouble occurred last February. Lawrenceburg business men and citizens generally held that they did not want to "wash Columbia's dirty linen." Lawrenceburg said it had "solved" its Negro problem by excluding Negroes from the town; now Columbia had had an interracial scrap and wanted to dump it in the lap of Lawrenceburg to be settled.

In this atmosphere the first legal skirmishes were held, with the defense lawyers, two colored and one white, being overruled and insulted on every point. In this atmosphere the selection of the jury began. It took five weeks. White veniremen paraded to the witness stand and asserted they were prejudiced, that they would take the word of a white man over that of a Negro, that they would not give a Negro a fair trial in a dispute with a white man. Defense counsel became so searching with their questions (searching, that is, to the locality, but in reality asking only the routine questions anyone would ask) that Judge Joe Ingram finally astounded the court and the public by announcing that he would take over the questioning of jurors.

THE BATTLE FOR A JURY

Typical of the examination of prospective jurors was that of Albert Patterson, former boss of a chain gang. Patterson testified that he would believe a white man before he would a colored man. Ransom asked Judge Ingram to excuse Patterson for cause. Ingram turned to Bumpus who declared Patterson was qualified. The judge upheld Bumpus. Under further questioning Patterson said:

"I worked a lot of colored men on the chain gang six years ago when I was a guard.

"The only colored people I ever dealt with were either criminals or criminally inclined."

"Do you think all Negroes are criminally inclined?" asked Patterson.

"Yes," replied Patterson.

Ransom again moved to challenge Patterson for cause, but was overruled by Judge Ingram. The defense was compelled to eliminate Patterson with a peremptory challenge.

The court also forbade defense attorneys to ask questions of prospective jurors on their membership in the Ku Klux Klan.

JUDGE VS. DEFENDANTS

From this point on the defense attorneys had to battle in a courtroom hostile to them personally as well as to the defendants. Maurice Weaver, the white NAACP attorney whose home is in Chattanooga, was the chief target of District Attorney Paul F. Bumpus, and his assistant prosecutor. Weaver to them was a traitor to the white race. Z. Alexander Looby, with his kindly voice, his sharp logic, his sarcasm and dry wit, and his fascinating West Indian accent drew many heated attacks from the red-faced prosecutors. As for Dr. Leon A. Ransom, his clear superiority as a lawyer, a strategist, and student of law, infuriated the opposition.

Bumpus used outrageous language in the courtroom. He threatened to "wrap a chair around his head"—meaning Ransom. He challenged Weaver to come outside the courtroom and fight. He called one defense attorney a sonofabitch in open court. Toward the end of the trial he turned purple language on Vincent Sheean who sat at the press table, whose syndicated articles on the trial enraged both Bumpus and Lynn Bomar, head of the state police. When Weaver asked Judge Ingram if he was going to permit such an attack in his court without rebuke, Ingram replied that it was a matter between Bumpus and Sheean!

A high point, illustrating not only the atmosphere in the courtroom, but the manner in which these defendants had been arrested, occurred during the testimony of Lynn Bomar, head of the state highway patrol. Bomar admitted on the stand that he had led state troopers into the homes of Columbia Negro citizens without a search warrant.

Q. Did you get Morton's permission to enter and search?

A. I just went right in.

Q. (By the court) Was the door open when you entered the house? Did you turn the knob?

A. I turned the knob and walked right in.

Q. Did anyone object?

A. I didn't wait to see. I knew a felony had been committed and I went in to get the guilty parties.

Bomar roared a denial when asked whether his men had ransacked and wrecked Negro property. Later he said he would enter Negro property again without a warrant if he wanted to do so.

GLOOM BEFORE VICTORY

In this atmosphere the trial dragged on. No defendant was identified as having fired a shot at the policemen who were wounded. In no manner whatsoever were any of the defendants connected with the crime except that one witness said she had walked with one of the defendants who had told her he was in Columbia on the night of the trouble. Mere presence in the town where the shooting had occurred thus became "proof" of guilt!

The defendants told their stories, and then came the summing up to the jury. District Attorney Bumpus and his assistant performed as was expected. The Vincent Sheean articles syndicated in daily papers throughout the country had roused the ire of Bumpus. He ranted at outsiders and newspaper writers. He raved about white supremacy. He called for the conviction of all 25 defendants.

On the speeches of the three defense lawyers to the jury, Sheean offers this description:

The three lawyers were excellent, each in a different way. Andy Ransom made the argument of reason and courtesy and common sense—deliberately appealing to those qualities in the jury, I mean. His was the first argument for the defense and had the effect (I believe) of reasonableness, the evocation of reasonableness. Then Weaver made his rather fiery speech, which could *not* have been made under the conditions by any Negro; he established the analogies to Nazi practise and made the appeal to historical conscience ("You are making history in this courtroom"). Then Looby made his searching appeal to their religious instincts. He had varicose veins badly and had to speak from a seated position with his right leg upon a cushion arrangement in front of him. His voice was better than it had been before, his manner and language simple, his argument less studded with legal authority than I had expected. His essential argument was of a purely religious nature and it was my impression that it reached home with that jury.

VICTORY—WHY?

Why was the surprising verdict rendered? No one will know unless the jurors themselves tell their reasons. Was this the way Lawrenceburg had of showing Columbia how distasteful the trial was—if you want these Negroes convicted you will have to do it yourself?

Did Bumpus and Judge Ingram overplay their hands? Did the judge muzzle the defense lawyers so obviously and so unfairly that even those Tennessee jurymen thought the Negroes were not getting a fair shake? Did Paul Bumpus stress the white supremacy argument too much even for rural Tennessee?

Did the defense lawyers by their courage, their brilliance, and their persistence under handicaps and discouragements capture the sporting fancy of the jury? Did the jury really mean to indicate that the South was ready to change its attitude and that hereafter Negroes could expect a fair deal?

The Optimists have seen a "new day" in the verdict, a sign that democracy is here for the Negro in the rural South. The cynics say the jury was just trying to wash its hands quickly of the Columbia "dirt."

But the truth would seem to be somewhere in between. The first round has been won. It may be that its winning will cause the state to drop all charges and close the book on the shameful chapter of the Columbia disturbance of last winter. Or, angered by the acquittal, District Attorney Bumpus may continue his fight. The defendants, their lawyers, and the thousands of Americans who contributed to the defense fund await his next move.

The two convicted defendants, John McKivens and Robert Gentry, were granted a new trial on October 26 by Circuit Judge Joe M. Ingram, who declared he was not satisfied with the evidence presented against them. The motion for a new trial was granted by Judge Ingram only ten minutes after it was presented by NAACP attorneys.

Newsweek, November 4, 1946

Trial and Terror

Floating face down in the sluggish waters of a bayou, the body of a small, 35-year-old Negro was found one day last July near Lexington, Miss. His name was Leon McAtee, and he had not died by drowning. The evidence was that his body had been thrown into the water from a car.

He had been working on the farm of Jeff Dodd. Questioned, the thin-faced, 57-year-old farmer had a lot to say about McAtee. Two days before a saddle had disappeared from Dodd's barn. He never thought twice. He knew McAtee had done time in the State penitentiary for stealing. He took him right into town and turned him over to the sheriff.

Still pretty mad, he'd got to talking with some of the boys. A hill-country farm like his took a lot of hard working for the $76 he put out for that saddle. A couple of boys pricked up their ears. Stole a saddle, huh? Done time? They had had saddles stolen too. How about getting that nigger out of jail and asking him a few questions?

Dodd went back to jail and fixed it up with the sheriff. Dodd withdrew the charges, paid the court costs, and the sheriff discharged McAtee in Dodd's custody. The men took McAtee out of town and asked him a few questions.

Last week Jeff Dodd and his son, Jeff Dodd, Jr., Dixie Roberts of Greenwood and his nephew, James Roberts, and Spencer Ellis faced a Holmes County jury. Sure, they had whipped Leon a little. Dodd explained: During the questioning McAtee "made a break at me and I hit him." He said the other four "hit him a few licks, I think, but I was so excited I don't know." The defendants testified that after the whipping, the last they saw of McAtee he was able to jump a fence and keep running.

But pretty, young Hazel Brannon, crusading editor of Lexington's weekly newspaper, *The Advertiser*, was not satisfied. She waylaid McAtee's widow, Henrietta, on her way out of the courtroom. Henrietta had been told not to talk to anyone about the case. But Miss Brannon got a story: "Henrietta McAtee, the Negro's wife, testified that she saw McAtee that afternoon with the five defendants. She said his lips were bruised, his eyes 'poppish,' and that his hands were bound with rope. Later, she said, she saw Ellis's pickup truck go by with McAtee doubled up in the back."

The all-white jury took only ten minutes to return a verdict: not guilty. As for Hazel Brannon, the judge cited her for contempt of court. And the case ended on this ironic note: McAtee's 16-year-old stepson confessed that it was he, not McAtee, who had stolen the saddle.

George Schermer

The Fairgrounds Park Incident: A Study of the Factors Which Resulted in the Outbreak of Violence at the Fairgrounds Park Swimming Pool on June 21, 1949

An Account of What Happened, and Recommendations for Corrective Action

EVENTS LEADING TO THE INCIDENT

The Division of Parks and Recreation had been following the practices of segregation in the playgrounds, community centers and swimming pools. Without express policies, without any planning or instruction of personnel, the handling of previous pressure situations was such as to encourage aggressive action. No efforts were being made without or within the Department to provide for the orderly transition of facilities from one type of use to another, or to prepare the people in borderline areas to accept a sharing of facilities. Playgrounds were shifted from white to Negro use under duress. Because playgrounds were numerous and of only local neighborhood concern, none of the tension which developed around specific playgrounds became of city-wide importance. Each tension situation grew, came to a crisis and subsided as a separate, isolated situation.

The outdoor swimming pools were a different matter. There were only two in the entire City of St. Louis. Both had been closed to Negroes.

It should be clear that in the summer months there is a decided difference between the indoor and outdoor swimming facilities, at least so far as children are concerned. There is considerable more exhilaration in swimming in the open air under the blue sky as compared to swimming in an indoor pool.

Numerous persons testified that in previous years, small groups of Negroes had come to swimming pools, particularly Fairground Pool, and asked whether they would be admitted. There were varying stories as to how it was handled. Some of the persons interviewed said it was their instructions to bar Negroes from entering. Others said that they were instructed to say, "If you *really* want to swim, you can get in line."

It was reported by the Director of Public Welfare that for at least a a couple of months prior to the opening of the pools, the Commissioner of Parks had been asking him for instruction as to what to do about the pools. At the outset, his response was, "Why do you ask this question? What is the problem?" He quoted the Commissioner as replying, "It's a question that comes up every year that is difficult to handle and we ought to decide on a policy." The Director of Welfare explained, "Frankly, I didn't know what to do. I couldn't see where there was any basis for excluding Negroes under the law. I kept postponing giving an answer. I really thought that the man who had been the Commissioner of Parks for a long time should know what to do. Finally, on the Friday before the pools were to open, the Commissioner once more asked me if I had come to a decision, so I told him I could see no basis for keeping Negroes out of the pools. They are citizens like everybody else and have every legal right to enter any public facility."

From that point until Monday afternoon, the course of events is still cloudy. At first officials avoided the question of how they handled the situation. Later the Commissioner stated that he had issued an order that under instructions from the Director of Public Welfare, if Negroes requested admittance to swimming pools, they were to be admitted. As far as can be determined, no instructions as to how to handle the situation were issued swimming pool personnel. Apparently no instructions were issued to park guards. Apparently there was no consultation with the Chief of Police, nor were the police in any way notified.

On Sunday, June 19, in suburban Webster Groves, a new public swimming pool was opened. Certain Negro residents of that suburban community sought admittance to the pool and were denied. The metropolitan press reported this and that the Negroes involved had threatened civil suit. On Monday afternoon, a *Post-Dispatch* reporter got word that the Director of Welfare had issued an order that Negroes were to be admitted to the pools. In company with a *Globe-Democrat* reporter, he asked the Director for a statement. The Director subsequently reported that he denied that he had issued an order that Negroes and whites were to swim together and explained that he had instructed the Park Commissioner that Negroes were to be admitted if they requested. He states further that the reporters responded by saying, "We must construe that as an order." A few minutes later, the reporters went to see the Mayor and thereafter the Mayor asked the Director to come over and the nature of his order was once more confirmed.

At this point there needs to be some clarification as to the interpretation of this order. There is a difference between an order which says, "If Negroes request admittance, they are to be permitted to enter," and an order which says, "The swimming pools are open to all that come, and Negroes and whites alike are invited." The real import of the order was to the effect that an old practice of questionable legality barring Negroes was to be eliminated. At that point there was present no overt effort to bring whites and Negroes together into the same pool.

Realizing that if the order received special attention in the press public reaction might follow, the Mayor consulted with a number of advisors. It was decided to contact all the editors of the papers, requesting that the story be given only factual and routine coverage. However, in at least one case, top level management could not be reached, although some promise of careful handling is said to have been made.

As far as can be determined, even at this point there was no consultation with the police. Later in the evening, the *Globe-Democrat* was issued with a front page story headlined "Pools and Playgrounds Open to Both Races." Opening paragraphs ran as follows: "Negroes and whites hereafter may swim together in all the City's nine pools and use the same thirty-five playgrounds, Director of Public Welfare John J. O'Toole announced yesterday. O'Toole thus opened the pools to members of both races in an order to Park Commissioner Palmer B. Baumes. The order read, 'If Negroes apply for admission to municipal pools, they are not to be refused.'"

This order was also given frequent attention on radio news broadcasts.

EVENTS OF TUESDAY, JUNE 21

On Tuesday, June 21, Negro children appeared at three swimming pools formerly reserved for whites. At the Mullanphy Community Center indoor pool, the pool opened at 9:00 A.M. There were no Negroes swimming until 1:30 P.M., when four Negro boys came in with the regular white crowd. At the second shift, starting at 2:45 P.M., there were about seventy-five Negroes and only fifteen white boys. At the third shift, at 4:00 P.M., there were about forty-seven white and twenty colored boys. No tension, name-calling or violence of any sort was noted or recorded.

At Marquette outdoor pool, in the course of the afternoon four Negro children swam with a large crowd of whites and no incident of any kind was noted or recorded.

At Soulard Playground, a number of Negro children went wading with white children and no incident of any kind was recorded as far as relationships between the children are concerned. There is one report indicating that some white parents came and objected to the supervisor.

It is difficult to reconstruct accurately the course of events at Fairgrounds pool. Drawing from a variety of testimony and ruling out the inconsistencies and contradictions, the following seems to be the story:

The pool opened for the first shift at 2:00 P.M. Customary procedure provided for boys to line up at a gate on one side of the entrance and girls at the other. Each gate led to separate lockers. There were several hundred boys lined up, most of them white, but approximately thirty of them Negro. There was a much smaller number of girls, all white. The boys filed in, took their lockers, changed clothes, took their showers and gathered in the "ready" area, and when the gates were opened, went swimming. There was a tendency for the Negro youths to gather in one part of the pool and for the whites to swim in another section. Within the group that went swimming, there was little or no evidence of feeling and no open incident of any kind.

One of the lifeguards reported that there was some discussion among the guards as to whether they should continue working under the new order, but it was agreed that they should. While this first shift was in swimming, a group of boys began to gather outside the enclosure and there were evidences of name-calling and threats. There was a shift change at 2:40 P.M., with the second shift going in at 3 o'clock. By that time, the group of boys outside the enclosure, with some adults interspersed, had grown in number and had become quite threatening in behavior. As a result, the custodial worker instructed the Negro boys to stay inside until all were dressed, while he let the white boys out. Some of the white boys went their way, while others stayed behind to join with those gathered outside. He then requested that the police escort the Negro boys out of the park so as to prevent injury to them. There were no Negro children in the second shift and there were no other Negroes who entered into the pool enclosure later that day (except as noted later two were taken there for protection by the police in the evening). This seems to be the sum of information available from swimming pool personnel.

Police reports and statements from Lieutenant Nicholas J. Kube, who was in command at the Fifth District on the afternoon of the incident, indicate the following:

There is normally one park guard and one City policeman stationed at the pool during the swimming season. On the morning of June 21, Captain Thomas Dirrane detailed some additional officers to the pool, inasmuch as he had noticed the announcement of change in policy in the paper and surmised that there might possibly be some difficulty arising at Fairground Park. At 2:30 P.M., Lieutenant Kube reported for duty at the Fifth District to relieve Captain Dirrane. As he talked to some officers prior to roll call, he was informed of some tension at Fairground Park and after a consultation with Captain Dirrane, it was decided to assign additional men to prevent trouble. According to Lieutenant Kube's report, the total number of officers assigned at that time included the regular man plus six extra uniformed officers in command of Corporal A. Havey and two plain-clothes men. A police report stated that three officers took a car out of service to keep the swimming pool located at Fairground Park under surveillance. They reported that upon their arrival, one hundred to two hundred white children had gathered around the scene and were shouting to the colored children. When the swimming period was over, at about 3:00 P.M., these officers, assisted by three others, then escorted the various Negroes from the park at the request of the Negro children. These officers report that they observed no fights or destruction of property. There were, however, reports of fights and of harassment of Negroes in nearby areas.

Various eyewitness accounts have been obtained from persons who were present, particularly newspaper reporters and photographers. One witness stated that he arrived about 2:30 P.M. and noted Negro children swimming in the pool, and later noted the Negro children leaving under police escort. He said there were only two or three officers and no effort was made to group the children together. He saw that white children who were following would dart in and strike the Negro children from time to time and noted that this was not prevented by police action. He reported that the police escorted the children five or six blocks beyond Natural Bridge Avenue and at that point stopped the white children who were following and shooed them back to the park. He states further that several other Negroes came to the park to swim, but each time were turned away and always escorted out by the police. There were a large number of white people, most of them teen-aged boys, but with many adults interspersed, and all of them displaying "nasty attitudes." He noted one older man, perhaps fifty years of age, making crude remarks to the children and using foul language, who encouraged the children to run the Negroes out of the park. This witness reported that he frequently heard remarks to the effect that a large number of Negroes had assembled at the west end of the park and were coming in to cause trouble. He did not see the group and did not verify the rumor.

Another witness reported that about 3:15 P.M. he saw several white boys smash three bicycles which were chained and locked to a tree. He learned later that the bicycles belonged to some Negro boys. One of the park officers chased the boys away, shouting, "Look here, what do you think you are doing?" The boys were not taken in custody. Later, other police officers escorted three Negro boys into the park while they obtained their smashed bicycles and then escorted them out. At about that time, he also noted a police officer stop a white boy who was carrying something under his arm, which was discovered to be a six-inch hunting knife. When questioned why he had taken the knife, the boy said that he had it "just in case." The officer took the boy's name and address, retained the knife, and said the boy should come to the station with his mother if he wished to have it returned. This witness described the crowd as consisting of boys ranging in age from fourteen to sixteen, most of them under sixteen. Nearly all of them were carrying baseball bats, sticks and clubs. All were highly excited and tense. They would gather in knots, converse briefly, and then run off in one direction or another, as it was reported that Negro boys were coming. This witness felt that the police were doing a good job of protecting Negro youngsters from injury but were doing nothing to disperse the white crowd.

At about 4:30 P.M., four Negro adults came to the park entrance and asked for the manager. They were told he wasn't there. One of the men said he was a war veteran who had fought for his country. In great anger, he stated, "My kid brother just got beat up by these ruffians." At another point, he said, "If you want a race riot, you'll have one." One of the newspaper reporters present suggested that if his brother had been hurt, the place to register a complaint was at the Fifth District Police Station. These men then left, probably going over to the Fifth District. Several reporters stated that they noticed the same man of about fifty years or a little older, in a white shirt and a straw hat, who seemed constantly to be encouraging the boys to attack the Negroes and also using foul language. Several also reported that while they saw the police officers confiscate some clubs and a knife, they saw none of them take baseball bats.

This concludes most of the events of the afternoon. There are numerous reports of scattered attacks in the neighborhood around Fairgrounds Park. The testimony as to whether police gave adequate protection to Negro children who were under attack is inconsistent. It appears that in some instances the police gave adequate protection against attack, and in other instances they did not. All of the evidence that can be obtained would indicate that there were not more than a dozen policemen assigned to the park during the afternoon, and that while the police tried to protect the Negro boys from injury, they were not discouraging or taking a firm hand with the white youths. The pool closed at 5:00 P.M. and most of the crowd dispersed at that time.

A reporter returning at about 6:00 P.M. reports, "There was a group of about fifteen white boys, none of them over fourteen, listening to two white agitators, and I am not using the word loosely. One was a man of about fifty-five and the other was a burly man of about thirty. When we came on them, they were saying, 'You want to know how to take care of them niggers? Get bricks and smash their heads, the dirty, filthy——.' One boy timidly said, 'The police might put us in jail for that kind of thing.' The younger man replied, 'No, they won't. Kill a nigger and you will make a name for yourself.' I called a policeman's attention to this lecture and he immediately dispersed them. I saw no more of the older man, but the younger man showed up constantly with the shout, 'Kill the black bastards.' " This same reporter states that he learned from another reporter that at about 6:20 P.M. the Mayor had rescinded the order opening the pools to Negroes. The pool custodian stated that he had not been so informed. At 6:49 P.M., John Turner, Superintendent of Recreation, arrived, and when told of [Mayor] Darst's action, called Commissioner Baumes for instructions. He then stated that Baumes had stated that he had not been informed of Darst's action and instructed Turner to open the pool in compliance with Monday's order.

Several witnesses are agreed that at about 6:45 P.M., there were a couple of hundred boys and young men and some young women who gathered in front of the pool waiting for the gates to open. There were no Negro girls present, but there were a number of Negro youths—estimates range from thirteen to thirty in number, although more of the witnesses hold to a number under twenty. Some witnesses report they heard no name calling at this point. Others state that they overheard whites saying, "You'd better get out of here if you don't want trouble."

Quoting from one eye-witness' report, "Starting at about 6:40 P.M., a constantly growing number of whites gathered at the east end of the pool. Many were carrying baseball bats. The atmosphere was extremely tense. Frequently, among them I heard comments such as these, 'This is a waiting party. Waiting until it gets dark.' 'I'll kill the bastards.' The tough ones and most blood-thirsty appeared to be in their late teens."

There is a ten-minute variation in the time quoted by various police officers and observers as to what happened next. Up until this time, there were not more than a dozen police officers on the scene.

At some time between 7:05 and 7:15 P.M., someone shouted, "There's some niggers." Some witnesses claim that they saw a number of Negroes approaching, perhaps as many as twelve or fifteen. Others insist that there were only three. Testimony from the Negro boys themselves would indicate there were four in the first group. In any event, the crowd surged around from the east to the south side of the pool and quickly gathered around three Negroes, all young men ranging in age from eighteen to twenty years. There were some sharp words and blows were struck. There were cries of, "He's got a knife." "He cut him."

One of the Negroes was observed to have a knife in his hand. Some of the whites were beating him with clubs, bats, bricks, sticks and their fists. He quickly went down. One officer went to his rescue, finally falling on top of him. While the Negro was down, he was kicked and beaten. It was simply impossible for the officer to protect him and keep the assailants away at the same time. One of the other Negro boys was receiving the same treatment a few feet away.

At about the same moment, a couple of Negro boys were seen at Natural Bridge on the bus and a crowd took after them. The boys raced away and the witness could not tell whether or not they were caught. Another Negro got off the streetcar at Natural Bridge and Grand and was immediately attacked and beaten. A cry surged through the park that a Negro had stabbed and killed a white boy.

At the outset, perhaps only five hundred people had gathered around the pool. However, there were several thousand people on the grounds that night. Six American Legion league ball games were in process. Another hardball game and five softball games were also being played. Twenty-four horseshoe courts were in use. There was a casting contest. There was perhaps heavier than normal traffic on Natural Bridge, which became jammed up as people stopped to see what was going on. Hundreds of people were getting off streetcars and buses on their way to Sportsmans Park to see the Cardinal game. All these factors will readily explain how a crowd of five thousand or more could have gathered quickly in response to a cry of racial violence.

The numerous attacks that occurred within the next half to three-quarters of an hour have been well described by the press and there are sufficient pictures to show that a number of Negroes were attacked, brutally beaten and hurt in that short period of time. A call was put in for police reinforcements and for ambulances. In a short time, in response to a riot call, more than one hundred fifty police officers had arrived; and the two Negro boys who had been beaten near the pool had first been taken into the enclosure and later loaded into a patrol wagon and taken to the hospital.

Shortly after the police arrived in large numbers, a semblance of order was established. Traffic was rerouted off Natural Bridge Avenue. Police were detailed to various streets leading to the park for the purpose of turning away any Negroes who might be approaching. Most of the observers agree that violence was checked mainly because there were so few Negroes within sight who could be attacked. This resulted in part from the precautionary action taken by the police in turning Negroes away. The fact that the crowd was not immediately under control is indicated by the fact that at about 8:45 P.M., five Negroes parked their two trucks on the opposite side of the park, on Kossuth Avenue. As they started to cross the park, they were set upon by the crowd. Four of them sought refuge in one of the trucks and were rescued by the police before being seriously injured. The other one sought refuge on a porch, was ordered off, and was very brutally kicked and beaten before police officers were able to rescue him. A few minutes later, the crowd began to wreck the trucks. It would appear that at about 9:30 P.M. order was restored, except for one attack which occurred an hour later some distance from the park. The crowd, however, did not disperse until several hours later.

The Negroes who were beaten can tell only sketchy stories of what happened, because they were caught by surprise and have only a general impression of cries, foul language and beating. The stories of two Negro witnesses are quite revealing. They are two young men, well educated and of good bearing. Their story follows:

"We were out riding with our wives. We were driving through the park on Vandeventer when we noticed a lot of cars and people, so we stopped and got out. Someone threw a brick at us. Three big boys came up and told us to get out of the park. We argued that we were citizens and had a right to be there. One of them said, 'There's a race riot over there (pointing) and if you don't get out you'll get killed.' Just then, some other young men came up with clubs and bricks. It looked to us like some of them had guns. They were about to attack when the first boy held them back, saying, 'Let them alone, they're going and they got their girl friends with them.' Then several police officers came up and asked if we were in trouble. We said, 'No, we're all right.' Then an officer said, 'What in hell do you come over to this park for?' We were walking to our car. The police walked with us. There was an older woman there with a gun she was half-hiding in her purse. She kept urging the boys to jump on us. The boys kept stepping on our heels, trying to start something. We got in our car and drove away. Those police certainly were acting as though what those boys were doing was all right."

There is incomplete information as to how many Negroes came to the park that afternoon and evening, whether they came in large groups, and whether some of the groups came armed for combat with clubs, bats, etc. Certain reports appear sufficiently consistent to indicate that groups of Negroes, youngsters, did form in the afternoon, some of them carrying clubs, approaching within a few blocks of the park, and in one instance, reaching the southwest corner of the park. Apparently, most of these groups dispersed of their own volition, or were turned back by the police. It appears quite evident that there was no concerted movement on the part of Negroes to retaliate in an organized manner.

William Gremley

Social Control in Cicero

On the morning of Friday, July 13, 1951, the press of America, and subsequently of the world, carried headline stories of a racial disturbance in Cicero, Illinois, U.S.A., a town with a population of 67,000 located immediately adjacent to, and west of, Chicago. The disturbance at that time centered around the move-in of a Negro family into a flat in Cicero. The actual beginning of the resultant disorders, however, can be dated five weeks earlier.

On June 8, Harvey Clark, Jr., a twenty-nine-year-old Negro war veteran, married, with two children, attempted to move his goods into a flat he had rented at 6139 19th Court, Cicero. According to Mr. Clark, as related in his official complaint to the Federal authorities, the following actions took place:

As he arrived at the building with the moving van, local police officials, including the Cicero police chief, stopped him from entering. When he protested, they informed him he could not move in without a "permit." Clark argued in vain against this edict and finally telephoned his solicitor, who assured him that there was no provision in local, state or Federal laws for any such "permit." The police officials then bluntly ordered him and the van away, threatening him with arrest if he failed to comply with their demand. Clark then left, after being man-handled and struck. While this action was taking place a group of residents gathered and observed the incident.

About two weeks later, through the aid of the National Association for the Advancement of Colored People (NAACP), Clark obtained an injunction from Federal District Judge John P. Barnes. The injunction, carrying the weight of the Federal government, restrained the Cicero police from interfering with Clark's moving into the building and ordered them to afford him full protection from any attempt to so restrain him.

The move-in, on Tuesday, July 10, was accomplished without incident except for the presence of residents of the area who stood across the street from the flat building and shouted derogatory racial epithets. On the evening of that day, a considerable crowd gathered in front of the building, again shouting abuse of a racial nature. Late in the evening, several in the crowd threw stones, breaking front windows in the Clark flat. The Clarks did not occupy the flat that night nor on the subsequent nights, having departed immediately after their goods had been moved into the third-story flat.

By Wednesday evening, July 11, the mob had attacked the building, which contains twenty flats in all, and had looted that of the Clarks' as well as some of those adjoining his. Mob members threw Clarks' furniture into the street, where others set it afire. During this time, these activities were not hampered nor restricted in any significant manner by the local police, who were present. Seven of the nineteen families in the building (all white) had moved by Wednesday morning and the remaining twelve evacuated on Thursday morning, July 12. By Thursday night, the mob was again completely out of control and directing its ire at the entire building. National Guard troops (home militia) were then dispatched to the scene by the Governor of the State of Illinois to quell the disorders.

There are numerous questions that may be raised as a result of this Cicero disturbance. Perhaps the most important, particularly to those not fully conversant with social and cultural concepts affecting Negro-white relationships in the United States, is the following: how was such racial violence possible in an urbanized Northern community?

According to Myrdal:

The American Dilemma . . . is the ever-raging conflict between, on the one hand, the valuations preserved on the general plane which we shall call the "American Creed," where the American thinks, talks, and acts under the influence of high national and Christian precepts, and, on the other hand, the valuations on specific planes of individual and group living, where personal and local interests; economic, social and sexual jealousies; considerations of community perstige and conformity; group prejudice against particular persons or types of people; and all sorts of miscellaneous wants, impulses, and habits dominate his outlook. . . .

The main conflict is between the ever-present equalitarian American Creed, on the one hand, and the caste interest, on the other (Myrdal, 1944, pp. xlvii, 899).

Mores which contain positive elements regarding this "American Creed" have, particularly in recent years and by many processes, to use Sumner's phrase, become "crystallized" into law. Some examples are recent U.S. Supreme Court decisions upholding the rights of persons regarding various aspects of racial segregation, denying court sanctions to restrictive covenants (property agreements restricting, on grounds of race, religion or national origin, the right of one to buy or rent property), and other matters; the existence of civil rights laws in many Northern states; the establishment of Fair Employment Practices Commissions and laws in several Northern states and cities to enforce equal employment opportunities; the establishment by law of official city and state agencies to deal with intergroup tensions and promote intergroup harmony, and the increasing enforcement by the Federal Government of Federal civil rights laws already in existence.

Existing side by side with these "positive" mores and the legal safeguards for the civil rights of Negroes are certain widespread beliefs about Negroes. Most of these beliefs are in contradiction to the "positive" mores, and, when they are acted upon, as in the Cicero incident, can lead to violations of the legal norms. . . .

Most if not all of the stereotyped beliefs may be found in Cicero, Berwyn and the violence area. Thus, as a Northern urbanized community, Cicero is also caught in the Dilemma. By itself, however, this does not completely explain the violence since these beliefs are everpresent in this and other communities where racial mob violence is infrequent or has never occurred. For other motivating factors we must turn to an analysis of the community itself.

The incident should properly be called the "Cicero-Berwyn" incident, because the building attacked by the mob is located on the Cicero side of the dividing line between Cicero and Berwyn, a community of 51,000 immediately to the west. About 10 per cent of those arrested lived in Berwyn and there seems to be little doubt that the Berwyn proportion of the mob was at least equal to that from the town of Cicero. Consequently, any sociological description of the community should be considered in "Cicero-Berwyn" terms. Berwyn is similar to Cicero in most respects with the exception that it is not so highly industrialized. Cicero and Berwyn are primarily middle middle-class urban communities with the same diversity of ethnic groups making up their population as is found in most Northern urban areas of similar size.[1] The specific violence area consisted of about *two* square miles of the total *nine and one-half* square miles within the boundaries of the two towns, an area populated by a variety of ethnic groups and with an ecological pattern which has taken the form of nuclei of subcommunities in which people of one particular national group live within an area of one or two square miles.

While no statistics on ethnic composition are available for the small area being discussed, available data indicate that the dominant ethnic group in this particular area is Czech with Poles in second place. These same sources also indicate that persons of foreign parentage predominate as family heads over foreign-born or 2nd and 3rd generations.

Of primary significance in understanding the violence is the fact that it was widely believed by the residents of the community that no Negroes lived in Cicero. 1950 Census figures indicate, however, a total of 31 Negroes were living there at the time the census was taken. It is highly probable that some if not all of that number were still residents of Cicero at the time of the violence a year later. There is no way of determining whether such residents are tenants, home-owners or servants living on the premises of employers.

This sub-community is primarily an area of small homes, some two and three-flat buildings, and a lesser number of multi-flat buildings. A wide variety of trades and professions is represented with factory-workers, white-collar workers, and owners of small businesses predominating over others. A two-block square factory of one of the world's largest manufacturers of telephone equipment, the Western Electric Company, is located in Cicero about two miles from the area involved, and employs a considerable number of residents. Many other large factories are also located nearby. Two blocks south of the building attacked lies 22nd Street or Cermak Road, a main business artery linking Cicero with Chicago in an east-west direction. Small and large stores of all types line both sides of the street on which run main lines of public transportation.

The primary religious group in the violence area is Roman Catholic; approximately 60 per cent of the area's population is Catholic. The balance of the church-going population is composed chiefly of adherents of the following denominations (apart from church-going residents who worship outside the area): Christian Reformed (Calvinist), Reformed,

1. The 1950 Census reported that slightly over 20 percent of Cicero's population was foreign-born.

Presbyterians, and United Lutherans. There are three Christian Re-
formed churches and one each of the other denominations.

The social framework of this community as given above contains
strong elements of stability as represented by home-owning and religious
traditions. Yet violence and a breakdown of law and order resulted as
an outgrowth of the negative appraisals of the Negro in this area. Thus
a basic question is posed—why should racial violence occur in such a
community?

Before discussing this question in detail some insights into a possible
answer may be obtained by the results of a survey of eighty families
taken before, during, and immediately after the disturbance. This was
an independent interview house-to-house survey taken by a member of
a religious interracial organization. Because it was not a carefully
planned or scientifically oriented survey carried out by a trained interviewer, no conclusive findings can be based on it. One qualifying aspect
of this report should be noted. The interviewer stated that two-thirds
of those interviewed were housewives since the survey was made during
the daytime working hours. A summary of the report follows:

The survey was made withi a four-block radius of the riot scene. It began on
July 5 and ended July 12. About 10 interviews a day were accomplished.

About half of those questioned were homeowners. The community is made
up chiefly of Czechs, Poles and Slovaks. The greater number are Catholics.

The questions asked, with their answers immediately following, are as follows:

1. How do you feel about the Clarks moving into the neighborhood?

(a) During the first four days of the survey, 20 responded with mention of a
"Communist invasion." These persons were certain that the Clarks were Communists and were more upset by this belief than the fact that the Clarks
were Negroes.

(b) About 10 felt bitter over the move-in and expressed strong anti-Negro
sentiments.

(c) Five said they were glad to hear that coloured people were moving into
the neighborhood. All five were employed or involved in interracial contact
situations.

d) The greater majority of the people were unhappy about the move-in but
were resigned to it.

The next questions were varied according to the responses to the first
question.

2. Do you think this is the Christian attitude?

About 35 were asked this. All avoided this question with such responses as:

"The neighborhood would become a slum area if Negroes moved in."

"Negroes should move to some coloured area and keep to themselves."

"The presence of Negroes would decrease property values."

"If Negroes live in the area, white children will intermarry with them."

3. Are you planning on selling your home? (asked of 40).

Five replied affirmatively, the rest negatively.

4. What difference does it make if the value of your property drops when
you have no intention of selling?

Ten were asked this and could not answer. Each returned again to the idea that they did not want Negroes living in the area.

5. How do your neighbors feel about the Clarks' moving in?

About 30 said that their neighbors shared their opinions.

6. Do you think violence should be used to keep the Clarks out?

About 40 were asked this question. All stated that violence should not be used to exclude the Clarks.

For further insights into basic causes of the incident we can now consider the Cicero governmental structure, its relationship to the various laws applicable to the violence, and the social interpretations of those laws themselves.

As of this time of writing, the Cicero police chief is under indictment by the State of Illinois and awaiting trial on charges of failure to enforce state laws prohibiting gambling. He is also under indictment by the Federal Government, together with the town president, town attorney (solicitor), fire chief, and three Cicero policemen for violations of the Federal Civil Rights statute in connection with his role in the disturbance.

The police officials of Cicero are expected to act officially as enforcers of state and local laws. Unofficially, however, they also act as representatives of a political machine as well as reflectors of public opinion in any given issue as they may define it. If, as Clark alleges, the Cicero police chief actually barred him from entering premises which he had a legal right to enter, then we have a subversion of the legal rights of a person by the state itself. On the surface this would seem a most complete breakdown of control as understood in terms of legal rights in American society.

Underlying it, however, is a basic conflict of roles regarding the actions of the Cicero police. While on the one hand these officials have a sworn responsibility to uphold legal rights; on the other, we can assume that the Chief of Police believed he was expressing, in his actions, the sentiments of the community and acting as a mediator or even "protector" of community mores, thus crystallizing the state into an instrument to enforce mores contrary to the law of the state. The reluctance of the Cicero police to act vigorously to prevent the violence that followed also reflects this conflict of roles.

It is obvious, though, that such mob members would be quite aware they were breaking *some* laws concerning violence and property damage. What is important to a basic understanding as to why this violence happened in this community are the attitudes of mob members towards such laws whether or not they knew specifically of them.

Some insight into this question may be derived from the reaction of the community to the decision of the Governor of Illinois to send National Guard troops to the scene. This action, of course, illustrated the inviolate right of the state to suppress what it defines as a "riotous situation." When this definition was made and troops dispatched, it did not mean that full community consensus existed for such action. Various eyewitness reports indicated that the troops were subjected to strong insults at the time they arrived, and during the course of the interviews accomplished for this paper, much disapproval was voiced by some residents of the presence of troops at the time. Many people felt that the state, as represented by the State of Illinois, had no "right" to interfere with what they termed a "legitimate" expression of community sentiments and expressed the opinion that the Governor would suffer political reprisals at the next gubernatorial election for his action.

For a fuller understanding, perhaps, as to why violence occurred in this community and laws were not a deterrent to the violence, the words of the noted American jurist, Roscoe Pound, may have some relevance:

Popular impatience of restraint is aggravated in the United States by political and legal theories of "natural law." As a political doctrine, they lead individuals to put into action a conviction that conformity to the dictates of the individual conscience is a test of the validity of the law. . . . In the same spirit a well-known preacher wrote not long since that a prime cause of lawlessness was enactment of legislation at variance with the law of nature. . . . In the same spirit the business man may regard evasion of statutes which interfere with his carrying on business as he chooses as something entirely legitimate. In the same spirit public officials in recent addresses have commended administrative violations of the legal rights of certain obnoxious persons, and one of the law officers of the federal government has publicly approved of mob violence toward such persons (Pound, 1922, p. 15).

It may be safely assumed that behaviour in line with the mores of this community governing Negro-white relationships appear to residents of the area as "natural rights," and that the Clarks were "obnoxious" persons to the mob-members. If the Clarks' allegation of threats and manhandling by the local police is true, another illustration of Pound's analysis is at hand, and we can merely substitute "local" for "federal" government in his last sentence.

When viewed as "natural rights," it is clear that such mores not only transcend laws in importance as factors of social control but actually displace those laws. Since the community interpreted the violation of those "rights" as a greater threat to the community than the violation of laws governing mob action, it was considered "lawful" to exclude the Clarks by any means whatsoever. Thus violence, along with the anti-Negro mores and the whole institutional structure of the area, functioned as a means to achieve social control as defined by the norms of this particular community. For a further implementation of this point we shall now turn to a more intensive analysis of that institutional structure which embodies the basic mores.

THE ECONOMIC AND RELIGIOUS NEXUS
AND ETHNIC SOLIDARITY

Seen from the perspective of the Cicero home owner, the disturbance was a battle in defence of property values. The fury of the community action can only be understood against the peculiar economic and ethnic structure of the area.

Persons and groups of Czech or Polish ethnic derivation have a virtual monopoly of the building and loan associations as well as the real estate firms in the Cicero area as a whole. It appears that this monopoly is linked with strong home-owning traditions in the violence area.

Property beliefs are set in an almost sacred frame of reference. Property rights are held to be almost inviolate and the needless destruction or abuse of property, as well as careless maintenance, is practically a moral concept, equivalent to those regarding behaviour deviations such as crime or adultery.

In addition, thrift and property investment have been linked with religious norms of the community. As it grew from the early 1890's on, the building and maintenance of churches, particularly among the Roman Catholics, rivalled in importance and perseverance the building of homes. This gave a secular tradition, thrift and home-building, a distinct religious connotation. Thus, when the "threat" to this tradition became imminent—when the Clarks finally appeared on move-in day, July 10, after weeks of rumours and counter-rumours—the opposition, in the form of the mob action, had almost a religious fervour underlying it.

Of four Roman Catholic churches one has long been a centre of Czech social and cultural traditions and, as such, has been one of the primary forces in the maintenance of cultural solidity in the community. According to one Czech-descent informant, this solidity or "in-group" feeling was so strong at one time that when the first German-descent Catholic family moved into the neighbourhood some twenty-five years ago parishioners held a meeting in protest against their attendance at church before the family was finally admitted to worship. Of late years, however, the influence of this one church as a factor for cultural unity has diminished considerably, assimilation having affected the role of the church in this respect. At one Mass each Sunday, however, the sermon is still preached in Czech for, as the informant stated, "the old people." The three other Catholic churches in the area, while not primarily centers of Czech culture, retain strong "in-group" feelings among the Czech, Polish, German, and other ethnic group communicants.

The Protestant composition of the area, while secondary to that of the Roman Catholic, is still of significant importance as a factor influencing community behaviour. There is some indication that Protestant conformity to the prevailing anti-Negro attitude exists. Some two weeks prior to the move-in, July 10, the Church Federation of Greater Chicago, a centralized body of various Protestant denominations in the Chicago metropolitan area, was informed of the growing tension in the community. On June 28, the Federation contacted the Protestant churches in Cicero and Berwyn by letter and urged the pastors to exhort their parishioners, through sermons as well as any other possible means, to refrain from acts of violence in the situation. Although individual pastors may have taken private action, there is no available record that any minister in either locality complied with the Federation's appeal for pulpit sermons on the two Sundays following the June 28 letter and prior to the July 10 move-in. Such sermons have become a standard technique for dealing with local racial tensions.

Following the violence, a group of eleven Protestant pastors from Cicero and Berwyn met on July 19 to consider action that they, as spiritual leaders, could take. An unpublished Federation report of this meeting, dated July 31, indicates that considerable circumspection was observed by those present. Beliefs were voiced that the root of the present problem was in the long-standing political corruption in Cicero, and grave doubts were raised that any effective attempt could be made at the present time to work against the Cicero political machine. Moreover, the majority present seemed to feel that any overt action by either the group or any single minister would, in the first case, be wholly ineffectual, and, in the second, inevitably result in that minister losing his community leadership and, possibly, his church.[2] . . . Since that meeting and up to the present time of writing, no further organized attempt has been made by either this group or any other of the Protestant ministers of Cicero and Berwyn to deal with the situation.

When considering the religious mores of this community, it should be stressed that they are in opposition to the anti-Negro mores and to violence if they are viewed as purely religious. Among the Catholic group religious values are rigid and authoritarian; among Protestants they are perhaps equally or even more so among the Calvinists and Lutherans as contexts of moral values. The obvious question as to the ineffectiveness of these religious values as deterrents to prejudice and violence can be answered in only one way—such values are subordinate to the nonreligious cultural and group values and mores already discussed.

It would be an oversimplification, however, to consider the religious values as purely religious. The purely social activities of a church, the nonreligious attitudes and beliefs of pastors and prominent lay leaders, all have significance in the interpretation of religious values as they relate to community behaviour patterns. If it may be concluded that "in-group" feelings and activities of a non-religious nature are amply present in this community, of a Czech, Polish or other ethnic character,

2. The ministers did, however, issue a joint statement "deploring" violence.

then it can be assumed that the church, for the church-going elements of the population, is a focal point for expression of such feelings and activities and of significance in this regard.

For another major factor of importance in explaining why violence took place in this community, we can now turn to the role of youth in the disturbance, and prevalent family structures in the community.

THE ROLE OF YOUTH IN THE VIOLENCE

The general beliefs about the place of the Negro and his effect on property values, together with other factors, created a permissive atmosphere in which the youth were able to take an active part in the rioting. An eyewitness has reported as follows:

There were approximately 1,000 people on this corner when I arrived. The "milling" process was evident. The crowd seemed reasonably good-natured. There was a heavy percentage of teenagers in this group, and there was much fraternization between the crowd and the police present.

The youthful elements were composed of two types: (1) a group that could be described as clean-cut, fresh-looking, and apparently residents of the area, and (2) a distinctly different type, harder and tougher-looking and far more dangerous-appearing than the other. It did not appear that the latter were from the immediate neighborhood. Subsequent events proved, however, that both types participated equally in the vandalism that ensued.

I observed a space on the prairie in front of the building being cleared from which to hurl bricks and rocks. Boys and girls, ranging from twelve years to late teens, were collecting stones and breaking bricks in half, with the older boys then hurling the bricks. Two youths broke open the door of a nearby police car, twisting the handle, and turned the spot light on windows of the building so that rock-throwers could have more visibility. There was much camaraderie among all and it was apparent they were having a good time.

Early in the evening, while at the western intersection, I observed two young girls deploring the fact that nothing was happening, saying: "Things seem to be kind of dull around here." An adult man of about forty overheard them, turned and said: "Well, you kids should know how to take care of that. You know how to start things if you want to." The girls then giggled to each other and coyly turned away.

Much has been said of the ineptness of the police in handling the situation. I believe that to be true for the fraternization and sympathy of the police with the mob was most evident. I overheard one policeman tell a group of teenagers, "Why don't you go away and come back when you will be able to have more success?"

A clue to the permissive atmosphere in which youthful elements of the mob acted during the violence may be found in the family structure of the community. Czech and Czech-descent families predominate and, on the whole, conform to the Central European strong paternalistic pattern as opposed to the "companionship" type now emerging as a type-conception from within the amalgamated American culture pattern. There is, however, at least one interesting departure in Czech families from this paternalistic pattern.

From the sources contacted, this departure rests on the fact that most foreign-born family heads either resist or are indifferent to the assimilation of their children into an American culture context. However, for most ethnic groups, by the time the first generation offspring is a family head, such assimilation is generally welcomed for 2nd generation siblings. This, of course, means a breakaway from or dissipation of the original family cultural background: the native language is forgotten, old folkways are discarded, and old festivities such as grape or harvest festivals become childhood memories. The cultural framework of the term "American" then takes on meaningful aspects and becomes more strongly reinforced with each succeeding generation.

It seems, however, that this process, as described, applies to a lesser degree in the case of the Czech national group as compared to other ethnic groups. A lack of interest or encouragement concerning such cultural assimilation often extends to the 2nd and 3rd generation in city areas and, in some rural areas, even to the 4th generation. In practical terms this means that the survival of cultural bonds among youths of Czech descent, such as language, participation in Sokols or Czech athletic organizations, Czech folkways or social events or other indices of culture are encouraged and strengthened. Quite naturally such efforts at encouraging cultural survival take place mostly in the home or school, or in social groups of which the family is a member. This process, however, cannot be accomplished without a slowing up of the assimilation by the youth of certain phases of American cultural concepts. It is here that a clue to the actions of the teenagers, at least of the Czech if not those of other ethnic groups as well, during the disturbance may be found.[3]

One aspect of contemporary American culture as applied by educational processes to youths is that body of techniques dealing with the promotion of concepts which embody respect for the individual regardless of race, colour, creed or national origin. Human relations workshops for teachers, specialized high school and college courses in race and nationality studies, the establishment in recent years of official city and state agencies for the purpose of dealing with intergroup problems, the

3. From all competent observers on the scene from the beginning, it has definitely been established that there were few "outsiders" present during the early phases of the incident. These observers agree that the great majority of the mobs on Tuesday and Wednesday were area residents and that "outsiders" did not appear in any large numbers until press and radio media gave the situation widespread publicity Thursday morning. Cicero officials have declared that the violence was principally caused by "outsiders' and point to arrest lists which show that only one-fourth of those arrested came from Cicero and Berwyn, and over one-half from Chicago. There were no arrests made by the Cicero police, however, until Thursday night when mass media brought thousands of thrill and curiosity seekers as well as vandal elements to the scene from elsewhere.

emergence of the human relations profession with skilled and professional personnel, and mass advertising techniques promoting intergroup harmony are some examples of this growing body of concern for human relations in general.

In cultural terms, this body of activities is becoming an integral part of an American culture matrix. Like all aspects of culture, however, it must have persons to affect. Unless a youth is exposed, both in the home and school, to some activities of this nature—and, in particular, to those involving personal contact with or direct knowledge of different racial, religious or ethnic groups—he or she will not likely absorb a feeling or understanding regarding basic human respect for people despite intergroup differences. It may be inferred, therefore, that if the youth has had no chance to absorb such feelings or respect for others, he or she will, psychologically, be more affected in a time of racial crisis by the mechanics of mob psychology than otherwise. Thus, the youth will have no deterrents within to prevent an emotional arousal leading to vandalism.

From all evidence and sources contacted, it is apparent that the development described above can be applied to the youth of Czech descent who participated in the violence, and to a lesser degree, to those of other ethnic groups. The strong cultural solidity and "in-group" feelings, combined with suspicion of the "out-group," have reacted to shield the youth in the community from the positive concepts mentioned. In addition, we can assume that many of the sex mores of these young people are in the monogamous paternalistic family tradition. When such mores are reinforced by beliefs about the amorality of an "out-group" as mentioned earlier, another "protection" motivation for racial violence is thus established.

Another factor which may provide an insight into the actions of teenagers during the disturbance is the release of adolescent repressions in a time of crisis. It is reasonable to assume that a paternalistic family pattern may produce feelings of repression in siblings, particularly with reference to social and peer group activities. Such feelings, in general, can most satisfactorily be released by aggressive physical behaviour of one kind or another. If, in such a time of racial crisis, an object such as a building or person exists and is available as a target for physical behaviour, acts of vandalism against that object can be more easily understood. Also, such an "escape valve" for these feelings is more readily utilized when adult or parental-figure approval of the aggressive behaviour is present. From the evidence we have, it is clear that adult approval of the vandalism committed was not only present but, in some cases, took on the form of an actual urging or initiating of the aggression. It is also, of course, a commentary on the willingness of the more socially mature adult to permit a substitute figure to act out adult aggressions.

CONCLUSION

Before concluding, certain comments are necessary to complete this discussion of basic factors contributing to the Cicero racial violence. The most important concerns the configuration of Cicero in relation to the whole of the metropolitan Chicago area. An extensive treatment of this relationship is not possible in this paper but it may be useful to present the major aspect of this configuration.

The Cicero disturbance was not a unique situation in the Chicago metropolitan area. Within the past five years there have been five major racial mob incidents in the city of Chicago[4] and numerous others where adequate police action prevented the formation of extensive mobs. All of these incidents involved either the actual move-in of new Negro residents to the community or a fear that such a move-in was to take place. Two of the five, Fernwood and Airport Homes, equalled Cicero in the size of mobs and a third, Peoria Street, involved intense anti-Semitic and anti-Communistic mob sentiments as well as anti-Negro bias.

Such incidents illustrate that Negro population movements are operative above all other motivations in racial violence in the Chicago area. . . . One of the directions Negro population movements are presently taking in Chicago is toward the northern and eastern boundaries of Cicero, and has reached a point where Negro residents live only two miles from the boundary line between Chicago and Cicero. Because of this fact, many Cicero residents feel that the Clark move-in was only an "advance guard" of what they fear will eventually be a mass movement of Negroes to the town.

Recent census figures released for the city of Chicago indicate the extent of Negro population movements. The Chicago Negro population grew from 277,731 in 1940 to 494,225 in 1950, an increase of 77 per cent. In a number of communities the percentage increase amounted to over 500 per cent and there are today numerous areas in the city considered "mixed" which were not so labelled in 1940. . . .

A comment on possible specific incitement factors at the time of the disturbance may also be useful. In a sense, much of the presentation already given contains such factors, but there are others which may be mentioned although considerable study is necessary before accepting them as valid.

COMMUNIST PARTICIPATION

On Wednesday, July 11, one person was arrested in the area for allegedly distributing pamphlets carrying the label of the Communist Party of

4. Airport Homes, Nov. 15–17, 1946; Fernwood Homes, Aug. 12–15, 1947; St. Lawrence Avenue, July 25–29, 1949; Peoria Street, Nov. 9–12, 1949; St. Lawrence Avenue, Aug. 11–14, 1950.

Illinois. The pamphlets were supposed to have urged the residents to refrain from violence and accept the Clarks as neighbours. Other than this incident, there is no direct evidence to sustain the charge by Cicero town officials that Communists instigated the violence.

Open Anti-Negro Propaganda

One eyewitness reported the presence on Wednesday night of Joseph Beauharnais of the White Circle League. It was alleged that Beauharnais was making inflammatory remarks and urging the mob to further violence. He was also supposed to be distributing membership blanks of his organization. The White Circle League is a small group that believes in complete segregation of the Negro and white peoples and has openly distributed literature charged to be racially inflammatory. Beauharnais was arrested, tried, and convicted in the Chicago Municipal Court for allegedly distributing in a public place this literature. He appealed the case to the Supreme Court of the United States which, in a 5 to 4 decision on April 28, 1952, upheld his conviction.

Press, Radio and TV

The role of mass media in contributing to the severity of racial violence situations is extremely complex. Cicero was perhaps the most widely publicized racial incident of recent times in the Chicago area or perhaps in the United States. Yet, no consensus exists, either among human relations observers or mass media personnel, as to the extent publicity numerically increases mobs or contributes to further violence. Undoubtedly many persons came to the scene after reading of it in the press, hearing it on radio or seeing it on TV, but whether such persons actually became mob members committing vandalism, and if so, how many, is a matter for considerable study.

For the first time a racial incident in the Chicago area was filmed on TV. This was not a "live" TV presentation but films of the scene made by a TV cameraman and presented over a TV news show two or three hours later. As with press and radio the incitement index of this medium is unknown.

In conclusion, we have attempted to present an analysis of some of the basic considerations that will aid in understanding why this incident took place in a Northern urban area. It is not a complete analysis by any means for research of a far more intensive nature is necessary for a complete picture.

8

MASSIVE ASSAULT UPON THE ACCOMMODATIVE STRUCTURE AND THE VIOLENCE OF THE SIXTIES 1955–1969

As Negro disillusionment with the outcome of the Supreme Court school desegregation decision grew in the latter half of the Fifties, black people began to turn to more direct confrontations with the accommodative structure. Sit-ins, boycotts, and marches began to emerge as modes of direct protest action. Some changes resulted, most notably in access to public facilities, but also in some extension of the franchise. This protest activity, much of which took place in the South, was accompanied by violence of varying degrees—civil rights workers were slain, sit-in demonstrators were hosed down or attacked by police dogs. Some of this violence is described in the first selection in this chapter which deals with "routine" violence in the South.

During the current decade there have been a number of changes; the most important of these has been the occurrence of very large-scale riotous disorders. These were preceded by a shift of earlier direct confrontation tactics to Northern cities, particularly in attempts by blacks to gain some control over schools and over policing in black neighborhoods. No one yet knows whether the pattern of urban rioting that began in 1964 resulted from heightened frustration over the too modest successes with direct confrontation techniques or whether there were indeed tactical decisions made by black leaders; if the latter was the case, there clearly was dissension among these leaders themselves. Some of this discussion of causation is included in later chapters. In this chapter I have included the sections from the report of the National Advisory Commission that treat descriptively the Newark and Detroit disturbances. The final two selections, which anticipate some later theoretical issues, were written by Tomlinson and by Murphy and Watson as parts of a large, integrated research investigation into the events, causes, and consequences of the Watts riots.

"Routine" Violence in the South—1963

BEATINGS

Many of the reported cases of beatings were in some way connected with the movement of Negroes to eliminate segregation; thus demonstrators were the main targets of those opposed to their activities. Prominent among these opponents were officers of the law, who were brutal before, after, and during arrests. Cases of such brutality before arrests may be cited. At Plaquemine, Louisiana, mounted police and State Troopers scattered 150 Negroes with electric cattle prods, and horses "trampled, kicked and hospitalized children," it is reported. State Troopers drove 300 Negro demonstrators from the Etowah County Courthouse lawn with electric prod poles, and men and women were "beaten to the ground." In Birmingham, the police used dogs and high powered water hoses to disperse groups. One man was wrestled to the ground by police officers and a dog and handcuffed. Other reports of brutality of police before arrest came from Savannah, Georgia, and other places.

Police brutality was evident while officers were making arrests. A fourteen-year-old girl in Americus, Georgia, was struck on the head during a demonstration; Jackson, Mississippi, policemen charged adults and teenagers, who reportedly were jeering and chanting "we want freedom" on the porch of a Negro home. They were clubbed into submission and a white Tougaloo Southern Christian College sociology professor who was with them was felled. At Hampton, Virginia, police threw a juvenile bodily from a drug store during a sit-in demonstration and charged him with assault and battery.

While lodged in jail, police brutality was continued against demonstrators. A Negro comedian reported he was whipped in a Birmingham jail. The Department of Justice accused five men, including the Sheriff and Chief of Police of Winona, Mississippi, of beating or directing the beating of five Negro prisoners, including three women. Other cases of police brutality against demonstrators came from St. Augustine, Florida; Brownsville, Tennessee; Danville, Virginia; Albany, Georgia; and Jackson, Mississippi, where a Negro woman was reportedly taken from her cell and beaten for no apparent reason.

Other prisoners, as in the past, felt the brutality of police officers. Atlanta's Chief of Police admitted a Negro suspect who was being transported to jail was "worked over" by policemen. A man accused of stealing a car at Lebanon, Tennessee, was "beaten in the face with a lantern" by the Sheriff. The car belonged to his brother. At Houston, Texas, two policemen were indicted for assaulting two Negro youths, whom they accused of attempting to enter the car of one of the officers' wives. The boys were hitching a ride to Galveston. From Dublin, Georgia, New Orleans, Louisiana, and Beckley, West Virginia, came reports of extreme cruelty. Other beatings were reported from Louisville, Kentucky, and Washington, D. C.

Demonstrating Negroes and their white supporters were assaulted by individuals and groups other than policemen. At High Point, North Carolina, a white picket was beaten and a minister struck in the face by a white man who at first pretended to shake hands with him. Demonstrators were attacked while being served at a lunch counter at Anderson, South Carolina; and were beaten and doused with catsup and mustard while sitting-in at Jackson, Mississippi. A crippled boy was clubbed on the main street of Danville, Virginia, and a young girl in the same city was thrown downstairs three times. In Atlanta, Georgia, three Negroes and two whites who sought service at a cafeteria "were pummeled and pushed" by two white men; another was "knocked down" while sitting at the Trailways Bus Terminal in Montgomery, Alabama. A nineteen-year-old youth, a Negro, was beaten and kicked at a city park in Pine Bluff, Arkansas.

Persons were attacked while using or attempting to use other public facilities. A Negro girl who refused to move to the back of a Columbia, South Carolina, bus was slapped by a white man; a bus driver attacked a minister while he was enroute to Griffin, Georgia; an eighteen-year-old girl and three companions were beaten by whites for refusing to leave the white waiting room at the McComb, Mississippi, railroad terminal; another was beaten for trying to use a white restroom at Clarksdale in the same state; and in addition, was arrested for disturbing the peace. Two ministers were beaten by a white mob for trying to enter the Anniston, Alabama, library for whites.

Other persons were beaten while attempting to vote or while helping others to register to vote. Such beatings occurred at Brandon, Mississippi, Americus, Georgia Selma, Alabama, and at many other localities. The Voter Education Project, sponsored by the *Southern Regional Council,* released on March 31 a chronological listing of sixty-four acts of violence and intimidation against Negroes in Mississippi since January, 1961. Almost all of the incidents are directly related to efforts by Negroes to register to vote. The last item listed is that for March 27 when Greenwood, Mississippi, policemen and their dogs dispersed Negro voter registration applicants and jailed voter registration workers.

Negroes and whites were beaten for a variety of other reasons connected directly or indirectly with race. Twenty white men beat three students from Ghana and two whites who were with them near Tuscaloosa, Alabama, for no given reason; a Negro barmaid died of a stroke after being knocked unconscious by a rain of blows about the face and shoulders at Baltimore, Maryland. She was too slow in bringing a wealthy farmer a drink. A Negro man in Atlanta, Georgia, was dragged from his home by two whites and carried to a lonely spot and beaten. He was accused of hi-jacking a load of whiskey. Six white Florida youths admitted a series of "clubbings" of Negroes in Atmore, Alabama; a Negro man was knocked down by a group of Maryland youths when he reproached them for making racial remarks to a Negro woman at an eating place. A Catholic priest in New Orleans, Louisiana, was attacked and his eye blackened by a man who protested an integrated instructional class. A policeman was beaten and disarmed by whites in an alley near a desegregated Birmingham school.

BOMBING

Bombings in 1963 were reported from the States of Alabama, Arkansas, Florida, Georgia, Louisiana, Mississippi, South Carolina, and Virginia. Houses, churches, businesses, a school and persons were the targets of terrorists acting on behalf of segregation.

The homes of integrationists were among the main objectives of bombers. In almost each instance recorded, the owners or dwellers had participated in some action intended to break down the South's segregated social structure. In Birmingham, Alabama, the home of a prominent Negro minister, the brother of the Rev. Martin Luther King, Jr., was virtually demolished. He had led demonstrators in the streets of Birmingham. The home of an outstanding civil rights attorney, also a Negro, was bombed twice. His wife was injured in the second incident and his home badly damaged. The home of a wealthy businessman was bombed as integration of public schools pended.

In St. Augustine, Florida, bombs were thrown at the home of a couple whose children were in the first Negro group who attended integrated classes; at Macon, Georgia, a bomb was placed in the Mayor's mail box because three white youths did not like his policies about integrating a public park. Metal fragments capable of killing were scattered over a 100-foot area.

In Mississippi, a number of homes were bombed. At Clarksdale, a fire bomb crashed through the window of the home of an integration leader where a Negro congressman was asleep. Two whites were arrested. One was acquitted; charges against the other were dismissed. At Jackson, a bomb exploded in the carport of the home of Medgar Evers, integration leader, causing damage. At Lexington, a fire bomb was thrown at the home of the first Negro to register during a voter registration drive by Negroes.

At Columbia, South Carolina, the home of an eighteen-year-old girl scheduled to enter the University of South Carolina was attacked by bombers. She originated the court suit which ended with the order for the University to desegregate. The home of a Negro family at Arlington, Virginia, was the target of a bomb thrown by white youths who sped away, police reported.

Bombs exploded twice near a dormitory of the University of Alabama at Tuscaloosa. The only Negro student at the University, a woman, resided there; and, at the University of Mississippi at Oxford a bomb exploded breaking windows at one of the mens' dormitories.

Churches in Birmingham, Alabama, and at Pine Bluff and Gillet, Arkansas, were bombed. Bethel Baptist Church in Birmingham had been bombed twice before 1963. Homes nearby were damaged. The Sixteenth Street Baptist Church, long an important religious institution in the city, and the main rallying ground for demonstrators against racial segregation during the "massive civil rights struggle" was made unsafe for use by bombing. Not only that, but the lives of four little girls, the victims of Southern prejudice, were snuffed out as they attended Sunday School there. Twenty-three other persons were injured. As of November 30 no one had been apprehended in connection with the bombing.

At Gillet, Arkansas, no reason was given for dynamiting a rural church; and at Pine Bluff, Arkansas, an incendiary bomb set the AME church afire. Its pastor was one of the advisors to Negro students conducting sit-ins at segregated lunch counters.

Businesses which were the targets of bombers were located in Birmingham, Alabama, in Greenwood and Gulfport, Mississippi, and in Charleston, South Carolina. The A. G. Gaston Motel, headquarters for civil rights leaders during demonstrations in the city, was badly damaged. Several persons were injured. Tear gas bombs were dropped on the first floor of Loveman's Department Store, and twenty-two persons there were overcome with fumes. Four white youths in Greenwood, Mississippi, tossed tear gas grenades on the sidewalk in front of a Negro cafe and grocery. They were fined $100 each and given thirty-day suspended sentences upon stipulated conditions being met by their parents. Aerial flash bombs shattered the plate glass window and scattered debris throughout the office of a physician, a leader in the civil rights movement at Gulfport, Mississippi; and at Charleston, South Carolina, the Club Jamaica was bombed. The only person present was not injured.

The new wing of a desegregated Catholic school at Buras, Louisiana, was ripped in a midnight gasoline explosion. Bombs were placed in Negro neighborhoods in Birmingham and Tuscaloosa, Alabama. In the first instance, two bombs were placed at the intersections of several streets in the Southside Negro residential section. The first exploded fifteen minutes before the second and fifteen feet away. They "appeared to have been arranged to draw the sleeping community outside their homes where flying shrapnel 'could cut them down.'" The shrapnel riddled a half-dozen homes, damaged an automobile and toppled a telephone pole. In Tuscaloosa, no damage was reported from a bomb placed in the Negro section there.

INCENDIARISM

Fires were used by whites as a means of expressing distaste for Negroes who sought citizenship equality, and by Negroes in retaliation against white terrorists. Birmingham Negroes set fire to businesses of whites in Negro neighborhoods, once in retaliation for the bombing of homes and other property owned by their group, and the second time for the bombing of the Sixteenth Street Baptist Church. In Greenwood, Mississippi, four Negro businesses were burned to the ground by whites on the same day a *Student Non-Violent Coordinating Committee* registration worker received a telephone call telling him he would not be going there (to the office building) any more. In Sumter, Georgia, the home of a Negro who was active in the voter registration drive was burned; the St. Paul AME Church at Palmetto, Georgia, was burned four times leaving it "gutted, windowless and stripped of all of its fixtures and furnishings." The congregation could give no reason for the fires, neither could the police come up with any leads. In Rosman, North Carolina, a youth camp was burned—the gymnasium was set on fire and gasoline was poured on the lake and set ablaze. The campers were charged with "nudism, immorality and integration."

RIOTING

Rioting, too, resulted from Negroes' demands for their rights as citizens. Two riots occurred in Birmingham. The May 12 riot took place after the bombing of the home of a minister, a leader in the integration struggle, and of the A. G. Gaston Motel. Buildings and a taxicab were burned, the taxicab driver beaten, and a patrolman stabbed in fighting that spread over an eight block area. Firemen responding to calls were pelted with rocks.

On September 4, rioting was again sparked by the bombing of the home of a Negro attorney who had handled many school and civil rights cases. Hundreds of Negroes rioted in protest. One was fatally shot and at least twenty injured "in a pitched battle with police."

In Savannah, Georgia, on July 10, more than 1,000 Negroes, including a prominent integration leader had been arrested. Six were convicted on anti-trespass charges. Negroes had demanded desegregation of "a sweeping number of businesses," fair employment practices, more responsible public jobs for Negroes, and that all charges against Negroes who participated in anti-segregation demonstrations be dropped. After police used tear gas bombs to rout the demonstrators, they roamed the city slashing automobile tires, and smashing windows of stores and cars. Three policemen and several Negroes were injured. More than 100 State Troopers "bolstered" local police efforts.

At Cambridge, Maryland, also the site of a struggle of Negroes against continued segregation, there was rioting. The immediate cause was the beating by white patrons of six white and Negro sit-in demonstrators at a segregated lunch counter; 200 Negroes staged a protest march to the county jail where twenty Negroes were held. Mobs formed in both white and Negro sections. Bands of whites and Negroes sped through the city shooting at people not of their race. National Guard troops, withdrawn from the city after twenty-five days in town, were ordered back to restore order.

North Carolina was the scene of riots at Lexington, Oxford, and Williamston. On June 6, at Lexington, a few Negroes tried to obtain service in restaurants, a theatre, and a bowling alley. This caused a riot involving about 500 whites and 150 Negroes. One white man was killed; another wounded. Twenty-eight persons were convicted of engaging in rioting. The whites received jail sentences ranging from three to sixteen months the Negroes from six months to seven years. Between June 19 and June 22, rioting involved some 300 whites and Negroes at Oxford. At Williamston, in August, there were two racial eruptions within two days, two squads of highway patrolmen were ordered into the city.

At Danville, Virginia, Negroes demanded a bi-racial committee, the lowering of color bars at public eating places, and the hiring of colored policemen, meter readers, stenographers and other City Hall workers, as well. Thirteen Negro leaders were indicted by a grand jury for participating in demonstrations which led to rioting.

A riot was averted on July 11 in Jackson, Mississippi, by an attorney for the United States Department of Justice after a "mourning march" for Medgar Evers, assassinated Negro leader. He persuaded Negroes to put away bottles and bricks they were about to use as weapons. On this occasion, twenty-seven persons were arrested, a number clubbed by policemen and a woman bitten by a police dog. Other accounts of near riots came from Nashville, Tennessee, and Charleston, South Carolina.

SHOOTINGS

Police officers killed or wounded Negroes with gunfire for various reasons. At Andalusia, Alabama, an off-duty State Trooper killed a Negro because his car was blocked by the Negro's automobile. At Americus, Georgia, a thirty-year-old Negro was killed for threatening to kill his former employer. He is said to have attacked the employer and a policeman with an ax and butcher knife. A workman was shot to death when he picked up a small billy club to fight policemen while in the Fort Valley, Georgia, jail; a twenty-four-year-old youth was killed for interfering in the questioning of an elderly man by a Savannah, Georgia, patrolman and his partner. In the same Georgia city, a policeman "accidentally shot" a fifteen-year-old Negro boy to death as he sought to escape being apprehended in the act of burglary. At LaFayette, Georgia, a teenager was shot when he "pulled a knife." He with others was watching a Halloween street dance given on the town square for white teenagers.

Many voter registration workers were fired upon as they peacefully went about their business in their homes or as they rode in cars on the streets or highways. Such instances were reported from Wilcox County, Alabama, and Itta Bena, Greenwood, Jackson, Kosciusko, and Yazoo City, in Mississippi.

Integration leaders other than those working with voter registration drives were the targets of bullets. Among these were two martyrs of the civil rights cause—William L. Moore, killed near Attalla, Alabama, on a one-man "Freedom Walk" to Mississippi; and Medgar Evers, Field Secretary of the NAACP, of Jackson, Mississippi. He also was shot to death from ambush, as he left his car to enter his home. In Florida, whites shot into the home of a prominent Negro physician at Ocala, and into the home of a dentist at St. Augustine. Two integrationists at Albany, Georgia, reported "four or five shots" were fired into their bedroom. The home of the parents of James H. Meredith was fired on at Kosciusko, Mississippi. At Monroe, North Carolina, the home of a white integration leader was fired on; so was the home of the Vice-President of the Nashville, Tennessee, *Christian Leadership Council;* as well as a Negro attorney as he was driving near the Shelby-Fayette County line in the same State.

Negroes were shot as a result of other matters related to race. In Birmingham, Alabama, on September 16, a sixteen-year-old white boy killed a thirteen-year-old Negro youth, and another Negro was wounded in the arm by a white man following a church bombing on the same date. At Gainesville, Florida, a Negro was shot in the aftermath of a week-end demonstration; a nineteen-year-old Marine at Albany said he "just had to shoot a Negro" after brooding over recent racial unrest. In Savannah, Georgia, shots were fired into a Negro family's home and into two cars. Five Negroes at Canton, Mississippi, were wounded near a hall where an integration rally was in progress.

In a few cases, whites were shot by Negroes. This occurred mainly as a result of the segregation-desegregation controversy, as at Cambridge, Maryland, when a twenty-three-year old Negro shot five whites, including two National Guardsmen and a boy. Two State Troopers said they were fired on in the Negro section of Gadsden, Alabama; and two white men were shot by the father of four Negro children who were enrolled in a desegregated school in Caswell County, North Carolina. He claimed his life was threatened and he had been "harassed and reviled" by groups of whites. In Danville, Virginia, a gunman shot at a patrol car in which two policemen were riding after they had arrested a Negro for being drunk.

The segregation-desegregation issue caused the Negro section outside of the City of St. Augustine, Florida, to be attacked. Two night spots, a food market and two homes were shot up after the funeral of a white man killed while driving through the Negro section in the city. Three Negroes were fired on from a car carrying five white youths in St. Louis, Missouri, and one Negro youth at Crystal City, in that state, was shot in the leg for ordering a sandwich at a tavern. Four teenagers were wounded by gunshot near a recently integrated theatre in Asheboro, North Carolina. The home and car of the Negro family whose children desegregated the DeKalb County, Tennessee, school were struck by gunfire; and a former Major-General of the United States Army, famed for his connection with the University of Mississippi student riots in 1962, reported being shot at while sitting in his home. At Savannah, Georgia, a sixteen-year-old Negro youth was killed when a white man is said to have "fired at the pavement" from a passing car. Arrested, he was charged with disorderly conduct and released on a $50 bond.

One of three Negroes in Americus, Georgia, was killed when their car pulled in front of one owned by a white man, nearly causing an accident. They are also said to have called the man "white trash." Six white youths at Savannah, Georgia, shot a Negro fireman in the stomach as he guarded a fire alarm box to prevent false alarms; and a seventeen-year-old youth was killed in Crittenden County, Arkansas, when accused of attempting to assault a white school girl near her home. His killing was termed "excusable."

STABBING AND STONING

Many stabbing incidents were connected with the integration movement. Stabbings of whites by Negroes were reported after a bombing and other acts of violence in Birmingham. The uncle of a Negro girl who entered the desegregated school at Dollarway, Arkansas, was arrested for "assault with intent to kill' when a white boy at the school was stabbed. He said his niece had been abused at the school and the windows of his car broken when he came to school to take her home. At both Atlanta and Macon, Georgia, Negroes were stabbed by whites. In the former case, an unidentified white man knifed a seventeen-inch gash in the back of a fifteen-year-old boy during a sit-in demonstration; in the latter, a Negro leader was stabbed by whites as a result of pressing for the desegregation of a city-owned park.

Stones were used as weapons during clashes between whites and Negroes and during clashes between Negroes and the police—an after-

math of demonstrations. White motorists complained that their automobiles were stoned as they drove through sections occupied by
Negroes. Two Negro girls reported stones were hurled at them as they
left a newly integrated school. A nineteen-year-old Negro was charged
with throwing a stone which critically wounded a white youth; and the
home of a white minister was pelted with stones. He had recommended
attendance of Negroes at his church. A group of stone-throwing white
youths chased Negro demonstrators from a store to a church. Accounts
of stoning came from Birmingham and Linden, Albama; Albany, Colum-
bus and Savannah, Georgia; Shreveport, Louisiana; Cambridge, Maryland; Jackson, Mississippi; St. Louis, Missouri; Cleveland, Lexington,
Thomasville, Goldsboro, Smithfield and Wilson, North Carolina; Charleston, South Carolina; and Nashville, Tennessee.

OTHER ACTS OF VIOLENCE

The listings of acts of violence above are by no means all the incidents that took place, but are typical of what happened. A few unusual
incidents may also be noted. About twenty-five Negroes fled from a
segregated Pine Bluff, Arkansas, hamburger stand when a white youth
tossed ammonia into the small building; a white man tossed a tear gas
canister down an aisle of a theatre and fled out of a side exit; three
white boys in Atlanta, Georgia, charged with tossing a snake into a
Negro group were sentenced to work week-ends in the snake house of
the park zoo; in Albany, Georgia, a white grocer in a Negro neighborhood who refused to hire a Negro girl as cashier suffered a smashed
window and a loss of customers. The finding of the "castrated and
mutilated" body of Sylvester Maxwell, a twenty-four-year-old Negro of
Canton, Mississippi, was termed a "probable lynching."

A white man in Chapel Hill, North Carolina, drove his car through
a line of 200 white and Negro pickets; and five integrationists were
struck by cars as they picketed a supermarket and the funeral home of
a Negro in Dunn, North Carolina. The Negro owner said the pickets
had the notion he was an "Uncle Tom."

Death threats and vandalism were directed at teachers of the *Prince
Edward Free School Association* and at their relatives at Farmville,
Virginia, causing an investigation by the local police and by the FBI.

Newark

The last outburst in Atlanta occurred on Tuesday night, June 20. That same night, in Newark, N.J., a tumultuous meeting of the planning board took place. Until 4 A.M., speaker after speaker from the Negro ghetto arose to denounce the city's intent to turn over 150 acres in the heart of the central ward as a site for the State's new medical and dental college.

The growing opposition to the city administration by vocal black residents had paralyzed both the planning board and the board of education. Tension had been rising so steadily throughout the northern New Jersey area that, in the first week of June, Col. David Kelly, head of the state police, had met with municipal police chiefs to draw up plans for state police support of city police wherever a riot developed. Nowhere was the tension greater than in Newark.

Founded in 1666, the city, part of the Greater New York City port complex, rises from the salt marshes of the Passaic River. Although in 1967 Newark's population of 400,000 still ranked it 30th among American municipalities, for the past 20 years the white middle class had been deserting the city for the suburbs.

In the late 1950's, the desertions had become a rout. Between 1960 and 1967, the city lost a net total of more than 70,000 white residents. Replacing them in vast areas of dilapidated housing where living conditions, according to a prominent member of the County Bar Association, were so bad that "people would be kinder to their pets," were Negro migrants, Cubans, and Puerto Ricans. In 6 years, the city switched from 65 percent white to 52 percent Negro and 10 percent Puerto Rican and Cuban.

The white population, nevertheless, retained political control of the city. On both the city council and the board of education, seven of nine members were white. In other key boards, the disparity was equal or greater. In the central ward, where the medical college controversy raged, the Negro constituents and their white councilman found themselves on opposite sides of almost every crucial issue.

The municipal administration lacked the ability to respond quickly enough to navigate the swiftly changing currents. Even had it had great astuteness, it would have lacked the financial resources to affect significantly the course of events.

In 1962, seven-term Congressman Hugh Addonizio had forged an Italian-Negro coalition to overthrow longtime Irish control of the city hall. A liberal in Congress, Addonizio, when he became mayor, had opened his door to all people. Negroes, who had been excluded from the previous administration, were brought into the government. The police department was integrated.

Nevertheless, progress was slow. As the Negro population increased, more and more of the politically oriented found the progress inadequate.

The Negro-Italian coalition began to develop strains over the issue of the police. The police were largely Italian, the persons they arrested were largely Negro. Community leaders agreed that, as in many police forces, there was a small minority of officers who abused their responsibility. This gave credibility to the cries of "brutality!" voiced periodically by ghetto Negroes.

In 1965, Mayor Addonizio, acknowledging that there was "a small group of misguided individuals" in the department, declared that "it is vital to establish once and for all, in the minds of the public, that charges of alleged police brutality will be thoroughly investigated and the appropriate legal or punitive action be taken if the charges are found to be substantiated."

Pulled one way by the Negro citizens who wanted a police review board, and the other by the police, who adamantly opposed it, the mayor decided to transfer "the control and investigation of complaints of police brutality out of the hands of both the police and the public and into the hands of an agency that all can support—the Federal Bureau of Investigation," and to send "a copy of any charge of police brutality . . . directly to the Prosecutor's office." However, the FBI could act only if there had been a violation of a person's federal civil rights. No complaint was ever heard of again.

Nor was there much redress for other complaints. The city had no money with which to redress them.

The city had already reached its legal bonding limit, yet expenditures continued to outstrip income. Health and welfare costs, per capita, were 20 times as great as for some of the surrounding communities. Cramped by its small land area of 23.6 square miles—one-third of which was taken up by Newark Airport and unusable marshland—and surrounded by independent jurisdictions, the city had nowhere to expand.

Taxable property was contracting as land, cleared for urban renewal, lay fallow year after year. Property taxes had been increased, perhaps to the point of diminishing return. By the fall of 1967, they were to reach $661.70 on a $10,000 house—double that of suburban communities.[1] As a result, people were refusing either to own or to renovate property in the city. Seventy-four percent of white and 87 percent of Negro families lived in rental housing. Whoever was able to move to the suburbs, moved. Many of these persons, as downtown areas were cleared and new office buildings were constructed, continued to work in the

---

1. The legal tax rate is $7.76 per $100 of market value. However, because of inflation, a guideline of 85.27 percent of market value is used in assessing, reducing the true tax rate to $6.617 per $100.

city. Among them were a large proportion of the people from whom a city normally draws its civic leaders, but who, after moving out, tended to cease involving themselves in the community's problems.

During the daytime Newark more than doubled its population—and was, therefore, forced to provide services for a large number of people who contributed nothing in property taxes. The city's per capita outlay for police, fire protection, and other municipal services continued to increase. By 1967 it was twice that of the surrounding area.

Consequently, there was less money to spend on education. Newark's per capita outlay on schools was considerably less than that of surrounding communities. Yet within the city's school system were 78,000 children, 14,000 more than 10 years earlier.

Twenty thousand pupils were on double sessions. The dropout rate was estimated to be as high as 33 percent. Of 13,600 Negroes between the ages of 16 and 19, more than 6,000 were not in school. In 1960 over half of the adult Negro population had less than an eighth grade education.

The typical ghetto cycle of high unemployment, family breakup, and crime was present in all its elements. Approximately 12 percent of Negroes were without jobs. An estimated 40 percent of Negro children lived in broken homes. Although Newark maintained proportionately the largest police force of any major city, its crime rate was among the highest in the nation. In narcotics violations it ranked fifth nationally. Almost 80 percent of the crimes were committed within 2 miles of the core of the city, where the central ward is located. A majority of the criminals were Negro. Most of the victims, likewise, were Negro. The Mafia was reputed to control much of the organized crime.

Under such conditions a major segment of the Negro population became increasingly militant. Largely excluded from positions of traditional political power, Negroes, tutored by a handful of militant social activists who had moved into the city in the early 1960's, made use of the antipoverty program, in which poor people were guaranteed representation, as a political springboard. This led to friction between the United Community Corporation, the agency that administered the antipoverty program, and the city administration.

When it became known that the secretary of the board of education intended to retire, the militants proposed for the position of city budget director a Negro with a master's degree in accounting. The mayor, however, had already nominated a white man. Since the white man had only a high school education, and at least 70 percent of the children in the school system were Negro, the issue of who was to obtain the secretaryship, an important and powerful position, quickly became a focal issue.

Joined with the issue of the 150-acre medical school site, the area of which had been expanded to triple the original request—an expansion regarded by the militants as an effort to dilute black political power by moving out Negro residents—the board of education battle resulted in a confrontation between the mayor and the militants. Both sides refused to alter their positions.

Into this impasse stepped a Washington Negro named Albert Roy Osborne. A flamboyant, 42-year-old former wig salesman who called himself Colonel Hassan Jeru-Ahmed and wore a black beret, he presided over a mythical "Blackman's Volunteer Army of Liberation." Articulate and magnetic, the self-commissioned "colonel" proved to be a one-man show. He brought Negro residents flocking to board of education and planning board meetings. The Colonel spoke in violent terms, and backed his words with violent action. At one meeting he tore the tape from the official stenographic recorder.

It became more and more evident to the militants that, though they might not be able to prevail, they could prevent the normal transaction of business. Filibustering began. A Negro former State assemblyman held the floor for more than 4 hours. One meeting of the board of education began at 5 P.M., and did not adjourn until 3:23 A.M. Throughout the months of May and June, speaker after speaker warned that if the mayor persisted in naming a white man as secretary to the board of education and in moving ahead with plans for the medical school site, violence would ensue. The city administration played down the threats.

On June 27, when a new secretary to the board of education was to be named, the state police set up a command post in the Newark armory.

The militants, led by the local CORE (Congress of Racial Equality) chapter, disrupted and took over the board of education meeting. The outcome was a stalemate. The incumbent secretary decided to stay on another year. No one was satisfied.

At the beginning of July there were 24,000 unemployed Negroes within the city limits. Their ranks were swelled by an estimated 20,000 teenagers, many of whom, with school out and the summer recreation program curtailed due to a lack of funds, had no place to go.

On July 8, Newark and East Orange police attempted to disperse a group of Black Muslims. In the melee that followed, several police officers and Muslims suffered injuries necessitating medical treatment. The resulting charges and countercharges heightened the tension between police and Negroes.

Early on the evening of July 12, a cabdriver named John Smith began, according to police reports, tailgating a Newark police car. Smith was an unlikely candidate to set a riot in motion. Forty years old, a Georgian by birth, he had attended college for a year before entering the Army in 1950. In 1953 he had been honorably discharged with the rank of corporal. A chess-playing trumpet player, he had worked as a musician and a factory hand before, in 1963, becoming a cabdriver.

As a cabdriver, he appeared to be a hazard. Within a relatively short period of time he had eight or nine accidents. His license was revoked.

When, with a woman passenger in his cab, he was stopped by the police, he was in violation of that revocation.

From the high-rise towers of the Reverend William P. Hayes housing project, the residents can look down on the orange-red brick facade of the Fourth Precinct Police Station and observe every movement. Shortly after 9:30 P.M., people saw Smith, who either refused or was unable to walk, being dragged out of a police car and into the front door of the station.

Within a few minutes, at least two civil rights leaders received calls from a hysterical woman declaring a cabdriver was being beaten by the police. When one of the persons at the station notified the cab company of Smith's arrest, cabdrivers all over the city began learning of it over their cab radios.

A crowd formed on the grounds of the housing project across the narrow street from the station. As more and more people arrived, the description of the beating purportedly administered to Smith became more and more exaggerated. The descriptions were supported by other complaints of police malpractice that, over the years, had been submitted for investigation—but had never been heard of again.

Several Negro community leaders, telephoned by a civil rights worker and informed of the deteriorating situation, rushed to the scene. By 10:15 P.M., the atmosphere had become so potentially explosive that Kenneth Melchior, the senior police inspector on the night watch, was called. He arrived at approximately 10:30 P.M.

Met by a delegation of civil rights leaders and militants who requested the right to see and interview Smith, Inspector Melchior acceded to their request.

When the delegation was taken to Smith, Melchior agreed with their observations that, as a result of injuries Smith had suffered, he needed to be examined by a doctor. Arrangements were made to have a police car transport him to the hospital.

Both within and outside of the police station, the atmosphere was electric with hostility. Carloads of police officers arriving for the 10:45 P.M. change of shifts were subjected to a gauntlet of catcalls, taunts, and curses.

Joined by Oliver Lofton, administrative director of the Newark Legal Services Project, the Negro community leaders inside the station requested an interview with Inspector Melchior. As they were talking to the inspector about initiating an investigation to determine how Smith had been injured, the crowd outside became more and more unruly. Two of the Negro spokesmen went outside to attempt to pacify the people.

There was little reaction to the spokesmen's appeal that the people go home. The second of the two had just finished speaking from atop a car when several Molotov cocktails smashed against the wall of the police station.

With the call of "Fire!" most of those inside the station, police officers and civilians alike, rushed out of the front door. The Molotov cocktails had splattered to the ground; the fire was quickly extinguished.

Inspector Melchior had a squad of men form a line across the front of the station. The police officers and the Negroes on the other side of the street exchanged volleys of profanity.

Three of the Negro leaders, Timothy Still of the United Community Corporation, Robert Curvin of CORE, and Lofton, requested they be given another opportunity to disperse the crowd. Inspector Melchior agreed to let them try and provided a bullhorn. It was apparent that the several hundred persons who had gathered in the street and on the grounds of the housing project were not going to disperse. Therefore, it was decided to attempt to channel the energies of the people into a nonviolent protest. While Lofton promised the crowd that a full investigation would be made of the Smith incident, the other Negro leaders urged those on the scene to form a line of march toward the city hall.

Some persons joined the line of march. Others milled about in the narrow street. From the dark grounds of the housing project came a barrage of rocks. Some of them fell among the crowd. Others hit persons in the line of march. Many smashed the windows of the police station. The rock throwing, it was believed, was the work of youngsters; approximately 2,500 children lived in the housing project.

Almost at the same time, an old car was set afire in a parking lot. The line of march began to disintegrate. The police, their heads protected by World War I-type helmets, sallied forth to disperse the crowd. A fire engine, arriving on the scene, was pelted with rocks. As police drove people away from the station, they scattered in all directions.

A few minutes later, a nearby liquor store was broken into. Some persons, seeing a caravan of cabs appear at City Hall to protest Smith's arrest, interpreted this as evidence that the disturbance had been organized, and generated rumors to that effect.

However, only a few stores were looted. Within a short period of time the disorder ran its course.

The next afternoon, Thursday, July 13, the mayor described it as an isolated incident. At a meeting with Negro leaders to discuss measures to defuse the situation, he agreed to appoint the first Negro police captain, and announced that he would set up a panel of citizens to investigate the Smith arrest. To one civil rights leader, this sounded like "the playback of a record," and he walked out. Other observers reported that the mayor seemed unaware of the seriousness of the tensions.

The police were not. Unknown to the mayor, Dominick Spina, the Director of Police, had extended shifts from 8 hours to 12, and was in the process of mobilizing half the strength of the department for that evening. The night before, Spina had arrived at the Fourth Precinct Police Station at approximately midnight, and had witnessed the latter half of the disturbance. Earlier in the evening he had held the regularly weekly "open house" in his office. This was intended to give any person who wanted to talk to him an opportunity to do so. Not a single person had shown up.

As director of police, Spina had initiated many new programs: police-precinct councils, composed of the police precinct captain and business and civic leaders, who would meet once a month to discuss mutual problems; Junior Crimefighters; a Boy Scout Explorer program for each precinct; mandatory human relations training for every officer; a Citizens' Observer Program, which permited citizens to ride in police cars and observe activities in the stations; a Police Cadet program; and others.

Many of the programs initially had been received enthusiastically, but —as was the case with the "open house"—interest had fallen off. In general, the programs failed to reach the hard-core unemployed, the disaffected, the school dropouts—of whom Spina estimates there are 10,000 in Essex County—that constitute a major portion of the police problem.

Reports and rumors, including one that Smith had died, circulated through the Negro community. Tension continued to rise. Nowhere was the tension greater than at the Spirit House, the gathering place for Black Nationalists, Black Power advocates, and militants of every hue. Black Muslims, Orthodox Moslems, and members of the United Afro-American Association, a new and growing organization that follows, in general, the teachings of the late Malcolm X, came regularly to mingle and exchange views. Antiwhite playwright LeRoi Jones held workshops. The two police-Negro clashes, coming one on top of the other, coupled with the unresolved political issues, had created a state of crisis.

On Thursday, inflammatory leaflets were circulated in the neighborhoods of the Fourth Precinct. A "Police Brutality Protest Rally" was announced for early evening in front of the Fourth Precinct Station. Several television stations and newspapers sent news teams to interview people. Cameras were set up. A crowd gathered.

A picket line was formed to march in front of the police station. Between 7 and 7:30 P.M., James Threatt, executive director of the Newark Human Rights Commission, arrived to announce to the people the decision of the mayor to form a citizens group to investigate the Smith incident, and to elevate a Negro to the rank of captain.

The response from the loosely milling mass of people was derisive. One youngster shouted "Black Power!" Rocks were thrown at Threatt, a Negro. The barrage of missiles that followed placed the police station under siege.

After the barrage had continued for some minutes, police came out to disperse the crowd. According to witnesses, there was little restraint of language or action by either side. A number of police officers and Negroes were injured.

As on the night before, once the people had been dispersed, reports of looting began to come in. Soon the glow of the first fire was seen.

Without enough men to establish control, the police set up a perimeter around a 2-mile stretch of Springfield Avenue, one of the principal business districts, where a band of youths roamed up and down smashing windows. Grocery and liquor stores, clothing and furniture stores, drugstores and cleaners, appliance stores and pawnshops were the principal targets. Periodically, police officers would appear and fire their weapons over the heads of the looters and rioters. Laden with stolen goods, people began returning to the housing projects.

Near midnight, activity appeared to taper off. The mayor told reporters the city had turned the corner.

As news of the disturbances had spread, however, people had flocked into the streets. As they saw stores being broken into with impunity, many bowed to temptation and joined the looting.

Without the necessary personnel to make mass arrests, police were shooting into the air to clear stores. A Negro boy was wounded by a .22 caliber bullet said to have been fired by a white man riding in a car. Guns were reported stolen from a Sears, Roebuck store. Looting, fires, and gunshots were reported from a widening area. Between 2 and 2:30 A.M. on Friday, July 14, the mayor decided to request Gov. Richard J. Hughes to dispatch the state police and National Guard troops. The first elements of the state police arrived with a sizable contingent before dawn.

During the morning the Governor and the mayor, together with the police and National Guard officers, made a reconnaissance of the area. The police escort guarding the officials arrested looters as they went. By early afternoon the National Guard had set up 137 roadblocks, and state police and riot teams were beginning to achieve control. Command of antiriot operations was taken over by the Governor, who decreed a "hard line" in putting down the riot.

As a result of technical difficulties, such as the fact that the city and state police did not operate on the same radio wave-lengths, the three-way command structure—city police, state police and National Guard —worked poorly.

At 3:30 P.M. that afternoon, the family of Mrs. D. J. was standing near the upstairs windows of their apartment, watching looters run in and out of a furniture store on Springfield Avenue. Three carloads of police rounded the corner. As the police yelled at the looters, they began running.

The police officers opened fire. A bullet smashed the kitchen window in Mrs. D. J.s' apartment. A moment later she heard a cry from the bedroom. Her 3-year-old daughter, Debbie, came running into the room. Blood was streaming down the left side of her face: the bullet had entered her eye. The child spent the next 2 months in the hospital. She lost the sight of her left eye and the hearing in her left ear.

Simultaneously, on the street below, Horace W. Morris, an associate director of the Washington Urban League who had been visiting relatives in Newark, was about to enter a car for the drive to Newark Airport. With him were his two brothers and his 73-year-old stepfather, Isaac Harrison. About 60 persons had been on the street watching the looting. As the police arrived, three of the looters cut directly in front of the group of spectators. The police fired at the looters. Bullets plowed into the spectators. Everyone began running. As Harrison, followed by the family, headed toward the apartment building in which he lived, a bullet kicked his legs out from under him. Horace Morris lifted him to his feet. Again he fell. Mr. Morris' brother, Virgil, attempted to pick the old man up. As he was doing so, he was hit in the left leg and right forearm. Mr. Morris and his other brother managed to drag the two wounded men into the vestibule of the building, jammed with 60 to 70 frightened, angry Negroes.

Bullets continued to spatter against the walls of the buildings. Finally, as the firing died down, Morris—whose stepfather died that evening—yelled to a sergeant that innocent people were being shot.

"Tell the black bastards to stop shooting at us," the sergeant, according to Morris, replied.

"They don't have guns; no one is shooting at you," Morris said.

"You shut up, there's a sniper on the roof," the sergeant yelled.

A short time later, at approximately 5 P.M., in the same vicinity, a police detective was killed by a small caliber bullet. The origin of the shot could not be determined. Later during the riot, a fireman was killed by a .30 caliber bullet. Snipers were blamed for the deaths of both.

At 5:30 P.M., on Beacon Street, W. F. told J. S., whose 1959 Pontiac he had taken to the station for inspection, that his front brake needed fixing. J. S., who had just returned from work, went to the car which was parked in the street, jacked up the front end, took the wheel off, and got under the car.

The street was quiet. More than a dozen persons were sitting on porches, walking about, or shopping. None heard any shots. Suddenly several state troopers appeared at the corner of Springfield and Beacon. J. S. was startled by a shot clanging into the side of the garbage can next to his car. As he looked up he saw a state trooper with his rifle pointed at him. The next shot struck him in the right side.

At almost the same instant, K. G., standing on a porch, was struck in the right eye by a bullet. Both he and J. S. were critically injured.

At 8 P.M., Mrs. L. M. bundled her husband, her husband's brother, and her four sons into the family car to drive to a restaurant for dinner. On the return trip her husband, who was driving, panicked as he approached a National Guard roadblock. He slowed the car, then quickly swerved around. A shot rang out. When the family reached home, everyone began piling out of the car. Ten-year-old Eddie failed to move. Shot through the head, he was dead.

Although by nightfall most of the looting and burning had ended, reports of sniper fire increased. The fire was, according to New Jersey National Guard reports, "deliberately or otherwise inaccurate." Maj. Gen. James F. Cantwell, Chief of Staff of the New Jersey National Guard, testified before an Armed Services Subcommittee of the House of Representatives that "there was too much firing initially against snipers" because of "confusion when we were finally called on for help and our thinking of it as a military action."

"As a matter of fact," Director of Police Spina told the Commission, "down in the Springfield Avenue area it was so bad that, in my opinion, Guardsmen were firing upon police and police were firing back at them . . . I really don't believe there was as much sniping as we thought. . . . We have since compiled statistics indicating that there were 79 specified instances of sniping."

Several problems contributed to the misconceptions regarding snipers: the lack of communications; the fact that one shot might be reported half a dozen times by half a dozen different persons as it caromed and reverberated a mile or more through the city; the fact that the National Guard troops lacked riot training. They were, said a police official, "young and very scared," and had had little contact with Negroes.

Within the Guard itself contact with Negroes had certainly been limited. Although, in 1949, out of a force of 12,529 men there had been 1,183 Negroes, following the integration of the Guard in the 1950's the number had declined until, by July of 1967, there were 303 Negroes in a force of 17,529 men.

On Saturday, July 15, Spina received a report of snipers in a housing project. When he arrived he saw approximately 100 National Guardsmen and police officers crouching behind vehicles, hiding in corners and lying on the ground around the edge of the courtyard.

Since everything appeared quiet and it was broad daylight, Spina walked directly down the middle of the street. Nothing happened. As he came to the last building of the complex, he heard a shot. All around him the troopers jumped, believing themselves to be under sniper fire. A moment later a young Guardsman ran from behind a building.

The director of police went over and asked him if he had fired the shot. The soldier said yes, he had fired to scare a man away from a window; that his orders were to keep everyone away from windows.

Spina said he told the soldier: "Do you know what you just did? You have now created a state of hysteria. Every Guardsman up and down this street and every state policeman and every city policeman that is present thinks that somebody just fired a shot and that it is probably a sniper."

A short time later more "gunshots" were heard. Investigating, Spina came upon a Puerto Rican sitting on a wall. In reply to a question as to whether he knew "where the firing is coming from?" the man said: "That's no firing. That's fireworks. If you look up to the fourth floor, you will see the people who are throwing down these cherry bombs."

By this time, four truckloads of National Guardsmen had arrived and troopers and policemen were again crouched everywhere, looking for a sniper. The director of police remained at the scene for three hours, and the only shot fired was the one by the guardsman.

Nevertheless, at six o'clock that evening two columns of National Guardsmen and state troopers were directing mass fire at the Hayes Housing project in response to what they believed were snipers.

On the tenth floor, Eloise Spellman, the mother of several children, fell, a bullet through her neck.

Across the street, a number of persons, standing in an apartment window, were watching the firing directed at the housing project. Suddenly, several troopers whirled and began firing in the general direction of the spectators. Mrs. Hattie Gainer, a grandmother, sank to the floor.

A block away Rebecca Brown's 2-year-old daughter was standing at the window. Mrs. Brown rushed to drag her to safety. As Mrs. Brown was momentarily framed in the window, a bullet spun into her back.

All three women died.

A number of eyewitnesses, at varying times and places, reported seeing bottles thrown from upper story windows. As these would land at the feet of an officer he would turn and fire. Thereupon, other officers and Guardsmen up and down the street would join in.

In order to protect his property, B. W. W., the owner of a Chinese laundry, had placed a sign saying "Soul Brother" in his window. Between 1 and 1:30 A.M., on Sunday, July 16, he, his mother, wife, and brother, were watching television in the back room. The neighborhood had been quiet. Suddenly, B. W. W. heard the sound of jeeps, then shots.

Going to an upstairs window he was able to look out into the street. There he observed several jeeps, from which soldiers and state troopers were firing into stores that had "Soul Brother" signs in the windows. During the course of three nights, according to dozens of eyewitness reports, law enforcement officers shot into and smashed windows of businesses that contained signs indicating they were Negro-owned.

At 11 P.M., on Sunday, July 16, Mrs. Lucille Pugh looked out of the window to see if the streets were clear. She then asked her 11-year-old son, Michael, to take the garbage out. As he reached the street and was illuminatd by a street light, a shot rang out. He died.

By Monday afternoon, July 17, state police and National Guard forces were withdrawn. That evening, a Catholic priest saw two Negro men walking down the street. They were carrying a case of soda and two bags of groceries. An unmarked car with five police officers pulled up beside them. Two white officers got out of the car. Accusing the Negro men of looting, the officers made them put the groceries on the sidewalk, then kicked the bags open, scattering their contents all over the street.

Telling the men, "Get out of here," the officers drove off. The Catholic priest went across the street to help gather up the groceries. One of the men turned to him: "I've just been back from Vietnam 2 days," he said, "and this is what I get. I feel like going home and getting a rifle and shooting the cops."

Of the 250 fire alarms, many had been false, and 13 were considered by the city to have been "serious." Of the $10,251,000 damage total, four-fifths was due to stock loss. Damage to buildings and fixtures was less than $2 million.

Twenty-three persons were killed—a white detective, a white fireman, and 21 Negroes. One was 73-year-old Isaac Harrison. Six were women. Two were children.

The National Advisory Commission on Civil Disorders

Detroit

On Saturday evening, July 22, the Detroit Police Department raided five "blind pigs." The blind pigs had had their origin in prohibition days, and survived as private social clubs. Often, they were after-hours drinking and gambling spots.

The fifth blind pig on the raid list, the United Community and Civic League at the corner of 12th Street and Clairmount, had been raided twice before. Once 10 persons had been picked up; another time, 28. A Detroit vice squad officer had tried but failed to get in shortly after 10 o'clock Saturday night. He succeeded, on his second attempt, at 3:45 Sunday morning.

The Tactical Mobile Unit, the Police Department's crowd control squad, had been dismissed at 3 A.M. Since Sunday morning traditionally is the least troublesome time for police in Detroit—and all over the country—only 193 officers were patroling the streets. Of these, 44 were in the 10th precinct where the blind pig was located.

Police expected to find two dozen patrons in the blind pig. That night, however, it was the scene of a party for several servicemen, two of whom were back from Vietnam. Instead of two dozen patrons, police found 82. Some voiced resentment at the police intrusion.

An hour went by before all 82 could be transported from the scene. The weather was humid and warm—the temperature that day was to rise to 86—and despite the late hour, many people were still on the street. In short order, a crowd of about 200 gathered.

In November of 1965, George Edwards, Judge of the United States Court of Appeals for the Sixth Circuit, and Commissioner of the Detroit Police Department from 1961 to 1963, had written in the *Michigan Law Review* Edwards 1965):

It is clear that in 1965 no one will make excuses for any city's inability to foresee the possibility of racial trouble. . . . Although local police forces generally regard themselves as public servants with the responsibility of maintaining law and order, they tend to minimize this attitude when they are patrolling areas that are heavily populated with Negro citizens. There, they tend to view each person on the streets as a potential criminal or enemy, and all too often that attitude is reciprocated. Indeed, hostility between the Negro communities in our large cities and the police departments, is the major problem in law enforcement in this decade. It has been a major cause of all recent race riots.

At the time of Detroit's 1943 race riot, Judge Edwards told Commission investigators, there was "open warfare between the Detroit Negroes and the Detroit Police Department." As late as 1961, he had thought that "Detroit was the leading candidate in the United States for a race riot."

There was a long history of conflict between the police department and citizens. During the labor battles of the 1930's, union members had come to view the Detroit Police Department as a strike-breaking force. The 1943 riot, in which 34 persons died, was the bloodiest in the United States in a span of two decades.

Judge Edwards and his successor, Commissioner Ray Girardin, attempted to restructure the image of the department. A Citizens Complaint Bureau was set up to facilitate the filing of complaints by citizens against officers. In practice, however, this Bureau appeared to work little better than less enlightened and more cumbersome procedures in other cities.

On 12th Street, with its high incidence of vice and crime, the issue of police brutality was a recurrent theme. A month earlier, the killing of a prostitute had been determined by police investigators to be the work of a pimp. According to rumors in the community, the crime had been committed by a vice squad officer.

At about the same time, the killing of Danny Thomas, a 27-year-old Negro Army veteran, by a gang of white youths had inflamed the community. The city's major newspapers played down the story in hope that the murder would not become a cause for increased tensions. The intent backfired. A banner story in the *Michigan Chronicle,* the city's Negro newspaper, began: "As James Meredith marched again Sunday to prove a Negro could walk in Mississippi without fear, a young woman who saw her husband killed by a white gang, shouting: 'Niggers keep out of Rouge Park,' lost her baby.

"Relatives were upset that the full story of the murder was not being told, apparently in an effort to prevent the incident from sparking a riot."

Some Negroes believed that the daily newspapers' treatment of the story was further evidence of the double standard: playing up crimes by Negroes, playing down crimes committed against Negroes.

Although police arrested one suspect for murder, Negroes questioned why the entire gang was not held. What, they asked, would have been the result if a white man had been killed by a gang of Negroes? What if Negroes had made the kind of advances toward a white woman that the white men were rumored to have made toward Mrs. Thomas?

The Thomas family lived only four or five blocks from the raided blind pig.

A few minutes after 5 A.M., just after the last of those arrested had been hauled away, an empty bottle smashed into the rear window of a police car. A litter basket was thrown through the window of a store. Rumors circulated of excess force used by the police during the raid. A youth, whom police nicknamed "Mr. Greensleeves" because of the color of his suit, was shouting: "We're going to have a riot!" and exhorting the crowd to vandalism.

At 5:20 A.M., Commissioner Girardin was notified. He immediately called Mayor Jerome Cavanagh. Seventeen officers from other areas were ordered into the 10th Precinct. By 6:00 A.M., police strength had grown to 369 men. Of these, however, only 43 were committed to the immediate riot area. By that time, the number of persons on 12th Street was growing into the thousands and widespread window-smashing and looting had begun.

On either side of 12th Street were neat, middle-class districts. Along 12th Street itself, however, crowded apartment houses created a density of more than 21,000 persons per square mile, almost double the city average.

The movement of people when the slums of "Black Bottom" had been cleared for urban renewal had changed 12th Street from an integrated community into an almost totally black one, in which only a number of merchants remained white. Only 18 percent of the residents were homeowners. Twenty-five percent of the housing was considered so substandard as to require clearance. Another 19 percent had major deficiencies.

The crime rate was almost double that of the city as a whole. A Detroit police officer told Commission investigators that prostitution was so widespread that officers made arrests only when soliciting became blatant. The proportion of broken families was more than twice that in the rest of the city.

By 7:50 A.M., when a 17-man police commando unit attempted to make the first sweep, an estimated 3,000 persons were on 12th Street. They offered no resistance. As the sweep moved down the street, they gave way to one side, and then flowed back behind it.

A shoe store manager said he waited vainly for police for 2 hours as the store was being looted. At 8:25 A.M., someone in the crowd yelled, "The cops are coming!" The first flames of the riot billowed from the store. Firemen who responded were not harassed. The flames were extinguished.

By midmorning, 1,122 men—approximately a fourth of the police department—had reported for duty. Of these, 540 were in or near the six-block riot area. One hundred eight officers were attempting to establish a cordon. There was, however, no interference with looters, and police were refraining from the use of force.

Commissioner Girardin said: "If we had started shooting in there . . . not one of our policemen would have come out alive. I am convinced it would have turned into a race riot in the conventional sense."

According to witnesses, police at some roadblocks made little effort to stop people from going in and out of the area. Bantering took place between police officers and the populace, some still in pajamas. To some observers, there seemed at this point to be an atmosphere of apathy. On the one hand, the police failed to interfere with the looting. On the other, a number of older, more stable residents, who had seen the street deteriorate from a prosperous commercial thoroughfare to one ridden by vice, remained aloof.

Because officials feared that the 12th Street disturbance might be a diversion, many officers were sent to guard key installations in other sections of the city. Belle Isle, the recreation area in the Detroit River that had been the scene of the 1943 riot, was sealed off.

In an effort to avoid attracting people to the scene, some broadcasters cooperated by not reporting the riot, and an effort was made to downplay the extent of the disorder. The facade of "business as usual" necessitated the detailing of numerous police officers to protect the 50,000 spectators that were expected at that afternoon's New York Yankees-Detroit Tigers baseball game.

Early in the morning, a task force of community workers went into the area to dispel rumors and act as counterrioters. Such a task force had been singularly successful at the time of the incident in the Kercheval district in the summer of 1966, when scores of people had gathered at the site of an arrest. Kercheval, however, has a more stable population, fewer stores, less population density, and the city's most effective police-community relations program.

The 12th Street area, on the other hand, had been determined, in a 1966 survey conducted by Dr. Ernest Harburg of the Psychology Department of the University of Michigan, to be a community of high stress and tension. An overwhelming majority of the residents indicated dissatisfaction with their environment.

Of the interviewed, 93 percent said they wanted to move out of the neighborhood; 73 percent felt that the streets were not safe; 91 percent believed that a person was likely to be robbed or beaten at night;

58 percent knew of a fight within the last 12 months in which a weapon had been employed; 32 percent stated that they themselves owned a weapon; 57 percent were worried about fires.

A significant proportion believed municipal services to be inferior: 36 percent were dissatisfied with the schools; 43 percent with the city's contribution to the neighborhood; 77 percent with the recreational facilities; 78 percent believed police did not respond promptly when they were summoned for help.

U.S. Representative John Conyers, Jr., a Negro, was notified about the disturbance at his home a few blocks from 12th Street, at 8:30 A.M. Together with other community leaders, including Hubert G. Locke, a Negro and assistant to the commissioner of police, he began to drive around the area. In the side streets, he asked people to stay in their homes. On 12th Street, he asked them to disperse. It was, by his own account, a futile task.

Numerous eyewitnesses interviewed by Commission investigators tell of the carefree mood with which people ran in and out of stores, looting and laughing, and joking with the police officers. Stores with "Soul Brother" signs appeared no more immune than others. Looters paid no attention to residents who shouted at them and called their actions senseless. An epidemic of excitement had swept over the persons on the street.

Congressman Conyers noticed a woman with a baby in her arms; she was raging, cursing "whitey" for no apparent reason.

Shortly before noon, Congressman Conyers climbed atop a car in the middle of 12th Street to address the people. As he began to speak, he was confronted by a man in his fifties whom he had once, as a lawyer, represented in court. The man had been active in civil rights. He believed himself to have been persecuted as a result, and it was Conyers' opinion that he may have been wrongfully jailed. Extremely bitter, the man was inciting the crowd and challenging Conyers: "Why are you defending the cops and the establishment? You're just as bad as they are!"

A police officer in the riot area told Commission investigators that neither he nor his fellow officers were instructed as to what they were supposed to be doing. Witnesses tell of officers standing behind saw-horses as an area was being looted—and still standing there much later, when the mob had moved elsewhere. A squad from the commando unit, wearing helmets with face-covering visors and carrying bayonet-tipped carbines, blockaded a street several blocks from the scene of the riot. Their appearance drew residents into the street. Some began to harangue them and to question why they were in an area where there was no trouble. Representative Conyers convinced the police department to remove the commandos.

By that time, a rumor was threading through the crowd that a man had been bayoneted by the police. Influenced by such stories, the crowd became belligerent. At approximately 1 P.M., stonings accelerated. Numerous officers reported injuries from rocks, bottles, and other objects thrown at them. Smoke billowed upward from four fires, the first since the one at the shoe store early in the morning. When firemen answered the alarms, they became the target for rocks and bottles.

At 2:00 P.M., Mayor Cavanagh met with community and political leaders at police headquarters. Until then there had been hope that, as the people blew off steam, the riot would dissipate. Now the opinion was nearly unanimous that additional forces would be needed.

A request was made for state police aid. By 3 P.M., 360 officers were assembling at the armory. At that moment looting was spreading from the 12th Street area to the other main thoroughfares.

There was no lack of the disaffected to help spread it. Although not yet as hard-pressed as Newark, Detroit was, like Newark, losing population. Its prosperous middle-class whites were moving to the suburbs and being replaced by unskilled Negro migrants. Between 1960 and 1967, the Negro population rose from just under 30 percent to an estimated 40 percent of the total.

In a decade, the school system had gained 50,000 to 60,000 children. Fifty-one percent of the elementary school classes were overcrowded. Simply to achieve the statewide average, the system needed 1,650 more teachers and 1,000 additional classrooms. The combined cost would be $63 million.

Of 300,000 school children, 171,000, or 57 percent, were Negro. According to the Detroit superintendent of schools, 25 different school districts surrounding the city spent up to $500 more per pupil per year than Detroit. In the inner city schools, more than half the pupils who entered high school became dropouts.

The strong union structure had created excellent conditions for most working men, but had left others, such as civil service and Government workers, comparatively disadvantaged and dissatisfied. In June, the "Blue Flu" had struck the city as police officers, forbidden to strike, had staged a sick-out. In September, the teachers were to go on strike. The starting wages for a plumber's helper were almost equal to the salary of a police officer or teacher.

Some unions, traditionally closed to Negroes, zealously guarded training opportunities. In January of 1967, the school system notified six apprenticeship trades it would not open any new apprenticeship classes unless a large number of Negroes were included. By fall, some of the programs were still closed.

High school diplomas from inner-city schools were regarded by personnel directors as less than valid. In July, unemployment was at a 5-year peak. In the 12th Street area, it was estimated to be between 12 and 15 percent for Negro men and 30 percent or higher for those under 25.

The more education a Negro had, the greater the disparity between his income and that of a white with the same level of education. The income of whites and Negroes with a seventh-grade education was about equal. The median income of whites with a high school diploma was $1,600 more per year than that of Negroes. White college graduates made $2,600 more. In fact, so far as income was concerned, it made very little difference to a Negro man whether he had attended school for 8 years or for 12. In the fall of 1967, a study conducted at one inner-city high school, Northwestern, showed that, although 50 percent of the dropouts had found work, 90 percent of the 1967 graduating class was unemployed.

Mayor Cavanagh had appointed many Negroes to key positions in his administration, but in elective offices the Negro population was still underrepresented. Of nine councilmen, one was a Negro. Of seven school board members, two were Negroes.

Although Federal programs had brought nearly $360 million to the city between 1962 and 1967, the money appeared to have had little impact at the grassroots. Urban renewal, for which $38 million had been allocated, was opposed by many residents of the poverty area.

Because of its financial straits, the city was unable to produce on promises to correct such conditions as poor garbage collection and bad street lighting, which brought constant complaints from Negro residents.

On 12th Street, Carl Perry, the Negro proprietor of a drugstore and photography studio, was dispensing ice cream, sodas, and candy to the youngsters streaming in and out of his store. For safekeeping, he had brought the photography equipment from his studio, in the next block, to the drugstore. The youths milling about repeatedly assured him that, although the market next door had been ransacked, his place of business was in no danger.

In midafternoon, the market was set afire. Soon after, the drug store went up in flames.

State Representative James Del Rio, a Negro, was camping out in front of a building he owned when two small boys, neither more than 10 years old, approached. One prepared to throw a brick through a window. Del Rio stopped him: "That building belongs to me," he said.

"I'm glad you told me, baby, because I was just about to bust you in!" the youngster replied.

Some evidence that criminal elements were organizing spontaneously to take advantage of the riot began to manifest itself. A number of cars were noted to be returning again and again, their occupants methodically looting stores. Months later, goods stolen during the riot were still being peddled.

A spirit of carefree nihilism was taking hold. To riot and to destroy appeared more and more to become ends in themselves. Late Sunday afternoon, it appeared to one observer that the young people were "dancing amidst the flames."

A Negro plainclothes officer was standing at an intersection when a man threw a Molotov cocktail into a business establishment at the corner. In the heat of the afternoon, fanned by the 20 to 25 m.p.h. winds of both Sunday and Monday, the fire reached the home next door within minutes. As residents uselessly sprayed the flames with garden hoses, the fire jumped from roof to roof of adjacent two- and three-story buildings. Within the hour, the entire block was in flames. The ninth house in the burning row belonged to the arsonist who had thrown the Molotov cocktail.

In some areas, residents organized rifle squads to protect firefighters. Elsewhere, especially as the wind-whipped flames began to overwhelm the Detroit Fire Department and more and more residences burned, the firemen were subjected to curses and rock-throwing.

Because of a lack of funds, on a per capita basis the department is one of the smallest in the nation. In comparison to Newark, where approximately 1,000 firemen patrol an area of 16 square miles with a population of 400,000, Detroit's 1,700 firemen must cover a city of 140 square miles with a population of 1.6 million. Because the department had no mutual aid agreement with surrounding communities, it could not quickly call in reinforcements from outlying areas, and it was almost 9:00 P.M. before the first arrived. At one point, out of a total of 92 pieces of Detroit firefighting equipment and 56 brought in from surrounding communities, only four engine companies were available to guard areas of the city outside of the riot perimeter.

As the afternoon progressed, the fire department's radio carried repeated messages of apprehension and orders of caution:

There is no police protection here at all; there isn't a policeman in the area. . . . If you have trouble at all, pull out! . . . We're being stoned at the scene. It's going good. We need help! . . . Protect yourselves! Proceed away from the scene. . . . Engine 42 over at Linwood and Gladstone. They are throwing bottles at us so we are getting out of the area. . . . All companies without police protection—all companies without police protection—orders are to withdraw, do not try to put out the fires. I repeat—all companies without police protection orders are to withdraw, do not try to put out the fires!

It was 4:30 P.M. when the firemen, some of them exhausted by the heat, abandoned an area of approximately 100 square blocks on either side of 12th Street to await protection from police and National Guardsmen.

During the course of the riot, firemen were to withdraw 283 times.

Fire Chief Charles J. Quinlan estimated that at least two-thirds of the buildings were destroyed by spreading fires rather than fires set at the scene. Of the 683 structures involved, approximately one-third were residential, and in few, if any, of these was the fire set originally.

Governor George Romney flew over the area between 8:30 and 9:00 P.M. "It looked like the city had been bombed on the west side and there was an area two-and-a-half miles by three-and-a-half miles with major fires, with entire blocks in flames," he told the Commission.

In the midst of chaos, there were some unexpected individual responses.

Twenty-four-year-old E. G., a Negro born in Savannah, Ga., had come to Detroit in 1965 to attend Wayne State University. Rebellion had been building in him for a long time because,

You just had to bow down to the white man. . . . When the insurance man would come by he would always call out to my mother by her first name and we were expected to smile and greet him happily. . . . Man, I know he would never have thought of me or my father going to his home and calling his wife by her first name. Then I once saw a white man slapping a young pregnant Negro woman on the street with such force that she just spun around and fell. I'll never forget that.

When a friend called to tell him about the riot on 12th Street, E. G. went there expecting "a true revolt," but was disappointed as soon as he saw the looting begin: "I wanted to see the people really rise up in revolt. When I saw the first person coming out of the store with things in his arms, I really got sick to my stomach and wanted to go home. Rebellion against the white suppressors is one thing, but one measly pair of shoes or some food completely ruins the whole concept."

E. G. was standing in a crowd, watching firemen work, when Fire Chief Alvin Wall called out for help from the spectators. E. G. responded. His reasoning was: "No matter what color someone is, whether they are green or pink or blue, I'd help them if they were in trouble. That's all there is to it."

He worked with the firemen for 4 days, the only Negro in an all-white crew. Elsewhere, at scattered locations, a half dozen other Negro youths pitched in to help the firemen.

At 4:20 P.M., Mayor Cavanagh requested that the National Guard be brought into Detroit. Although a major portion of the Guard was in its summer encampment 200 miles away, several hundred troops were conducting their regular week-end drill in the city. That circumstance obviated many problems. The first troops were on the streets by 7:00 P.M.

At 7:45 P.M., the mayor issued a proclamation instituting a 9:00 P.M to 5:00 A.M. curfew. At 9:07 P.M., the first sniper fire was reported. Following his aerial survey of the city, Governor Romney, at or shortly before midnight, proclaimed that "a state of public emergency exists" in the cities of Detroit, Highland Park and Hamtramck.

At 4:45 P.M., a 68-year-old white shoe repairman, George Messerlian, had seen looters carrying clothes from a cleaning establishment next to his shop. Armed with a saber, he had rushed into the street, flailing away at the looters. One Negro youth was nicked on the shoulder. Another, who had not been on the scene, inquired as to what had happened. After he had been told, he allegedly replied: "I'll get the old man for you!"

Going up to Messerlian, who had fallen or been knocked to the ground, the youth began to beat him with a club. Two other Negro youths dragged the attacker away from the old man. It was too late. Messerlian died 4 days later in the hospital.

At 9:15 P.M., a 16-year-old Negro boy, superficially wounded while looting, became the first reported gunshot victim.

At midnight, Sharon George, a 23-year-old white woman, together with her two brothers, was a passenger in a car being driven by her husband. After having dropped off two Negro friends, they were returning home on one of Detroit's main avenues when they were slowed by a milling throng in the street. A shot fired from close range struck the car. The bullet splintered in Mrs. George's body. She died less than 2 hours later.

An hour before midnight, a 45-year-old white man, Walter Grzanka, together with three white companions, went into the street. Shortly thereafter, a market was broken into. Inside the show window, a Negro man began filling bags with groceries, and handing them to confederates outside the store. Grzanka twice went over to the store, accepted bags, and placed them down beside his companions across the street. On the third occasion he entered the market. When he emerged, the market owner, driving by in his car, shot and killed him.

In Grzanka's pockets, police found seven cigars, four packages of pipe tobacco, and nine pairs of shoelaces.

Before dawn, four other looters were shot, one of them accidentally while struggling with a police officer. A Negro youth and a National Guardsman were injured by gunshots of undetermined origin. A private guard shot himself while pulling his revolver from his pocket. In the basement of the 13th Precinct Police Station, a cue ball, thrown by an unknown assailant, cracked against the head of a sergeant.

At about midnight, three white youths, armed with a shotgun, had gone to the roof of their apartment building, located in an all-white block, in order, they said, to protect the building from fire. At 2:45 A.M., a patrol car, carrying police officers and National Guardsmen, received a report of "snipers on the roof." As the patrol car arrived, the manager of the building went to the roof to tell the youths they had better come down.

The law enforcement personnel surrounded the building, some going to the front, others to the rear. As the manager, together with the three youths, descended the fire escape in the rear, a National Guardsman, believing he heard shots from the front, fired. His shot killed 23-year-old Clifton Pryor.

Early in the morning, a young white fireman and a 49-year-old Negro homeowner were killed by fallen power lines.

By 2:00 A.M. Monday, Detroit police had been augmented by 800 State Police Officers and 1,200 National Guardsmen. An additional 8,000 Guardsmen were on the way. Nevertheless, Governor Romney and

Mayor Cavanagh decided to ask for Federal assistance. At 2:15 A.M., the mayor called Vice President Hubert Humphrey, and was referred to Attorney General Ramsey Clark. A short time thereafter, telephone contact was established between Governor Romney and the attorney general.[1]

There is some difference of opinion about what occurred next. According to the attorney general's office, the governor was advised of the seriousness of the request and told that the applicable Federal statute required that, before Federal troops could be brought into the city, he would have to state that the situation had deteriorated to the point that local and state forces could no longer maintain law and order. According to the governor, he was under the impression that he was being asked to declare that a "state of insurrection" existed in the city.

The governor was unwilling to make such a declaration, contending that, if he did, insurance policies would not cover the loss incurred as a result of the riot. He and the mayor decided to re-evaluate the need for Federal troops.

Contact between Detroit and Washington was maintained throughout the early morning hours. At 9:00 A.M., as the disorder still showed no sign of abating, the governor and the mayor decided to make a renewed request for Federal troops.

Shortly before noon, the President of the United States authorized the sending of a task force of paratroops to Selfridge Air Force Base, near the city. A few minutes past 3:00 P.M., Lt. Gen. John L. Throckmorton, commander of Task Force Detroit, met Cyrus Vance, former Deputy Secretary of Defense, at the air base. Approximately an hour later, the first Federal troops arrived at the air base.

After meeting with state and municipal officials, Mr. Vance, General Throckmorton, Governor Romney, and Mayor Cavanagh, made a tour of the city, which lasted until 7:15 P.M. During this tour Mr. Vance and General Throckmorton independently came to the conclusion that— since they had seen no looting or sniping, since the fires appeared to be coming under control, and since a substantial number of National Guardsmen had not yet been committed—injection of Federal troops would be premature.

As the riot alternately waxed and waned, one area of the ghetto remained insulated. On the northeast side, the residents of some 150 square blocks inhabited by 21,000 persons had, in 1966, banded together in the Positive Neighborhood Action Committee (PNAC). With professional help from the Institute of Urban Dynamics, they had organized block clubs and made plans for the improvement of the neighborhood. In order to meet the need for recreational facilities, which the city was

1. A little over two hours earlier, at 11:55 P.M., Mayor Cavanagh had informed the U.S. Attorney General that a "dangerous situation existed in the city." Details are set forth in the final report of Cyrus R. Vance, covering the Detroit riot, released on September 12, 1967.

not providing, they had raised $3,000 to purchase empty lots for playgrounds. Although opposed to urban renewal, they had agreed to cosponsor with the Archdiocese of Detroit a housing project to be controlled jointly by the archdiocese and PNAC.

When the riot broke out, the residents, through the block clubs, were able to organize quickly. Youngsters, agreeing to stay in the neighborhood, participated in detouring traffic. While many persons reportedly sympathized with the idea of a rebellion against the "system," only two small fires were set—one in an empty building.

During the daylight hours Monday, nine more persons were killed by gunshots elsewhere in the city, and many others were seriously or critically injured. Twenty-three-year-old Nathaniel Edmonds, a Negro, was sitting in his backyard when a young white man stopped his car, got out, and began an argument with him. A few minutes later, declaring he was "going to paint his picture on him with a shotgun," the white man allegedly shotgunned Edmonds to death.

Mrs. Nannie Pack and Mrs. Mattie Thomas were sitting on the porch of Mrs. Pack's house when police began chasing looters from a nearby market. During the chase officers fired three shots from their shotguns. The discharge from one of these accidentally struck the two women. Both were still in the hospital weeks later.

Included among those critically injured when they were accidentally trapped in the line of fire were an 8-year-old Negro girl and a 14-year-old white boy.

As darkness settled Monday, the number of incidents reported to police began to rise again. Although many turned out to be false, several involved injuries to police officers, National Guardsmen, and civilians by gunshots of undetermined origin.

Watching the upward trend of reported incidents, Mr. Vance and General Throckmorton became convinced Federal troops should be used, and President Johnson was so advised. At 11:20 P.M., the President signed a proclamation federalizing the Michigan National Guard and authorizing the use of the paratroopers.

At this time, there were nearly 5,000 Guardsmen in the city, but fatigue, lack of training, and the haste with which they had had to be deployed reduced their effectiveness. Some of the Guardsmen traveled 200 miles and then were on duty for 30 hours straight. Some had never received riot training and were given on-the-spot instructions on mob control—only to discover that there were no mobs, and that the situation they faced on the darkened streets was one for which they were unprepared.

Commanders committed men as they became available, often in small groups. In the resulting confusion some units were lost in the city. Two Guardsmen assigned to an intersection on Monday were discovered still there on Friday.

Lessons learned by the California National Guard two years earlier in Watts regarding the danger of overreaction and the necessity of great restraint in using weapons had not, apparently, been passed on to the Michigan National Guard. The young troopers could not be expected to know what a danger they were creating by the lack of fire discipline, not only to the civilian population but to themselves.

A Detroit newspaper reporter who spent a night riding in a command jeep told a Commission investigator of machine guns begin fired accidentally, street lights being shot out by rifle fire, and buildings being placed under siege on the sketchiest reports of sniping. Troopers would fire, and immediately from the distance there would be answering fire, sometimes consisting of tracer bullets.

In one instance, the newsman related, a report was received on the jeep radio that an Army bus was pinned down by sniper fire at an intersection. National Guardsmen and police, arriving from various directions, jumped out and began asking each other: "Where's the sniper fire coming from?" As one Guardsman pointed to a building, everyone rushed about, taking cover. A soldier, alighting from a jeep, accidentally pulled the trigger on his rifle. As the shot reverberated through the darkness, an officer yelled: "What's going on?" "I don't know," came the answer. "Sniper, I guess."

Without any clear authorization or direction, someone opened fire upon the suspected building. A tank rolled up and sprayed the building with .50-caliber tracer bullets. Law enforcement officers rushed into the surrounded building and discovered it empty. "They must be firing one shot and running," was the verdict.

The reporter interviewed the men who had gotten off the bus and were crouched around it. When he asked them about the sniper incident, he was told that someone had heard a shot. He asked "Did the bullet hit the bus?" The answer was: "Well, we don't know."

Bracketing the hour of midnight Monday, heavy firing, injuring many persons and killing several, occurred in the southeastern sector, which was to be taken over by the paratroopers at 4:00 A.M., Tuesday, and which was, at this time, considered to be the most active riot area in the city.

Employed as a private guard, 55-year-old Julius L. Dorsey, a Negro, was standing in front of a market when accosted by two Negro men and a woman. They demanded he permit them to loot the market. He ignored their demands. They began to berate him. He asked a neighbor to call the police. As the argument grew more heated, Dorsey fired three shots from his pistol into the air.

The police radio reported: "Looters, they have rifles." A patrol car driven by a police officer and carrying three National Guardsmen arrived. As the looters fled, the law enforcement personnel opened fire. When the firing ceased, one person lay dead.

He was Julius L. Dorsey.

In two areas—one consisting of a triangle formed by Mack, Gratiot, and E. Grand Boulevard, the other surrounding Southeastern High School—firing began shortly after 10:00 P.M. and continued for several hours.

In the first of the areas, a 22-year-old Negro complained that he had been shot at by snipers. Later, a half dozen civilians and one National Guardsman were wounded by shots of undetermined origin.

Henry Denson, a passenger in a car, was shot and killed when the vehicle's driver, either by accident or intent, failed to heed a warning to halt at a National Guard roadblock.

Similar incidents occurred in the vicinity of Southeastern High School, one of the National Guard staging areas. As early as 10:20 P.M., the area was reported to be under sniper fire. Around midnight there were two incidents, the sequence of which remains in doubt.

Shortly before midnight, Ronald Powell, who lived three blocks east of the high school and whose wife was, momentarily, expecting a baby, asked the four friends with whom he had been spending the evening to take him home. He, together with Edward Blackshear, Charles Glover, and John Leroy climbed into Charles Dunson's station wagon for the short drive. Some of the five may have been drinking, but none was intoxicated.

To the north of the high school, they were halted at a National Guard roadblock, and told they would have to detour around the school and a fire station at Mack and St. Jean Streets because of the firing that had been occurring. Following orders, they took a circuitous route and approached Powell's home from the south.

On Lycaste Street, between Charlevoix and Goethe, they saw a jeep sitting at the curb. Believing it to be another roadblock, they slowed down. Simultaneously a shot rang out. A National Guardsmen fell, hit in the ankle.

Other National Guardsmen at the scene thought the shot had come from the station wagon. Shot after shot was directed against the vehicle, at least 17 of them finding their mark. All five occupants were injured, John Leroy fatally.

At approximately the same time, firemen, police, and National Guardsmen at the corner of Mack and St. Jean Streets, 2½ blocks away, again came under fire from what they believed were rooftop snipers to the southeast, the direction of Charlevoix and Lycaste. The police and guardsmen responded with a hail of fire.

When the shooting ceased, Carl Smith, a young firefighter, lay dead. An autopsy determined that the shot had been fired at street level, and, according to police, probably had come from the southeast.

At 4:00 A.M., when paratroopers, under the command of Col. A. R. Bolling, arrived at the high school, the area was so dark and still that the colonel thought, at first, that he had come to the wrong place. Investigating, he discovered National Guard troops, claiming they were pinned down by sniper fire, crouched behind the walls of the darkened building.

The colonel immediately ordered all of the lights in the building turned on and his troops to show themselves as conspicuously as possible. In the apartment house across the street, nearly every window had been shot out, and the walls were pockmarked with bullet holes. The colonel went into the building and began talking to the residents, many of whom had spent the night huddled on the floor. He assured them no more shots would be fired.

According to Lieutenant General Throckmorton and Colonel Bolling, the city, at this time, was saturated with fear. The National Guardsmen were afraid, the residents were afraid, and the police were afraid. Numerous persons, the majority of them Negroes, were being injured by gunshots of undetermined origin. The general and his staff felt that the major task of the troops was to reduce the fear and restore an air of normalcy.

In order to accomplish this, every effort was made to establish contact and rapport between the troops and the residents. Troopers—20 percent of whom were Negro—began helping to clean up the streets, collect garbage, and trace persons who had disappeared in the confusion. Residents in the neighborhoods responded with soup and sandwiches for the troops. In areas where the National Guard tried to establish rapport with the citizens, there was a similar response.

Within hours after the arrival of the paratroops, the area occupied by them was the quietest in the city, bearing out General Throckmorton's view that the key to quelling a disorder is to saturate an area with "calm, determined, and hardened professional soldiers." Loaded weapons, he believes, are unnecessary. Troopers had strict orders not to fire unless they could see the specific person at whom they were aiming. Mass fire was forbidden.

During five days in the city, 2,700 Army troops expended only 201 rounds of ammunition, almost all during the first few hours, after which even stricter fire discipline was enforced. (In contrast, New Jersey National Guardsmen and state police expended 13,326 rounds of ammunition in three days in Newark.) Hundreds of reports of sniper fire—most of them false—continued to pour into police headquarters; the Army logged only 10. No paratrooper was injured by a gunshot. Only one person was hit by a shot fired by a trooper. He was a young Negro who was killed when he ran into the line of fire as a trooper, aiding police in a raid on an apartment, aimed at a person believed to be a sniper.

General Throckmorton ordered the weapons of all military personnel unloaded, but either the order failed to reach many National Guardsmen, or else it was disobeyed.

Even as the general was requesting the city to relight the streets,

Guardsmen continued shooting out the lights, and there were reports of dozens of shots being fired to dispatch one light. At one such location, as Guardsmen were shooting out the street lights, a radio newscaster reported himself to be pinned down by "sniper fire."

On the same day that the general was attempting to restore normalcy by ordering street barricades taken down, Guardsmen on one street were not only, in broad daylight, ordering people off the street, but off their porches and away from the windows. Two persons who failed to respond to the order quickly enough were shot, one of them fatally.

The general himself reported an incident of a Guardsman "firing across the bow" of an automobile that was approaching a roadblock.

As in Los Angeles 2 years earlier, roadblocks that were ill-lighted and ill-defined—often consisting of no more than a trash barrel or similar object with Guardsmen standing nearby—proved a continuous hazard to motorists. At one such roadblock, National Guard Sgt. Larry Post, standing in the street, was caught in a sudden crossfire as his fellow Guardsmen opened up on a vehicle. He was the only soldier killed in the riot.

With persons of every description arming themselves, and guns being fired accidentally or on the vaguest pretext all over the city, it became more and more impossible to tell who was shooting at whom. Some firemen began carrying guns. One accidentally shot and wounded a fellow fireman. Another injured himself.

The chaos of a riot, and the difficulties faced by police officers, are demonstrated by an incident that occurred at 2:00 A.M., Tuesday.

A unit of 12 officers received a call to guard firemen from snipers. When they arrived at the corner of Vicksburg and Linwood in the 12th Street area, the intersection was well-lighted by the flames completely enveloping one building. Sniper fire was directed at the officers from an alley to the north, and gun flashes were observed in two buildings.

As the officers advanced on the two buildings, Patrolman Johnie Hamilton fired several rounds from his machinegun. Thereupon, the officers were suddenly subjected to fire from a new direction, the east. Hamilton, struck by four bullets, fell, critically injured, in the intersection. As two officers ran to his aid, they too were hit.

By this time other units of the Detroit Police Department, state police, and National Guard had arrived on the scene, and the area was covered with a hail of gunfire.

In the confusion the snipers who had initiated the shooting escaped.

At 9:15 P.M., Tuesday, July 25, 38-year-old Jack Sydnor, a Negro, came home drunk. Taking out his pistol, he fired one shot into an alley. A few minutes later, the police arrived. As his common-law wife took refuge in a closet, Sydnor waited, gun in hand, while the police forced open the door. Patrolman Roger Poike, the first to enter, was shot by Sydnor. Although critically injured, the officer managed to get off six shots in return. Police within the building and on the street then poured a hail of fire into the apartment. When the shooting ceased, Sydnor's body, riddled by the gunfire, was found lying on the ground outside a window.

Nearby, a state police officer and a Negro youth were struck and seriously injured by stray bullets. As in other cases where the origin of the shots was not immediately determinable, police reported them as "shot by sniper."

Reports of "heavy sniper fire" poured into police headquarters from the two blocks surrounding the apartment house where the battle with Jack Sydnor had taken place. National Guard troops with two tanks were dispatched to help flush out the snipers.

Shots continued to be heard throughout the neighborhood. At approximately midnight—there are discrepancies as to the precise time—a machinegunner on a tank, startled by several shots, asked the assistant gunner where the shots were coming from. The assistant gunner pointed toward a flash in the window of an apartment house from which there had been earlier reports of sniping.

The machinegunner opened fire. As the slugs ripped through the window and walls of the apartment, they nearly severed the arm of 21-year-old Valerie Hood. Her 4-year-old niece, Tonya Blanding, toppled dead, a .50-caliber bullet hole in her chest.

A few seconds earlier, 19-year-old Bill Hood, standing in the window, had lighted a cigarette.

Down the street, a bystander was critically injured by a stray bullet. Simultaneously, the John C. Lodge Freeway, two blocks away, was reported to be under sniper fire. Tanks and National Guard troops were sent to investigate. At the Harlan House Motel, 10 blocks from where Tonya Blanding had died a short time earlier, Mrs. Helen Hall, a 51-year-old white businesswoman, opened the drapes of her fourth floor hall window. Calling out to other guests, she exclaimed: "Look at the tanks!"

She died seconds later as bullets began to slam into the building. As the firing ceased, a 19-year-old Marine, carrying a Springfield rifle, burst into the building. When, accidentally, he pushed the rifle barrel through a window, firing commenced anew. A police investigation showed that the Marine, who had just decided to "help out" the law enforcement personnel, was not involved in the death of Mrs. Hall.

R. R., a white 27-year-old coin dealer, was the owner of an expensive, three-story house on L Street, an integrated middle-class neighborhood. In May of 1966, he and his wife and child had moved to New York and had rented the house to two young men. After several months, he had begun to have problems with his tenants. On one occasion, he reported to his attorney that he had been threatened by them.

In March of 1967, R. R. instituted eviction proceedings. These were still pending when the riot broke out. Concerned about the house, R. R. decided to fly to Detroit. When he arrived at the house on Wednesday, July 26, he discovered the tenants were not at home.

He then called his attorney, who advised him to take physical possession of the house and, for legal purposes, to take witnesses along.

Together with his 17-year-old brother and another white youth, R. R went to the house, entered, and began changing the locks on the doors. For protection they brought a .22 caliber rifle, which R. R.'s brother took into the cellar and fired into a pillow in order to test it.

Shortly after 8 P.M., R. R. called his attorney to advise him that the tenants had returned, and he had refused to admit them. Thereupon, R. R. alleged, the tenants had threatened to obtain the help of the National Guard. The attorney relates that he was not particularly concerned. He told R. R. that if the National Guard did appear he should have the officer in charge call him (the attorney).

At approximately the same time, the National Guard claims it received information to the effect that several men had evicted the legal occupants of the house, and intended to start sniping after dark.

A National Guard column was dispatched to the scene. Shortly after 9:00 P.M., in the half-light of dusk, the column of approximately 30 men surrounded the house. A tank took position on a lawn across the street. The captain commanding the column placed in front of the house an explosive device similar to a firecracker. After setting this off in order to draw the attention of the occupants to the presence of the column, he called for them to come out of the house. No attempt was made to verify the truth or falsehood of the allegations regarding snipers.

When the captain received no reply from the house, he began counting to 10. As he was counting, he said, he heard a shot, the origin of which he could not determine. A few seconds later, he heard another shot and saw a "fire streak" coming from an upstairs window. He thereupon gave the order to fire.

According to the three young men, they were on the second floor of the house and completely bewildered by the barrage of fire that was unleashed against it. As hundreds of bullets crashed through the first- and second-story windows and richocheted off the walls, they dashed to the third floor. Protected by a large chimney, they huddled in a closet until, during a lull in the firing, they were able to wave an item of clothing out of the window as a sign of surrender. They were arrested as snipers.

The firing from rifles and machine guns had been so intense that in a period of a few minutes it inflicted an estimated $10,000 worth of damage. One of a pair of stone columns was shot nearly in half.

Jailed at the 10th precinct station sometime Wednesday night, R. R. and his two companions were taken from their cell to an "alley court," police slang for an unlawful attempt to make prisoners confess. A police officer, who was resigned from the force, allegedly administered such a severe beating to R. R. that the bruises were visible 2 weeks later.

R. R.'s 17-year-old brother had his skull cracked open, and was thrown back into the cell. He was taken to a hospital only when other arrestees complained that he was bleeding to death.

At the preliminary hearing 12 days later, the prosecution presented only one witness, the National Guard captain who had given the order to fire. The police officer who had signed the original complaint was not asked to take the stand. The charges against all three of the young men were dismissed.

Nevertheless, the morning after the original incident, a major metropolitan newspaper in another section of the country composed the following banner story from wire service reports:

DETROIT, *July 27 (Thursday)*.—Two National Guard tanks ripped a sniper's haven with machine guns Wednesday night and flushed out three shaggy-haired white youths. Snipers attacked a guard command post and Detroit's racial riot set a modern record for bloodshed. The death toll soared to 36, topping the Watts bloodbath of 1966 in which 35 died and making Detroit's insurrection the most deadly racial riot in modern U.S. history. . . .

In the attack on the sniper's nest, the Guardsmen poured hundreds of rounds of .50 caliber machine gun fire into the home, which authorities said housed arms and ammunition used by West Side sniper squads.

Guardsmen recovered guns and ammunition. A reporter with the troopers said the house, a neat brick home in a neighborhood of $20,000 to $50,000 homes, was torn apart by the machine gun and rifle fire.

Sniper fire crackled from the home as the Guard unit approached. It was one of the first verified reports of sniping by whites. . . .

A pile of loot taken from riot-ruined stores was recovered from the sniper's haven, located ten blocks from the heart of the 200-square block riot zone.

Guardsmen said the house had been identified as a storehouse of arms and ammunition for snipers. Its arsenal was regarded as an indication that the sniping—or at least some of it—was organized.

As hundreds of arrestees were brought into the 10th precinct station, officers took it upon themselves to carry on investigations and to attempt to extract confessions. Dozens of charges of police brutality emanated from the station as prisoners were brought in uninjured but later had to be taken to the hospital.

In the absence of the precinct commander, who had transferred his headquarters to the riot command post at a nearby hospital, discipline vanished. Prisoners who requested that they be permitted to notify someone of their arrest were almost invariably told that: "The telephones are out of order." Congressman Conyers and State Representative Del Rio, who went to the station hoping to coordinate with the police the establishing of a community patrol, were so upset by what they saw that they changed their minds and gave up on the project.

A young woman, brought into the station, was told to strip. After she had done so, and while an officer took pictures with a Polaroid camera, another officer came up to her and began fondling her. The negative of one of the pictures, fished out of a wastebasket, subsequently was turned over to the mayor's office.

Citing the sniper danger, officers throughout the department had taken off their bright metal badges. They also had taped over the license plates and the numbers of the police cars. Identification of individual officers became virtually impossible.

On a number of occasions officers fired at fleeing looters, then made little attempt to determine whether their shots had hit anyone. Later some of the persons were discovered dead or injured in the street.

In one such case police and National Guardsmen were interrogating a youth suspected of arson when, according to officers, he attempted to escape. As he vaulted over the hood of an automobile, an officer fired his shotgun. The youth disappeared on the other side of the car. Without making an investigation, the officers and Guardsmen returned to their car and drove off.

When nearby residents called police, another squad car arrived to pick up the body. Despite the fact that an autopsy disclosed the youth had been killed by five shotgun pellets, only a cursory investigation was made, and the death was attributed to "sniper fire." No police officer at the scene during the shooting filed a report.

Not until a Detroit newspaper editor presented to the police the statements of several witnesses claiming that the youth had been shot by police after he had been told to run did the department launch an investigation. Not until 3 weeks after the shooting did an officer come forward to identify himself as the one who had fired the fatal shot.

Citing conflicts in the testimony of the score of witnesses, the Detroit Prosecutor's office declined to press charges.

Prosecution is proceeding in the case of three youths in whose shotgun deaths law enforcement personnel were implicated following a report that snipers were firing from the Algiers Motel. In fact, there is little evidence that anyone fired from inside the building. Two witnesses say that they had seen a man, standing outside of the motel, fire two shots from a rifle. The interrogation of other persons revealed that law enforcement personnel then shot out one or more street lights. Police patrols responded to the shots. An attack was launched on the motel.

The picture is further complicated by the fact that this incident occurred at roughly the same time that the National Guard was directing fire at the apartment house in which Tonya Blanding was killed. The apartment house was only six blocks distant from and in a direct line with the motel.

The killings occurred when officers began on-the-spot questioning of the occupants of the motel in an effort to discover weapons used in the "sniping." Several of those questioned reportedly were beaten. One was a Negro ex-paratrooper who had only recently been honorably discharged, and had gone to Detroit to look for a job.

Although by late Tuesday looting and fire-bombing had virtually ceased, between 7:00 and 11:00 P.M. that night there were 444 reports of incidents. Most were reports of sniper fire.

During the daylight hours of July 26, there were 534 such reports. Between 8:30 and 11:00 P.M., there were 255. As they proliferated, the pressure on law enforcement officers to uncover the snipers became intense. Homes were broken into. Searches were made on the flimsiest of tips. A Detroit newspaper headline aptly proclaimed: "Everyone's Suspect in No Man's Land."

Before the arrest of a young woman IBM operator in the city assessor's office brought attention to the situation on Friday, July 28, any person with a gun in his home was liable to be picked up as a suspect.

Of the 27 persons charged with sniping, 22 had charges against them dismissed at preliminary hearings, and the charges against two others were dismissed later. One pleaded guilty to possession of an unregistered gun and was given a suspended sentence. Trials of two are pending.

In all, more than 7,200 persons were arrested. Almost 3,000 of these were picked up on the second day of the riot, and by midnight Monday 4,000 were incarcerated in makeshift jails. Some were kept as long as 30 hours on buses. Others spent days in an underground garage without toilet facilities. An uncounted number were people who had merely been unfortunate enough to be on the wrong street at the wrong time. Included were members of the press whose attempts to show their credentials had been ignored. Released later, they were chided for not having exhibited their identification at the time of their arrests.

The booking system proved incapable of adequately handling the large number of arrestees. People became lost for days in the maze of different detention facilities. Until the later stages, bail was set deliberately high, often at $10,000 or more. When it became apparent that this policy was unrealistic and unworkable, the prosecutor's office began releasing on low bail or on their own recognizance hundreds of those who had been picked up. Nevertheless, this fact was not publicized for fear of antagonizing those who had demanded a high-bail policy.

Of the 43 persons who were killed during the riot, 33 were Negro and 10 were white. Seventeen were looters, of whom two were white. Fifteen citizens (of whom four were white), one white National Guardsman, one white fireman, and one Negro private guard died as the result of gunshot wounds. Most of these deaths appear to have been accidental, but criminal homicide is suspected in some.

Two persons, including one fireman, died as a result of fallen powerlines. Two were burned to death. One was a drunken gunman; one an arson suspect. One white man was killed by a rioter. One police officer was felled by a shotgun blast when a gun, in the hands of another officer, accidentally discharged during a scuffle with a looter.

Action by police officers accounted for 20 and, very likely, 21 of the deaths; action by the National Guard for seven, and, very likely, nine; action by the Army for one. Two deaths were the result of action by storeowners. Four persons died accidentally. Rioters were responsible for two, and perhaps three of the deaths; a private guard for one. A white man is suspected of murdering a Negro youth. The perpetrator of one of the killings in the Algiers Motel remains unknown.

Damage estimates, originally set as high as $500 million, were quickly scaled down. The city assessor's office placed the loss—excluding business stock, private furnishings, and the buildings of churches and charitable institutions—at approximately $22 million. Insurance payments, according to the State Insurance Bureau, will come to about $32 million, representing an estimated 65 to 75 percent of the total loss.

By Thursday, July 27, most riot activity had ended. The paratroopers were removed from the city on Saturday. On Tuesday, August 1, the curfew was lifted and the National Guard moved out.

T. M. Tomlinson

The Development of a Riot Ideology among Urban Negroes

For the most part, the substance of this paper uses a data base provided by a study of the Los Angeles riot of 1965.[1] In that study a random probability sample of 585 Negro respondents residing in the 182 census tracts which made up the riot curfew area were interviewed by indigenous Negro interviewers. The interviewers were located, hired, and trained by the survey staff; they entered the field within two months after the riot and completed their task six months later. A sample of whites, similar in size and stratified by socioeconomic status and racial composition of the area (integrated and non-integrated) was gathered at the same time from areas outside of the curfew zone.

An omnibus interview schedule was used which covered mainly social-

1. The survey was carried out by several members of the sociology and psychology faculty at U.C.L.A., but the data reported here stem mainly from reports prepared by Vincent Jeffries, Richard Morris, David O. Sears, and T. M. Tomlinson. Copies of the reports may be obtained by writing to the project coordinator, Nathan Cohen, Institute of Government and Public Affairs, University of California, Los Angeles.

economic-political issues and riot participation and evaluation. The interviews were generally long, usually requiring upwards of two hours for completion. Respondent cooperation was very good, and interviews were seldom halted for reasons of attention or cooperation lag. The coded data were analyzed by conventional cross-tabulation and statistical techniques (chi square) in the computer facilities available at U.C.L.A.

Although the conclusions of this paper are based on data drawn principally from the Los Angeles riot survey, it should be kept in mind that the sense of those data are essentially duplicated by several other riot studies, most notably the one following the Detroit riot of last summer, 1967.[2] Thus the generalizations which follow will describe a set of conditions that exists in most Northern centers.

SOME CONCLUSIONS FROM THE LOS ANGELES STUDY

In describing the results of the Los Angeles study, it is appropriate to begin by dispelling some myths that persist in the minds of many whites, a large number of public officials, and some Negroes.

1. It is a myth that only a tiny fraction (3% to 5%) of the Negroes living in the riot zone(s) participated in the riots. The best estimates indicate that upwards of 15% of the people interviewed in Los Angeles (and Detroit) claim to have participated actively in the riot. Measures of participation were made from a number of direct and indirect angles, and each time the rate was about the same.
2. It is a myth that an overwhelming majority of the Negro community disapproves of those who supported the riots. At least 34%, and perhaps as high as 50%, express a sympathetic understanding of the views of the supporters.
3. It is a myth that most of the Negro community views the riot as a haphazard, meaningless event whose thrust was a disregard for law and order. On the contrary, 62% saw it as a Negro protest, 56% thought it had a purpose, and 38% described the riot in revolutionary rhetoric (revolt, insurrection, revolution). And it was a justifiable protest; 64% of the respondents who said it was a protest also said the victims deserved attack.
4. It is a myth that Negroes expect and are afraid of white retaliation and a decline in the quality of the relations between blacks and whites. Favorable effects were expected by 58% of the Negroes; unfavorable effects by only 18%.

In sum, participation in and support of riots in the Negro community

2. I am indebted to Phillip Meyer of Knight Publications (Detroit Free Press) and the Detroit Urban League for the materials from the Detroit riot study of 1967.

is by no means the position of a tiny minority of malcontents. The riot in the eyes of a large proportion of Negro citizens was a legitimate protest against the actions of whites, and the outcomes are expected to produce an improvement in the lot of Negroes and their relations with whites.

Departing from the context of mythology, two additional important points should be noted:

1. Of the 56% who claimed the riot had a purpose, each cited one or another of the following goals of the riot: (a) to call attention to Negro problems, (b) to express Negro hostility to whites, or (c) to serve an instrumental purpose of improving conditions, ending discrimination, or communicating with the "power structure." In all cases these responses give justification to the action, whether it be a release of pent-up frustration or simply making the point that injustice and inequality exists among Negroes in America. The riot has been assigned the purpose of letting whites know "how it is" for Negroes in this country.

2. The second point deals with the fear the events of the riot generated in a majority of the Negro citizens. No matter the justifications for the event, 71% of the sample expressed dismay about the burning, destruction, and killing. Louis Harris' riot survey also describes the stark terror in his respondents as they talked about the fires. Thus political purpose is involved in riots, but the response of the citizens is also one of fear following its events.

MILITANCE AND RIOT IDEOLOGY

Probing the data a bit deeper, an attempt was made to find out who was most likely to view the riot positively, to participate, and to expect a positive outcome. To this end the sample was divided into three parts based on the respondents' expressed sympathy with radical militant Negro organizations. Those who sympathized were called *militant,* those who were antagonistic were called *conservatives* (or more precisely, counter-radicals) and those who had no pro or con position were called *uncommitted.* Rather than describe each of these groups, this paper will concern itself with the characteristics of the militants compared to the non-militants. The data support the following conclusions:

1. Militants, those identified by their radical sympathies, make up 30% of the sample and are most often found among male youth. They are more likely to be brought up in an urban setting, somewhat better educated, relatively long-term residents of the city (over ten years), more involved in religion, and in possession of a more positive self-image. They are equally likely to be working and tend to be

more sophisticated politically than the non-militants. In short, they are the cream of urban Negro youth in particular and urban Negro citizens in general.[3]

2. Militants are the most deeply aggrieved and claim to have had higher rates of personal contact with the police under conditions usually described as police misbehavior.

3. They are more likely to view the communication media as unfair in their portrayal of Negro problems.

4. They are not markedly anti-white, but they are considerably more disenchanted with whites than the non-militants.

5. They are the most active politically and more likely to endorse the advancement of the Negro cause by any method necessary; they will endorse all conventional civil rights activity and in addition will lend disproportionate approval to use of violent means. Three times as many militants (30%) as non-militants endorse the use of violence as a legitimate last resort.

6. In describing the riot, the militants are more likely to use a term from the revolutionary lexicon than the non-militants. By a ratio of almost 2 to 1 they claim to have participated actively in the riot. They were much more favorable to the riot and its events than the non-militants, and project that view onto the community at large by claiming larger rates of community support for the riot. They are more hopeful of positive change in race relationships (which under-cuts the notion that they are clearly antagonistic to whites, i.e., they look for and apparently desire an improvement in Negro-white relations).

7. Finally the militants place the responsibility for change clearly in the laps of the whites. The non-militants tend to take the view that both races must change to achieve rapprochement, but the militants clearly ascribe the locus of change to whites.

Now where does this take us? In the first place, it must be continuously kept in mind that the differences between militants and non-militants are those of proportions; more militants feel this way than non-militants. It does not mean that only militants feel this way. A majority of the entire Negro population is aggrieved, angry and disaffected. For example, compared to whites in the Los Angeles study, there are dramatic differences in the level of trust of elected officials and police by Negroes. Negroes express far higher rates of perceived political disenfranchisement and impotence to bring about change. At the same time, however, they appear to be deeply committed to bringing about change. The picture therefore is one of intense political concern combined with felt impotence to exert influence on the political structure, and that is a cornerstone of social unrest.

3. These conclusions are similar to those of Gary Marx, 1967.

Thus the climate which fosters riots is endemic in American society and in the Northern urban centers particularly. The Los Angeles riot took the lid off by disinhibiting a riot response to the conditions of Negro life that had always existed. The response of the Negro ghetto residents suggests that a sufficient proportion of them view the riot as a justifiable protest form to account for the absence of counter-riot behavior on the part of the Negro community. What then are the implications of these data for the future of urban violence in America?

It would seem that a sort of simplified riot ideology has taken form, and riots today have assumed the shape of a popular movement. Support, or at least sympathetic understanding, of the purpose of riots characterizes a large segment of the Negro population. Within this segment are imbedded a group of sophisticated, activist young people who have provided the riot with political interpretations of purpose. They have created a riot ideology, and this ideology has infected the thinking of other less sophisticated but equally disaffected individuals. It should be emphasized that this is not a description of a conspiracy. It is a description of a portion of the population that for a variety of historical and current reasons are susceptible to the idea of violent protest. That idea emerged in its clearest form in the aftermath of the Los Angeles riot and has been blown across the country on the winds of pervasive Negro discontent.

The creation of a riot ideology has a number of implications for this society. In the first place, it does not allow one to cite the actions of "agents provocateurs" in accounting for the occurrence of a riot, unless one is willing to call the mood of the people by that name. Second, and most important, it implies that nothing can be done to stem the tide of urban disorders until they run their course. There are no immediate responses within the repertoire of any agency or person which are sufficient to expunge the outrage that gives birth to Negro violence, except the Negroes' own fear of the burning and killing, and that comes only after the riot has occurred.

Now it may appear that this is an unnecessarily pessimistic position (assuming the foregoing is interpreted as being pessimistic), or perhaps it appears that other equally plausible, but less stark, views of the underpinnings of urban riots have been overlooked. Let us examine some of the other possibilities.

Riots have occurred in cities with every type of administrative structure. They have occurred in model cities; indeed Detroit was a well known "model city." They have occurred in cities receiving relatively large sums of poverty money, and ones receiving relatively small amounts. They have occurred in cities with compact ghetto enclaves and in cities in which the ghetto was distributed over a large area. They have occurred in cities with relatively high Negro employment and wage rates (Detroit) and in cities with relatively low rates (Watts). They have occurred in cities with relatively large proportions of Negroes and cities with relatively low proportions.[4]

Clearly what produces riots is not related to the political or economic differences between cities. What produces riots is the shared agreement by most Negro Americans that their lot in life is unacceptable, coupled with the view by a significant minority that riots are a legitimate and productive mode of protest. What is unacceptable about Negro life does not vary much from city to city, and the differences in Negro life from city to city are irrelevant. The unifying feature is the consensus that Negroes have been misused by whites, and this perception exists in every city in America.

Thus it is the thesis of this paper that urban riots in the North will continue until the well of available cities runs dry. They will continue because the mood of many Negroes in the urban North demands them, because there is a quasi-political ideology which justifies them, and because there is no presently effective deterrent or antidote.

DETERRENTS AND ANTIDOTES

There are a number of approaches to riot control, none of which, if the thesis of this paper is correct, will serve to foreclose the occurrence of

---

4. They have not occurred in the modern South or in cities with Negro mayors. The data aren't in on the latter category yet, but they may provide a clue about the necessary change in the political structure, i.e., the assumption of political power by Negroes may be necessary to foreclose riots. Time will tell.

Two things operate to maintain calm in the South: a history of repression and high out-migration of young Negroes. What this means is that there is a low frequency of the population which is most susceptible to the riot mood of the Northern Negro. Such of that mood as exists takes form in a context which has traditionally and violently inhibited its expression.

There is, however, one important characteristic of Northern cities which serves to distinguish them from those in the South; they have received the influx of Negroes who have migrated out of the South and now live in the urban ghettos of the North. But the data from the riot surveys lend no credence to the notion that riots are a product of recent migrants from the South who have failed to adjust to city ways or who have brought traditions of violence. Quite the contrary, the average rioter has lived ten years or more in the city of his choice. As Williams (1967) has pointed out, the riot data do however support the hypothesis that rioters are typical second-generation youth. Traditional behavior by other migrant groups has seen crime rates of the first generation holding at the rate of the country of origin, but sharply increasing with the second generation. About one generation of "new" Negroes exists in this country. By "new" I mean the generation which has seen the development of the Negro drive for equality. We are now faced with the second generation who, unlike their parents, are unwilling to settle for the luxury of being an American and the token gestures of gradualism. And so instead of, or perhaps in addition to, high crime rates, we see high riot rates, and the participants are most likely to be those late teen and early twenties youth who are the second-generation offspring of those migrants from the South. But discontented youth per se are not the cause of riots, nor do they account for all Negroes who are discontented.

popular riots. Nevertheless it is worth discussing some of these approaches simply to buttress the assertion that even if something could be done, nothing will be.

Taking non-repressive methods first, where does the War on Poverty fit into all of this? The answer at present is nowhere. Congress, reflecting the attitudes of whites in this country, has already made it clear that it is not interested in using the poverty program to ameliorate, not to mention remove, the causes of urban violence. It recently appropriated a mere 1.733 billion dollars for the poverty program, and that only after a long and desperate fight by the proponents of the program. Little has been said by the political leaders of this country which would indicate both an awareness of the social causes of riots and a receptive position to costly but nonrepressive methods of riot control. Quite the contrary, the public position of the Administration is that riots, for whatever reason or whatever legitimate grievance, will not be tolerated. But this position simply reflects the position of the bulk of white Americans, and represents an awareness by the country's leaders that it is impolitic to suggest that whites be prepared to make a personal sacrifice to remove the conditions of Negro life that generate a riot response.

The problem of white reaction must also be faced by any investigative body appointed by the Administration, in this particular case the National Advisory Commission on Civil Disorders. Advisory commissions are appointed by the President (or in a given state by a Governor), and their recommendations, so far as they are taken seriously, require the support and advocacy of the appointing figure. When the issue is explosive and when the truth is unlikely to be palatable to the majority of the electorate, the commission is in a ticklish political position. Its recommendations must not offend the negatively disposed (white) majority or their elected representatives (Congress), because then the appointing leader (President or Governor) is placed in the embarrassing and impolitic position of having to support recommendations which almost surely will alienate him from a significant proportion of the electorate and the legislature. Thus the real disaster of the situation is that the Commission on Civil Disorders must be responsive to the political realities of the country. In this context it cannot deliver the full message if by doing so it stands to antagonize a substantial number of voters. The voters, directly or through their representatives, would reject both the recommendations and those who made them and support them—i.e., the recommendations would not be implemented, and of those who advocate them, the politically vulnerable would be turned out of office.

Thus it is inconceivable that politically sensitive appointed groups would be free to issue a report which had the potential to be violently unpopular among a majority of the citizenry. The Commission is bound by political considerations to make a statement which, from the viewpoint of practical politics, is both feasible and palatable. And when the issue is Negro behavior in the face of white racism, and when historically such commissions have dealt with this issue by making "half-a-loaf" recommendations, it seems unlikely that a full loaf will be requested by a politically sensitive body faced with overt white hostility to precisely the measures the Commission must advocate. Thus it seems implausible to expect the Civil Disorders Commission to recommend much beyond what it is feasible for the Administration to expect the country to tolerate.[5] The recommendations may go beyond others, e.g., the McCone report following the Los Angeles riot, but once again whites will be able to avoid a confrontation with the realities of Negro life and once again the Negro ghetto dweller will feel that he has been sold out. And if this analysis is correct and predictive, it will indeed be sad, because for the first time in the history of this country, a national body of powerful men has been given access to the full body of data, and they will have once again concluded that the data and the required response to that data are, for reasons of political security, too explosive to allow an official utterance which truly "tells it like it is."

What then is left? Restraints imposed by the Negro community on its brothers? Not likely in consideration of the mood among the Negro populace which justifies riots, and since the conditions which provide that justification will continue in the absence of the economic wherewithal to change them.

The police? They might, but even at best that will involve incredible cost in lives and property. Furthermore, it is already clear that counter-violence by the police, national guard, or any other agency of the public control exerts no deterrent effect; it helps to stop or control riots once they have ignited, but it does not apparently deter the impulse to ignition. It appears, however, that it is the police that the society is banking on. The police are the "patsies" for a country which seems to feel that it is cheaper to kill Negroes for burning and looting than it is to spend the money and create the climate which might produce a life situation which obviates these responses.

And so popular riots will continue and nothing of significant worth will have been done to relieve their causes. And because nothing is being done now to alter the situation, the future is bleak. Popular riots may run their course, but what will take place after they cease if the

5. At the time this paper was deing drafted (December, 1967), the Advisory Commission on Civil Disorders was engaged in behavior which was difficult to interpret except in terms of the half-a-loaf, classic-politics-of-compromise, thesis. For example, it seems at this date that an interim-report, part of which was entitled the "Harvest of American Racism," has been put aside. But by the time this paper is published the "facts" about the internal workings of the Commission will only be of historical concern (although the ramifications of its action may reverberate for some time to come). What will stand over time is the realization of the half-a-loaf argument, and that this investigative body, as others with political liabilities, will not have faced up to the hard reality of stating the truth about the racism embedded in the character of this country or the economic and attitudinal sacrifice that whites must make to restore the health of the society.

country decides against the necessary sacrifices now on behalf of the Negro ghetto dweller?

After the popular riots are over, probably in a few years, there will be a retrenchment by both blacks and whites. If at this point nothing is done by way of relieving the conditions which foster the riots, then it is entirely conceivable that politically-motivated black organizations, both public and clandestine, may indeed actively foment civil disturbance. Then there may well be the generation of formal revolutionary groups, whose cause, however futile, will be violent harassment, if not outright destruction of the urban centers, and with them the character of American society.

How can this be averted? A number of events occurring in concert might serve to reduce the possibilities of this outcome. Among them are the following:

Belatedly, and perhaps too late, *massive infusions of money and industrial resources into the ghetto*. White society simply must realize that this is essential for their own and the total society's welfare. They must realize that, if for no other reason, it is in their best long-range economic interests to make a relatively short-range financial sacrifice.

The unification of the street militant and the Negro middle class in the common cause of Negro development. This may or may not happen. If money is available to make it possible and justifiable for the Negro middle class and the militants to coalesce and to work toward a common goal, then the development of the entire Negro population toward equality and affluence may take place. But as of now, there is no reason for the two to combine forces, and even if they should want to (and the burgeoning ethnic character of the Negro movement united by the commonality of skin color suggests that such an event is possible) they have no point or purpose around which to unite except protest. Therefore the Negro must be given the chance to organize around economic and political projects that provide for the unification of the factions within the Negro community and allow all Negroes to pursue the constructive goals of political and economic power.

White society must demonstrate faith in the concept of Negro equality, i.e., that the whites are truly willing for the Negroes, as Negroes, to enter into a society which is black and white. Negroes have lost faith. They no longer believe that whites will allow them to take their place in this society regardless of what they might do by way of "proving themselves." For the Negro to stop rioting, he must first feel that honest and legitimate action will be sufficient to gain entry. Thus, the country must enact open housing laws, open its trade unions, provide equal access to the courts, and strike all the other overt and covert devices which serve to keep the Negro "in his place." The point of this is twofold: there is no place in a democracy for institutionalized discrimination, and there is no other way to restore the faith of the Negro

American in this quasi-democracy save by demonstrating to him that it is a true democracy worthy of his commitment. The Negro must believe it is worth his time to work and achieve. He must believe that the trappings of affluence will come as easily to him as they appear to come to most whites. He must be able to say to himself, "Nothing is keeping me here except the absence of my own industry." As it stands now, there are ample real justifications for erratic behavior and disaffection. The myths and stereotypes still exist in the minds of whites about the nature of the Negro American. Whites still justify their actions in terms of fanciful or superficial beliefs about Negro behavior. These beliefs are prevalent in white liberals, and they are endemic in the average citizen. Neither Negro behavior nor white attitudes will change until the Negro is given a true chance to develop his potential. And he will not have a true chance until the country decides to make available to him the climate and resources which lead to the outcome which we all presumably want. Self-help projects in the face of legal and extra-legal restraints are a lie. If the Negro is to do what whites evidently want him to do—namely, become like them—they must accept two facts: the Negro is black and will remain so, and self-help is a hypocritical sham if whites refuse to provide equal access to "their" society.

Raymond J. Murphy and James M. Watson

Ghetto Social Structure and Riot Support: The Role of White Contact, Social Distance, and Discrimination

Race riots in America in the late nineteenth century and the first half of the twentieth century were confrontations between groups of whites and Negroes. Unlike these "classical" American race riots, the urban riots of the 1960's have been actions of destruction and looting taken by Negroes *within* the ghetto.

It is this self-destructive character that lends justification to describing such acts of violence as revolts rather than as riots But this does not mean that racial factors have not been involved in the recent riots. In Los Angeles (as in other cities with recent riots), the selective nature of the burning and looting, especially in the riot's early stages, indicates that white merchants were a prime target. The verbal abuse of the police and the arrest that triggered the riot point to the police as another major target.

Undoubtedly, such revolts have their roots in the problems of poverty and discrimination that form the heritage of the American Negro. Research findings from the riots of the 1960's, however, indicate that these most obvious causes of unrest do not exhaust our understanding of the motivations of rioters, nor do many of the findings "make sense" in a purely economic or discrimination framework. Data from Detroit and Los Angeles, for example, indicate that the most active participants in riots in those cities were likely to be employed rather than unemployed. Little evidence exists that the rioters were newly arrived persons, uprooted in a cold hostile urban environment. Participants seem to represent the relatively well educated along with the illiterate and dropout populations. Support for violence seems to be far more widespread than the educated guesses of the social scientists or the observations of public officials would lead us to expect. It seems evident that many more questions will have to be asked and answered before we can understand the complexities of contemporary urban racial violence.

The present paper represents an attempt to raise questions concerning an area of long-standing sociological interest—the role of interracial contact in mitigating sentiments and acts of militance. Since the liberal stance of sociologists has affirmed and reaffirmed the utility and social value of interracial contact as an aid to understanding and a necessary ingredient in the reduction of prejudice, such an examination seems timely and worthwhile.

The sample of respondents upon which our analysis depends was selected as part of the Los Angeles Riot Study conducted at U.C.L.A. following the August riots in 1965. A total of 586 respondents were selected from the "Curfew Zone"—an area designated by Acting Governor Glenn Anderson in the aftermath of the rioting. This 46.5 square-mile area included not only the Negro ghetto in South Central Los Angeles, but surrounding areas of mixed racial populations as well. Respondents were selected on the basis of a probability sample of addresses in the designated area. Quota techniques permitted an age-sex distribution approximating that reported in the 1960 census tabulations.

A common assumption of those who have shown concern for reducing tensions between whites and Negroes in American society is that an increase in equalitarian interracial contacts will lead to a reduction in prejudice and outgroup hostility. This theme is particularly prominent in the sizeable literature on intergroup relations that was produced during the 1940's and 1950's. White liberals placed great hope on education and voluntary social contact as crucial factors in improving race relations. As Robin Williams noted:

"Contact brings friendliness." This is the extreme and unqualified phrasing of a general assumption manifest in a great many current activities . . . The great amount of effort currently devoted to arranging special occasions for intergroup association would hardly be expended except for the assumptions that (a) the experience changes behavior, and (b) there is a transfer of the changed behavior to other, more usual, types of situations (Williams, 1947, pp. 15–16. The bibliography in this source lists studies and articles dealing with intergroup relations).

Social scientists in the 1940's and 1950's studied in some detail the effects of interracial association on the reduction of prejudice. The extensive literature on this topic indicates that equal status contact is associated with relatively low anti-Negro prejudice among whites and, although less research has been done among Negro populations, the available literature suggests that equalitarian contact leads to a reduction in antiwhite prejudice as well (for a summary of the studies of the effects of equal-status contact on the attitudes of the white majority, see Wilner, Walkey, and Cook, 1955, esp. pp. 155-161. For an example of a study dealing with the attitudes of Negroes as affected by contacts with whites, see Works, 1961, pp. 47-52). One of the most comprehensive studies of this problem is that prepared at Cornell University by Robin Williams and his associates. Utilizing data derived from the white and Negro populations of four middle-size American cities, the authors investigated the role of social contact and social distance in the reduction of intergroup tensions and prejudice. After a review of the findings, Williams concludes:

We have seen that close interethnic contacts in the communities studied are relatively rare and that they tend to attract the less prejudiced on both sides. Within each ethnic grouping, there is associational inbreeding, both by reason of positive preferences and by reason of defensive withdrawal against feared outgroup relationships. But when there is repeated interethnic associations, the statistically dominant outcomes are relatively friendly interaction and reduced prejudice, at least in the context in which the interactions occur. We did find some exceptions, but the dominant uniformity is surely quite impressive and not at all to be taken for granted. (Williams *et al.*, 1964, pp. 215-216. For an additional discussion based on the same data, see Noel and Pinkney, 1964, pp. 609-622).

The researchers are careful to point out, however, that prejudice can best be reduced through conditions of contact which are truly equalitarian, which occur in a supportive normative environment, and when interaction is focused on common goals and interests.

If one accepts the proposition that equalitarian social contact with whites reduces antiwhite prejudice among Negroes, it seems to follow that persons with such contact will tend to display fewer sentiments of hostility against white institutions and symbols of white authority. Accordingly, we would expect those in our present sample who have experienced social contact with whites to be less active and supportive of the riot. Data from our larger study, however, showed no relationship between social contact and riot participation [1] or favorability.[2]

1. In order to measure the degree to which respondents in the sample were active in the riot two questions concerning riot participation were included in the interview guide. The more direct of these questions simply asked the respondent, "We are not interested in the details of what you actually did, but just generally, would you say that you were: very active, somewhat active, or not at all active?" The other less direct question asked the respondent whether or not he had personally witnessed such events as shooting, stones being thrown, looting of stores, stores being burned, and crowds of people.

A dichotomous measure of activity was constructed by classifying respondents as active if they reported themselves to be "very active" or "somewhat active" and as not active if they reported themselves to be "not at all active." Thus, activity, as operationally defined in this report, is entirely based on the single item which asks for a self-report of the respondents' participation in the riot.

Clearly, we cannot have complete assurance that the self-reported activity item is valid unless it can be supported by other measures of riot activity. It was for this reason that the less direct activity question was asked concerning what events the respondent had personally witnessed. This question was asked much later in the interview than was the self-reported activity item and was intended to be used as a check on the validity of the latter.

The results of correlating the two measures of activity are reassuring. Those who rate themselves as active are more likely to report having seen stones thrown, stores burned and looted, and crowds than are those who claimed to have been inactive. For example, 44% of those calling themselves "very or somewhat active" saw shooting while only 16% of those who said they were "not active" saw shooting; and again, 54% of the self-reported "active" saw stones being thrown as contrasted to 25% of the self-reported "inactive." Results for the other items concerning events witnessed showed similar magnitudes of difference between the self-reported active and inactive.

A further check on the validity of the self-reported activity measure was made possible because in addition to the probability sample employed in this study a sample of arrested persons was also interviewed with the same schedule and was asked the same questions about their activity in the riot. A comparison of probalility sample respondents with the arrestees that were interviewed should constitute a check on the validity of the self-participation measure of activity. Even if some of the arrestees were innocent of all involvement in the riot it is a fair presumption that the arrestees as a group were more involved and participated more than the probability sample who were selected by random procedures to represent the general population of the entire Los Angeles ghetto area.

The comparison of the probability sample with the arrestee sample leads further support to the self-reported activity measure of participation. Of most importance is the fact that 62% of the arrestees, as opposed to 22% of the probability sample respondents, reported that they were either "very" or "somewhat" active. It should also be pointed out that the items concerning events witnessed indicate large differences between the arrestees and the probability sample. Whereas only 20% of the probability sample saw shooting, close to half of the arrestees (48%) reported seeing shooting. Even larger differences resulted from comparisons on some of the other items. For example, 29% of the probability sample reported seeing stones thrown as contrasted with a full 67% of the arrestees claiming to have seen stones thrown.

It is axiomatic that no single item can hope to be a perfectly satisfactory measure of a complex social fact which involves many factors and facets. It appears, nevertheless, that the "self-reported participation" measure of activity described above can be counted on for the purposes of tabular analysis to yield a relatively stable and meaningful dichotomy.

2. The term "riot favorability" as used in this report designates the extent to which respondents approved or disapproved of the riot. Since the degree of approval which a person may feel about such a complex event as a riot is made up of many, sometimes contradictory, components, it was decided that the best way to tap the favorability dimension was by means of a series of open-ended questions.

One reason for this lack of relationship may be that social contact is a function of the socioeconomic level of the respondent, that is, persons in lower socioeconomic levels in the community have fewer social contacts with white persons. All of our measures of socioeconomic status and life style show that this is indeed the case. The strong relationship between socioeconomic level and social contact may thus confound the relationship between contact and riot participation and support. A more adequate test of the hypothesis that social contact reduces riot support would be provided by controlling for our various measures of socioeconomic level. We have done this and have presented all controls (except for education) in dichotomous form.[3] The relationship between social contact and each of our two measures of riot support has been re-examined and the results are presented in Tables 1 and 2. Table 1 shows that for each of our three socioeconomic controls (employment status, occupation and education), there is no significant relationship

---

Three items were designed to assess the degree of attitudinal support among the persons interviewed. The first of these asked: "Some people supported the riot-revolt-insurrection (the interviewer was instructed to use whatever term the respondent himself spontaneously chose) and others were against it. What were the main differences between the kinds of people who supported it and the kinds of people who were against it?" The second item asked more directly about the respondent's own personal feelings about the riot. It asked respondents to state: "What did you like about what was going on and what did you dislike about what was going on?" Finally, the third item asked for the most direct expression of personal feeling of any of the three questions. It asked: "Now that the (riot-revolt-insurrection) is over, how do you feel about what happened?"

Each of the three questions was coded in accordance with the same set of standard instructions. Coders were asked to rank individual responses in terms of both the content of the remarks made and the degree of affect that accompanied them on a five point scale ranging from "very favorable" through "neutral or ambivalent" to "very unfavorable." For example, if someone said he liked everything about the riot except that not enough stores had been burned, he was coded as 'very favorable." If the respondent said the riot had set the Negro back 100 years and that he deplored the burning and shooting, he was assigned to the "very unfavorable" category.

For codes involving riot favorability where coders were required to make judgments concerning degree of affect (i.e., the direction and degree of feeling implicit in the response), three coders made independent ratings of the same material. For each of the three codes concerning favorability the percentage of consistency among the coders' ratings was calculated and was found to be at least .95 or better. In those few cases of complete disagreement among the coders the coding supervisor was asked to make the final decision.

Since each of the three questions designed to measure "riot favorability" were positively related to each other they have been combined into an index of overall riot favorability. Numeric scores were assigned to each of the response categories so that a total score could be calculated for each individual by simply summing his scores on each of the individual items. The five categories of response were assigned the following values: 4 for "very favorable," 3 for "somewhat favorable," 2 for "ambivalent or neutral," 1 for "somewhat unfavorable," and 0 for "very unfavorable." The resulting distribution of total scores ranging from 0 to 12 was dichotomized, for the purposes of the present report, at the median. Respondents whose total score added to six or above were classified as "favorable"; respondents considered "unfavorable" were those whose scores added to five or below.

3. Occupations semiskilled and below were classified as "low," skilled and above as "high."

between participation in the riot and social contact with white persons. Table 2 indicates that there is no significant relationship between favorability toward the riot and social contact with whites when socioeconomic status level is controlled.

Table 1. Activity in Riot and Social Contact with Whites, Controlled for Employment Status, Occupation, and Education (in Percentages)

Riot Activity   EMPLOYMENT STATUS

		UNEMPLOYED		EMPLOYED	
		Social Contact	*No Social Contact*	*Social Contact*	*No Social Contact*
% Active		28.6%	33.7%	26.3%	20.2%
	N	70	86	137	129
		Gamma = −.12		Gamma = .17	
		$X^2 = 0.48$ 1df p $<$.50		$X^2 = 1.39$ 1df p $<$ .30	

OCCUPATIONAL LEVEL

		LOW OCCUPATION		HIGH OCCUPATION	
		Social Contact	*No Social Contact*	*Social Contact*	*No Social Contact*
% Active		24.7%	19.5%	24.5%	23.2%
	N	77	118	143	99
		Gamma = .15		Gamma = .03	
		$X^2 = 0.74$ 1df p $<$ .50		$X^2 = 0.05$ 1df p $<$ .95	

EDUCATIONAL LEVEL

	LESS THAN HIGH SCHOOL		HIGH SCHOOL		SOME COLLEGE	
	Social Contact	*No Social Contact*	*Social Contact*	*No Social Contact*	*Social Contact*	*No Social Contact*
% Active	24.1%	17.6%	25.9%	28.1%	21.4%	23.3%
N	83	131	85	96	70	43
	Gamma = .20		Gamma = −.06		Gamma = −.05	
	$X^2 = 1.35$ 1df p $<$ .30		$X^2 = 0.11$ 1df p $<$ .90		$X^2 = 0.05$ 1df p $<$ .95	

In Tables 3 and 4, the same relationships are examined, using two measures of life style; area of residence, and condition of home as controls.[4] Both tables show that social contact and riot support are unrelated.

4. In order systematically to study the internal structural differences within the Curfew Area, we divided the curfew zone into four homogeneous socioeconomic areas. This was done by ranking the 114 census tracts used for our sample fom high to low in terms of three variables—median education, median income, and percent white-collar workers as reported in the 1960 tract data for the Los Angeles Standard Metropolitan Statistical Area. These median figures and percentages were standardized and summed for each tract, giving equal weight to each of the three variables. The resultant array of tracts was then divided into quartiles, regardless of their geographical location within the curfew zone. The resultant distribution, however, displayed a clear geographical pattern.

Each interviewer was instructed to rate the household of each respondent by the degree of order and neatness as well as by the quality and condition of the interior furnishings. This technique was used to provide an additional measure of the socioeconomic level of the respondent, to give some indication of life style as a supplement to data on educational attainment and occupational level.

Table 2. *Favorability Toward Riot and Social Contact with Whites, Controlled for Employment Status, Occupation, and Education (in Percentages)*

Riot Favorability   EMPLOYMENT STATUS

	UNEMPLOYED		EMPLOYED	
	Social Contact	No Social Contact	Social Contact	No Social Contact
% Favorable	56.7%	52.6%	51.6%	55.5%
N	67	76	124	110
	Gamma = —.08		Gamma = .07	
	X² = 0.24 1df p < .70		X² = 0.35 1df p < .70	

OCCUPATIONAL LEVEL

	LOW OCCUPATION		HIGH OCCUPATION	
	Social Contact	No Social Contact	Social Contact	No Social Contact
% Favorable	56.5%	53.1%	52.3%	55.4%
N	69	98	128	83
	Gamma = —.07		Gamma = .06	
	X² = 0.20 1df p < .70		X² = 0.19 1df p < .70	

EDUCATIONAL LEVEL

	LESS THAN HIGH SCHOOL		HIGH SCHOOL		SOME COLLEGE	
	Social Contact	No Social Contact	Social Contact	No Social Contact	Social Contact	No Social Contact
% Favorable	48.7%	43.6%	52.6%	62.3%	53.2%	50.0%
N	78	117	76	77	62	38
	Gamma = —.10		Gamma = .20		Gamma = —.07	
	X² = 0.50 1df p < .50		X² = 1.46 1df p = .30		X² = 0.19 1df p < .70	

Therefore, we find no relationship between social contact with whites and participation in and favorability toward the riot when we employ our various measures of socioeconomic position and life style as controls. If riot support implies hostility toward whites, our data indicate that its magnitude is unaffected by contact with white persons.

Another, more direct, measure of attitude toward white persons is provided by a social distance item used in our study. This is an item which inquires whether or not the respondent would find it distasteful to go to a party where the majority of persons were white. We have treated this item as an indication of the desire for white contact. Williams and his associates used the same item as a measure of "negative feeling toward whites." (Williams, 1964, pp. 29-30.)

Data from our larger study indicate that social distance is significantly related to riot participation and favorability among our respondent. What we would like to know, however, is whether this significant relationship holds up when we control for our measures of socioeconomic level and life style. Does this relation exist for persons at all levels of the community structure, or is the social distance-riot support relationship a function of one's stratification position? Some evidence that social distance is class linked is provided by the Williams study:

Table 3. *Activity in Riot and Social Contact with Whites, Controlled for Area of Residence and Condition of Home (in Percentages)*

Activity		AREA OF RESIDENCE			
		LOW		HIGH	
		Social Contact	*No Social Contact*	*Social Contact*	*No Social Contact*
% Active		25.0%	21.1%	19.6%	25.3%
	N	124	166	92	83
		Gamma = .11		Gamma = −.16	
		$X^2 = 0.62$ ldf p $<$ .50		$X^2 = 0.83$ ldf p $<$.50	

Activity		CONDITION OF HOME			
		POOR		GOOD	
		Social Contact	*No Social Contact*	*Social Contact*	*No Social Contact*
% Active		28.0%	27.4%	19.8%	14.0%
	N	107	146	126	114
		Gamma = .02		Gamma = .21	
		$X^2 =0.01$ ldf p $<$.90		$X^2 = 1.42$ ldf p $<$ .30	

Table 4. *Favorability Toward Riot and Social Contact with Whites Controlled for Area of Residence and Condition of Home (in Percentages)*

Riot Favorability		AREA OF RESIDENCE			
		LOW		HIGH	
		Social Contact	*Social Contact No*	*Contact Social*	*No Social Contact*
% Favorable		55.8%	52.3%	40.5%	46.9%
	N	113	151	84	64
		Gamma = −.07		Gamma = .13	
		$X^2 = 0.31$ ldf p $<$ .70		$X^2 = 0.61$ ldf p $<$ .50	

Riot Favorability		CONDITION OF HOME			
		POOR		GOOD	
		Social Contact	*No Social Contact*	*Contact Social*	*No Social Contact*
% Favorable		53.0%	54.7%	49.5%	45.3%
	N	100	28	111	95
		Gamma = .03		Gamma = −.09	
		$X^2 = 0.06$ ldf p $<$ .80		$X^2 = 0.38$ ldf p $<$ .70	

The great reservoir of social-distance prejudice against whites is found among the uneducated Negroes who have no close social contacts with white persons. Such persons typically have been restricted to low-paid, low-prestige occupations. As a usual thing they have been brought up in segregated environments . . . Their experiences with white people have included instances of severe frustration, deprivation, insult, and hurt. They have been compelled to suppress or repress their aggressive reactions. They are often both fearful and resentful. In any event, they do not feel adequate to cope with hypothetical situations of close informal associations with whites. Bitter and withdrawn, they often look upon the prevailing prejudice and discrimination manifest among whites with an attitude of hopeless resentment. (Williams, 1964, pp. 292-293.)

Table 5 shows the relationship between social distance and riot participation with controls for each of our socioeconomic variables. For our data to be in support of Williams' position, we would have to find that those in low socioeconomic positions with high social distance responses would be most bitter and resentful toward whites and thus be most likely to have participated in the riot. Instead, we find that the highest levels of activity appear when high social distance is coupled with *high* socioeconomic position. In addition, Table 5 shows that the relationship between social distance and activity is significant only among those in the higher socioeconomic level. Table 6 shows the relationship between riot favorability and social distance with the same controls. Here, as contrasted with activity, we find that the socioeconomic controls do not differentiate either the magnitude of favorability or the strength of the relationship between negative feeling toward whites and riot

Table 5. Activity in Riot and Social Distance, Controlled for Employment Status, Occupation, and Education (in Percentages)

Riot Activity		EMPLOYMENT STATUS			
		UNEMPLOYED		EMPLOYED	
		Low Social Distance	*High Social Distance*	*Low Social Distance*	*High Social Distance*
% Active		28.0%	31.6%	20.2%	35.6%
	N	107	38	188	59
		Gamma = .09		Gamma = .37	
		$X^2 = 0.17$ 1df p $<$ .70		$X^2 = 5.84$ 1df p $<$ .02	

		OCCUPATIONAL LEVEL			
		LOW OCCUPATION		HIGH OCCUPATION	
		Low Social Distance	*High Social Distance*	*Low Social Distance*	*High Social Distance*
% Active		16.5%	27.3%	21.5%	37.7%
	N	139	44	172	53
		Gamma = .31		Gamma = .38	
		$X^2 = 2.49$ 1df p $<$ .20		$X^2 = 5.64$ 1df p $<$ .02	

		EDUCATIONAL LEVEL					
		LESS THAN HIGH SCHOOL		HIGH SCHOOL		SOME COLLEGE	
		Low Social Distance	*High Social Distance*	*Low Social Distance*	*High Social Distance*	*Low Social Distance*	*High Social Distance*
% Active		18.6%	14.3%	21.5%	41.7%	18.5%	44.4%
	N	145	49	135	36	81	27
		Gamma = −.16		Gamma = .45		Gamma = .56	
		$X^2 = 0.48$ 1df p $<$ .50		$X^2 = 6.06$ 1df p $<$ .02		$X^2 = 7.26$ 1df p $<$ .01	

Table 6. *Favorability Toward Riot and Social Distance, Controlled for Employment Status, Occupation, and Education (in Percentages)*

Favorability

EMPLOYMENT STATUS

	UNEMPLOYED		EMPLOYED	
	Social Low Distance	*High Social Distance*	*Low Social Distance*	*High Social Distance*
% Favorable	45.0%	77.1%	46.8%	73.5%
N	100	35	171	49
	Gamma = .61		Gamma = .52	
	X² = 10.76 1df p < .01		X² = 10.88 1df p < .001	

OCCUPATIONAL LEVEL

	LOW OCCUPATION		HIGH OCCUPATION	
	Low Social Distance	*High Social Distance*	*Low Social Distance*	*High Social Distance*
% Favorable	45.3%	73.2%	46.5%	75.0%
N	117	41	157	44
	Gamma = .53		Gamma = .55	
	X² = 9.46 1df p < .01		X² = 11.20 1df p < .001	

EDUCATIONAL LEVEL

	LESS THAN HIGH SCHOOL		HIGH SCHOOL		SOME COLLEGE	
	Low Social Distance	*High Social Distance*	*Low Social Distance*	*High Social Distance*	*Low Social Distance*	*High Social Distance*
% Favorable	38.2%	67.4%	48.7%	76.5%	43.6%	77.8%
N	131	46	115	34	78	18
	Gamma = .54		Gamma = .55		Gamma = .64	
	X²=11.71 1df p<.001		X² = 8.18 1df p < .01		X² = 6.84 1df p < .01	

favorability. In both low and high socioeconomic levels, we find significant differences between low and high social distance and support for the riot. We feel that the lack of structural differentiation in the case of favorability is due to the fact that this is an attitudinal rather than behavioral variable. Our data indicate that attitudinal support for the riot is widespread in the community and thus overrides any effects that structural differences may produce.

Thus our data do not support Williams' conclusion. Favorability is unrelated to socioeconomic level, and activity is significantly related to high social distance only in the higher (rather than lower) economic levels of our sample population.

Let us now consider our measures of life style. Table 7 shows that by far the greatest amount of activity is reported by those who enjoy higher life styles and have high social distance feelings. The relationship between social distance and activity is insignificant among those in the low areas and those with poor housing, but highly significant among those with higher life styles. Table 8 presents data on the relationship

Table 7. Activity in Riot and Social Distance, Controlled for
Area of Residence and Condition of Home (in Percentages)

Activity		AREA OF RESIDENCE			
		LOW		HIGH	
		Low Social Distance	*High Social Distance*	*Low Social Distance*	*High Social Distance*
% Active		19.5%	23.9%	18.0%	43.3%
	N	200	71	133	30
		Gamma = .13		Gamma = .55	
		X^2 = 0.63 1df p < .50		X^2 = 8.92 1df p < .01	

Activity		CONDITION OF HOME			
		POOR		GOOD	
		Low Social Distance	*High Social Distance*	*Low Social Distance*	*High Social Distance*
% Active		24.4%	26.6%	15.0%	32.5%
	N	180	64	173	40
		Gamma = .06		Gamma = .46	
		X^2 = 0.11 1df p < .80		X^2 = 6.63 1df p < .01	

Table 8. Favorability Toward Riot and Social Distance, Controlled for
Area of Residence and Condition of Home (in Percentages)

Favorability		AREA OF RESIDENCE			
		LOW		HIGH	
		Low Social Distance	*High Social Distance*	*Low Social Distance*	*High Social Distance*
% Favorable		45.0%	69.7%	36.1%	79.2%
	N	180	66	119	24
		Gamma = .48		Gamma = .74	
		X^2 = 11.79 1df p < .001		X^2 = 15.06 1df p < .001	

Favorability		CONDITION OF HOME			
		POOR		GOOD	
		Low Social Distance	*High Social Distance*	*Low Social Distance*	*High Social Distance*
% Favorable		44.4%	71.7%	41.9%	77.4%
	N	160	66	155	31
		Gamma = .52		Gamma = .65	
		X^2 = 13.02 1df p < .001		X^2 = 13.04 1df p < .001	

between social distance and favorability toward the riot, controlled for
life style. As with our controls for socioeconomic level, we find that in
both life style levels the relationship between favorability and social
distance is significant. This time, however, the relationship is stronger
in the higher area of residence and among those living in better-kept

homes. Among those expressing high social distance, 69.7% in the low area report support for the riot and in the high area, 79.2% are favorable.

Thus our findings, controlled for differences in life style, again contradict the conclusion of Williams that there is a close relationship between high social distance and latent hostility or aggressiveness against whites among the lower segments of the Negro community. If we can assume that a massive outburst of violence presents the opportunity for such resentment to be aired, then it appears from our data that this resentment is just as, or more, likely to find expression in riot participation by those who are better off than by those who are disadvantaged.

Indeed, we may hypothesize from our data that racial animosity is a prime factor in the motivations of persons in higher levels of the community to participate in and give support to violence against the symbols and institutions of the white-dominated society.

An indication of the pressures and psychological difficulties experienced by those Negroes who have achieved modest success and aspire to greater participation and acceptance by whites is indicated by Clark:

Middle-class Negroes do not generally react with the overt, active hostility prevalent in many members of the "working class," but they, too, are often hostile, in ways similar to the larger pattern of white middle-class competitiveness, yet complicated by the persistent problems of racial anxiety, hyper-sensitivity, and defensiveness . . . The middle-class Negro is demanding the right to share in the status symbols of personal success—quality education for his children; white collar, managerial, or executive jobs ;a fine home in one of the better neighborhoods. Having accepted the same value system which the middle-class whites live by, middle-class Negroes are forced to compete with them even at th risk o fconflict . . . That Negroes continue to seek to imitate the patterns of middle-class whites is a compliment, not the threat it may seem, but a compliment in large part undeserved, and the scars inflicted upon Negroes who are constantly confronted by the flight of those they encounter are deep and permanent. The wounded appear to eschew bitterness and hatred, but not far below the often genial, courteous surface lies a contempt that cannot easily be disguised (Clark, 1965, pp. 59-62).

Our data indicate that social distance is less closely related to riot participation and support among lower status Negroes than it is among those in the relatively higher levels of the ghetto community. We must therefore look to other factors as more salient in the motivations for violence among those in the lower segments of the social structure. James Q. Wilson, in his discussion of Negro politics, has suggested that the goals of Negroes can be classified analytically as "status goals" and "welfare goals." (On this distinction, see Wilson, 1960, Chapter 8.) The status goals of Negroes center around integration and greater mobility opportunities in the broader society. As such, Wilson indicates, they are most important to middle-class Negroes. Welfare goals, on the other hand, represent demands for an improvement in the day-to-day living conditions of persons in the ghetto—better teachers, more and better jobs, decent housing, hospitals in the community, etc. Such considerations are more salient to lower or working class Negroes. Accordingly, we might hypothesize that those lower in the social structure of the community were motivated to riot participation and support by factors indicative of economic hardship rather than by frustrations accompanying competition with whites for greater participation in the broader society. Although we do not have a direct measure of the salience of economic hardship as it was perceived by respondents, an indirect test of this hypothesis may be undertaken through the use of our measure of perceived discrimination. We feel that this is appropriate inasmuch as the majority of our respondents reported that jobs represented the type of discrimination most frequently experienced and those in low residential areas and with poorly kept homes had experienced significantly more discrimination than those who enjoyed higher life style.

Table 9 shows the relationship between perceived discrimination and

Table 9. Activity in Riot and Perceived Discrimination, Controlled for Area of Residence and Condition of Home (in Percentages)

Activity		AREA OF RESIDENCE			
		LOW		HIGH	
		Low Discrimination	*High Discrimination*	*Low Discrimination*	*High Discrimination*
% Active		15.5%	29.5%	25.2%	19.0%
	N	148	139	111	58
		Gamma = −.39		Gamma = .18	
		$X^2 = 8.06$ ldf p $< .01$		$X^2 = 0.84$ ldf p $< .80$	

Activity		CONDITION OF HOME			
		POOR		GOOD	
		Low Discrimination	*High Discrimination*	*Low Discrimination*	*High Discrimination*
% Active		23.7%	33.1%	16.4%	18.2%
	N	131	127	140	88
		Gamma = −.23		Gamma = −.06	
		$X^2 = 2.81$ ldf p $< .10$		$X^2 = 0.12$ ldf p $< .95$	

riot activity when controlled for area of residence and condition of home. This table shows that in the low areas of residence in the ghetto, those who perceive high discrimination report significantly more participation in the riot than do those who sense less discrimination. No significant relationship between discrimination and activity exists among those in the higher residential areas. Similarly, persons with high discrimination perception living in poorly kept homes are more likely to indicate participation in the riot than are those who feel less discrimination. Again, no relationship can be found between perceived discrimination and participation among those who live in well kept homes.

Table 10. Favorability Toward Riot and Pereceived Discrimination, Controlled for
Area of Residence and Condition of Home (in Percentages)

Favorability	AREA OF RESIDENCE			
	LOW		HIGH	
	Low Discrimination	High Discrimination	Low Discrimination	High Discrimination
% Favorable	40.3%	64.8%	30.9%	56.2%
N	139	122	94	48
	Gamma = .46		Gamma = .48	
	X^2 = 15.58 1df p < .001		X^2 = 8.58 1df p < .01	

Favorability	CONDITION OF HOME			
	POOR		GOOD	
	Low Discrimination	High Discrimination	Low Discrimination	High Discrimination
% Favorable	37.2%	66.4%	38.8%	59.2%
N	121	113	121	71
	Gamma = .54		Gamma = .39	
	X^2 = 19.92 1df p < .001		X^2 = 7.42 1df p < .01	

Table 10 presents data on the relationship between favorability toward the riot and perceived discrimination with the two controls for life style. We see that in both low and high life style groups, there is a significant relationship between perceived discrimination and favorability. In both levels, those perceiving higher discrimination are more likely to indicate a favorable reaction to the riot. In terms of the magnitude of support, however, we note that among those sensing high discrimination, persons in the low residential areas are somewhat more likely to indicate favorability (64.8%) than those living in higher residential areas (56.2%). The same pattern holds for condition of home: those perceiving high discrimination who live in poorly kept homes report greater support (66.4%) than those perceiving equally high discrimination living in well kept homes (59.2%). Thus, the evidence in these tables seems to uphold the hypothesis that riot support is associated with economic hardship.

Several findings stemming from our research require special emphasis. First, it is important to note that a high level of discontent seems to pervade the entire curfew community. This is particularly striking in the light of the often repeated refrain that problems of police brutality and exploitation by merchants are essentially confined to the poorer segments of the segregated community. Silberman, for example, argues that "squalid housing, a narrow range of job possibilities, frequent unemployment, low pay, exploitation (whether real or imagined) by landlords, shopkeepers, and employers, police brutality—these are the

grievances that animate the Negroes that live in the big city slums."
(Silberman, 1964, p. 138.)

We have found that these grievances are indeed salient for the
Negroes in Los Angeles and are related to support for the riot and
participation in it, but they are not limited to those who form the
"underclass" of the Negro community. Evidence of a class link is shown
only in perceived discrimination.

Second, we have presented indirect but compelling evidence that the
motivations of persons supporting the riot vary with their relative positions in the structure of the community. Those who are better off seem
to evidence considerable antiwhite sentiment which is significantly related to their participation in violence. Those less fortunate rebel against
discrimination and appear to be motivated mainly by economic discontent. Mistreatment or exploitation by whites (merchants and police)
seems to be a source of riot support for all levels in the ghetto. Such
evidence of differential motivation points to the hypothesis that the
more fortunate members of the community compare themselves with
the white majority and feel frustrated at their inability to gain benefits
in keeping with their status aspirations. Such persons have made social
and economic gains, but along with their mobility have gone rising
levels of expectation. We have seen that the amount of social contact
with whites increases with improvements in socioeconomic status. But
we have also seen that discontent increases as social contact increases.
We would expect that continued contact with white persons by those
Negroes who have made economic gains would serve to increase their
impatience and frustration at not being able to enjoy the same freedom
of movement and opportunity taken for granted by white persons in
their quest of "the American dream." We suspect that many white
persons have viewed the middle-class Negro group as a moderating influence in the racial struggle. The "better element," it is often argued,
will be responsible and orderly and understand the necessity for a
gradualist solution to the Negro problem. Furthermore, such sensible
and enlightened elements in the community will serve as models for
their less fortunate brothers.

We find little room for such an optimistic appraisal. If our analysis
is correct, the problems of urban life for the Negro, even in the palm-
lined spaciousness of Los Angeles, have grown acute and a significant
number of Negroes, successful or unsuccessful, are emotionally prepared
for violence as a strategy or solution to end the problems of segregation,
exploitation, and subordination.

PART II

Patterns in American Racial Violence

9

PATTERNS IN AMERICAN RACIAL VIOLENCE

Chapters 10 through 12 attempt to bring some kind of intellectual order out of the violent events previously described. For Chapter 10 I have chosen selections which have the modest goal of isolation of repeated patterns in American racial violence. In the first paper I have attempted to gain a perspective on patterns of violence in this country by comparing our racial violence with that which has begun to occur in Britain in the past decade. This is followed by two of my own papers on patterns in police behavior and on the ecology of rioting.

The chapter continues with selections dealing with the characteristics of those who get caught up in violent disorders. Akers and Fox analyzed the characteristics of rioters convicted and imprisoned after the 1943 Detroit riot. A chapter of the National Advisory Commission report was devoted to describing riot participants, as was a supplemental study undertaken by Fogelson and Hill for the Commission. These three selections are followed by another brief piece in which I try to untangle some of the conflicting views of black response to current disorders.

The final three selections include a piece by Weisberg on the interaction of law and law enforcement with violence related to civil rights activities, a summary of patterns of disorder discerned by the National Advisory Commission in its work, and a paper by Spiegel in which he attempts to delineate patterns in preconditions, chronologies, and aftermaths of riots.

Allen D. Grimshaw

Factors Contributing to Color Violence in the United States and Britain

Anthony Richmond, in a 1954 monograph, examined patterns of relations between West Indian Negroes in England and other English groups in an attempt to see whether a general theory of intergroup relations based on American experience could illuminate that of Britain (Richmond, 1954). He observed that different historical and cultural factors in the two countries might be expected to produce significant contrasts but felt that similar patterns appearing in different social contexts could provide more convincing confirmation of a general theory than further re-examination of American materials. The purpose of this paper is to carry such comparative study a step further, through examination of a particular variety of intergroup relations in the United States and England—relations culminating in social racial violence. There are marked differences between historical patterns of colored-white conflict in the two countries, particularly those differences generated by a briefer history of a much smaller (both in absolute and in relative size) colored community in Britain. Similarities confirming a general theory of racial conflict are, however, no less remarkable.

Violence is social when it is directed against an individual or his property solely or primarily because of his membership in a social category. Thus if a West Indian or West African in Britain or a white Anglo-Saxon Protestant in the United States is assaulted because he is a West Indian or a West African or an Anglo-Saxon Protestant, this is social violence. If, on the other hand, he is the random victim of armed robbery because he happens to be in the right place at the right time, or if his home or place of business is randomly vandalized, there is violence, but not social violence. Group violence against persons because of color, whether or not it is mutual, is particularly noticeable because of the saliency of the social characteristic involved and, in the United States, has been of great social cost.

Research on urban race riots in the United States resulted in two findings which are of relevance for general interpretations of intergroup relations (Grimshaw, 1959a and 1961. Both articles are reproduced in this volume.). The first is essentially confirmed by more limited English experience, the second cannot be tested with any assurance because of insufficient data. Both findings seem banal once stated; neither has been stated with sufficient emphasis in the research literature.

The first was that urban racial social violence in the United States has resulted not from conscious policy decisions of either the white or

254

the Negro group, but rather from reactions of the dominant group to real or perceived assaults upon the accommodative structure. There may have been occasional instances when whites, for political purposes, manufactured threats by Negroes against the *status quo* or where particularly militant members of the minority have espoused violence against whites as a tactical policy. In the large, however, when the Negro has "stayed in his place" Negro-white violence has been very rare. This has been true not only during the current century, with widespread urban rioting in northern states, but in all historical periods of Negro-white violence in the United States.

With the exception of a brief period after the Civil War, the pattern closely approximated the classic accommodative pattern of superordination-subordination, with the whites a continually dominant group. The most savage oppression, whether expressed in rural lynchings and pogroms or in urban race riots, has taken place when the Negro has refused to accept a subordinate status. The most intense conflict has resulted when the subordinate group has attempted to disrupt the *status quo* or when the superordinate group has defined the situation as one in which such an attempt is being made (and British experience confirms the American, that the reality of such an attempt is irrelevant, belief in it alone being sufficient to generate conflict). Conflict in Negro-white relations in the United States has been conflict generated by the breakdown of an essentially unstable accommodative pattern, essentially unstable because the subordinated group has refused to accept its status and has had increasing power with which to challenge it.

Two obvious differences between colored-white relationships in Britain and in the United States are suggested in the paragraph above. The first is that Britain, unlike the United States, has no history of a "color problem" of any magnitude prior to the First World War.[1] Britain's experience since then has been similar to that of the United States, but conflicts have occurred on a much smaller scale and the development of intergroup relationships, including patterns of prejudice and discrimination, has occurred at a different pace. The lack of a long tradition of conflict and violence in England has given the colored community a fund of goodwill and tolerance which, in the view of many American whites, never existed or was long ago exhausted by Negroes in America. The second difference, of course, is the much smaller size of the colored community in Britain. Even the highest estimate of the size of the group places its number at around 200,000—substantially

1. This is true in spite of occasional reports of disturbances in dockland areas or references to colored "gangs" at very early periods. Such instances were small in scope and affected a minimal proportion of England's white population.

In the years since this article was written (1961), the racial situation in Britain has continued to deteriorate. Recent attempts to legislate "bars" against immigration and even the encouragement of "repatriation" are apparently only the more public manifestations of fundamental stresses on British society. No attempt has been made to update this article, however, because it is the author's belief that the basic description and interpretation are still sound.

less than 1 per cent of the total population (see, among others, Wickenden, 1958 and Glass, 1960). The total nonwhite population of the United States (constituted largely of Negroes) is slightly over 10 per cent of the population and is probably close to 20,000,000. There are several cities in the United States with nonwhite populations greater than 200,-000, some with Negro populations larger than those of smaller African states. Colored people in the United States can, with increasing effectiveness, show the power necessary to challenge their subordinated status. Events of recent years, such as the nonviolent demonstrations of power in the Deep South, show the Negro population of the United States unwilling to wait for spontaneous concessions from the majority community. The colored community in Britain is too small and too weak to challenge the accommodative structure so sharply as to generate violence comparable to that which has occurred in the United States.

The second major finding of the research on American race riots was a reaffirmation of the importance of external forces of constraint in the determination of the occurrence or nonoccurrence of social violence. This conclusion is also obvious once stated, though perhaps less obvious from the perspective of events in Britain. British students of intergroup relations who have attempted to isolate the relationships among prejudice and discrimination and conflict have found the assertion that discriminatory behavior is merely the acting out of prejudiced attitudes to be, at best, an oversimplification. In the research on urban racial violence in the United States an attempt was made to analyze factors involved in the development of "violence-proneness" (see, e.g., Grimshaw, 1962a). In addition to a review of the many causal allegations about urban race riots, this required a careful examination of relationships among prejudice, discrimination, social tension and social violence. If the concepts of prejudice, discrimination, social tension and social violence represent real phenomena, it should be possible to state relationships among the variables which are so labelled. Relationships between prejudice and discrimination have frequently been stated and attempts have been made to isolate relationships between social tension and social violence. Systematizing of the interrelationships among all four phenomena simultaneously had not been done (an attempt to do this is made in Grimshaw, 1961, *op. cit.*). It was from such an attempt that this second major conclusion emerged.

. . . When social tension occurs it is not automatically followed by violence. Nor, on the other hand, is social violence always preceded by a period in which there is a gradual build-up of social tension. Readers will be familiar with instances where organizations with a monopoly of the legal use of force (police or the military) have prevented, by a firm stance, the eruption of violence between categories defined by social characteristics.[2]

2. This is the role claimed by Britain in the months of communal strife preceding independence in India and Pakistan.

British readers may be less familiar with instances in which the police, because of partisanship or inefficiency, have been unable to control violence.[3] They will also recall instances in which violence, perhaps spontaneously generated, quickly becomes social violence in the sense of this paper (for some illustrations see Grimshaw, 1961, *op. cit.*). The claim has been made that major racial violence in the United States has occurred only when the police have been corrupt, partisan, ineffective, or some combination of these three characteristics (such a claim fails to explain, of course, why violence has *not* occurred in some cities). The appearance of any of these characteristics, of course, is likely to be followed by the others. If the English constabulary is as stouthearted and honest as it is generally believed to be (by Americans, who must make comparisons with the frequently scandalous actions of their own police), large-scale racial violence is not likely to occur. It is not likely, however, that British police will be put to the test. Events of 1958 notwithstanding, there have been no major outbreaks of racial violence in England. Banton remarks, of the events in Nottingham and North Kensington, "The disturbances were widely described as 'race riots,' an expression which may cause people to overlook the fact that no one was killed and no one—apparently—severely disabled" (Banton, 1959). The small size of the colored community in Britain and its relatively great dispersion makes unlikely the occurrence of the widespread violence which characterized major riots in the United States (such as those of Chicago in 1919 and Detroit in 1943, in both of which several dozen persons were killed and hundreds injured).

. . . In this paper attention will be focused on factors which contribute to social tensions and to generally more moderate forms of social conflict, erupting only occasionally as social violence. Here there is a very high degree of comparability between British and American experience. The factors which have contributed to rising racial tensions in England have also been important in the creation of "violence-proneness" in the United States. Additional factors in the latter country, however, have received less attention in England and have been of less importance.

Causal analysis of social conflict and of social tensions underlying conflict can take place on three levels. In the most fundamental sense, all general historical trends; changes in intellectual *milieux;* changes in economic organization; changes in international relationships; urbanization and industrialization, have contributed to the development of social situations conducive to social conflict. A second variety of causal analysis, microsocial rather than macrosocial, involves the isolation and analysis of specific incidents which provide occasions for social disturbances. Given a sufficient level of social tension and/or a sufficiently low level

3. References to such cases appear with some frequency, however, in the *Summary of Press News and Comment,* published by the Institute of Race Relations until December 1960.

of efficiency in agencies of external control, any one of a variety of incidents can initiate conflict processes. Finally, a third set of factors consists of the characteristics of relations between conflicting groups; in which an opposing group is identified, in which accommodative relations are strained and in which there are gradual increases in social tension and violence-potential. In these sets of relationships there are marked similarities between American and English experience.

These factors vary in degree of specificity as to time and locale. They are commonly characterized by identification of opposing groups. They may be distinguished by the type of intergroup contact which they involve. Most notable, in both countries, are those areas of interaction where contact is direct and assault upon the *status quo* therefore most noticeable. While smaller numbers of whites have been involved in Britain than in the United States, direct contacts between white and colored persons have occurred in housing, in employment and in recreation. Processes of segregation, invasion, succession and re-segregation have characterized patterns of colored housing in both countries. Both mixed (Stepney) and segregated (Cardiff) patterns of occupancy can be found in Britain, but disputes have frequently occurred in areas where a transition from segregated to mixed patterns has begun. The most publicized events in the northern states since the Second World War (in Cicero, Illinois; Trumbull Park in Chicago, Illinois; and in Levittown, Pennsylvania) have all followed the appearance of Negroes in previously all-white areas. Housing disputes were of great importance in the generation of social tensions which culminated in the Chicago riot of 1919, one of the bloodiest twentieth-century disturbances in the United States (Chicago Commission on Race Relations, 1922).

A complex of personal, cultural, social and economic variables raise housing to a position of great importance in the determination of patterns of prejudice and tension in intergroup relations. In the United States, as in England, "a man's home is his castle." But it is more than this. In most instances it is his single most valuable economic possession, and any perception of threat to its value, whether warranted or not, is a threat to himself. In so far as colored persons are conceived of as having inferior status, living in the same neighborhood with them will, many whites believe, cause their own status to deteriorate. The cultural differences of white and colored, in social activities, conceptions of morality and the like when for example, he discovers his hours of sleep do not coincide with those of his new neighbors, frequently cause the white person to feel personally attacked. It is true, furthermore, that when genuine housing shortages exist, colored movement into a neighborhood may cause some deterioration. Landlords, knowing the greater difficulty in finding housing which confronts the colored person, will charge him greater rent for equivalent or even less desirable housing. The higher rent, frequently coupled with lower income, can cause one of two patterns to develop—both of which serve to cause housing quality to be damaged. The first is a fragmentation of dwelling units in which more and more persons are crowded into a single dwelling. The second is one in which so great a portion of the tenant's income must be spent on housing that he is unable to maintain the property. Where other housing, either public or private, is not obtainable some landlords are content to let properties deteriorate knowing that their tenants will have to stay in them and that municipalities cannot condemn the buildings because no alternatives are available. Thus we find an instance of the "self-fulfilling prophecy," and neighborhoods do deteriorate and values do fall.

Another area of interaction in which there is direct contact and in which social tensions have been generated in both Britain and the United States is that of work. Here, however, the differences in historical background in the two countries and differences in the size and character of the labor forces involved, have interacted to produce a situation in contemporary Britain, which while superficially similar to that in the United States is in reality not.

Large-scale violence over colored labor occurred a century ago in the United States and in the years after the Civil War colored participation in the labor force continued to be a source of social tensions (see Grimshaw, 1959a, reproduced in this volume, p. 000). Negroes were denied the right to engage in some kinds of employment, in both the north and south, and were often paid lower wages for performing the same tasks as whites. At the time of the First World War, however, labor shortages in northern industry precipitated very substantial migration of colored persons to northern cities and factories. Some of the large-scale disturbances which occurred in the years during and immediately after the First War, in East St. Louis and Chicago, had disputes over jobs as an important contributory cause.

In the years after the war, the complexion of the labor problem in the north changed. In a context of unionism quite different from that in Britain, Negroes had developed a not unwarranted suspicion of and hostility toward unions. Experiences with unions had meant one thing to the colored community, a reification of barriers to the industrial progress of the Negro laborer. While some Negro leaders, a small but vociferous minority, insisted that salvation lay within the union, Negroes as a group were anti-union and remained so. As industrial unionism developed in the thirties, however, white labor leaders saw that as long as Negroes constituted a large bloc of anti-union labor it would be relatively easy for large employers to break strikes through the importation and employment of Negro workers. A Negro labor force which had moved north in response to wartime needs had stayed on to be used by employers to stave off the encroachments of union power. Packing and steel strikes in the twenties and automotive and rubber strikes in the thirties forced unions to bring in colored workers. These men stayed in unions and became good union men, in spite of frequent protests from the white rank and file. Frequently, however, official policies were honored only in the breach by union locals and, in spite of activities of the Federal Government, Negroes continued to be last hired and first fired.

As the Second World War approached, and industry stepped up its pace, Negroes again found themselves in an increasingly tenuous situation. Defence industry was in desperate need of trained personnel and the Government undertook the responsibility of providing much of this training. In spite of some of the gains of the interwar period most of this training was provided for whites only and Negroes found themselves systematically excluded from opportunities for training and subsequent skilled employment. Concurrently, northward migration of southern whites into industrial areas such as Detroit, began to undermine the position even of those Negroes who were unionized. The period prior to the Detroit riot of 1943 was punctuated by a series of wild-cat strikes in the Detroit area directed against the upgrading of Negroes.

With increased employment—for whites—at the beginning of the Second World War, and a subsequent closing down of Federal work programmes, Negroes again made up the bulk of relief cases and of the unemployed. They were taken into the military arms on a quota basis; were not incorporated into training programmes; and were last hired. Murmurs of Negro protest, never completely stilled, grew to an almost strident roar and Negro leaders asked publicly why they should fight a "white man's war to maintain Jim Crow." In 1940 and 1941 there emerged from the protest the March on Washington Committee, an all-Negro movement unprecedented in its inclusion of Negroes and Negro organizations from across the whole spectrum of militancy.[4] While the later activities of the March on Washington Movement did not culminate in unqualified success, partly at least because some of the government officials involved were either unsympathetic or felt that rigid enforcement of nondiscriminatory practices might hurt the war effort, the activities of the M.O.W.C. either coerced President Roosevelt into issuing Executive Order 8802 appointing the Committee on Fair Employment Practices or made it politically possible for him to do this.

Commentors have not agreed in the evaluation of the effectiveness of F.E.P.C. Some have emphasized its success, particularly in increasing Negro employment in government agencies. Others have claimed that the incorporation of colored persons in the labor force, particularly in defence industries, resulted from the very real exigencies of a war-time labor market. Negroes and other colored persons were initially hired when there were no whites available, they claim, and once employed unions were compelled to organize them. By the time the war was over certain types of employment, usually dirty jobs, had become identified as "ethnic jobs" and colored persons were so firmly entrenched in them

4. An excellent study of the activities and achievements of the M.O.W.C. and its successor organization the M.O.W.M. is to be found in Garfinkel, 1959.

that it was not possible to displace them (this, of course, is merely another form of segregation).[5]

Whatever the precise interaction of causal variables may have been, by the middle of the fifties the position of the Negro in the labor movement in the northern and western United States seems to have become that of earlier migrant groups. Many of the craft unions, long the strongholds of anti-Negro sentiment, are now agreed at least in principle to equal rights for all employees. Most of the gains made by colored labor in the war were maintained, although Negroes still hold a disproportionate share of "dirty" jobs. Negroes, as a group, have not attained job parity with white fellow workers; findings of the United States Civil Rights Commission and current activities of the Negro Labor Congress (within the A.F.L.-C.I.O.) do not permit such an interpretation. Nonetheless it is here, as in probably no other area of race relations in the United States, that Negroes have been able to break down the color bar and become not only assimilated, but partly integrated as well. There have been no expressions of public concern by the leaders of organized labor, in the years since the Second World War, over too rapid incorporation of Negroes into the labor force, nor any suggestion that they should not be employed when whites are not. Pressure has come, rather, from Negro leaders, who point to the higher rates of unemployment and the lower ratings of Negroes. George Meany, the President of the A.F.L.-C.I.O. has criticized A. Philip Randolph, the major Negro leader in organized labor, for pressing too hard; but concedes the right of Negroes to full and equitable employment under identical work rules.

The review above of the labor history of colored Americans is, perhaps, suggestive of British parallels. Differences between the two countries will be more instructive in a look toward the future than will be similarities. The history of colored participation in the work force in Britain covers a scant four decades. The traditions of British trade unionism are, in the large, more liberal than those of much of the American labor movement, although Britain too has had its craft snobbery. More important, perhaps, is the much smaller relative and absolute size of the colored minority in Britain as contrasted to that in the United States.

Colored workers in Britain first appeared in any numbers at all during the period of the First World War, in response to pressures similar to those which precipitated northward migration of southern American Negroes. They were engaged then, as they are to a certain extent to the present, in the maritime trades and in longshore work. During the period following the war, and through the interwar years, there were occasional clashes, frequently generated by allegations that

5. See Greer, 1959. Perhaps the most interesting aspect of Greer's study is his demonstration of the manner in which organizational structure and environment operate to constrain the antidiscriminatory activities of even those most militantly committed to equality. It is interesting to note, incidentally, that some positions in public transportation in Britain are apparently coming to be defined as "colored jobs."

colored workers undercut white wages. The numbers involved were small, the Government acted in what has been labelled a discriminatory manner (Aliens Order of 1920 and Special Restriction Order of 1925) and exposure to conflict was limited, both geographically and socially. With the onset of the Second World War a series of immigration schemes were initiated with the joint purposes of relieving unemployment in the West Indies, providing labor for British war industries, and "strengthening the bonds between Great Britain and the West Indies." The workers who came under these schemes, along with postwar immigrants from both the West Indies and West Africa, have been those involved in the tensions and disputes of the last decade and a half. These workers have had more varied participation in the labor force and in some instances have been highly skilled. It is an interaction between claims of discrimination made by these men and claims that they have taken away jobs from British workers that is at the root of current difficulties. That there has been discrimination is clear, both from statements of individual employers and from statistics of unemployment which consistently show colored workers to be disproportionately unemployed. British writers have observed that here, as in the case of housing, a complex of factors: personal (prejudice), social (fear of status-deprivation on the part of whites, extreme sensitivity on the part of colored persons), economic (threats of loss of income), and cultural (lack of preparation for life in England, differences in work and consumption patterns, and the like) interact to contribute to the increase of social tensions.

The discussion above notwithstanding, from an American perspective it seems unlikely that there will be substantial increases in the magnitude of social frictions generated in the area of employment of colored labor. This will be true even in the event of a major increase in unemployment due to recession, which seems unlikely in the years ahead. The reason for this can be found in the essential powerlessness of the colored working force in Britain. Even if it were possible for the sub-groups within the colored minority to come together and agree to act as a bargaining unit, it would not be possible for them to substantially alter current patterns of accommodation. There is no prospect of a war-time labor shortage similar to that of the early forties developing again— and even if there were, a threat by the group to withhold their labor would be an inconvenience rather than a disaster. Similarly, a threat to organize against the trade unions—as strike breakers—would be of little effect outside of a limited number of industries, which would doubtless reject such offers even if they were made, in fear of long-term consequences. If, as seems to be likely, colored persons in Britain gain increasingly diversified employment, major attacks on the *status quo* would be even more improbable. Government antidiscrimination legislation might have the effect of temporarily increasing prejudice and tension in the dominant group; this would have little impact on long-range possibilities of overt conflict. If, as seems to be the case, West Indian authorities are more carefully preparing their emigrants to be aware of the hardships which may await them in Britain and if control over dishonest travel agents is asserted, increases in friction will be even less likely. Individual problems will continue, and some muttering from both white and colored persons can be expected. Major disorders seem very unlikely.

A final area of direct contact should be mentioned. The problem of access to recreational and other public facilities has generated more social tension in Britain than it has in the United States (although recently lunch-counter "strikes," other "sit-downs," "wade-ins," and "Freedom Rides" have shown a changing emphasis in this country). Paradoxically, it has been the smaller size of the community, along with its social-demographic composition, which has been responsible for the greater importance of access to public facilities as a tension-producing factor in England. A consequence of segregation of absolutely large Negro and colored populations in the urban centers of the northern United States has been the development of autonomous sub-cities, with all-Negro recreational institutions. In England, on the other hand, no cities, except perhaps those with the largest colored population, can support such segregated facilities, even were they considered desirable. A result has been that colored and white persons have been thrown into close contact, frequently in those situations which may be most prone to misunderstandings and conflict. Several of the disturbances which have occurred in Britain since the war have occurred in public houses or in the streets outside public houses at closing time.

Other disturbances have occurred at public dance halls. Problems have been generated here which can be directly traced to the tremendously high sex ratio of the colored community. It has been only in recent years that whole families and single unattached women have joined in the stream of immigrants to Britain from the West Indies. The West African immigrants have continued to be largely males and the same holds, with some exceptions, for the Pakistani and Indian immigrants. Understandably, these unattached males have sought female companionship. Collins notes that colored men are resented when they consort with white women, as miscegenation is considered a challenge to white supremacy (Collins, 1957). Richmond claims that, with the possible exception of employment, the area of most intense prejudice against West Indian Negroes is that of sexual relations (Richmond, 1954). Most students of race relations in Britain have emphasized the low social and economic status of the women who become involved with colored males. It seems likely that for many of these women, intermarriage and inter-cohabitation serve as a route to security which would otherwise not be available. But both the women and their colored consorts have been subjected to public vilification and abuse, and occasional physical violence.

It is difficult to determine the precise sources of antipathy over this social mixing of colored males and white females. While there has been a residue of colonial attitudes reminiscent of Kipling, it seems probable that more direct competition for female companionship is also involved. During the war, and to a lesser extent in the post-war years, American Negro soldiers in Britain have had, because of their somewhat higher incomes, an advantage in competition. The determination of these men to seek out white female companionship was not lessened by the stereotyped expressions which were brought to England by white American soldiers. Several dance halls closed their doors to American Negro soldiers and West Indians alike during the war on the grounds that there would otherwise be violence. There seems to be some element of punitiveness in the response of West Indian males to the discomfort of whites in this area, and there have been expressions which suggest that sexual relations with white women have been interpreted as assault on the *status quo* by colored as well as white persons. In spite of all this, and in spite of the occasionally deprived socio-economic backgrounds of white females who become involved with colored males, many of the relationships show remarkable stability and several students have noted that the women frequently identify with their colored consorts and in the case of women who have married Muslims have often converted to Islam. As the colored population grows in size its demographic composition will become more normal and more marriage will take place within the community. Nonetheless, interracial relationships will continue. Whether or not they will be the cause of antipathies which are further heightened can be doubted; it seems probable that when intergroup sexual relations are emphasized as a source of conflict, such attribution may screen more basic economic and social competition.

Two further areas of high direct contact have been influential in patterns of intergroup relations in the United States; public transportation and education. These two areas have been of less impact on relations between colored and white people in Britain than employment, housing and sexual relations. Nor have areas of indirect contact been of substantial importance in British race relations. In labor and employment, in housing, in recreation, in public transportation, and in the school there is continual evidence of direct assault upon the *status quo*. Another set of factors show the influence of activities either by colored persons or white who may not be involved in any contact whatsoever, or in very little contact. Most whites, in England and to a somewhat lesser extent in the United States, continue to have little contact with Negroes, and the conflicts which occur seem remote.

In the United States several factors have influenced patterns of intergroup relations in ways which have been less evident in Britain. Colored participation in politics, the treatment of the Negro in the white press and of whites in the Negro press, and Negro involvement in crime and in relations with the police have all contributed to social tension in the two communities.

An apparently unanticipated consequence of segregated Negro housing and a concentration of Negroes in limited geographical areas in the urban north of the United States has been a sharp growth in Negro political power. It has been claimed that if Negroes vote as a bloc they can control national elections. One thing is certain. No administration in a northern city with a sizable Negro population can ignore the importance of the Negro vote. In the long run, of course, this fact has ramifications in the areas of direct contact already examined.

In the South, particularly in the past but to a certain extent even today, the very act of voting by a Negro was a breach of "racial etiquette" and a cause for concern and occasional violence. Several major riots in the south grew, either directly or indirectly, out of Negro political activity. Some of the current tensions in the American South has developed directly from attempts by Negroes to gain, or regain, the franchise, and some Negro leaders feel that the franchise is more important than access to schools, transportation, or other public facilities. The small size and relatively great dispersion of the colored community in Britain makes unlikely the development of political participation as an issue in intergroup relations.

The role of the press in race relations is problematical. While there is virtually no colored press in Britain, several authors have emphasized the role of the press in the creation of anxieties and tension and, in the case of the 1958 disturbances, the spread of violence. The study of urban race riots in the United States included conclusions on the role of the press. Both the Negro and the white press have "slanted" news presentation; however, this may result from a reflection of readers' attitudes, as seen by editors, rather than from conscious policy. Studies in this area frequently fail to study the dimensions of attitudes and fail to make explicit the link between attitude and behavior. Biased news presentations probably reach already prejudiced individuals and reinforce rather than mold attitudes. Such reinforcement may raise levels of social tension; it is doubtful that this alone would create a situation of "violence-proneness"; there are other networks of communications (note, however, the discussions of the press, in Wickenden, *op. cit.,* and Glass, *op. cit.,* and the coverage of press reports in the summaries published by the Institute for Race Relations).

Examination of available British materials suggests no major changes in this evaluation of the importance of the press. Wide newspaper (and television) coverage of events in Nottingham and Notting Hill and references to "Teddy Boys" may have had some influence on suggestible youth. The influence of the mass media, however, was probably more in determining when disturbances took place than in whether they would take place at all. Similarly, agitation, whether by the Ku Klux Klan and the

White Defence League or by Communists, can be discounted as having any major influence in creation of social tensions leading to violence. Given sufficiently high social tension a variety of events could precipitate violence. It can be seriously doubted, however, that mass media coverage alone is responsible for major increments in tension. While the role of the mass media might be greater in England because of the reduced impact of other variables, it is also true that the press has taken a generally more responsible and less inflammatory position in Britain than it has historically in the United States.

Negro crime and Negro relations with the police have been major, if unmeasurable, influences in the creation of social tensions between the white and colored communities in the United States. Richmond and Collins both state that police in England remark on a relative absence of adult crime and juvenile delinquency among the colored minority in Britain and emphasize that a small segment of the community is responsible for a major portion of law-breaking.[6] This has not been true in the United States. Negro rates of crime, no matter how carefully defined and standardized, are consistently greater than those for whites. The causes may well lie in differential treatment of the Negro and in patterns of widespread social deprivation. The causes, however, are irrelevant and whites respond to reported Negro crime with a generalized fear and antipathy. Negroes, in turn, expect differential and unfair treatment from law-enforcing agencies; are therefore more likely to resist arrest, are therefore more roughly handled—another example of reflexive prophecy. Reports of incidents of racial violence in England suggest that colored persons have more frequently been arrested and that police have not always acted with complete impartiality. Nonetheless, it is doubtful that there is as widespread distrust and suspicion by the colored minority—nor as warranted—of the police in Britain as is true in the United States. While the situation may change, it is probably fair to say that these two problems, Negro crime as creating apprehension in the white community and Negro relations with the police as creating social tensions among members of the colored community, will not be of great import in race relations in Britain at least for the next few years.

In the pages above an attempt has been made to trace out the influence of several factors involved in the building up of racial tensions. No attempt has been made to assess weights of importance for the various factors, though it would seem that in England some of them, for reasons specified, are of less importance than they are in the United States. References have been made to the essential irrelevance of incidents actually precipitating overt conflict—the claim has been made that

6. *Op. cit.* The later numbers of the Institute summaries carried a warning that reports of colored crime and difficulties with the police should be used with great caution.

given a sufficient level of tension almost any incident could serve to set off a disturbance.

In concluding, attention is directed to three problems which cannot be treated here because of limitations of space, but which are nonetheless of considerable importance in an understanding of problems of intergroup relations in Great Britain and in the United States. The first of these has to do with major changes in the form of assaults upon the *status quo* of race relations in the United States which have occurred in the last few years. The second has to do with possible interactions of events and publicity of these events of racial conflict in the two countries—e.g., the coverage of the 1958 disturbances in Nottingham and North Kensington in the American press and British news on American events. Finally, some of the difficulties inherent in forecasting patterns of interracial adjustment and conflict can be noted.

In early 1960 racial conflict in the United States appeared in a previously unexperienced form. Demonstrations by Negro youth, largely students, were directed first against segregation in public eating facilities and then in public transportation. These demonstrations differ from previous patterns in the characteristics of the protestors, who are middle-class and respectable; and in the tremendous restraint with which the Negro participants have acted, even when subjected to considerable physical abuse by white youth (e.g., the dropping of lighted cigarettes down the backs of Negro students seated at lunch counters in a silent request for service) and the quiet acceptance, even courting, of arrest. In view of the historical patterning of race relations in the American South, the restraint and apparent impartiality of *most* municipal officials and police is also remarkable. Almost equal numbers of whites and Negroes, for example, have been taken into custody. The long-range consequences of these activities, along with major and again self-conscious, assaults on the accommodative structure through legal pressures, cannot as yet be discerned. Social tensions have certainly increased, but changes in behavior are also taking place.

Press coverage, it has been suggested above, has less influence on shaping racial attitudes within a country than is sometimes thought. It would be difficult to deny, however, that events of racial conflict in England have gained support for ardent anti-Negroes in the United States (and probably also in South Africa). It seems clear that the American press, including the mass-circulation news weeklies, overplayed the significance of events in Britain. There were substantial tones of "cast out the mote in thine own eye" in American coverage. *Time* magazine reproduced, apparently with approval, a cartoon by Cummings from the *Daily Express* with the caption, "Now, perhaps, the English will stop giving us that 'More anti-colour bar than thou' stuff" (8 September, 1959). It is probably true that demonstrations of racialism anywhere in the world will be seized upon by anticolored groups wherever they are.

Considerable courage, even foolhardiness, would be required to forecast major racial violence as a result of current events in the American South or north or in England, or even of patterns of continuing tension. It is possible, nonetheless, to note areas of change in the general patterning of race relations which may affect probabilities (Grimshaw, 1960). The forecasting of racial violence requires knowledge of the history and current status of three factors:

1. The mode and pattern of the assault upon the *status quo;* its direct or indirect nature, the militancy with which it is pressed, and the areas in which it occurs. If, as has been asserted, violence results not from conscious policy of the majority or minority groups, the militancy with which claims for equal treatment are pressed will be of great importance. In England, of course, the size of the communities involved will be important in the perception by the majority of the assault. The appearance of new tactics of non-violence makes even more difficult the forecasting of events in the arena of social conflict.

2. The attitude and actions of agencies of external control. There is no direct relation between the level of social tension and the eruption of social violence. Social tension in England, as in the United States, will continue to be generated by assaults on the *status quo.* In Britain it seems probable that police impartiality will restrain *major* violence. Changes in the attitudes (or at least behavior) of American police have had an undeniable influence in reducing the possibilities of violence in the current American "sit-down" and "Freedom Ride" campaigns, though some large southern cities (e.g., Birmingham, Alabama) could still experience large-scale violence.

3. The nature of the accommodative structure itself. In the United States Negro participation is now grudgingly accepted in areas previously forbidden. At the same time areas considered secure in past interaction are being redefined. Some barriers of the *status quo,* previously unthreatened, are now becoming more rigid. Similarly, changes in the *status quo* will frequently have the effect of raising colored aspirations, then new rebuffs generate greater tensions. The same processes of redefinition can be expected to be important in the further development of patterns of race relations in Britain.

A comparison of colored and white relations in Britain and in the United States and their potentials for social racial violence seems generally to add support to general interpretations of intergroup relations and to theories of prejudice. Social tensions in Britain, as in the United States, can be seen to be generated by assaults on the *status quo,* namely, to be generated by the social structure itself. Some sources of social tension in intergroup relations in the United States are not found in England; it can be shown that these differences result from the size and historical backgrounds of the communities in the two countries. It seems unlikely, furthermore, that the colored community in Britain will be able, in the years immediately ahead, to wield sufficient power to threaten the social structure to a point where heightened social tensions make possible the occurrence of major violence. On the other hand, this same impotence makes unlikely major shifts in patterns of intergroup relations without the intervention of government authority. Implications for policy, however, are not properly examined in a paper such as this.

Allen D. Grimshaw

Actions of Police and the Military in American Race Riots

A by-product of the increasing urbanization of American society is the concentration of social control functions in formalized agencies (Turner and Killian, 1957). In a situation of anonymity and a complex division of labor, police forces increasingly lose the ability to apply informal sanctions for the enforcement of behavior to meet the normative demands of the larger society, and more and more are pressed to rely on secular rule by force. At the same time, while communications patterns with societal subgroups may become more and more attenuated, such formal police forces retain the ideological orientations of the groups from which they themselves are recruited.

Lambert found, in his study of communal violence in India (Lambert, 1951), that as an accompaniment to broad changes in the social organization of the Indian polity in the period immediately preceding Independence, there was a breakdown in the formal system of social controls. Policemen came to be regarded, not as neutral arbiters of social disputes operating within a system of legal redress for grievances, but rather as armed representatives of the communities from which they were originally recruited. This interpretation of their role was accepted by members of the rival community, by members of their own community, and increasingly, by the policemen themselves. When this occurred the usefulness of the police in social control was sharply reduced and, in some cases, police activities contributed to further disruption of social organization.

The role played by police forces in urban race riots in the United States has not been uniform. In at least a few cases the situation, as defined both by the police and the conflicting racial groups, has been similar to that described above as having been endemic in India at the time of Independence. In other cases, prompt and non-partisan police action has been effective in either preventing the eruption of major interracial disturbancs or in confining them and bringing them to a prompt close. Formal agencies of social control have played a pivotal role in the history of social interracial violence in this country (Grimshaw, 1961). Action or inaction of individual police officers has determined, at times, the occurrence or nonoccurrence of racial violence. In the Chicago riot of 1919, the refusal of a white police officer to arrest a white person accused of throwing the rock responsible for the drowning of the first victim of the riot, followed by his later arrest of a Negro on the complaint of a white person, is alleged to have been the precipitating cause of the riots.

Analysis of the activities of the police has been made by police officials, as in Detroit (1943), or by organizations highly hostile to the police in Detroit and in other areas. It is not surprising that estimates of the efficiency and partisanship of police forces vary sharply. White policemen have refused to protect Negroes and in some cases have actually joined in attacks on Negroes. On the other hand, although every riot has produced allegations of misbehavior on the part of individual police officers, in some disturbances police forces have acted so as to gain the approbation of leadership elements of both the white and Negro communities. This was true, for example, of the activities of the New York Police Department in the Harlem disturbances of 1943.

Federal or state troops, national guardsmen, state militia and state troopers have all been called on to participate in riot control activities. A search for consistencies in the behavior and utilization of these organizations shows no more regular patterns than those to be found in an examination of the role of police departments. The effectiveness of these troops has been determined by the attitudes of the troops themselves and their leaders, by the character of the relationships between military and civilian leadership, and by patterns of utilization by civil authorities. In the East St. Louis riots (1917), troops allowed their weapons to be taken away from them to be used in firing on Negro victims of the mob. The leadership of these troops was branded as ineffective by both white and Negro leaders and a full-scale investigation of their participation resulted in a sharp indictment of the officer commanding them. On the other hand, the action of troops in Omaha (1919), Chicago (1818), and Detroit (1943), under more effective leadership, and with clearer chains-of-command and communications with civilian authorities, met with the approval of the most diverse elements within those communities.

In the case of both police and military participation in riot and anti-riot activities, it may be that partisan activity by troops or by police is unexpected and hence more attention-catching than similar activities of individuals in other categories. Such a qualification is less clearly applicable to the activities of municipal and state civilian authorities. Opinion has been divided on the activities of agencies of the civil arm of government, but, in most cases, heavy criticism has been levelled against these bodies and charges made both of ineffectiveness and of partisanship. Only in the Harlem disturbance of 1943 has a municipal administration been given a clean bill for its riot activities (*viz.*, by "action" agencies).

In a situation characterized by the breakdown of formal social controls and widespread disruption of communications patterns, rioters and looters are not the only persons engaged in collective behavior. The individuals and groups who take over the functions of policing and protection and engage themselves in the task of re-establishing patterns of communication and social control are also participating in collective behavior. Novel behavior patterns appear as official and unofficial leadership attempts to reconstruct organization out of disorganization, and a new social structure with new norms, however temporary it may be, emerges.

This paper is devoted to a discussion of a variety of anti-riot activities by external forces of control, *viz.*, police and the military, and of municipal government authorities.[1]

Mark Twain, writing about lynching in the United States, expressed the belief that few people really want to participate in lynchings, and that lynchings would not occur if a few martial personalities could be found who would face mobs without flinching (Twain, 1946). Major emphasis is placed on the role of external forces of control throughout this paper. It has been claimed that the presence of strong police forces could prevent race rioting. Unfortunately, few cases of "prevented" riots come to the attention of students of interracial violence. There is agreement, however, that in almost every major riot local police forces have been ineffective and inefficient. In this section, documentation of claims of police ineffectiveness and partisanship will be briefly examined.

The indictment of police forces and their activities which resulted from postriot investigations on the East St. Louis riots undertaken by a Special Committee of the United States House of Representatives (1918), is typical. It reads, in part:

When the lawlessness began to assume serious proportions on July 2, the police instantly could have quelled and dispersed the crowds, then made up of small groups; but they either fled into the safety of a cowardly seclusion, or listlessly watched the depredations of the mob, passively and in many instances actively sharing its work.

The testimony of every witness who was free to tell the truth agreed in condemnation of the police for failure to even halfway do their duty. They fled

1. Grimshaw, 1959, includes a discussion of development of spontaneous nonofficial anti-riot activities and activities of established institutional bodies (e.g., the American Legion and churches).

the scene where murder and arson held full sway. They deserted the station house and could not be found when calls for help came from every quarter of the city. The organization broke down completely; and so great was the indifference of the few policemen who remained on duty that the conclusion is inevitable that they shared the lust of the mob for negro blood, and encouraged the rioters by their conduct, which was sympathetic when it was not cowardly.

Some specific instances will be given in proof of the above conclusions:

After a number of rioters had been taken to the jail by the soldiers under Colonel Clayton, the police deliberately turned hundreds of them loose without bond, failing to secure their names or to make any effort to identify them.

In one instance the mob jammed policemen against a building and held them while other members of the gang were assaulting unoffending negroes. The police made no effort to free themselves and seemed to regard the performance as highly humorous.

The police shot into a crowd of negroes who were huddled together making no resistance. It was a particularly cowardly exhibition of savagery (Special Committee Report, East St. Louis Riot, 1918, p. 8). [Extensive excerpts from this Report are included in this volume, pp. 000-000.—A. D. G.]

After citing a number of specific cases of police ineffectiveness and complicity with the rioters, the House Committee concluded:

Many other cases of police complicity in the riots could be cited. Instead of being guardians of the peace they became a part of the mob by countenancing the assaulting and shooting down of defenseless negroes and adding to the terrifying scenes of rapine and slaughter (p. 9).

The Chicago Commission on Race Relations, in its moderate and reasoned examination of the activities of the Chicago police during the Chicago rioting of 1919, first noted that the police labored under two major handicaps. These were the hostility of the Negro population to the police and a "lack of sufficient numbers adequately to cope with the situation" (Chicago Commission on Race Relations, 1922. Some recent writers have given a more critical evaluation of the Commission's report, see, e.g., Waskow, 1966). As in the case of the East St. Louis riots, the Commission was able to give a number of specific cases of police law violations and of differential treatment of Negroes during the rioting. The conclusions which they drew of police ineffectiveness and harsher treatment of Negroes were in agreement with those of the grand jury and the coroner's jury, as well as of Herman M. Adler, State Criminologist of Illinois, who testified that the police showed more readiness to arrest Negroes than whites because the officers thought they were "taking fewer chances if they 'soaked' a colored man." During the Chicago riot the police forces, operating under the command of Chief of Police Garrity, were concentrated in the "Black Belt," thereby leaving other sectors of the city practically without protection. Negro casualties were highest, not in the area where police were concentrated, but in the almost unprotected "Stockyards District" (Grimshaw, 1960, pp. 109-119). Garrity ordered the establishment of a "barred zone," across which neither whites nor Negroes were permitted to go, and closed saloons and cabarets. "A general policy was adopted of search and seizure of persons suspected of carrying weapons on the street, and of houses from which firing came" (Chicago Commission, 1922, p. 37). While no police records existed of "flying squadrons of police," some such bodies seem to have been operating. Yet, in spite of these actions taken by police command personnel, the riot continued over an extensive time period and with great numbers of casualties to both racial groups, ceasing only with the introduction of state militia into the situation. It seems likely that in many cases the intent of higher echelon police command was either wrongly interpreted or ignored by individual officers.

The Commission noted several cases of individual brutality and neglect on the part of police officers. One such case was reported with which a policeman approached a Negro victim of mob attack with the words, "Where's your gun, you black —— of a ——? You damn niggers are raising hell." He then struck the wounded Negro and allegedly robbed him after he became unconscious. Another Negro was "rescued" from a mob by being ordered by a white officer to leave a street car in the words, "Come out of there, you big rusty brute you. I ought to shoot you." He was then struck on the head and forced into a patrol car, and held incommunicado from July 28 to August 4. None of the white rioters involved was arrested.

As in the East St. Louis riots, policemen were accused of leaving the scene of rioting on questionable grounds. Considerable indifference on the part of a police captain to lawlessness during the riot and to the post-riot investigation was shown in the following excerpt from the inquest of the coroner's jury. The officer involved had been in command of twelve mounted and between sixty-three and one hundred foot patrolmen during a clash between the police and a Negro mob. The Commission observed that the officer left before firing began, but the building he had been in was struck by bullets:

Q. What time did the shooting take place at the building known as the Angelus Building? What time did that occur? Was there any shooting at that building?
A. Not that I heard.
Q. Had there been any shooting done there that evening . . . before you left?
A. Not to my knowledge.
Q. When was the shooting done, and where were you?
A. What do you mean by shooting? (Chicago Commission, 1922, pp. 40-41. Words slightly altered for purposes of condensation.)

This captain had been in command of the police who had killed two men and inflicted wounds on others before the Negroes had run in order to escape the police advance.

The activities of the Chicago Police Department came in for sharp criticism by Walter White, then the Executive Secretary of the National Association for the Advancement of Colored People, in an article in *Crisis*, the official organ of that organization. He wrote (White, 1919, p. 295):

During the riot the conduct of the police force as a whole was equally open to criticism. State's Attorney Hoyne openly charged the police with arresting colored rioters and with an unwillingness to arrest white rioters. Those who were arrested were at once released. In one case a colored man who was fair enough to appear to be white was arrested for carrying concealed weapons, together with five white men and a number of colored men. All were taken to a police station; the light colored man and the five whites being put into into one cell and the other colored men in another. In a few minutes the light colored man and the five whites were released and their ammunition given back to them with the remark, "You'll probably need this before the night is over."

It should be noted that one dissenting opinion on the activities of the Chicago police can be found. In an article published in *The Survey*, Graham Taylor asserted,

Great credit is given the police by Negro citizens, with very few exceptions, for standing up to their duty, especially when and where contending with the very insufficient force against overwhelming odds in the midst of mobs of infuriated blacks and whites numbering as many as three thousand. This is the more creditable since many of them are Irishmen and had to contend with the most aggressive element from an Irish district bordering the Negro quarter.

It will be recalled that the greatest number of Negro casualties occurred in just that Irish district inhabited by the "most aggressive element" (Taylor, 1919, pp. 695-697).

In an eyewitness report published in *The Outlook*, within a few weeks after the Washington, D. C. riots of 1919, the observation was made (Anonymous, 1919, p. 533):

Failure of the police to check the rioters promptly, and in certain cases an attitude on their part of seeming indifference, filled the mob with contempt of authority and set the stage for the demonstration of the following night. In behalf of the police, it may be said that their number—about eight hundred and forty to a population estimated by the Census authorities a year ago at four hundred and one thousand—has long been complained of as wholly inadequate. Fully a third of the force, moreover, are new men, chiefly discharged soldiers and unfamiliar with their new duties.

In the early hours of Monday morning the attacks on Negroes were carried into sections where the black population is heavy. The whole Negro element of Washington became suddenly aware of a war on their race, which spared no man of color and stopped not to determine whether or not he belonged to the large class of industrious and orderly Negroes in the city. Always more or less suspicious of the white police . . . and believing that a Negro on arrest is treated more harshly than a white man, by Monday night the colored population held themselves to be without police protection. The mob elements among the blacks then armed for war, while many of the better element of their race armed in obedience to the first law of nature.

Herbert Seligman, writing in the *New Republic*, spoke even more critically of the Washington police (Seligman, 1919, p. 49):

It is hardly necessary to characterize the protection afforded Negroes by the Washington police. There need have been no widespread disorders after the first Saturday and Sunday rioting. . . . But on those first nights the police gave the impression both to Negroes and white men that they would be the allies of white men. Although the aggressors were white mobbists led by white men in uniforms of the United States, ten Negroes were arrested for every white man arrested.

Similar criticisms have been levelled against police forces in almost every major riot. In one of the sharpest attacks on the police, Thurgood Marshall, formerly chief legal counsel for the NAACP, wrote in *The Crisis* (Marshall, 1943, p. 232, reprinted in this volume, pp. 140-143):

When disorder starts, it is either stopped quickly or permitted to spread into serious proportions, depending upon the actions of the local police.

Much of the blood spilled in the Detroit riot is on the hands of the Detroit police department. In the past the Detroit police have been guilty of both inefficiency and an attitude of prejudice against Negroes. Of course, there are several individual exceptions . . .

In the June riot of this year, the police ran true to form. The trouble reached riot proportions because the police once again enforced the law with an unequal hand. They used "persuasion" rather than firm action with white rioters, while against Negroes they used the ultimate in force: night sticks, revolvers, riot guns, sub-machine guns, and deer guns.

The NAACP claimed to have collected a large number of affidavits from Negroes concerning police brutality during the riot (see, e.g., T. Marshall, 1943; and White and Marshall, 1943). In addition, it was claimed that rather than protecting stores and preventing looting, the police drove through the troubled areas, occasionally stopping their vehicles, jumping out, and shooting whoever might in a store. Police "would then tell Negro bystanders to 'run and not look back.' On several occasions persons running were shot in the back." According to Marshall, the police treated all Negroes on Hastings Street as "looters." Another claim made by Marshall was that Negroes driving automobiles were forced to detour into Woodward Avenue, a thoroughfare where violence against Negroes was particularly intense. Marshall felt that police action at any one of a number of junctures could have prevented the spread of violence, but that the police policy of inaction, in accord with Mayor Jeffries' refusal to make decisions, allowed violence to get out of hand. He concluded, "The responsibility rests with the Detroit police."

Even in those situations where individual policemen have acted in violation of the law or have failed to fulfill their duty in protecting the

Negro populace, actions of police officials usually have been directed toward some control of violence. The major tactical goal of police officials, once riots began, seems to have been the sealing off of access between the two racial groups. This has been undertaken in two ways. The first, and most frequent, has been the establishment of "barred zones" or "deadlines." Cordons of police have been thrown along so-called dividing lines, such as Wentworth Avenue in Chicago, or around the entire Negro community, as in Detroit in 1943, and in Harlem in the same year. The other attempt to prevent contact between the conflicting racial groups has focussed on the isolation and "preventive detention" of the Negro population. In Tulsa in 1921, all Negroes, either refugees from the burning Negro section or captured combatants, were gathered and placed in detention camps, first in the city's convention hall and later, when that edifice overflowed, in the city baseball park. Large numbers of Negroes were given temporary protection in public buildings in East St. Louis at the time of the major outbreaks in that city.

A second major tactical policy has been the establishment of temporary curfews and the barring of sales of alcoholic beverages. Sometimes, as in the Chicago riot of 1919, this curfew has been established by the local authorities. At other times, curfews and the prohibition of the sale of "intoxicating beverages" have been instituted by troop commanders who have come in and established virtual martial law. It is difficult to tell how successful such edicts have been in stopping or curtailing social violence. It is hardly necessary to tell proprietors whose places of business are being threatened to close their shops. On the other hand, those who have participated in social violence, and particularly that which is manifested in looting and in the variety of forms of property assault noted above, seem to have been little influenced by such regulation. While it is possible that "whiskey courage" may be important in building up a situation which culminates in the first outbreaks of major racial violence, it seems unlikely that much alcohol is needed to sustain the rioting, once it has begun.

Three facts characterize every outbreak in which there have been major interracial clashes. (The Harlem riots were not "major interracial clashes.") In every case the police have claimed to be understaffed. This claim has been concurred in by observers of the East St. Louis, Chicago, Washington, Tulsa, and Detroit riots. An added claim made by Negroes has been that of underrepresentation of their race on these police forces. Almost all the major riots of this century have occurred either in wartime or during periods in which wars have taken place and the police forces, therefore, have been depleted.[2] Whether or not any qualitative depreciation in police forces has accompanied this depletion during these periods would be difficult to establish. The fact is clear, however,

2. The Springfield riot in 1908 and the Atlanta "massacre" of 1906 are exceptions to this "wartime' rule. [This article was published before the disturbances of the Sixties began. The Vietnam War has not noticeably "depleted" police forces—A.D.G.]

that allegations of illegal police practices and of partisanship toward white rioters and differential and discriminatory treatment of Negro rioters and of Negro nonrioters seem fairly well substantiated. Post-riot investigations in the East St. Louis, Chicago, Tulsa, and Cicero disturbances established the fact that not only were police discriminatory in their treatment of Negroes, but that at least a few policemen in the forces of these communities had been engaged in a variety of forms of illegal behavior, ranging from participation in the sale of stolen cars in Tulsa (*New York Times*, 70:23,164, June 26, 1921), to widespread protection of gambling and organized vice in Chicago (Chicago Commission, 1922) and East St. Louis (Special Committee Report . . . East St. Louis riots, 1918).

Finally, an examination of materials on the major racial outbreaks of this century shows that the police departments of the communities involved have had no plans for the suppression of civil racial violence [3] and that in times of race rioting police officials have used only two tactics consistently, with, it may be added, little notable success. These tactics have been the attempts to separate the warring factions by isolation of the Negro community, and the establishment of curfews and prohibition of the sale of alcoholic beverages. Police mobilization has been inefficient and the disposal of police forces has been ineffective.

While there has been widespread criticism of the actions, or inactions, of local police forces during race riots, troops have generally been praised for their decorum and for their impartial enforcement of the law.[4] With the exception of the East St. Louis riots, where the troops were alleged to have been cowardly and themselves to have participated in anti-Negro violence, reports on the behavior of troops by both Negro and other observers have been positive evaluations. The major complaint about the use of troops has been that municipal authorities have waited too long before calling on troops for help or that troops were available only after considerable delay.

In the Chicago riot of 1919, strong representations were made to the Chief of Police that he request aid from the militia because of the insufficiency of the police forces. The course of events is summarized by the Chicago Commission on Race Relations in the following passage:

Chief Garrity steadily refused to ask for troops, in spite of his repeated statement that the police force was insufficient. He gave as his reason the belief that inexperienced militiamen would add to the deaths and disorders. Mayor Thompson supported the chief's refusal until outside pressure compelled him to ask the governor for aid. On the other hand the chief deputy of police was

3. Until the post-World War II period. It was less true in 1963, when this article was originally published. By 1968 every major urban center in the United States has detailed plans for actions in event of large-scale racial disturbances—plans which include use of Federal forces.
4. This was written before the "hot summers" of the Sixties. National Guardsmen have been severely criticized in recent summers, particularly for their actions in Detroit in 1967.

quoted by State's Attorney Hoyne as having said at the outbreak of the riot that the police would not be able to handle the situation and that troops were needed. In this he was supported by Mr. Hoyne. From observation of conditions on the first three days of the riot, the chief of staff of the troops, . . . concluded that the police were insufficient in numbers and that no improvement was apparent in the general situation, and that therefore the troops were necessary. He saw no reason, however, for putting the city under martial law. Other military men were of the same opinion (p. 40).

When the governor was finally asked for troops, he responded promptly. Of the troops the Commission said:

The troops themselves were clearly of high caliber. . . .
The militia discipline was of the best. Not a single case of breach of discipline was reported to the regimental commanders. . . .
The militia had been given special drills in the suppression of riots and insurrections for a year and a half previous to this occasion.
Distribution of troops was determined not by the militia command but by the police, because the city was not under martial law, the civil authority being insufficient, not broken. . . .
The orders under which the militia operated did not have the authority of martial law. The purpose of the orders was to effect a thorough cooperation with the police only, and not to take over any duties other than the preservation of law and order. . . . Persons arrested by the militia were turned over to the police.
Responsibility for the preservation of law and order rested on the regimental commanders. Careful instructions were given troops for preventing violence: they were to act as soldiers in a gentlemanly manner; they were furnished with arms to enable them to perform their duties; they were to use the arms only when necessary; they were to use bayonet and butt in preference to firing, but if the situation demanded shooting, they were not to hesitate to deliver an effective fire. Above all, the formation of mobs was to be prevented (pp. 40-42).

The militia were generally well received. Expressions of hostility came largely from hoodlums and the organized gangs which participated widely in the rioting. Some expressions of disdain came from volunteer ex-servicemen and from deputy sheriffs who had been mobilized for riot duty. Most of the activities of the militia were directed against the gangs of hoodlums composed of white youths. It prevented outbreaks of violence by dispersal of incipient mobs and by taking stations at critical points before raids could take place. The Commission concluded:

There was a marked contrast between the militia and the police. The troops were under definite orders: Commanders had absolute control of their forces and knew at all times where and how many effectives were available. Precision and promptness of movement was the rule. Reserves were always at hand. Discipline was always good. Only one person, a white man, was killed by the troops. Whatever other restraining causes contributed, it is certain that the riot was not revived after the troops were posted (p. 42).

The findings of the Chicago Commission on Race Relations on the activities of militia during the Chicago riot are in sharp contrast to those of the United States House of Representatives Special Committee on the East St. Louis disturbances. Were it not for the tragic consequences which resulted from the ineffectiveness of troops in that disturbance, the Committee report, particularly its comments on the officer commanding, would make amusing reading. The Committee describes the preparations made by Colonel Tripp, after his receipt of orders to take charge in East St. Louis and subsequent to the request of Mayor Mollman for assistance, in the following paragraph (Special Committee Report, East St. Louis riots; 1918, pp. 20-21):

When the adjutant general's office summoned Col. Tripp in the early hours of the morning he answered the call to duty arrayed in a seersucker suit and a dainty straw hat, after having, as he informed your committee, hastily packed his hand bag with a lot of toilet articles. Thus ready for any emergency he took the first train for East St. Louis. He brought no uniform with him and, although it was his duty to face and quell a riotous mob, at no time was he garbed as a soldier.

After repeating Colonel Tripp's description of his own acts of heroism, on which they comment, "Your committee was unable to find any evidence to confirm this valiant deed of the redoubtable colonel, where he practically mastered hundreds of infuriated rioters; but, as he states it to be a fact, it must be true," they conclude with an evaluation of his leadership:

It is the unanimous opinion of every witness who saw Col. Tripp on that fateful day that he was a hindrance instead of a help to the troops; that he was ignorant of his duties, blind to his responsibilities and deaf to every intelligent appeal that was made to him (pp. 20-21).

They continue by remarking that the State itself, and its various official bodies, must share the responsibility. After commenting favorably on Colonel C. B. Clayton, the officer next in command to Tripp, they continue with details on the conduct of the troops themselves:

The conduct of the soldiers who were sent to East St. Louis to protect life and property puts a blot on that part of the Illinois militia that served under Col. Tripp. They were scattered over the city, many of them being without officers to direct or control them. In only a few cases did they do their duty. They seemed moved by the same spirit of indifference or cowardice that marked the conduct of the police force. As a rule they fraternized with the mob, joked with them and made no serious effort to restrain them.

Following are a few of the many instances testified to by responsible witnesses:

A negro, unarmed, making no resistance, and trying to escape the fury of the mob, was knocked down and cruelly kicked and beaten. His condition was so pitiable that a soldier said to the rioters, "Boys, he has suffered enough; let him alone." For answer one of the mob drew his pistol and shot the Negro

five times, one bullet plowing through his brain. The soldier then put his
gun on his shoulder and calm (sic!) walked away, making no arrests.

A number of soldiers openly stated that "they didn't like niggers" and would
not disturb a white man for killing them.

Three soldiers and two policemen were ordered to close a negro saloon.
On their approach two Negro men ran, and the soldiers and policemen shot
and killed both, although neither had committed any offense . . .

Paul Y. Anderson, reporter for the St. Louis Post-Dispatch, testified that he
heard a soldier tell a white man who was loading a revolver "to kill all the
negroes he could, that he didn't like them either."

A member of the Sixth Illinois Infantry boasted that he had fired his gun
17 times during the riot and every time at a "black target." . . .

It was a common expression among the soldiers: "Have you got your nigger
yet?" (pp. 21-22).

The Committee report continues with other cases of alleged law violations by the militia. It further concludes that the Governor of the State
of Illinois and the military officials of the State had been lax in their
responsibility for investigating the activities of the militia.

The most complete take-over by military authorities in an event of
interracial violence occurred in Omaha, Nebraska, in 1919. Secretary of
the Army Baker directed General Leonard Wood to proceed to Omaha
and establish order. Specific orders issued to Wood by Chief of Staff
March commanded him to go to Omaha and "restore and maintain
order regardless of the cost." A *New York Times* report included the
following description (68:22,530, October 1, 1919):

With the advent of General Wood and his staff the city took on the aspect of
an armed camp. Machine guns were posted before the City Hall, the wrecked
courthouse and at several other points. Soldiers were bivouacked in the ro-
tundas of many large buildings. Guards patrol the downtown streets as well as
the Negro section. A gathering of more than two people is challenged by the
first guard which passes. Army trucks are at strategic points, ready to rush
reinforcements wherever needed. Artillery, hand grenades, and other fighting
material are banked around the City Hall. An observation balloon keeps watch
over the city.

An official statement by Wood made clear his position on further
disturbances:

"I would suggest that all meetings and large public gatherings be prohibited,"
said the General. "If this is not done, the 4,000 Federal troops now on guard
here will be ordered to take drastic action to put down and prevent any
repetition of the disorders. If this should occur, it is altogether probable that
many deaths might occur before the disturbances could be quieted."

There is no case other than that of Omaha where the military took over
the complete administration and control of an American municipality.
The police command was turned over to the army, news was censored
by General Wood when he prevented the local newspapers from print-

ing a story, which he felt was both questionable and inflammatory, of a second alleged rape and the army itself arrested violators and rioters and was apparently prepared to assist in their prosecution.

The 1943 Detroit race riot was another which saw participation of federal troops. Debate on the participation of these troops focused not on their behavior and decorum but on the series of events which culminated in their final arrival on the scene. Municipal and state authorities claim that the accessibility of these troops had been misrepresented to them or, at the very least, that they had not been correctly informed about the procedures necessary to obtain federal aid in the suppression of civil disturbance. Commissioner Witherspoon and Mayor Jeffries both claimed that the troops were not forthcoming as they had been promised and that the disorders were already under control by the time troops appeared on the streets of Detroit (Rushton, *et al.*, 1943). Other nonofficial versions claim that these two men, along with Governor Kelly, were remiss in their failure to heed the requests of various groups within the city for troop protection (Lee and Humphrey, 1943, and reports of various "action" agencies such as the Urban League and the National Association for the Advancement of Colored People). These nonofficial sources also claim that the disturbances ceased only when troops appeared and when an alleged "shoot to kill" order by the officer commanding received wide publicity.[5] As in the Chicago riot, once the troops appeared no complaints were raised about their performance. They appeared in strength and there were indications that their behavior was to be completely impartial and that in conjunction with the civil authorities they would brook no violations of the law. Over six thousand troops armed with rifles and machine guns were temporarily in the city. They were equipped with weapons carriers and with armored cars. These troops were maintained in the city for approximately two weeks, being utilized to protect Negroes during the graduation ceremonies of a Detroit high school (*New York Times*, 92:31,147, June 24, 1943) and, later, to guard places of public recreation. There were no major outbreaks after the arrival of the troops, although the situation remained tense. At no time was martial law declared. The municipal authorities were in command at all times.

Lambert, drawing on his observation of communal violence and rioting in India, particularly as manifested at the time during which external controls were breaking down, suggested the following propositions concerning the relationships between actions of external agencies of control exemplified in force and the appearance or nonappearance of violence (Lambert, 1950):

1. A highly visible display of overwhelming force at command of government decreases likelihood of violence.

5. The writer was told this several times in private conversations in Detroit as late as June, 1958.

2. In absence of such power, patterns of social control rather than objective strength of force is the important factor:

a. the longer the time required to visibly dominate the situation, the greater the likelihood of violence

b. the greater the susceptibility of civil government to public criticism, the greater the likelihood of violence

c. the greater the degree of violence in process of suppression (harsher aggression), the less the likelihood of violence

d. the greater the uniformity of application of control, the less the likelihood of violence

e. the greater the comprehensiveness and harshness of punishment after disturbances, the less the probability of future violence.

3. The more frequently a pattern or agency of government control is used, the less effective becomes its deterrent value.

4. In the face of increasing numbers of riots stability can be restored by:

a. increasing the strength of the forces

b. varying one or more of the elements in the control pattern

5. In the use of forces to control riots, increments in force are more important than the intial engagement, of superior forces.

There has been no American city which, as in the case of some Indian centers, has experienced series of riots continuing over numbers of years.[6] For this reason it is difficult to attempt the validation of some of the above propositions, particularly the third and fourth. However, indirect confirmation of several of these propositions can be essayed by utilizing materials on the riots which have served as a data base for this paper.

It is difficult to determine which of several factors suggested in these propositions have operated in the termination of some of the riots discussed. For example, in the termination of the Detroit riot of 1943 it was claimed by many observers that it was the appearance of the disciplined and nonbiased federal troops, under instructions to put down civil violence "at all costs," which brought the rioting to a close. Here the emphasis is on the factor of the lack of susceptibility of the troops to criticisms based on presumed partisanship (Prop. 2b., Lambert, *op. cit.*). On the other hand, it could also be claimed that the appearance of weapons carriers, armored cars and large numbers of armed troops constituted a "highly visible display of overwhelming force." Lohman has suggested that it is in the period prior to the outbreak of actual violence that a show of force is important. He writes (Lohman, 1947, p. 103):

If an unruly crowd has gathered, it should be possible to mobilize adequate numbers of police, quickly and without delay. A *show of force* is preferable to a belated and tragic exercise of force. It is well to recognize that an incident

6. Although high racial social tension and frequent skirmishes have characterized Chicago. Since 1963 tension and at least minor violence have become endemic in many urban centers.

which has passed beyond the control of the police can only with great difficulty be again brought under control. As a cardinal principle, it may be noted that a situation should never be permitted to develop in which control has passed out of the hands of the police authority.

He continues by noting the necessity for a plan of reinforcing officers by sending squad cars or even whole platoons of police to the scene of a conflict. Such a program has been instituted in Chicago and was used, apparently with some success, at the time of the Trumbull Park disturbances. This program calls for the progressive commitment of police forces (see Proposition 5) in such a way that police at the scene of the difficulties can call for plans (in this case by number) and receive pre-arranged assistance.

It seems probable that such exhibitions of force, in overwhelming strength, have prevented outbreaks on numerous occasions. The efficacy of such displays, however, can only be inferential since it is not known how many riots have been prevented by such action. It can be seen, however, that in those cases where riots have occurred, the social factors included in the other propositions have been operative. Thus, in every case where major interracial rioting has occurred, considerable time has elapsed between the initiating incident and the institution of strong external controls.[7] It will be recalled that in both the Chicago and Detroit disturbances, perhaps the most sanguinary of this century, police and other municipal authorities were reluctant to call for additional forces. In both these cases also, the administration of the police and the civil government generally, was distrusted by the Negro communities involved. Similarly, the municipal government of East St. Louis was trusted by neither whites nor Negroes; further, in the East St. Louis case it was suspected by the white community that in any application of formal controls there would be a differential treatment of whites and Negroes, favorable to their own group.

There is little evidence that either case proves or disproves the propositions related to the degree of violence in suppression of violence or the comprehensiveness and harshness of punishment. While there have been statements made frequently during the actual course of interracial

7. Through the summer of 1967, this continued to be true. It is expected that this situation will change sharply in 1968 and subsequent summers.
[There was no major race-related violence during the summer of 1968. There were large numbers of National Guardsmen mobilized *before* the bloody events during the Democratic convention in Chicago. During the spring of 1969 we have seen large contingents of law-enforcement officers and National Guardsmen brought to university communities like Berkeley and Greensboro. Observers in Berkeley have commented that National Guard maneuvers in that city seem to be dress rehearsals for control of any variety of urban-centered disturbances. The first air attacks on American cities (helicopters dropping CS tear gas at Berkeley and Greensboro) seem to give credibility to a belief that police and military agencies are not only prepared to more quickly institute control but also to use increasingly severe repressive measures in attaining that "control." During the weeks (May, 1969) in which galley proofs for this book were being read we were several times forced to stop working because of tear gas attacks on the university or forced evacuation by police.—A. D. G.]

violence that law violators will be arrested and convicted, in some cases presumably for murder, few post-riot events have taken place which would be likely to coerce potential rioters. Threats made in Omaha, which had the townspeople anxious in the days during which Wood was in control, were never followed up by large-scale legal action against offenders in that disturbance. There is only one major interracial outbreak in this century in which great harshness was used in suppression and in which harsh punishments were administered after the termination of social violence. This was not an urban race riot but a rural "insurrection" of Negroes—that of the "Elaine Massacre" in 1919. This rural rebellion was suppressed with great harshness on the part of the authorities and many Negroes received stiff sentences when convicted of various crimes in the court trials which immediately followed the suppression of the disorders. There were no further outbreaks of this nature, but in the absence of information on conditions in other areas and at other times it is difficult to attribute this lack of further violence to the utilization of harsh control patterns. There is, further, no evidence to suggest that punishments have become sharper over the years since the turn of the century.[8] It is possible that there has been greater uniformity in the application of control. In all the major riots which have been discussed in this paper, Negroes were arrested and convicted with much greater frequency than whites. More recently, police forces in those major metropolitan areas in the North, which might presumably be the scene of interracial violence, increasingly have arrested whites and Negroes without distinction in those situations which might have led to interracial outbursts.[9] These arrests have not, it is true, been followed with a high incidence of convictions and commitments. Nonetheless, the greater uniformity of application of police controls as exhibited, for example, in Chicago, might have acted to prevent large-scale eruptions in Northern cities since World War II. The major disturbance in a Northern city since the war, in Cicero, was marked by a lack of uniformity in the application of external controls, a long lapse of time prior to the introduction of strong forces which could dominate the situation, considerable susceptibility of civil government to public criticism, and a low degree of harshness and aggression in the process of suppression. Other situations which have nearly erupted into large-scale rioting have

8. The question legitimately could be raised as to whether the prospect of harsh punishment for riot participation would deter such activity. Much riot behavior would seem to be analogous to "crimes of passion," particularly certain varieties of homicide. While dissenting opinion in the dispute over the concept of deterrence as related to capital punishment can still be heard, most professional criminologists are agreed that harshness does not deter. See the whole issue of the *Prison Journal*, Vol. 38, No. 2 (1958), devoted to capital punishment, especially the extensive bibliography appended to an article by Hugo A. Bedau (pp. 41–45). See also Thorsten Sellin (ed.), "Murder and the Penalty of Death," *Annals of the American Academy of Political and Social Science*, 284 (1952).

9. See, *e.g.*, the data on arrests in the Chicago Commission on Human Relations publications on Trumbull Park.

been characterized by factors which fit one or another of the propositions. In the St. Louis swimming pool incidents (1950), for example, considerable time elapsed before the police acted in such a way as to dominate the situation and there was no highly visible display of force during the beginnings of the disturbance (Grimshaw, 1962a, pp. 146-58).

Proposition 5, which deals with the process of commitment of forces, suggests that gradual increments in force are more effective than the initial engagement of superior forces once rioting has begun. This proposition seems at least partly antithetical to the first proposition, which emphasized the importance of a display of overwhelming force. In the Trumbull Park disturbances, the police, because of considerable reserve power, were able to bring increasingly larger forces to bear, thus creating the impression of a limitless supply of reinforcements. That the ultimate limits of these forces were known, however, can be seen from the editorial maneuvering of the community newspapers, which attempted to bring pressure for the removal of the police by noting deficiencies in police coverage in other areas of the city. The question can be raised whether the initial commitment of a larger portion of the over fifteen hundred policemen eventually concentrated in the Trumbull Park area might not have prevented such violence as did occur. In the Detroit riot, with a limited number of police reserves, almost the entire force was concentrated in the areas of violence soon after the rioting started. It seems doubtful that holding back reserves for later commitment would have been very effective in the control of that disturbance. Both of these propositions (1 and 5) assume the availability of rather extensive forces for the control of eruptions of social violence. In most race riots in this century, such forces simply have not been available. In New York, with a much more sizable police force and with reserves of a large variety, police officials and other municipal authorities have been able either to display overwhelming force in a highly visible manner or to progressively commit increments of force. Both of these techniques have been successful to a certain extent. The display of force decreases the possibility of violence itself; the technique of increments of force is important if rioting has actually begun.

There has been no urban center in this country which, like Bombay or Calcutta, has experienced a series of major eruptions of social violence increasing in number over time. In only one Northern city is evidence available which indicates that social violence, of greater or lesser intensity, is an almost continuous phenomenon. This is Chicago. It has been suggested that Chicago's apparently greater incidence of social racial violence may be a reflection of superior reporting. It is clear, however, that the flexibility of police control practices, as spelled out particularly by Lohman, has acted to prevent any of these disturbances from culminating in full-scale rioting in recent years. In almost every major race riot which has been studied, two major tactical goals have been apparent. These have been suggested above: the closing of access to inter-group contacts and the use of curfews. It is probable that the area in which flexibility of elements in control pattern would be possible is in the utilization of varying techniques for achieving the first of these goals.

Two major theses have been developed from work on racial social violence in the urban centers of the northern United States. The first has been that racial social violence has resulted, in this country, from the reactions of the dominant group (whites) to assaults upon the accommodative structure by the subordinate group (Negroes) (Grimshaw, 1959a, b). The second major thesis has asserted that the background factors of prejudice, discrimination, and social tension are present in all urban centers in the North with relatively or absolutely great Negro populations in a degree sufficient to permit the development of situations characterized by "violence-proneness" (Grimshaw, 1961 and 1962a). The eruption or non-eruption of interracial violence is determined, it has been claimed, by the character of external forces of constraint and control, especially the police forces. Sufficient evidence is available to validate the assertion that prejudice, discrimination and social tensions are present in every major urban center with a large Negro population. No such evidence can be adduced to validate the assertion of the primary importance of external control factors. Validation of this assertion would require data on four types of situations:

Riots occurring in situations of high social tension with strong social controls.
Riots not occurring in sitautions of high social tension with strong social controls.
Riots occurring in situations of high social tension with weak social controls.
Riots not occurring in situations of high social tension with weak social controls.

The thesis on the importance of external controls, as stated, would predict only situations 2 and 3. If data were available, over time, for all major Northern cities with large Negro populations, the thesis could be adequately tested. With the data available it is not, however, possible to determine whether there may not be situations of high social tension with weak social controls which have not erupted into major interracial disturbances. Similarly, the lack of outbursts of interracial violence cannot be taken as proof that strong external controls have existed. On this point there is at least indirect evidence, such as the example of Washington (at the time of the swimming pool openings) where strong external controls have prevented the occurrence of major social violence. The data available support the conclusion that in every case where major rioting has occurred, the social structure of the community has been characterized by weak patterns of external control. Final validation or rejection of the thesis of the importance of strong external controls must await intensive examination of the police and other agencies of external constraint in those urban centers which have not experienced major outbursts of interracial social violence.

Allen D. Grimshaw

Urban Racial Violence in the United States: Changing Ecological Considerations

Urban racial social violence has occurred in every geographic region of the United States. It has not occurred in every city in every area. Certain similarities in background and social context are found in the cities which have had major race riots.[1] East St. Louis, Washington, Chicago, Tulsa, and Detroit all had sharp increases in Negro population in the years immediately prior to major interracial disturbances, and there were accompanying strains in the accommodative structure, generated in part by the Negroes' assaults on it and in part by the sheer pressure of population on facilities.

Accounts of urban race riots which are in sharp disagreement on other details consistently converge in descriptions of their ecology.[2] Ecological patterns are found in reports of individual incidents which did not lead to riots.

Without doing too great an injustice to the data, it is possible to specify roughly four patterns of urban racial violence:

1. Spontaneous brawls over an immediate disturbance, among bystanders.

   1. The question of why some cities have had riots and others not cannot be fully answered until data have been collected on four types of urban areas: those characterized by combinations of high or low social tensions with weak or strong external forces of constraint. It will then be possible to isolate peculiarities of cities that have had riots. There has been no agreement as to what is decisive in causing outbreaks of violence.
   2. Other consistent patterns in major urban racial disturbances can be isolated. In view of the acknowledged defects in the materials and their frequently partisan nature, however, considerable caution is necessary in drawing conclusions about "patterns" (cf., e.g., the conclusions on the Detroit riot [1943] of the "Dowling Report" [Rushton *et al.*, n.d.] and of various "action" agencies, such as the Urban League and the National Asssociation for the Advancement of Colored People).

2. The "mass, unco-ordinated battle" occurring when groups of one race attack usually isolated members of the other. Mobs of one race seldom engage mobs of the other race in open battle.

3. The "urban pogrom," which is the full-scale assault of one group, almost always white, upon Negroes and which has occurred particularly where whites have assumed the tacit approval of government. These "pogroms" have resulted in the flight of large numbers of the minority community.

4. Stray assaults and stabbings on the part of individuals or small groups of one race upon individuals of the other.[3]

Three varieties of expression of social violence may be distinguished: physical assault, including lynching and other homicide; arson, bombing, and like forms of attack upon property; and looting. These occur with differential frequency and intensity in the four patterns of urban racial violence noted above and in the following types of ecological areas: (a) Negro residential areas with no, or a minimal number of, business establishments (usually the upper or middle strata of the Negro population); (b) white middle-class residential areas; (c) Negro residential areas of high density, serviced largely by white businesses; (d) "stable" mixed neighborhoods; (e) neighborhoods previously dominated by whites, now undergoing a transition in occupancy (called "contested area" in Chicago Commission on Race Relations, 1919); (f) white-dominated areas not contested by Negroes; and (g) white-dominated central business districts.[4]

The importance of other sites within a city, such as recreational areas and, more recently, lunch counters or schools, is determined partly by their location relative to the seven types of ecological areas and partly by the local potential for violence.[5] In major riots occurring before and up to the end of World War II, two other types of locations were of particular importance in the ecology of major disturbances: public transportation facilities, particularly transfer points, and government buildings. Finally, either natural or man-made boundaries (e.g., bodies of water or large parks and large industrial complexes or railroad yards) have confined or determined the path of violence.

3. These four categories are a paraphrase and condensation of a typology of social violence developed by Richard D. Lambert in his study, "Hindu-Muslim Riots" (Lambert, 1951, pp. 217–21). Marked parallels and some significant differences emerge from comparison of Hindu-Muslim and Negro-white violence.

4. Obviously these ecological areas do not *cause* variant manifestations of social violence. It would be more precise to say that patterns of social organization or disorganization which are local characteristics are more likely to be associated with some outbreaks of violence than with others. For heuristic purposes, however, it is convenient to bypass the well-documented social characteristics of the areas and speak of the areas themselves as experiencing the varying manifestations.

5. While two of the bloodiest riots in this century, Chicago's in 1919 and Detroit's in 1943, started in recreational facilities, combat quickly moved away from the site of the original incident and thereafter conformed to the ecological patterns described below.

The purpose of this paper is to determine whether patterns of urban racial violence (brawls, etc.) and particular expressions of violence (physical assaults, etc.) are differently manifested in different types of ecological areas. Data are drawn from accounts of major urban race riots up to and including the Detroit riot of 1943. While no attempt has been made to integrate materials on the ecology of the violence of the Sixties, it may be mentioned that these events closely parallel the patterns discussed in the section below on Negro slums.[6]

ECOLOGICAL CONSISTENCIES IN URBAN RACIAL VIOLENCE THROUGH THE WORLD WAR II PERIOD

During the first forty-five years of the twentieth century the United States experienced a large number of major interracial outbreaks and, particularly in the years following World War I, a host of lesser disturbances (a typology of periods of racial violence in the United States is suggested in Grimshaw, 1959a). Excepting certain differences between "northern" and "southern" styles of race riots, they show a remarkable degree of ecological consistency (Grimshaw, 1959a, p. 65; Grimshaw, 1959b, pp. 36-37, 178).

NEGRO RESIDENTIAL AREAS WITH NO, OR
A MINIMAL NUMBER OF, BUSINESS ESTABLISHMENTS

Where they have existed, these Negro residential areas contain populations which, in income, in years of education completed, and in occupational status, are above the norms for the larger Negro population. These neighborhoods had few incidents. The absence of non-residential property meant an absence of opportunity for looting. Lower population density and less likelihood of large gatherings made rioting on a large scale unlikely. It is also possible, although no evidence can be found to support the claim, that the higher social and economic status of the residents enabled them to enjoy better police protection than was provided in other Negro areas.

Two varieties of racial violence might be expected to occur in these neighborhoods: arson and bombing and related forms of assault on property, and attacks on persons. In Chicago, where bombings and arson were used to intimidate real-estate dealers of both races from selling properties in "exclusive" areas, trouble might have been anticipated where middle-class Negroes were concentrated; however, there is no

6. When this paper was originally published, it included discussions of changes in patterns of urban racial violence in the years between 1943 and 1960 and an attempt to delineate problems in forecasting the future of racial social violence.

evidence that these neighborhoods were singled out or that they suffered from "raids" directed randomly by white hoodlums either during the major riot or in times of relative peace. It can only be concluded that insufficient evidence documents the local violence; there may have been incidents, but too few to attract the attention of authorities, or the characteristics of the neighborhoods and residents may have reduced the likelihood of incidents. In the absence of adequate documentation it seems reasonable to accept the second interpretation.

WHITE HIGHER-CLASS RESIDENTIAL NEIGHBORHOODS

The experience of white residential neighborhoods, particularly those more distant from central business districts with residents of relatively high socioeconomic characteristics, was similar to that of Negro residential neighborhoods. The more isolated they were from centers in which violence occurred, the more likely they were to escape trouble, except during major outbursts of race rioting.

The single pattern of racial violence reported for such neighborhoods reflected the higher social and economic status of their white residents, many of whom employed Negro domestics.[7] During the course of several major riots such domestics were attacked by white gangs, frequently while waiting for buses or streetcars. Large mobs seldom gathered in such neighborhoods, removed as they were from the areas where rioting was concentrated, but youths frequently prowled in automobiles in search of stray Negroes,[8] and many frightened white employers kept their domestics at home until violence came to an end.

NEGRO SLUMS

Violence in time of major race riots has been concentrated in Negro slums, which in many cities were served largely by white businesses. Casualties and fatalities occurred most often in slums or along their fringes,[9] and destruction of property, particularly looting, was greatest

7. With recent changes in the American social and economic structure, there have been fewer domestics. During the waves of riots during the two world wars, however, domestic service accounted for a large proportion of all Negroes who worked, particularly of Negro women.

8. It would be interesting to see how the wider distributions of automobile ownership has spread racial disturbances to areas more remote from city centers. With television carrying news of incipient disturbances (see, e.g., Gremley, 1952), and cars available to carry people to the scene (as in the case of a Negro "move-in" in Levittown, Pennsylvania), the time may be ripe for an examination of "modern technology and the diffusion of racial disturbances." While it is too early to tell, it seems likely that the spread of the current "lunch counter" strikes is related to the wide coverage of news by television.

9. The Chicago riot of 1919 was an exception.

there. Three subvarieties of social racial violence have occurred in Negro slums.

In a number of race riots of the "southern" style, attaining the intensity of urban "pogroms" or of mass racial war, Negro slums were completely or partially destroyed. In the Springfield, Illinois, riot of 1908, forty Negro homes were destroyed and an estimated two thousand Negroes were driven from the town by rioting whites. In the riot in East St. Louis in 1917, the Negro section was invaded, Negro residences and businesses were set on fire, and Negroes were shot down in large numbers as they attempted to flee from the burning buildings. In these, and in equally bitter disorders in Tulsa in 1921, violence was confined to Negro areas and their boundaries; however, in each case, fighting began in the central business district. Negroes then retreated to their own sections, and attacks were launched against them there by large white mobs. In Springfield there was little fighting back; in Tulsa, on the other hand, the white attackers were resisted in strength and, for a time, repulsed. In these cases, and in similar "southern" riots, all three varieties of violence occurred, although looting was minimal and was often only in the form of breaking into pawnshops and hardware stores in search of weapons and ammunition. Casualties were heavy and fatalities high, Negro victims accounting for the largest share. Arson was endemic; in Tulsa and East St. Louis the Negro sections were almost totally destroyed.

No northern city experienced racial strife in which "all-out" attacks such as these were made on Negro sections (Alfred McClung Lee and Norman Daymond Humphrey assert that one was narrowly averted in Detroit in 1943 [Lee and Humphrey, 1943, pp. 39-40]). The two Harlem disturbances of 1935 and 1943 were completely limited to the Negro slum; on other occasions riots in Negro sections occurred in conjunction with more widespread violence.

The Harlem disturbance differed from other riots because of the sheer size of the local Negro population. A major invasion was inconceivable without a fairly well-equipped army, and only police forces were equipped in a manner in any way adequate to cope with the 1943 disorders. On the other hand, whites in the area were relatively few and, when outbreaks occurred, were either able to flee or to find Negroes willing to give them shelter. There were few occasions for Negro-white contacts, and physical clashes were usually between the resident population and the police. Most of the violence was in the form of looting of stores and general destruction of property. While some evidence suggests white property was singled out for attack, enough Negro establishments were attacked to leave open the question whether the violence was racial.

In other northern urban race riots Negro sections have shared in physical social violence as well as being the centers of property damage and looting. Physical assault may be by Negroes on whites passing through their neighborhoods in automobiles, on public vehicles, or on foot, or on whites who found themselves in the area when major rioting began; or there may be conflict between Negroes and the police, the Negroes frequently being armed and, according to the police, initiating violence by assault or by resisting arrest; or, finally, there may be conflict following the invasion of Negro neighborhoods by bands of armed whites, most frequently making forays by automobile. In both the Chicago riot of 1919 and the Detroit riot of 1943, the Negro slum or the immediately contiguous areas experienced the greatest number of casualties. Over half the fatalities in the Detroit riot occurred in Paradise Valley. According to the reports filed by the police department, seventeen of thirty-four deaths in the riot were caused by justifiable shooting by the police (Rushton *et al., op. cit.,* Exhibits 18, 19. Considerable caution is needed in interpreting the findings of this report).

With two exceptions, physical violence in these areas was usually visited by mobs of one race upon isolated members of the other. One exception involves large numbers of police engaged in battle with mobs of Negroes: in both the Chicago and the Detroit riots they waged pitched battles. The other exception has occurred when large numbers of Negroes have caught and engaged raiding parties of whites invading Negro sections. A more frequent occurrence than either of these, however, was that in which white motorists passing through Negro areas, in some cases unaware of the rioting, were stoned by Negroes or in which whites were pulled from buses and beaten or otherwise assaulted.

Assaults on property have taken three forms. In the Chicago riot, arson was fairly common in the Negro section, allegedly committed by members of white gangs and "athletic clubs." Arson and bombings were not frequent in other major northern riots; more frequent was the looting of places of business by Negroes who engaged in general destruction of property of whites. Destruction of automobiles was incidental to assaults on white motorists.

"STABLE" MIXED NEIGHBORHOODS

The term "stable mixed neighborhood" has, conveniently, no precise meaning. In discussions of race riots the term has come to mean, residually, neighborhoods in which no social violence occurred. The implied meaning, however, seems to be that neighborhoods so labeled are characterized by unchanging patterns of occupancy, whatever the proportion of whites to Negroes. If this is the case, there is indirect confirmation that violence is less likely there. Studies like that of Kramer (Kramer, 1950) have demonstrated that more favorable interracial attitudes are to be found in such neighborhoods.

Direct evidence is more problematical. Lee and Humphrey (1943, p. 17) state that students reported that there was no violence in mixed neighborhoods during the Detroit riot.[10] The characteristics of these neighborhoods were not specified, either in their volume or in other writings on the Detroit riot where similar statements were made. On the other hand, in the Chicago riot of 1919 violence directed against Negroes occurred even in areas of long-established Negro occupancy, while other "adjusted" areas remained quiet (e.g., the North Side [see Chicago Commission on Race Relations, *op. cit.*, pp. 108-113, 119]). If there were any residential areas in northern cities where Negroes and whites had lived amicably for long periods, they were probably few and far between, and any assertions about a lack of violence there should be looked upon with caution (there were "nonadjusted" neighborhoods which experienced no violence [Chicago Commission on Race Relations, *op. cit.*, pp. 114-115]). Areas where patterns of occupancy remained relatively unchanged over long periods of time, where friendly or, at the least, cordial relations prevailed between the two races, probably had the same experience during race riots as did the Negro residential and white middle-class neighborhoods: violence, such as it was, resulted from invasions from outside, not from the explosion of local social tensions. As in the case of Negro and white middle-class residential areas, however, there is insufficient data to state positively that "stable" neighborhoods were characterized by particular patterns of violence, during periods either of actual rioting or of relative peace.

"CONTESTED AREAS"

The term "contested area" was used by the Chicago Commission on Race Relations to describe areas previously dominated by whites but undergoing transition and those which, although not yet penetrated, are in the line of movement of the Negro population and anticipating invasion. The latter differs from the next ecological type in that the areas discussed in the next section, although close to centers of Negro population, are not contested by Negroes.

Opposition to Negro in-movement has been expressed in both an organized and a non-organized fashion. Much of the interracial conflict in periods of relative harmony occurred there, and much of it was, and is, organized in the form of "neighborhood improvement" or "property-owners" associations. These usually disavowed, at least verbally, violence of any variety, although the claim has been made that their publicity was often inflammatory. Whatever their official views toward violence

10. They claimed that violence did not occur in mixed neighborhoods, among mixed groups of students, or among whites and Negroes who worked together in war plants.

may have been, it was in contested areas, where Negroes had already moved in, that incidents of violence most frequently occurred in periods when there were no actual riots. The incidents largely involved property, either destruction of Negro-occupied property or harassment of the owners by minor damage. Long and Johnson (1947) have noted that both the Chicago and Detroit riots were preceded by violence over the entrance of Negroes into white neighborhoods. Such areas, in a pattern that continues today, also provided the scene for physical assaults.

In view of the concentration of violence in these contested areas in periods when other parts of the city were enjoying relative peace, it might be anticipated that in times of actual race rioting they would have been the focal point of violence. This is not the case; the Negro slum suffered more casualties and, in at least one major riot, that in Chicago in 1919, the highest number of casualties reported was in an area with no Negro residents. Some violence did occur in these areas, particularly along their borders and at transfer points in public transportation. In 1943, Woodward Avenue in Detroit served as a boundary line between the major concentration of Negroes in that city and an area of low-class white residence which included a large number of rooming houses. Lee and Humphrey, in their volume on the Detroit riot of 1943, include a "battle map" of major points of overt conflict. Two were located at Woodward Avenue and main cross-streets in the Mack-Davenport area and at Vernor Highway where the sharpest fighting, involving large mobs of whites, took place. Whites stoned automobiles with Negro passengers, dragged Negroes from buses, and beat them. At other points up and down Woodward Avenue, Negroes occasionally took the initiative and attacked whites. However, there was no major invasion across this line, and, although some Negro penetration had occurred in areas west of Woodward Avenue, there was no major violence there. However, violence also occurred around a smaller concentration of lower-income Negroes along Michigan Avenue. Here again, the violence occurred on the peripheries rather than in surrounding contested areas.

The reason for the lack of major violence in contested areas during major race riots is not clear. A possible answer may lie in the implicit observation made by the Chicago Commission on Race Relations that the neighbors of Negro in-movers were infrequently involved in attacks upon the new tenants. It is possible that most of the violence visited upon new Negro residents is the work of individuals not themselves local residents. In its investigation of bombings the commission heard testimony of one victim that the police believed that the bombings were being done by a gang of young white "roughnecks" who were under police surveillance (Long and Johnson, 1947).[11] If this was true, and if similar acts of violence directed against property have been committed

11. Observers in Levittown, Pennsylvania, noted that most of the opposition to the Meyers family moving in was by persons not resident in the immediate neighborhood.

not by neighbors but by "outside fanatics," [12] it becomes easier to understand why these sectors saw less violence during actual rioting. The perpetrating individuals or groups were, during major riots, more likely to be found where there was more action. Violence in these areas during major rioting was probably more likely to occur as a result of chance encounters or of a concentration of people, not specifically gathered for the purpose, for instance, at bus transfer points.

Except in the peak periods of major race riots, contested areas were the centers of most racial violence in northern cities through World War II. In cities which experienced no major race riots, almost all violence occurred there or in areas, such as recreation centers, with unusually high potential for trouble.

WHITE-DOMINATED AREAS NOT CONTESTED BY NEGROES

In their discussion of Negro residence areas in Chicago, the 1919 Commission on Race Relations described adjusted and nonadjusted areas. The second category consisted of areas of organized opposition and of unorganized opposition. The report presented materials on areas of organized opposition; of one variety of unorganized opposition, the commission said:

There are residence districts of Chicago adjacent to those occupied by Negroes in which hostility to Negroes is so marked that the latter not only find it impossible to live there, but expose themselves to danger even by passing through. There are no hostile organizations in these neighborhoods, and active antagonism is usually confined to gang lawlessness. . . . In the section immediately west of Wentworth Avenue and thus adjoining the densest Negro residence area in the city, practically no Negroes live. . . . Wentworth Avenue has long been regarded as a strict boundary line separating white and Negro residence areas. The district has many "athletic clubs." The contact of Negroes and whites comes when Negroes must pass to and from their work at the Stock Yards and at other industries located in the district. It was in this district that the largest number of riot clashes occurred. Several Negroes have been murdered here, and numbers have been beaten by gangs of young men and boys. (Chicago Commission on Race Relations: 1922, p. 155.)

Of those reported injured in the Chicago riot, 34 per cent received their wounds in the "Black Belt" itself, and 41 per cent in the stockyards district of the Southwest Side.

It is difficult to find neighborhoods which have been as vehement in

12. A recent study in a Kansas City residential area found that whites were, at the least, resigned to an in-movement of Negro residents (Community Studies, Inc., n.d., undertaken at the request of the Kansas City, Missouri, Commission on Human Relations). When a bomb was exploded in the neighborhood, it was interpreted as the work of a fanatic, not a resident (personal communication from W. H. Gremley, executive secretary, Kansas City, Missouri, Commission on Human Relations).

hostility to Negroes as the stockyards area of Chicago. Even today, the district west of Wentworth in Chicago has remained one of minimal Negro residence.[13] In 1910, Wentworth Avenue was the east-west dividing line between the Negro and white populations. Between 1910 and 1950 the Negro population increased from slightly under fifty thousand to a little over five hundred and eighty-six thousand. (The best ecological and demographic study of the Negro population of Chicago or, for that matter, of any northern city, is Duncan and Duncan, 1957.) Squeezed between Wentworth Avenue and the lake front, they spread throughout the South Side and into enclaves in western sections. The stockyards district has remained essentially white in the face of tremendous pressures of the Negro population.

Under ordinary circumstances, Chicago Negroes in 1919 would have avoided the stockyards district. They passed through it on their way to and from their work in the yards and packing houses and other industries but did not linger; as noted above, prior to the riot several Negroes had been murdered there by gangs of young men and boys. If the situation had been normal, no Negroes would have been found there during the riot, with the possible exception of small "raiding" parties. However, the riot coincided with a major strike of Chicago's transportation lines. Negroes found themselves stranded at work; some stayed, others attempted to go home. Whether it was to protect their families or to engage themselves in rioting, or whether they did not know about the riot, is unimportant: what matters is that they got caught in the very locality most notorious for hostility to them. Many were beaten, and several slain.

No other major urban race riot has taken place where a white neighborhood characterized by such intense prejudice immediately abutted on the central concentration of Negroes. If, in Chicago, it had not been for the transportation strike, it is doubtful whether so much of the violence would have occurred where it did. More probably, battles would have been concentrated, as elsewhere, along the boundary lines. However, tension was high in the areas of Detroit immediately west of Woodward Avenue, which, however, was a contested area even in 1940; and, as has been observed, violence was largely concentrated along the dividing line itself.

13. Between the Chicago River and Fifty-fifth Street. This neighborhood, like Cicero and Trumbull Park, scenes of more recent disorders, has a Polish, Bohemian and Slavic population. The residents are too poor and many are too foreign to go elsewhere. They are neither geographically nor socially mobile.

[The area immediately west of Wentworth Avenue and Fifty-fifth Street was settled by Eastern Europeans, mostly Lithuanians and Poles with smaller blocs of Italian, Yugoslavian, and German working classes and almost entirely Roman Catholic Bohemians well-concentrated northwest of the River in Pilsen. (Source: University of Chicago 1951 study)—A. D. G.]

WHITE-DOMINATED CENTRAL BUSINESS DISTRICTS

With the exception of the Harlem disturbances, highly distinctive in many of their characteristics, in every important interracial disturbance in both northern and southern cities, Negroes were the victims of mobs in the white-dominated central business districts. In those cases where few Negroes were so assaulted, it was because the Negro population, forewarned, had not ventured downtown. Violence in central business districts took the form of physical assault and usually involved large mobs of whites and individual Negroes or small groups of them. In the Chicago riot it was reported that the white gangs of soldiers and sailors who raided the Loop, the central shopping district, in search of Negroes, "in the course of their activities . . . wantonly destroyed property of white business men." (Chicago Commission on Race Relations: 1922, p. 7.) This, as in other cases, was largely incidental to the main purpose of catching and assaulting Negroes. No major outbreaks of looting directed at white property were reported resulting from white mob activity.

The largest mobs of whites have usually been those which gather in the central business district. Lee and Humphrey report a mob of "10,000 people jammed around the Woodward and Davenport-Mack intersections on the northern edge of the downtown district. Cadillac Square—between City Hall and the County Building—was packed with milling murderous thousands, especially at the City Hall end." (Lee and Humphrey, 1943, p. 36.) The mobs engaged in a variety of types of assault, from the stoning of Negro automobiles and their occupants, to the invasion of theaters in search of Negroes. Army officers saw, from windows of the Federal Building in downtown Detroit, a mob estimated at five hundred pursuing a lone Negro on Fort Street from Woodward. Similar events occurred in every major riot.

SPECIAL ECOLOGICAL FACTORS

Two types of ecological locations warrant special mention. Violence in northern urban race riots occurred frequently at transfer points of public transportation lines, particularly where members of one race had to pass through the territory of the other. A comparison of maps noting transportation contacts between Negroes and whites with spot maps of injuries and deaths in the Chicago riot of 1919 is instructive.[14] A

14. See the numerous maps accompanying the report of the Chicago Commission on Race Relations. Note also the special exhibits on incidents on the Detroit Street Railway (Rushton, *et al., op. cit.*).

general strike on surface and elevated lines after the second day of the rioting magnified the importance of transportation, for, with the stopping of the street cars, a new source of danger arose to those who attempted to walk to their places of employment. Even on the first day of the riot, however, "attacks on street cars provided outstanding cases, five persons being killed and many injured" (Chicago Commission on Race Relations: 1922, p. 17).

In the Detroit riot, both whites and Negroes were pulled from street cars and beaten or otherwise assaulted. The same thing occurred in the East St. Louis and Washington riots, Negroes being the major victims. Incidents in Harlem have been recorded in which white employees of the transportation systems were assaulted by Negro passengers, although this was important in neither of the major disturbances in Harlem.

Public transportation provides an opportunity to catch isolated individuals and attack them without fear of immediate reprisal. Another scene of violence is government buildings, attacks on which have occurred when it is believed that Negroes have sought shelter there or because Negroes are known to work there. Negro municipal employees were evacuated from the City Hall in Detroit when the building was threatened by white mobs. Other locations of interracial violence in major northern urban race riots have been highly specific. The rioting in Detroit began on the Belle Isle Bridge and became general apparently only after a much publicized announcement at a Negro night club. That location (Belle Isle) was on the very periphery of the Negro concentration in Detroit and fits none of the ecological classifications of areas suggested above. Once the riot was under way, activity in the original area became minimal.

*Elmer R. Akers and Vernon Fox **

The Detroit Rioters and Looters Committed to Prison

Race riots have occurred many times in the United States, but the conviction and sentence to prison of a hundred and more of the participants is unprecedented in its volume. On March 9, 1944, we had received in the State Prison of Southern Michigan at Jackson 105 of the defendants who had been tried on charges growing out of the Detroit race riot of June 21-22, 1943. Others are still being tried or are awaiting trial.

Already there have been written several reams concerning the race riot in Detroit. Newspaper and magazine articles, editorials, pamphlets, surveys of opinion, reports of lawyers' and other associations, and reports by psychiatrists, police commissions, and various city officials have been published. Probably the most important publication has been a small book by Alfred McClung Lee and Norman D. Humphrey of Wayne University (1943). This volume contains a rather objective journalistic report and sociological interpretation of the riot.

The present article is concerned, not with the Detroit race riot itself, but with that group of men convicted of felonies and incarcerated in State Prison as a result of it. The investigators are interested in the social and psychological background and equipment of the men that induced them to participate in activities connected with mass race violence, and for which they were convicted of felonies. As far as the writers can discover, this particular phase has not heretofore been attacked.

METHOD OF PROCEDURE

The records of the State Prison of Southern Michigan were used as the source of data. These records include with regard to each man the Michigan State Police report, a copy of the Court's Indeterminate Sentence Record, Probation Officer's report, educational and psychological examinations, medical report, and a social history. In some cases, these records are supplemented by letters from the man's relatives, former employers, from schools he has attended and from institutions both penal and eleemosynary, which have had contact with the prisoner himself and with other members of his family.

All of the men who were sentenced to prison for crimes directly connected with the Detroit race riot were studied and the records compiled on them were the source of the data used in this paper. There were ninety-seven Negroes and eight white men in the group,[1] a total of 105 cases. As will be pointed out in greater detail later in the paper, the majority of this group were not rioters as such, but looters and carriers of concealed weapons. Most of the actual rioters, the participants in acts of violence, were convicted on charges of assault and battery, disorderly conduct, and/or other misdemeanors. These misdemeanants, or active rioters, were in the main sentenced to the Detroit House of Correction

---

* The authors of this paper, who are, respectively, the Sociologist and Psychologist on the staff of the Southern Michigan prison at Jackson, are reporting the results of their studies of the Detroit rioters who have been committed to the State Prison. The riot itself appears not to be simply a symptom of race feeling.—Editor.

1. A similar disproportion occurred in the Chicago race riot of 1919. See the report of the Chicago Commission on Race Relations, 1922.

for periods varying from thirty to ninety days. Although there were thirteen perpetrators of violent crimes sent to prison, only three were actually charged with rioting. For purposes of this study, however, the group of men convicted for crimes directly connected with the riot are hereafter called the riot group.

It was noted that each man in the riot group had been tried and sentenced at Recorder's Court in Detroit. A control group of ninety-seven Negroes and eight white men was selected at random from the men received at the State Prison of Southern Michigan from Recorder's Court during the months of May and June, 1943, immediately preceding the riot. Frequency distributions were set up for the riot group and the control group on the basis of age of offenders, intelligence quotient, nativity and length of residence in Michigan, grade placement in school as indicated by individual results on the New Stanford Achievement Test, history of drug addiction, and venereal condition. Statistical analyses were made on each of these sets of distributions. Further analyses were made of the riot group alone on the basis of industrial skill, marital status, previous criminal record, and the specific crimes for which the men were convicted.

NATIVITY

Only fourteen of the riot group were born in the State of Michigan, and but twenty-one of the control group were born in this state. Thirteen of the rioters had lived in Michigan less than one year, eleven less than two years; fourteen had been in this state from three to four years, thirteen others had been here from five to ten years, and forty had been here eleven years or more. The states contributing most heavily to the riot group were, in descending order of importance, the following:

Georgia, 22; Alabama, 18; Michigan, 14; Tennessee, 11; Mississippi, 8; total of all other states, 32; grand total, 105. A statistical analysis indicated that there was no significant difference between the riot and control groups as to whether the men were natives of Michigan or from other states. Most of the men in both the riot and control groups had come from other states. The mean length of residence in Michigan of the non-native riot and control groups were 10.6 ± 0.9 and 12.0 ± 0.9 respectively. A critical ratio of 0.3 indicates that no significant difference exists between the two groups of men as to their length of residence in Michigan.

Tabulation and analysis of members of the riot and control groups as to whether they were natives of southern states or northern states yielded rather interesting results. The Mason and Dixon line was selected as a rough dividing line between the northern and southern states. The following table may be helpful in visualizing the differences in nativity of the two groups:

	RIOT GROUP		CONTROL GROUP	
Nativity	*Expected*	*Observed*	*Expected*	*Observed*
Natives of Northern States	24	16	24	32
Natives of Southern States	81	89	81	73

The chi-square test indicates that a difference exists that reaches the one per cent level of significance. Therefore, a significantly larger group of men in the riot group than would be expected were natives of the southern states.

AGE

The mean age of the riot group was found to be 28.2 ± 0.9, as compared with 26.7 ± 0.9 for the control group. A critical ratio of 3.6 between the distribution indicates that the riot group is significantly older than the control group. Lee and Humphrey indicate that ". . . it is well to remember that those hurt and those arrested were probably the less agile persons and, in most cases therefore, not as young as those who got away" (Lee and Humphrey, 1943, p. 83). On the other hand, it is known that persons convicted of individual assaultive crimes, including sex assaults, are on the average significantly older than those convicted for all other crimes.[2] The investigators have no substantial evidence at this time to prove that a difference in age exists between participants in individual assault and in mob violence. The group that was imprisoned as a result of the riot were, as has been mentioned before, generally not those who actually participated in assault, but the looters, and those convicted of carrying concealed weapons. Burglary and concealed weapons have been found to be crimes of younger men.[3] It is not unexpected, then, to find that the group of men convicted of looting and weapons charges resulting from the riot are significantly younger than the control group.

INTELLIGENCE

The mean intelligence quotient of the riot group is 81.0 ± 0.6. This is very significantly below the mean of intelligence quotient of 83.8 ± 0.8 of the control group, as is evidenced by the critical ratio of 7.3. Both groups are very significantly below the prison population mean of 87.7 ± 0.1. The intellectual classifications of the rioters and control group are as follows:

2. Vernon Fox; "Intelligence, Race, and Age as Selective Factors in Crime," 1943, an unpublished report to Michigan's Director of Corrections, p. 18.
3. Ibid., pp. 19–20.

Classification	Riot Group	Control Group
Very superior	0	0
Superior	2	3
Average	21	24
Dull	23	29
Borderline defective	40	37
Feebleminded	19	12

ACADEMIC GRADE PLACEMENT

According to the results of the New Stanford Achievement Test, Form D, the mean average grade placement of the riot group was 4.3 ± 0.3. The mean average grade placement of the control group was found to be 5.2 ± 0.2. The critical ratio of 4.4 between these distributions indicates that the riot group is significantly inferior to the control group as to education.

FURTHER DESCRIPTION OF RIOT GROUP

Of the riot group, ninety-seven were vocationally unskilled. Eight could be called semi-skilled. There was not a skilled worker in the group. Twenty-nine of the men were unemployed at the time of the riot, despite the fact that war industry at that time was able to use all available manpower. Very few of these unemployed men had been out of work for more than a few days, a situation which suggests that the riot group represents an area of society where a high motility of labor exists. Only fourteen men had been on only one job during the year prior to the riot; as mentioned above, twenty-nine were unemployed at the time of the riot; the remaining sixty-two had been on their jobs for periods ranging from a few days to several months, but none had been employed at one place for a year. Vocational instability or a high motility of unskilled labor was the rule.

The marital status of the riot group is as follows: Common-law relationship, 41; single, 34; married by ceremony, 19; separated, 8; divorced, 3. The high proportion of common-law relationships is not entirely unexpected, since the larger proportion of the riot group are southern Negroes. This group of people includes a large number who have continued the more primitive conjugal union which was general in slavery days, but now may represent cultural lag.

It is noteworthy that only twenty-seven of the riot group had had no previous police record. Twenty-three had had only jail records. Sixteen others had been convicted of felonies and had been given probation or suspended sentences. Twenty-three had served prison terms; fifteen of this number had had but one previous incarceration, four had been imprisoned twice, three had been sentenced three times previously, and one had had four previous prison terms and is wanted by the Alabama State Penitentiary for escaping. Sixteen of the men with previous police records had also been subjected to juvenile institutionalization. Seventy-four per cent of the rioters, then, had previously been in conflict with law-enforcement agencies.

Earlier in this paper it was mentioned that the majority of the men convicted of felonies as a result of the Detroit race riot were not rioters as such, but looters and carriers of concealed weapons. The crimes for which the men were sentenced, together with the number of offenders in each category are as follows:

Crime	Number of Men
Entering without breaking in the daytime	38
Carrying concealed weapons	37
Larceny from a store	16
Felonious assault	4
Rioting	3
Resisting arrest	2
Larceny of an automobile	1
Malicious destruction of property	1
Armed robbery	1
Negligent homicide	1
Manslaughter	1
Total	105

It will be noticed that thirteen of the crimes, including armed robbery, may be considered violent ones. Ninety-two of the men were convicted of relatively non-violent crimes, such as stealing small articles from a store or walking into it after the windows had been broken by a prospective misdemeanant. Thirty-seven were convicted of carrying concealed weapons. Many of these men said they were convicted of carrying knives that they habitually carried, but for which they had never before been arrested. At any rate, an unexpectedly small proportion of men were imprisoned for actual and active rioting.

SUMMARY

In summary, the following conclusions may be drawn with regard to the men who were imprisoned for felonies directly connected with the Detroit race riot:

1. The men convicted of felonies as a result of the riot were disproportionately from states south of the Mason and Dixon line.

2. The mean age of the riot group was significantly older than the control group.

3. The riot group was very significantly inferior to the control group with regard to general intelligence.

4. The riot group was educationally inferior to the control group.

5. There was no significant difference between the riot group and control group with regard to venereal condition.[4]

6. No significant difference with regard to history of drug addiction existed between the two groups.[4]

7. The riot group were in the main unskilled workers with high vocational motility.

8. The riot group has a very high proportion of common-law relationships.

9. Seventy-four per cent of the riot group had previously been in conflict with the law-enforcing agencies. Twenty-three of this number had prison records.

10. Most of the men sentenced to prison for crimes directly connected with the riot were looters and carriers of concealed weapons, and not active and violent participators in the riot. Only thirteen men were sentenced for violent crimes.

The National Advisory Commission on Civil Disorders

The Riot Participant

It is sometimes assumed that the rioters were criminal types, overactive social deviants, or riffraff—recent migrants, members of an uneducated underclass, alienated from responsible Negroes, and without broad social or political concerns. It is often implied that there was no effort within the Negro community to attempt to reduce the violence.

We have obtained data on participation from four different sources:

Eyewitness accounts from more than 1,200 interviews in our staff reconnaissance survey of 20 cities;

Interview surveys based on probability samples of riot area residents in the two major riot cities—Detroit and Newark—designed to elicit anonymous self-identification of participants as rioters, counterrioters or noninvolved;

Arrest records from 22 cities; and

A special study of arrestees in Detroit.

4. Data have not been reproduced here but can be found in the article as originally published.

[The interested reader should refer to the *Report* itself for substantial documentation of the information on participants recorded in this section.—A. D. G.]

Only partial information is available on the total numbers of participants. In the Detroit survey, approximately 11 percent of the sampled residents over the age of 15 in the two disturbance areas admittedly participated in rioting; another 20 to 25 percent admitted to having been bystanders but claimed that they had not participated; approximately 16 percent claimed they had engaged in counterriot activity; and the largest proportion (48 to 53 percent) claimed they were at home or elsewhere and did not participate. However, a large proportion of the Negro community apparently believed that more was gained than lost through rioting, according to the Newark and Detroit surveys.

Greater precision is possible in describing the characteristics of those who participated. We have combined the data from the four sources to construct a profile of the typical rioter and to compare him with the counterrioter and the noninvolved.

THE PROFILE OF A RIOTER

The typical rioter in the summer of 1967 was a Negro, unmarried male between the ages of 15 and 24. He was in many ways very different from the stereotype. He was not a migrant. He was born in the state and was a lifelong resident of the city in which the riot took place. Economically his position was about the same as his Negro neighbors who did not actively participate in the riot.

Although he had not, usually, graduated from high school, he was somewhat better educated than the average inner-city Negro, having at least attended high school for a time.

Nevertheless, he was more likely to be working in a menial or low status job as an unskilled laborer. If he was employed, he was not working full time and his employment was frequently interrupted by periods of unemployment.

He feels strongly that he deserves a better job and that he is barred from achieving it, not because of lack of training, ability, or ambition, but because of discrimination by employers.

He rejects the white bigot's stereotype of the Negro as ignorant and shiftless. He takes great pride in his race and believes that in some respects Negroes are superior to whites. He is extremely hostile to whites, but his hostility is more apt to be a product of social and economic class than of race; he is almost equally hostile toward middle class Negroes.

He is substantially better informed about politics than Negroes who were not involved in the riots. He is more likely to be actively engaged in civil rights efforts, but is extemely distrustful of the political system and of political leaders.

THE PROFILE OF THE COUNTERRIOTER

The typical counterrioter, who risked injury and arrest to walk the streets urging rioters to "cool it," was an active supporter of existing social institutions. He was, for example, far more likely than either the rioter or the noninvolved to feel that this country is worth defending in a major war. His actions and his attitudes reflected his substantially greater stake in the social system; he was considerably better educated and more affluent than either the rioter or the noninvolved. He was somewhat more likely than the rioter, but less likely than the noninvolved, to have been a migrant. In all other respects he was identical to the noninvolved.

CHARACTERISTICS OF PARTICIPANTS

RACE

Of the arrestees 83 percent were Negroes; 15 percent were whites. Our interviews in 20 cities indicate that almost all rioters were Negroes.

AGE

The survey data from Detroit, the arrest records, and our interviews in 20 cities, all indicate that the rioters were late teenagers or young adults. In the Detroit survey, 61.3 percent of the self-reported rioters were between the ages of 15 and 24, and 86.3 percent were between 15 and 35. The arrest data indicate that 52.5 percent of the arrestees were between 15 and 24, and 80.8 percent were between 15 and 35.

Of the noninvolved, by contrast, only 22.6 percent in the Detroit survey were between 15 and 24, and 38.3 percent were between 15 and 35.

SEX

In the Detroit survey, 61.4 percent of the self-reported rioters were male. Arrestees, however, were almost all male—89.3 percent. Our interviews in 20 cities indicate that the majority of rioters were male. The large difference in proportion between the Detroit survey data and the arrestee figures probably reflects either selectivity in the arrest process or less dramatic, less provocative riot behavior by women.

FAMILY STRUCTURE

Three sources of available information—the Newark survey, the Detroit arrest study, and arrest records from four cities—indicate a tendency for rioters to be single. The Newark survey indicates that rioters were single —56.2 percent—more often than the noninvolved—49.6 percent.

The Newark survey also indicates that rioters were more likely to have been divorced or separated—14.2 percent—than the noninvolved— 6.4 percent. However, the arrest records from four cities indicate that only a very small percentage of those arrested fall into this category.

In regard to the structure of the family in which he was raised, the self-reported rioter, according to the Newark survey, was not significantly different from many of his Negro neighbors who did not actively participate in the riot. Twenty-five and five-tenths percent of the self- reported rioters and 23 percent of the noninvolved were brought up in homes where no adult male lived.

REGION OF UPBRINGING

Both survey data and arrest records demonstrate unequivocally that those brought up in the region in which the riot occurred are much more likely to have participated in the riots. The percentage of self-reported rioters brought up in the North is almost identical for the Detroit survey—74.4 percent—and the Newark survey—74 percent. By contrast, of the noninvolved, 36 percent in Detroit and 52.4 percent in Newark were brought up in the region in which the disorder occurred.

Data available from five cities on the birthplace of arrestees indicate that 63 percent of the arrestees were born in the North. Although birthplace is not necessarily identical with place of upbringing, the data are sufficiently similar to provide strong support for the conclusion.

Of the self-reported counterrioters, however, 47.5 percent were born in the North, according to the Detroit survey, a figure which places them between self-reported rioters and the noninvolved. Apparently, a significant consequence of growing up in the South is the tendency toward noninvolvement in a riot situation, while involvement in a riot, either in support of or against existing social institutions, was more common among those born in the North.

RESIDENCE

Rioters are not only more likely than the noninvolved to have been born in the region in which the riot occurred, but they are also more likely to have been long-term residents of the city in which the disturbance took place. The Detroit survey data indicate that 59.4 percent of the self-reported rioters, but only 34.6 percent of the noninvolved, were born in Detroit. The comparable figures in the Newark survey are 53.5 percent and 22.5 percent.

Outsiders who temporarily entered the city during the riot might have left before the surveys were conducted and therefore may be underestimated in the survey data. However, the arrest data, which is contemporaneous with the riot, suggest that few outsiders were involved: 90 percent of those arrested resided in the riot city, 7 percent lived in the same state, and only 1 percent were from outside the state. Our interviews in 20 cities corroborate these conclusions.

INCOME

In the Detroit and Newark survey data, income level alone does not seem to correlate with self-reported riot participation. The figures from the two cities are not directly comparable since respondents were asked for individual income in Detroit and family income in Newark. More Detroit self-reported rioters (38.6 percent) had annual incomes under $5,000 per year than the noninvolved (30.3 percent), but even this small difference disappears when the factor of age is taken into account.

In the Newark data, in which the age distributions of self-reported rioters and the noninvolved are more similar, there is almost no difference between the ritors, 32.6 percent of whom had annual incomes under $5,000, and the noninvolved, 29.4 percent of whom had annual incomes under $5,000.

The similarity in income distribution should not, however, lead to the conclusion that more affluent Negroes are as likely to riot as poor Negroes. Both surveys were conducted in disturbance areas where incomes are considerably lower than in the city as a whole and the surrounding metropolitan area. Nevertheless, the data show that rioters are not necessarily the poorest of the poor.

While income fails to distinguish self-reported rioters from those who were not involved, it does distinguish counterrioters from rioters and the noninvolved. Less than 9 percent of both those who rioted and those not involved earned more than $10,000 annually. Yet almost 20 percent of the counterrioters earned this amount or more. In fact, there were no male self-reported counterrioters in the Detroit survey who earned less than $5,000 annually. In the Newark sample there were seven respondents who owned their own homes; none of them participated in the riot. While extreme poverty does not necessarily move a man to riot, relative affluence seems at least to inhibit him from attacking the existing social order and may motivate him to take considerable risks to protect it.

EDUCATION

Level of schooling is strongly related to participation. Those with some high school education were more likely to riot than those who had only finished grade school. In the Detroit survey, 93 percent of the self-reported rioters had gone beyond grade school, compared with 72.1 percent of the noninvolved. In the Newark survey the comparable figures are 98.1 and 85.7 percent. The majority of self-reported rioters were not, however, high school graduates.

The counterrioters were clearly the best educated of the three groups. Approximately twice as many counterrioters had attended college as had the noninvolved, and half again as many counterrioters had attended college as rioters. Considered with the information on income, the data suggest that counterrioters were probably well on their way into the middle class.

Education and income are the only factors which distinguish the counterrioter from the noninvolved. Apparently, a high level of education and income not only prevents rioting but is more likely to lead to active, responsible opposition to rioting.

EMPLOYMENT

The Detroit and Newark surveys, the arrest records from four cities, and the Detroit arrest study all indicate that there are no substantial differences in unemployment between the rioters and the noninvolved.

Unemployment levels among both groups were extremely high. In the Detroit survey, 29.6 percent of the self-reported rioters were unemployed; in the Newark survey, 29.7 percent; in the four-city arrest data, 33.2 percent; and in the Detroit arrest study, 21.8 percent. The unemployment rates for the noninvolved in the Detroit and Newark surveys were 31.5 and 19.0 percent.

Self-reported rioters were more likely to be only intermittently employed, however, than the noninvolved. Respondents in Newark were asked whether they had been unemployed for as long as a month or more during the last year. Sixty-one percent of the self-reported rioters, but only 43.4 percent of the noninvolved, answered, "yes."

Despite generally higher levels of education, rioters were more likely than the noninvolved to be employed in unskilled jobs. In the Newark survey, 50 percent of the self-reported rioters, but only 39.6 percent of the noninvolved, had unskilled jobs.

ATTITUDES ABOUT EMPLOYMENT

The Newark survey data indicate that self-reported rioters were more likely to feel dissatisfied with their present jobs than were the noninvolved.

Only 29.3 percent of the rioters, compared with 44.4 percent of the noninvolved, thought their present jobs appropriate for them in responsibility and pay. Of the self-reported rioters, 67.6 percent, compared with 56.1 percent of the noninvolved, felt that it was impossible to obtain the kind of job they wanted. Of the self-reported rioters, 69 percent, as compared with 50 percent of the noninvolved, felt that racial discrimination was the major obstacle to finding better employment. Despite this feeling, surprising numbers of rioters (76.9 percent) responded that "getting what you want out of life is a matter of ability, not being in the right place at the right time."

RACIAL ATTITUDES

The Detroit and Newark surveys indicate that rioters have strong feelings of racial pride, if not racial superiority. In the Detroit survey, 48.6 percent of the self-reported rioters said that they felt Negroes were more dependable than whites. Only 22.4 percent of the noninvolved stated this. In Newark, the comparable figures were 45 and 27.8 percent. The Newark survey data indicate that rioters wanted to be called "black" rather than "Negro" or "colored" and were somewhat more likely than the noninvolved to feel that all Negroes should study African history and languages.

To what extent this racial pride antedated the riot or was produced by the riot is impossible to determine from the survey data. Certainly the riot experience seems to have been associated with increased pride in the minds of many participants. This was vividly illustrated by the statement of a Detroit rioter:

Interviewer: You said you were feeling good when you followed the crowds?
Respondent: I was feeling proud, man, at the fact that I was a Negro. I felt like I was a first-class citizen. I didn't feel ashamed of my race because of what they did.

Similar feelings were expressed by an 18-year-old Detroit girl who reported that she had been a looter:

Interviewer: What is the Negro then if he's not American?
Respondent: A Negro, he's considered a slave to the white folks. But half of them know that they're slaves and feel that they can't do nothing about it because they're just going along with it. But most of them they seem to get it

in their heads now how the white folks treat them and how they've been treating them and how they've been slaves for the white folks. . . .

Along with increased racial pride there appears to be intense hostility toward whites. Self-reported rioters in both the Detroit and Newark surveys were more likely to feel that civil rights groups with white and Negro leaders would do better without the whites. In Detroit, 36.1 percent of the self-reported rioters thought that this statement was true, while only 21.1 percent of the noninvolved thought so. In the Newark survey, 51.4 percent of the self-reported rioters agreed; 33.1 percent of the noninvolved shared this opinion.

Self-reported rioters in Newark were also more likely to agree with the statement, "Sometimes I hate white people." Of the self-reported rioters, 72.4 percent agreed; of the noninvolved, 50 percent agreed.

The intensity of the self-reported rioters' racial feelings may suggest that the recent riots represented traditional interracial hostilities. Two sources of data suggest that this interpretation is probably incorrect.

First, the Newark survey data indicate that rioters were almost as hostile to middle-class Negroes as they were to whites. Seventy-one and four-tenths percent of the self-reported rioters, but only 59.5 percent of the noninvolved, agreed with the statement, "Negroes who make a lot of money like to think they are better than other Negroes." Perhaps even more significant, particularly in light of the rioters' strong feelings of racial pride, is that 50.5 percent of the self-reported rioters agreed that "Negroes who make a lot of money are just as bad as white people." Only 35.2 percent of the noninvolved shared this opinion.

Second, the arrest data show that the great majority of those arrested during the disorders were generally charged with a crime relating to looting or curfew violations. Only 2.4 percent of the arrests were for assault and 0.1 percent were for homicide, but 31.3 percent of the arrests were for breaking and entering—crimes directed against white property rather than against individual whites.

POLITICAL ATTITUDES AND INVOLVEMENT

Respondents in the Newark survey were asked about relatively simple items of political information, such as the race of prominent local and national political figures. In general, the self-reported rioters were much better informed than the noninvolved. For example, self-reported rioters were more likely to know that one of the 1966 Newark mayoral candidates was a Negro. Of the rioters, 77.1 percent—but only 61.6 percent of the noninvolved—identified him correctly. The overall scores on a series of similar questions also reflect the self-reported rioters' higher levels of information.

Self-reported rioters were also more likely to be involved in activities associated with Negro rights. At the most basic level of political participation, they were more likely than the noninvolved to talk frequently about Negro rights. In the Newark survey, 53.8 percent of the self-reported rioters, but only 34.9 percent of the noninvolved, said that they talked about Negro rights nearly every day.

The self-reported rioters also were more likely to have attended a meeting or participated in civil rights activity. Of the rioters, 39.3 percent—but only 25.7 percent of the noninvolved—reported that they had engaged in such activity.

In the Newark survey, respondents were asked how much they thought they could trust the local government. Only 4.8 percent of the self-reported rioters, compared with 13.7 percent of the noninvolved, said that they felt they could trust it most of the time; 44.2 percent of the self-reported rioters and 33.9 percent of the noninvolved reported that they could almost never trust the government.

In the Detroit survey, self-reported rioters were much more likely to attribute the riot to anger about politicians and police than were the noninvolved. Of the self-reported rioters, 43.2 percent—but only 19.6 percent of the noninvolved—said anger against politicians had a great deal to do with causing the riot. Of the self-reported rioters, 70.5 percent, compared with 48.8 percent of the noninvolved, believed that anger against the police had a great deal to do with causing the riot.

Perhaps the most revealing and disturbing measure of the rioters' anger at the social and political system was their response to a question asking whether they thought "the country was worth fighting for in the event of a major world war." Of the self-reported rioters, 39.4 percent in Detroit and 52.8 percent in Newark shared a negative view. In contrast, 15.5 percent of the noninvolved in Detroit and 27.8 percent of the noninvolved in Newark shared this sentiment. Almost none of the self-reported counterrioters in Detroit—3.3 percent—agreed with the self-reported rioters.

Some comments of interviewees are worthy of note:

"Not worth fighting for—if Negroes had an equal chance it would be worth fighting for."

"Not worth fighting for—I am not a true citizen so why should I?"

"Not worth fighting for—because my husband came back from Vietnam and nothing had changed."

Robert M. Fogelson and Robert B. Hill

Who Riots? A Study of Participation in the 1967 Riots *

A great many public figures—including the mayors and the governors of the stricken areas—have already given their views on the 1960's riots. This was their privilege and responsibility. That they have disagreed sharply on a number of crucial issues—among them, the degree of organization and advanced planning, the amount of violence and destruction, the conditions in the Negro ghettos, and, perhaps most important, the implications for public policy—is not surprising (*New York Times*, June 30, July 12, 16, 19, 20, 22, 24-28, 1967). The differences between California Governor Ronald Reagan and New Jersey Governor Richard J. Hughes and between former Acting-Mayor of New York Paul Screvane and the late Los Angeles Police Chief William H. Parker were marked. And so were the differences between the Los Angeles (1965), Newark (1967), Detroit (1967), and Washington, D. C. (1968), riots, on the one hand, and the Rochester (1964), Chicago (1965), San Francisco (1966), and Boston (1967) riots, on the other. What is surprising is that most of these public figures (and, as the public opinion surveys reveal, most of their constituents) have agreed substantially on probably the most perplexing question raised by the 1960's riots: who riots?

Their answer is what we refer to as the "riffraff theory" of riot participation (Fogelson, 1967, p. 342). At the core of this "theory" are three distinct, though closely related, themes. First, that only an infinitesimal fraction of the black population (2 per cent according to some, including several prominent Negro moderates, and 1 per cent according to others) actively participated in the riots. Second, that the rioters, far from being representative of the Negro community, were principally the riffraff—the unattached, juvenile, unskilled, unemployed, uprooted, criminal—and outside agitators. Indeed, many public figures have insisted that outside agitators, especially left wing radicals and black

* The Fogelson-Hill study became available after the manuscript for this volume had been completed. If it had been available earlier, I would have wanted to include selections from the materials which they provide to refute each of the three themes of the "riffraff theory." I urge the interested reader to examine their study in the fuller detail available in National Advisory Commission on Civil Disorders *Supplemental Studies*, 1968, pp. 221-248. I felt that even if the entire report could not be presented, this statement of the relevant qustions should be.

Other authors have reached conclusions similar to those of Fogelson and Hill. The interested reader should see, particularly, the more detailed paper by Sears and Tomlinson, 1968. This excellent paper also became available only after the manuscript had been completed.

nationalists, incited the riffraff and thereby provoked the rioting. And third, that the overwhelming majority of the Negro population—the law-abiding and respectable 98 or 99 per cent who did not join in the rioting—unequivocally opposed and deplored the riot (*New York Times,* July 16, 20, 22, 26, 1967; *New York Times,* July 22, August 4, 1964; *Newark Evening News,* July 20, 1964; New York *Journal-American,* July 26, 1964. Some officials, like former Detroit police chief Ray Girardin, rejected the riffraff theory).

For most white Americans the riffraff theory is highly reassuring. If, indeed, the rioters were a tiny fraction of the Negro population, composed of the riraff and outside agitators and opposed by a large majority of the ghetto residents, the riots were less ominous than they appeared. They were also a function of poverty, which, in American ideology, is alterable, rather than race, which is immutable; in which case too, they were peripheral to the issue of white-black relations in the United States. Again if the riffraff theory is correct, the riots were a reflection less of the social problems of modern black ghettos than of the personal disabilities of recent Negro newcomers. And the violent acts—the looting, arson, and assault—were not political protests, but rather, in the words of the McCone Commission, "formless, quite senseless," and, by implication, "meaningless" outbursts (*Violence in the City—An End or a Beginning? A Report by the Governor's Commission on the Los Angeles Riots,* 1965, pp. 4-5). Lastly, if the prevailing view of riot participation is accurate, future riots can be prevented merely by elevating the riffraff, and by muzzling outside agitators, without transforming the black ghettos. Without, in other words, radically changing the American metropolis by thoroughly overhauling its basic institutions or seriously inconveniencing its white majority.

In view of the profound implications of the riffraff theory, it is disconcerting that very few of its adherents have offered solid supporting evidence. Their estimates of participation were based largely on the impressions of subordinates, who had good reason to play down the rioting, and not on interviews with lower-class and working-class Negroes. Their descriptions of the rioters were drawn primarily from personal observations and, in a handful of cases, casual, and often poorly informed, glances at arrest statistics. Their opinions about ghetto attitudes were formed mainly from cursory soundings of moderate Negroes, who strongly opposed the rioting, and not of militant blacks (*New York Times,* June 30, July 22, 26-28, 1967; Rustin, 1966, pp. 29-35; Blauner, 1966, p. 3). The adherents of the riffraff theory have also overlooked a good deal of evidence which sharply questions and sometimes directly contradicts their position. For example, unless the police caught most of the rioters—which is highly unlikely—the large number of arrests alone indicates that more than 1 or 2 per cent of the Negroes participated. The written and graphic descriptions of the riots reveal that many working- and middle-class blacks joined in the looting and assaults (if not the burning). And the remarks of Negroes during and after the rioting suggest that many who did not themselves participate tacitly supported the rioters anyway (Sears, 1966, pp. 1-2; Governor's Commission on the Los Angeles Riots, Archives, II, in the University of California Library, Los Angeles [hereafter referred to as the McCone Archives]).

Why, then, has the riffraff theory been so widely adopted to explain the 1960's riots? Why was it adopted to explain the Harlem riots of 1935 and 1943 and many earlier riots in America as well? The answer, we believe, can be traced to the American conviction that no matter how grave the grievances there are no legitimate grounds for violent protest—a conviction shared by most whites that reflects the nation's traditional confidence in orderly social change. To have accepted the possibility that a substantial and representative segment of the Negro population participated in or supported the riots would have forced most Americans to draw one of two conclusions. Either that the long-term deterioration of the black ghettos has destroyed the prospect for gradual improvement and provided the justification for violent protest, or that even if conditions are not so desperate a great many Negroes believe otherwise. Neither conclusion could have been reconciled with the commitment to orderly social change; either one would have compelled most Americans to reexamine a fundamental feature of the ideology of their race, class, and country. And, not surprisingly, they were no more inclined to do so than previous generations of Americans.[1]

Hence it was not until 1966, when the U.C.L.A. Institute of Government and Public Affairs released a survey of participation in the Los Angeles riots of 1965 and the California Department of Justice issued a report on the persons arrested therein, that the riffraff theory was even questioned. And it was not until 1968, when the University of Michigan's Survey Research Center, the Governor of New Jersey's Select Commission on Civil Disorder, and the U.S. Department of Labor completed similar studies of the Newark and Detroit riots of 1967, that the theory was seriously challenged (Sears, 1966; Bureau of Criminal Statistics, California Department of Criminal Justice, 1966; Governor's Select Commission on Civil Disorder, State of New Jersey, 1968; U.S. Department of Labor, Manpower Administration, 1968; Caplan and Paige, see data on Newark and Detroit Negro residents in the *Report, of the National Advisory Committee on Civil Disorders,* [hereafter referred to as the *Kerner Report*] Chapter 2, fn. 111-143, pp. 171-178). Although these studies did not employ precisely the same methods or

1. Silver, 1968; Hartz, 1955, Chapter One. It must be noted, however, that this tendency on the part of officials to dismiss rioters as "riffraff" or "criminals" is not unique to America. Rude has shown that similar terms were used by both French and British officials during the eighteenth century and nineteenth century European riots. His statistical analysis of the social characteristics of the rioters demonstrated that such descriptions were unfounded. Rude, 1959 and Rude, 1964.

arrive at exactly the same findings, they did reach certain conclusions which contradict one or more of the three central points of the riffraff theory. First, that a substantial minority of the Negro population, ranging from roughly 10 to 20 percent, actively participated in the riots. Second, that the rioters, far from being primarily the riffraff and outside agitators, were fairly representative of the ghetto communities. And third, that a sizable minority (or, in some cases a majority) of the Negroes who did not riot sympathized with the rioters (*Kerner Report,* Chapter 2; California Advisory Committee to the U.S. Commission on Civil Rights, 1966; Blauner, 1966; Scoble, 1966; Oberschall, 1968).

These conclusions have very different implications than the riffraff theory. If the rioters were a substantial and representative segment of the Negro population, widely supported in the black communities, the riots were every bit as ominous as they seemed. They were also a manifestation of race more than poverty. Indeed, there is considerable evidence that working- and middle-class Negroes resent the indignities of ghetto life as much as, if not more, than lower-class Negroes do; thus, the riots were central to the relationship of whites and blacks in America (McCone Archives, III, Testimony of Councilman Thomas Bradley, 29-36; V, Testimony of John A. Buggs, Executive Director of the Los Angeles County Human Relations Commission, 18-23; VI, Testimony of Assemblyman Mervyn M. Dymally, 48-49; VIII, Testimony of Congressman Augustus F. Hawkins, 82-85; X, Testimony of Councilman Billy G. Mills, 9-10). If these conclusions are warranted, the riots were a reflection of social problems endemic to the black ghettos and not of personal disabilities peculiar to the Negro newcomers from the South. And the violent acts were indeed political protests against ghetto conditions. Finally, if the revisionist view of riot participation is valid, future riots can only be prevented by transforming the black ghettos and, by implication, the white metropolises. If for no other purpose than to test the riffraff theory, then, an investigation of riot participation is very much in order.

Allen D. Grimshaw

Black Response to Contemporary Urban Violence:
A Brief Note on the Sociology of Poll Interpretation

White Americans, particularly politicians and policy makers, have understandably been very interested in how black Americans "feel about" the violence of recent years. Black Americans presumably know, although there is evidence that there is no monolithic opinion within the community on this any more than there is opinion within the community on other matters, or any more than there is on important issues which divide the white majority. Some pundits have hastened to reassure the white American majority that the violence has aggrieved and alarmed the majority of the black community, that the violence itself has involved only a miniscule proportion of all blacks. Other observers have "viewed with alarm" the fact that substantial proportions of the black community have actually participated in the disorders and that among those who have not participated many approve, or at least feel that only through such cataclysmic disturbances can racial progress be achieved. Some of the reasons for such differing perspectives are discussed below in the paper on "Three Views of Urban Violence."

A SAMPLING OF REPORTED OPINIONS

Four studies in the last several years have reported opinions on the violence reported by black respondents.[1] The questions, unfortunately, are not comparable. They are similar enough, however, that the different patterns which emerge raise some interesting questions about interpretation.

1. Murphy and Watson (1967), in their thorough study of social structural variables affecting response (of a probability sample of interviewees in the affected areas) to the Los Angeles riot, have reported the interesting finding that a substantial number of their respondents disapprove

1. After the completion of the manuscript for this volume, a fifth study became available comparable in rigor of research design and in carefulness of interpretation to the Murphy-Watson study (1967), although once again the questions were not exactly comparable. This study, by Campbell and Schuman (1968), prepared for the National Advisory Commission, reports findings on surveys of fifteen cities (white and black respondents, riot and non-riot cities). They do not report on "approval" of the disturbances but do report that over one-third of their black respondents (riot and non-riot cities, riot and non-riot zones within cities) said that the disturbances helped the Negro cause, that one half were sympathetic (even while they might not all participate), and that nearly six respondents out of ten stated that the disturbances were principally a protest against unfair conditions.

of the violence, but that at least some of the respondents who disapprove also believe that the riot helped the cause of the Negro.

2. The Detroit Urban League-Survey Research Center (University of Michigan)-Detroit Free Press Survey, *The People Beyond Twelfth Street* (Meyer, 1967), reported that slightly more than half of their black respondents (in a probability sample of the affected area) believed that Negroes had more to lose than to gain by "resorting to violence" and that slightly over one quarter believed that they had more to gain.

3. A Yankelovich survey, supported by *Fortune* magazine (Beardwood, 1968), reported that thirty-five per cent of slightly more than 300 Negroes in thirteen cities felt that violence is necessary to achieve Negro objectives while sixty-two per cent disagreed. The survey also reported, however, that only fourteen per cent of the respondents characterized the violence and rioting which had already occurred as "essentially good" while fifty-eight per cent labeled it as "essentially bad" and twenty-eight percent made mixed judgments.

4. Louis Harris and Associates reported (on the basis of a survey done on August 9, 1967, almost immediately after the Detroit rioting) that twelve per cent of their Negro respondents believed that the riots of that summer had helped the cause of civil rights for Negroes while sixty per cent felt that the cause had been damaged. In the same survey, however, sixty-eight per cent of the Negro respondents reported that Negroes would lose by resorting to violence while fifteen per cent felt that more would be gained (Harris results are from Erskine, 1968).

Watson and Murphy found that approximately one quarter of their female and one third of their male respondents approved the riot but that over half of both males and females reported that the riot had at least some beneficial effects. These results suggest a considerably more positive reaction than is true of any of the other three studies mentioned above. There are several reasons for these differences, some quite clear, others somewhat more ambiguous.

In the ambiguous category is the possibility of shifting reactions within the black community over time.[2] There are two time dimensions which should be considered. First, it can be noted that the Watts dis-

2. Ambiguous in the sense of the problematic nature of interpretation of findings only, however. Responses clearly do shift. This is perhaps most clearly demonstrated by the changes in reply to the question, "Do you think the riots that have taken place . . . have helped or hurt the cause of Negro rights or don't you think it makes much difference?" In the summer of 1966 the Harris organization had asked the same question (Brink and Harris, 1967). The results then were far more "favorable" to the rioting: Thirty-four per cent of the Harris national sample felt that the riots had helped while only twenty per cent felt that they had hurt (seventeen per cent responded that they had not made much difference and twenty-nine per cent were not sure). As Watson pointed out in a personal communication, the Harris (1966) figures for the non-South are very close to those which he and Murphy obtained in their study of the Los Angeles rioting. Watson felt that the earlier Harris figures, closer in time to the study he and Murphy had done, validated the Watts study without definitively answering the questions about shifts in response patterns over time or apparent differences in studies done within shorter time periods.

turbances occurred in 1965 and that the Watts riot was the first really large-scale urban explosion. It is possible that initial enthusiasm and hope has given way to a realization (or belief) that violence is no more productive of social change than other modes of action. Second, the several surveys have been taken at different time periods after the disturbances to which they refer. The Harris survey and the Detroit Urban League survey came immediately after the Detroit riot of 1967; the *Fortune* study and the Murphy-Watson study were done some months after the actual violence had occurred. There may be tendencies to re-evaluate, though the direction of such re-evaluation is not clear from the evidence available. Another ambiguity producing difference in the surveys is the fact that different types of respondent populations were questioned. The Los Angeles study and the one done in Detroit were directed to people resident in the riot areas or very close by. The *Fortune* survey included respondents from a number of different cities (with unreported or unknown riot experience) and the Harris poll presumably reflects some sort of national sample. It is not clear how propinquity might effect responses. Moreover, it seems likely that there is some interaction effect between propinquity and time.

Murphy and Watson employed local blacks, including dissident youth, in their survey; the Detroit Urban League used Negroes (largely school teachers); the *Fortune* survey was done by "Negroes" (without further identification); there is no information on the Harris poll. On issues of such sensitivity we can be sure that there will be some kind of "interviewer effect," and we simply can't identify it without controlled research designs. Similarly, the questions were asked in different ways. Only in the Murphy-Watson study do we have a number of questions directed to different facets of the problem of evaluative response, in some instances further combined into indices. The Detroit survey asked only whether there was more to gain or to lose by violence and whether or not more violence was necessary. The Harris questions are fairly clear but leave no leeway for qualifications and, if probing was done, it is not reported. *Fortune* magazine reports only summary statements and will release neither data tables nor questionnaire items. There are, thus, problems of equivalence of meaning in interpreting reported results.

Finally, while confirmation is not possible, it seems likely that differences in procedures of analysis influence reported results. Many studies seem to have good, bad, and mixed response categories. It might be that in all surveys on this topic raw distributions will show that approximately thirty per cent are highly favorable or slightly favorable, approximately thirty percent highly unfavorable or slightly unfavorable, and that the remaining forty per cent are neither favorable nor unfavorable but report, rather, both positive and negative outcomes. In some instances, it seems, mixed favorable and unfavorable responses have been added to favorable and in others to unfavorable. It is only reasonable to expect that there is considerable ambivalence among black respondents, perhaps particularly those who are middle class in their socioeconomic characteristics. Differences in results reported may perhaps be an artifact of the lesser ambivalence of analysts.

Black attitudes on violence must, in these days of violence, be highly unstable. Quite clearly, events like the assassinations of King and Kennedy (or of Evers) will affect the uncommitted. Quite clearly, the occurrence of violence on one's own block will affect the uncommitted. Quite possibly, substantial attempts by the Federal government to redress grievances may affect both the committed and the uncommitted. Changes such as these aside, there is some significant information available to us. If even fifteen percent of the black population of the United States approves violence or believes violence to be necessary in order to achieve needed social change, this means three million Americans. This should be a cause for some concern. Finally, it seems clear, particularly from the analysis presented by Murphy and Watson, that whatever attitudes may emerge can be most efficiently explained by reference to social structure rather than to individual idiosyncracies.

Bernard Weisberg

Racial Violence and Civil Rights Law Enforcement

The history of racial violence in the United States, filled with accounts of costly race riots and lynchings, is uncomfortably familiar.[1] Increasingly urgent is the question whether a great body of civil rights law must remain unenforced because of the spectre of such violence.[2]

The practical problems of law enforcement have been thrown into sharp relief by postwar agitation for civil rights legislation and by recent decisions which have seriously weakened the constitutional founda-

1. Consult G. Myrdal, 1944; Chicago Commission on Race Relations: 1922; Lee and Humphrey, 1943; Raper, 1933.

Racial violence is usually treated as an unmitigated evil. However, some observers feel that it may have positive value as a catalyst for progress in race relations (Myrdal, 1948, pp. 196, 208). It may also provide an opportunity for minority group resistance to aggression, thus encouraging minority group members to establish positive identification with their group through collective action (Fisher, 1947, pp. 17, 18; Johnson, 1943, pp. 313–315. Compare Sartre, 1948, pp. 59–141 and Broyard, 1950, p. 56).

2. Mangum, 1940, p. 26 ff. contains a summary of the civil rights legislation passed in many northern states after post-Civil War federal civil rights legislation was held unconstitutional. Much of the state legislation has ample enforcement provisions. An Illinois statute, e.g., provides that all persons are entitled to full and equal enjoyment of establishments maintained for public use (hotels, restaurants, department stores,

tions of racial segregation. *Sweatt* v. *Painter, McLaurin* v. *Oklahoma State Regents,* and *Henderson* v. *United States,* all decided in 1950 by the Supreme Court, represented the most sustained attack yet made on the principle of racial segregation, constitutionally embodied in the "separate but equal" doctrine. The decisions attenuated that doctrine and further vitiated what remains of the principal case under attack, *Plessy* v. *Ferguson.*

But it is clear that the passage of civil rights legislation and the judicial extension of constitutional protections are but first steps toward vitalizing democratic principle in the field of race relations. Even if an asserted right to be free from segregation is given legal recognition, proof of its infringement may be so difficult that the right is effectively denied. Or the right can be made a dead letter if government fails to provide for vigorous law enforcement.

This note focuses on one aspect of the problem of enforcing civil rights law. The concrete question is whether racial violence is an inevitable consequence of protecting individual rights which come into conflict with established patterns of racial segregation.[3] The question calls for an examination of recent situations in which the problem has arisen and a consideration of new developments in the arts of law enforcement.[4]

---

railroads). Ill. Rev. Stat.: 1949 c. 38, section 125. Remedies include (1) recovery of damages by persons aggrieved by violations of the statute, *ibid.,* at section 126; (2) criminal penalties, *ibid.,* at section 126; and (3) the declaration of establishments violating the statute to be public nuisances whose operations can be enjoined, *ibid.,* at section 128a.

3. The proponents of segregation make two arguments connected with violence. The first, dealt with here, is that disturbing existing patterns of segregation is likely to lead to violence. The classic rebuttal of the second notion, that segregation tends to prevent racial conflict, remains Justice Harlan's dissent in *Plessy* v. *Ferguson,* 163 U.S.: 1896, p. 537, 552, 560. See also Edgerton, J., dissenting in *Hurd* v. *Hodge,* 162 F. 2d 233, 242, 243 (App. D.C, 1947), whose view was later upheld by the Supreme Court in *Hurd* v. *Hodge,* 334 U.S. 24 (1948). In passing on the eligibility of Negroes to hold public office, a Georgia court once said that "If . . . laws are unfair, unjust, unequal, they will breed discontent and disorder, and it is better for the peace and good order of society that all shall have equal rights." *White* v. *Clements,* 39 Ga. 232, 269 (1869). See also *Hurd* v. *Hodge,* 334 U.S. 24 (1948), Brief for Petitioners at 68–71.

That segregation tends to promote tension and violence seems clearest in the case of housing (Weaver, 1944, pp. 183, 187, 189, 193). Reporting on the 1943 Detroit race riot, a Wayne University sociologist observed that interracial neighborhoods were conspicuously free from disturbances (Lee and Humphrey: 1943, pp. 17, 97, 116, 130, 140). Specialists agree that tensions are likely to run highest along the borders of residential ghettos (Lohman, 1947, pp. 21, 22).

4. Although the unity of the enforcement problem is stressed here, for other purposes it may be important to distinguish the different contexts in which the law bears on segregation: (1) law which directly compels segregation, for example "Jim Crow" legislation; (2) law which directly forbids segregation, for example a great deal of civil rights legislation and situations in which the Fourteenth Amendment is construed so as to find segregation per se a denial of equal rights; and (3) areas in which the law appears to be neutral. "Neutrality" may take two forms. Legal relief may be denied to persons attacking the segregation or the emphasis may be on the denial of legal remedies to persons seeking to maintain segregation (as when the courts refuse to enforce restrictive covenants).

In recent years many American communities have faced the danger of racial violence when existing patterns of segregation were challenged. The experiences of St. Louis, Washington, D. C., and Chicago illustrate the complexity of the problems involved.

ST. LOUIS

Until 1949, the use of city owned and operated outdoor swimming pools in St. Louis, Missouri, was denied to Negroes, although this segregation found "No authority in ordinance, statute, or the Constitution of Missouri." [5] Responding to continued protests against this policy, the Director of Public Welfare decided in June 1949, shortly before the beginning of the swimming season, that there was no legal basis on which the use of these pools could be denied to Negroes and announced that they would henceforth be open to all citizens regardless of race. Soon after the pools opened, Fairgrounds Park was the scene of a major disturbance in which a crowd of several hundred persons gathered and many Negroes were assaulted. The Mayor immediately ordered reimposition of the segregation policy. The St. Louis Council of Human Relations was created to study the problem and set up a program designed to win public acceptance of the use of all city-owned recreation facilities on a non-segregated basis. The Director of the Mayor's Interracial Committee of Detroit, invited by the Council to study the situation, issued an extended report on the Fairgrounds Park riot (Schermer, 1949) in which he concluded that the step to break the segregation custom was taken too hastily. There had been none of the necessary advance planning with other government agencies and private groups, nor was it clear that the police were utilized effectively.[6]

5. Draper v. St. Louis, 92 F. Supp. 546, 548 (E.D. Mo., 1950).
6. It is difficult to evaluate the work of the St. Louis Police Department in the Fairgrounds Park disturbance. The Schermer report noted complaints about discriminatory police action (*Ibid.*, at pp. 24–26, 30, 35, 39). It was also stated that the police were given no advance notice of the decision to open the pools to Negroes at the beginning of the 1949 season (*Ibid.*, at p 34). The President of the St. Louis Board of Police Commissioners makes the same statement but goes on to say that the police were on notice in 1950 when a federal court injunction again ended the segregation (Communication from W. Holzhausen, November 13, 1950). However, the decision to open the pools to Negroes in 1949 was publicized at least one full day before they were due to open. Nevertheless it was reported that early on the day of the opening there were only a few extra officers at the Fairgrounds Park pool, those having been sent by a district officer who thought there might be trouble. The day was filled with sporadic incidents reported to the police. Yet that evening, when a crowd of several hundred was gathered in front of the pool, there were only a dozen police officers on the scene (Schermer, *op. cit. supra* note 5, at pp. 22, 27).
As to whether the police had received adequate training in race relations problems, there is also conflicting evidence. Commissioner Holzhausen states that "For several years, the Police Department in St. Louis has been laying heavy emphasis on the human relations factors involved in police work." He describes a series of panel discussions in an in-service training program in which representatives of local religious

In April 1950, the Council recommended that segregation be ended at two additional indoor swimming pools but that the opening of all other recreational facilities (notably the desirable outdoor pools) be accomplished gradually and only after an educational program had been conducted by the Council. In accepting its report, the Mayor stated to the Council that "Public safety demands the approach you have outlined." In June, the outdoor pools opened for 1950, again segregated. In the same month, Negro citizens, denied admission to the pools solely because of their race, sought an injunction in the federal courts compelling the city to discontinue its segregation policy. The principal defense raised by the city was that its attempt to eliminate the segregation as "expeditiously as public feeling will permit" would "tend to prevent interracial friction." [7] In granting the injunction, Hulen, J., branded this contention "as a proposition of law . . . a new and novel theory" and stated that "The law permits of no such delay in the protection of plaintiffs' constitutional rights." [8]

On July 19th the injunction took effect and St. Louis' outdoor swimming pools were again unsegregated.[9] For the rest of the summer, the pools remained open to all citizens and no major violence occurred. However, in order to prevent an outbreak, the police found it necessary to assign as many as 175 men to handle hostile crowds ranging up to 350. Early in August, when primary elections reduced the number of policemen available for this duty, the pools were closed for three days so as to prevent any disturbance. The pools were boycotted by their usual patrons. On a warm Sunday, when normally attendance at the

---

and public service organizations discuss "In the frankest possible terms, the minorities in the community, a philosophy of dealing with them as well as the obligation of police in a free democratic society to treat and handle them regardless of race, national origin or any other presumably identifiable characteristics" (communication from William Holzhausen, November 13, 1950) However, a staff member of the *St. Louis Post Dispatch*, writing of the Fairgrounds Park violence, concluded that the lack of proper training in race relations was an important factor in preventing full utilization of the police force in handling the disturbance.

7. *Draper* v. *St. Louis*, 92 F. Supp. 546, 549 (E.D. Mo., 1950).

8. *Ibid.*, at p. 549. The court held that the denial of publicly supported facilities to Negroes, solely because of their race, deprived them of their right to equal protection of the laws under the 14th Amendment and violated the Civil Rights Statute, 8 U.S.C.A. section 43.

The significance of the decision lay largely in the breadth of the reasoning with which a finding of discrimination was made. The defendants had testified as to the imminent completion of an outdoor pool which was to be open to Negroes. The court, having already observed that the McLaurin case appeared to narrow the meaning of "substantial" in the "substantially equal" formula to a very fine line, stated that "Even when completed such a pool may mitigate discrimination, but it will not validate it as to other sections of the city." *Draper* v. *St. Louis*, 92 F. Supp. 546, 550 (E.D. Mo., 1950). The court found that the plaintiffs had shown no pecuniary loss to support a claim for compensatory and punitive damages. *Ibid.*, at 550.

9. The *St Louis Post Dispatch* editorialized that the city's action for a last minute stay of execution before the injunction took effect "Seems to be evidence that it is little better prepared now than it was for the opening of the Fairgrounds Park pool in June of 1949." (*St. Louis Post Dispatch*, July 18, 1950. Section B, p. 2, col. 3).

Fairgrounds Park pool might have reached 4,000, there were 129 Negroes and twelve whites swimming. On July 30th, the *St. Louis Post Dispatch* reported that Negro men and boys, "go to and from the pool between two lines of policemen, who face outward, separating the swimmers from a crowd of several hundred white men, women and children. Most of the whites make no secret of their hatred of what they regard as an intrusion. The policemen, backed by a fleet of motorcycles and scout cars, quickly shift position when necessary to head off sudden movements of the crowd." [10]

WASHINGTON

In June 1949, Washington, D.C., was the scene of two days of sporadic fighting between Negroes and whites after an Interior Department order had re-affirmed a formal policy of non-segregation and after mixed groups attempted to enter a swimming pool previously used only by whites. Secretary Krug ordered the pool closed on the second day of violence and so it remains for the rest of the summer. Soon afterward a race relations specialist was called in to discuss the problem of handling such disturbances with the Capital Parks police and Interior Department officials. Criticism of Secretary Krug's action was voiced in Congress where Representative Williams of Mississippi declaimed that "The Secretary . . . had but to look to similar occurrences . . . to know that such an order would bring bloodshed and race riots." And further: "I think that the Secretary is expecting a race riot as a result of his action in doing away with segregation at the swimming pools." Representatives Rankin of Mississippi, Davis of Georgia, and Hoffman of Michigan concurred.

In March 1950, Secretary Chapman announced that the Anacostia pool, closed in 1949 because of racial disorders, would be reopened in 1950 to all citizens without any distinction. He went on to state that the Department of the Interior would be prepared to enforce the pool regulations by police action and protection if that became necessary. Amid predictions of violence, arrangements were made for training the National Capital Parks police, pool personnel, and government officials

10. *St. Louis Post Dispatch* (July 30, 1950, section C, p. 1, col. 2). The President of the St. Louis Board of Police Commissioners states that a sizeable force was necessary only in the early stages of the situation to preserve order, and that the police detail was gradually reduced to a normal one at the pool. However, reserves were always standing by in the vicinity, subject to immediate call in the event of a disturbance. In a communication from William Holzhausen, November 13, 1950, Mr. Holzhausen emphasizes the fact that the pool at Fairgrounds Park is located in a large recreational area which attracts several thousand persons on weekends. However, this also appears to be the case at Anacostia Park in Washington, D.C., where no sizeable police detail was found necessary in a similar situation. Most importantly, there is no explanation as to why the St. Louis police did not attempt to disperse any crowds which gathered around the swimming pool.

in methods of handling racial tensions. Meanwhile, the Interior Department publicized its decision and emphasized the fact that the law would be enforced and that the policy of non-segregation was going to "stick." [11] In June, before the pools opened, the Superintendent of the Washington Metropolitan police announced that he would back up the Capital Parks police in preserving order, even if that required using all of the men on his force.

The results were in sharp contrast to the situation in St. Louis. There was no disorder throughout the summer, nor was it found necessary to station a large force of police at the pools to prevent an outbreak. Attendance at the pools did drop during 1950. However, cold weather, a polio epidemic and the reluctance of parents to send their children swimming when violence was feared were seen as important contributing factors. Although the *Washington Post* had joined those predicting violence after Secretary Chapman's April statement, September found the *Post* glad to acknowledge its error and the success of the nonsegregation policy. An editorial stated that the absence of any disorder was due in large part to effective police action and concluded that "Trouble is likely to arise only if, as was the case in 1949, some organized group attempts to foment it" (*Washington Post*, September 10, 1950, section M, p. 12, col. 2).

CHICAGO

Racial tensions run high in our society not only when people are competing for the use of public facilities, but also when jobs and housing are at stake. The Supreme Court's decision in the 1948 *Restrictive Covenant* cases (*Shelley* v. *Kraemer*, 334 U.S. 1 [1948]; *Hurd* v. *Hodge*, 334 U.S. 24 [1948]) may have spelled an end to the support of racially segregated housing in the United States by legal sanctions. (Ming, 1948, pp. 203, 216-224). If so, serious problems are raised about the extralegal means which may be used to prevent Negroes from breaking out of tightly closed and overcrowded ghettos in cities like Chicago where the pattern of housing segregation is well established.[12]

In Chicago, during November 1949, the rumor that a Negro had purchased property in a "white" residential neighborhood near the notorious south side "black belt" was a factor in bringing about a riot in which a crowd of several hundred persons destroyed property and

11. Although the newspapers treated the Interior Department action as settling on a policy of nonsegregation, the position of the Department was that there was no new policy involved, rather that the law which had no provision for segregation was to be enforced as it should have been in prior years.

12. Housing is particularly important because of the way in which it serves as the basis for other patterns of segregation (e.g., schools, social facilities) in communities where these are neither compelled nor permitted by law (See Weaver, 1948).

assaulted innocent individuals for five successive nights before being dispersed by the police.[13]

Tension generated by the rumor erupted into violence on November 8th when a recently settled resident on Peoria Street entertained in his home a group of visiting labor union officials and fellow union members, a group which included eight Negroes. A crowd gathered outside the home, protesting the presence of Negroes and threatening their white host. During the following four nights large crowds assembled in the area, no action being taken by the police to disperse them. During this time, the disturbance assumed an anti-Semitic and anti-communist as well as an anti-Negro flavor.[14] The property of the individual who had entertained Negroes in his home was damaged by the rioters who later turned to beating persons found in the area who were thought to be Jewish or were identified as "outsiders" and communists. On the fifth night of violence, after the crowd threatened to spill over onto a nearby business street, the police, who by that time had turned out in force under an emergency riot control plan, closed off the area and systematically attempted to disperse the mob.

Despite pressure from many private organizations and individuals during the rioting, the Mayor had refused to issue a statement. On November 18th, he made his first statement, blaming the disturbance on subversive groups, thus giving credence to the slogans of the rioters. Twelve days later this statement was "amplified" and Chicago's citizens were told that the "Police have definite orders to disperse any crowd gathering for the purpose of harassing citizens" and that "Law and order must and will be preserved in this community." A circular from the Police Commissioner, dated December 2, 1949, outlined procedures for immediately dispersing crowds gathering at a point of disorder.[15]

There was strong criticism of the action of the city administration, particularly of the police department. Familiar complaints were voiced

13. Versions of the Peoria Street violence vary widely. An extended report was issued by the Chicago Commission on Human Relations (Dec. 10, 1949). The Commission, because of its position as an agency of the city government, has been criticized for a "conservative" attitude in these situations. The facts as here reported are therefore drawn largely from the Commission report, treating that report as a kind of "irreducible minimum" version of what actually happened. For examples of stronger criticism of the police and the Mayor, see Jack, 1949; Peters, 1950.

14. The *Chicago Daily News* reported that "A policeman explained to one of our reporters that one batch [of persons] were properly beaten because they were Communists." "How do you know they were Communists?" the reporter inquired. "Because they were Jews," explained the policeman (*Chicago Daily News,* Nov. 16, 1949. Section I, p. 24, col. 1).

15. Report of the Chicago Commission on Human Relations 42 (December 10, 1949). Such incidents were not new to postwar Chicago. In 1946, when Negroes moved into Airport Homes, a publicly owned and operated housing project, there was a major disturbance. In 1947, a similar situation in the Fernwood community led to violence which was suppressed by one of the largest concentrations of police manpower ever seen in Chicago (Martin, 1949, p. 199). A running account of attacks on property and individuals symptomatic of racial tensions is to be found in the monthly reports of the Chicago Commission on Human Relations in the section titled "Law and Order."

about discriminatory police action, in this instance based on evidence that some policemen were in direct sympathy with the mob. Prominent among the demands made upon the Mayor after the riot was the recommendation that Chicago's Metropolitan Police receive training in the techniques for preventing future outbreaks of this kind.

The immediate results of the police training, the policy of immediate dispersal of disorderly crowds, and the Mayor's statement indicate the importance of informed government action in situations where racial violence is a danger. Several incidents occurring during 1950 which might have developed into major violence were handled with dispatch by the officials concerned and, significantly, relations between the Chicago Commission on Human Relations and the police, almost at the breaking point during the Peoria Street riot, improved greatly.[16]

While the complexity of these situations is such that no simple lessons are to be learned from them, they do suggest that the problem of racial violence can be effectively dealt with on a practical level. Responsible government officials must first of all decide to enforce relevant laws vigorously and protect the rights of individuals despite pressure from hostile members of the community. Equally important is skilled police work based on an understanding of the unique problems of predicting and preventing racial disorders.

. . . It is suggested that further investigation will bear out the hypothesis here advanced: that racial violence can be prevented even where the enforcement of civil rights law involves direct attack on established patterns of racial segregation. The key to such successful law enforcement is decisive and informed government action.

The rhetoric of violence has been an important part of the rationale of racial segregation in the United States; it has often swayed courts as well as legislatures. In this context, the violence threat appears not only as a possible obstacle to effective law enforcement but, what is more important, as one of the costs of eliminating segregation. There is the cost of violence which is not prevented, as well as the physical cost of preventive measures (as when a sizeable police force is found necessary) [17] and the sacrifice of the psychological and economic stake which certain groups have in the *status quo*. On the other hand, there is evidence that most, if not all, racial violence can be prevented by well-advised government action. The expense of preventive measures may itself be due to

16. During the Peoria Street riots, the Police Commissioner angrily refused to confer in the future with representatives of the Commission on Human Relations. Commission report 23 (Dec. 10, 1949). Indications of the improvement are seen in the description of the working liaison now existing between the police and the Commission. Consult Commission reports: 14-19 (July, 1950); 14-17 (Aug., 1950).

17. Compare the policy of the London police department when post-war anti-Semitic riots found both communists and fascist organizations attempting to battle on the streets (West, 1948a, p. 24 and 1948b, p. 26). As to whether the duty of the state is the same even when the protection of individual rights would involve an extraordinary allocation of resources, it appears that the problem simply does not arise in such form.

delay and inefficiency in using them. And the disturbance of established expectations is a cost of any major social change. It is outweighed by the moral, psychological and economic costs connected with the institutions of segregation.

It is in this context that the soundness of the *Draper* v. *St. Louis* decision becomes clear. Judicial approval of racial segregation, based on the fear that recognition of a competing civil right would provoke costly violence, is unwise. The violence question is best decided by government officials responsible for law enforcement. Such judicial action is also undesirable since it reduces what should be a constant pressure on government to develop and utilize the most efficient techniques of law enforcement. If the danger of violence in any particular case is so great as to constitute a major threat to the security of the community, the worst result will be a practical limitation on individual rights. Such unenforced civil rights law is not a new phenomenon. Its very existence emphasizes the importance of formally recognizing individual rights even where their immediate exercise is beset with practical difficulty. For only if this is done can citizens press for vigorous law enforcement.

Thirty-four years ago, in passing on the constitutionality of a municipal ordinance requiring residential segregation, the Supreme Court indicated what the attitude of the courts should be towards the question of racial violence.

It is urged that this proposed segregation will promote the public peace by preventing race conflict. Desirable as this is, and important as is the preservation of the public peace, this aim cannot be accomplished by laws or ordinances which deny rights created or protected by the Federal Constitution (*Buchanan* v. *Warley*, 245 U.S. 60, 81 [1917]).

Courts and legislatures, called upon to weaken further the institutions of segregation, may be reassured by substantial progress made since then in the arts of law enforcement and by important shifts in social sentiment.

The language of race relations discussion has shifted significantly during the past four decades. Waning in importance, but still important, are arguments based on the impossibility of "legislating social equality" and a supposed "right" to be prejudiced. Here, as elsewhere, social movement and the process of discussion have produced ever-changing formulations of the issues. Now it is said that there is no "right" to be prejudiced insofar as prejudice is expressed in overt acts which deprive other individuals of their rights. It is argued that few laws of any kind are ever made which do not conflict with the sentiments of some group in the community (compare McWilliams: 1944). And it is urged that legally sanctioned segregation has been a major cause of the prejudices which are said to make effective legal action impossible.[18] Finally, as

18. See especially, Myrdal, 1944, pp. 75-78, recalling Justice Harlan's famous phrase about permitting "the seeds of race hate to be planted under the sanction of law." (*Plessy* v. *Ferguson*, 163 U.S. 537, 560 [1896]).

the functions of government in modern society expand, the role played by government agencies in race relations problems emerges as a central focus of debate.[19]

The change in rhetoric is never ending. However, the process serves to remind that exorcising the spectre of racial violence is a matter of redefining the larger issues of freedom and equality as well as obtaining effective enforcement of civil rights law.

The National Advisory Commission on Civil Disorders

Patterns of Disorder

Based upon information derived from our surveys, we offer the following generalizations:

1. No civil disorder was "typical" in all respects. Viewed in a national framework, the disorders of 1967 varied greatly in terms of violence and damage: while a relatively small number were major under our criteria and a somewhat larger number were serious, most of the disorders would have received little or no national attention as "riots" had the nation not been sensitized by the more serious outbreaks.

2. While the civil disorders of 1967 were racial in character, they were not *inter*racial. The 1967 disorders, as well as earlier disorders of the recent period, involved action within Negro neighborhoods against symbols of white American society—authority and property—rather than against white persons.

3. Despite extremist rhetoric, there was no attempt to subvert the social order of the United States. Instead, most of those who attacked white authority and property seemed to be demanding fuller participation in the social order and the material benefits enjoyed by the vast majority of American citizens.

4. Disorder did not typically erupt without pre-existing causes as a result of a single "triggering" or "precipitating" incident. Instead, it

19. Compare the treatment of government action in Weaver, 1948 with that in Ross, 1948, and Johnson, 1943, pp. 323-324. The broadened scope of govenmental action is particularly important in the light of the "public-private" distinction which has limited the application of the Fourteenth Amendment. That the distinction is in the process of drastic redefinition is shown by comparing its treatment in the Restrictive Covenant Cases, 334 U.S. I (1948) with the extensions suggested by Ming, 1948, and by the discussion in Race Discrimination in Housing 57 *Yale L. J.* 426, 456, 457 (1948).

developed out of an increasingly disturbed social atmosphere, in which typically a series of tension-heightening incidents over a period of weeks or months became linked in the minds of many in the Negro community with a shared reservoir of underlying grievances.

5. There was, typically, a complex relationship between the series of incidents and the underlying grievances. For example, grievances about allegedly abusive police practices, unemployment and underemployment, housing, and other conditions in the ghetto, were often aggravated in the minds of many Negroes by incidents involving the police, or the inaction of municipal authorities on Negro complaints about police action, unemployment, inadequate housing or other conditions. When grievance-related incidents recurred and rising tensions were not satisfactorily resolved, a cumulative process took place in which prior incidents were readily recalled and grievances reinforced. At some point in the mounting tension, a further incident—in itself often routine or even trivial—became the breaking point, and the tension spilled over into violence.

6. Many grievances in the Negro community result from the discrimination, prejudice and powerlessness which Negroes often experience. They also result from the severely disadvantaged social and economic conditions of many Negroes as compared with those of whites in the same city and, more particularly, in the predominantly white suburbs.

7. Characteristically, the typical rioter was not a hoodlum, habitual criminal or riffraff; nor was he a recent migrant, a member of an uneducated underclass or a person lacking broad social and political concerns. Instead, he was a teenager or young adult, a lifelong resident of the city in which he rioted, a high school dropout—but somewhat better educated than his Negro neighbor—and almost invariably underemployed or employed in a menial job. He was proud of his race, extremely hostile to both whites and middle-class Negroes and, though informed about politics, highly distrustful of the political system and of political leaders.

8. Numerous Negro counterrioters walked the streets urging rioters to "cool it." The typical counterrioter resembled in many respects the majority of Negroes, who neither rioted nor took action against the rioters, that is, the noninvolved. But certain differences are crucial: the counterrioter was better educated and had higher income than either the rioter or the noninvolved.

9. Negotiations between Negroes and white officials occurred during virtually all the disorders surveyed. The negotiations often involved young, militant Negroes as well as older, established leaders. Despite a setting of chaos and disorder, negotiations in many cases involved discussion of underlying grievances as well as the handling of the disorder by control authorities.

10. The chain we have identified—discrimination, prejudice, disadvantaged conditions, intense and pervasive grievances, a series of

tension-heightening incidents, all culminating in the eruption of disorder at the hands of youthful, politically-aware activists—must be understood as describing the central trend in the disorders, not as an explanation of all aspects of the riots or of all rioters. Some rioters, for example, may have shared neither the conditions nor the grievances of their Negro neighbors; some may have coolly and deliberately exploited the chaos created by others; some may have been drawn into the melee merely because they identified with, or wished to emulate, others. Nor do we intend to suggest that the majority of the rioters, who shared the adverse conditions and grievances, necessarily articulated in their own minds the connection between that background and their actions.

11. The background of disorder in the riot cities was typically characterized by severely disadvantaged conditions for Negroes, especially as compared with those for whites; a local government often unresponsive to these conditions; Federal programs which had not yet reached a significantly large proportion of those in need; and the resulting reservoir of pervasive and deep grievance and frustration in the ghetto.

12. In the immediate aftermath of disorder, the *status quo* of daily life before the disorder generally was quickly restored. Yet, despite some notable public and private efforts, little basic change took place in the conditions underlying the disorder. In some cases, the result was increased distrust between blacks and whites, diminished interracial communication, and growth of Negro and white extremist groups.

John Spiegel

Hostility, Aggression and Violence

For the past year, the staff of the Lemberg Center for the Study of Violence has been studying the process associated with outbreaks of racial violence and rioting in a number of Northern cities. The investigation has been directed toward discovering what factors among whites and blacks account for a massive, hostile outburst occurring in one city but not in another, given similar circumstances of racial components and tensions. We have compared attitudes of whites and blacks in three cities which have experienced a riot with those in three cities which might have but did not. In addition, we have also observed the behavior of city administrations, law enforcement personnel, and riot participants during the course of a riot. Finally, we have reviewed descriptions and analyses of previous cycles of riots which have occurred in the nineteenth and early twentieth centuries in our country.

. . . The riot process can be considered under three headings: (1) *Preconditions,* defined as the psychological and social factors which must be present in order for a riot to occur; (2) *The Phase Structure of the Riot,* or the plateaus of group behavior through which the riot moves in the course of its escalation; and (3) *The Aftermath,* the process of response in the city to the riot after it dies down which determines whether or not it will be repeated.

PRECONDITIONS

Value Conflicts

All riots stem from intense conflicts within the value systems which stabilize the social and political processes of a nation. There are two sorts of value conflicts, each of which gives rise to a different type of struggle.

Normative readjustment. In this case, the dominant values of a society are inequitably applied. Groups excluded from the application of the dominant values protest and if protest fails to attain readjustment, they riot. The anti-draft rioter at the time of the Civil War, for example, was protesting the plight of the common man who could not, like his wealthier compatriots, buy his way out of the draft. American egalitarian values were not being applied across the board. The readjustment came only after the intensity of the riots stimulated public concern to force a change. The anti-Negro riots of 1919-1920 grew out of the resentment of working-class whites toward the use of Negroes imported from the South for cheap labor and frequently as labor scabs. This resentment was amplified, of course, by racist sentiments, but the latter, acting alone, would not have brought about rioting.

The contemporary ghetto riots grow out of the failure of the civil rights movement in its attempt to achieve normative readjustment for black people through non-violent protest. This failure produces lines of cleavage which, if intensified, will result in the second type of value conflict, namely:

Value readjustment. In this case, the dominant values of the society are brought under severe pressure for change. The social movement which organizes the activities of an aggrieved sector of the population, having given up hope for benefiting from the going value system, sets up a new configuration of values. The movement now becomes revolutionary. When Americans gave up hope of benefiting from the English institutions of the monarchy and the colonial system, they set up their own egalitarian value system and staged a revolution which was seen by the British Crown as an insurrection.

Just now, the Black Power and Black Nationalist leaders are beginning to move in the direction of value readjustment. They are talking about organizing their people on the basis of separatist and collectivist values. They are moving away from the melting-pot, individualistic values of our country, which are not working for them.

How far and how rapidly they will move is anyone's guess. The President's Commission on Civil Disorders viewed this possibility with alarm in their recent report. It was perhaps the principal reason for their recommending massive economic assistance to relieve ghetto problems.

THE HOSTILE BELIEF SYSTEM

An aggrieved population always erupts into hostile outbursts on the basis of a pre-existing hostile belief system. During the anti-Catholic riots early in the nineteenth century, the rioters really believed that the Pope, in Rome, was trying to take over the country. The anti-Negro rioters in Chicago and East St. Louis (and even in Detroit in 1943) really believed that Negroes were trying to appropriate their jobs and rape their women and kill their men in dark alleys. Today, many rioters in black ghettos really believe in the malevolence of white society, its duplicity, and its basic commitment to oppressing Negroes. An important component of the hostile belief system is that the expected behavior of the identified adversary is seen as *extraordinary*—that is, beyond the pale of accepted norms. In the black ghettos, people are convinced, for example, that the police will behave toward them with extraordinary verbal incivility and physical brutality, far beyond the degrees of incivility and brutality displayed toward whites.

Hostile beliefs bear varying relations to "reality." Their systemization means that in some aspects they are incorrect exaggerations, in others, very close to the truth. In the 1830's, the Catholic Church wanted more power and influence locally, but it didn't, consciously, want to take over the country. Today, large numbers of white people want to keep Negroes about where they are by allowing them to advance at a snail's pace. But they don't, at least consciously, want to oppress them. That this policy, in the minds of Negroes, amounts to oppression is something whites have to learn. That whites, for the most part, don't consciously want to cause them suffering is something black people in the ghetto have to learn.

INADEQUATE COMMUNICATION

The value conflicts and the hostile belief system in which they are em-bodied tend to be maintained, in the course of any riot cycle, by a failure of communications between dissident and dominant groups. During the Civil War draft riots, poor laborers in the cities directed their anger toward the Republican leaders (and, eventually, toward any member of the Republican Party) who were thought responsible both for the war and for the draft. But these leaders had no idea how strongly the common man felt about their policy nor did they have lines of communication which could inform them of the feeling that existed. Today, many city administrations have no way of knowing how deep and intense is the resentment of black people in the ghetto. The politicians in city hall talk only to moderate Negro leaders who can't well articulate the feelings in the ghetto. Militant black leaders are discounted as "firebrands" or "Black Power Agitators." The press and the media of communication fail to report the facts of life in the ghetto and the white community, in general, remains ignorant or deluded, unconcerned or over-frightened about race relations. Therefore, when a riot breaks out in their city, they are surprised, or shocked, that such a thing could happen, or else blame it on the inevitable "outside agitator" or "the communist conspiracy."

SOCIAL CONTROL

Studies of past and present riots show that the immediate cause of the riot is a failure in social control. These failures are of two sorts, under-control and overcontrol. In the condition of undercontrol, law enforce-ment personnel are insufficiently active. The dissident group, noting the weakness of the authorities, seizes the opportunity to express its hostility. The inactivity of the police functions as an invitation to act out long-suppressed feelings, free of the social consequences of illegal behavior. In the condition of overcontrol, police, state troopers, or the National Guard are brought in too early, and make unnecessary arrests with unnecessary brutality.

In some communities, as in the recent Detroit riot, undercontrol during the opening phases of the riot leads to an efflorescence of looting and is then suddenly replaced with overcontrol. In other communities, overcontrol is instituted almost from the onset of the disturbance. Police and state troopers are rushed to the scene and begin to man-handle everyone in sight. Since the action is out of proportion to the event, it generates an intense reaction. If overcontrol is sufficiently repressive, as in the Milwaukee situation, where a 24-hour curfew was slapped down very quickly and the National Guard summoned in force, the disturbance is stamped out. Under these circumstances there can be no improvement in ghetto-City Hall communications. The consequences of such premature repression cannot yet be discerned. Short of the use of overwhelming force, overcontrol usually leads to increased violence. Black people in the ghetto see the police as violent and strike back with increasing intensity. In the majority of instances, police violence toward neighborhood personnel precedes and supersedes ghetto violence.

An adequate or optimum law enforcement policy requires an effective police presence when illegal activities, such as looting, take place. Arrests can and should be made, without cruelty. It is not necessary that all offenders be caught and arrested to show that authorities intend to maintain order. Crowds can be broken up or contained through a variety of techniques not based on clubbing or shooting. The avoidance of both under- and overcontrol is a matter of police training for riot control.

RIOT PHASES

We have found that a riot is a dynamic process which goes through different stages of development. If the preconditions described above exist, if a value conflict intensifies, hostile beliefs flourish, an incident which exemplifies the hostile beliefs occurs, communications are inadequate and rumor inflames feelings of resentment to a fever pitch, the process will get started. How far it will go depends upon the process of social control between the local authorities and an aroused community.

There are four stages within the riot process. Not all local civil disturbances go through all four stages; in fact, the majority do not reach Stage 3. It is still not certain at what point in the process it is appropriate to use the word "riot" to describe the event. We need more information about the process and better reporting of the phase structure itself.

PHASE 1. THE PRECIPITATING INCIDENT

How this phase fits into the hostile beliefs has already been mentioned. The precipitating trigger is always a concrete manifestation of some item of behavior already predicted by the hostile belief system. Up till now, the media and the press have been sluggish in reporting the details of the precipitating incident. In the main, they have tended to overemphasize versions of the incident put out by local authorities, thus losing credibility with ghetto residents and misleading the white community.

PHASE 2. STREET CONFRONTATION

Following the instigating incident, the local population swarms into the streets. A process of "keynoting" begins to take place. Potential riot promoters begin to articulate the rage accumulating in the crowd and vie with each other in suggesting violent courses of action. Others, frequently recognized ghetto leaders, suggest that the crowd disband to let tempers cool and to allow time for a more considered course of action. The well-known contagiousness of crowd behavior begins to manifest itself. Law enforcement officers appear and try to disrupt the "keynoting" process by ordering and forcing the crowd to disperse. Frequently, their behavior serves to elevate one or another hostile "keynoter" to a position of dominance, thus flipping the riot process into the next phase.

The outcome of Phase 2 is clearly of crucial importance. The temper of the crowd may dissipate spontaneously, or escalate explosively. The response of the city administration at this point is also crucial. If representatives of City Hall appear, listen to complaints and suggest some responsive method for dealing with them, the agitation tends to subside; a "let's wait and see' attitude takes over. If they fail to show up and are represented only by the police, who are already heavily involved in the hostile belief system, the level of agitation tends to rise.

PHASE 3. ROMAN HOLIDAY

If hostile "keynoting" reaches a sufficient crescendo, a quantum jump in the riot process occurs and the threshold of Phase 3 is crossed. Usually the crowd leaves the scene of the street confrontation and reassembles elsewhere. Older persons drop out for the time being and young people take over the acion. They display an angry intoxication indisinguishable from glee. They hurl rocks and bricks and bottles at white-owned stores and at cars containing whites or police, wildly cheering every "hit." They taunt law-enforcement personnel, risk capture and generally act out routine scenarios featuring the sortie, the ambush and the escape. These constitute the classic triad of violent action which they have seen whites go through endlessly on T.V. The youngsters set the stage for looting, but are usually too involved in "the chase" and are too excited for systematic plunder. That action comes later in Phase 3 when first younger, then older adults, caught up in the spirit of the Roman Holiday, and, angered by tales of police brutality toward the kids, join in the mood of righting ancient wrongs.

Phase 3 has a game structure. It is like a sport somehow gone astray but still subject to correction. Partly this openness derives from the "King-for-a-day" carnival climate. Partly it is based on the intense ambivalence of black people toward the white system and its symbolic representatives—its hated stores and their beloved contents, its despised police and their admired weaponry, its unregenerate bigots and its exemplary civil rights advocates, now increasingly under suspicion. Because of the ambivalence, action and motive are unstable. Middle-class, or upwardly mobile Negroes become militants overnight. Youths on the rampage one day put on white hats and armbands to "cool the neighborhood" the next. It is because of the ambivalence felt by Negroes, not only toward whites but toward violence itself, that so few Phase 3 disturbances pass over into Phase 4.

PHASE 4. SIEGE

If a city's value conflict continues to be expressed by undercontrol or overcontrol of the Roman Holiday behavior in the ghetto, the riot process will be kicked over into Phase 4. The adversary relations between ghetto dwellers and City Hall now reach such a degree of polarization that no direct communications of any kind can be established. Communications, such as they are, consist of symbolic, war-like acts. State troopers, National Guard, paratroopers are summoned for even more violent repression. A curfew is declared. The ghetto is subjected to a state of siege. Citizens can no longer move freely into and out of their neighborhoods. Forces within the ghetto, now increasingly composed of adults, throw firebombs at white-owned establishments, and disrupt firefighting. Snipers attack invading paramilitary forces. The siege runs its course, like a Greek tragedy, until both sides tire of this fruitless and devasting way of solving a conflict. It subsides when "order has been restored," meaning that black people and law enforcement personnel would rather get some sleep and city administrators decide to talk to ghetto leaders.

AFTERMATH

The value conflict, the hostile belief systems, communication and social control have different outcomes in different cities as a result of the riot. Speaking loosely, we might say that the riot can leave the pathology of race relations within the city unchanged, improved or worsened. We have been able to distinguish three types of response by city administrations to the events of the riot.

MASSIVE DENIAL

Cities that display massive denial refuse to admit or recognize the value conflict troubling black people in the ghetto. They claim that "their

Negroes" are relatively well off and satisfied and that they have done everything that needs to be done for them. Therefore, the riot could not have been due to frustration and widespread resentment. On the contrary, they maintain that rioting was the work of hoodlums and a small minority of lawless rabble, whipped up by outside agitators Therefore, the remedy consists of greatly strengthening law enforcement. Such communities spend large sums of money buying heavy weapons, armored cars and other forms of equipment designed to maximize the repressive capacity of the city. No productive communication takes place between City Hall and the ghetto leaders. As a result, the resentment in the ghetto hardens and the militant leadership goes underground. Under these circumstances, the possibility of a repetition of the riot and the continued eruption of smaller scale violence directed at the white establishment is high. The tension in the city is higher than before the riot.

INSINCERE RECOGNITION

In some cities, the administration seems to behave as if it had profited from the lessons of the riot. City leaders say that they had not realized how bad things were in the ghetto. They make an effort to talk to militant ghetto leaders but are quickly put off by the demands of these leaders. Subsequently, they continue to verbalize a recognition of ghetto problems and they may even claim with pride to have initiated attempts to improve conditions. Proposals and plans are announced with considerable publicity. However, little comes of these proposals, and, in the ghetto the city administration is perceived as engaged in a game of deceit. Under these circumstances, one may say that the pathology of the city remains unchanged and race relations are subject to future disturbances of unpredictable magnitude.

SINCERE RECOGNITION

In some cities, after the initial shock of the riot has died down, the city administration initiates a review of the causes of the riot and of possible remedies for the situation. Plans are drawn up which are related to correcting unjust practices and a serious attempt is made to implement them. For example, a Human Relations Commission is appointed with sufficient powers and staff to conduct hearings and to make findings in cases of discrimination in employment and housing. Or, a police-community relations program is instituted, with sufficient back-up from police administration and the mayor to guarantee its effectiveness. To overcome the communications problems some cities have instituted "vest-pocket" city halls, located in the ghetto, functioning much like branch libraries.

The steps which can be taken in this direction vary from city to city, depending upon its particular circumstances and resources, the imagination of city leaders and their capacity for innovation. But, given the high levels of grievance in all the ghettos all over the country, no city can afford to congratulate itself, no matter how sincere and extensive its efforts may be. Self-satisfaction and self-congratulation on the part of the mayor and his supporters are easily seen in the ghetto as political devices directed at impressing the voting public which may serve to increase rather than dispel resentment.

PART III

Causation:
Some Theoretical
and Empirical Notions

10

EMPIRICAL GENERALIZATIONS

Some of the more sophisticated attempts to use aggregated data in delineating empirical generalizations on racial violence are assembled in this chapter. The scarcity of such studies is caused more by the difficulties in obtaining comparable valid and reliable data than by the shortcomings of available statistical analysis techniques. Special efforts are now being made to generate usable comparative data and to provide for the collection of relevant statistics, and it is reasonable to expect that there will be a sharp increase in the quantity and quality of such studies in the years immediately ahead.

The four studies presented here represent pioneering attempts to invent modes of assembling and interpreting data in generating or testing hypotheses about collective violence. The Hovland and Sears article of three decades ago attempted to test the frustration-aggression hypothesis by correlating selected economic indices with lynchings. Some years later Mintz attempted to refine the Hovland-Sears findings through the application of more refined statistical analysis to the same data. In the early sixties Lieberson and Silverman attempted to sort out causal explanations of large-scale rioting through paired-comparison analysis of urban areas which had and had not experienced disorders; their conclusions must be seen as problematic since the number of cities which have not had rioting steadily decreases. The chapter ends with Gurr's interesting comparative study of civil strife in 114 nations, done in an attempt to isolate the influence of such variables as persisting deprivation, history of past strife, perceived legitimacy of government, and a number of mediating variables. He concludes that persisting deprivation has a direct and measurable effect on turmoil and speculates interestingly and cautiously on the meaning of his findings for understanding past and future events in the United States.

Minor Studies of Aggression: Correlations of Lynchings with Economic Indices

INTRODUCTION

It has been suggested elsewhere (Dollard, *et al.*, 1939) that the strength of instigation to an act of aggression following frustration varies not only with the strength of instigation to the frustrated goal-response (Sears and Sears, 1940), but also with the degree to which the goal-response suffers interference. It would be expected, for example, that if a hungry baby were forced to get its milk through a nipple with a very small hole, crying and general irritability would result and that the smaller the hole (i.e., the greater the interference with the goal-response, eating) the greater would be the irritability. The hypothesis may be stated formally as follows: *The strength of instigation to aggression varies directly with the amount of interference with the frustrated goal-response.*

Certain kinds of social statistics furnish excellent sources for the investigation of this principle. A comparison of the total amounts of social aggression during various phases of the economic cycle is an instance in point. If our hypothesis is correct, it would be expected that aggressive acts should be more numerous during years of depression than during years of prosperity, since economic conditions, in general, reflect the ease or difficulty with which the customary economic activities of the members of a group can be carried out, and low indices or bad economic conditions represent a greater interference with customary goal-responses than do high indices or good business conditions.

As a measure of aggression, the total number of crimes of violence would be satisfactory if the legal definition of "crime of violence" remained constant. Unfortunately for the present purpose, however, there have been marked changes during the past half century both in police and judicial interpretation of laws covering crimes of violence and in the laws themselves. The criteria of "property crimes with the use of violence" have remained somewhat more constant, and D. S. Thomas (1925) has shown that the numbers of these crimes correlate negatively with economic indices. But since crimes involving property might increase because of increased neediness during periods of poor economic conditions, and the aggression thus be only a by-product, this correlation is not completely convincing as a verification of the principle here postulated. Fortunately, however, in the case of one crime of violence, lynching, the criteria have remained quite constant during the past fifty or so years. Furthermore, lynchings do not arise out of an attempt to improve one's economic position during times of economic stress as in the case with property crimes. Statistics on the number of lynchings per year therefore constitute an excellent measure of aggression for our purpose. Consequently, in order to test the proposed hypothesis correlations were obtained between the number of lynchings and the concomitant indices of economic conditions during the last half century.

DATA AND RESULTS

SOURCES OF DATA

Economic indices which are to be used as a measure of the degree of interference with customary economic goal-responses must, obviously, refer to the economic activities of the group in which the measured aggression occurs. An analysis of 4,761 cases of lynching during the 49 years from 1882 to 1930 inclusive indicates that 3,386, or 71.1 per cent, were lynchings of Negroes (Work, 1931). Most of these cases occurred in the 14 Southern states in which, during that period, cotton was the basic commodity. Hence, as A. Raper (1933) has seen, the value of cotton crops is the index of greatest value in connection with Negro lynchings. The specific indices which were considered most relevant to the economic conditions of the group were: (a) the farm value of cotton, principally in the 14 Southern cotton states, and (b) the per-acre value of cotton in the same states. The farm value is the total value (price times yield) of cotton produced during a given year. The per-acre value of cotton was obtained by dividing the farm value for a given year by the total acreage for that year. The data on farm values of cotton and total acreage devoted to cotton were obtained from various volumes of the *Statistical Abstract of the United States.*

For the correlation with the total lynchings in the United States a composite economic index covering a large number of components seemed most suitable. The index chosen includes weighted individual measures of consumption, production, construction, imports, exports, and prices.

The number of lynchings which have occurred in any given year cannot be determined with absolute accuracy. Two factors make for difficulty in securing such information: (a) the censorship which is occasionally exerted over the reporting of such acts, and (b) some flexibility in the criteria for determining what constitutes a lynching. The data concerning the number of Negro lynchings and total number of lynchings are, naturally, fallible with respect to these factors. There is little reason to believe, however, that the censorship of lynching reports would vary systematically with economic indices, and in order to reduce the importance of the second factor, data have been used which were based on a consistent criterion and a uniform system of reporting for the entire period. The data were obtained from *The Negro Yearbook* (Work, 1931, p. 293) for all the years between 1882 and 1930 inclusive. Race riots and gang murders were not included in the computations. The distinction has been made between a lynching and a gang murder on the basis of the fact that, "whereas a gang murder is premeditated and carried out by a few people in conspired secrecy from constituted authorities, a lynching is usually spontaneous and carried out in a public fashion with scores, hundreds, and not uncommonly thousands of eye-witnesses. Gang murderers operate in secrecy to evade the law; lynchers operate in the open and publicly defy the law" (Southern Commission on the Study of Lynching, n.d., p. 73).

TREATMENT OF DATA

The data for both Negro and white lynchings and for farm value and per-acre value of cotton show pronounced trends from 1882 to 1930. In the case of the lynchings the trend line is downward, while in the case of the cotton values the trend is upward. The directions of the trends themselves follow the predicted relationship, i.e., there is a trend toward fewer lynchings with better economic conditions. This effect, however, might be due to some underlying general trend. The comparison of deviations from the trend line, from year to year, therefore gives a more critical test of the hypothesis. The values for the entire period from 1882 to 1930 were consequently first fitted to a straight line by the method of least squares. Deviations from this trend line were then computed and given the appropriate sign.

Tetrachoric correlations were computed between the deviations from the trend lines of the lynching data and of the economic indices. The tallies were placed in the appropriate cells simply on the basis of whether the deviations were above or below the trend line (+ or −). These correlations are given in Table 1. The approximation method discussed by H. E. Garrett (1937) and the Chesire, Saffir, and Thurstone graphic method (1933) were employed.[1] It will be observed that the results with the two methods are closely similar. The tetrachoric correlation method, using deviations from the trend line, appeared the most appropriate procedure for analysis, since in this way the trend itself does not affect the correlation and for preliminary study more exact correlations based on the extent of the deviations appeared unfeasible.

1. For further discussion of these methods see Henry E. Garrett, *Statistics in Psychology and Education*, New York: Longmans, Green, 1937, and Leone Chesire, Milton Saffir, and Louis L. Thurstone, *Computing Diagrams for the Tetrachoric Correlation Coefficients*, Chicago: The University of Chicago Press, 1933.

Table 1. *Tetrachoric Correlations Between Economic Indices*
and Lynching Data
(Data based on deviations from trend lines)

Variables	Garrett approximation Method	Saffir-Thurstone Chesire- graphic method
Composite Economic Index— Total lynchings	—.65	—.61
Per-acre value of cotton— Negro lynchings	—.63	—.61
Farm value of cotton— Negro lynchings	—.72	—.70

Another method of showing the relationship between the economic indices and the number of lynchings is to present graphically the comparable fluctuations in the two series. Figure 1 presents results in this way. Yearly variations of a composite economic index are plotted on the top line and the fluctuation from the trend line of the total number of lynchings on the bottom. To facilitate following of the relationship visually, the values for the lynching curve have been inverted. Thus when the two sets of data fluctuate inversely, the curves are parallel. Three-term smoothing of the values was employed, i.e., for the year 1905 the values for 1904, 1905, and 1906, were averaged, etc. Economic values were obtained for the years 1881 and 1931 to permit the use of the entire range from 1882-1930. Since comparable data on lynchings were not available for 1881 and 1931, the values for 1882 and 1930 were duplicated in the weighting for these years.

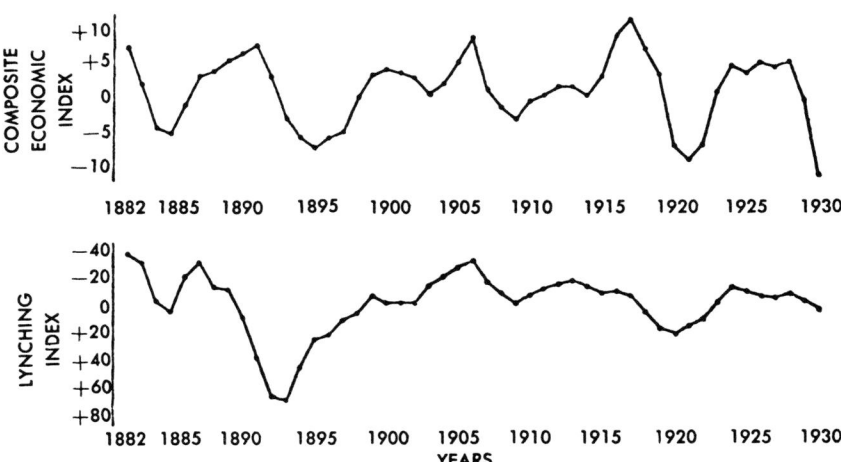

FIGURE 1.
Relation of Total Lynchings to a Composite Economic Index
Both curves represent the deviations from a trend (see text).

DISCUSSION AND CONCLUSIONS

It is evident from the correlations and the graphic presentation that the economic conditions of an area are intimately related to the amount of mass aggression displayed in that area as measured by lynchings. Our correlations are considerably higher than the one reported by Raper (1933) for the relationship between number of lynchings and per-acre value of cotton in nine Southern states, although it is not clear what method of correlation he employed. It is possible that the smaller sample he obtained by using only nine instead of fourteen states may have reduced this correlation. The verification of the general relationship is of particular interest in this instance because of the obvious lack of any causal relationship between the source of frustration and the objects toward which aggression is expressed. By no conceivable stretch of the imagination could the victims of lynchings, either Negro or white, be considered responsible for the value of cotton or the general level of business activity.

The reasons for this *displacement* of aggression are not hard to find. Although in any frustrating situation the strongest instigation is to acts of direct aggression against the agent perceived as the frustrator, such acts can occur only if the agent is available and if the act will not elicit too much counteraggression or punishment. In the present instance the frustrating agent is not readily available because it is not an object; one cannot be aggressive against a condition represented by index numbers. It is true, however, that certain individuals probably *represent* the condition symbolically, e.g., merchants, landlords, wealthy persons. These are individuals in a preferred and protected situation in society, however, and aggression directed toward them would elicit a relatively great amount of retribution (punishment). Hence, following the principle that anticipation of punishment inhibits acts of direct aggression and permits the occurrence of displaced aggression (Dollard, *et al.,* 1939), the aggression is directed toward persons in a less favorable and protected position who are unable to mobilize adequate retribution.

The majority of persons who are lynched, however, have actually been arrested, or are being sought, for a crime (Southern Commission on the Study of Lynching, 1932). It cannot be assumed, therefore, that these displays of group aggression are dependent on interference with economic activities alone. In point of fact, the object of aggression has already acted as a frustrating agent for the members of the group; he has interfered with their peaceful activity, comfort, and ideals of how society should operate, and has produced, by his acts, a threat to their future welfare. He is necessarily, then, the target of a certain amount of direct aggression. But according to the principle of summation of the strengths of instigation to aggression (Dollard, *et al.,* 1939), it would be expected that these persons would suffer more serious aggressions from the group when subsidiary frustrations, such as those represented by low economic indices, are operative. The increase in the number who are lynched verifies this expectation. It may be said, then, that individuals who arouse direct aggression suffer the additional effects of displaced aggression when the agent responsible for this latter is either not available or would retaliate with a great amount of punishment or counter-aggression. . . .

SUMMARY

The hypothesis that the strength of instigation to aggression varies directly with the amount of interference with the frustrated goal-response was tested through the use of social statistics. Tetrachoric correlations were computed between indices of the annual numbers of lynchings and of the economic conditions obtaining during the same period. The data cover the 49 years from 1882 to 1930.

The correlations between total lynchings in the United States and the composite index of economic activity were between —.61 and —.65. Slightly higher correlations were obtained when the comparison was made between the number of Negro lynchings and the farm value and per-acre value of cotton. Three-term smoothing of the curves for the economic index and the total number of lynchings shows the inverse relationship very clearly. During periods of depression the number of lynchings is high; during prosperity the number of lynchings declines. The results are discussed in terms of displacement of aggression and summation of instigation to aggression.

Alexander Mintz

A Re-Examination of Correlations between Lynchings and Economic Indices

INTRODUCTION

Hovland and Sears (1940) attempted to verify a causal relationship between economic frustration and aggressive behavior as expressed in lynchings by a statistical study. The statistical technique was as follows:

linear trends were computed for the numbers of lynchings reported for the years 1882 to 1930, inclusive, in the United States. Two figures were available for each year, the total number of lynchings in the United States, including both colored and white victims, and the number of lynchings of Negroes, most of them occurring in fourteen Southern states. Thus two trend equations were computed. The method of least squares was used in the computations. Similar computations were performed for the total value (in dollars) of cotton produced in fourteen Southern states and for the per-acre value of the cotton. The deviations of the numbers of lynchings and of the cotton value from the figures predicted by means of the trend lines were determined. In addition, an average index was computed for each year from monthly composite indices of economic activity. Thereupon a number of tetrachoric correlations were obtained by using two approximation methods:

Between composite index and deviations of total lynchings from
    linear trend (Garrett's Method):   —.65
Between deviations from trend lines of
    Negro lynchings and per-acre cotton value: —.63
    Negro lynchings and total cotton value: —.72

Almost identical tetrachoric correlations were obtained by the use of another approximation method. The correlations were impressively high and the authors viewed them as verifying the hypothesis according to which frustration tends to lead to aggressive behavior.

Hovland and Sears's results were favorably cited in several of the modern books dealing with social psychology. They are quoted as evidence by Britt in *Social Psychology of Modern Life,* by Cantril in *Psychology of Social Movements,* by Dollard, *et al.,* in *Frustration and Aggression.* Surprisingly, in all three books the nature of the correlations is inaccurately stated. None indicates that Hovland and Sears used deviations from trends in their correlations rather than actual numbers of lynchings or the value of cotton. The accounts implicitly attribute to Hovland and Sears an elementary error: Since both cotton value and frequency of lynchings are correlated with time, the presence of a correlation between them would be unsuitable as evidence about any possible causal relationship between them; all variables exhibiting marked time trends tend to be intercorrelated, *e.g.,* lynchings in the United States and birth rate in Germany, or the percentage of illiteracy in Russia, or the speed of transatlantic steamships.

Hovland and Sears had attempted to avoid this error by computing linear trends and using the deviations of their variables from the trends in their correlations. Unfortunately, an examination of their data suggested that in so doing they introduced another error; the trends exhibited by the data were not linear and some of their correlations seemed to be artifacts caused by the arbitrary choice of straight lines which were not appropriate to the data. In the course of computations performed in order to verify this suspicion, a second error was discovered: for one pair of variables, tetrachoric correlations as used by Hovland and Sears were seriously misleading. Their use presupposed normal distribution and homoscedasticity of the variables; apparently, these conditions were not fulfilled, inasmuch as a marked discrepancy between certain tetra- choric correlations and the corresponding more basic product-moment correlations was found to exist. . . .

Large discrepancies are apparent between the high correlations be- tween fluctuations of lynchings and of economic indices obtained by Hovland and Sears and the much lower correlations reported in this study. The discrepancies are due to two changes in statistical proce- dures: (1) the use of product-moment correlations instead of tetrachoric correlations, and (2) the subdivision of the time interval under investi- gation on the basis of inspection of the curves, and computation of linear trends for parts of the period rather than for the whole period. The advantages of the changes in the procedure remain to be discussed.[1]

1. The advantages of using product-moment correlations rather than tetrachoric can hardly be questioned. Tetrachoric correlations derive their validity entirely from the fact that they tend to approximate product-moment correlations under certain conditions, there being homoscedasticity and normal distribution of the variables. If a tetra- choric correlation fails to approximate the corresponding product-mo- ment correlation, it becomes meaningless. The inference is legitimate that the necessary conditions for the use of the tetrachoric formula are not fulfilled. Thus the product-moment correlations of the order of —.34, reported here, are clearly preferable to Hovland and Sears' tetrachoric —.62 as describing the relationship between the fluctuations of total lynchings and the composite economic index.

2. Hovland and Sears's use of one linear function as a descriptive of the trend exhibited by each of the variables over a 49-year period is an arbitrary procedure. Any analytical function—linear, polynomial, expo- nential, etc.—can be fitted to any set of data by the method of least squares. The choice of the function to be fitted may be determined by theoretical considerations or may be suggested by inspection of the data. Neither procedure requires the use of single linear trends for the 49- year period. Inspection of the curves of lynchings and of cotton values indicates that such linear trends are distinctly inappropriate. On theo- retical grounds, there seems to be no plausible basis for the choice of any particular analytical function rather than some other; it is even perfectly conceivable that, due to historical events, different functions are appropriate during different periods and that no single function of any

1. Details on data and methods used in calculating product-moment correlations and in subdivision of time intervals can be found in the originally published version of this article.

kind is applicable to the whole sequence of years. In case of Negro lynchings, a straight-line trend is theoretically improbable. Some function (or sequence of functions) giving first a rising trend (due to population growth, increased completeness of reporting, and other factors), then a drop, and and asymptotic approach to zero is more plausible.

The use of linear trends for parts of the period is arbitrary also. But the fit of the lines thus obtained is reasonably close. Inspection of the curves suggests that deviations of the variables from trend lines obtained by the use of other analytical functions fitted to similar periods, or by the computation of moving averages, would not have been markedly different. Consequently, while the procedure used in this study cannot be viewed as perfect, it appears to be a reasonable approximation and more trustworthy than the one used by Hovland and Sears; its advantage lies in the fact that the lengths of the segments of the curves to which linear trends were fitted were chosen on the basis of inspection rather than arbitrarily. On the basis of the above considerations, it was thought that the high correlations reported by Hovland and Sears are essentially statistical artifacts.

Two additional correlations are quoted by Hovland and Sears and by other authors in support of the theory according to which economic frustration leads to criminal aggression. According to A. F. Raper (1933), the correlation between lynchings and the per-acre value of cotton in nine states was -.532 for the years 1900-1930. D. S. Thomas (1925) reported, on the basis of English data between 1857 and 1913, a correlation of -.44 between fluctuations of the rate of property crimes with violence and an index of economic activity.

The significance of Raper's correlation cannot be evaluated. The author fails to state whether the variables correlated are raw data or deviations from trend lines. If the latter were used, it is unclear how **the curved lines representing** trends on the diagram in Raper's book were computed.

As far as the correlation reported by Thomas is concerned, it cannot be criticized on methodological grounds. Thomas used a method rather similar to the one in this investigation, but more elaborate. On the other hand, it is difficult to justify the choice of this particular correlation from Thomas' book. The correlation of the economic index with fluctuations of violence against persons was +.06, with malicious injury to property +.04. These crimes seem to represent aggressive behavior more clearly than do property crimes with violence. The increase of the latter during periods of depression may be due to inexperience of people who are driven into property crimes by bad economic conditions rather than to an increase of aggressive tendencies due to frustration. The clearly aggressive crimes are uncorrelated with economic conditions according to Thomas, which substantially agrees with the findings presented in the paper.

SUMMARY

The data used by Hovland and Sears in their study of lynchings as related to economic indices were re-examined, with the following results:

The trends exhibited by the numbers of lynchings of Negroes and by the total value of cotton were not found to be linear.

The total number of lynchings also suggests a nonlinear trend; but, due to greater irregularity of the data, the fit of a straight line does not seem to be much poorer than that of a curve.

After the curve of the Negro lynchings was divided into two portions and the cotton-value curve into three portions, linear trends were fitted to each portion. The product-moment correlation between the deviations of the variables from their trend lines was $+.014$; for 1882-1913 it was $-.25$. The corresponding correlation (tetrachoric, utilizing deviations from linear trends for the whole period 1882-1930) reported by Hovland and Sears was $-.72$.

Deviations of total number of lynchings from this linear trend for the whole period were found to correlate with the composite economic index to the extent of $-.34$ when the product-moment formula was used, as compared to a tetrachoric correlation of $-.65$ reported by Hovland and Sears. Dividing the period into three portions and using deviations from trends separately computed for each portion gave slightly lower negative correlations, $-.28$ by the product-moment, $-.55$ by the tetrachoric formula. The use of a parabolic trend for one of the periods resulted in a correlation (product-moment) of $-.33$.

The correlations reported here agree substantially with the correlations pertaining to British crime rates reported by D. S. Thomas, who used somewhat similar but more elaborate statistical procedures. The method is not viewed as perfect, but the correlations are considered to be closer approximations to the truth than those reported by Hovland and Sears.

Stanley Lieberson and Arnold R. Silverman

The Precipitants and Underlying Conditions of Race Riots

The immediate precipitants and underlying conditions of race riots in the U. S. during the past half century are the subject of this paper. Using both "hard" and "soft" data, employing journalistic accounts as well as census data, we consider in a somewhat more systematic fashion the influence of diverse factors suggested as causes of riots in sociological case studies and texts on collective behavior (Blumer, 1951, pp. 165-222; Chicago Commission on Race Relations, 1922, pp. 1-78; Grimshaw, 1963a, pp. 76-86 and 1962b, pp. 3-19 and 1960, pp. 109-119; Lang and Lang, 1961; Lee and Humphrey, 1943; Rudwick, 1964; Smelser, 1963; Turner and Killian, 1957; Turner and Surace, 1956, pp. 14-20). Riots, as distinguished from lynchings and other forms of collective violence, involve an assault on persons and property simply because they are part of a given subgroup of the community. In contrast, lynchings and other types of violence are directed toward a particular individual as a collective response to some specific act. In practice, this distinction is sometimes difficult to apply, particularly in deciding when a localized racial incident has become a riot.[1] We have excluded some of the housing "riots" from our analysis because they were directed specifically at Negroes attempting to move into an area rather than at Negroes *per se* or some other more generalized target.

Using the *New York Times Index* for the period between 1913 and 1963, we found 72 different events that might be properly classified as Negro-white race riots. Descriptions of riots in various editions of the *Negro Yearbook* supplemented some of the *New York Times* reports and also provided reports of four additional riots. In several instances, magazines and local newspapers were used for further information. Finally, we employed the sociological descriptions available for some race riots. Reliance on journalistic accounts for our basic sample of riots means the study is vulnerable to any selectivity in the riots actually reported in the newspaper. Our analysis of the immediate precipitants of race riots is similarly limited by the brevity of some of the descriptive accounts as well as by possible distortions in reporting (see, for example, Raoul Navroll, *Data Quality Control—A New Research Technique.* New York: Free Press, 1962). For the underlying community conditions of riots, we relied largely on census data.

---

1. Lynchings, for example, are sometimes followed by riots. No doubt we would have included some of these events and excluded others had more detail been available.

IMMEDIATE PRECIPITANT

As one might expect, race riots are usually sparked by a provocation involving members of the two races. At most only four of the 76 riots occurred without a precipitating event, and even in these few cases, the apparent lack of precipitant may be due to the scantiness of the accounts rather than the absence of an immediate cause. In riots, life and property are treated with an indifference and recklessness contrary to basic values in western society (except in wartime), and it is therefore important to ask what kind of events precipitate such an acute breakdown of social control, and whether these precipitants are uncommon occurrences of an exceptionally provocative nature.

Although lynchings are not riots, data gathered on the immediate causes of the 3,700 lynchings in the U.S. between 1889 and 1930 are illuminating. Of the known accusations, more than a third (37.7 per cent) were murder; in nearly a quarter (23.4 per cent) the accusation was rape or attempted rape; assault was the charge in 5.8 per cent and theft in 7.1 per cent (Raper, 1933, p. 36). Compared with the frequency of these felonies in the South, murder and rape—violations of strong social taboos—are greatly over-represented as precipitants of lynchings.

In the same fashion, we suggest, the immediate precipitants of race riots almost always involve some confrontation between the groups in which members of one race are deeply "wronged" in fact or in rumor by members of the other. Precipitants tend to be transgressions of strongly held mores by a representative of the other group. The difficulty is to obtain an independent judgment of the severity of offenses that precipitate riots.

For two rather frequent types of precipitants, we can offer some independent evidence of their intensity. First, riots are often precipitated in the U.S. by crimes—particularly alleged crimes against persons rather than property alone, or the public order. Murder, rape, assault, manslaughter, and theft by means of violence or intimidation arouse the greatest concern and receive the most publicity in the mass media (Clinard, 1957, p. 196). In 1950, the median sentence received by men found guilty of offenses against persons was 9.9 years, whereas it was 3.9 years for those charged with other felonies.[2] Even excluding murder, sentences for other felonies against persons were more than twice as long as those for offenses solely against property or the public order. Since punishment reflects the public's values with respect to the intrinsic "evil" of various acts, it is in this sense an independent measure of the severity of acts that precipitate race riots.

2. Based on data reported in Federal Bureau of Prisons, *National Prisoner Statistics: Prisoners in State and Federal Institutions, 1950,* Leavenworth, Kansas: U.S. Penitentiary, 1954, Tables 37 and 38. Determinate and maximum indeterminate sentences are combined.

Another class of events that apparently violates strongly held norms involve Negroes crossing the various segregation barriers erected against them. Particularly frequent as precipitants in recent years, these acts are "bad" only because Negro-white interaction occurs in a form generally prohibited, e.g., when Negroes use the same swimming pool as whites.[3]

Table 1. Immediate Precipitants of Race Riots, 1913–1963

Rape, murder, attack, or hold-up of white women by Negro men	10
Killings, arrest, interference, assault, or search of Negro men by white policemen	15
Other inter-racial murder or shooting	11
Inter-racial fight, no mention of lethal weapons	16
Civil liberties, public facilities, segregation, political events, and housing	14
Negro strikebreakers, upgrading, or other job-based conflicts	5
Burning of an American flag by Negroes	1
No information available	4
Total Number	76

We have classified the 72 riots for which data are available in terms of the nature of the immediate precipitant of the violence. (See Table 1.) The reader should recognize that it is not always clear which event triggered a riot, especially when a chain of inter-related events occurs. Not only is it difficult to specify where the riot begins and the precipitant ends, but often there are several precipitants. In these cases we have determined whether at least some of the events involve offenses against relatively sacred values.

A sizable majority of the precipitants do involve an actual or rumored violation of one group by a member of the other. The ten cases in which white women were attacked by Negro men are highly inflammatory; apparently these involve violations of an extremely strong taboo. Highly charged acts to begin with, the murder, rape, or assault of women is even more serious an offense when offender and victim are of different races. Negroes were almost half of all persons executed for murder by civil authorities in the United States between 1930 and 1952 and nearly 90 percent of those executed for rape.[4] In their analysis of the 1943 Los Angeles zoot-suiter riot, Turner and Surace describe sexual assault as the dominant trigger:

The most prominent charge from each side was that the other had molested its girls. It was reported that sailors became enraged by the rumor that zoot-

3. Myrdal hypothesizes a rank order of discrimination in which whites object most strongly to close personal contact with Negroes (Myrdal, 1944, pp. 6061). Although a follow-up study suggested some modifications of this thesis, the areas of highest white resistance to Negroes remained unaltered (Killian and Grigg, 1961, p. 238).

4. Federal Bureau of Prisons, *op. cit.*, pp. 30-31.

suiters were guilty of assaults on female relatives of servicemen." Similarly, the claim against sailors was that they persisted in molesting and insulting Mexican girls. While many other charges were reported in the newspapers, including unsubstantiated suggestions of sabotage of the war effort, the sex charges dominated the precipitating context (Turner and Surace, 1956, pp. 16-17).

The second type of precipitant, offenses committed by white law enforcement officials against Negroes, involves white transgression of norms no less sacred than those involved in the rape of white women by Negro men. The Harlem riot during World War II started when a Negro woman was arrested by a white policeman for disorderly conduct. A Negro soldier, on leave, tried to stop him and the ensuing fight ended with both men in the hospital, the policeman with a battered head and the soldier with a pistol wound in the shoulder. Of greatest interest here is the account of the incident that spread through the Negro community: a Negro soldier was said to have been shot in the back and killed by a white policeman in the presence of the Negro's mother (*Time,* August 9, 1943, p. 19; *New Republic,* August 16, 1943, pp. 220-222).

The Harlem riot of July, 1964, was precipitated by a demonstration protesting the slaying of a 15-year-old Negro boy by a white policeman, an act viewed as a wanton exercise of police brutality. The Bedford-Stuyvesant, Rochester, Jersey City, and Philadelphia riots of 1964—also outside the period covered in our study—were also precipitated by arrests or the presence of police (*New York Times,* September 27, 1964, p. 81).

Both the fatal shooting of the boy and the rumored treacherous shooting of a soldier during wartime, in front of his mother, are highly inflammatory acts because they arouse some of the strongest sentiments the population holds, and they are especially inflammatory because they were commmitted by members of one race against another. In addition, offenses committed by white law enforcement officials, highly inflammatory in themselves, are aggravated when they involve actual or alleged wrong-doing on the part of officials expected to uphold and administer the law in an impartial manner. A number of recent race riots over civil-rights issues have been precipitated by police behavior, particularly in breaking up demonstrations.[5] We shall have more to say about the role of the police in our discussion of the underlying conditions of race riots.

The next category of precipitants, "Other inter-racial murder or shooting," calls for little additional comment. The shooting of white policemen by Negro men (three cases), although intrinsically not as inflammatory as inter-racial offenses against women and children, nevertheless involves murder or attempted murder of a representative of the government. The rumored beating to death of a Negro boy in a

5. This is particularly evident in the South.

New York department store after he was seized for shoplifting, and the rumors of brutal assaults on women and children that circulated among both races during the Detroit race riot of World War II, are clearly in accord with our thesis that the precipitants tend to be violations of important mores. In two cases rumors of impending violence precipitated actual riots. In one instance there was a rumor of a forthcoming riot and in the other, anticipation of a lynching. In both instances, the rumors involved inter-racial violation of rights widely accepted as fundamental. Finally, two of the other four inter-racial murders or shootings were accompanied by Negro offenses against white women: as we noted earlier, more than one element may be involved in the precipitation of a race riot. In one of these incidents, a white man was murdered by three Negroes and a rumor arose that he had been trying to protect a white woman from these men. (New York Times, September 21, 1920, p. 1; Chicago Daily Tribune, September 21, 1920, pp. 1-2). In the other, a Negro had made derogatory statements about a white woman over whom a Negro had been lynched some weeks before (Work, 1921, p. 75).

Most of the 16 race riots precipitated by inter-racial fights without the use of lethal weapons do not appear to involve offenses of the most intense nature. One difficulty here is that the accounts of these riots are so scanty that we do not know whether rumors existed, over what issue the fights started, or other features that may have made the incident especially inflammatory, e.g., a young adult attacking an elderly person or a cripple. A fairly common element in riots with this type of precipitant is a chain of events in which members of each racial group come to the assistance of others already engaged in the fight. This tends to excite the onlookers who arrive after the initial provocation, particularly if members of one race appear to be receiving the worse part of the battle.

"Civil liberties, public facilities, segregation, political events, and housing" is a residual category involving diverse precipitants. Some of the precipitants fit the thesis that sacred values were violated. For example, a riot in upstate New York in the mid-thirties was precipitated by whites attempting to break up a meeting called to rally support for a Negro accused of attacking a white girl (New York Times, August 28, 1934, p. 3). From the white point of view this involves the not uncommon theme of sexual molesting; from the other side, it is a white attempt to prevent Negroes' efforts to insure fair treatment for a Negro accused of a provocative act. A riot in Athens, Ala. in 1946 involved whites protesting police favoritism after a brawl for which two whites had been arrested and a Negro escaped (Lawrence, 1947, pp. 253-254). But for the most part, it is difficult to establish conclusively the extent to which the precipitants in this caegory were offenses against inter-racial mores. In some cases we are tempted to say that they were— the two just mentioned, or the Negro boy attempting to dance with a white girl at a city-sponsored dance—but in others, we are less certain about the nature of the acts.

Of the five job-based riots, three involved the allegation that Negroes were or had been strike breakers, one was over the up-grading of jobs held by Negroes, and one was simply in an industrial setting. Taking a conservative stance, we would not be inclined to label these as violations of sacred norms.

Burning an American flag is a different type of offense, for it violates neither the person nor any segregation taboo, but it is clearly an offense against one of the nation's most sacred symbols. We shall say more about this type of precipitant, which is unusual for riots in the U.S., when we discuss racial and ethnic riots elsewhere in the world.

In brief, at least a sizable proportion of the immediate precipitants of race riots appear to involve inter-racial violations of intense societal norms. Noteworthy are the large number of events in which bodily injury is the precipitant as well as the smaller number of cases precipitated by violations of inter-racial segregation taboos.

UNDERLYING CONDITIONS

Applying Durkheim's typology, we observe that many of the immediate precipitants were acts that call for repressive sanctions, that is, they "consisted essentially in an act contrary to strong and defined states of the common conscience" (Durkheim: 1933, p. 105). Repressive sanctions are normally administered under penal law by courts in the U.S. For example, murder, rape, and other acts of physical violence are strongly disapproved and severely punished in our society. Many, though not all, of the violations of segregation taboos in the period studied were also punishable through law enforcement, but in these instances, at least some members of either or both racial populations were unable to accept the institutions normally used for handling such offenses. Instead a riot occurred, involving, by definition, a generalized response directed at a collectivity rather than the offender—indeed, the actual offender was often untouched.

Although the immediate precipitants were highly inflammatory, we may still ask why a riot occurred rather than the normal processes of arrest, trial, and punishment, for inter-racial friction occurs far more often than the small number of occasions that erupted into race riots indicates. Why did violence break out where it did rather than at other places where similar incidents occurred? Or to put it another way, the types of violation described earlier probably occur almost daily, yet in most instances they do not lead to collective violence. Are there special circumstances that increase or decrease the chances of a riot ensuing?

One possible interpretation of the location and timing of riots is simply that riots are randomly distributed. Any precipitating incident of this type increases the chances of a riot, but there is no systematic reason why riots occur when and where they do, other than possible differences among cities in the frequency of precipitating incidents. A second approach is based on the notion that certain social conditions in the community increase the probability that a precipitating incident will lead to a riot. From this persepctive, we can ask whether cities experiencing riots differ from other cities with regard to the institutional conditions suggested as increasing the chances of a riot.

Poisson distribution. To evaluate the first interpretation, that is, whether riots are randomly distributed in time and place, we used the Poisson distribution, which the low frequency of race riots (1.5 per year between 1913 and 1963) makes appropriate for comparing the actual frequency of riots with what would be expected in a random distribution.[6] Columns 2 and 3 of Table 2 show, respectively, the actual and expected number of riots per year in the 51 years from 1913 through 1963. Inspection indicates that the Poisson distribution yields a poor fit. For example, in 26 of the years no riot was reported though the theoretical distribution would lead us to expect only 11 such years. Applying the appropriate chi-square test for goodness of fit, we conclude that we cannot accept the assumption that the probability of riots is equal each year.[7]

Table 2. Race Riots : Actual and Expected Frequencies

	BY YEAR			BY CITY	
Riots per Year (1)	*Observed Frequency* (2)	*Poisson Frequency* (3)	*Riots per Year* (4)	*Observed Frequency* (5)	*Poisson Frequency* (6)
0	26	11.4	0	300	281.2
1	10	17.1	1	25	47.2
2	7	12.8	2	3	4.3
3	2	6.4	3	3	0.3
4	1	2.4	4	1	0.0
5	0	0.7	5–14	1	0.0
6	0	0.2			
7	2	0.0			
8	1	0.0			
9	1	0.0			
10	0	0.0			
11	1	0.0			
Total Years	51	51.0	Total Cities	333	333.0

In similar fashion, we can consider the concentration of riots in cities. Restricting ourselves to the 333 cities with 50,000 or more population

6. For discussions of the application of the Poisson distribution, see G. Udny Yule and M. G. Kendall, *An Introduction to the Theory of Statistics,* London: Charles Griffin, 1950, pp. 189-194; M. J. Moroney, *Facts From Figures,* Harmondsworth, Middlesex: Penguin Books, 1951, Ch. 8.

7. Our computation of chi-square is based on the adjustments suggested in Helen M. Walker and Joseph Lev, *Statistical Inference,* New York: Henry Holt, 1953, pp. 105-107.

in 1960, we have compared the actual and expected frequencies of cities experiencing a specified number of riots. There are more cities without any riots, and more with several, than would be expected on the basis of the Poisson distribution (columns 5 and 6): riots occurred in only 33 of these cities. The goodness-of-fit test confirms our impression that the theoretical distribution does not fit the actual distribution of riots in cities.

Two types of sampling bias may have influenced these results. First, newspapers probably fluctuate in their propensity to report riots, so that the frequency of riots at a given point in time increases the probability that riots occurring shortly afterwards will be reported. This is analogous to the tendency of newspapers to make the frequency of rapes or other events into a crime wave when in fact the major variable is the frequency of reporting such events (Medalia and Larsen, 1958, pp. 180-186). A second possible bias arises from the fact that our primary source is the *New York Times*. Milder forms of racial violence in metropolitan New York and the mid-Atlantic area are more likely to be covered than riots of equivalent severity elsewhere. This would lead to a distribution of repeated riots different from that expected on the basis of the Poisson formula. Also, note that our test refers only to riots, not to precipitating incidents *per se*. Therefore we can reach no conclusions with respect to the distribution of precipitants by time or place. These difficulties notwithstanding, the results give us no reason to think riots are random with respect to time and place.

A COMPARATIVE ANALYSIS

Since the type of event that precipitates riots is far more common than actual riots, we ask whether this form of collective violence is due to underlying conditions that keep at least one segment of the population from accepting the normal institutional response to a provocative incident. From this perspective, precipitants are a necessary but not sufficient cause of riots.

A rather wide-ranging array of interpretations have been advanced after the occurrence of riots in particular communities. Such factors as rapidly expanding Negro population, economic hardships, police brutality, job ceilings, Negro competition with whites, slums, unsympathetic city officials, contagion, communist elements, agitators, warm weather, unruly elements, and others have figured in popular and semi-popular interpretations of race riots. Although case studies of race riots are extremely valuable where they provide an accurate description of events before and during a riot, obviously it is impossible to determine which factors are critical on the basis of one city's experience.

When we move from the presentation of *plausible* reasons to a systematic empirical test of the actual importance of various attributes in increasing the chances of riots, we encounter serious difficulties. Not only do we have a plethora of independent variables, but their actual significance is very difficult to test. Quantitative data on many of these characteristics are scarce, and in any case it is difficult to know how much causal significance to attribute anyway. For example, a riot may occur in a city containing a Negro slum area. The cruel truth is that housing conditions for Negroes are inferior in virtually every city in the U.S. To infer a causal link, one must determine not whether Negro slums exist in the riot city, but whether that city is worse in this respect than others where no riots occurred. Similarly, in any large city unemployed whites and Negroes might respond to an opportunity for a racial riot. Again the question is whether an unusually large number of such people live in one community compared with another.

Our requirements for quantitative data covering at least part of a 50-year span limit the causal hypotheses we can test. For the most part we have relied on U.S. censuses of the past six decades for data bearing on some of the propositions encountered in case studies and popular interpretations of race riots. This part of our study, therefore, necessarily has a certain *ad hoc* quality.

Method. To examine the influence of variables others have suggested as underlying causes of race riots, we used a paired comparison analysis. Each city experiencing a riot was compared with a city as similar as possible in size and region which had no riot in the ten years preceding or following the riot date.[8] Preference was given to the city in the same state closest in population size, with the provision that it have at least half but no more than twice the population of the riot city. Where no such city existed we selected the city closest in size in the same subregion or region.[9] We compared the very largest cities, such as New York, Chicago, and Los Angeles, with other leading centers in the nation closest in population, regardless of region.

Using the nonparametric sign test, we evaluated the extent to which riot cities differ from their control cities in the direction hypothesized. When a given city experienced more than one riot, it was included as many times as the number of riots. Because census data by size of place and decade were not always available, our "N" in most cases is considerably less than the 76 riots discussed earlier. For convenience in presentation, we have divided the hypotheses into four major categories: population growth and composition; work situation; housing; and government.

8. For the most recent riots we could not apply the ten-year limit into the future in selecting control cities, but such cities were included in our analysis.

9. See U.S. Department of Commerce, *U.S. Bureau of the Census, 1960. Selected Area Reports, Standard Metropolitan Statistical Areas,* Washington, D.C., U.S. Government Printing Office, 1963, pp. xvi-xvii.

DEMOGRAPHIC FACTORS

The rapid influx of Negroes and sometimes whites into cities is certainly one of the most frequently cited reasons for the occurrence of race riots. Although large-scale migration is not usually viewed as a sufficient cause for a riot, it is commonly considered important because rapid influx disrupts the on-going social order and creates various problems in the Negro community. For 66 riots we could determine the growth of the Negro and white populations between the census years preceding and following the race riot, for each riot city and for a comparable community selected at the beginning of the decade. We thus have data for 66 pairs of cities, each pair consisting of a riot city and a control city.

In about half the cases, percentage increases in both total and white population were smaller in the riot cities than in the non-riot cities. Moreover, in 56 per cent of the comparisons the control cities experienced greater percentage increases in Negro population than the riot cities did. Our results clearly fail to support the contention that rapid population change accompanies riots. For the years between 1917 and 1921—a period marked by both Negro migration and numerous riots— we found no sizable difference between riot and control cities in their percentage gains in Negro population during the decades. Also contrary to expectation are the differences in racial composition of riot and control cities. Again for 66 pairs, we find that in exactly half the comparisons, the proportion of Negroes is smaller in the riot city than in its control city.

Since this comparative approach is used with succeeding hypotheses, we should consider briefly the implications of these findings. First, we draw no conclusions about whether Negro population growth in riot cities differs from its growth elsewhere in the U.S. Riot cities have experienced more rapid growth than the remainder of the nation simply because Negro population movement has been largely from rural to urban areas. Similarly, since our method is designed to compare riot cities only with other cities similar in size and region, we make no inferences about differences between riot cities and all other U.S. cities. What we do conclude is that riot cities do not differ from non-riot cities of the same size and region in their rates of population increase, and therefore that increases in population fail to explain the occurrence of outbreaks in one city rather than another.[10]

10. In a study based on a nationwide sample of cities, Williams (1964, pp. 135-137) found the general level of race conflict and tension no higher in cities with rapid population growth and high mobility than in those with relatively stable populations. In short, our method gets at the question of why riots occur in the particular cities they do, rather than in comparable urban centers.

WORK SITUATION

TRADITIONAL OCCUPATIONS

The occupational world of Negroes is far more restricted than that of whites. In particular, certain occupational pursuits have been more or less "traditional" for urban Negroes. These are generally lower in both status and income. Accordingly, wherever possible we determined the proportion of Negro men in the labor force who are employed either as laborers or in domestic and service occupations. Needless to say, we were forced to use some rather crude measures as well as broad categories which undoubtedly include some occupations outside the "traditional" rubric. A serious difficulty is created by contradictory hypotheses that depend on which group appears to be the aggressor. On the one hand, we might expect greater antagonism on the part of Negroes in cities where they are relatively restricted in occupational opportunities, i.e., where most Negroes are in traditional pursuits. On the other hand, we might well expect that where Negroes fare relatively well in their efforts to break through the job restrictions, whites' hostility might be greater and hence riots more likely to ensue.

For 43 riots we were able to determine the Negro occupational distribution in both the riot and control city during the closest census period. In 65 per cent of these paired comparisons (N=28), the percentage of Negro men holding traditional occupations is lower in the riot city (using a two-tailed test, p=.0672). This suggests that riots are due to the relative threat to whites where Negroes are less concentrated in their traditional pursuits. If such were the case, then we might expect the white and Negro percentages in these occupations to be more alike in the riot city than in the control city. This is precisely what we find: in 30 of the 43 paired comparisons, the *difference* between whites and Negroes, in proportions engaged in laboring, domestic, and service occupations, is smaller in the riot city (p=.0073, single-tailed test). The encroachment of Negroes in the white occupational world evidently tends to increase the chances of a riot, although we must also consider the possibility that Negro militancy increases as Negroes move out of their traditional niche.

STORE OWNERS

A more specific occupational factor sometimes associated with riots—particularly ghetto riots—is the low frequency of store ownership in Negro areas and the consequent resentment of white store owners in these areas. We are unable to get at these data directly. If we assume, however, that virtually all Negro store owners are located in the ghetto, then we can simply examine the percentage of employed Negro men who are self-employed in various facets of retail trade, such as store, restaurant, or tavern owners. Although differences between riot and control cities tend to be slight, nevertheless in 24 of 39 riots, the percentage of Negroes who are store owners is larger in the non-riot city. (These differences are significant at the .10 level.) Results might be even stronger had it been possible to subcategorize riots. For instance, the absence of Negro store owners would presumably contribute to Negroes' rioting but would contribute relatively little to white assaults.

UNEMPLOYMENT

As was the case for traditional occupations, unemployment presents contradictory possibilities, so that we might well expect riots when either Negroes or whites have relatively high unemployment rates. Our analysis is even cruder here, since unemployment is far more volatile from year to year, and we are able to use data only for the closest census year.[11] First, the white unemployment rate appears to have no influence on the likelihood of a riot. In 12 comparisons white unemployment rates were higher in the city experiencing the riot, and in 13 cases, higher in the control city. For Negro unemployment, results tend to run counter to what we might expect. Negro unemployment is higher in the control than in the riot city in 15 out of 25 comparisons. And Negro-white *differences* are lower in the riot than in the control city in 15 out of 25 comparisons (p=.212, single-tailed test).

These results do not confirm our expectations: high white unemployment apparently does not increase the chances of a riot, nor is high Negro unemployment associated with riots in the direction expected. On an aggregate basis, the number of riots during the Great Depression of the thirties was not unusually large. In view of the weakness of the data—particiularly the fact that we do not have unemployment rates for the specific year in which the riots take place—all we can conclude is that we have failed to confirm the hypothesis, not that we have disproved it.

INCOME

Since the influence of income on riots may reflect either group's position, our problem is similar to that discussed in connection with Negro occupational composition. Median income data are available for only 12 riots and their controls. In six comparisons Negro income is higher

11. Although data are available for other years, to our knowledge none can be obtained by race for specific cities.

in the control city and in the other six it is higher in the riot city. In 11 of the 12 cases, however, white income in the riot city is lower than in the control (p<.01, single-tailed test). The *difference* between Negro and white income was larger in the city without a riot in ten of the 12 cases (p=.038, two-tailed test). The small number precludes analysis of these findings in greater detail, but we can observe that riots tend to occur in cities where white income is lower than that of whites in comparable areas. The lower white income also means that Negro-white differences tend to be smaller in these cities than in the control areas. Thus, the results, though extremely limited in time and place, do not support the notion that race riots are a consequence either of low Negro income or of relatively large Negro-white discrepancies in income.

HOUSING

Ghetto riots in particular are often attributed to the poor housing conditions of Negroes, but our data fail to disclose any tendency whatsoever for housing to be of lower quality in cities that have experienced riots. For 20 paired comparisons we could determine which city had a larger percentage of Negro families in sub-standard housing (using the census categories of "dilapidated" in 1950 and 1960 and "needing major repairs" in 1940). In ten cases the non-riot city had poorer Negro housing than the riot city. Although obviously not all riots could be considered ghetto riots, surely we should find some tendency for Negroes in cities experiencing riots to have poorer dwellings than they do in cities without riots, if it were true that poorer housing quality increases the likelihood of a race riot. Very likely, Negro housing is poor in so many locales that it cannot distinguish cities experiencing riots from those that do not.

GOVERNMENT

POLICE

Local government is one of the most important institutions to consider in an analysis of race riots. Municipal policies, particularly with respect to police, can greatly influence the chances of a race riot. Earlier, we observed that many of the precipitating incidents involve white police behavior toward Negroes, and adequate police training and tactics often prevent incipient riots from developing (Lohman, 1947, pp. 80-93; Smelser, 1963, pp. 261-268). Moreover, police activities reflect the policies, sympathies, and attitudes of the local municipal government.

One often-cited factor in race riots is the lack of Negro policemen. First, one major complaint on the part of Negroes is that of white police brutality. So far as the police are Negroes, actual brutality will probably not arouse strong racial feelings. Second, police in some riots have encouraged or tolerated white violence toward Negroes, so that we might expect stronger police control where the force is mixed, as well as greater confidence in police protection among Negroes. Finally, since the number of Negro policemen is for the most part controlled by the city administration, the representation of Negroes is an indicator of city policies toward race relations in general.

Data are hard to obtain and for 1950 and 1960 we have been obliged to use census reports for entire metropolitan areas. Also for some decades policemen are not reported separately from closely related occupations such as sheriffs and marshalls. Nevertheless, of 38 pairs of cities, in 24 the city without the riot had more Negro policemen per thousand Negroes than did the matched city that experienced a riot ($p = .07$, single-tailed test). Although differences between riot and control cities are rather slight, these results do suggest that police force composition influences the likelihood of a riot.

CITY COUNCIL

We hypothesize that the manner in which councilmen are elected and the relative size of the city council will influence the occurrence of riots. Our reasoning is based on several assumptions. The election of councilmen at large gives numerically smaller groups a greater handicap in expressing their interests than they encounter in communities where councilmen are elected directly from spatial districts (Wilson, 1960, pp. 25-33). In cities where the average size of a councilman's constituency is small, we assume that representatives are more responsive to the wishes of the population and therefore that members of the community have a more adequate mechanism for transmitting their interests and concerns. This implies that more diverse interests will be expressed in the city's governing body.

Our hypothesis is that the more direct the relation between voter and government, the less likely are riots to occur. A more responsive government makes riots less likely because it provides regular institutional channels for expressing grievances. Small districts provide more responsive government than large districts, and large districts, more than elections at large. In comparisons between a city with a city-wide election system and one where councilmen are elected both at large and by district, we classified the latter situation as the less likely to lead to riots. Where both cities have the same form of election, we computed the mean population per councilman. (Comparisons involving Deep South cities were based on the white population only.) Thus, we gave form of election priority over size of constituency in our causal hypothesis.

In 14 of 22 pairs, population per councilman was larger in the city experiencing the riot than in the control city, or elections at large were used in the riot city and direct election of representatives in the control city. (Though p is not significant [.143], the relationship is in the predicted direction.) Considering our inability to take into account the degree of gerrymandering in cities with direct representation, these results offer an encouraging degree of support for our hypothesis.

DISCUSSION

Our analysis of the precipitating and underlying conditions of race riots suggests several generalizations about their evolution. First, precipitating incidents often involve highly charged offenses committed by members of one group against the other, such as attacks on women, police brutality and interference, murder, and assault. In recent years, violation of segregation taboos by Negroes as well as white resistance have been increasingly frequent precipitants. Riots are generalized responses in which there is categorical assault on persons and property by virtue of their racial membership. Such violence is not restricted and may even exclude the specific antagonists responsible for the precipitating event.

The diffuse response generated by the precipitating event, as well as the fact that often the alleged offenses are of the sort normally dealt with by appropriate communal institutions, suggests that additional factors channel the inflammatory act into a riot. Since there are usually a number of factors that could have contributed to a riot in any given community, we used a comparative approach to determine why riots occur in some cities and not in others of comparable size and location.

Going beyond our data and trying to place our findings in a broad framework, we suggest that riots are more likely to occur when social institutions function inadequately, or when grievances are not resolved, or cannot be resolved under the existing institutional arrangements. Populations are predisposed or prone to riot; they are not simply neutral aggregates transformed into a violent mob by the agitation or charisma of individuals. Indeed, the immediate precipitant simply ignites prior community tensions revolving about basic institutional difficulties. The failure of functionaries to perform the roles expected by one or both of the racial groups, cross-pressures, or the absence of an institution capable of handling a community problem involving inter-racial relations will create the conditions under which riots are most likely. Many riots are precipitated by offenses that arouse considerable interest and concern. When members of the victimized race are dubious about the intention or capacity of relevant functionaries to achieve justice or a "fair" solution, then the normal social controls are greatly weakened by the lack of faith in the community's institutions.

Our evidence supports the proposition that the functioning of local community government is important in determining whether a riot will follow a precipitating incident. Prompt police action can prevent riots from developing; their inaction or actual encouragement can increase the chances of a race riot. Riot cities not only employ fewer Negro policemen, but they are also communities whose electoral systems tend to be less sensitive to the demands of the electorate. Local government illustrates the possibility that riots occur when a community institution is malfunctioning, from the perspective of one or both racial segments.

Our finding that Negroes are less likely to be store owners in riot cities illustrates the problem arising when no social institution exists for handling the difficulties faced by a racial group. Small merchants require credit, skill and sophistication in operating and locating their stores, ability to obtain leases, and so on. To our knowledge no widely operating social institution is designed to achieve these goals for the disadvantaged Negro. Similarly, our finding that riots are more likely where Negroes are closer to whites in their proportions in "traditional" Negro occupations, and where Negro-white income differences are smaller, suggests that a conflict of interests between the races is inherent in the economic world.

Our use of significance tests requires further comment. Many of the relationships are in the direction predicted but fail to meet the normal standards for significance. Several extenuating circumstances help account for this. First, many of our hypotheses refer to specific types of riots: for example, some riots are clearly "white riots;" others, equally clearly, are Negro; and many are both, in the sense that extensive attacks are directed at both groups. Were the data in an ideal form, we could separate the ghetto riots, the white assaults, and the interracial warfare into separate categories, and then apply our hypotheses to specific subsets of riots. Because our sample is small and the accounts of many riots are very scanty, we are prepared to accept these weaker associations as at least consistent with our approach to the underlying conditions of race riots.

Several implications of our results are relevant to riots elsewhere. Racial and ethnic incidents in other parts of the world are also frequently precipitated by physical violence. Dahlke's description of the Kishinew pogrom in Russia ascribes considerable importance as a precipitant to the widespread legend that Jews anually kill Christian children, as a part of their religious rites (Dahlke, 1952, p. 421). The extensive riots in Ceylon in 1958 included a number of highly provocative rumors of inter-ethnic violations. For example, "a Sinhalese baby had been snatched from its mother's arms and immersed in a barrel of boiling tar" (Vittachi, 1958, p. 48). The Durban riots of 1949 were precipitated by an incident in which an African youth was knocked over by an Indian trader (Richmond, 1961, p. 123).

A number of other riots, however, are precipitated by violations of symbols rather than persons or taboos. The burning of an American flag by Negroes triggered a race riot in the United States. Our impression is that this type of precipitant is more common in some other parts of the world. Riots in Kashmir, West Bengal, and East Pakistan in late 1963 and early 1964, for example, were precipitated by the theft of a hair of the prophet Mohammed from a Mosque in Kashmir (*New York Times*, January 16, 1964, p. 17; January 19, p. 6; January 20, p. 6; January 24, p. 2; January 26, p. 15). One of the precipitants of the Chinese-Thai riots of 1945, the Yaorawat Incident, was the Chinese tendency to fly Chinese flags without also flying the Thai flag of the nation (Skinner, 1957, p. 279). Jews tore down the czar's crown from the town hall and damaged portraits of various rulers prior to Kiev's pogrom in 1905 (Shulgin, 1949).

Our results also suggest that race riots are frequently misunderstood. We have encountered a number of accounts in the popular literature attributing riots to communist influence, hoodlums, or rabble-rousers. Although lower-class youths and young adults are undoubtedly active during riots, potential participants of this type are probably available in almost any community. What interests us is the community failure to see the riot in terms of institutional malfunctioning or a racial difficulty which is not met—and perhaps cannot be—by existing social institutions. Many riots in other parts of the world revolve about national political institutions such that a disadvantaged segment is unable to obtain recognition of its interests and concerns through normal political channels. While this type of riot is not common in the U.S., the same basic conditions exist when either whites or Negroes are unable to use existing institutions to satisfy their needs and interests.

EDITOR'S NOTE—Three years after Lieberson and Silverman published the article produced immediately above, Milton Bloombaum (1968) published an article entitled, "The Conditions Underlying Race Riots as Portrayed by Multidimensional Scalogram Analysis: A Reanalysis of Lieberson and Silverman's Data." Multidimensional scalogram analysis is a nonmetric data analysis technique which permits comparison of matched sets; in this instance Bloombaum compared twenty-four cities in which Negro-white race riots occurred with twenty-four cities which did not experience racial violence. The riot and control cities were effectively partitioned with only small error although no one of the underlying conditions was strongly related to the occurrence or non-occurrence of riots. The conditions (demographic characteristics of the selected cities) also reflect temporal and regional differences; the analysis distinguished between Northern and Southern and pre- and post-World War II cities. Bloombaum's analysis tends to confirm Lieberson and Silverman through the use of a different technique rather than uncovering new relationships.

Neither Lieberson and Silverman nor Bloombaum claim that they have identified techniques through which prediction of violence can be essayed with a high probability of success. The techniques of analysis utilized in the two studies are probably considerably more powerful than the quality of the data available would seem to warrant. At the very least, great caution is necessary in accepting their findings and interpretations. These authors have made, however, a major contribution by pioneering attempts to move from anecdotal treatment to systematic and controlled analysis of clearly defined variables—A.D.G.

Ted Gurr

Urban Disorder: Perspectives from the Comparative Study of Civil Strife

I assume that the sources and dynamics of urban disorder in the United States are fundamentally comparable to those of civil violence throughout the world. American Negro rioters and their white antagonists seem to share one basic psychological dynamic with striking French farmers, Guatemalan guerrillas, and rioting Indonesian students: most of them feel frustrated in the pursuit of their goals, they are angered as a consequence, and because of their immediate social circumstances they feel free enough, or desperate enough, to act on that anger.

It is not a sufficient explanation to say that Negroes riot because all angry men have a propensity to violence, but it is a useful assumption on which to base explanation. There is considerable theoretical speculation about the psychological sources of aggression, some of which has been applied to civil disorder. The first section of this article summarizes briefly some concepts and propositions about psychological factors that dispose men to violence and suggests their implications for research on urban disorder. We also know from cross-national studies of civil strife that there are regularities in its occurrence and intensity, that certain kinds and patterns of social conditions seem regularly to lead to strife and that others tend to minimize it. In the second section of the article I report on a cross-national study that was designed to determine the effects of some social conditions on the outcome of discontent, and suggest some of the study's implications for the most recent phase of the American dilemma.

SOME PSYCHOLOGICAL SOURCES OF TURMOIL

The sociological and popular cliché is that "frustration" or "discontent" or "despair" is the root cause of rebellion. Cliché or not, the basic relationship appears to be as fundamental to understanding civil strife as the law of gravity is to atmospheric physics: relative deprivation, the phrase I have used, is a necessary precondition for civil strife of any kind, and the more severe is relative deprivation, the more likely and severe is strife.[1] Relative deprivation is not whatever the outside ob-

1. For a more detailed and systematic discussion of the psychological sources of civil strife, see Gurr, 1968a). The propositions in this article provide the theoretical basis for the cross-national research discussed in this paper, as well as for the proposed interpretations of the sources and consequences of discontent among American Negroes.

server thinks people ought to be dissatisfied with, however; it is a state of mind that can be defined as a discrepancy between people's expectations about the goods and conditions of life to which they are justifiably entitled, on the one hand, and on the other their value capabilities—what they perceive to be their chances for getting and keeping those goods and conditions. This is not a complicated way of making the simplistic and probably inaccurate statement that people are deprived and therefore angry if they have less than what they want. At least two characteristics of value perceptions are more consequential: what people think they *deserve,* not just what they want in an ideal sense, and what they think they have a chance of getting, not just what they have. They can have relatively little, but are likely to be relatively satisfied so long as they feel they are making satisfactory progress toward their goals. They feel deprived, and become angry, when they encounter or anticipate increased resistance. Since men live mentally in the immediate future as much as the present, *anticipated* frustration may be as important a cause of deprivation as actual frustration.

Underlying this relative deprivation approach to civil strife is a frustration-aggression mechanism, apparently a fundamental part of our psychobiological makeup. When we feel thwarted in an attempt to get something we want, we are likely to get angry, and when we get angry the most satisfying inherent response is to strike out at the source of frustration. Relative deprivation is, in effect, a perception of thwarting circumstances. *How* angry men become in response to the perception of deprivation seems determined partly by the nature of the expectations affected and partly by the kind and seriousness of interference with capabilities. The following propositions suggest some variables that affect the intensity of emotional response to the perception of deprivation.

The first proposition is that the greater the extent of discrepancy that men see between what they seek and what seems to be attainable, the greater their anger and consequent disposition to aggression. This variable is highly susceptible to change, for any increase in men's expectation levels, or any decrease in perceived capabilities, can increase this discrepancy. It is also one of the keys to the supposed paradox that dissatisfied people often (but by no means always) revolt just when things begin to get better: a little improvement accompanied by promises that much improvement is to come raises expectations, and if much improvement does *not* come when expected, perceptions of capabilities may drop, sometimes abruptly and sharply.

The proposition suggests a basic question for research on urban disorder in the United States: What has happened to levels of Negro expectations and to their perceptions of capabilities? The expectations of many Negroes have clearly increased, but how much, and why? Capabilities also seem to have increased for the majority, as suggested by the Brink and Harris survey finding that two-thirds of American Negroes felt that they were better off in 1966 than in 1963. But it may be that perceived capabilities are increasing less rapidly than expectation levels, so that the discrepancy, and consequently Negro anger, is still growing. Moreover, five per cent of Negroes feel that they are worse off now than they were. Who are they, and are they the potential extremists? (Brink and Harris, 1967, p. 258)

A second proposition relates to "opportunities": men who feel they have many ways to attain their goals are less likely to become angry when one is blocked than those who have few alternatives. The educated man has more skills, hence usually has more opportunities, than the uneducated. The city-dweller usually has more economic opportunities than the peasant, and thus the discontented peasant throughout the world often responds to the lack of rural opportunity by migrating to the city. For the unemployed Negro, the creation of job-training programs is presumably an expansion of opportunities. But this way there also may be dragons, since those who invest their energies in what appear to be opportunities but fail to make progress toward their goals tend to become more bitterly angry than those who do nothing. It is not entirely coincidental that Fidel Castro rebelled after his brief conventional political career was ended by the cancellation of elections, or that the young man now called Ho Chi Minh trained for service in a bureaucracy whose upper ranks were largely closed to Vietnamese, or that Job Corps drop-outs are found among riot leaders. Theory, along with popular liberal belief, suggests that expanding opportunities for goal attainment can be a crucial means of minimizing discontent. The qualification suggested here is that if what was promoted as opportunity proves just another dead end, the effects can be explosive. What the psychological effects of public and private efforts to expand opportunities for various groups of American Negroes have been I at least cannot say, but social researchers certainly have survey techniques that can provide some answers.

A third general proposition is that the greater the *intensity* of men's expectations, the greater their anger when they meet unexpected or increased resistance. By "intensity" is meant how badly they want whatever it is that they are seeking. The questions this poses for an analysis of Negro discontent are: Which groups of American Negroes have become more strongly motivated toward their economic and social goals in the past decade or so, and how much more strongly? One would predict that expectations are most intensely held among the young, among Northern Negroes, and among Negro leaders, the groups that have the greatest personal investment in alleviating or escaping from discrimination. These are in fact the groups that are most dissatisfied with the pace of improvement in Negro rights (*Ibid.*).

Another perceptual variable serves to control the effects of deprivation. The proposition is that if men think that deprivation is legitimate, i.e., justified by circumstances or by the need to attain some greater end, the intensity and perhaps the level of expectations decline and consequently deprivation tends to be accepted with less anger. This proposition seems applicable, for example, to the great personal sacrifices men sometimes will make in the service of revolutionary movements. It probably also helps explain why most Negroes, like most white Americans, accept tax increases and the risks of military service without open rebellion.

These comments are not designed to provide an explanation of urban disorder in the United States but to demonstrate that to assess any particular act of political violence, or the potential for it, social scientists should begin by getting answers to some specific questions about the extent, intensity, and character of discontent. We need to know which groups feel most deprived, for these are the people who are most likely to become alienated to the point of violence. We need to assess the intensity of their anger, because this is a major determinant of the intensity of their action. Most important for policy purposes we need to know—not just to assume that we know—the *content* of their deprivation, for effective solutions can be devised only on the basis of accurate diagnosis.

The four propositions outlined above specify one set of psychological variables that can be examined. There is empirical evidence for these propositions and a good deal of suggestive evidence, from studies of civil strife, that they operate among collectivities. But there is far too little evidence about the psyches of rebels for us to say generally how important one or another of the variables is, or how they interact, or whether they are the most consequential psychological factors in civil strife. Some others bear mentioning: civil violence is sometimes assumed to be a calculated strategy for getting what the participants want —which it certainly is for some men, angry or not. Some scholars suggest that discontented men rebel only when faced with a specific threat. Some, notably Fanon, interpret violence as a therapeutic assertion of self for the oppressed. Others of a Freudian or Lorenzian disposition suggest that aggression is a fundamental human drive, not necessarily a response to a specific kind of circumstance but a predisposition that seeks some kind of outlet and that will take violent forms if nonviolent channels are closed off (Fanon, 1963, 1966; Lorenz, 1966. See Gurr, 1968a for a critique of some alternative views of the sources of human aggression).

THE OUTCOMES OF DEPRIVATION:
A RECENT CROSS-NATIONAL STUDY

Despite these qualifications, one can accept for operational purposes the thesis that relative deprivation is a necessary condition for and a major source of civil strife. It also is evident that even when deprivation is intense and common to a large group, it is not a sufficient condition for strife. Patterns of social control and of facilitation have a great deal to do with the outcomes. Whereas psychological variables such as expectation levels are difficult to study directly on any large scale, the intervening social conditions that determine their outcomes are more amenable to comparative, cross-national study. The remainder of this article summarizes some results of one such study, especially as they relate to the problems of contemporary urban disorder.

THE STUDY DESIGN: MEASURES OF DEPRIVATION AND CIVIL STRIFE

The first operational task was to assess the relative extent and intensity of some common kinds of deprivation among the populations of 114 nations. The propositions described above suggested many conditions that are frequently associated with widespread discontent, and a variety of these conditions were indexed. Short-term and persisting deprivation were separately assessed. The extent of short-term economic and political deprivation in the late 1950's and early 1960's was inferred from the magnitude of short-term fluctuations in economic conditions and from politically repressive activities and value-depriving policies of governments, as determined by applying systematic coding procedures to news information. Persisting deprivation was indexed by constructing and combining measures of the extent of such conditions as economic and political discrimination, political separatism, religious cleavages, and lack of educational opportunity.[2]

Data on the types and characteristics of civil strife in all countries for the years from 1961 through 1965 were separately gathered from news sources. During these five years, incidentally, we found that only ten of the world's 114 largest polities appeared completely free of civil strife.[3] From these data we determined the approximate proportion of each nation's population that participated in strife; the total duration of strife; and its casualties proportional to total population. These measures were combined to obtain measures of "magnitude of strife," which was divided into separate measures of magnitude of turmoil, conspiracy, and internal war. Although the United States was not among the 24 polities that experienced what we defined as internal war, it ranked 15th among the 95 polities that experienced turmoil. (Turmoil was defined as relatively spontaneous, unstructured, mass strife, including demonstrations, political strikes, riots, political clashes, and localized rebellions.) The United States ranked 42nd among the 114 polities in total magnitude of strife. Although not all turmoil is urban, by far the

2. No comprehensive report on this research has yet been published. Some preliminary data and analyses are reported in Gurr, 1966 and Gurr and Ruttenberg, 1967. A summary description of all the measures referred to in this article appear in Gurr, 1968b.
3. All polities—nations and colonies—with more than one million people were included, except for five that were excluded because of insufficient data: North Korea, North Vietnam, Mongolia, Laos, and Albania.

larger part of it is, and the generalizations the study suggests about turmoil can be applied with some confidence to urban disorder.

THE INTERVENING VARIABLES

Theories about aggression, and about the conditions of revolution, suggested a number of variables that affect the outcome of deprivation. I decided to index, and determine the relative effects of, four kinds of conditions: the legitimacy of the political regime in which strife occurs, coercive potential, institutionalization, and social facilitation. I suggested above that if men feel that deprivation is legitimate they are likely to accept it with less anger. The legitimacy of a political regime is likely to have a comparable effect: insofar as people regard their political system as a proper one, they are likely to tolerate some kinds of deprivation—in particular those for which the government is held responsible—without taking violent action against it. Two characteristics were taken into account in devising an indirect measure of legitimacy: the length of time each political system had persisted without substantial, abrupt reformation; and the extent to which it was indigenously developed rather than borrowed or imposed from abroad.

Conventional wisdom and studies of strife both emphasize the importance of actual or threatened coercion on the outcome of deprivation. If men are sufficiently afraid of the consequences, the argument goes, they will not riot. But comparative studies of civil strife, and psychological theory, both suggest that the relationship is not so simple. Some kinds of coercion are more likely to increase than deter violence, specifically "medium" or sporadically-applied coercion, which seems to be associated with greater strife than either low or high coercion. Two measures were used to estimate some of these effects: one a measure of the relative size of military and police forces, proportional to population, the other a measure which took account both of the size of these forces and their past and concurrent (1961-65) loyalty to the regime.

Many social scientists have argued that strife is minimized to the extent that organizations like labor unions, political parties, and the government itself are broad in scope, command large resources, and are stable and persisting. The existence of such organizations may have several essentially psychological effects for the discontented. Men may see in them greater opportunities for satisfying their expectations. At the same time, they may be able to express their discontent through them in routinized and typically nonviolent ways; a strike vote or an antigovernment political rally can provide a safe outlet for considerable anger. To assess the effects of "institutionalization," a measure was devised that takes account of the relative strength of unions, the stability of the political party system, and the fiscal resources of government.

Legitimacy, coercion, and institutionalization are social variables that hypothetically serve in various ways to minimize or redirect the destructive consequences of deprivation. A great many conditions can have the opposite effect, to stimulate men to take violent action; for example, the presence of revolutionary organization and leadership, the availability of sanctuary or outside assistance, and beliefs in the rightness of violence. I devised measures for two different kinds of "facilitation." First, there are good historical reasons for assuming that in countries with a history of civil strife violence is likely to become an accepted way of responding to deprivation, i.e., that traditions of civil violence tend to develop and persist. To assess this effect, a measure was constructed of the relative levels of strife among the 114 nations for the years from 1946 through 1959. Second, a composite measure was developed of three kinds of conditions that seemed likely to facilitate strife directly in the early 1960's: the relative size and activity of Communist parties (excluding countries in which they were in power), the extent to which each country had rugged terrain that rebels could use for sanctuary, and the extent to which foreign countries gave direct assistance to rebels.

SOME RESULTS AND THEIR IMPLICATIONS FOR URBAN DISORDER

The measures of deprivation, of magnitudes of strife, and of the postulated intervening variables were correlated, with the results shown in Table 1.[4] All but one of the independent variables are significantly related to the measures of strife. The one exception is the size of coercive force, whose effects were anyway expected to be complex. This variable, and the measure combining size and loyalty, are plotted against the magnitude of turmoil in Figure 1. Large military and police forces alone appear to have no consistent deterrent effect on turmoil, at least at this very general level of comparison, and in some as yet undetermined circumstances turmoil tends to increase as the coercive forces increase in size.

The next step in analysis was to determine how much of the magnitude of turmoil is explained—in the statistical sense—by all the variables acting together.[5] Total magnitude of civil strife is remarkably well accounted for by the eight variables, as shown in Table 2: the multiple correlation coefficient is .806. Turmoil is less well accounted for, with an R of .533. The difference may be partly the result of the way in

---

4. Correlations with magnitudes of conspiracy and of internal war are not reported here, but are of similar order and significance. Separate measures of short-term economic and political deprivation were also used; the short term deprivation measure whose correlations are shown in Table 1 is the sum of those two measures and is reported here to simplify comparisons.

5. The "coercive force size" variable was eliminated from the regression analyses; the separate short-term political and economic deprivation measures were used rather than the summary measure.

Table 1. Correlates of Civil Strife

Variables	1	2	3	4	5	6	7	8	9
1　Short-term deprivation * (+)									
2　Persisting deprivation (+)	04								
3　Legitimacy (—)	—20	—04							
4　Coercive force size ** ±)	—07	—21	25						
5　Coercive force loyalty (—)	—42	—14	48	53					
6　Institutionalization (—)	—17	—37	02	27	41				
7　Past strife levels (+)	34	—04	—05	31	—14	—19			
8　Facilitation (+)	34	17	—15	04	—37	—40	41		
9　Magnitude of turmoil	32	27	—29	—01	—35	—26	30	30	
10　Total magnitude of strife	48	36	—37	—14	—51	—33	30	67	61

NOTE: The proposed relationships between the independent variables and the strife measures are shown in parentheses, + or —. The correlation coefficients are product-moment r's, multiplied by 100. Italicized r's are significant, for n = 114, at the .01 level. Correlations between 18 and 14, inclusive, are significant at the .05 level.

* In regression analyses, separate measures of short-term political and short-term economic deprivation were used. Their separate correlations with other variables are not significantly different from those of the summary short-term deprivation measure.

** This measure was not used in multiple regression analyses.

which turmoil was categorized. Equally important, a great many temporary and local conditions of kinds not represented in the summary measures of deprivation are probably responsible for much turmoil. The

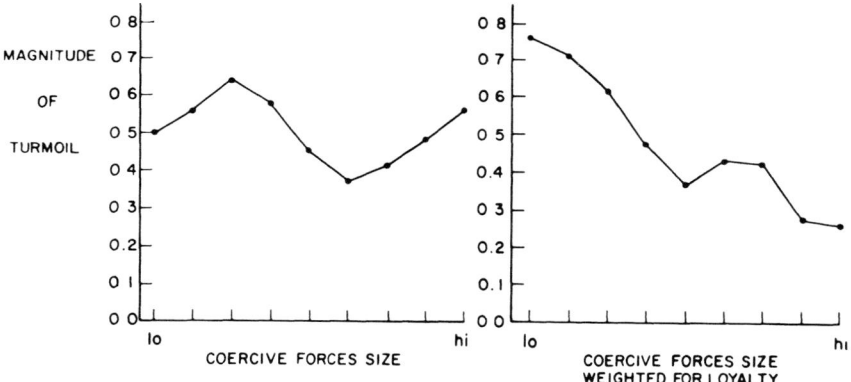

FIG. 1. COERCIVE FORCES AND MAGNITUDE OF TURMOIL

NOTE: The vertical axis gives the average magnitude of turmoil score for (left) deciles of countries with coercive forces of increasing size and (right) deciles of countries with increasingly large coercive forces relative to their loyalty. The range of turmoil scores for the 114 countries is 0.0 to 1.57, their mean is 0.52, their standard deviation 0.40. Units on the horizontal axis represent numbers of cases, not proportional increases in force size/loyalty. Only nine points are shown because the decile score curves were smoothed by averaging overlapping pairs of decile scores.

results are nonetheless significant enough to indicate that the variables represent some of the major sources of civil strife.

The next and most important step was to analyze the causal interrelationships among the variables. A basic supposition for evaluating proposed causal relationships is that if X is a cause of Z whose effects are mediated by an intervening variable Y, then if Y is controlled, the resulting partial correlation between X and Z should be approximately zero. The results of this analysis for magnitude of turmoil provide some surprises.

Remember that I suggested above that all the social conditions intervened between deprivation and strife. The causal model obtained by analyzing a series of partial correlation coefficients is summarized in Figure 2, and suggests a somewhat different sequence of events.[6]

Table 2. Determinants of Magnitude of Strife:
Multiple Regression Results

	DEPENDENT VARIABLES AND PARTIAL CORRELATIONS	
Independent Variables	Magnitude of Turmoil	Total Magnitude of Strife
Short-term deprivation:		
Economic	(07)	24
Political	(08)	(09)
Persisting deprivation	23	39
Legitimacy	—19	—26
Coercive forces loyalty	(—09)	—17
Institutionalization	(—05)	(07)
Past strife levels	21	(04)
Facilitation	(04)	55
Multiple R	.533	.806
Multiple R²	.284	.650

NOTE: Partial correlations represent the relative contribution of each independent variable to the explanation of the dependent variable when all the other variables are controlled. Those in parentheses are significant at less than the .05 level. Since these analyses are concerned with what is in effect the entire universe of polities, all the correlations are in one sense "significant," but those in parentheses are of considerably less consequence than the others.

Among nations generally—the qualification that applies to all these results—only three variables are direct and important causes of turmoil: long-term deprivation, a history of strife, and the legitimacy of the political system. These three variables control or mediate the effects of all

6. The fundamental arguments on which causal inference analysis is based are interpertations of the sources and consequences of discontent among American Negroes. summarized in Hubert M. Blalock, Jr., *Causal Inferences in Nonexperimental Research*, Chapel Hill, North Carolina: University of North Carolina Press, 1964. The brevity of this article precludes technical description of the calculations which suggested the relationships in Figure 2, but those who wish to reconstruct the analysis and to test the fit of alternative models to the data can do so on the basis of the correlation matrix in Table 1 and the data in Table 2.

others. It is important to recognize that this does not mean that short-term deprivation and institutionalization, for example, do not have anything to do with turmoil, but that "something happens" to them en route.

The "something" that happens to short-term deprivation is that its outcome is effectively controlled by three mediating conditions. If coercive forces are large and loyal, if few facilitative conditions are present, and most important if there is no tradition of civil violence, short-term deprivation is unlikely to lead to violence. If these intervening conditions are substantially different, however, even mild deprivation is likely to result in turmoil.

These general conclusions provide some basis for speculation about the United States. The economic and political measures show relatively little short-term deprivation in the United States during the late 1950's and early 1960's: economic conditions were generally good and improving, and there were few government actions that were likely to antagonize large numbers of citizens. The position of American Negroes may not be reflected in these aggregate measures, however. As a group they did not experience any absolute economic decline, but civil rights activism in the early 1960's began to meet increasingly hostile and often brutal responses

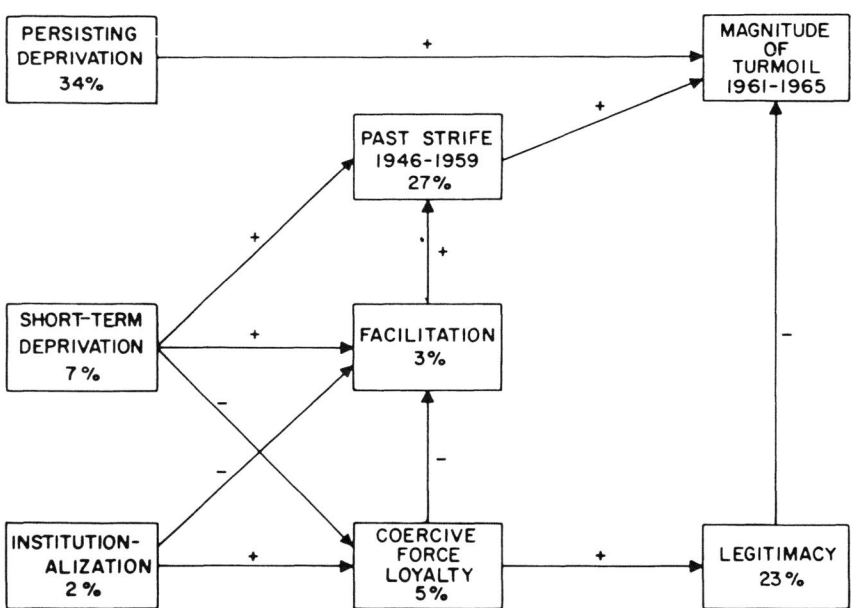

FIG. 2. SEQUENTIAL CAUSES OF TURMOIL

NOTE: The percentages are the proportions of explained variance accounted for by each variable when the effects of all others are controlled. Also see note 6.

at the local level, especially but not solely in the South. We have considerable evidence, comparative and specific, that police or military repression has effects similar to deprivation: it infuriates its victims, the more so to the extent that they believe their acts are legitimate, and their fury is likely to be contained only by the strongest of internal or external controls (See Gurr, 1968a for some evidence. Two recent papers that make this point with reference to specific cases include AlRoy, 1967, pp. 87-99, and Wedge, 1967). How strong external controls must be for containment can be suggested by examining the policies of the Soviet Union in the thirty years after the October Revolution, and of South Africa since the passage of apartheid legislation. The interpretation I am suggesting with specific reference to the United States is that police clubs falling on marchers' heads in Selma for a national television audience might as well have fallen on the heads of every American Negro, so far as their effect on Negroes' anger was concerned. The consequence, in the language of the theoretical model, was a sharp increase in short-term deprivation.

The three mediating conditions that affect the outcome of short-term deprivation seem at first to point, in the United States, to a minimization of turmoil. The military and police are numerous and unlikely to join in rioting. Extremist organizations were inconsequential in the early 1960's, and material foreign support for urban violence was and is nonexistent. But Americans are not, historically, as peaceful a people as they like to believe. Ethnic, religious, and labor violence are chronic in American history, and with reference to the late 1960's there is little doubt that a new pattern of racial violence as a response to deprivation has emerged, too new to be called a "tradition" but potent in its facilitative effects on deprivation in the future. When this new pattern is taken into account, in conjunction with the growth of extremist organizations that advocate covert and violent protest, the inference is that turmoil will be chronic in the near future. This interpretation—and it should be emphasized that it is only that—has some policy implications. Of the three intervening conditions that are generally relevant, it may be possible to minimize one kind of facilitation, that provided by extremist organization, but "traditions" are unalterable in the short run. Moreover, coercion seems to have no consistent effects on angry men: it may in fact impel them to violent resistance. One general policy based on these findings would be to minimize coercion and to eliminate the specific short-term deprivations that contribute to violence.

Institutionalization, as it was measured in the cross-national research design, does not generally have a direct controlling effect on short-term deprivation nor any separate effect on turmoil. Instead it seems to be an underlying cause of the other mediating conditions. Countries with large, stable unions, parties, and governments tend to have high coercive potential and few of the immediate conditions that facilitate strife. Extending these generalizations to the United States, institutionalization is relatively high—on this index the United States ranks 36th among all 114 nations in the study—but such summary statistics conceal major internal variations. Negroes in many regions tend to be underorganized and underserved by local government. Moreover, the first major riot in the 1960's, that of Watts, occurred in a community in which by contemporary accounts associational activity and poverty programs had been less effective than those of almost any other large Negro community. Whether degrees of institutionalization are a major factor in American urban disorders is one of the many questions that needs to be studied on a city-by-city, or better, neighborhood-by-neighborhood, basis.

Legitimacy seems to be causally related to strife in the 114 polities, independent of either deprivation or the other intervening variables. About half of the initial correlation between legitimacy and strife is the result of the apparent causal relation between legitimacy and coercive force loyalty: not surprisingly, large and, most importantly, loyal military and police establishments are characteristic of legitimate regimes. Separately from this, however, high legitimacy is an important and independent source of low turmoil. The implication is that political legitimacy is itself a desired value, one so consequential that its absence constitutes a deprivation that incites men to violent political action. One implication for urban racial violence in the United States can be drawn from this. Although most Americans regard their political system as a legitimate one, a growing minority of Negroes say they do not because of what they regard as its deliberately dilatory progress toward racial equality. Whatever the merit of their judgment, it seems likely to persist; and insofar as the general principle applies to the United States, higher levels of turmoil can be expected as a consequence.

The most striking result of the cross-national analysis is that the extent of persisting deprivation has a major, direct effect on the magnitude of turmoil. There seems to be a certain inevitability about the association of such conditions as systematic discrimination, political separatism, religious cleavages, and lack of educational facilities, on one hand, and the extent of strife, on the other. No patterns of societal arrangements nor coercive response seem to have any consistent effect on its impact. (The same relationship holds between persisting deprivation and the magnitudes of conspiracy, internal war, and total civil strife.) [7] If the general relationship holds for the United States, then the country is likely to be afflicted by racial turmoil so long as racial discrimination persists. The potential for turmoil has existed since the founding of the Republic. Why so much of it has exploded in *this* decade is suggested by

7. The inconsequential correlation shown in Table 1 between persisting deprivation and past civil strife is a consequence, first, of the fact that in many countries "persisting" depriving conditions have changed—typically decreased—between the 1940's and the 1960's; and second, that during the 1940's and 1950's reported strife in most traditional and colonial polities was minimal, although objectively they had many of the conditions that led to violence, once their inhabitants were caught up in the "revolution of rising expectations."

some of the preceding interpretations, to the effect that deprivation has intensified and that social conditions increasingly facilitate its violent manifestation. But the results of the research I have summarized give no general theoretical or empirical reason to believe that turmoil based on pervasive inequality can be permanently deterred or diverted. The only effective and enduring solution seems to be to remove its causes.

11

THEORY: TAXONOMIC, EXOTIC, PSYCHOLOGICAL, AND SOCIOLOGICAL

The distinctions made in assigning selections to Chapter 10 (Patterns), 11 (Empirical Generalization), or 12 (Theory) are in some ways arbitrary; none of the selections in 10 and 11 are atheoretical (since classificatory theories inform taxonomies), and several of the selections in the "theory" chapter include data. But I have attempted in this chapter to include selections which span the range of theoretical perspectives on racial violence, though by no means all viewpoints are represented.

As I suggested in the Introduction, there are two principal perspectives which inform attempts to explain violence, one focusing on the individual and the other on the social structure within which individual behavior occurs. In the initial selection I have tried to show how the location of an individual within the social structure can influence the perspective he chooses; the paper combines taxonomic and social structural interpretation.

Following a classificatory paper by Dahlke, are four papers representing various psychological perspectives. Sterba's paper represents a psychoanalytic position, the papers by Clark and by Clark and Barker represent social psychology from the psychological wing of that perspective, and Ransford's paper represents the analytical perspective of sociological social-psychological study of attitudes.

In the next two papers, I have attempted to show the central importance of the posture and strength of external agencies of control in the occurrence or nonoccurrence of social violence. Waskow, basing his analysis on a review of historical evidence has attempted to show ways in which changes in those external agencies have been occurring and the consequences of these changes for changes in modes of assault upon the accommodative structure by black people. Finally, two brief selections from the theoretical chapter of Williams' excellent study, *Strangers Next Door* (1964), have been included to indicate the directions which theory-building in the study of social conflict and social violence might take.

Allen D. Grimshaw

Three Views of Urban Violence:
Civil Disturbance, Racial Revolt, Class Assault

Aside from some spectacular happenings in the world of sport and the continuing conflict in and about Vietnam, it is probable that no topic has been more discussed in the year drawing to a close [1967] than that of urban violence. Events of the last four summers have left behind over a hundred dead, thousands injured, property damage which can simply not be calculated, and a population schizophrenically both outraged and conscience-stricken. Researchers—scholarly, journalistic and governmental—have prowled the stricken cities like Graves Registration Units after military combat, and have come up with causal explanations ranging from the standards of unemployment and bad living conditions to the more specialized interpretations of insufficient socialization and the decline of religious values. The researchers have been both preceded and followed by right and left and white and black extremists; these observers have their explanations and their recommended solutions. Embarrassed liberals find themselves accused either of having capitulated to extremist "black power" or of being, when the chips are down, "white racists." Embarrassed traditional spokesmen of the minority community find themselves out of contact with the masses they claim to represent, under parliamentary attack in their own organizations, and threatened with physical attack by adversaries who claim that they have "sold out to whitey." Government officials variously increase funds for the war on poverty (or cancel the war on rats), increase funds for law enforcement, and create new commissions for "study of the problem." Black leadership castigates the mass media; the mass media responds in kind. The urban violence is linked, by various people in various ways, to violence in Vietnam. Confusion, good intentions and recrimination are equally rampant; only the foolhardy make predictions—except to state that, troubled as the situation is, there are no prospects for immediate improvement.

The period of "classic" race rioting in the United States, which dates from about the time of the First World War, was one in which whites responded to Negro "insubordination" and "pushiness" by direct assault upon the minority—direct assault in which mobs of white civilians took part (see, e.g., Grimshaw, 1963a). In these riots a difference emerged from earlier "pogroms" in that Negroes fought back, and in some instances racial mobs attacked smaller groups or individuals of the other group. The Detroit "race riot" of 1943 was such a case, one in which large mobs of whites and Negroes directly confronted members of the opposite group in a pattern of racial warfare (Grimshaw, 1960). The most immediately obvious difference between the Detroit disturbances in 1943 and those in 1967 is that in the latter there were no significant cases in which black and white civilians directly attacked members of the other race. Indeed, while the significance of such activity has been overestimated, whites and Negroes occasionally cooperated in attacks upon the police and upon commercial establishments. Moreover, there were not in 1967, as there had been in the earlier vieolence, widely circulated rumors in each of the groups about cross-racial assaults upon women and children.

The pattern in Detroit in 1967 closely parallels those other urban disturbances of the Sixties which involved the Negro minority: Philadelphia, Rochester, Bedford-Stuyvesant, Watts, and Newark to name some major instances. In their lack of direct confrontation between civilian whites and Negroes they also parallel the Harlem disturbances of 1935 and 1943, although in the latter instances there had been rumors of heinous cross-racial assault (upon Negroes). The two Harlem riots and the riots of the Sixties may also differ from earlier riots in that, while there was improper behavior by police and other control agencies, it never compared to that of earlier riots—for example, in East St. Louis in 1917 formal control agencies actively participated in large-scale assault upon the minority group (Grimshaw, 1963b). Furthermore, while much of the mass media has been critical of the black community for being insufficiently grateful for changes which have already taken place and for endangering future improvements by "hoodlumism," media treatment—both in news reporting and in editorial posture—has generally been far more sympathetic than was true in the past.[1] In this greater sympathy they have either led or followed a greater sympathy and concern in substantial sections of the dominant white community.

The large-scale urban violence of the first half of the century clearly had economic overtones. The rhetoric, however, was racist, and racial identity was the prime factor in determining attitudes and behavior alike. Disputes over housing and recreational facilities in the decade following World War II and, in the latter part of that decade, dis-

1. For some notion of these changes, compare current editorials in the New York Times with these comments on the riots in Washington in 1919 (July 23, 1919):

"The majority of the negroes [sic] in Washington before the great war were well behaved . . . Most of them admitted the superiority of the white race, and troubles between the two races were undreamed of. Now and then a negro intent on enforcing the civil rights law, would force his way into a saloon or a theatre and demand to be treated the same as whites were, but if the manager objected he usually gave in without more than a protest.

"Nevertheless, there was a criminal element among the negroes, and as a matter of fact nearly all the crimes of violence in Washington were committed by negroes. Had it not been for this fact, the police force might well have been disbanded, or at least reduced to very small proportions."

putes over educational desegregation were clearly racial (see, e.g., Grimshaw, 1962a and Grimshaw, 1963a). In contrast to the earlier riots, the events of the 1960's have a complexity of motivation and of relations to the larger social structure which eludes any easy interpretation. Again in contrast to earlier violence, events of the last few years have been the focus of a large variety of formal studies and of interpretations from within and without the affected communities in which it is difficult to find a common thread of explanation.[2] In the remainder of this paper I will identify three main sets of interpretations of the occurrences of the last four years, identify principal proponents of the several perspectives, and attempt to relate the various explanations to the locations of their proponents within the social structure. The three interpretations can be most easily identified by using the labels for the violence given by their adherents: civil disturbance, racial revolt, class assault.

A number of social characteristics and several ill-defined variables are involved in the process by which individuals and groups label the violent events of recent years. Some of these, such as race and involvement (whether as rioter or as official), have a more obvious bearing than others. The interplay of motivation and of structural constraints which culminates in a labelling decision is, however, no less complex and difficult to unravel than the "causation" of the urban eruptions themselves. Moreover, if it is not at all clear what the long-range consequences of the disturbances may be, it is certainly clear that the process of labeling and of the emergence of one or another set of labels as predominant will have consequences for the future events. To oversimplify, if society at large (or significant and powerful segments of the society) agrees with linguistic labeling of events as "criminal" and "rebellious," then an atmosphere will be created in which pleas for the strengthening of police (and other agencies with legal monopolies of force) and for "stricter law enforcement" will strike a responsive chord. If, on the other hand, identification of the same events as "a legitimate revolt against impossible conditions" is accepted, then people will be predisposed to accept solutions which attack sources of the behavior rather than solely problems of control. Similarly, certain critics have claimed that characterization of the events as an expression of "class assault" will have the result of arousing fears of "Communism" and related threats with the consequence of producing still another response.

Race and involvement were suggested above as social characteristics with obvious influence on labelling perspectives. Related to involvement is the question of the official position of the labeler: is he an elected or

2. See, especially, the publications of the Los Angeles Riot Study undertaken by the Institute of Government and Public Affairs of the University of California, Los Angeles. Probably the most useful of these studies for purposes of this paper is Murphy and Watson, 1967. Two other major studies, still in the data analysis state, are those of Dr. John Spiegel of Brandeis (the six-city study) and the ongoing study sponsored by the Detroit Urban League and Michigan's Survey Research Center. This has been partially published. See Meyer, 1967.

appointed official; is his constituency formal or informal; is his primary responsibility for social control or for welfare, and so on. These questions lead in turn to a consideration of perceptions: is the threat seen as immediate or remote; is the activity seen, for example, as legitimate or criminal; and so on. Reporters on the scene may witness "criminal behavior" while editorial writers may have in mind statistics about unemployment and poor housing. On the other hand, reporters may witness "unnecessary use of force" by police while editorial writers may have in mind the passage of civil rights legislation and the changing pattern of court decisions. Middle-class Negroes in the area of violence may be subjected to police insult or threats to their own property while middle-class Negroes who live away from the ghetto may, in the first instance, see legal improvements and ameliorative programs and, in the second, have in mind the same statistics about unemployment and poor housing. White liberals living in insulated small towns and protected college communities will respond differently from those in urban areas who can see the flames and hear the shots and sirens. Ecological and social distance from the actual events will both have an influence on perceptions.

Perspectives in labeling are also influenced by ideological postures and, given ideological positions, by tactical considerations. Some few observers have been ideologically neutral and have simply chronicled events (an excellent and generally "neutral" study done by a journalist is Robert Conot, 1967). Most, however, fall somewhere on a "right-left" continuum—or rather on continuua, since there are different meanings to "right-left" within the white and Negro communities. Right-left categorizations are made more difficult by the presence of different strategic orientations within the several groups and by preferences for legalistic as contrasted to amelioristic strategies and, in the left groups, by disagreements over the primacy of political and social as contrasted to welfare goals.

Tactical perspectives are, of course, related to ideology. A wish to deny the race and/or class aspects of the events or to minimize the magnitude of the importance of such characteristics may lead to relatively neutral labeling of them as disturbances or disorders. Someone sharing the same general ideological perspective, however, but wishing to maximize the legal aspects—whether or not concerned with race and class aspects—may label the same events as lawlessness or insurrection. More generally, labelling may represent threatening as contrasted to conciliatory tactics. Thus "tough" military men and "hard" policemen may join not only with political rightists but also with black militants in labeling disturbances as "revolt," "rebellion," or "warfare." Similarly, elected officials oriented to the *status quo*, as well as sections of the mass media, may join with more moderate Negro leaders (the old-line, "Negro" leaders as contrasted to "black" leaders) and with white liberals in assigning more neutral and conciliatory labels such as "disturbance" or "disorder." In these instances those who use the same labels may have very different purposes in mind: "enforcement" types want rigorous suppression of the "revolt," "black power" advocates are seeking recruits for the overthrow of the current social structure; white liberals and moderate Negroes want ameliorative social changes; some officials who talk about disorders want, immediately, to "cool" the situation, although they may also be sincerely interested in improvements in the conditions of minority group members.

The several variables suggested above are all of importance in influencing perspectives in labeling. Whatever their interaction, however, and whatever the weights of their mutual influence, there is another variable which in many instances may out-weigh even ideological posture and immediacy of threat. This variable, which is of importance not only in the selection of an original position but also in its maintenance or rejection, is that of social supports and relevant reference groups. It is not yet clear what the boundaries will be of the new conflict groups emerging in American society. It *is* clear that processes of boundary definition are in operation. Insofar as the boundaries become more clearly defined and rigid and as the society becomes more polarized, there will be strong pressures on individuals to choose "for" or "against" ideological and tactical positions. Thus, apparently, white "liberals" attending last summer's National Conference for a New Politics were constrained to accept more and more "extreme" positions and labeling in order to maintain an even grudging acceptance from their black colleagues. Thus, before a large public audience Dick Gregory can castigate the whites (much to their apparent pleasure) and can then ask Negro students to rise, following this with the directive, "All of you who don't think there wasn't enough burning last summer sit down" —and can thereby manipulate social structure so as to coerce a public acceptance or rejection of a "militant" stance. Thus, "white, liberal, so-called intellectuals" who have long identified with the aspirations of the Negro revolution are constrained to give up their status as objective observers and to accept the interpretations and verbalizations of black militants uncritically, or else to face complete rejection—a quandary which leaves some of them immobilized, others emasculated, others schizophrenic and still others driven into retreat from the situation.

Two further points may be made. First, labeling perspectives may be somewhat less stable than is the case with some other emotionally and politically important attitudes. There is evidence that there have been shifts in perception as a consequence of peer pressures, of superordinate policy shifts, of information on the scope and magnitude of events. Thus, some elected officials may in anger initially condemn rioters as "hoodlums" engaged in criminal violence. Their characterization may shift (perhaps in response to a review of the full political implications of their position) to one which labels the events as civil disturbances generated by impossible conditions. On the other hand, the *New York Times,* which initially emphasized the conditions which "caused" the riots, shifted as the summer of 1967 wore painfully by to a position where they stated editorially (July 25, 1967), "the arsonists and looters have to be dealt with as the criminals they are (whatever the root causes)."

The second point to be made now is that while the variables discussed operate in complex ways, they have influences on some more mundane and measurable characteristics of persons who ultimately do the labeling. Negroes with different sex, age, occupational, class, and educational characteristics do respond differently to queries about the meanings and reasons of the riots and about their possible consequences for the Negro "cause." Middle-, lower- and working-class Negroes do have different sets of complaints and different perspectives on goals as well as on tactics. They also have differential access to the opportunity structure and differential exposure to social slight and insult. Differences in responses by age categories can clearly be linked to differences in the experiences of different generations. Other papers will document differences on the basis of these more traditional socioeconomic variables; I simply want to underline the fact that behind the distribution of responses, there is a complex interplay of structural features of the social system with individual attributes.

CIVIL DISTURBANCE AND/OR INSURRECTION

"open rebellion . . . criminal insurrection . . . an atrocity . . . plain and simple crime and not a civil rights protest."

> New Jersey Governor Richard J. Hughes on the August, 1967, "disturbances" in Newark.

Victims of civil disorders report here . .

> Notice outside of office of municipal social service agency, Detroit, 1967.

Both radical rightists and elected moderates have chosen to label events of recent summers as if there were no racial overtones, although in detailed exposition both sets of observers have referred to the fact that most of those involved have, indeed, been Negroes. The rightists have chosen to keep their labels racially neutral for two reasons. First, they have chosen to depict the disturbances as resulting from leftist agitation and from a general breakdown of the normative order, and they see the agitation and breakdown as characterizing the entire society with Negroes being only somewhat more susceptible because of the fact that they can't or won't "make it" in American society. Second, because in spite of their ideological predispositions they are politically sensitive to growing sympathies which exist, at least in the abstract, for the Negro plight. Thus, while in many instances they have referred to "ingratitude" and to the fact that "appeasement" will only lead to more violence and to further inflated demands, they are cautious about alienating possible sources of support in the larger community.

Elected officials like Governor Hughes have responded viscerally during the actual eruption of violence and have generally moderated their characterizations in the post-riot period. Many of them, and I single Hughes out only because of the widespread attention given to his pronouncements, are fundamentally sympathetic to the situation of the Negro, but are simply unable to understand why Negroes are not aware of "what is being done for them." They *do* want peace and order but at the same time they want to avoid racial labeling because of the dangers of either white or black "backlash," or both. They *are* concerned about conditions in the ghetto and may in some instances use racially neutral euphemisms because they do not want to endanger programs directed to improving those conditions. Some officials, moreover, may choose to use racially neutral terms because of the implications which admission of racial meaning of the disturbances might have for the conduct of American foreign policy.

Individual police officers and many enlisted military personnel doubtless see the disturbances as race riots, "pure and simple." Law enforcement officials and many military officers, on the other hand, have responded to disorder in the abstract and have seen the events simply as problems of law enforcement and peace maintenance and have seen their duty simply as that of restoring law and order. While many are doubtless sympathetic, and while others may be strongly prejudiced, they have been preoccupied with questions of logistics and tactics and only after disturbances have been quelled (or have simply run down out of inertia) have they moved from control problems to interpretation of causes. Thus, the reflections of at least some officials have been directed to the relative merits of different patterns of the commitment of police officers and/or troops, the advantages of containment as contrasted to dispersal, and the effectiveness of tear gas as compared to that of night stick or bullet.

RACIAL REVOLT

. . . If you know the culture and gain access to the heart of the community, you come up with one astounding pattern and that is, they hate Whitey—they literally hate Whitey, all of them. And even with the middle class Negroes— you're not going to get them to say, "Let's go and kill Whitey." or something like that, you're not going to get that—but I'll tell you what. Try talking to them about their jobs. Where the highest level among many of them is to get to be some kind of bullshit supervisor, and they know damn well they're smarter than the honky who's over them. Get them talking about that some time. . . . Everybody, well, not everybody, but particularly the liberals do not want to face the aura of hate that is inside the community. They don't want to deal with it. They don't want to deal with the tremendous racial aspect of what has happened. It's just too ugly.

From an interview with a Negro intellectual, Detroit, August, 1967.

Particularly since the events of the summer of 1967, Negroes of every political persuasion and of every ideological hue have increasingly identified the current activities as "the Negro Revolt" or, in some instances, "the black revolt." These terms have superseded the earlier label of "Negro Revolution" which had, in spite of its implications for a complete restructuring of society, come to be identified as a peaceful revolution which would use the courts and the ballot as well as non-violent confrontation as tactics. The term "revolt" is used in its dictionary meaning as "a renunciation of allegiance and subjection to a government; rebellion; insurrection."

In the case of the militant blacks (and they by no means constitute an ideologically homogeneous bloc), the label is used descriptively and also as a rallying cry and a coercive linguistic weapon in the definition of the boundaries of a conflict group. The threat, however, is not directed against whites or the white Establishment or its mercenaries—for there is an attitude that there is little to be gained from Whitey, that his institutions will respond only to forceful change and that white reaction will be the same no matter what labels are used or what tactics adopted. The threat is, rather, directed to moderate Negroes and more traditional leaders—"Join with us or see your organization wiped out—and we can't promise safety for you!"

For some traditional-style leaders this threat has been enough; they choose to adopt the militant "black" rhetoric as a mode of organizational and, perhaps, even personal survival. Others, however, accept the labeling primarily in order to use it as a threat to the white Establishment. Thus, national leaders have stated that the labels are descriptively correct, that the reasons for the emergence of militant revolt lie in a failure of the Establishment to fulfill the more moderate requests that they have been making over the years. They state, "Meet the kinds of demands that we have been making or you will have to deal with wild-eyed radicals and guerrilla warfare in the streets, rather than with intelligent and reasonable men like ourselves." These leaders are in a far more difficult situation than the black militants. They are dealing with multiple constituencies and must, while publicly calling for reason and for peaceful solutions, privately mobilize the entire battery of threats which the militants imply in their labels. They must also, somehow, adopt enough of the militant rhetoric in dealing with dissidents within their own organizational structures to disarm them while not losing credibility with the white Establishment.

It has been suggested above that some whites have, in order to maintain access to the militant movement, also accepted its rhetoric (as at the NCNP). There are other whites, however, who have insisted on the continuing importance of racial factors in the etiology of violence. This has been true even of scholars who have found significant class aspects in the violence. Thus, for example, the Murphy-Watson study of Watts found that middle-class Negroes were even more hostile to whites than the very poor, who were primarily angered about "welfare" issues (*op. cit.*). The same hostility is suggested in the quotation which introduced this section, and which is accompanied by the question, "Just what the hell do we have to do in order to be accepted? We've done everything that has been demanded of us in terms of obtaining education and acting like middle-class people—but we're still subjected to continuing insult and social exclusion."

Thus, in this case and in that of those labeling the disturbances in racially neutral terms, a wide variety of perspectives, motives and tactical outlooks is involved.

CLASS ASSAULT

Initially, I like to term this thing as an economic revolt. Initially, it had no racial overtones at all. It was just the looting, etc., and as you know there was integrated looting in the 12th Street area. I saw integrated couples over there. No one said anything. Whites and colored were standing on the corner together. It started out, as I said, like an economic revolt. . . .

Really, on the racial overtones, I think the police and the National Guard brought this in. . . . Some of us said (at that time) if you bring in the National Guard, you'll bring in the racial connotation that heretofore there has not been. As you know, the National Guard and the police with their brutality, etc., have done this, people who were not angry before are—because of what happened—because of this hotel-motel thing.

. . . .

It's being played up by some people that there's this schism between lower and middle-class Negroes and there is this class type thing. . . . I know that there is a lot of feeling in the community now—not only in Detroit—but all over the country that middle-class folk have not done as much as they can for the brethren. I'm sure that you've heard the expression many times that, 'When he gets into the system, he becomes whiter than Whitey.'

From an interview with a Negro activist, Detroit, 1967.

This is one of the major problems on reporting. Everybody from the newspaper reporters to these so-called intellectuals, they come on with their preconceived notions. The newspapers have their side and their specific interests within the framework of the entire control process, so they report it in a certain way. Intellectuals and social scientists usually have theoretical fancies which they use phenomena to support—they have certain ways of looking at things . . . A reporter, if he is to have veracity, cannot have any preconceived notions.

From an interview with a Negro intellectual, Detroit, August, 1967.

Three sets of commentators have emphasized the class and economic aspects of the summer violence. Committed leftists, including theoretically oriented socialists as well as activist Communists, are influenced by ideological concerns in their search for understanding of the events. Poverty workers are influenced by the obvious economic disadvantages of ghetto residents and may be more likely to notice the "economically rational" behavior which accompanied simple cathartic or more punitive destructiveness. Some social scientists and journalists in their emphasis on class aspects of the riots may be influenced by the sharp differences in behavior patterns which have distinguished the disturbances of the Sixties from those of 1943 and earlier (with the aforementioned exception of the two major Harlem disturbances in 1935 and 1943).

Some of these differences were mentioned above, particularly that in which, in contrast to earlier riots, those of the Sixties were characterized by an absence of direct confrontation between large groups of civilians of the two communities. But there have been other, more subtle differences as well. Williams, in his studies in smaller communities done in the Fifties, reported that militancy (as measured by fairly routine types of civil rights goals) was higher among the educated, young and middle-class Negroes—but that prejudice toward whites was also lower in this group (Williams, *et al.*, 1964. Also see, more recently, Marx, 1967). It seemed likely that as militancy became redefined—and it clearly has—the middle-classes might lose their role as militant leaders to new leaders with greater demands, but that at the same time they would remain lower in prejudice toward whites. There was evidence that although progress was slow, an increasing number of Negroes could be characterized as middle-class. The overall gap in education between whites and Negroes narrowed; and although the income gap increased, this was more a function of larger proportions of Negroes who had in some sense dropped completely out of the economic structure than it was of continuing discrimination on a large scale against Negro professionals and others with middle class occupations. Indeed, as was suggested in the interview quoted above, some middle-class Negroes were being coopted out of the Negro community. If anything, then, it seemed likely that as middle-class Negroes became more successful and lower-class Negroes less, it could be anticipated that there would be a growing estrangement between the two class groups within the minority community.

Moreover, there had been some evidence that, as ties between class groups within the community became attenuated, new linkages might grow up between the underclasses of each of the two communities—in other words, that lower-class whites and lower-class Negroes, both victims of economic exploitation and of diminishing opportunities in a social world demanding, for example, increasing education, might act together in common cause. Thus, while middle-class Negroes continued to be victims of discrimination (as suggested in the quote at the beginning of the section on racial revolt) and subject to police indignities and social affront, at the same time they would increasingly identify with the white Establishment while their less successful brethren would begin to see the identity of their interests with those of unsuccessful lower-class whites. This set of events did occur; and Bayard Rustin, among others, began to suggest that there were identities of interest amongst all the very poor. It began to look as if there might be processes in motion which would establish new group boundaries and new conflict alignments in American society (for a fuller review of some of these changes, a review now in need of substantial revision, see Grimshaw, 1965).

These trends, if they existed, were essentially cut off by the course of actual events. It is clear that while the initiating incidents in the disturbances of the Sixties were frequently if not always racial in character, nonetheless, the events that initially followed showed a reaction to economic conditions as well as to discrimination. Moreover, at least in Detroit, there were cases of cross-racial solidarity. However, as the disturbances were drawn out, the role of the police and of the National Guard was such that middle-class Negroes, whatever their initial feelings about the rioting, were sharply reminded of their racial identity and of their common cause and fortune with their brethren.

Murphy and Watson in their careful survey of Watts in the aftermath of that catastrophe were somewhat surprised to find that middle-class Negroes were more rather than less hostile and prejudiced toward whites than their less successful fellow community members (*op. cit.*). Lower-class Negroes were preoccupied with "welfare" problems, poor housing, jobs, education, high prices and bad food. Middle-class Negroes reported anger and hostility toward whites. It would be interesting to know what kinds of responses these same middle-class Negroes would have given to the same sets of questions prior to the riot, and what role the behavior of police and the National Guard had in redefining their attitudes. Quite clearly, such redefinitions did take place during the course of the rioting in Detroit; it can be assumed that similar redefinition took place elsewhere.

SUMMARY AND CONCLUSIONS

As is the case with every pattern of social behavior, there are no simple explanations of the terror we have witnessed through the last four summers. This is clearly *not* a case of conflict between well-bounded and homogeneous groups. Lower-class Negroes and lower-class whites have been brutalized by the police and have been victims of an exploitative or indifferent economic system. More militant blacks, however, have little sympathy for lower-class whites because, no matter what their difficulties, they have the advantage of being white and yet can't "cut it" in a society where skin color is the most important characteristic a man has. Middle-class Negroes, on the other hand—who, as some felt, were slipping into white society—have had the importance of their color driven sharply home not only by recent events, but also by a continuing pattern in which they have not moved successfully within the white Establishment and where they have frequently witnessed more rapid advancement of whites whom they feel are substantially less qualified. The situation is further complicated by the fact that while all Negroes are angry at "whitey"; some are more concerned about social slights and some more concerned about welfare issues, the nitty-gritty of jobs, housing, bad food and wretched schools. Even among those who agree on goals, there are sharp differences on tactics. Perhaps one of the things which has prevented greater success of the Negro Revolution is the multiplicity of factions within the Black Community. There are more complicated dimensions to this issue than to any other I have ever examined in my role as a sociologist.

The situation is not simple. The events *are* disorders and they *have* involved criminal elements. There *are* clear elements of revolt against the economic power structure which can be seen in the pattern of attacks upon merchants in the ghetto and upon those identified as mercenaries of that structure, namely, the police and the National Guard. However, as a consequence of questionable practices by the police and by the National Guard there is, at least in Detroit and probably in other major cities as well, a growing increase in the strength of the previously attenuated solidarity between the Negro middle- and lower-classes. There is probably, at the same time, a decrease in whatever bonds may have been growing up between the Negro proletariat and the lower-class white "honkies." As a consequence, we may conclude that there is some accuracy in each of the three perspectives from which people, located differently in the social structure, see urban disorder. As has already been suggested, selection of one or another of these labels by policy-makers in our society will have major consequences both for the immediate possibilities of improvement and for the likelihood of recurrence or nonrecurrence of major urban violence.

Race and Minority Riots—A Study in the Typology of Violence

A constructed type is an exaggeration of actuality. Certain aspects of an historical event are abstracted in accordance with certain hypotheses. In this study we will attempt to delineate a pattern of social action in which violence is one of the essential attributes by asking: What are the essential elements of a race or minority riot? Under what conditions do these elements combine to produce the series of actions in the total event which is labled a riot?

The underlying assumption in this study is the principle that valuations of the person and of the group organize social relations. Such valuations have been characterized as personal or categoric, intrinsic or extrinsic (Hiller, 1947, pp. 191-218, 631-650). In those instances where intrinsic valuations in terms of respect, accountability, and inviolability are withheld, social relations are utilitarian or dissociative. Such social relations are reinforced if the content of the extrinsic categorizations is negative. These assessments, moreover, may be of long historical standing, a fact frequently overlooked, and they may become strengthened in a period of transition. When a series of negative evaluations impinges upon a group, then its situation, in the absence of mitigating norms of justice and humanitarianism, becomes extremely precarious. Violent expression of disesteem on the part of the superordinate group may readily result. Violence is more likely to occur when the minority group is not content to accept the assignment of low rank from the so-called majority group [1] and when it attempts a redefinition of the situation which will bring about assimilation or at least equal status without assimilation. This means that a redistribution of power and of opportunities is to be effected. This struggle will bring forth the opposition of the superordinate group.

Instead of defining the term riot and then finding examples to illustrate the definition we shall examine two historical events which have been defined by participants and bystanders as riots. The construction of a riot type obviously could involve many more instances. Improvement and modification of the construct arrived at in this preliminary study could be made by reference to the Nazi persecution of Jews and other groups, Polish pogroms, the Armenian pogrom in Tur-

---

1. The utility of the terms "minority group" and "majority group" is greatly limited if the terms are thought of quantitatively. Whites have frequently been dominant minorities. The crux of the matter lies in the relationship of domination and submission with the supporting valuations and power techniques.

key, the Huguenot massacre in France, Luddite riots in England, the recent riots in the Union of South Africa, communal riots in India, riots against Protestants in Mexico, the zoot suit riots in California, and others.

HISTORICAL CONDITIONS

KISHINEW RIOT OF 1903

A Russian official stated the case against the Jews as follows: "What can we do with them? They are the racial antithesis of our nation. A fusion with us is impossible, owing to religious and other disturbing causes. They will always be a potential source of sectarian and economic disorder in our country. We cannot admit them to equal rights of citizenship for these reasons, and, let me add, because their intellectual superiority would enable them to gain possession of most of the posts of the civil administration. . . . They are the active propagandists of the Socialism of Western Europe in our borders. Their discontent is a menace to us along the Austrian and German frontiers. The only solution to the problem of the Russian Jew is departure from Russia" (M. Davitt, 1903, pp. 65-66). In this statement there is a fairly complete negative assessment of the Jew. Various groups shared and supported this extreme disesteem, i.e., the government and especially the lower ranking officials of the political bureaucracy; the Russian Orthodox Church which was the established church; students and seminarists in the royal schools and gymnasia; the small merchant, petty trader, and working man.

This assessment, moreover, became institutionalized in a great variety of discriminatory statutes and administrative decrees. In the royal schools and gymnasia, Jews were restricted to five per cent or ten per cent of the total school population. From 1882 to 1903 a series of laws and administrative decrees limited property holding among Jews, restricted access to occupations, restricted education, forced unequal military service, and segregated them to the so-called Pale of Settlement.[2] These laws plus numerous local administrative decrees inhibited the economic and social development of the Jews. They furthermore made Jews prey to the exactions of local petty officials and police. The *sous prefect* of police in Bessarabia in which Kishinew is located apparently was an expert at this. The May law of 1882 which segregated all Jews to the Pale, i.e., from the land and villages to the towns, was not put into full effect until 1891 when the procurator of the Holy Synod, M. Podedonostev, forced the issuance of the imperial decree compelling the

---

2. These laws and decrees are summarized in *Die Judenpogrome in Russland,* Zionistischen Hilfsfond in London von der zur Erforsachung der Pogrome Einge-setzten Kommission, Judischer Verlag (1910) pp. 97-133. (Referred to hereafter as *Die Judenpogrome.*)

enforcement of the 1882 laws. Many of the fliers distributed around Kishinew advocating violence against Jews were printed by the press of the Holy Synod of St. Petersburg and passed by the church censor.

Putting into effect the May law of 1882 had certain population and social consequences. These laws required that all Jews settle within the Pale, a series of provinces along the western frontier extending from Riga to the Black Sea. These laws also excluded from agriculture all Jews except those already so engaged. Confined to the towns, the Jews had recourse only to industrial, service, and trade opportunities. Since Russia at this time was in process of becoming industrialized, occupational opportunities in industry were relatively meager. It has been estimated that 1,300,000 Jews or about one-third of the total Jewish population, were forced from the land and villages into the towns (Kulischer, 1943, p. 23). Three out of five inhabitants in urban centers of the Pale provinces were Jews (Davitt, 1903, p. 38). In Bessarabia Jews composed 38 percent of the population. This population influx tended to increase the struggle for self-maintenance for both Jews and non-Jews, particularly among the small shopkeepers, petty middlemen, and artisans. Jews resorted to almost any means to keep themselves on a bare subsistence level.[3] To do so they had to resort to extralegal and illegal means which augmented the parasitic demands of police and other officials of the bureaucracy. Extensive smuggling, for example, was one means and became so prevalent, including the entailed bribery and corruption, that Jews were forbidden to live within a stretch 35 to 40 miles from the western frontier.

Not only were Jews segregated by being forced to live in the Pale but they also tended to live in special districts within the urban centers. This local segregation apparently was on economic lines, with poor Jewish traders, shopkeepers, and laborers living close together. The more wealthy Jewish merchants and bankers had residences in the better sections of the towns. Such concentration of despised populations limits to a few focal points the outbreak of violent attacks.

A traditional anti-Jewish story, which was a very important element in the Kishinew riot, was the murder-ritual legend. This originated in the middle of the thirteenth century and spread all over Europe. This legend held that there was an annual killing of Christian children by Jews as part of the Blood Atonement in Hebrew Paschal rites (Bloch, 1922, pp. 611-634). The story emphasized the out-group nature of the Jew and evidently was firmly established in the cultures of Europe despite Jewish efforts to disavow it.

Social unrest, existing in many groups in Russia at this time, was

3. This aspect is understated in *Die Judenpogrome*, particularly the relations of workers and petty traders. Davitt emphasizes this aspect as important. The amount of competition varied, it would seem, in the various pogrom centers. I do not intend to overemphasize this economic factor, as the matter of religious difference was of equal, if not of greater, importance. The propaganda attack was especially based on religious differences.

attacked by the government with increasingly repressive measures. Although Jews played a role in certain movements and demonstrations, their role was exaggerated by constituted authorities as the dominant role. This repressive role of the government was expressed in the tremendous increase in death sentences for political activities, deportation to Siberia, and other tactics (*Die Judenpogrome*, 1910, p. 231 and footnote p. 232). The fiasco of the Russo-Japanese war brought out the inefficiency and corruption of the government. In this situation Jews furnished a convenient scapegoat.[4]

Pogroms were not new in Russia. There were two large pogrom periods, the first from 1881 to 1883, and the second from 1903 to 1906. The first period involved 8 provinces and 224 pogroms; and the second, 12 provinces and 690 pogroms (*Die Judenpogrome*, I, pp. 189, 190-191). Kishinew ushered in the pogroms of the second period. Local pogroms had taken place as early as 1821 in Odessa. Several isolated pogroms took place between 1884 and the second major period (*Die Judenpogrome*, p. 14–15). A pattern of violence against Jews was evidently an integral part of the culture.

Detroit Riot of 1943

The Negro came in large numbers to Detroit during tense periods, World War I and World War II. The town itself had grown meteorically, particularly after the establishment of the automobile industry. It had a large foreign-born population, including a strongly anti-Negro Polish district of around 50,000. It was estimated that 50,000 Negroes migrated to Detroit between June 1940 and June 1943, resulting in a total Negro population of about 210,000. An estimated 500,000 southern whites were living in Detroit and adjacent areas (Brown, 1944, p. 506; Bureau of Census Series CA-3: 1944, pp. 7-8). The non-white population was 11 per cent of the city's population in 1940 and 13 per cent in 1944. The influx of Negroes and southern whites into Detroit is similar to the migration of the Jews into the Pale, except that the American migration was largely unplanned, except for the labor recruiting programs of corporations.

Just as Jews were concentrated in their ghetto in Kishinew, the Negroes were jammed into their thirty-block ghetto of Paradise Valley. This area, congested for years, had to bear the brunt of the wartime influx, and increase in population of around 33 per cent. That the Negro was not content with this type of living was expressed in his effort to secure federal housing and this attempt culminated in the Sojourner

---

4. (Stahlin, 1939, p. 655). The unsettled conditions in Russia, indicating a lack of consensus, struggle at new definitions of the situation (pp. 599-686). *Die Judenpogrome*, I, pp. 267-292, discusses the organization of pogroms as part of the function of the Russian bureaucracy as a means of intimidating revolutionary activities.

Truth Project. Bad housing, however, was not merely a Negro problem. Competition for services in housing, transportation, recreation, education, the problem of the cost of living, were common to all. All these factors, compounded with the tensions and anxieties of the war, may have interacted to lower the threshold of control and excitability. The struggle for the allocation of goods and services may have intensified the unstable relation of domination and unwilling submission between whites and Negroes.

The Negro coming to the North discovered shackles slightly less onerous than those he was trying to escape (Bontemps and Conroy, 1945, pp. 147-162 and 213-239). He found himself living among groups emphasizing emotionality and hate. The apocalyptic religion of the South found expression in numerous small groups. Brown estimated about 2,500 active southern-born evangelists (*op. cit.*, p. 8). In addition to the small fry evangelists there were the blood, sweat and fear virtuosos such as the Rev. Gerald L. K. Smith, the Rev. J. Frank Norris, the pistol-packing parson, and others. Of the many non-religious groups indulging in violence, threats, and expressions of hate, the most notorious was the Black Legion. When this group was broken up under FBI investigation, it diversified into many other groups, such as the Black Guards, Bullet Club, and Modern Patriots (Bontemps and Conroy, 1943, p. 224; Carlson, 1943 and 1946).

Relations between Negroes and city officials, especially police officers, were unfavorable. There was a negative relation with those Negro leaders who endeavored to improve the lot of their group, and an essentially corrupt and parasitic relation with those Negroes involved in the policy and numbers racket. Negro arrests and treatment by police also developed mutual attitudes of suspicion and fear. Discussing the 1943 riot, Commissioner of Police Witherspoon frequently referred to this hostile relation between his department and the Negro, the perpetuation of which he blamed on the Negro (Lee and Humphrey, 1943, p. 53).

Lynchings are almost past history in this country, but riots are not, and they may in the future substitute for lynchings. The struggle with regard to superordination and subordination is thus carried from the country into the urban centers where it continues on a group rather than on an individual basis. The first series of major riots involving the Negro occurred during the period of World War I, with riots in Chicago (1919), East St. Louis (1917), and Washington, D.C. (1919). Detroit had a minor riot over Negroes in the Sweet case of 1926. Harlem broke loose in 1935 and in 1943. It was during the second World War that relations between whites and non-whites became much worse. *The Negro Handbook* (Murray, 1944) lists seven military riots, several civilian riots, and three industrial hate strikes or sit-downs in 1942; in 1943, five military riots, nine civilian riots, five industrial hate strikes and/or riots. Mass violence against the Negro and others was nothing new to this country.

EVENTS LEADING TO THE RIOT

IN KISHINEW

The vice-governor of Bessarabia conducted an informal and active persecution of Jews on his own account for several years prior to the 1903
pogrom. He and his sub-officials traveled through Bessarabia and under
any pretext or excuse or interpretation of laws and administrative
decrees, they would extort money from the Jews, close their business or
synagogue, or drive them away. Vice-governor Ostrogoff thus gave an
apparent official sanction to Jewish persecution, and his attitude and
actions encouraged the lower ranks of the bureaucracy to indulge in
petty persecutions of their own.

The accusation of ritual-murder was made once in 1902 and twice in
1903. The local paper had to print a retraction of its charges but the
retraction implied that Jews were securing special privilege and protection in their attacks on Christians. Fearing outbreaks, the rabbi of
Kishinew asked the leading Greek bishop to issue an episcopal assurance that Jews did not practice ritual-murder and that Jews were not
responsible for the local deaths. The bishop refused, implying that there
were some Semitic sects that did practice such a ritual.

Six years before the riot the local paper was revived as a most violent
anti-Semitic paper. As censor, the vice-governor Ostrogoff, a regular
contributor under a pseudonym, could have curtailed the paper's violence on grounds of public safety and welfare. For five years the
Bessarabetz fulminated against the Jews as swindlers, liars, parasites,
and exploiters of the Christian population, ritual-murderers, etc. and
continuously called upon the Christian population to rise and strike
down the Jews. Since it was the only paper in Kishinew, counter-propa-
ganda by the Jews was almost impossible. Articles in the paper were
directed to the police, soldiers, workingmen, seminarists, and to the
minor employees of the post office, telegraph, and other public departments. Articles were headed: "Death to the Jews," "Crusade against
the Hated Race," "Down with the Disseminators of Socialism." The
editors of the paper also organized a pure Christian Welfare society. Its
members bought weapons and printed handbills and posters which were
distributed in great quantities. One of these stated that on the basis of
an ukase of the Tsar, Christians were permitted to hold a judgment of
blood over Jews during the three Easter holidays.

IN DETROIT

Contributing to the development of the riot of 1943 was a series of
minor riots. During 1941 there was an anti-Negro strike at the Ford

River Rouge Plant, a student strike and fracas against Negroes at the Northwestern High School, and a series of fights between Polish youths and Negroes. The Sojourner Truth Project riot occurred in 1942. Federal troops guarded the entrance of Negroes into this housing project. This riot was not wholly spontaneous and unplanned. Local authorities, moreover, did not push an investigation, and no convictions resulted from detained "key" persons. Between March and the end of May 1943, there were hate strikes against Negroes in five different industrial plants. In the next month the major riot broke out.

DURATION OF THE RIOT

IN KISHINEW

From noon, Sunday, April 5 to Monday 5:00 p.m., April 6.

IN DETROIT

From Sunday, 10:30 p.m., June 20, to Monday, 11:00 p.m., June 21.

PERSONNEL

IN KISHINEW

Rioters included soldiers, policemen, civil servants, priests, peasants, laborers, students and seminarists, petit bourgeois, and a group of imported pug-uglies. Members of polite society, professional groups, and upper bourgeois participated primarily as spectators, but at times taking some of the loot, at times encouraging the rioters. With few exceptions, soldiers and policemen sided with the rioters. Peasants were especially imported from the countryside to participate. Rioters were predominantly from lower strata and their attacks were directed primarily against lower strata and moderately wealthy Jews. Rich Jews purchased immunity with bribes paid to both military and police officials. Actual leaders of the rioters were youths in the late teen ages and early twenties.

IN DETROIT

Both Negro and white were rioters. Both sexes were included, though the greatest proportion was male. According to the prosecutor's report, 35 per cent detained in the riot were under 21 years and 63 per cent under 31 years of age. Of detained Negroes, 23 percent were under 21 years and of white 48 percent were under 21 years (Lee and Humphrey, 1943, p. 82). Youthful whites were also the leaders of mob groups, egged on in many cases by vociferous white females. Police were either help-less or negligent and on the whole took the side of the whites as demonstrated in the ratio of arrests, 12 Negro to 1 white (Murray, 1944, p. 44).

ORGANIZATION OF THE RIOT

In Kishinew

The pogrom was organized by a group of citizens of Kishinew with the tacit approval and support of governmental officials. Actual leaders of the riots were students and seminarists disguised as laborers and strangers. The riot began when a gang of 10 to 15 year old boys began to attack and molest Jews to test the reaction of the police. Since the police merely dispersed the gang without making any arrests, the action was interpreted favorably. Three hours later about two hundred men wearing red shirts (a working class symbol) split up into 24 sections composed of 10 to 15 men. Jewish quarters then were attacked simul-taneously in 24 parts of the city. The first effort was directed to the looting and destruction of Jewish homes and shops. In the evening a group of peasants was imported. Then all Jewish homes and stores were marked with white chalk, a process in which some policemen assisted. A system of communication between the various gangs was established with students and seminarists on bicycles. A new attack began at 3:00 a.m. on Monday. The gangs were composed of 10 to 20 persons, these numbers occasionally swelling to 80 or 100. This time not only looting, destruction, and plundering took place, but attacks on persons of all ages and sexes, murder, beating, and rape became common until the riot gradually played out, and martial law was declared.

In Detroit

The most accepted version is that the riot was precipitated by a fist fight between a Negro and a white man at Belle Isle. The major part of the rioting was concentrated in a two-mile area. In this riot, crowds of whites and crowds of Negroes fought each other, or an individual of either color would be set upon by a group of opposite color. Looting, plundering, and pillaging involved both white and Negro stores. These stores, however, were in the Negro area. Since Negroes were so con-centrated, whites marched and rode in from other areas of the city to participate in the rioting. Groups gathered at street car lines, the-atres, schools, and other strategic points. Actual leadership was taken over by teenage boys, who were egged on by older men. Pitched battles were fought between police and Negroes, one at the Frazer Hotel and the other at a three-story apartment building.

METHODS OF CONTROL

IN KISHINEW

Jews tried unsuccessfully to secure the intervention of officials and of the Greek bishop in curtailing rumors and the attacks of the *Bessarabets*. Provincial officials grudgingly agreed to furnish some protection. City officials ignored the requests of Jewish delegations. Even though the criminal code granted the governor discretion to use soldiers as a supplementary force to the police, an appeal to him on the morning of the riot was fruitless. His excuse was that he had received no order from Petersburg to use troops. The governor then forbade the sending of private telegrams and turned over the administration of the province to his assistant Ostrogoff. A telegram finally declaring martial law arrived too late.

IN DETROIT

As in Kishinew the police were either helpless, negligent, or actual participants in furthering the riot. Efforts of the police were predominantly directed against the Negro. Press and radio reports added to the general excitement rather than endeavoring to induce calm. Appeals by Mayor Jeffries, small neighborhood groups, Negro pastors, and leading labor officials came to nothing. Rioting stopped only when federal troops went into action. The securing of federal troops was unduly delayed because the governor did not want to declare martial law and state and city officials were hazy as to the procedure in securing troops. Police leadership appeared equally inept. The police commissioner refused to swear in Negro deputies and declared the riot under control when it was actually becoming worse.

RESULTS

IN KISHINEW

Killed—44; seriously wounded and injured—583; houses wrecked—700; shops and small stores looted and damaged—600; people requiring relief—10,000; families ruined in business and employment—2,000. The economic activities of the town were almost paralyzed for several days.

Ensuing trials did not result in any marked convictions. Judges and the state's attorney put all blame on the Jews. Official statements by the Russian government also placed all blame on the Jews.

IN DETROIT

Killed—34 (25 Negro, of which 17 were killed by the police); several hundred persons more or less seriously wounded; two million dollars property damage.

All official government reports, whether issued by the city or state government, blamed the Negroes for causing the riot. They also exonerated the police and state militia and the city and state officials for the way in which they handled the riot.

CONCLUSION

We conclude that if the conditions specified below are present, then the likelihood of rioting and violence is very high. If there is an alteration in any of these conditions, the likelihood is less; and it is even less if several of these phases are absent.

1. *Historical context.* A transitional period, such as industrialization, or a period involving unusual stresses and strains, such as a major war; within this period considerable horizontal and vertical mobility; a history of violence against the subordinate group.

2. *The role of the subordinate group.* An outstanding trait or characteristic, such as religion or color, which serves as a focal point for negative assessments, and minor constellations of value judgments and traditional negative beliefs; the subordinate group is regarded as an undesirable competitor for services, goods, control of market, and the allocation of occupations; the group is officially or unofficially segregated; the group is engaged in a struggle for subsistence or is struggling to improve its status against historical traditions and controls which hold it in an inferior status.

3. *The role of established authorities and law.* Law assigns the minority group a second or third rate role as citizen, and the group attempts to change this legal status; violence or incipient violence (on the part of constituted authorities) is either officially approved or tacitly supported either on top levels or in some lower ranks where such sponsorship may be open and unabashed; there is a relation of hatred and suspicion between minority group and authorities; and a pattern of petty exaction, bribery and corruption; authorities do not want to assume responsibility for control of a riot or there is administrative confusion as to the control of a riot.

4. *The role of associations.* There are one or more associations whose

major function is devoted to propaganda, defamation, and advocation of violence against the minority group.

5. *Role of press and other means of communication.* The press as official or covert policy indulges in race-minority baiting, or in general reports the group in an unfavorable way, i.e., reinforces prevailing negative assessments; the minority does not have or has limited access to the agencies of mass contact, particularly those reaching the members of the dominant group.

6. *Personnel.* Upper class, professionals, and more wealthy merchants contribute indirectly through the circulation of rumors, and some may participate more actively in the organization of a riot if they have an opportunity to gain by the elimination of competition; as a rule they will be morbid bystanders or by voice and gesture encourage rioters; students and marginal employed workers in the late teens and early twenties are the leaders and active participants, i.e., an older youth phenomenon; older rioters are primarily of the same social stratum as those against whom they are rioting, laborers against laborers, shop-keepers against shopkeepers, etc.

In a general way we know already the major phases given above from some studies made of riots in our country, but many of these studies deal with one incident. The significance of the cross-cultural comparison lies in a check on these findings, and this comparison corroborates them.

The race-minority riot as a type consists of the six enumerated points. The construct refers to a confluence of actions that end in violence. It is the working together of these various actions that logically culminates in a riot. These actions expressed in the many propositions about a riot pattern can be subsumed under three principles of social interaction. We understand and explain riots in the interrelation of these principles: (1) deliberately maintained opposite inclinations; (2) the augmentation of negative relations; (3) dissociative complementary inclinations (Hiller, 1947, pp. 179-180). These relations are buttressed by negative extrinsic valuations and the withholding of intrinsic valuations. When these apply to the racial or minority groups within a particular society, one possible and very likely consequence is a riot.

Richard Sterba

Some Psychological Factors in Negro Race Hatred and in Anti-Negro Riots

In this paper I shall make no attempt to explain fully the phenomena of race antagonism and of race hatred, since I feel myself inadequate to this task. A complicated and deeply rooted phenomenon such as that of race hatred has multiple causes, many of them in the sociological and economic fields and I am not able to deal with this problem from these angles. The excellent study by Gunnar Myrdal, *An American Dilemma,* shows the complexity of the phenomenon and multiplicity of those factors that produce it and illuminate its importance. My contribution will be limited to the psychological field. The material was gathered from patients, particularly during the Negro race riots in Detroit during June of 1943. This clinical material obtained from analyses, together with well-known facts concerning the race riots, made it possible to draw conclusions as to some deeper and unconscious motivations which lead to the constant antagonism against Negroes on the part of many white people, as well as to exacerbation into the form of the group-psychological phenomenon of the Negro race riots. The results fitted so well into the hypothesis that psychoanalysis, or rather Freud, had developed with regard to the origin of human groups that the communication of these observations and thoughts seemed further justified from the theoretical standpoint. . . .

From the clinical material obtained in our practical analytic work we are forced to conclude that the negative attitude toward Negroes has a twofold origin, and that it therefore manifests itself in two different forms of hatred and aggression. The first form is the constant and general antagonism against the Negroes, and includes all members of the race. It is expressed in the general trend of many white people to "draw the color line," i.e., either to keep or to drive the Negro out of the community, of the social circle, of particular jobs or of certain localities. Negroes are considered, or better, experienced emotionally, as unwelcome intruders. The mere idea that they could be accepted by members of the social group, to which the antagonistic white person belongs, creates horror and most irrational and violent reactions, which, through their very violence and lack of reason, betray their origin in parts of the mind that are not controlled by reason, consideration and altruism, but by vehement, impetuous desires such as we find in the unconscious, or the id, that "cauldron of seething excitement" (Freud, *A New Series of Introductory Lectures on Psycho-*

analysis). Locked up through repression, and preserved through the lack of participation in the development of the rest of the personality, these desires retain in the unconscious their infantile character and aims, since the main repressions take place in early childhood. The primitive mechanism of displacement, i.e., the substitution of another object for that originally tied up with the infantile emotional desire, enables the repressed tendencies even in the adult person to find some outlet with the substitute object. The irrationality and impetuosity of the emotional reaction, and the flimsy rationalizations by which it is explained are indications of its infantile origin in the unconscious.

We know of a specific infantile reaction that shows this characteristic of intense hostility and this tendency to keep out or to drive out, which is re-enacted with Negroes as substitute objects. It is the reaction to the arrival of a newcomer into the family, an infant brother or sister. The older child develops extreme jealousy of the younger sibling, often openly shows his disapproval, or his hatred and disgust, and has only one desire: to do away with the newcomer, or to shut him out from acceptance by the family. Whoever has observed children, or has analyzed adults and their infantile reactions to younger siblings as they are preserved in the unconscious, is deeply impressed by the intensity of the negative reaction of the older child to the new member of the family. It often expresses itself in direct aggression against the baby, and only gradually and not without repeated relapses is this jealousy overcome and replaced by more friendly feelings. The hostility is repressed, but preserved in the unconscious, and then directed against the Negroes as a substitute object. In this respect the Negroes signify *younger siblings*. As such they are unwelcome, and every attempt is made to keep them out of the social group of white people, which represents an enlarged family. Out of many dreams of patients I choose two which are very revealing in this respect. The first patient's dream occurred at a time when his hostility against his younger brother was the main subject of the analytic investigation, and it ran as follows:

The patient is in his parents' house. A group of Negroes are attacking the house, and are ready to set it on fire. This danger is all of a sudden removed by a magical procedure; the Negroes are all transformed into small balls of protoplasm which are contained in a bottle, so that they can easily be disposed of by emptying the bottle into the sink.

It can easily be recognized that the Negroes are re-converted into ovula in the womb, and the dreamer indicates that in this way he can get rid of them, in that the womb is emptied. Their significance as younger siblings is clear from the dream and from the analytic material of sibling rivalry during which the dream occurred.

The second patient's dream occurred at a time when the patient had signed affidavits for a refugee family in Europe, who were distant relatives of his, so that they could obtain immigration visas for the United

States. He felt obliged to do this at the request of his family, but inwardly resented it and was afraid that his dominating position in the family might be threatened, since this refugee family consisted of the patient's family. After signing the affidavits the patient dreamed:

A big boat approaches New York harbor. The patient is on a small raft nearby. Some Negroes jump from the porthole of the boat into the water. The patient drives his raft toward them and crushes the Negroes between his raft and the side of the big boat.

The patient, who was the oldest of six children, had in his childhood reacted with violently aggressive wishes against each of his newly-arrived siblings. The big ship symbolizes the mother's body, while the jumping into the water typically signifies giving birth to younger siblings, represented in the dream by Negroes. The patient was a violent Negro hater. The newcomers, his younger siblings and Negroes can easily be recognized as identical in this dream. . . .

The *general negative reaction* to and hostility against the Negro race is directed equally against both sexes. Male as well as female Negroes are to be kept out of the family, since in the unconscious they represent unwanted younger siblings. Here lies the cardinal difference from the second unconscious emotional motive for Negro hatred on the part of many white persons, which manifests itself in the *Negro race riot* and is directed against male Negroes only. The deeply emotional and unreasonable origin of this mass psychological phenomenon is obvious to anybody who is not forced by his own unconscious drives to participate in this mass psychological reaction. The race riots in Detroit in June, 1943, provided an excellent opportunity for studying the unconscious motives of white patients in analysis. The findings were surprisingly consistent with some of Freud's theoretical ideas in connection with the primitive group and its development which will therefore be presented in this discussion.

The male Negro as he appeared in dreams of white people even before the race riots often had to be recognized as representative of the dreamer's father, particularly the father at night or in his nocturnal activities. Many dreams of being threatened by a Negro were understood as the expression and repetition of the dreamer's infantile fears of his father. After having recognized this deep-seated equation of Negro with father one is able to understand much better the emotional reactions during the race riots with regard to their unconscious significance. Our attitude in childhood toward our own father is neither exclusively positive nor exclusively negative, but is mixed, and reveals components of love as well as hatred. Such feelings, composed of positive and negative attitudes and tendencies are called *ambivalent*. In the immature and infantile mind they can easily remain and be expressed beside one another, until the growing organization of the conscious personality does away with emotional contradictions and ambivalence through repression of one component; as a rule, in the case of the emotional attitude toward the father, it is the negative one. It disappears from consciousness and can find expression only in disguised form and with substitute objects, if the positive relationship to the father gains the upper hand, which it does in most persons. . . . The violence of the hatred against the Negro, the lack of justification for this hatred in many individuals who have never had unpleasant experiences with Negroes, and the mass psychological implications can be partially understood if we consider the unconscious origin of these strong emotions in the infantile hatred against the father. . . .

Psychologically, Negro race riots are violent outbreaks of infantile father hatred. Negro hatred has its origin in the South, where many white children were and are brought up by a Negro "mammy," toward whom they often develop feelings like those toward a mother. Due to the development of the oedipus complex, the male Negro is then naturally brought into the position of the hated father. The South furnishes the classical example of the race riot in the form of lynching. The rebellious sons unite against the hated father substitute with the aim of killing and castrating him. The inhumanity, cruelty, and brutality with which they proceed reveals the origin of this conduct in the most primitive and barbaric layers of our minds, where it is otherwise buried in the unconscious and is brought forth only under the mass psychological conditions of the riot. The fact that the Negro riot regularly breaks out through the rumor that a Negro has raped a white woman confirms our opinion about its patricidal origin. Almost without exception the riot is then the revenge for the alleged sexual assault upon a white woman by a Negro. We have mentioned that the original father hatred of the little boy in the oedipal situation is the reaction to the sex relations between the parents, which the child considers as acts of violence on the part of the father against the mother. The little boy's aggression against the father's penis and his castrative tendencies are the expression and result of his inferiority feelings concerning the smallness of his own penis. The larger size of the Negro's penis and legends about it seem to play an equally important role in the unconscious emotional reactions leading to race riots. It was interesting to observe that among the most embittered white participants in the race riots in Detroit were adolescents, many of southern origin. Their own sexual immaturity and insecurity made them particularly vicious in their patricidal impulses. The castrative tendency expresses itself either in a direct way during the process of lynching in the South, where not infrequently the genitals of the lynched Negro are cut off, or more often it finds symbolic expression: in the South the victim of the riot is tarred and feathered, which means that he is turned into a bird, and then killed. The bird is an ubiquitous penis symbol (cf. the vulgar term "cock"; or the vulgar German term for intercourse, "vogeln," which literally means "to bird"). In northern parts of the country in accordance with the higher degree of technical development and the higher standard of civilization, the aggression against the Negro's penis is expressed against a penis symbol detached from the victim, namely against the automobile, which stands for the penis in numerous dreams and jokes. The burning automobiles of Negroes on Woodward Avenue during the race riots in Detroit were a ghastly picture of primitive aggression directed against symbolic substitutes at a time when automobiles were not produced due to wartime restrictions, and their loss was irreparable. . . .

. . . Dreams related above [*not included in this abridgement*] make the psychological identity of group hunting and Negro race riots obvious. People who observed the race riots in Detroit from their downtown office windows above the streets where the riots occurred had the definite impression that the Negro was hunted. When he attempted to escape in one direction he was met by a group of white people who chased him back to his first persecutors, or in another direction where he met a third group of "hunters," until he was cornered like an animal and knocked down. The way in which the persecutors shouted at one another, such as "There's one! Get him!" definitely reminded the spectators of hunting scenes. It corresponds to the hunting rituals and to their archaic origin that no Negro women were attacked, and that only males were allowed to be the victims.[1] Hunting and Negro riots, therefore, have the same unconscious origin in patricidal impulses. They both represent repetitions of father murder as it occurred among archaic tribes.

The mass psychological phenomena of the race riots in Detroit are those described as characteristic of short-lived groups in LeBon and Freud. The Detroit race riots showed all the earmarks of regression from individual to most primitive group psychology. Temporary and fleeting leadership was exercised by individuals. In the short-lived groups that were formed during the race riots in Detroit it was noteworthy that they lacked strong leadership, which is otherwise so characteristic of group formations, even of a temporary kind. It may be that the innermost emotional motives for the group formation, namely collective father murder, influenced the structure and character of the groups. It was precisely this fleeting character that contributed to the nervousness and excitement in the city during the riots.

Some pictures taken during the riots and reproduced in newspapers and magazines (*Life,* July 5, 1943) showed very clearly the man-hunting character of the riots, the intensity and viciousness of the aggression and the satisfaction over the injury or slaughter of the victim. Groups standing around a Negro lying on the ground, their faces still wild with aggressive excitement, can easily be taken as revivification of the

---

1. We assume that the same unconscious motives were active in Negroes persecuting white men during the riots, but we have no material available to prove this assumption.

sons of the primitive group standing around the primal father whom they had murdered.

Kenneth B. Clark and James Barker

The Zoot Effect in Personality: A Race Riot Participant

This case is presented and analyzed for the following reasons:

1. It vividly illustrates the impact of racial prejudice and social isolation upon the personality of an individual who is a victim of such circumstances.

2. Through an understanding of this case it is possible to observe some implications of the pathology of racial prejudice not only in reference to its effects upon the individual but also in reference to the stability of the society as a whole.

3. It presents a clear picture of a personality undergoing a process of disintegration. Similar case studies might lead to insights concerning ways to check these patently disintegrative processes and stabilize the personality.

4. When racial problems and conflicts are seen in the light of their effects upon individual persons rather than in broad, general, detached statistical terms, their psychological significance becomes clearer and the practical implications for an applied social psychology become inescapable.

DESCRIPTION OF RESPONDENT

R. is a dark-brown-skinned Negro, 18 years old. He was born in New York City. For the past two years he has lived alone in a rooming-house in the center of Harlem. His mother, who is separated from his father, does not have "enough room" for him to live with her, although she visits him frequently "to see how he was getting along."

He was attending a vocational high school irregularly before he was notified by his draft board that he would be inducted into the Army. Then he decided to stop school and "have some fun" before his induction.

His recreational activities were limited to attending moving pictures, occasional nonmembership contacts with the community YMCA, and membership in a neighborhood "cellar club" or gang.

When asked whether he attended church, he replied: "Yeah, I go to the Baptist Church once a year, Christmas."

Comic books (particularly *Bat Man*) and the New York *Daily News* dominate his reading.

It is the opinion of the interviewer that this respondent was one of the brightest members of a group of Civilian Defense messengers with whom he had periodic contact. He not only appeared to be superior in intelligence but also definitely possessed qualities of leadership.

At the time that R. was interviewed he was dressed in his usual manner: He wore rusty brown shoes, striped blue socks, extremely pegged pants (narrow at ankles and wide at knee), a quite long jacket, a worn white shirt with open collar, no tie, and a hat with an extremely wide brim. These complied with the basic requirements of the "zoot suit" styles.

When the interviewer saw him for the first time on the evening of the interview he was engaged in animated conversation with two other members of his CD messenger unit. He was telling his audience what he was going to do when he got into the Army—that he wanted to be assigned to the cavalry unit so that he could ride a horse. His demonstrations and acting which accompanied his conversations indicated genuine talent. He often changed his voice to make a narrated conversation sound more realistic. A sawed-off broomstick which he held in his hands was used as a convenient prop, sometimes as a nightstick and sometimes as a rifle.

During the course of this conversation, R., *unprompted by the interviewer, began to discuss the 1943 Harlem riot and his role in it.* The riot had taken place about a month before this. The interviewer, realizing that this was an excellent opportunity to obtain a case record from an active participator in the riot, desired to take notes on his conversation as he talked, but realized that this might inhibit him, and therefore decided against it.

After he finished his account to the group, the interviewer casually said to R., "You ought to write a book." He replied (probably because he knew that the interviewer was a college student), "Why don't you— are you going to write a book?" This gave the interviewer an opportunity to tell him that he would like a record of his account of his experiences in the riot. He readily agreed to cooperate and the interviewer immediately made arrangements to interview him in a private office.

During the interview he was anxious to have every word recorded just as he said it. He was proud to be interviewed and was extremely entertaining and cooperative. He walked, sometimes stalked, up and down as if he were imitating the behavior of big business men dictating to their secretaries, as portrayed in the moving pictures. Every now and then he would stop and say: "What you got there?", "Read it back to me." At the end of the interview he said, "Lemme know how your book comes out."

INTERVIEW IN SUBJECT'S OWN WORDS

The following excerpts are indicative of R.'s rejection of ordinary social values; the complete absence of sympathy in observing physical brutality inflicted upon other individuals and the absence of guilt feelings in reference to his own participation in antisocial behavior:

1. Before the riot starts I was in the Harlem Dump Theater, where the bed-bugs and roaches and rats and cats run across the floor. (*This statement appears to indicate some insight into and resentment of the ghetto-like deprivation of his environment. It is of interest, however, that no similar statement recurs in the rest of the interview.*) Some two-by-four motherfucker runs in there and says that: "Harlem is on fire!" The niggers jump up half full of juice and running for the goddam door, me leading of course. As we got out the door a sawed-off son-of-a-bitch runs by with 15 of Crawford's and Howard's suits, and pegged pants, a root suit with a reet pleat, and a stuffed cuff started the shit off. By this time the niggers have tored-off half of Harlem. So as the friend of mine that's writing this sweet line of B.S., the shit roves from 11 o'clock that nite 'til about 5 o'clock next morning. By this time half a Harlem is on fire.

2. The riot started when a colored man got shot. About half hour later the riot was goin' full blast, and the people was going 'round stores. They was fucking up the place. Quite naturally the party writing this was in it. They fucked up '25th St. badly. They hit shoe stores, beat the shit out of a cop standing there unmercifully. A 16-year-old boy hit a 'fay (*White*) boy with glasses on— blast his fucking head off. While they bashed his head in unmercifully, the party that you're writin' about goes in a store and helps himself to the man's cash register. The store next to the A & P—goes in there. There was nothin' there. While I goes in there a lady was stealin' a man's big half-a-cow. While she was comin' out a cop was askin' her "where in the hell she was goin'"— she said: "Kiss my ass!"

Back on '25th Street. They steals the man's goddam material—beats the shit out of a coupla cops—which was great for me. As I was coming out some son-of-a-bitch busses a window and a piece of glass catches my leg (*showed gash*). Then I really got mad.

R.'s attitude toward social authority, police, and the army is revealed by paragraphs 3, 4, and 5 of his interview. His complete disregard for the ordinary social prestige values of a stable society is particularly evident in his phantasy description of the incident involving the mayor's attempt to restore order.

3. P.S. I lef' out a little bit. I jumped in a fur store, got myself $300 in cash, was on my way out the mother-fuckin' store. A big white bastard stood up in

front of the door, cop of course, hit me in my head with that big ass night-stick, which really rocked my brains, and told me to empty out my pockets. He found $300 on me and called another cop. Then the other cop tells the cop that hit me to let the black bastard go—takin' the $300 and puttin' it in his pocket.

4. Whoever is goin' to read this little letter of introduction, let him know it was hell down here. By time you read this I will be fighting for Uncle Sam, the bitches, and I do not like it worth a dam. I'm not a spy or saboteur, but I don't like goin' over there fightin' for the white man—so be it.

5. Well, John the Man *(Mayor LaGuardia)* comes over; he jumps up and hollers, "Good people of Harlem," and before he could get the rest of the words out of his mouth a brick smacked him up side his head. He jumps down, jumps in his car and goes to his Castle-a-Bunk-a *(home)*, knocks himself out some shut-eye, has three or four Johns *(policemen)* outside of his door to keep the niggers from runnin' cross his ass while he is sleep. The next morning he jumps out his Castle-a-Bunk-a and hollers: "Good people of Harlem, restore order!" Well if you do not know the rest, any time you wish to see a riot start it up again.

Further evidence of R.'s rejection of socially accepted values and his acceptance of values peculiar to a restricted, distorted, antisocial environment and perspective is to be found in his description of the riots in paragraphs 6, 7, 8, and 9. That his callous, unsympathetic attitude is not restricted to whites but extends to Negroes and even to himself is also evident in these excerpts and in the interview as a whole.

6. P.S.S. (stands for P.S.): Well as I was runnin' up 8th Ave. cops was whipping guys' asses left and right. Well I managed to miss an ass whippin' 'til I got to 125th Street and Lenox Ave. Just as I get to Lenox Ave. and '25th Street a white man was comin' down the street toward the subway, which he couldn't get into. Some young colored hoodlums beat the shit out of him, bashin' his glasses into his head. The man takes his hand and put it into his pocket and emptying his pocket into the street with the little money he had, which wuz a damn dumb thing to do. Back up to St. Nicholas Ave. and 125th Street. The colored people of Harlem, evil as they are, got mad. A trolley car comes along packed with 'fay people *(white people)* and a few colored people grabbing the trolley and the conductor to keep him from drivin' the trolley, while other people throw rocks and stones into the window causing serious accidents. Half-juiced *(half-drunk)* the rest of the people grabs the trolley and begins lifting it into the air while the other people that was in the trolley climbs the window. By this time everybody was in a panic and I ain't kidding. Liftin' the trolley considerably in the air, the cops run over to the scene of the crime and start whippin' asses like hell, beats one colored man dam near to death before he let go the trolley.

7. B.S.: One boy broke into Busch, located 125th Street and 7th Avenue. A flatfoot with a sawed-off rifle watches the boy when he enters the store, waits 'til the boy comes out, draw the bead on the boy an' begins to fire. A colored lady jumps in front of the cop, turns her black ass up the cop and tells him: "Why don't you shoot me in the back?" The cop gets excited when the rest of the crowd begins to walk over, puts the rifle down, lowered it rather, and

walks away. By this time there's more blood—blue blood—in the streets of Harlem. Tired as I am from runnin', I decides to go home. Tired of gettin' my ass whipped. Goes upstairs bloody as a bat, tries to knock myself a little shut-eye.

8. Well I have told my story as I see it. I hope that it will do you some good, cause it meant my ass gettin' whipped. That's why I'm here to tell you. B.S.: As I was stealin' I had a croaker-sack *(burlap bag)* load with soup to nuts. I have a radio in the bottom of the sack. Coming along half-juiced and half-so, more juiced than ever, some son-of-a-bitch—can't steal around Harlem without gettin' some stole from you—cuts the bottom of the croaker-sack and helps himself to my radio.

Walkin' a little ways, they caught a 'fay, beatin' the hell outa him half to death. The man pulls the same shit that the other one did, throwing the money into the air and runnin' like hell. The boys was fightin' left and right for a two dollar bill, tearin' it in half; one of the boys say: "You gimme your half!", the other one says: "You gimme your half!" Stubborn as they was, neither one of them gave in. As tired as I was I was scuffling, I gets myself $50.

Grabbing a white man and using him for a block buster, heaves his ass through a big grocery store winda, cut the man considerably. Along comes Johnny Bull *(policemen)* marchin' him and his bloody ass off to the hospital.

B.S.: A cop was runnin' along whippin' the hell outa colored man like they do in slaughter pen. Throwin' him into the police car, or struggle-buggy, marchin' him off to the jail. That's that! Strange as it may seem, ass whippin' is not to be played with. So as I close my little letter of introduction, I leave this thought with thee:

Yea, so it be
I leave this thought with thee
Do not attempt to fuck with me.
(An expression of manifest defiance even though stated in characteristic humorous vein)

Yours truly,
? ? ? ? ?
P.S., B.S.

Voluntary after-thoughts in R.'s own words:

Remember the picture in the newspapers of those boys in the top hats and full dress coats with sleeves down to here *(demonstrates)*? Well, I know one of them and I told him he'd better take 'em off. He said: "Aw, man, I'm havin' fun." I know his brother, too. Well that bastard is makin' time in jail now.

People was fittin' on shoes and stuff. One old bastard was juiced, and he was sittin' down with some new shoes. And he had a bottle between his legs like this *(demonstration)*. I saw one dummy where the vest was glued on. A son-of-a-bitch took the whole goddam dummy into a hallway and stripped it. I had a fine pair of Florsheim bantam weights, but niggers grabbed one of them. I was goin' to hock that shit, sell it, or wear it. The only thing I took wuz money. The rest of that shit was too hot. I wasn't figurin' on spending no time in jail. I saw a nigger with a big slab o' bacon on his shoulder that night. Man I went out and had a bacon sandwich. I ain't lyin'. I saw one bastard breakin' his back with a sack of flour. I didn't steal no dam food. One woman was sendin' her daughter out and tellin' her that if anyone troubled her to say: "I sent you out." I was eatin' and eatin'. I grabbed a hunk of bologna and just chewed it all the way down on one side *(this was demonstrated with the stick representing the bologna).* They messed up in sugar, walking in it, pissed in it, and one woman come up there with a bag and just pushed the messed up sugar aside with her hands and filled up her bag. She said: "Sugar is scarce, you know." I said: "Yes ma-a-am."

"Is there anything else you would like to say?" the interviewer asked at the close of the free interview.

"No."

"Anything you want to emphasize?"

"PEACE! for it is truly wonderful. It's a old sayin' of Father Divine."

SUMMARY IMPRESSIONS

R.'s account of the events of the Harlem riot cannot be approached as if it were a description of these events as they actually occurred. There are many statements of this respondent which cannot be reconciled with the objectively determined facts of this incident. The significance of this interview is to be found in its psychological implications; what it reveals about R.'s phantasies, desires, perspective, and the pattern of distortion of a personality which becomes compatible with proud participation in acts of racial group violence.

The major indices of distortion, if not disintegration of the personality of this respondent, are:

1. There is a complete lack of manifest guilt feelings in reference to his own participation in antisocial acts.

2. There is an habitual, seemingly deliberate, disregard of even the simple rules of grammar in his ordinary speech—probably a specific indication of a generalized defiance of the larger society.

3. There is an excessive use of profanity in ordinary conversation even in the presence of individuals whom he obviously respects—indicating the possibility that these words have been used with such frequency by the individual that they either become meaningless or are another symptom of habitual social defiance and cynicism. They become "normal" for his rigidly restricted ideational and behavioral sphere.

4. A complete lack of manifest sympathy, sorrow, or other human feelings in observing and reporting acts of brutality inflicted upon another or even upon himself. This cannot be ascribed to the objectivity of his report since it is certainly not objective. Further, this index is consistent with the overall pattern of his personality as indicated in the specific interview situation and as observed in general.

5. A general tendency to engage in exhibitionistic exaggeration, bordering upon phantasy, in descriptions of events in which he was

allegedly involved. The same exhibitionism is shown in his general language and in his dress.

6. A definite rejection of social authority, *i.e.*, prestige of public administrators and police.

This manifest process of distortion and disintegration in a personality who otherwise could be described as "intelligent" and having "qualities of leadership" and who shows by his description of the riot in which he participated a subtle sense of humor demands some clarifying dynamic interpretation.

The peculiar structure of R.'s personality and perspective as revealed by this interview seems best described by the term, "the zoot effect." [1] The "zoot effect" in American culture appears to manifest itself when the human personality has been socially isolated, rejected, discriminated against, and chronically humiliated. It is the consequence of the attempts of the individual to stabilize himself and maintain some ego-security in the face of these facts. It is not primarily a racial phenomenon since a given person of any race who is subjected to the determining conditions may manifest this effect in personality structure.

It appears evident that the degree to which this effect exists as a part of total personality pattern may vary from individual to individual —from zero to complete saturation.

Together with the obvious characteristics of R. outlined above, this "zoot effect" may involve other expressive characteristics also found in R.; *i.e.*, modifications of language (deliberately ungrammatical), high saturation of slang or profane words in ordinary speech, manner and inflection of speech, swagger or exaggeration of some aspect of style of walking, and, more obvious and widely recognized, manner of dress. In short it appears to represent an observable deviation in style of life (veering toward the asocial, or toward those areas which permit within the larger social framework certain exhibitionistic patterns) of many individuals living within, but not a part of, the larger cultural and societal context.

The distortions in perspective and social values which seem inevitably to accompany the "zoot effect" may best be interpreted as follows: The generally accepted social values have definite meaning and stabilizing function for only those individuals who are a part of, and permitted free interaction with, the larger unrestricted social field. These values seem to have little meaning or function for the individual who has been deliberately and involuntarily isolated and rejected from the functions and benefits of the society as a whole. Socially desirable values, there-

1. The choice of this term represents an attempt to get a clear, summary term which would indicate a complicated process of personality organization within a given set of field forces. It should not be interpreted as implying any narrow social evaluative connotation. The term "zoot suit" has had widespread use with definite disparagement and ridicule. It is again emphasized that no such meaning is implied by the use of the term "zoot effect."

fore, having no meaning and function for such an individual who is forced to develop within a humiliating, contracted social field, are discarded. The individual appears then to construct for himself or to acquire from his restricted field new values which are appropriate to his restricted status. These new values may be antisocial but it appears that the important factor for such an individual is not the larger social acceptability of his values or perspective, but rather whether they serve the function of stabilizing his ego which had been threatened by the larger society, and whether they tend to give him some security, relative prestige and status in the restricted caste to which he has been relegated and therefore forced to seek his primary social adjustment.

It seems probable that the "zoot effect" also involves a pattern of conscious or unconscious protest against society-at-large which has imposed restrictive and humiliating conditions upon individuals and groups. It is clear that many of the facets of the "zoot effect" are antisocial—unconcern for the value of human personality as such or for property rights. It may be that the disregard of property rights stems out of a basic desire for revenge and incipient aggression against this seemingly very important aspect (property) of the larger society. This may also be one of the symbolic attempts—conscious or unconscious—of the individual further to stabilize himself and seek ego-security by indicating to a society which he perceives as rejecting him that he in turn has rejected this larger society, its values, its ideals, and its property. Further it seems that what appears to be a permeating cynicism and callous indifference to the human and material values of the larger society is essentially an imperative mechanism of the individual, utilized for the purpose of concealing a deep-seated hurt or scars in his personality.

Racial stereotyping and concepts of inherent antisocial tendencies of certain races are clearly incompatible with the above interpretation. Rather it suggests that the stability of the individual personality and the stability of the larger society are inextricably interrelated and therefore the socially accepted dehumanization of an individual or group must inevitably manifest itself in societal disturbances.

Kenneth B. Clark

Group Violence: A Preliminary Study of the Attitudinal Pattern of Its Acceptance and Rejection
A Study of the 1943 Harlem Riot

THE PROBLEM

There have been few psychological studies of the nature of the individual's motivational pattern which would determine participation in violent group behavior. Meier, Menninga and Stolz (1941) attempted to deal somewhat with this problem when they asked 79 male and 45 female college students to answer questions as, "Would you join a mob if you knew you would not be punished?" They found that 12 per cent of their subjects stated that they would have joined under any circumstances, and 72 per cent would not—while the remainder would have joined conditionally. The authors conclude on the basis of Bernreuter responses the participators are more extroverted and that "early religious training is a dominant drive to deterrence of mob action." There will be reason to discuss this later conclusion below.

Many investigations have shown that interracial riots and mob action are related to certain social inadequacies suffered by both the white and colored groups, e.g., poor housing, poor recreational facilities, transportation inadequacies, discrimination in housing and employment, discriminative higher prices in Negro neighborhoods, etc. These factors are undoubtedly important in understanding the social context within which violent group behavior develops and manifests itself. A subsidiary, transitional area must be explored, however, in order to obtain a more complete understanding of the psychology of group violent behavior. While it is obviously true that the stated environmental inadequacies are causally related to interracial violent group behavior, this relation is clearly not an immediate, direct one. Their causal impact occurs through the mediation of groups of individuals, who are similarly affected and react in concert. In the final analysis and immediate acts, it is people—not conditions—who riot. What are the changes, therefore, that have been brought about in these conditions, in the motivational pattern of people, which make them riot? What are the changes in values and patterns of attitudes which result in the ability of an individual to participate in or condone violent group behavior? What is the difference, if any, in the pattern of attitudes and social values of those who participate in riots (or condone them) from those who condemn or reject this type of violence. These seem to be pertinent questions for psychologists to attempt to answer. An exhaustive, definitive study of this problem would have to include as subjects those individuals who actually participated in riots. It would be desirable to obtain as subjects those people who were detained by the police as riot participants. For the present analysis, this procedure was impossible so therefore the following method of investigation was adopted.

PROCEDURE

Within a month after the Harlem riots a group of social science students interviewed residents and storekeepers of the Harlem area.[1] An attempt was made to approximate a representative sample of individuals. Upon the basis of the interviewer's response to the first question he was classified into one of three groups as follows: (a) Accepted (or condoned), (b) Rejected (or condemned), the riots, or (c) neither accepting nor rejecting.

Table 1 presents the total number of subjects according to percentage of those accepting or rejecting group violence with a breakdown according to sex.

Table 1. Total Negro N = 67: Male 33; Female 34

	ACCEPTED			NEITHER			REJECTED	
N	20		N	7,		N	40	
%	30		%	10		%	60	
Sex	M	F		M	F		M	F
N	13	7	N	4,	3	N	16	24
%	65	35	%	57	43	%	40	60

Interviewees were classified as accepting or rejecting this riot as a form of group protest. The specific problem of this preliminary investigation is, therefore, to what extent is there a demonstrable difference in certain background factors and relevant attitudinal pattern between the group which rejected or condemned and the group which verbally, at least, accepted or condoned this riot?

RESULTS

It can be seen from an analysis of Table 1, that the majority (60 per cent) of the total group of Negroes interviewed rejected and condemned the riot while 30 percent accepted or justified it. An examination of

1. Colored students interviewed colored residents; white students interviewed the white storekeepers. Only the responses of colored residents are reported in this paper.

the protocols indicated a marked divergence in emotional tone of these differentiating responses.

Among the responses of the rejectors there is a strong pattern of personal guilt feelings which seem to play an important part in the expressed attitudes. These guilt feelings, as expressed by such responses as "disgrace to race" or "an awful thing," "a terrible thing," are obviously not found among the acceptors, since this was one basis of differentiating the two groups. The difference between the two groups is not one of degree or quality of emotionality since both groups appear equally emotional.

The major aspects of the general attitude of the rejectors toward the riot is expressed in the following evaluations, "disgrace to the race," "awful—terrible," "senseless—stupid," "ridiculous—silly," "does no good for race," "an opportunity to loot," "unfortunate, pathetic, sorrowful."

More detailed analysis of the responses of the rejectors reveals that those who rejected the riots as being a "disgrace to the race" appeared to be reacting with personal guilt feelings and personal shame. It can be seen from their verbatim reports that they identified themselves (because of racial similarity) with the participants in the riot. They used the first person plural for the most part, giving responses such as "set *us* back."

On the other hand the rejectors who characterized the riots as "awful —terrible" or "senseless—stupid," "ridiculous—silly," do not indicate by their responses any dynamic identification of themselves with the riot participants. They for the most part use the third personal plural ("*they* only hurt themselves") or project the guilt on "Southerners," "vandals," or "conspirators." In fact it is clear that when these moralistic evaluative judgments are made they occur with the attempts of the respondent to dissociate himself completely from the people involved in the riot—in spite of racial similarity.

Examining the responses of the acceptors or condoners of the riot, it is seen that their reactions range from "strong enthusiastic-ecstatic approval" through to "approval for trivial personal benefit." The majority of the acceptors reacted to riot in terms of its being an expression of the pent-up resentment of the Negro—retribution and revenge for their having been cheated. It will be seen that many rejectors mention this point but not in this context. The fact that the rejectors did not mention this point in their response to this initial question, while the acceptors did, developed to be a significant point of difference between these two groups. The further fact that many of the rejectors mention this point later in their interview (Item B, Table 10) is one of the significant areas in which these two groups appear to be quite similar. This peculiar pattern, at the one time involving differences and similarities, can be interpreted only in the light of assuming a differential perspective, and a difference in attitudinal and value weight for a given awareness which is held equally by both groups. This postulate is essential to an interpretation of the results of this report as a whole and must be referred to frequently in this analysis.

COMPARATIVE ANALYSIS OF BACKGROUND MATERIAL OF EACH GROUP

Tables 2 through 8 are practically self-explanatory. The results which

Table 2.

Age	Accepted N	Rejected N	Accepted N	%	Rejected N	%
Above 50	1	4				
46-50	2	1	6	30	7	17.5
41-45	2	2				
36-40	3	7	5	25	10	25.0
31-35	2	3				
26-30	1	5	6	30	14	35.0
21-25	5	9				
16-20	3	9	3	15	9	22.5
Total	20	40				

they present suggest that many of the common sense beliefs concerning the characteristics of the "militant" Negro are open to question. While these are preliminary results in the light of the admitted inadequacies of this study—the fact that the "acceptors" are not actually "participators"—they reveal suggestive information concerning the comparative characteristics of the "militant" vs. the more "conservative" Negro. For this analysis it is assumed that the acceptors or condoners are more militant while the rejectors are more "conservative." An examination with respect to the general tone of the complete interviews of each group indicates that this assumption is not unwarranted.

As can be seen from these tables (2-9) in no area are the differences strikingly marked. However, there are some differences which are of interest because they all appear to be contrary to "common sense" expectations.

Age. Results presented in Table 2 indicate that the younger respondents tend to be more conservative, while the older group is more "militant." It is of interest that in the age groups from 20-30 and from 30-40 there are no differences. It is difficult to reconcile explanation of racial unrest and tensions as due to the increased militance of "younger Negroes" and the stereotype of the "satisfied older Negro" with these results. Rather, these results suggest an increase in militancy in the Negro with an increase in age. This may reflect a crystallization of cumulative social disillusionment into a more structured resentment as the individual grows older.

Education. There is a higher percentage of respondents who *claim* some college training among the more militant group than among the rejectors. On the other hand there is a higher percentage of lower education status among the more conservative (rejectors) group.

Table 3.

Education	ACCEPTED		REJECTED	
	N	%	N	%
Grade	4	20	12	30
High school	9	45	18	45
College	7	35	10	25

Table 4.

Church Attendance	ACCEPTED		REJECTED		Accepted	Rejected
	N	%	N	%		
Never	2	10	1	2.5		
Seldom	9	45	13	32.5	55%	35%
Frequent	4	20	18	45.0	45%	65%
Every Sunday	5	25	8	20.0		

Church Attendance. As can be seen from Table 4 there is a tendency for those who "seldom" or "never" attend church to be somewhat more militant. Those who attend "frequently" or "every Sunday" are more conservative. This finding would tend to support Meier, Menninga and Stolz's conclusion that religious training is a deterrent to mob action. It must be repeated, however, that the acceptors (militant group) are not actual participators or even necessarily would-be participators. Further it should be pointed out, in the light of these results, that religious training as reflected in stated frequency of church attendance does not appear to be an absolute basis (or even an acceptably stable one) of differentiating between "militant" and "conservative" Negroes. Relevant to this point is the fact that a higher percentage (25 per cent) of the acceptor (militant) Negroes state that they attend church every Sunday than do the (20 per cent) rejectors (conservative).

Place of Birth. Table 5 indicates that there is slight tendency for the West Indian Negro, the native New York Negro,[2] and the Southern

Table 5.

Place of birth	ACCEPTED		REJECTED	
	N	%	N	%
Native New York City	4	20	10	25.0
North	5	25	5	12.5
West Indies	4	20	11	27.5
Puerto Rico	1	5	—	—
			*1	no inf.

2. Age factors probably reflected here since this group tends to be younger.

Negro to be conservative in the presented order. The Northern born non-native New Yorker is comparatively the most militant as a group. These tentative results seem contrary to the often stated belief that racial unrest in the north is primarily due to the influx of Southern Negroes "who mistake freedom for license" or that "the West Indian Negro is more radical than the American Negro." It does, however, tend to support the contention that native New Yorkers are likely to be more conservative.

Newspapers Mentioned as Read. As can be seen from Table 6, there is general similarity between the percentage of each group claiming to read each of the listed newspapers, with the exception of *PM* and the *Journal American* readers. *PM,* a crusading newspaper devoting more than the usual amount of space to focus social issues with emphasis upon spotlighting social injustices, had, as would be expected, a higher percentage of claimed readers among the "militant" group. It should be emphasized, however, that of all the respondents who mentioned *PM,* the majority were in the conservative group. Ironically, the one subject who claimed to be a reader of the *Daily Worker,* Communist Party newspaper, was classified among the conservatives. Of the 10 claimed readers of the *Journal American,* a Hearst newspaper, nine were classified among the conservatives and one was classified as "militant." The practically complete identity of the percentage of "militants" and percentage of "conservatives" reading the other papers would indicate that these figures merely reflect circulation and appear in no way related to the attitudinal pattern of "acceptance" or "rejection" of group violence.

Table 6.

Newspapers mentioned as read	ACCEPTED		REJECTED	
	N	%	N	%
News	13	65	27	67.5
P.M.	9	45	13	32.5
Times	8	40	16	40.0
Telegram	3	15	6	15.0
Tribune	3	15	5	12.5
Post	3	15	6	15.0
Mirror	2	10	5	12.5
Journal American	1	5	9	22.5
Sun	1	5	1	2.5
Daily Worker	—	—	1	2.5

Percentages do not add up to 100 because many mention several papers.

Negro Newspapers. Table 7 presents results which indicate that, contrary to some prevalent opinion, the Negro press does not appear to be a significant factor in developing a pattern of attitudes which would

Table 7. *Negro Newspapers*

	ACCEPTED		REJECTED	
	N	%	N	%
A. *Originally and spontaneously mentioned*				
PV	3	15	7	17.5
Amst. News	2	10	10	25.0
Afro.-Amer.	—	—	1	2.5
B. *Mentioned only when specifically prompted*				
PV	8	40	15	37.5
Amst. News	8	40	16	40.0
Pitts. Courier	3	15	3	7.5
Afro.-Amer.	2	10	1	2.5

lead to the acceptance of group violence among Negroes. It is seen that a higher percentage of "rejectors" (conservative) spontaneously mention a Negro newspaper when asked what newspapers they read. These results in terms of the incidence of unprompted mention of a Negro newpaper seem a more basic indicator of the degree to which a Negro newspaper is read and accepted than are the responses obtained after specific prompting (presented in B of Table 7).

Relatives in Army. Table 8 indicates that there is little difference between the "militant" and the "conservative" group in this area. What slight difference exists is in the direction of a larger percentage of the militant group having relatives in the army.

Table 8. *Relatives in Army*

	ACCEPTED		REJECTED	
	N	%	N	%
Yes	15	75	26	65
In North	6	30	4	10
South or overseas	9	45	22	55
None	5	25	14	35

COMPARATIVE ANALYSIS OF GENERAL ATTITUDE PATTERN OF EACH GROUP

Explanations of Cause of Riot. An examination of the response presented in Table 9 reveals a difference in the pattern of types of causes of the riot presented by the "acceptors" as contrasted to those of "rejectors." In spite of this general difference in pattern of ascribed causes, it is of interest to point out that the majority of the rejectors (32.5 per cent) believe the riot was due to "general racial tensions . . . and resentment of injustices. . . ." This reason was also offered by the majority (45 per cent) of the "acceptors."

A total of 35 per cent of the "rejectors" ascribed the riots to various reasons not mentioned by any of the "acceptors." As can be seen in Table 10, these reasons tended to be generally more specific—isolated from the general context of racial attitudes, e.g., "violence and looting for own sake," citing the specific precipitating incident, "the policeman and the soldier," or transferring the blame to "out of towners."

Characterization of Riot Participants. The responses to this question (answers tabulated in Table 10) may logically be considered an aspect of the basis of differentiating the two groups and not a probable independent aspect of relevant attitudes. It appears likely that an evaluation (acceptance or rejection of riot as a whole) would include inevitably a consistently positively related attitude toward the participants of the riot. In fact the answer to this question may well be considered a check on the reliability of the responses found in Table 2. The marked disparity in the responses presented in Table 10 should therefore be expected.

Table 9. Judgment of Cause—Reasons Given
(Why do you think it happened?)

		ACCEPTED		REJECTED	
		N	%	N	%
A.	Bad treatment of soldiers	3	15	2	5.0
B.	High prices (discriminatory)	1	5	1	2.5
C.	Generalized racial tensions and resentment of injustices	9	45	13	32.5
D.	Because of poverty of people	1	5	1	2.5
E.	No reason—baseless rumors	2	10	5	12.5
F.	Because of Detroit riot	1	5	4	10.0
G.	God	1	5	—	——
H.	Anti-semitism	2	10	—	——

Reasons found only among rejectors

J.	Violence and looting for own sake	5	12.5
K.	Specific incident (policeman and soldier)	4	10.0
L.	Planned by out of towners	2	5.0
M.	Mayor's leniency	1	2.5
N.	Shortage of transportation	1	2.5
O.	Have not least idea	1	2.5

It can be seen from these results that practically all of the "acceptors" had a tendency to describe the participants in positive evaluative terms. They felt for the most part that the riot participants were "not unusual," "average Americans," "were all right" (expressed approval and sometimes enthusiastic approbation), or "not hoodlums" (in manifest contradiction to the general newspaper characterization of the rioters).

The majority (45 per cent) of the "rejectors" on the other hand condemned the riot participants as "hoodlums—vandals—degraded—looters—and criminals," or as "spiteful—stupid—or fools." It seems of significance to point out that only 12.5 per cent of the "rejectors" did not characterize the rioters in these negatively evaluative terms.

Anticipated Consequences of Riot. The results in Table 11 indicate

Table 10. Evaluation of Rioters
(What do you think of the people who were in it?)

	ACCEPTED		REJECTED	
	N	%	N	%
A. All types of people—not unusual average Americans	5	25	1	2.5
B. All right (positive evaluation)	6	30		
(with moral qualifications)	3	15	4	10.0
C. Not hoodlums	3	15	—	—
D. Kids—young people	1	5	1	2.5
E. Lower classes	2	10	3	7.5

Answers found only among rejectors

	ACCEPTED		REJECTED	
F. Hoodlums, vandals, degraded, looters, criminals			18	45.0
G. Distinction between rioters and looters			5	12.5
H. Unfair, spiteful			2	5.0
J. Stupid, fools			2	5.0
K. Agitated by press			1	2.5
L. Felt sorry for them			1	2.5
M. Don t know			2	5.0

Table 11. Immediate Consequences of Violence
[What do you think will be the result (outcome)?]

	ACCEPTED		REJECTED	
	N	%	N	%
A. Good	6	30	1	2.5
B. More good than bad	1	5	6	15.0
C. No change	4	20	4	10.0
D. More bad than good	—	—	6	15.0
E. Bad	2	10	15	37.5
F. Don't know	3	15	7	17.5
Hope good	1	5	1	2.5
G. More riots	3	15	—	—

that a majority of the "acceptors" anticipate some *good* to result from the outbreak while a majority of the "rejectors" expect some *bad*. These results are in agreement with the expected.

Verbalized Praticipation in Group Violence. It can be seen from Table 12 that 60 per cent of the "acceptors" state that they would not have participated in the riots if they "had been around when it started"; 15 per cent of them "don't think" that they would participate; while 25 per cent of them stated that they would. The reasons given for each category of answer may be seen by observing Table 12; 95 per cent of the "rejectors," on the other hand, would not have participated, while a surprising 5 per cent of these "rejectors" claimed that they would have participated for reasons of "personal gain."

Again in an analysis of the differential responses to this question a consistent difference between "acceptors" and "rejectors" manifests it-

Table 12. Verbalized Participation in Group Violence
(If you had been around when it started would you have joined in?)

	ACCEPTED		REJECTED	
	N	%	N	%
No				
Fear	3	15	8	20.0
Moral disapproval	3	15	11	27.5
Believe in law and order	1	5	6	15.0
Was not a race riot	1	5	—	——
No reason	4	20	3	17.5

Reason found only among rejectors

	ACCEPTED		REJECTED	
Dumb, stupid, senseless,				
hurt Negroes	—	—	10	25.0
Total No	12	60	38	95.0
Yes				
For personal gain	2	10	2	5.0
To destroy—but not steal	1	5	—	——
To protect race	1	5	—	——
Actually participated	1	5	—	——
Total Yes	5	25	2	5.0
Don't Think So	3	15	—	——

Table 13. Anticipation of Riot
(Did you expect a riot to happen here?)

	ACCEPTED		REJECTED	
	N	%	N	%
Yes	11	55	17	42.5
No	7	35	20	50.0
Don't know	2	10	3	7.5

self: the "rejectors" clothe their reasons and attitudes in more moralistic and strongly (negative) evaluative terms.

Anticipation of Riot. As may be seen in Table 13 the responses to this question offer a slight basis for discriminating between "acceptors" and "rejectors." There is a tendency for a higher percentage of "acceptors" to have expected a riot while there is a tendency for a higher percentage of "rejectors" not to have expected one. This may indicate a higher level of racial sensitivity among the "acceptors."

TREATMENT OF NEGRO SOLDIERS

If responses A and B in Table 14 are combined it will be seen that there is no difference whatsoever in the two groups as far as response to this question is concerned. An equal percentage of each group feels that Negro soldiers as a *whole* are unjustly treated in the army or that

Table 14. Treatment of Negro Soldiers
(Have you been hearing about how Negro soldiers get along in the Army)

		ACCEPTED		REJECTED	
		N	%	N	%
A.	Unjustly treated—discriminated	16	80	27	67.5
B.	Some treated all right—others not	3	15	8	20.0
C.	No stated answer	1	5	—	——

Answers received only from rejectors

D.	Don't know			3	7.5
E.	Like it			2	5.0

some are unjustly treated. The responses to this question—an indication of subjective knowledge or attitude about the treatment of Negroes in the army—in no way discriminate between "acceptors" or "rejectors" of group racial violence.

.   .   .   .

SUMMARY AND CONCLUSIONS

In a preliminary attempt to determine whether there existed certain background factors or relevant attitudinal dynamics, which would make it possible to discriminate between individuals who would participate in or condone group violence from those who would condemn such violence, 67 Negro residents of the Harlem area were interviewed by Negro interviewers within a month after the August, 1943, Harlem riots. The following results were obtained:

1. While 60 per cent of the respondents rejected, or condemned the riots, 30 per cent accepted or condoned the riots.

2. Of those who condoned the riots a higher percentage were males; of those who condemned the riots a higher percentage were females.

3. The condoners (acceptors) tended to be concentrated among the older respondents while among the condemners (rejectors) there was a somewhat higher percentage of younger respondents.

4. There is a tendency for a higher percentage of the condoners (acceptors) to have a stated higher educational level—while a higher percentage of the condemners (rejectors) have a stated lower educational level.

5. There is a tendency for the rejectors (condemners) to be more regular church goers than the acceptors—although the difference between these two groups is quite small when extremely frequent church attendance ("every Sunday") is compared.

6. Negligible differences exist between these two groups as to place of birth of respondents, except that there is a higher percentage of northern born non-New Yorkers found among the condoner group

and a slightly higher percentage of the native New Yorkers found among the condemner group.

7. Newspapers stated as read show no differences between these two groups, with the following exceptions: comparatively there is a higher percentage of *PM* readers among the condoner group while there is a comparative and absolute greater number of *Journal-American* (Hearst newspaper) readers among the condemner groups. This latter is the most marked difference found in this section of the analysis.

8. There is a tendency for the condemners (rejectors) to be more habitual readers of Negro newspapers.

9. There is a tendency for the higher percentage of the acceptors (condoners) to have close relatives in the army—while there is a tendency for a higher percentage of the rejectors to have no relatives in the army.

10. The rejectors give a somewhat different pattern of reasons in attempting to account for the riot and tend to characterize the participants generally more negatively and with more moralistic evaluative statements than do the acceptors.

11. A higher percentage of rejectors believe that the immediate consequences of the riots will be detrimental in contrast to a higher percentage of acceptors who believe these consequnces will be "good."

12. A strikingly higher percentage of rejectors stated that they would have participated in group violence "under no circumstances"; 25 per cent of them characterize it as "dumb—stupid—senseless, etc." while some of the "acceptors" so described it; 25 per cent of the acceptors stated that they would have, or did participate in the riot— while 5 per cent of the rejectors so stated.

13. There was a slight tendency for the acceptors to be generally more sensitive in terms of having expected a riot.

14. In the following dimensions of general attitudinal pattern there appears to be no significant basis in the obtained results for discriminating between these two groups: (a) subjective knowledge or attitude concerning the treatment of Negro soldiers in the army; (b) general attitude toward the army; (c) optimism or pessimism in reference to the post-war status of the Negro; (d) general projected morale level as indicated by response to the question: "Are Negroes in general all out for this war?" [3]

Upon the basis of the results of this preliminary investigation it seems advisable to make the following negative conclusion awaiting verification from a more extensive and controlled study.

That aside from the suggestive trend differences in some of the more concrete background factors presented above, the rejectors and acceptors of group racial violence can best be discriminated in terms

3. Data on these questions has not been reproduced here but can be found in the original article.

of the fact that the negations of group violence by the rejectors are couched in moralistic, ethical, and evaluative terms indicating a strong sense of a "superego" which appears to be the determinant of their attitude toward group violence in general—and strong enough to outweigh any other relevant and specific aspects of general attitude pattern which might exist.

The acceptors, on the other hand, show no such general social-ethical concern but rather appear to be strongly and emotionally oriented to the more specific and relevant determinants of the nature of the group violence themselves. Wherein the rejectors are emotional in their concern about the observance of general social ethics, the acceptors are emotional about their concern about what they consider specific social or "racial" injustice.

These two groups cannot be differentiated in terms of their responses which indicate the pattern of their relevant general racial attitude. From these data each group appears to have the same general level of morale as indicated by their attitude toward the treatment of Negro soldiers in the army, attitude toward the army in general, optimism or pessimism concerning the post-war future of the Negro, and general attitude of Negroes toward the war. This fact may suggest that the acceptance or rejection of group violence by an individual is not determined by the nature of his relevant general attitude as much as it is determined by his general perspective—or frame of reference within which this general attitude pattern gets its meaning. If this frame of reference is a broad social-ethical or superego determined one, it is likely to lead to a categorical rejection of group violence even if this appears consistent to the more relevant general attitude. If this frame of reference is a more restricted one, primarily concerned with a specific subjective social injustice, it is likely to lead to the acceptance of group violence as a means to the end of rectifying the specific injustice. In this instance it appears that there is no subjective awareness of an incompatibility of violence with broad or narrow social ethics. But rather this violence appears to be conceived by its acceptors as an instrument for the establishing of a specific socially desirable and ethical end.

H. Edward Ransford

Isolation, Powerlessness, and Violence: A Study of Attitudes and Participation in the Watts Riot

Since the summer of 1965, it is no longer possible to describe the Negroes' drive for new rights as a completely nonviolent protest. Urban ghettos have burst at the seams. Angry shouts from the most frustrated and deprived segments of the Negro community now demand that we recognize violence as an important facet of the Negro revolution.

In attempts to understand the increase in violence, much has been said about unemployment, police brutality, poor schools, and inadequate housing as contributing factors (see, e.g., Governor's Commission on the Los Angeles Riots, 1965). However, there are few sociological studies concerning the characteristics of the participants or potential participants in racial violence.[1] Little can be said about which minority individuals are likely to view violence as a justifiable means of correcting racial injustices. It is the purpose of this paper to identify such individuals—specifically, to identify those Negroes who were willing to use violence as a method during a period shortly after the Watts riot.

A THEORETICAL PERSPECTIVE

Studies dealing with political extremism and radical protest have often described the participants in such action as being isolated or weakly tied to the institutions of the community (see, e.g., Kornhauser, 1959, pp. 182-223; Lipset, 1960, pp. 94-130; and Kerr and Siegel, 1954, pp. 189-212). Kerr and Siegel (1954) demonstrated this relationship with their finding that wildcat strikes are more common among isolated occupational groups, such as mining, maritime, and lumbering. These isolated groups are believed to have a weak commitment to public pressures and the democratic norms of the community. Thus, when grievances are felt intensely and the bonds to the institutions of the community are weak, there is likely to be an explosion of discontent (the strike) rather than use of negotiation or other normative channels of expression.

More recently, mass society theory has articulated this relationship

---

1. One of the very few studies of the potential participants in race violence was conducted by Kenneth B. Clark, shortly after the Harlem riot of 1943 (see Clark, 1944), pp. 319-337; see also Lee and Humphrey, 1943, pp. 80-87.

between isolation and extremism (Kornhauser, 1959; and Bramson, 1961, p. 72). The mass society approach sees current structural processes —such as the decline in kinship, the increase in mobility, and the rise of huge bureaucracies—as detaching many individuals from sources of control, meaning, and personal satisfaction. Those who are most isolated from centers of power are believed to be more vulnerable to authoritarian outlooks and more available for volatile mass movements. Indeed, Kornhauser instructs us that the whole political stability of a society is somewhat dependent upon its citizens being tied meaningfully to the institutions of the community (Kornhauser, 1959). He suggests that participation in secondary organizations—such as unions and business groups—serves to mediate between the individual and the nation, tying the individual to the democratic norms of the society.

The relationship between structural isolation and extremism is further accentuated by the personal alienation of the individual. Isolated people are far more likely than nonisolated people to feel cut off from the larger society and to feel an inability to control events in the society.[2] This subjective alienation may heighten the individual's readiness to engage in extreme behavior. For example, Horton and Thompson find that perceived powerlessness is related to protest voting.[3] Those with feelings of political powerlessness were more likely to be dissatisfied with their position in society and to hold resentful attitudes toward community leaders. The study suggests that the discontent of the powerless group was converted to action through the vote—a vote of "no" on a local bond issue being a form of negativism in which the individual strikes out at community powers. Alienation as a force for protest is consistent with the original Marxian view of the concept in which alienation leads to a radical attack upon the existing social structure (Fromm, 1962, pp. 56-73).

In summary, there are two related approaches commonly used to explain participation in extreme political behavior. The first deals with the degree to which the individual is structurally isolated or tied to community institutions. The second approach deals with the individual's awareness and evaluation of his isolated condition—for example, his feeling of a lack of control over critical matters or his feeling of discontent due to a marginal position in society. Following this orientation, this research employs the concepts of racial isolation, perceived powerlessness, and racial dissatisfaction as theoretical tools for explaining the participation of Negroes in violence.

---

2. E.g., Neal and Seeman found that isolated workers (nonparticipants in unions) were more likely to feel powerless to effect outcomes in the society than the participants in unions (Neal and Seeman, 1964, pp. 216-226).

3. Horton and Thompson, 1962, pp. 485-493. For another report on the same study, see Thompson and Horton, 1960, pp. 190-195.

STUDY DESIGN AND HYPOTHESES

In the following discussion, the three independent variables of this study (isolation, powerlessness, and dissatisfaction) are discussed separately and jointly, as predictors of violence participation.

RACIAL ISOLATION

Ralph Ellison has referred to the Negro in this country as the "invisible man" (Ellison, 1952). Although this is a descriptive characterization, sociological studies have attempted to conceptualize more precisely the isolation of the American Negro. For example, those studying attitudes of prejudice often view racial isolation as a lack of free and easy contact on an intimate and equal status basis.[4] Though the interracial contact may be frequent, it often involves such wide status differentials that it does not facilitate candid communication, nor is it likely to give the minority person a feeling that he has some stake in the system. In this paper, intimate white contact is viewed as a mediating set of relationships that binds the ethnic individual to majority-group values— essentially conservative values that favor working through democratic channels rather than violently attacking the social system. Accordingly, it is reasoned that Negroes who are more racially isolated (by low degrees of intimate contact with whites) will have fewer channels of communication to air their grievances and will feel little commitment to the leaders and institutions of the community. This group, which is blocked from meaningful white communication, should be more willing to use violent protest than the groups with greater involvement in white society.

POWERLESSNESS AND RACIAL DISSATISFACTION

In contrast to structural isolation, powerlessness and racial dissatisfaction are the subjective components of our theoretical scheme. A feeling of powerlessness is one form of alienation. It is defined in this research as a low expectancy of control over events (this definition of subjective powerlessness is taken from the conceptualization proposed by Seeman, 1959). This attitude is seen as an appropriate variable for Negroes living in segregated ghettos; that is, groups which are blocked from full participation in the society are more likely to feel powerless in that society.

4. Many studies have brought forth the finding that equal status contact between majority and minority members is associated with tolerance and favorable attitudes. For the most recent evidence of the equal status proposition, see Williams *et al.*, 1964. For an earlier study, see Deutsch and Collins, 1951.

Powerlessness is also a variable that seems to have a logical relationship to violent protest. Briefly, it is reasoned that Negroes who feel powerless to change their position or to control crucial decisions that affect them will be more willing to use violent means to get their rights than those who feel some control or efficacy within the social system. For the Negro facing extreme discrimination barriers, an attitude of powerlessness is simply a comment on the society, namely, a belief that all channels for social redress are closed.

Our second attitude measure, racial dissatisfaction, is defined as the degree to which the individual feels that he is being treated badly because of his race. It is a kind of racial alienation in the sense that the individual perceives his position in society to be illegitimate, due to racial discrimination. The Watts violence represented an extreme expression of frustration and discontent. We would expect those highly dissatisfied with their treatment as Negroes to be the participants in such violence. Thus, the "highs" in racial dissatisfaction should be more willing to use violence than the "lows" in this attitude. In comparing our two forms of subjective alienation (powerlessness and racial dissatisfaction), it is important to note that, although we expect some correlation between the two attitudes (a certain amount of resentment and dissatisfaction should accompany the feeling of powerlessness), we propose to show that they make an independent contribution to violence.

UNIFICATION OF PREDICTIVE VARIABLES

We believe that the fullest understanding of violence can be brought to bear by use of a social-psychological design in which the structural variable (racial isolation) is joined with the subjective attitudes of the individual (powerlessness and dissatisfaction).

In this design, we attempt to specify the conditions under which isolation has its strongest effect upon violence. It is reasoned that racial violence should be most important for determining participation in violence (a) when individuals feel powerless to shape their destiny under existing conditions or (b) when individuals are highly dissatisfied with their racial treatment. Each of the attitudes is seen as a connecting bridge of logic between racial isolation and violence.

For the first case (that of powerlessness), we are stating that a weak attachment to the majority group and its norms should lead to a radical break from law and order when individuals perceive they cannot effect events important to them; that is, they cannot change their racial position through activity within institutional channels. Violence, in this instance, becomes an alternative pathway of expression and gain. Conversely, racial isolation should have much less effect upon violence when persons feel some control in the system.

For the second case (racial dissatisfaction), we believe isolation should have a far greater effect upon violence when dissatisfaction over racial treatment is intense. Isolation from the society then becomes critical to violence in the sense that the dissatisfied person feels little commitment to the legal order and is more likely to use extreme methods as an outlet for his grievances. Statistically speaking, we expect an interaction effect between isolation and powerlessness, and between isolation and dissatisfaction, in the prediction of violence.[5]

METHODS

Our hypotheses call for measures of intimate white contact, perceived powerlessness, and perceived racial dissatisfaction as independent variables, and willingness to use violence as a dependent variable. The measurement of these variables, and also the sampling techniques, are discussed at this time.

SOCIAL CONTACT

The type of social contact to be measured had to be of an intimate and equal status nature, a kind of contact that would facilitate easy communication between the races. First, each Negro respondent was asked if he had current contact with white people in a series of situations: on the job, in his neighborhood, in organizations to which he belongs, and in other situations (such as shopping). After this general survey of white contacts, the respondent was asked, "Have you ever done anything social with these white people, like going to the movies together or visiting in each other's homes?" (this question was taken from Williams *et al.*, 1964). The responses formed a simple dichotomous variable: "high" contact scores for those who had done something social (61 per cent of the sample) and "low" contact scores for those who had had little or no social contact (39 per cent).[6]

_____

5. In contrast to the mass society perspective, in which structural isolation is viewed as a cause of subjective alienation, we are viewing the two as imperfectly correlated. For example, many Negroes with contact (nonisolates) may still feel powerless due to racial discrimination barriers. We are thus stressing the partial independence of objective and subjective alienation and feel it necessary to consider both variables for the best prediction of violence.

6. As a further indication that this measure was tapping a more intimate form of interracial contact, it can be noted the 88 per cent of those reporting social contact with whites claimed at least one "good friend" ("to whom you can say what you really think") or "close friend" ("to whom you can talk over confidential matters"). Only 10 per cent of those lacking social contact claimed such friendships with white people.

POWERLESSNESS

Following the conceptualization of Melvin Seeman, powerlessness is defined as a low expectancy of control over events (Seeman, 1959). Twelve forced-choice items were used to tap this attitude (the powerlessness scale was developed by S. Liverant, J. B. Rotter, and M. Seeman in Rotter, 1966). The majority of items dealt with expectations of control over the political system. The following is an example:

_____ The world is run by the few people in power, and there is not much the little guy can do about it.

_____ The average citizen can have an influence on government decisions.

After testing the scale items for reliability (using the Kuder-Richardson test for reliability, a coefficient of .77 was obtained for the twelve items), the distribution of scores was dichotomized at the median.

RACIAL DISSATISFACTION

The attitude of racial dissatisfaction is defined as the degree to which the individual feels he is being treated badly because of his race. A five-item scale was developed to measure this attitude. The questions ask the Negro respondent to compare his treatment (in such areas as housing, work, and general treatment in the community) with various reference groups, such as the southern Negro or the white. Each of the five questions allows a reply on one of three levels: no dissatisfaction, mild dissatisfaction, and intense dissatisfaction. Typical of the items is the following: "If you compare your opportunities and the treatment you get from whites in Los Angeles with Negroes living in the South, would you say you are much better off_____ a little better off_____ or treated about the same as the southern Negro_____?" After a reliability check of the items, replies to the dissatisfaction measure were dichotomized into high and low groups (Kuder-Richardson coefficient of .84). The cut was made conceptually, rather than at the median, yielding 99 "highs" and 213 "lows" in dissatisfaction.[7]

VIOLENCE WILLINGNESS

The dependent variable of the study is willingness to use violence. Violence is defined in the context of the Watts riot as the willingness to

7. With a cut at the median, a good many people (N=59) who were mildly dis-
1944 disatisfied on all five items would have been placed in the "high" category. It was decided that a more accurate description of the "high" category would require the person to express maximum dissatisfaction on at least one of the five items and mild dissatisfaction on the other four.

use direct aggression against the groups that are believed to be discriminating, such as the police and white merchants. The question used to capture this outlook is, "Would you be willing to use violence to get Negro rights?" With data gathered so shortly after the Watts violence, it was felt that the question would be clearly understood by respondents (as an indication that the question was interpreted in the context of participation in violence of the Watts variety, it can be noted that our question was correlated with approval of the Watts riot [$\phi=.62$]). At the time of data collection, buildings were still smoldering; violence in the form of looting, burning, and destruction was not a remote possibility, but a tangible reality. The violence-prone group numbered eighty-three.

A second measure of violence asked the person if he had ever used violent methods to get Negro rights.[8] Only sixteen respondents of the 312 reported (or admitted) that they had participated in actual violence. As a result of this very small number the item is used as an indicator of trends but is not employed as a basic dependent variable of the study.

SAMPLE

The sample was composed of three hundred and twelve Negro males who were heads of the household and between the ages of eighteen and sixty-five. The subjects responded to an interview schedule administered by Negro interviewers. They were chosen by random methods and were interviewed in their own homes or apartments. Both employed and unemployed respondents were included in the sample, although the former were emphasized in the sampling procedure (269 employed in contrast to 43 unemployed). The sample was drawn from three major areas of Los Angeles: a relatively middle-class and integrated area (known as the "Crenshaw" district) and the predominantly lower-class and highly segregated communities of "South Central" and "Watts." The sample could be classified as "disproportional stratified" because the proportion of subjects drawn from each of the three areas does not correspond to the actual distribution of Negroes in Los Angeles. For example, it was decided that an approximate fifty-fifty split between middle- and lower-class respondents would be desirable for later analysis. This meant, however, that Crenshaw (middle-class) Negroes were considerably overrepresented, since their characteristics are not typical of the Los Angeles Negro community as a whole, and the majority of Los Angeles Negroes do not reside in this, or any similar, area.

8. The question, "Have you ever participated in violent action for Negro rights?" was purposely worded in general terms to avoid accusing the respondent of illegal behavior during the Watts violence. However, racial violence in the United States was somewhat rare at that time, so it is likely that most of the sixteen respondents were referring to participation in the Watts violence.

Table 1. *Percentage Willing to Use Violence, by Social Contact,*
Powerlessness, and Racial Dissatisfaction

Variables	Not Willing (%)	Willing (%)	Total (%)
Social contact: *			
High	83	17	100 (N = 192)
Low	56	44	100 (N = 110)
Powerlessness: †			
High	59	41	100 (N = 145)
Low	84	16	100 (N = 160)
Racial dissatisfaction: ‡			
High	52	48	100 (N = 98)
Low	83	17	100 (N = 212)

* $x^2 = 24.93, P < .001.$
† $x^2 = 22.59, P < .001.$
‡ $x^2 = 30.88, P < .001.$

NOTE.—In this table and the tables that follow, there are often less than 312 cases due to missing data for one or more variables.

RESULTS

We have predicted a greater willingness to use violent methods for three groups: the isolated, the powerless, and the dissatisfied. The data presented in Table 1 confirm these expectations. For all three cases, the the percentage differences are statistically significant at better than the .001 level.

The empirical evidence supports our contention that Negroes who are more disengaged from the society, in the structural (isolation) and subjective (powerlessness and racial dissatisfaction) senses, are more likely to view violence as necessary for racial justice than those more firmly tied to the society.

It is one thing to establish a relationship based on action willingness and quite another thing to study actual behavior. Unfortunately, only sixteen of the 312 respondents (5 per cent) admitted participation in violent action for Negro rights. This small number did, however, provide some basis for testing our hypotheses. Of the sixteen who participated in violent action, eleven were isolates while only five had social contact. More impressive is the fact that fifteen of the sixteen "violents" scored high in powerlessness, and thirteen of the sixteen felt high degrees of dissatisfaction. Even with a small number, these are definite relationships, encouraging an interpretation that those who are willing to use violence and those who reported actual violent behavior display the same tendency toward powerlessness, racial dissatisfaction, and isolation.

The next task is to explore the interrelationships among our predictive variables. For example, we have argued that powerlessness has a specific meaning to violence (a low expectancy of changing conditions within the institutional framework) that should be more than a generalized disaffection; that is, we expected our measures of powerlessness and racial dissatisfaction to have somewhat unique effects upon violence.

The data indicated an interaction effect (interaction $\chi^2 = 7.85$; $P < .01$) between the two attitudes. The feeling of powerlessness is a more relevant determiner of violence for the highly dissatisfied or angry Negro. Similarly, racial dissatisfaction is far more important to violence for those who feel powerless. In sum, the data suggests that the powerless Negro is likely to use violence when his feelings of powerlessness are accompanied by intense dissatisfaction with his position. It can be noted, however, that, even among those who were relatively satisfied with racial conditions, powerlessness had some effect upon violence (a 13 per cent difference, $\chi^2 = 5.41$; $P = .02$). Presumably, a low expectance of exerting control has a somewhat unique effect upon violence.

As a second way of noting an interrelationship between our predictive variables, we turn to the more crucial test of the isolation-extremism perspective in which the effect of racial isolation upon violence is controlled by powerlessness and dissatisfaction.[9] It will be recalled that we expected the isolated people (with a lower commitment to democratic norms and organized channels) to be more violence-prone when these isolated individuals perceive they cannot shape their destiny within the institutional framework (high powerlessness) or when they perceive differential treatment as Negroes and, as a result, are dissatisfied. It is under these subjective states of mind that a weak attachment to the majority group would seem to be most important to extremism. Table 2, addressed to these predictions, shows our hypotheses to be strongly supported in both cases.

Table 2. Percentage Willing to Use Violence, by Social Contact Controlling for Powerlessness and Racial Dissatisfaction

PERCENTAGE WILLING TO USE VIOLENCE

	Low Power-lessness (%)	*High Power-lessness* (%)	*Low Dis-satisfaction* (%)	*High Dis-satisfaction* (%)
Low contact	23 ($N = 31$)	53 ($N = 78$)	23 ($N = 47$)	59 ($N = 63$)
High contact	13 ($N = 123$)	26 ($N = 66$)	15 ($N = 158$)	26 ($N = 34$)
χ^2	$P < .20$	$P < .01$	$P < .20$	$P < .01$

NOTE.—The interaction χ^2 between powerlessness and contact: $P < .05$. The interaction χ^2 between dissatisfaction and contact: $P < .01$.

Among the powerless and the dissatisfied, racial isolation has a strong effect upon violence commitment. Conversely, the data show that isola-

9. The independent variables are moderately intercorrelated. For isolation and powerlessness, the ø correlation is .36 $P < .001$; for isolation and dissatisfaction, the ø is .40, $P < .001$; for powerlessness and dissatisfaction, the ø is .33, $P < .001$.

tion is much less relevant to violence for those with feelings of control in the system and for the more satisfied (in both cases, significant only at the .20 level) (the .05 level is considered significant in this analysis).

The fact that isolation (as a cause of violence) produces such a small percentage difference for the less alienated subjects calls for a further word of discussion. Apparently, isolation is not only a stronger predictor of violence for the people who feel powerless and dissatisfied, but is *only* a clear and significant determiner of violence for these subjectively alienated persons. For the relatively satisfied and control-oriented groups, the fact of being isolated is not very important in determining violence. This would suggest that a weak normative bond to the majority group (isolation) is not in itself sufficient to explain the participation of the oppressed minority person in violence and that it is the interaction between isolation and feelings of powerlessness (or racial dissatisfaction) that is crucial for predicting violence.

A final attempt at unification involves the cumulative effect of all three of our predictive variables upon violence. Since it was noted that each of the three predictive variables has some effect upon violence (either independently or for specific subgroups), it seemed logical that the combined effect of the three would produce a high violence propensity. Conceptually, a combination of these variables could be seen as ideal types of the alienated and non-alienated Negro. Accordingly, Table 3 arranges the data into these ideal-type combinations.

The group at the top of the table represents the one most detached from society—individuals who are isolated and high in attitudes of powerlessness and dissatisfaction. The group at the bottom of the table is the most involved in the society; these people have intimate white contact, feelings of control, and greater satisfaction with racial conditions. The middle group is made up of those with different combinations of high and low detachment. Note the dramatic difference in willingness to use violence between the "ideal-type" alienated group (65 per cent willing) and the group most bound to society (only 12 per cent willing). The "middles" in alienation display a score in violence between these extremes.

Table 3. Percentage Willing to Use Violence, by the Combined Effect of Social Contact, Powerlessness, and Racial Dissatisfaction

	Not Willing (%)	Willing (%)	Total (%)
Ideal-type alienated (low contact, high powerlessness, and high dissatisfaction)	35	65	100 (N = 51)
Middles in alienation	76	24	100 (N = 147)
Ideal-type non-alienated (high contact, low powerlessness, and low dissatisfaction)	88	12	100 (N = 107)

Note.—$x^2 = 49.37$; $P < .001$ (2 d.f.).

SPURIOUSNESS

It is possible that the relationship between our predictive variables and violence is due to an intercorrelation with other relevant variables. For example, social class should be related both to violence and to our isolation-alienation measures. In addition, we could expect a greater propensity toward violence in geographical areas where an extreme breakdown of legal controls occurred, such as the South Central and Watts areas (in contrast to the Crenshaw area, where no rioting took place). In such segregated ghettos, violence may have been defined by the inhabitants as a legitimate expression, given their intolerable living conditions, a group definition that could override any effects of isolation or alienation upon violence. In short, it seems essential to control our isolation-alienation variables by an index of social class and by ghetto area. Age was also considered as a control variable but was dropped when it was discovered that age was not correlated with violence or the independent variables.

Because of the rather small violent group, it is necessary to examine our predictive variables separately in this analysis of controls. Table 4 presents the original relationship between each of the independent variables and violence, controlled by two areas of residence: the South Central-Watts area, at the heart of the curfew zone (where violence occurred), and Crenshaw area, on the periphery (or outside) of the curfew zone (where violent action was rare). In addition, Table 4 includes a control for education, as a measure of social class.[10]

Table 4. Percentage Willing to Use Violence by Contact, Powerlessness, and Racial Dissatisfaction, Controlling for Two Geographical Areas and Education

Independent Variables	NEIGHBORHOOD		EDUCATION	
	South Central-Watts	Crenshaw	Low (High School or Less)	High (Some College)
Low contact	53** (N = 62)	33** (N = 45)	52** (N = 77)	24* (N = 33)
High contact	27 (N = 83)	10 (N = 109)	26 (N = 86)	10 (N = 105)
Low powerlessness	22** (N = 73)	11* (N = 88)	19** (N = 67)	14 (N = 93)
High powerlessness	55 (N = 77)	25 (N = 68)	51 (N = 100)	18 (N = 45)
Low dissatisfaction	26** (N = 81)	12** (N = 130)	22** (N = 96)	12 (N = 114)
High dissatisfacticon	53 (N = 68)	39 (N = 28)	59 (N = 73)	17 (N = 24)

* $P < .05$.   ** $P < .01$.

NOTE.—Interaction x^2 between contact and neighborhood: P is not significant. Interaction x^2 between powerlessness and neighborhood: $P < .02$. Interaction x^2 between dissatisfaction and neighborhood: P is not significant. Interaction x^2 between contact and education: P is not significant. Interaction x^2 between powerlessness and education: $P < .02$. Interaction x^2 between dissatisfaction and education: $.05 < P < .10$.

10. For this sample, education was believed to be superior to other indexes of class. It is an index that is freer (than either occupation or income) from the societal restrictions and discrimination that Negroes face. Also, it was discovered that Negro occupations in the more deprived ghetto areas were not comparable to the same occupations listed in standardized scales, such as the North-Hatt or Bogue scales.

When the ghetto residence of the respondent is held constant, it appears that our independent variables are important in their own right. Education (social class), however, proved to be a more powerful control variable. Among the college educated, only isolation persists as a predictor of violence; powerlessness and racial dissatisfaction virtually drop out. Yet each variable has a very strong effect upon violence among the high school (lower-class) group. In other words, we do not have an instance of spuriousness, where predictive variables are explained away in both partials, but another set of interaction effects—attitudes of powerlessness and dissatisfaction are predictors of violence only among lower-class respondents. These results may be interpreted in several ways. Persons higher in the class structure may have a considerable amount to lose, in terms of occupational prestige and acceptance in white society, by indorsing extreme methods. The college educated (middle-class) may be unwilling to risk their position, regardless of feelings of powerlessness and dissatisfaction. These results may further indicate that middle-class norms favoring diplomacy and the use of democratic channels (as opposed to direct aggression) are overriding any tendency toward violence (for a discussion of class norms, see Lipset, 1960). An extension of this interpretation is that middle-class Negroes may be activists, but non-violent activitists, in the civil rights movement. Thus, class norms may be contouring resentment into more organized forms of protest.

CONCLUSIONS

In an attempt to locate the Negro participant in violence, we find that isolated Negroes and Negroes with intense feelings of powerlessness and dissatisfaction are more prone to violent action than those who are less prone to violent action than those who are less alienated. In addition, isolation has its strongest effect upon violence when individuals feel powerless to control events in the society or when racial dissatisfaction is intensely felt. For those with higher expectations of control or with greater satisfaction regarding racial treatment, isolation has a much smaller and non-significant effect (though in the predicted direction) upon violence. That is, a weak tie with the majority group, per se, appeared insufficient to explain wide-scale participation in extreme action. This study indicates that it is the interaction between a weak bond and a feeling of powerlessness (or dissatisfaction) that is crucial to violent participation.

Viewed another way, the combined or tandem effect of all three predictive variables produces an important profile of the most violence-prone individuals. Negroes who are isolated, who feel powerless, and who voice a strong disaffection because of discrimination appear to be an extremely volatile group, with 65 per cent of this stratum willing to use violence (as contrasted to only 12 per cent of the "combined lows" in alienation).

Ghetto area and education were introduced as controls. Each independent variable (taken separately) retained some significant effect upon violence in two geographical areas (dealing with proximity to the Watts violence) and among the less educated respondents. Powerlessness and dissatisfaction, however, had no effect upon violence among the college educated. Several interpretations of this finding were explored.

Applying our findings to the context of the Negro revolt of the last fifteen years, we note an important distinction between the non-violent civil rights activists and the violence-prone group introduced in this study. Suggestive (but non-conclusive) evidence indicates that the participants in organized civil rights protests are more likely to be middle-class in origin, to hold considerable optimism for equal rights, and to have greater communication with the majority—this represents a group with "rising expectations" for full equality. (See Searles and Williams, 1962; Ransford, 1966; and Gore and Rotter, 1963.) In contrast, this study located a very different population—one whose members are intensely dissatisfied, feel powerless to change their position, and have minimum commitment to the larger society. These Negroes have lost faith in the leaders and institutions of the community and presumably have little hope for improvement through organized protest. For them, violence is a means of communicating with white society; anger can be expressed, control exerted—if only for a brief period.

Allen D. Grimshaw

Relationships Among Prejudice, Discrimination, Social Tension, and Social Violence

If the concepts of prejudice, discrimination, social tension and social violence represent real phenomena, it should be possible to state relationships among the variables which are so labeled. Relationships between prejudice and discrimination have been stated. Attempts have been made to state relationships between social tension and social violence. There has been no attempt, however, to state the relationships among all four of these phenomena taken simultaneously. In this paper a method for studying these relationships is suggested and some tentative conclusions are briefly discussed.

As part of a larger project on social violence as manifested in urban race riots in the United States, the writer undertook the analysis of general trends and factors involved in the development of "violence-proneness" (Grimshaw, 1959b, chap. IV-VI). In addition to a review of the many causal allegations about urban race riots, this required a careful examination of relationships among prejudice, discrimination, social tension and social violence.

Two major findings emerged from the larger research. The first was that urban racial social violence in the United States has resulted not from conscious policy decisions of either the white or the Negro group, but rather from reactions of the dominant group to real or perceived assaults upon the accommodative structure. In brief, if the Negro "stays in his place," there is unlikely to be Negro-white violence. This has been true not only during periods of urban racial violence in the North but in all historical periods of Negro-white violence in the United States (Grimshaw, 1959b).

The second major finding was the reaffirmation of the importance of external forces of constraint in the determination of the occurrence or non-occurrence of social violence. This documentation of a sociological truism came about through attempts to discern relationships among the variables to be discussed.

INTERRELATIONSHIPS

The four possible relationships resulting from combinations of prejudice and discrimination are shown in Chart I. Merton, among others, has

CHART 1

RELATIONSHIPS BETWEEN PREJUDICE AND DISCRIMINATION

	No Prejudice	Prejudice
No Discrimination		
Discrimination		

noted that there can be prejudice without discrimination, that there can be discrimination without prejudice, and that each of these phenomena can act in causing the other (Merton, 1948). Prejudiced employers do not discriminate when such discrimination may mean legal penalties or the loss of government contracts. Professional sociologists do not discriminate when such discrimination may bring the disapproval of fellow sociologists. Non-prejudiced college deans in the South do not hire Negro professors when such a hiring policy may mean the withdrawal of financial resources. Examples of prejudiced non-discriminators and non-prejudiced discriminators come easily to mind.

Social violence is defined as attacks upon individuals or their property solely or primarily because of their membership in social groups or categories. The basic relationships between social tension and social violence are shown in Chart II. There may be high social tension and no

CHART II

RELATIONSHIPS BETWEEN SOCIAL TENSION AND SOCIAL VIOLENCE

	No Violence	Violence
No Tension		
Tension		

outbreak of social violence. Conversely, social violence may occur when there is relatively little *social* tension. Little Rock provides an example of high social tension without social violence. In that case, strong police forces (after Federal intervention) prevented outbreaks. On a less spectacular level, police controls prevent the outbreak of fights and brawls after sports contests involving traditional rivals.

On the other hand, examples of social violence without specifically related tensions can be found in spontaneous brawls of a wide variety. During World War II, incidents were frequently reported of brawls between servicemen of different branches. Men could be sitting in a bar, enjoying the company of other servicemen, without any sign of social tension. Then a chance remark would precipitate battles drawn along lines of service membership. Student disturbances provide another example of social violence without prior building up of social tensions. The tension which produces student riots is an individual rather than a social variety of tension (in that students are concerned about whether they, as individuals, will pass their exams), although once police arrive the violence which follows may be social in nature.[1]

Again, brawls between traditionally rivalrous groups can frequently develop with tremendous speed in what may have seemed to observers to be situations characterized by amicability. In most cases where there is social tension, there is perceived to be discrimination. Nonetheless, violence can and does occur in the absence of prejudice, discrimination, or tensions demonstrably related to group memberships.

1. Reference is to student disturbances in this country. In Latin America and in other parts of the world, student disturbances have more frequently arisen directly from social tension.

INTERACTIONS

It would seem then, that all of the cells in Charts I and II are easily filled. However, the apparent simplicity of the relationships shown in these two charts is spurious. An attempt to elaborate the interaction of all four variables, using even their current broad definitions, uncovers a wide range of problems. Row I of Chart III recapitulates the stated relationships between prejudice and discrimination and Column I, the relationships between social tension and social violence. Seen in this new context, the relationships take on deeper and more complex dimensions. To say, for example, that there are discriminating and non-discriminating prejudiced individuals is not precisely the same thing as saying there can be discrimination without prejudice or prejudice without discrimination.

Given the occurrence of a "Northern style race riot" (Grimshaw, 1959b), the student might reason as follows: Prejudice encourages discrimination; discrimination produces tension; tension can cause violence. If this were actually the case, however, and the appearance of each of the phenomena under discussion required the prior occurrence of variables with a lower position on a presumed continuum, only five cells in Chart III would be filled. The first would be that representing the "Utopian" state in which none of the phenomena were present, that is, where there was no prejudice, or discrimination, or social tension, or social violence. Others would be those with prejudice alone, prejudice with discrimination, prejudice with discrimination and tension, and all four concurrently. In the absence of intervening variables of external

CHART III

RELATIONSHIPS AMONG PREJUDICE, DISCRIMINATION,
SOCIAL TENSION AND SOCIAL VIOLENCE

	No Discrimination and No Prejudice	Discrimination	Prejudice	Discrimination and Prejudice
No Social Tension and No Social Violence				
Social Tension				
Social Violence				
Social Tension and Social Violence				

constraint it seems highly likely that the eruption of violence *would* follow such a pattern. In the actual event other cells *are* filled, and a number of legal, social and political controls prevent the free operation of the variables.

Let us return briefly to the cases of the non-prejudiced discriminating person and the non-discriminating prejudiced person. The former discriminate only because of external constraints. Most often their discrimination consists of passive acceptance of established patterns of discrimination, such as segregation in the American South, rather than in any initiation of differential treatment. The sociologist who uses segregated eating facilities and hotels in the South does not by virtue of such acts alone prove himself to be prejudiced.

In the case of the non-discriminating prejudiced persons there are two possible explanations. One is that external pressures prevent the expression of discriminatory behavior (as in the case where judicial injunctions or a display of military force prevent such expression). The other is that the individual or individuals involved have internalized norms which prohibit him or them from expressing their prejudices in discriminatory behavior.[2] It should be noted, however, that while prejudice is spoken of as if it were a "free-floating" group phenomenon, as an attitude it is ultimately an attribute, located in individuals.

One comment should be made relative to the designation of prejudice as an "attitude." A difficulty encountered in the use of the pairs of concepts—prejudice and discrimination and social tension and social violence—stems from the fact that in each set there are differences in the dimensions of action to which the concepts refer. Prejudice and tension are individual attributes, people *are* prejudiced or tense. Prejudice and tension require objects, but do not imply action (except in the sense of individual psychology and personality systems). To discriminate or to participate in social violence, however, is to *act* toward an object or objects.

APPARENT PARADOXES

It will not suffice, unfortunately, to label prejudice simply as a "predisposition" to discriminate and social tension as a "predisposition" to engage in social violence. Prejudice can be expressed in other ways than in discriminatory behavior. Discrimination is no more the sole expression of prejudice than social violence is the only form of conflict resolution. We do know that non-prejudiced persons do discriminate and

---

2. The discussion of the individual psychological aspects of relationships among phenomena labeled by those concepts is not within the scope of this note. I would suggest, however. an extremely thoughtful review to be found in Roger W. Brown (1954.)

conversely that prejudiced persons do not always discriminate. Explanation of these apparent paradoxes in behavior requires recourse to a fuller investigation of relationships among all four phenomena.[3]

An inference to be drawn from the preceding discussion is that there is no discrimination where there is not some prejudice. The discriminating individual himself may not be prejudiced, however prejudice is defined, but the individuals whose position in the power structure permits them to define situations in which interaction characterized by discriminatory behavior takes place *must* be prejudiced. It is theoretically possible, of course, that the individuals who are at the apex of the power structure are not actually themselves prejudiced but perceive the situation to be one in which they can only maintain themselves in power through acting as if they were, indeed, prejudiced. To suggest an example—it is possible that some educated leaders in the South are not themselves anti-Negro but feel that they cannot keep themselves in positions of power if they do not *act* as if they were anti-Negro. Whatever their motivations or rationalizations may be, the net effect is the same as if they were prejudiced.

EXTERNAL CONSTRAINTS

Free operation of the variables under discussion is hindered by the interference of intervening forces of constraint. Prejudice, discrimination (real or perceived) and social tension characterize patterns of Negro-white relationships in virtually every Northern city with a relatively or absolutely great Negro population. Social violence occurs either when social tension reaches a sufficiently high level or when external controls are ineffective. Parenthetically, it may be noted that it is theoretically feasible to assert that there is some absolute threshold of social tension above which social violence *must* occur. However, a ceiling on the effectiveness of external controls seems a more likely limit to the suppression of violence. External controls enter the definition of the situation on two levels. The first is in the prevention of expressions of prejudice in discriminating behavior. The second is the prevention of the eruption of social tensions in social violence. Chart IV suggests possible sequential relationships among these variables with the inclusion of intervening variables of external control.[4]

The last two columns of this chart represent situations where external constraints prevent discrimination but where there is a variation in the

3. Similar conclusions, based on desegregation research in Virginia, have been reached by Johan Galtung. He suggests analysis of these phenomena based on a distinction of manifest and latent attitudinal and expressive behavior on individual and collective levels (Personal communication, 1959).

4. Suggestions for the extension of this paradigm, particularly as it is relevant to the current desegregation controversy, have been made by Kenneth B. Clark.

CHART IV

SOME POSSIBLE SEQUENTIAL RELATIONSHIPS OF PREJUDICE,
DISCRIMINATION, SOCIAL TENSION AND SOCIAL VIOLENCE

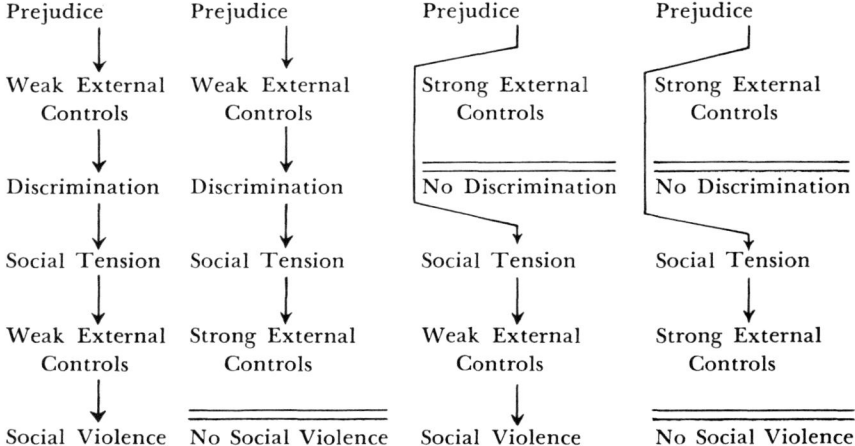

effectiveness of police controls. (The term police here could refer to any organized body authorized to use force.) An example can be found in the 1942 struggle over the occupancy of the Sojourner Truth Housing Project in Detroit. In that conflict, political and legal decisions prevented discrimination. Social tension in the majority community resulted from disruption of the accommodative pattern and the entire power structure of the community became involved.

A first attempt to move Negroes into the project met with social violence, which prevented the settlement of Negro tenants. The attitude of the local police was clearly shown by the fact that although whites were the principal law violators and the Negro tenants were being moved under auspices of Federal agencies, most of those arrested were Negroes. After this initial incident, there was considerable struggle in the political arena and a Negro occupancy pattern was reaffirmed. A second attempt to establish Negro occupancy followed. This second attempt was made under the protection of 800 troops. There was no further violence.

It has been shown that external forces are influential on two levels. It has been noted above that large numbers of prejudiced whites can be found in every urban area with substantial Negro population. In many instances this prejudice is expressed in discriminatory behavior. However, external constraints in the form of legal decisions and anti-discrimination legislation can prevent this discriminatory behavior. This prohibition of discrimination, when coupled with continuous Negro assaults upon the accommodative structure, is the cause of increased social tension in the white community. In situations of high social tension external factors again become crucial, this time in the determination of the occurrence or non-occurrence of social violence.

VIOLENCE AND FORCE

While discrimination is prevented by judicial or legislative action, the prevention of social violence is a function of military and quasi-military agencies which have a monopoly of the legitimate use of force. In recent years, police departments have been increasingly concerned with police-minority relations and with "preventive policing." Considerable attention has been directed toward the instillation of "professional" attitudes in policemen with the intention of increasing police effectiveness in interracial situations.

Westley has recently published a most suggestive volume on the formation, nature and control of crowds (Westley, 1955). He has shown that most police departments have orientations favoring either force or persuasion in the control of crowd behavior. As a means of external constraint in situations of high social racial tension, it seems probable that persuasion would be less effective than force. In cases of racial disturbances there is extremely high group identification. In situations of high racial social tension leadership which is willing to deal with the other group or with presumably neutral authorities is likely to lose control.

Labor identification may be high in the case of strikes. But at the same time, the leadership of the union seeks rational goals and can deal with the police and with other authorities. It is for this reason that police have more difficulty with wild-cat strikes than with organized bonafide activities of the union. Where group values of greatest importance are at stake, "moderate" leadership tends to lose control (Myers, 1948, pp. 57-67). Examination of materials on American race riots shows this to be the case in social racial violence. When social tensions reach the point where social violence can occur, persuasion and negotiation with community leadership, either white or Negro, is unlikely to be effective. But force, or a clear demonstration of the ability to apply it, can effectively cut off racial disturbances in their earliest stages. More effective ultimately, of course, are attacks upon the sources of social tension.

Chart III will take on added meaning if it is examined first with the assumption of weak external controls and then with the assumption of strong external controls. Only through the introduction of variables of external control is it possible to specify, even on a primitive level, the relationships among prejudice, discrimination, social tension and social violence.

TENSION AND PREJUDICE

Systematic examination of Charts III and IV suggests some important problems: Does tension presuppose prejudice? Is prejudice possible without some tension? Answers to these questions are not obvious. The question arises: Can tension be felt by only one collectivity in an interactive situation or must it be reciprocal in order to be labelled tension? Ramification of this question raises still other problems: What is the direction of prejudice, of discrimination, of social tension or of social violence? These questions are important, and it is my belief that answers to them and to related queries must be found before any systematic theorizing can be done in the field of race relations.

Similar questions must be answered relative to industrial violence and to conflict patterns generally. Answers to these questions, however, require the resolution of a more fundamental problem. This is the problem of the definitions of, and the boundaries of the definitions of, the variables themselves. The simple juxtaposition of terms in a chart does not resolve problems of definition. Nonetheless, the use of this device, in conjunction with the primitive definitions already in use, has served both to uncover the presence of intervening variables which must be considered in isolating relationships among these phenomena and to point the direction which refinements of the definitions must take.

Phenomena analogous to prejudice and discrimination and varieties of social tension and social violence are important in defining areas other than that of Negro-white relations. Most sociologists seem to have assumed a direct relationship between social tension and social violence. From such an assumption has come a belief in the necessity for and efficacy of "barometers" of racial tension. The discovery that no such direct relationship existed came from research on communal violence in India (Lambert, 1951).

The writer hopes to do research on industrial social violence and on other varieties of social violence both in the United States and in other areas. Social violence does occur without the existence of prejudice, at least as we usually define it. Group violence frequently occurs as a result of individual tensions. Definition of the meaning of the terms we use and a search for similar patterns in other varieties of group behavior will make easier an understanding of the social problems, and of the social processes, involved in violence.

Allen D. Grimshaw

Negro-White Relations in the Urban North:
Two Areas of High Conflict Potential

In recent years students of race relations have witnessed a shift in public interest in Negro-white relations. Dramatic events which followed the Supreme Court decisions of 1954 and 1956 and the more recent "sit-down" and "Freedom Ride" movements have drawn the attention of "liberals" and "anti-liberals" alike away from the continuing problem of Negro assimilation into the Northern metropolis. There have been no major race riots in Northern cities since 1943. There has been a continuing eruption of racial tensions in sporadic violence, reminding us that the work of interracial commissions and other agencies is not yet completed. Almost all of the Negro-white violence which has occurred since World War II has resulted from incidents in the areas of housing and recreation.

The following discussion of these two violence-prone areas of interaction rests on three assumptions (Grimshaw, 1961).

1. That Negro-white conflict and Negro-white violence in the United States have resulted from real or perceived assaults upon the accommodative structure, by Negroes, and not from any policy decisions, conscious or unconscious, by the leadership of either group.

2. That these assaults are more public and more obvious to the dominant group in some areas than in others. Thus, "move-ins" in housing and attempts to gain access to recreational facilities, since they are accompanied by actual contacts of large numbers of whites and Negroes, have a more "public" character than events which occur in areas where there is less interaction. Conveniently, these areas are also more amenable to some kinds of measurement.

3. That there is no direct relation between the level of social tension and the occurrence or nonoccurrence of social violence. Thus, tension may be very high and violence not occur or violence may occur even where tension is not high. While other factors are doubtless of importance in this apparent anomaly, the exercise of police controls appears to be most influential.

Housing: The present century has witnessed a mass movement of the American Negro population from the rural South to the urban North.[1] With few exceptions, Negroes appearing in Northern metropolises have confronted highly restricted residential choices. Most of them have

---

1. Changes in the distribution of the Negro population have been among the most marked demographic phenomena in the United States in this century. See Taeuber and Taeuber, 1958, pp. 109-111.

found their homes in urban slums. These "black ghettos" have expanded their boundaries at a pace too slow to keep up with population increases. White Americans have not welcomed Negro Americans as neighbors.

Students of race relations in Northern urban areas attach central importance to problems of housing. Privately supported research organizations, "action" agencies and a wide variety of governmental bodies have shared an interest in housing conflicts. In those cases where housing tensions have culminated in social violence they have shared this interest with an attentive and occasionally "outraged" public and press. Agencies working in the area of intergroup relations have devoted particular attention to the problem of housing integration and there is no need to review the voluminous literature in this place.

"INVASION"—A SOCIOLOGICAL DEFINITION

Stated in its simplest form, the sociological explication of the process of "invasion" runs as follows.[2] Negroes, because of prejudice and because of their identifiability, are unable to utilize their economic resources to rent or buy housing that whites of similar economic status can obtain. Increasing "pressure" of population and housing income forces up rent and sales prices in Negro areas. The ceiling ultimately becomes so high that whites, in either immediately contiguous or more remote areas, are forced (by the profit motive) to open up units of housing to Negroes. Once an initial Negro move-in occurs there is flight from the area by white residents, based in part on an unwillingness to live with Negroes, in part on a fear of loss of status, in part in acquiescence to pressures from friends and relatives, and in part on a fear of declining real estate values and a loss of equity. Negroes move in to replace the fleeing white residents. In order to pay the higher rents now placed on housing, a process of fragmentation of housing units occurs. This, along with the fact that the lower income of Negroes prevents them from spending as much on improvements and maintenance, precipitates a pattern of neighborhood deterioration. The remaining whites (who are able) then leave, and consolidation of the neighborhood is completed. This is followed by further "piling up" and the neighborhood becomes saturated. Competition for available housing within the area becomes sharper, prices are driven up and, ultimately, a new area is opened up and the process begins anew.[3]

Supplementing studies of the mechanics of changing occupancy pat-

2. Attention in this paper is devoted to urban housing; consideration of events in suburbs and developments will be incidental. Comprehensive attention to *privately developed interracial housing* can be found in the publications of the Commission on Race and Housing. See also Grier and Grier, 1960.

3. Duncan and Duncan, 1957 trace the cycle of "penetration," "invasion," "consolidation," and "piling-up" in convincing detail.

terns is a rich research literature on residential contact as a determinant of attitudes toward Negroes. Perhaps the best known are the studies on segregated and nonsegregated public housing done at the Research Center for Human Relations of New York University.[4] Kramer,[5] in research in areas on the periphery of Chicago's "Black Belt" attempted to more precisely delineate the statuses of those involved in contact. He concluded that prejudice against Negroes was least manifest where there was most and least residential contact with Negroes and most prevalent where there was a medium amount of contact. However, some of the more spectacular cases of housing violence (or near violence) in recent years have occurred at the time of initial move-ins. It was in such circumstances that violence occurred in Cicero and in Trumbull Park[6] and was threatened in Levittown, Pennsylvania.[7]

Information helpful toward understanding of Negro-white housing conflict is available in: (1) careful studies of demographic and ecological processes involved in Negro residential movement; (2) numerous investigations of the attitudinal aspects of that movement; and (3) reports of specific instances of social racial violence arising from Negro move-ins. Unfortunately, the precise delineation of processes leading to racial violence remains unfinished. Specification of these processes necessitates the simultaneous investigation of pressure on housing, resistance to that pressure and the interplay of pressure and resistance in the creation of social tension and violence-proneness.

PRESSURE

In an entirely free housing situation, cost per space unit of housing is determined by the size of the population to be housed, the amount of housing available to that population, and the income available (for housing) to the population under consideration. Assuming a constant amount of housing available and an increasing population or increasing available income for housing, the cost per space unit of housing will increase. Assuming a constant amount of total space available for an

4. See Deutsch and Collins, 1951; and Wilner, Walkey and Cook, 1955. It was a conclusion of both studies that contact does, indeed, reduce anti-Negro attitudes.
5. Kramer studied private housing (Kramer, 1950). Further studies of private housing can be found in Grier and Grier, 1960, and in volumes of the Commission on Race and Housing series.
6. Gremley, 1952 provides an excellent description and analysis of the Cicero incident. For Trumbull Park see Chicago Commission on Race Relations, n.d. The American Friends Service Committee also has prepared a series of reports on the Trumbull Park disturbances.
7. Bressler, 1960. In personal conversation Bressler observed that while some of Myers' neighbors participated in the harassing action which went on during the first weeks of his residence, most of the demonstrators were visitors who originally appeared on the scene as "sightseers" and paraded by his residence in automobiles. When parking was restricted for several blocks around the affected area most of the demonstrations ceased. The tactical implications seem clear.

increasing population with constant per capita housing income, fragmentation of dwelling units will follow. An approximation of the pressure on housing can be obtained by multiplying the population by its per capita expenditure on housing (for some time unit) and dividing this figure by the product of housing space units times cost per unit. Statement of this rough index as a relative can be done by dividing total housing income by total housing cost. An excess of housing income would create pressure on housing.

The artificial restrictions on the housing market which are a characteristic of segregated housing prevent the free operation of these variables in determining pressure on housing. Given a restricted amount of available housing and a fairly constant per capita income available for housing, a rising Negro population will create pressure on housing. This pressure is temporarily alleviated by increases in per unit cost and by fragmentation of dwelling units within the "ghetto." Both these expedients have occurred in Negro housing in Northern urban areas. A point is reached, however, where the cost per space unit in Negro areas is so much greater than for equivalent housing units in white areas that Negroes can no longer, or refuse to, increase their expenditures for housing.[8]

RESISTANCE

Resistance by white residents to Negro pressure on white housing is the source of social tensions which can be productive of social violence. This resistance is a result of the effective Negro pressure on white housing, itself a product of the combination of Negro pressure on Negro housing and of white pressure on white housing. Resistance is a residual factor. Its intensity can be measured only inferentially. When there is high pressure on both Negro and white housing and Negro movement into white areas occurs, resistance must be relatively low. If, however, Negro pressure on housing is high and white pressure on housing is low and no Negro in-movement occurs, resistance must be high. If all other variables could be held constant, in-movement of Negroes would occur in areas where: (a) Negro population is increasing; (b) Negro per capita housing income is increasing; (c) Negro housing space units available decrease (as in some slum clearance programs); (d) white population is decreasing; or (e) resistance is decreasing.

The situation in Northern urban areas has not been one in which all other variables are constant. The mass media, action agencies, both

8. It will be seen that this interpretation would not be relevant to an understanding of housing problems in an area, such as the Union of South Africa, where government policy explicitly forbids the settlement of Africans in white areas. Where pressures become too great in the Union, further in-movement by Negroes is prohibited and the surplus forced to return to the Reserves.

official and private, and the public attitudes of government officials all have important but unmeasurable influences on resistance. Whites may over- or under-estimate Negro pressures on housing and Negroes may perceive resistance as being stronger or weaker than it is in reality. These "definitions of the situation" have an important but unknown influence in speeding up or slowing down changes in occupancy patterns.

The cycle may be precipitated by an initial out-movement of whites followed by a rush of Negro in-movement. The pressure required for move-ins may decline as aspirations of Negroes, particularly of higher socio-economic brackets, are raised. Similarly, Negro expectations of freedom of movement may lower the threshold of pressure required for in-movement. Purchase by proxy or through the application of law may open areas far from concentrations of Negro population. These factors do influence the rate and ease of Negro movement into white areas. Nonetheless, the bulk of such movement can be explained by the interplay of variables within the essentially economic model outlined above —with the proviso that when the model doesn't work, it is the variable of white resistance which intervenes.

Resistance can be expressed in a number of ways other than overt aggression and violence. "Restrictive covenants" and "neighborhood improvement associations" are defensive in nature and, until the Supreme Court declared them unenforceable by government agencies, the former constituted an effective form of legal resistance. Bombings, arson, vandalism and physical assault are direct and aggressive forms of resistance. Where economically able, whites show their dissatisfaction with the in-movement of Negroes by flight from "penetrated" neighborhoods.

Resistance, in the form of attempts at legal discrimination or violence, and flight are attributable to one or both of two causes. Many, perhaps most, northern whites have anti-Negro prejudices. But other individuals, who may consider themselves "liberals," or who at least feel that Negroes are deserving of rights under the Constitution, may resist or flee because of a genuine fear of economic consequences of Negro in-movement. That their fears may be unfounded is beside the point. They act, as do prejudiced persons, to resist or flee Negro residential movement.

It is not necessary to analyze prejudice or the attributes of the prejudiced person in order to understand resistance. In the case of the individual who wishes to flee from an area undergoing "invasion" (whatever his reasons), residual community ties or, more likely, economic disability may make such flight difficult. External constraint in the form of judicial decisions has weakened the expression of resistance in discriminatory covenants. Such constraint may contribute to an increase of social tension. The presence of individuals in a neighborhood who are highly prejudiced or who fear economic damage from in-movement but are unable to move also contributes to sharp increases in social tension. This heightening of social tensions, if strong external constraint in the form of police power is not present, can cause eruptions of overt social violence.

VIOLENCE

However, in many areas changing neighborhood patterns, even in the absence of strong police control, have not increased social tensions to a point where social violence has occurred. Mayer's study of changes in the residential pattern of Russell Woods shows a sub-community in which in-movement caused some flight, but one also in which remaining residents did not define the situation as one calling for action. (Mayer, n.d. [mimeo]. This study was done for the Commission on Race and Housing.) Propaganda of action agencies has come to be widespread in recent years, as represented by the movement in which residents have been encouraged to post their houses with signs reading: "Not for Sale: Either My House or My Principles." Numerous studies have found people giving at least lip service to the principle that everyone, no matter what his race or creed, has the right to live wherever he can afford to, provided only that he behaves properly. Individuals who are sharply anti-Negro in their attitudes may be increasingly reluctant to express their views as they perceive changes in the general climate of race relations.

Such violence as does occur may be less representative of majority community opinion than was true in the past. A study in Kansas City, Missouri, found whites resigned to an ongoing in-movement of Negroes into a previously all white residential area (Community Studies, Inc., n.d.). In spite of this finding, a bomb was exploded in the neighborhood. The bombing was interpreted as being the work of a "fanatic" not resident in the neighborhood (William Gremley, personal communication, October 23, 1957).

Although individual Negro residents have occasionally been accepted, postures of resistance and considerable social tension historically have characterized the situation in most areas threatened by changes in residential patterns. Even in middle-class white residential neighborhoods where the higher cost of housing prohibits the in-movement of substantial numbers of Negroes, white fears or expectations of such in-movement are accompanied by a rise in social tension. Latent fears of economic loss are encouraged by both white and colored real estate operators. The appearance of substantial Negro populations in Northern urban areas has almost universally been accompanied by the appearance of "improvement" and "protective" associations. In many cases the neighborhood press has taken a strong stand for preserving the "character" of a neighborhood. In every case of heightened racial social tension the occurrence or non-occurrence of social racial violence is dependent on the perceived or actual strength and attitude of external forces. In the actual event, this can be read as strength and attitude of the police.

The importance of external police forces (external to individuals and groups immediately involved) can be demonstrated by comparing situations where external constraints prevent discrimination but where there are variations in the strength of police controls. One such example can be found in the 1942 struggle over the occupancy pattern of the Sojourner Truth Housing Project in Detroit (reviewed in Grimshaw, 1961). More recent examples can be found in the Cicero and Trumbull Park incidents. In both cases Negroes moved into predominantly white areas, in both cases there was widespread hostility to the in-movement on the part of large proportions of the resident population. Flight was not feasible for the lower-middle-class home owners in these neighborhoods. Legal discrimination was not possible in the State of Illinois. The press was openly hostile. Social violence occurred in Cicero, aided and abetted by the police. Agents of local law enforcement agencies calmly observed substantial property violence and listened to threats of physical assault without taking any action. When it became obvious that the situation had gotten out of hand, National Guard troops were dispatched to the scene by the governor of Illinois. The chief of police and other city officials were later indicted for their role in the disturbances (and for other alleged malfeasance in office).

In sharp contrast, while incidents did occur at the time of the Trumbull Park move-ins, social violence was contained. Over a five year period the Chicago Police Department, with a complex riot-control program and under the watchful eye of the Chicago Commission on Human Relations, saturated the area with police and prevented mobs from getting out of control. Ranking Chicago police officers, while publicly stating their sympathies with white residents of the area in their antagonisms toward Negroes, at the same time insisted that the law would be upheld.

RECREATION [9]

Disputes over the use of recreational facilities have twice provided the spark touching off major race riots. Two of the most savage interracial outbursts of the current century, the Chicago riot of 1919 and that in Detroit in 1943, both started in public recreational facilities. Since World War II there have been disputes over the use of swimming pools in St. Louis, Youngstown, Ohio, and Washington, D.C., and a number of other interracial conflicts have involved recreational facilities. Such facilities are scarce in all urban areas, particularly in areas of deteriorating housing and in slums. These areas may have various types of com-

9. The best single discussion of recent events in this area of Negro-white relations is found in Weisberg, 1951.

mercialized recreation, including that commonly labeled as "vice," but share in common a shortage of "family" facilities, recreational outlets for young adults and outside play areas for groups of all ages. The pattern of Negro "pressure" on facilities, of white "pressure," and of the interplay of those pressures in the development of "resistance" on the part of members of the dominant community, closely parallels that described in housing.

The meaning, to Negroes and whites, of first attempts at penetration seems to have changed over the last four decades. Since World War II, it appears that Negro penetration of previously all-white recreation areas has been a self-conscious assault upon established accommodative patterns. The pattern of attack has been formalized and to an increasing extent preceded by attempts to "soften up" white resistance through recourse to political and more particularly legal maneuvering. Test cases have questioned the legality of segregated swimming pools, golf courses and similar facilities when they have been supported through a tax structure imposed on whites and Negroes alike. In the North, picketing and boycotts have been directed against privately owned corporations maintaining segregated facilities. In the South, this has occasionally meant the closing of the facilities. In the North, cities have had to purchase private recreational facilities, which have then become "Negro." In Philadelphia, for example, after boycotting of the Crystal Pool (a "club" facility operated by a private corporation) drove attendance down, the management threatened to close the pool. It was purchased by the city and became a "Negro" pool until closed by other building activity.

The North, in the last decade, has seen occasional eruptions of social violence. Minor violence followed integration of previously white swimming pools in St. Louis and Youngstown, and had it not been for the activities of action agencies and of the police, might have developed into more widespread difficulty.

THE USUAL PATTERN

Once initial penetration has been accomplished, with or without political and legal coercion, a familiar pattern frequently recurs. The success of the initial Negroes brings others, whites panic and some flee, in many cases the facility becomes completely Negro in its usage. In part this is a result of the tremendous backlog of Negro pressure on available recreational opportunities. In part it may be a reflection of changes in the occupancy patterns of the neighborhood in which the facility is located. It may be noted that the ecological succession can become even more complicated when early Negro users of a facility flee it as it becomes inundated with Negroes of lower socioeconomic status, as happened with the Kelly Olympic Pool in Philadelphia.

Violence is by no means an inevitable accompaniment of Negro penetration nor is it true that when violence does occur it occurs only during this stage. The report of the Chicago Commission on Race Relations, which gave considerable weight to recreational disputes as a background factor in the Chicago violence of 1919, nevertheless noted many instances of relatively peaceful integration of playgrounds or at least of peaceful "co-existence" within playground facilities. The incidents on Belle Isle which precipitated the Detroit riot of 1943 occurred at the end of the ecological cycle rather than at the beginning. Negroes were in an overwhelming majority in the throngs seeking relief from the heat on the June Sunday the riot started. It probably should be concluded, on the basis of the variety of situations in which disputes over recreational facilities occur, that it is not solely the stage of change in composition of the population using the facility that determines whether or not violence occurs. While it is true that many of the violent incidents have occurred during the period of initial penetration, at that time when the assault upon the accommodative pattern is most noticeable, it is the factor of external controls which is determinative of the actual eruption of social violence.

There are, in every interracial situation in any Northern city, some prejudiced white persons. Even individuals who do not possess anti-Negro attitudes of high intensity would probably be more comfortable in situations where discrimination, whether based on some legal fiction or on "custom," segregates whites and Negroes and reduces cross-racial contacts. In most cases of interracial contact the tension roused in prejudiced whites by Negro assault on the accommodative structure is augmented by the "anxiety" of other whites who, while not actively anti-Negro, would prefer to withdraw from potentially "uncomfortable" situations.

THE CRUCIAL FACTOR: EXTERNAL CONTROLS

When contact occurs, either because of Negro pressure on available facilities or because of legal or political decisions which prevent discrimination, social tension increases. Whether or not this tension erupts is dependent on external power, ultimately that of police control. In the Chicago riot of 1919 a strongly anti-Negro policeman refused to take action against whites alleged to have thrown a stone which felled the first victim of the riot, a drowned Negro boy. This refusal, in conjunction with the later attempts to arrest Negroes, caused Negroes to start the assaults which grew into the Chicago riot. In Detroit, in 1943, the police force was unable to contain early violence. In sharp contrast, has been the successful action of the Chicago police during the last five or six years in cutting off a series of incidents in the tension-laden South Side in their beginning stages. The parallel to the housing situation is marked. The interacting pressures of the Negro and white groups on available facilities and the varied activities of the courts and of municipal administrations and action agencies are clearly important in defining the level of violence-proneness. It is the strength and attitude of available police forces which determine whether or not violence occurs.

Clear-cut examples are again available. In Washington, D.C., the *Washington Post* predicted major rioting on the opening of swimming pools to Negroes in 1950. In 1949 the Secretary of the Interior had closed the pools when sporadic fighting between Negroes and whites occurred in a first attempt to desegregate the pools. In March, 1950, Secretary Chapman announced that the pools would be open to all citizens during the coming summer. He added that the Department of the Interior was prepared to enforce pool regulations by police action and protection, should that be necessary. Personnel who would be involved were given training in the handling of racial tensions. Just before the pools were opened, the Superintendent of the Washington Metropolitan Police announced that order would be preserved, even if it required the use of every policeman on the force. No violence occurred. Nor was it even necessary to station large numbers of police officers at the pool through the summer.

In 1949 the threat of violence caused the Washington swimming pools to be closed. In the same year, violence occurred when an attempt was made to desegregate pools in St. Louis and the pools remained segregated. In St. Louis when the pools were opened to all in 1950, police planning failed to show the firmness which was exhibited in Washington. Although the pools were opened, it was necessary to maintain large forces of police officers at the pools and incidents occurred. The Washington case suggests that St. Louis might have avoided much of its difficulty by initially taking a firm stance.[10]

Another factor in recreational disputes is the purely mechanical one of sufficient numbers. To say that social violence cannot occur in a demographic vacuum is to state the obvious. The critical number of individuals in either one or both racial categories which must be present before violence can occur is unknown. That there is some minimum number is clear (see Kephart's interesting and suggestive work, 1954).

SUMMARY

If discrimination is prevented by legal or other action, some individuals, even though prejudiced, will resign themselves to the situation. If the

10. A decade later St. Louis continued to have its problems. Although an antidiscrimination ordinance was passed in early 1961, a Negro registrant at professional meetings (the Society for the Study of Social Problems and the American Sociological Association) was refused admission to the swimming pool in the conference hotel. A threat to cancel the meetings, in conjunction with pressure from municpal agencies caused the management to capitulate.

law says they cannot discriminate, they will not discriminate. Other individuals, however, whose prejudice or suggestibility may be higher, may become involved in extralegal activity which can culminate in violence. Whether or not this violence occurs depends less on the level of social tension than on the strength and posture of police forces.

A crude model of Negro and white pressures on available facilities and of resultant white resistance has been suggested as a base for an understanding of housing conflicts. It has been suggested that the same model can roughly be extended to recreational disputes. Other approaches can be developed for the analysis of situations where the assault on the accommodative structure is more subtle and less public. In any case, however, this writer agrees with Weisberg, ". . . racial violence can be prevented even where the enforcement of civil rights law involves direct attack on established patterns of racial segregation. The key to such successful law enforcement is decisive and informed government action" (Weisberg, 1951).

Arthur I. Waskow

From Race Riot to Sit-In: 1919 and the 1960's

[1919]

An examination of the five major responses to the 1919 riots shows that several of them see changes in the behavior of the police as a way of preventing future riots. Looked at in terms of their views on the role of the police, the five responses cluster into three different positions. The first of these looked toward increasing the power of the police so that they could smash opposition to the established order, whether expressed in violent riots or disorderly protest. The second looked toward making the police more neutral as between the parties in conflict, more single-mindedly committed to preventing or punishing violence by whomever used, and more prepared to accept as legitimate any attempts by weaker parties to disturb the established order by means other than violence. The third approach tended to ignore the police and to concentrate instead on changes in the values and beliefs of American society.

The first view, favoring a more powerful police, was held both by those who demanded a return to racial hierarchy in American life and those who demanded the re-establishment of "law and order." In the first case, hierarchists deplored what they called the "mildness" that police in many cities had shown toward Negro rioters, and also demanded tough federal police action against the "radicalism" and "Bolshevism" they thought had helped incite the Negro mobs. Among those who wanted a return to "law and order" without specifying what sort of established order they had in mind, the idea seems to have been not suppression of Negroes by superior police power, but suppression of anyone, white or black, who disturbed the political system. The "law and order" school seemed to hope that whenever racial conflict became disorderly or violent, government would make authoritative decisions settling the conflicts and then enforce these decisions with a heavy hand. Despite the difference between the two groups over the kind of "order" to be enforced, both were prepared to enforce order with overwhelming power.

The approach that looked toward a neutral police force, oriented to the prevention of violence without the suppression of conflict, was exemplified by the campaign for a federal law against lynching and by the logic of the Supreme Court in the Arkansas cases. In both these instances, the argument was that the federal government could and should insist that no local mob or police force use violence on behalf of one of the parties to racial conflict. In both cases—specifically in the Arkansas cases, by clear intent in the anti-lynching campaign—this approach would have extended federal protection to such activities as the creation of Negro pressure groups and unions, no matter how "disorderly" and outrageous such activities were considered in a particular locality. But this approach would not have meant federal enforcement of a new established order of racial equality. In short, these proposals looked toward the creation of a neutral police oriented solely to the prevention of violence, not toward the increase of police power to the point where it could smash all disturbers of the established order.

The third approach to the role of the police, which tended to focus away from them and toward changing basic values in the community, was taken by those who wanted to move toward racial equality and those who supported a policy of "accommodation." Unlike supporters of racial hierarchy, supporters of racial equality did not urge the use of a powerful police force to establish and uphold their favorite version of order and to suppress their opponents. Although at first glance it may seem surprising that between believers in racial hierarchy and believers in racial equality there is so little symmetry on the question of a proper role for the police, the asymmetry seems less surprising if the facts of relative power in 1919 are taken into account. The hierarchists were entrenched in power in much of the United States (not only in the South), and could easily imagine a policy of suppression carried on by "their" police forces. The equalitarians, on the other hand, had little real power anywhere in the United States except a partial veto, and an indefinite appeal to the consciences of some of those who did hold power. It might have been hard for them to imagine, and certainly would have been absurd of them to urge, that the local and federal police power be used to uphold a new order of racial equality.

As for the "accommodationists," many of them were more cautious believers in an ultimate racial equality and many were working within the context of extremely hierarchist societies, in the South. For them the enforcement of even moderate racial change by overwhelming police action would have seemed impossible, and instead they urged the semi-official discussion and adjustment of particular issues.

Both groups therefore emphasized the need for major changes in the values held by Americans, before their values should be translated into enforceable law.

These three different approaches to the role of police—the call for a more powerful police to uphold order, the call for a more neutral police that might permit disorder without violence, and the call for a change in values before the police were asked to enforce any standard—can be developed for analytical purposes into three different basic ways of exercising political authority over a society within which there was intense political conflict carried on by powerful groups over basic issues strongly felt. These three forms of political authority might for the sake of convenience be called those of "church," of "state," and of "government."

A "church" is an institution that focuses and creates shared values by moral suasion, rather than force or coercion. Although we are used to thinking of churches as separate from the government, there are many elements of presidential and congressional authority that are symbolic rather than coercive and many aspects of court decisions on great issues that go beyond immediate, coercively enforceable decrees into the creation of a new consensus on basic values. In this sense some writers have spoken of the "religions" of democracy or of nationalism, and it is the institutionalization of such "religions" within some parts of the federal authority that is meant here by the word "church," rather than any particular religious body. In a society that had a single major "church," there would be no serious political conflicts; almost all the people would agree on political values and purposes. In a society where several "churches" or none existed, there might be intense political conflict, it would be hard to establish a single "church" or to keep an existing one legitimate. The argument for a new "church" on racial issues was expressed in 1919 by those who hoped for racial equality or accommodation to be achieved by a change in American values.

A "state," to use—and deliberately misuse—Max Weber's definition, is an institution that has a monopoly on legitimate violence and the power to prevent or punish illegitimate violence. Weber did not mean by defining a "state" in this way to suggest that a "state" did not have other powers as well. But let us, for the sake of convenience in discussing different sorts of political authority, turn Weber's definition around and call a "state" that sort of institution which can *only* forbid private, illegitimate violence—and which can use its own legitimate violence *only* to enforce that prohibition. In a society where there were intense political conflicts, but a "state" existed, the conflicts would be likely to be fought out with no outright violence, by "disorderly" methods. In a society beset by conflicts in which there was no "state," the conflicts would be extremely likely to erupt into violence. In 1919, those who called for a neutral police system and the prohibition of violence on racial issues were demanding what we are now calling a "state."

A "government," finally, is an institution that intermixes the functions of "church" and "state." A true "government" both sets forth values and prepares to enforce them with all the legitimate violence necessary. In doing so, a "government" creates something totally new: *law* in the strict sense, which first sets forth the acts people should perform or avoid and then prescribes the use of police power to punish those who fail to obey. In a society where a strong "government" operated and true law existed on all issues, political processes would be extremely "orderly," and change might be slow and hard to bring about from the bottom, but easy to command from on high. Those who in 1919 wanted forceful police measures taken to restore "law and order" or to uphold racial hierarchy were calling for the creation of a "government" on the race question.

These "ideal types" of political authority are, of course, convenient ways to categorize political behavior, rather than descriptions of actual political institutions operating in the pure forms as set forth here. But a particular political institution may act much more like one than another of these ideal types. Or, on a particular issue over which there is intense conflict, a given political institution may act like one of these forms—whereas on another issue over which there is little conflict, the same political institution may act much more like another of the "ideal types." This last, on the racial issue, has been precisely the case with the United States Government in Washington. On many questions, for many decades, it has acted like a true "government"; on the race question, it has not.

Indeed, in 1919 the United States had no single "church," no "state," and no single "government" as regards the race question (though it did, on the local level, have an ill-defined and inchoate set of "governments," mostly committed to racial hierarchy). In response to the 1919 race riots, there began to grow the seeds of an American "state" on the race question—an institution, or set of institutions, that outlawed violence from either side but did not try to settle the basic conflicts that led to violence. The way in which the United States Army behaved in most of the riot situations it entered and the way in which the Supreme Court acted when the Arkansas cases reached it are the indications that the seeds had begun to grow. But they were only seeds, and not until the racial crisis of the 1960s did the notion of an American "state" on the race question begin to flower.

.   .   .   .

[THE 1960's]

. . . All three forms of politics as used by the civil rights movement were concerned with bringing about change. But there was a difference in the extent to which people using the different forms tended to focus on the changes to be achieved, to the exclusion of focusing on the rules of the system that was to be changed or on those who defended that system. In the politics of order, people divide their attention between the changes to be accomplished and the accepted rules of society about the "legitimate" ways of bringing about change. In the politics of violence, people divide their attention between the changes to be accomplished and those powerful people who get in the way of change—the enemy. In the politics of disorder, people tend to reduce greatly their interest in both the given rules and the enemy; instead they focus very strongly on the changes to be accomplished. To oversimplify a bit: in the politics of order, men follow the rules; in the politics of violence, they attack their enemies; in the politics of disorder, they pursue change.

It can be argued that the civil rights movement of the 1960s actually accomplished more change in race relations than did either the politics of violence in 1919, 1943, and since, or the politics of order in 1866 and 1875 (the years of the first civil rights acts) and 1954 (the year of the Supreme Court's school desegregation decision). If so, the reason may well be that in focusing on the achievement of change rather than on the rules or the enemy, "disorder" in the racial struggle has actually brought about more change.

To the degree that the politics of disorder is aimed at bringing about change, it is generally invented by people who are "outside" a particular system of political order, and want to bring change about so that they can enter. In doing so, they tend to use new techniques that make sense to themselves out of their own experience, but that look disorderly to people who are thinking and acting inside the system. The Negroes were by no means the first to initiate this process. For example, in the seventeenth and eighteenth centuries, urban lawyers and merchants who could not get the entrenched politicians to pay attention to their grievances (and who were scarcely represented in Parliament) used the illegal and disorderly device of political pamphleteering against the established order. In the same way, nineteenth-century workers who could not get their employers or the elected legislators to pay attention to their demands used unionization and the strike—which at first were illegal—to call attention to their grievances. In both these cases, using the politics of disorder not only got the users accepted into the political order and got their immediate grievances looked after, but also got the new techniques accepted into the array of authorized and approved political methods. In short, the system of "order" was itself changed. Thus the "criminal libel" of political pamphleteering was enshrined as freedom of the press, and the "criminal conspiracy" of striking was enshrined in the system of free labor unions. One century's disorder became the next century's liberty under ordered law. Whether this will occur with the forms of creative disorder used by Negro Americans in their movement for racial equality has yet to be decided; but there are many indications that the process has begun.

. . . The seeming paradox that both racial equalitarians and racial hierarchists could on occasion believe themselves "outside" the legitimate political order and therefore [be] forced to use "disorderly" forms of politics is in reality no paradox at all. During the 1960s one of these groups which had long been securely within the political order—the hierarchists and segregationists—was slowly being pushed outside it. At the same time, the equalitarians and integrationists, or at least the bulk of the Negroes among them, who had long been excluded from the political order, were slowly being included for the first time. During the transition period, both groups had reason to feel like "outsiders" and to use the methods of disorder.

During this period of sustained disorder from both sides in the racial conflict, the federal government moved further than it had during the brief period of violence in 1919 toward acting like a "state." Because both of those groups using the politics of disorder were so powerful and because opinion in the society at large remained so deeply divided over the values of racial hierarchy as against racial equality, during the early 1960s there was strong pressure on practically all American political institutions to tolerate disorder when used by either side on the racial question, so long as violence was avoided; to prevent, halt, and punish violence by either side; and to draw back from what would have been a truly "governmental" act, the police enforcement of either side's view of the race question. Even then, there was difficulty in bringing an American "state" on the race question to full fruition. Attorney General Kennedy's difficulty in distinguishing a "state" from a "government," as when he opposed the original Title III of the civil rights bill for fear that a "national police force" could not simply prevent violence but would have to conquer the South, was one measure of the difficulty. But the growing strength of the "state" position can be seen from the desire of congressmen to enact Title III and from the position taken by the Justice Department in its *amicus* brief for the Supreme Court on the sit-in cases.

In both of these instances, unlikely organs of government were defending the notion that federal power should be exerted to protect disorder without violence. Obviously, neither the Justice Department nor members of Congress came easily to the position that the protection of disorder was more desirable than the establishment of a new order; their institutional roles require both of them to fear disorder and insist on the value of order. But because of the depth and intensity of the conflict over racial equality or hierarchy, both came to believe that an attempt to impose order might result instead in violence, and disorder should therefore be permitted and protected so long as it did not become violence. The transformation of disorder into order would have to await the creation of a much broader agreement on which "order" should be upheld.

As for the "church" aspects of federal authority, it could be argued that the 1954 Supreme Court decision on school segregation was the crucial event in beginning to establish official values based on racial equality. Although in several instances direct violations of court orders for school desegration were confronted by federal enforcement of the orders, the court decision had far more impact in the realm of values and morality—for example, in raising the expectations of young Negroes that finally erupted in the sit-ins—than it did in establishing directly enforceable law. And it is important to note that despite its high permanent prestige as an American "church," the Supreme Court from almost the moment of its decision began to suffer vigorous attacks, which demonstrated the absence of any real national consensus and the resistance to any single national "church" on the race question.

It was not really until the Civil Rights Act of 1964 was passed that the aspects of the "state" on racial issues that the Federal government had begun to take on in response to the 1919 riots and the aspects of the "church" on racial issues that it had begun to take on in 1954 were merged effectively into new law. Thus not until 1964 can there be said to have emerged the beginnings of an American "government" on the race question.[1]

What is likely to happen to that "government," barely born in 1964, and what may happen to the politics of order, disorder, and violence as they have been used in the racial conflict? To the extent that the Civil Rights Act of 1964 created a "government" on the race question, it is only a weak and tentative government. As the Negroes of Mississippi and Harlem—more generally speaking, the Deep South, most rural and most repressive, and the Deep North, most urban and most desperate— made clear as soon as the act was passed, it did not meet their problems. It would take new acts of "government" to bring Harlem and Mississippi fully into the American political system. And if the past is any indication of the future, such acts of new "government" are more likely to occur if they have been demanded by those who are still outside the political system, through acts of creative disorder.

What then is likely to be the future of the politics of disorder within

1. An abortive effort at creating a true federal "government" on the race question was made during Reconstruction, but soon failed.

the movement for racial equality? Will the new political forms wither away if equalitarians win more and more victories, or will the techniques outlive the particular issues? Which of the techniques are likely to prove most effective and creative? Is disorder often likely to escalate from the boycott or the sit-in to full-scale social disruption, or will the hostility to this form of attack prevent its being often used?

The answers to these questions will depend mostly upon two factors: the response of political authorities to the use of controlled forms of disorder as ways of attracting public attention to and bringing about a resolution of particular conflicts; and the degree of inventiveness and self-discipline in the Negro community as it tries to create new techniques to cope with whatever failures may occur in the use of controlled disorder.

As to the political authorities: if the local police try to smash equivalents of a "riot" that use no violence, they are much more likely to find real riots blossoming before them, or perhaps efforts at general social disruption. Even if the police attack, not the organized, deliberate equalitarian movements that are using creative disorder (as the police more frequently do in the South), but instead a number of unorganized, individual, "troublesome" Negroes (as they more frequently do in the North), they may find the Negro community ready to boil over into riots. If, on the other hand, all the governments concerned, local and national, step back and allow sit-ins, boycotts, and rent strikes to be "fought out" just as most labor strikes and lock-outs are, so long as neither side uses violence, and if local and national authorities act to punish violence used by either side in the racial conflict, then it is unlikely that efforts at creative disorder will degenerate into rioting. But a movement in this direction would require from the federal government the imagination necessary to build the kind of federal police force that could check and prevent particular acts of violence against Negroes, even violence by local police, without taking over entire cities or states.

It is not only deliberate police action to smash controlled creative disorder that may result in its degeneration into violence or disruption. If political authorities simply ignore attempts to use controlled disorder, its users may try the more threatening techniques. Limited forms of disorder seem less able to attract attention and disturb the authorities in a great and complex northern metropolis than in a middle-sized southern town or the rural Black Belt. Frustrated protestants in the northern cities who see their efforts at controlled disorder going for nought might well keep on trying such generally disruptive techniques as the World's Fair stall-in or blocking New York's Triborough Bridge, especially since the greater complexity of metropolitan society is likely to make it more vulnerable to small but carefully chosen acts of social disruption. Or if the failure of controlled creative disorder disillusions and discourages large numbers of urban Negroes, they may become ready tinder for a spark of riot. On the other hand, forms of limited disorder might become accepted throughout the United States as reasonable methods for persuading legislators and officials to change their minds—akin to free speech, in other words. If this is the direction of change—if the Congress and local governments fully accept sit-ins, marches, boycotts, and rent strikes as legitimate expressions of public desires and change their behavior accordingly—then it is rather unlikely that disorder will escalate into efforts at social disruption, or into rioting.

As to the degree of inventiveness in the Negro community: The question will be whether there is in existence a leadership that is committed to avoiding violence, that is capable of creating new forms of disorder without violence, and that can keep in close touch with its constituents in the Negro population. If so, the chances for riot would decrease, as compared to the chances of new forms of disorder. So far, Negro leaders in the North seem to have had difficulty in inventing new forms of disorder that would appeal to one specific and extremely important group: adolescent youths and young men without jobs or education. The southern sit-ins and marches have evidently appealed to some of the same qualities of masculinity and physical courage that make many young men good soldiers. But the northern rent strike and economic boycott seem to appeal to or be activities more easily carried out by quieter, older people. Although school boycotts and job blockades may appeal to the young, they cannot easily involve those who have already quit school or those who do not have the skills necessary to hold existing jobs; and it is exactly these men who are most likely to resort to violence. In the absence of new inventions in creative disorder that appeal to young men in the North, therefore, riots there may become more likely.

. . . The two sets of changes that from the discussion above seem to be necessary if violence and social disruption are to be avoided can be summed up as, first, the bringing to fruition of an American "state" on racial questions; and second, the invention and legitimation of a number of new techniques of controlled creative disorder. The first of these means that some form of federal police force must be created to prevent violence from being used by either side in the racial conflict, including violence that takes on the color of legitimacy because it is carried on by local police who are in fact merely acting on behalf of one side or the other. Such a force would have to be carefully aimed at the protection of creative disorder used by either side in the racial conflict, and would have to be carefully restricted from itself defending one view or the other of racial justice. Indeed, it would probably be wise to set up a separate force for this purpose, so as to avoid involving those enforcement officers who carry out "governmental" mandates to the degree that they exist on the racial issue—for example, the public accommodations provisions of the Civil Rights Act of 1964.

Conceivably, such a force might be most effective if there were also created a system for managing and coping with particular disorderly techniques used in racial conflict, just as the Wagner Labor Relations Act created ways of recognizing certain agents of labor and management as legitimate conflict organizations, approving some forms of labor-management disorder, ruling others out of bounds, and encouraging bargaining between the parties. If American society were to achieve new levels of consensus on new aspects of the race question, through the clash of ideas and power involved in creative disorder, then new enforceable "law" would presumably be created and the responsibility for dealing with the areas covered by the new laws would shift from agencies behaving like a "state" to agencies behaving like a "government."

The second of what seem to be the crucial prerequisites to avoiding racial violence—the invention and legitimation of new forms of controlled creative disorder that would be applicable to new areas of racial conflict—may have some implications and effects that go beyond the racial arena. As in the extension of the legitimacy of the free press beyond the issues and social groups for which it was first espoused to new issues and other social groups, so it is possible that some forms of creative disorder invented by Negroes in the movement for racial equality will become legitimate for other social groups as well. For example, it is not impossible to imagine some of the white miners of eastern Kentucky, many of whom have been without jobs from many years, sitting-in on federal unemployment compensation offices. It is not impossible to imagine school boycotts by students protesting the firing of a professor, or protesting against their schools being put on a split-shift schedule. In other words, if the new forms of disorder become legitimate there is no reason to expect that only Negroes will find them useful and necessary.

Robin M. Williams, Jr.

Strangers Next Door: Ethnic Relations in American Communities

THE CASE OF RELIGIOUS AFFILIATIONS IN A MULTIGROUP SOCIETY

Many general points find concrete illustrations in the instance of inter-faith relations in the United States. Most of our attention in the present volume has been directed to racial relations. But the basic concepts and the underlying model of a social system are adaptable to other types of intergroup relations. Let us illustrate the approach by examining briefly some of the main social features of interreligious relations in the United States.

A long-standing, if imprecise, hypothesis concerning social conflict has been that a society riven by many cleavages is in less danger of violent disruption than one in which a single massive division runs across the population (Williams, 1947, p. 59). Investigation of this notion takes on sharpened social relevance in view of our present understanding of the inevitability of *some* cleavages. Cleavages between groups exist in society as the simple "obverse of consensus within groups." This means that the question for analysis is not *why* is there cleavage, but *what* are the lines of potential cleavage in society, and what are the consequences of one configuration rather than another (Coleman, 1956, p. 53.)?

Among the categorical bases for group formation in the United States are: race, religious affiliation, language, region, socioeconomic stratum, ethnic origin, political affiliation. Let us imagine that these attributes are invariably associated in such a way that only the following three clusters occur, with approximately the same numbers of persons in each: What would be the outcomes of this situation? We may be sure that a society made up in this way would not be anything like the United States we now know. Nor would any of the major factors listed have its present significance.

CLUSTERS

Category	I	II	III
Race	White	Negro	Chinese
Religion	Protestant	Catholic	Buddhist
Language	English speaking	Spanish speaking	Bilingual: Chinese-English
Region	New England	South	West
Class	Upper class	Middle class	Lower class
Ethnic origin	British	Gold Coast	China
Political party	Republican	Democrat	Socialist

OVERLAPPING OF RELIGIOUS MEMBERSHIP WITH OTHER SOCIAL CHARACTERISTICS

Notice that in this hypothetical society there is *no overlapping of the several crucial social attributes*. This characteristic makes for maximum likelihood of divergent interests and for maximum clarity of group membership. If groupings of this kind are in contact and *if* they are competitive, the likelihood is great that some form of conflict will emerge. Thus we may arrive at this hypothesis: "Group conflicts are at their strongest, are most likely to develop and least easily dissipated, when no conflict is felt within the person." (*Ibid.*, 46.) Another way of stating the point is to say that a major factor in reducing conflict *between* groupings is the maximizing of cross pressures within individuals through multiple, overlapping group memberships.

We may say, therefore, that:

1. Maximum potentiality of large-scale group conflict is present when the *major structural* categories of social differentiation coincide to form a small number of massive social categories, whose members nevertheless are competitively interdependent in economic and political subsystems.

2. Major structural categories of great importance in any society are (a) territorial community; (b) social class; (c) ethnic grouping; (d) race; (e) religion; (f) political affiliation.

3. A society faces maximum likelihood of massive conflict (or of political disruption) when the various lines of differentiation of values, interests, and collectivity memberships coincide among the same population aggregates. In contemporary United States, the various major bases for collectivity memberships crisscross in a most complicated fashion. Very different are the consequences to be expected from a cumulative coincidence of all these lines of differentiation.

If the points thus far made are valid, it is a reasonable supposition that differences in religion will be least disruptive in a multigroup society when they are not systematically associated with other important bases of divergence in values and interests. (A conspicuous example of a modern religious sect that is radically alienated from the environing society is that of Jehovah's Witnesses. Like other alienated [proletarian] movements, it emphasizes a "cataclysmic end of the world with a millennium following," a system of esoteric knowledge, a doctrine of sharp rejection of the world, and a vision of a future utopia. Cf. Cohn, 1955.) In Underwood's study of an overwhelmingly Catholic city in northeastern United States (1957), it was observed that religious cleavage had been accentuated by the correlation of class and ethnic lines with religious affiliation, partly because this very association tended to reinforce stereotyped preconceptions and antipathies. Protestants were primarily of Yankee background and middle- and upper-middle-class position; Catholics derived more largely from later immigration and tended on the whole to occupy the lower socioeconomic strata.

The hypotheses just discussed can be put into testable forms. Establishment of the conditions under which they are valid, would, presumably, be of great permanent interest.

A more positive source of social solidarity arises from the multiplicity of interests and values in the overlapping memberships that bind men together in a pluralistic society. Each man can have the security of diversified economic, political, and other socio-emotional investments: he has not committed all his eggs to one basket. Conflicts of economic interest, of status aspirations, or even of religious views do not, therefore, have the desperate urgency that comes from staking everything on a single commitment (Cf. Wood, 1960, p. 194). This hypothesis is somewhat imprecise, and it will not hold without qualification under any and all circumstances. But the truth it contains becomes evident when we see the consequences of a threat to a single group membership upon which depends all the major values of a man's life. Whether the membership in question be that of clan, tribe, church or nation, any severe threat to an all-inclusive bond of membership must necessarily arouse great fear. The most powerful and elemental reactions to great fear are two, namely, flight or attack. And if flight is impossible, fear can lead to the deepest rage and the most complete and merciless conflicts. These are underlying elements in the ferocity of blood feuds, religious wars and totalitarian civil wars.

CONDITIONS LEADING TO CONFLICT OR ACCOMMODATION AMONG
RELIGIOUS GROUPINGS

In all relations of members of one religious body to those of another, there is the possibility of active disagreement concerning genuine questions of ultimate values (Williams, 1956, pp. 12-20). What we are increasingly discovering, however, is the great extent to which strictly religious differences need not interfere with peaceful coexistence, *if* certain other conditions are present. Again for illustration only, we cite a few additional hypotheses.

The likelihood of overt conflict between any two religious collectivities within a given social system would appear to be reduced by any one of the following conditions, or by any combination of them:

1. Low intensity or salience of belief in the exclusive validity of a highly specific, institutionalized belief system on the part of a high proportion of the members of both the religious groupings in question.

2. Frequent personal association of members of the religious collectivities in secular activities involving shared goals and cooperative action.

3. Presence of an outside collectivity perceived as competing with or actively threatening the power position and other interests and values of both of the religious collectivities.

4. Multiple, overlapping membership (on the part of a large proportion of members of both religious groupings) in other collectivities.

5. A stable balance of power, which may be either a traditionalized situation of accommodation to marked inequality or a situation of such perceived equality that neither party sees any possibility of dominance save at prohibitive cost.

This limited examination suggests that further systematic and objective study of interreligious relations would be likely to produce results of great theoretical as well as practical importance.

.   .   .   .

ON INTEGRATION

A human community or society exists as a complex structure of relationships. The main bases upon which a community or a society can function as a going concern are not too difficult to identify in a general way, no matter how hard it is to specify concretely how they work. The primary classes of factors in the coordination of behavior within social aggregates as *systems* are:

1. Mutual advantage
   (a) internal protection, exchange, and facilitation
   (b) external defense and aggression
2. Consensus
   (a) on values
   (b) on goals
   (c) on norms
   (d) on interpersonal liking-disliking
3. Power
4. Technical capacities for communication
5. Various social mechanisms for settling conflicts, restricting conflict, and producing consensus

A multigroup society can continue to operate as a system with a low degree of consensus in some respects if it is a society with high mutual advantage, effective means of communication, and some minimal unitary exercise of order-maintaining power. It will be driven more and more toward reliance upon power, the less consensus there is concerning the distribution of rewards and concerning the basic rules for settling conflicts.

Ethnic relations represent problems of consensus and dissensus. To the extent that prejudice and discrimination are sources of tension, discord and open conflict, to that extent there is a dissensus that raises the question of relative power to control the settlement of demands and claims. Conflicting claims in the absence of agreement on specific norms mean the exercise of power. Unless there is somewhere a stopping point at which *legitimacy* comes in—that is, where a source of power is invoked that represents a focus of value consensus—one can predict that there will be increasing disorder and the resort to increasingly drastic means.

Once a specific conflict has been precipitated, many forces may be evoked that were not a part of the original sources of the outbreak. Conflict is a vortex. Into it are drawn diverse elements not intrinsic to the initial causes of the conflict. The quality of this process is well suggested by Simmel's comment on the American Civil War:

The moment, however, the situation took on the color of war, it itself turned out to be an accumulation of antagonisms, of attitudes of hatred, newspaper polemics, frictions between private persons, frictions at the borders, and reciprocal moral suspicions in areas outside the central point of conflict (Simmel, 1955, pp. 109-110).

The precipitating situation is permeated with a variety of latent conflicts of interests, of differences of values, of suppressed antipathies, of interpersonal alienation. Once the situation becomes one of open conflict, three things of decisive importance immediately occur: (1) the suppressive and repressive forces that have partially controlled tensions are weakened or removed; (2) latent threats become actual, and new threats emerge, both polarized along the cleavage of the conflicting groups; (3) the axis of social approval and disapproval shifts, so that acts which formerly were antisocial now become virtuous, thus placing the superego energies in direct alignment with a wide range of hostile and aggressive urges.

If a community or a society wishes (that is, if enough of its more powerful and responsible members wish) to control conflict, the time to do it is before the conflict starts, or at least before it begins to take on a breakaway momentum. In modern American society the relative lack in interethnic relations of social controls that derive either from personal reciprocities or from mutual dependence on the same concrete leaders, authorities, patrons, etc., removes an important network of containing and mediating relationships. The phenomena of race riots, juvenile gang warfare, vigilante activity, and diffuse terrorism illustrate the problem.

The most certain way to maximize conflict is to give one's opponent only the choice of conflict versus certain defeat, deprivation, or subordination; the most certain way to maximize violence is to leave to the opponent violence as the only alternative to his own destruction (or, to the same effect, the destruction of his most cherished objects of value).[1]

Furthermore, the greater the number of relationships affected by any change in the relationships of two or more individuals, or two or more social roles, and the more important the values affected, the greater the likelihood that there will be intervention by some kind of third party. Considering the importance of ethnic relationships in a society like ours, it would be surprising were law and political authority generally not invoked to deal with conflicts of claims and breaches of order. Settlement of conflicts inevitably creates norms, and the creation and enforcement of legal norms is a decisive mode of securing consensus in complex sociocultural systems.

. . . .

Change through legal means under American conditions is typically

---

1. Zawodny, 1961, p. 24. For a striking case in point: "The ebb and flow of membership in sabotage and guerrilla units is not related to the number of tactical victories of these units, to their losses, nor even to the prospects for success. The rate of recruitment is positively correlated with the intensity of terror applied by the enemy in suppressing the movement."

a gradual and uneven process. Far from being revolutionary, it is the essence of established procedure and orderly development. Nevertheless, we would regard legal action through the courts and administrative action in business, education, government, and religious organizations as major avenues of realistic efforts to alter systems of discrimination and prejudice. These avenues are congruent with the dominant value systems and with the character of the complex social structure that has developed. And law and law enforcement are great agencies of public education.

The slowness of change put up against the moral claims of minorities for equality of rights necessarily maintains high tension. Furthermore, it cannot be assumed that any and all types of industrialization and urbanization will lead to a decrease in discrimination or to a narrowing of occupational and income differentials between whites and Negroes. For instance, under conditions of plentiful labor and weak unions (or with segregated monopoly-oriented white unions), differential job and wage opportunities may be maintained even with large industrial growth. Blalock has presented data for Southern counties that suggest that Negro-white differentials in levels of living probably are not less in the highly urban areas than in the less urbanized, even though levels for both Negroes and whites are higher in the more urbanized counties (Blalock, 1959, pp. 146-151). In Northern and Western cities, segregation and discrimination in housing remain crucial areas of tension, not only in relation to Negroes but also in relation to Puerto Ricans, Jews, Mexicans, and others. Social exclusion and discrimination in education and employment affect large numbers of Jewish persons, and, in less well-known degree, Catholics in some areas and Protestants in others. Many political and civil rights are widely denied to members of ethnic minorities, especially to Negroes in the South.

Thus, the pluralism of American society continues to be a changing and conflictful condition. As a total social system, the political society of the United States has been unable to establish or guarantee political and civil equality of protection and opportunity to ethnic minorities. Yet it is equally unable to renounce the universalistic norms and democratic goals. It cannot settle for a caste system, nor for a mosaic society of separate cultural segments. Its nominal ideal is an emancipated order of low prejudice, and minimal segregation and discrimination. Resistances to changes in the direction of public equality and public integration often touch off overt conflict. Looking simultaneously at prejudice and at segregation, there are these possibilities:

		SEGREGATION	
		Slight	*Great*
PREJUDICE	*Low*	Emancipated	Mosaic Pluralism
	High	Mass Conflict	Stressful Caste-like

Great pressures exist to move the society toward social integration of ethnic minorities, the emancipated outcome. Great resistances are thereby aroused. One key to the understnding of resistance on the part of dominant ethnic groupings is the recognition that resistance derives from a sense of threat. One key to understanding a sense of threat is to be found in answers to the questions: what is threatened? And how? We already have suggested some partial and tentative answers. We would propose as especially important the following hypothetical propositions:

1. The extent and intensity of resistance to increased rights (or privileges) of any ethnic (racial, religious) segment of the society will increase directly with the degree to which the present or prospective change is perceived by persons in other ethnic categories as a direct threat to their own long-term future prestige ranking, as determined by the evaluations of other persons who are in a position to importantly affect that ranking.

In short, resistance will increase directly with perceived threat to prestige status.

2. More specifically, resistance will vary directly with the perceived threat from the reactions of others within the dominant ethnic segment who have economic or political power, religious authority, or other indirect sanctioning power (for example, the ability to influence community evaluations of the person). That is, anticipated sanctions from persons of power and authority are especially threatening.

3. Whatever the perceived threat to status, it will be the more powerful, the less possibility there is for alternative ways of maintaining status, once the prospective change has occurred. Feeling trapped tends to produce panic.

Although prestige status is the subject of these three propositions, they are expected to apply to any other threatened values.

What factors encourage sense of threat in the first instance? We suggest, by way of examples, that under present conditions in the United States,[2] the sense of threat among persons in a dominant ethnic category facing potential change will be the greater: (1) the less the concrete knowledge of the beliefs, values, and motivations of the aspirant or rising subordinates; (2) the less knowledge there is of the effects of the potential change in actual experience elsewhere; (3) the greater the *actual* likelihood that the potential change will damage the dominant group's interests.

We have suggested that political authority is one of the primary necessary and important factors in determining the balance of ethnic relations in our society. From any point of view the political element, in the

---

2. The essential fact behind the qualifying phrase, "under present conditions in the United States" is that all the ethnic minorities have limited goals that are far short of those fantasied for them by uninformed members of dominant groupings. For instance, what Negroes actually want, at the level of realistic action, is much different from the social equality feared by some white people

widest sense, must be prominent in any appraisal of societal conflict and integration. As American Negroes become able to secure equal rights, including the vote, the possibility of protecting *other* rights will increase.

The divisiveness of prejudices and the discontinuities of experience and communication that are generated by group segregation and discrimination are extensively documented by data presented at various points throughout this book. Inevitably, reflection upon the facts of ethnic separateness has raised the basic question: in the face of group divisiveness, how are pluralistic social systems maintained? To answer this question is one of the most important tasks of the entire body of the social sciences, not an assignment to be handily completed in a single work on intergroup relations. Nevertheless, we must perforce make a few additional observations dealing with the issue. At the risk of inappropriate simplification, let us list certain other major factors as we have sensed them in the communities here studied at first hand.

First, as we see Hometown or Southport, Valley City or Steelville at the point in time in which our surveys were conducted, the communities as units are crucially dependent upon the larger society in which they are embedded. However vaguely this interdependence may be sensed (actually it is sometimes recognized quite clearly by the man in the street), every major economic or political event brings it home to at least some of the community's members. Livelihood and safety—survival itself—depend upon the adequate functioning of a division of labor and of systems of communication and order extending far beyond the control or detailed comprehension of local residents. Such interdependence need not, and often does not, lead to sentiments of solidarity. Indeed, recognition of dependence on outside groups often provokes feelings of resentment and frustration. But the dependence is *there*—it is *objective* —in the sense that any real attempt to break the chain of linkages with the larger economic and political orders quickly and painfully shows the real and immediate costs of removal from the environing systems of relationships.

The impersonal network of trade and power relations exists also within the community. And at this local level also people may accept their interdependence, and the limited associations it necessitates, without developing sentiments of solidarity or diffuse reciprocities of concern and obligation. A man can say, "I don't like having those damn X's around here, but we need them as workers." A political worker can say, "I never invite one of them to my home—but their votes are always welcome."

At the local level, in common with the societal, there is, second, the community that is formed by the recognized sharing of common beliefs and values. The communities we studied may seem to have enough of antipathies and to be severely fragmented by differences in values and beliefs. They are, indeed, socially divided, when seen up close under the microscope. But from a more extended perspective each of the ethnic, racial, or religious groupings in each of the local communities tended to hold in common with all the other local groupings a vast store of shared culture. This commonality tends to be taken for granted and to be ignored in much of the intergroup relations of ordinary daily life. In the present studies we have very little direct evidence concerning its exact part in intergroup solidarity and conflict. We must note the possibility, however, that a wider comparative study would show this shared culture to be of decisive importance in setting the limits of group relations, in defining the terms of conflict (as well as those of cooperation), and in channelizing the possibilities of social change.

Third, the maintenance of a local social system extending across ethnic-racial-religious lines is affected profoundly by the kinds of arrangements that have developed for group insulation, through both psychological defenses and the restriction of the qualities of interaction, and for the resolution of frictions. To these arrangements or mechanisms we have repeatedly called attention in earlier discussions.

Fourth, there are sources of resiliency or tolerance of imperfection that result in the absorption by individuals and groups of frustrations, deprivations, and other stresses including those growing out of intergroup relations—stresses that would otherwise be more productive of conflict (and probably of social change). These sources of adjustive capacities are concretely very diverse, but consist primarily of adequate levels of gratifications secured in the total round of social life, on the one hand, and of socially induced capacities for affection and compassion, on the other, which cushion and mediate the harshness of systems of discrimination and segregation. We are here referring to personality resources of the social system, or to speak even more loosely, but perhaps more communicatively, to a surplus of affective capacities permitting toleration of others, even in undesired roles. To say that this happens is not necessarily, of course, to unconditionally approve it.

Finally, we believe that the total body of evidence we have reviewed overwhelmingly supports the view that cooperation and solidarity among persons who differ in ethnic membership is fostered by any arrangements that produce joint action toward shared objectives. From a variety of approaches and theoretical suppositions one finds suggestions that *social solidarity among individuals or groups is enhanced by recognition of the sharing of a positive and noncompetitive regard for a common object of concern.*

PART IV

The Changing Meaning
of "Racial" Violence

12

THE CHANGING MEANING OF "RACIAL" VIOLENCE

A chapter entitled "Changing Meaning of 'Racial' Violence" seems presumptuous indeed, particularly when it concludes a volume in which literally dozens of interpretations have been suggested by careful scholars from a number of different disciplines. Yet, as I suggested in the Preface, the professional student has citizen obligations to his society as well as scholarly obligations. The three papers that constitute this final chapter each grew out of ameliorative concerns.

My first paper was prepared for presentation to nonprofessionals who were interested in explanations for various types of violence that began to emerge in this country during the current decade. As a sociologist I was concerned with an intellectual ordering of an extremely complex set of events; as a citizen I hoped to suggest points of leverage for viable response to legitimate revolutionary goals. I believe that some of the questions I raised were meaningful; I am also aware that some of my conclusions have already become obsolete.

Janowitz's paper is more frankly programmatic. He undertakes to explain the failures of past efforts at social control and to suggest more effective modes of response to what he has labeled "escalating" violence. Whether or not the reader agrees with his suggestions, the motivations are clearly those of the professional who wishes to utilize his professional skills in an attack upon social problems.

It is difficult for the professional social scientist to divest himself of the "objective" posture which is a major goal of much of our professional graduate school socialization. Yet we have values about the desirable society, as do all our fellow citizens. It is difficult to make these values explicit, even to ourselves, and it is even more difficult to exhort others to accept our values. The final paper in this book was written for a nonprofessional journal, whose editor insisted that I make evaluative judgments and raise moral issues. I have done just that.

487

Allen D. Grimshaw

Changing Patterns of Racial Violence
in the United States

I

Since Americans have all had experience, either direct or more remote, with problems of race, there is some tendency to believe that we know the dimensions of this domestic difficulty and could find solutions except for the obstinacy of certain people. Who is perceived as obstinate depends, of course, on where one stands. Where one stands depends, in turn, on one's personal history and degree of awareness of the complexity of detail historically and in contemporary developments. Too many concerned people have tended to look upon the history of race relations in this country as the simple unfolding of a drama moving toward its inevitable conclusion in today's conflict—too many people see all of today's events as being part of one massive struggle, with clearly defined issues and homogeneous opposing parties. These oversimplified views do little to increase prospects for viable solutions.

. . . Since 1948 the range of institutional areas under assault has broadened to include every aspect of social life. Similarly, a vastly increased variety of modes of attack upon the accommodative structure has been used by Negroes in their quest for equal rights as citizens. And, as partial successes have been attained, aspirations and demands have themselves increased in magnitude (see Grimshaw, 1962a, 1960 [concluding section], 1962b [concluding section]). As a consequence of all these changes, there have been both quantitative and qualitative changes in interpretation of and attitudes about the "Negro revolution." The issue of civil rights and equal opportunities has, in the minds of most Americans, replaced all other problems as the major domestic policy concern. At the same time, there have been subtle changes in the ideological dialogue over these rights—there has been a sharp decrease in the use of sacred themes of "protection of white womanhood" and the like, even among the most unreconstructed Southern white opponents to desegregation. Even Governor Wallace now insists that "all" Americans should have the right to vote—concern is expressed, however, about states' rights, constitutional issues, individual freedoms (of whites) and control of communist subversion. Finally, and the importance of this fact must not be underestimated, there have been demonstrable changes in the posture and behavior of external agencies of constraint. Local police forces and the federal government have both

488

increasingly supported the minority position—however flagrant the activities of some local law enforcement officers may be, however slowly the majesty of federal power may move.[1]

While any attempt to classify events of recent years meets with tremendous obstacles, some sense of chronology can perhaps be retained. At the beginning of this period there was a combination of legal and political activity directed toward fairly limited goals. Incidents occurred which, had it not been for the presence of better police controls than existed in the past, might have erupted into large-scale racial social violence. In the North, these incidents tended to cluster into two categories: (1) those related to Negro invasion of white residential areas and (2) those over use of public facilities, particularly recreational facilities. Near riots, now receding in memory in the face of more recent and more spectacular events, occurred over the use of swimming facilities in St. Louis, Youngstown and Washington. A litany of place names—Cicero, Trumbull Park, Levittown—marked the course of change in housing occupancy patterns.

The decade of the fifties saw a renewed and increased vigor in the use of the courts, particularly in the area of school desegregation, and in the South as well as in the North (these events have been chronicled in great detail in the *Southern School News* and *Race Relations Law Reporter*). Eruptions of violence occurred in Southern communities where court orders to integrate were greeted by organized resistance by sectors of the white community. It was a new era, with federal troops and Citizen's Councils, expanding militance and exotic attempts to stem the tide (whatever happened to John Kaspar?).

The most dramatic change in the pattern of intergroup relations has been the introduction of various techniques of direct action. The Congress on Racial Equality had sponsored some "sit-ins" in the 1940's, the first direct action occurring in 1942. The real impetus to direct action came, however, from the successful bus boycott in Montgomery in 1955. In this decade such activity has crescendoed, with a proliferation of organizations, *e.g.*, the Southern Christian Leadership Conference, the Student Nonviolent Coordinating Committee, etc., participating in a growing variety of direct action—"freedom rides," "sit-ins," "kneel-ins," "wade-ins," "prayer vigils" and currently culminating in the massive demonstrations in Selma (whoever heard of Selma?) and the march to Montgomery.[2] Each of these new techniques of direct action has elicited countertechniques from the white segregation establishment. An initial response was one of kidnapping and summary "execution" or of sudden assault in a fashion reminiscent of Northern gang warfare of the Thirties

1. For a study of the importance of law enforcement agencies, see Grimshaw, 1961. For a study of actual behavior of such agencies, see Grimshaw, 1963b. For a study of the philosophies of preventative action, see Grimshaw, 1963c.

2. The NAACP has not been explicitly mentioned here but has had a major role in all of these events.

or of post-Civil War "night-riding" activities. Similarly, there have been and continue to be widespread attempts at terrorization through arson and bombings. With increasing involvement, an interesting shift occurred with Southern areas appealing for judicial protection through injunction. Finally, we have the erratic pattern of direct counteraction by local law enforcement officers (or even state troopers) as in Selma, alternating with pleas for peaceful civic behavior (by governors) and protection for demonstrators from these same law enforcement agencies. Response behavior by the white resistance has become disorganized, almost to the point where it is random, with continual inability to stem the tide of change. This lack of pattern will continue, and further violence can be expected.

Two other sets of events have drawn national and worldwide attention. These are the internal struggle going on within the Black Nationalist movement and the explosions of violence which occurred in the summer of 1964 in Northern urban areas. These events require the addition of new dimensions to the analysis of Negro-white relations and do not easily fit into the chronology outlined above. There is not sufficient space here to discuss the internal struggle, but the violence of 1964 will serve as a fulcrum for discussion of new directions in violence in the concluding section. At this point, however, it may be worthwhile to state some generalizations based on the chronological discussion just completed.[3]

With the exception of a brief period after the Civil War, the pattern of American Negro-white relationships, especially in the American South, has closely approximated the classic accommodative pattern of superordination-subordination, with the whites a continually dominant group. The most savage oppression, whether expressed in rural lynchings and pogroms or in urban race riots, has taken place when the Negro has refused to accept a subordinate status. The most intense conflict has resulted when the subordinate minority group has attempted to disrupt the accommodative pattern or when the superordinate group has defined the situation as one in which such an attempt is being made. Conflict in Negro-white relationships in the United States has been conflict generated by the breakdown of an essentially unstable accommodative pattern, essentially unstable because the subordinated group has refused to accept its status and has had sufficient power to challenge it.

At a recent panel on violence, a speaker talked about violence as a "mystery," and attacked the problem of the "moral foundations" of violence. Violence is not a mystery to the sociologist. It is simply one of several modes of conflict resolution. The choice of this rather than other modes need not be a mystery; reasons are to be found within the structural arrangements of society itself. For the same reason, sociological explications of social violence need not be predicated on any grasp of

3. The chronology of events prior to 1948 has been dropped from this version of this paper. See, however, Grimshaw, 1959a, reprinted in this volume, pp. 14-28.

moral meanings, though questions of responsibility and guilt are of interest to the citizen and the philosopher of ethics.

Sociologist Georg Simmel, generally considered to be the first "formal sociologist," insisted that it was possible to examine certain "forms" of social interaction (or social processes) and to discuss these in the abstract, without reference to specific content. Thus, said Simmel, we can study that particular variety of accommodative relationship which we identify as the pattern of superordination-subordination. In this relationship, whether actual incumbents are priest and parishioner, master and slave, officer and enlisted man or psychiatrist and patient, there will be an asymmetry in interaction. Guidance, advice, directives and commands flow in one direction; deference, obedience and compliance flow in the other. From the sociological perspective, it is expected that similar patterns can be discerned in the process of social conflict and its particular subtype, social violence.

From this point of view there is no need to argue whether or not violence is consciously selected as instrumental. Most social violence, possibly excluding wars of conquest and similar adventures, is probably reactive rather than consciously instrumental. Social violence in the United States has seldom resulted from a conscious decision to follow a policy of violence.[4] Such violence has been, rather, a response of dominant groups to either real or perceived assaults upon the accommodative structure, the *status quo*. This has been true for Negro-white relationships throughout American history, though actual expressions of violence have varied. A similar interpretation holds for other varieties of social violence, ethnic, religious or labor-management in this country, and seems applicable, moreover, to patterns of social violence which have occurred elsewhere, *e.g.*, Hindu-Muslim violence in India (see Lambert, 1951).

No claim is made that social violence can be explained by a simple stimulus-response formula, with assault on the accomodative structure as stimulus and social violence as response. In the real world of Negro-white relations there is a complex interaction of prejudice, discrimination, social tension and social violence. There is no simple and direct relationship with an increase in social tension automatically increasing the probability of social violence. Agencies of external constraint (the judiciary, local police, federal troops) intervene to reduce the likelihood of violence in some cases—and to increase it in others. In an increasingly complex society the activities of agencies in possession of monopolies of the legal use of force can be crucial factors in determination of the occurrence or non-occurrence of violence—Selma provides a typical case.

---

4. There have, of course, been instances where sectors of one or the other community have adopted such a policy, or where leadership has appeared to give tacit approval by failure to publicly disavow violence. (Even in the late 1960s there are very few leaders, white or black, who have advocated that their followers should *initiate* violence.)

II

Some readers have some awareness of the history of racial violence in this country. Somewhat fewer are familiar with analysis of social violence from the perspective of attacks upon the *status quo*. More readers, even if simply through following current events in the mass media, will be aware that new patterns of intergroup relations and new modes of attempting to induce change are reflected in changing characteristics of participants. Some people, however, seem to have the view that participation patterns are pretty much the same now as they always have been, and that participants in racial conflict comprise criminal elements (Negro), good but gullible colored people, "bad niggers" (including those corrupted by Communists), "Reds" and good, Christian white men, upholders of the social order. As has been suggested, this oversimplification leads to difficulties in attempting to understand the phenomena of violence under consideration.

Although evidence is scanty for events prior to the twentieth century, there is considerable information on the socioeconomic characteristics of participants in the violent behavior of the period since the beginning of World War I. The most thoroughly documented material is that on characteristics of victims and offenders in the Detroit race riot of 1943, but there are journalistic and quasi-scholarly accounts of lynchings and of other urban racial disturbances. Few people who have written on race riots have failed to express strong opinions about the characteristics of rioters. While there is divergence of opinion in these reports, ranging from publications of action agencies such as the NAACP or the careful study of the Chicago Commission on Race Relations to the most journalistic news articles or to militant pamphlets prepared by left wing organizations, there is also considerable agreement. Almost all of the literature on race riots notes the greater participation of some categories of individuals than others. Categories frequently mentioned, other than the police, include criminals, youth (including organized gangs), women, servicemen (in wartime riots) and in some cases a variety of bourgeois elements. Other writers have claimed a heavy participation by agitators of the extreme right or left.

Criminal activity may have been great in urban race riots, but such participation is probably a consequence of the fact that rioting has been concentrated in the same areas of the city where criminal elements are ecologically centered. Organized criminal activity has not been a concommitant of interracial violence. While criminals are surely drawn to situations where formal controls have broken down, it is doubtful on the basis of available data whether any riot in this country has ever been started by criminals for the express purpose of gaining cover for criminal behavior. Characterization of all rioters as criminals or hoodlums is inaccurate. It is true, however, that criminals are more likely than others to be among those picked up during riots.[5]

The youth of many race rioters has been noted in most studies, professional or journalistic, of Northern riots. In the South the "bourbon" lynching, with its sacred overtones, was a serious business in which adult male members of the white community participated as a "social duty"; younger people frequently were spectators and even participants in less austere ceremonials. In the Detroit riot of 1943 over a quarter of all those arrested were in the age group 17-20 (Rushton, *et al.*, n.d.). While there are many reports of youths and even preadolescents being encouraged to participate in riotous behavior by older, nonparticipating adults, there is evidence that many young people in such disturbances have been caught up in a spirit of "carnival." The intensity of this carnival spirit is exemplified in the killing of Moses Kiska, an elderly Negro, in the Detroit riot. Four white teenage boys killed this man, unknown to them, because ". . . other people were fighting and killing and we felt like it too" (Lee and Humphrey, 1943). Clark presented a case study of a Negro youth, a participant in the 1943 Harlem disturbance, who utilized the general confusion to "have a holiday" and also to express pent-up aggressions against all manifestations of authority (Clark and Barker, 1945). It is unsafe to generalize from the meager data available, but there seems to have been, in riotous disturbances, a general crumbling of inhibitions in which youth expressed ordinarily repressed behavior patterns.

Limitations of space prevent the discussion of participation of all other special categories of people in racial violence. Suffice it to say that there are two possible, though not contradictory, interpretations. One is that certain types of participants mentioned have particularly high visibility, which is further enhanced because their presence and participation is not expected. The other is that there are particular gains for such participants, *e.g.*, women, normally required to play a more passive role, who used the situations of normlessness prevalent in periods of interracial violence to express inhibited aggressive impulses. In actuality, the facts of the case probably lie somewhere between the two alternative explanations.

Assertions have been made, and continue to be made, that subversive agitators of the extreme right or extreme left have played a major role in incitement to violence. There is no documentation for any such claims. Indeed, the Mayor's Commission on Conditions in Harlem, in its report on the 1935 disturbance, concluded in reference to claims blaming the Communists, "the Communists . . . deserve more credit than

---

5. This happens in other types of disturbances as well. During a "panty raid" at a midwestern university in 1951, staff from the office of the Dean of Men stood quietly on staircases and at doors, letting all students go by except those who had previously found their way into the Dean's office for disciplinary action. These "prior record" students were picked up and detained.

any other element in Harlem for preventing a physical conflict between whites and blacks" (Mayor's Commission on Conditions in Harlem, see *The New York Amsterdam News,* July 18, 1936).

The Communists, on the other hand, made accusations that World War II riots were "Axis-inspired," and there are people in Detroit today who noted activity of the KKK and other native Fascist groups in the city immediately preceding that riot. There is no evidence, however, that agitators ever did any more than perhaps to encourage violence that had already started. It must be concluded for these riots, as the FBI has concluded about the 1964 disturbances, that allegations of organized leadership by Communists or rightists remain unproved.

In the last analysis it is difficult to avoid the conclusion that persons who participated in the large-scale urban violence of the past were drawn largely from the areas where rioting was concentrated and that their social, psychological and demographic characteristics reflect those of populations resident in those areas. Older persons were somewhat more likely to stay indoors and not to participate. Women may have generally followed role prescriptions, but some women did participate and their participation drew the attention of observers. If there were more persons characterized by unemployment, low education, low intelligence, possible psychiatric defects, prior criminal records and other indicators of social debility participating and being apprehended in riots, it was because those individuals lived largely in those areas.

During the last few years sharply different patterns have emerged in the composition of groups participating in the broad arena of the civil rights struggle.

Anyone who has followed events of the voter registration drive in the mass media cannot fail to realize that recruits in that effort vary sharply in their characteristics from those involved in any earlier attempts to change the traditional pattern of superordination-subordination. From the time of the bus boycott in 1955 and the earliest "sit-ins," events in the South have had a strong religious flavor. Both the SCLC and the SNCC have made religious appeals throughout their campaigns. This may explain why in the South they have been successful in uniting lower-class Negroes who had previously been either terrified or apathetic and an increasingly discontented, articulate and deeply religious middle class. In many ways Martin Luther King's particular mixture of Gandhian nonviolence and Christian theology has had the potency of fundamental revivalism.

But this is a fundamental revivalism which has attracted a heterogeneous following. While clergymen and religious leaders of many faiths have been involved in events of the drive, particularly in the spring of 1965, we are witnessing the interesting spectacle of mass involvement of nonbelievers in a civil rights crusade explicitly organized around religious as well as political premises. The "civil rightsniks" are familiar with the solidarity gospel because of fairly long involvement in the movement. It is doubtful, however, whether they or the much more sedate middle-class students and academic types are typically religious. Statistics are not, of course, available, but there is something incongruous about Jews, Catholics, Protestants, atheists and agnostics joining in common ceremony before an "altar" on the statehouse steps in a political move to achieve a secular goal.

There will be a continuing debate over the tactical wisdom of the March on Montgomery. There will be speculation over the motivations of some participants—there may well be elements of "liberal catharsis," "bandwagon psychology," or even of the carnival atmosphere mentioned above in the discussion of violence. It seems, however, that the very heterogeneity of participants and the apparent incongruities of events have served to confuse and disorganize segregationist resistance. Whites from Alabama did participate in the March. Violence was not met with violence, although after the first bloody Sunday there were restrained threats. It is difficult to find any real analog to this mass social movement. Violence there will be—but racial social violence on a large scale in urban areas will not become endemic in the South.

Limitations of space prevent any full discussion of the other two groups manifesting disaffection of different sectors of the Negro minority—the Black nationalists and participants in the violence of the Sixties.[6] It may be noted, however, that both are, in contrast to that in Selma, solely Negro and almost totally lower-class or, in the case of some sectors of the Black Nationalists, lower-middle-class. In the concluding section an attempt will be made to gain some perspective on the events of the "long hot summer" of 1964 and of characteristics of participants in those disorders.

III

Without denying that events of last summer in Harlem, Bedford-Stuyvesant, Rochester, Chicago and New Jersey represent manifestations of a deep social unrest in the largest American minority, it can be said that they did not represent outbreaks of major racial violence. Nor, for that matter, did they represent the aspirations and modes of attaining goals defined as acceptable by the bulk of that minority. The incidents labeled as race riots which occurred in urban areas in the northern United States in the summer of 1964 were neither race riots in the proper usage of that term, nor were they part of the mainstream of civil rights agitation which has been going on in this country since the 1954 Supreme Court decision on school desegregation.[7]

There were two main themes in the discussion of the events of last summer. One of them, predictably, had strong political overtones, and

6. See, however, selections on participant characteristics in Chapter 10, of this volume.
7. By the middle of 1968 this assertion *may* no longer be true.

was directed to an analysis of the so-called "white backlash," sometimes with a certain smug satisfaction and with apparent hopes that this phenomenon could be used politically in the attempt to change the party in power. Among those holding this general orientation were analysts who claimed to find in the disturbances sinister evidence of Communist conspiracy, widespread dope addiction and crime, a failure of sincere attempts to meet Negro "demands" through such palliatives as the then new Civil Rights Act—a palliative, as often as not, rejected by these experts when it was under discussion. These people admitted, albeit with some reluctance, the fact that the Negro has been denied full citizenship. They insisted, however, that the minority must be satisfied with gradual gains as they were conceded by the majority, that civil disobedience could under no circumstances be tolerated, even if in a righteous cause, and they recommend harsh represession as a technique of control.

Their motto was—and is—"no negotiation while disturbances continue." In this they demonstrate one of the major fallacies of their position, an assumption that those with whom they negotiate have the power to control the Negro rioters who were involved in the disturbances. They see the civil rights protest movement, indeed, the Negro community as a whole, as a monolithic, organized antiwhite conspiracy. In this view they err in two matters of substance. In the first place, even within the "respectable" civil rights movement there is no monolithic hierarchy of control. There is a schism and disagreement on both tactics and long-range strategy among the leaders of the middle-class movement, men like King and Wilkins and Farmer. Nor are the organizations which these men lead monolithic. Both Wilkins and Farmer, for example, have had difficulty in retaining control of more militant leaders of local organizations. In any event, these leaders were agreed in condemnation of disturbances such as those in Harlem last summer as being tactically in error. To a certain extent they were swept up in the concern about the "backlash," while some of their subordinates have the attitude that "backlash" or no, the only way to gain full rights is to keep pressing.

The other error of substance is the assumption that the disturbances were indeed a part of the fabric of the larger civil rights struggle. In point of fact, this was not and will not be the case. The Negroes who engaged in riotous behavior, antipolice activity and looting are not the same Negroes as those who have peacefully picketed and who have gone into the South to participate in voter drives—or who marched on Washington.[8] They are the lower-class apathetics, the new style indifferents, who have been outside the movement, skeptical of any success in dealing with "the man," or with the society itself. These people are not students and the respectable middle classes. They are permanently dispossessed, the urban Negro poor, unemployed or underemployed, peo-

8. By the middle of 1968 this assertion *is* no longer true.

ple on relief, people with little to live for and with little expectation of any improvement in their life chances—whatever the success or failure of the larger "Negro Revolution." [9] What we saw last summer was not race warfare but a phenomenon of class expression, the Negro undersociety expressing its hatred of a class system which makes it permanently deprived. Expressions about civil rights are only tags which the more sophisticated among this unorganized mass have learned to use, hoping to acquire some facade of reasonableness in their protest—if not of acceptability. It is no accident that most of the violence which took place was directed against property or against the police, representatives of the class system and of property. When actual interracial clashes occurred in these disturbances it was usually because whites appeared in these areas or because whites have, themselves, been representatives of the propertied classes (*e.g.*, in the case of shopkeepers).

The second major theme is a more continuing one which appeared before the drastic events of last summer. This has been the continuing examination and re-examination, by participants in and friends of the general movement toward full equality, of the short and long term goals of the "Negro Revolution" and of the most efficient manner in which to move toward these goals. Over the last decade, civil rights activity has been concentrated primarily in four areas. These have been education, housing, the franchise and the use of public facilities. Through the same period there has been continuing but less organized activity in the areas of employment and of relations with law enforcement agencies. Events of last summer underlined again the question of priorities of goals, and of different priorities for different sectors of the Negro community.

Throughout the post-World War II period, up until last summer, the most dramatic events in the civil rights contest occurred in the areas of housing, education and access to public facilities. The long-drawn-out struggle in Chicago over a mixed occupancy pattern in Trumbull Park, the confrontation of federalized troops with militant segregationists in Little Rock, the looks of hatred on the faces of the mothers of white schoolchildren threatened with integration, the "sit-ins," "wade-ins" and "pray-ins"—these activities have been colorful and newsworthy. With the exception of the struggle over public facilities and of this year's voter registration drive, however, they actually involve relatively small numbers of Negroes. Most of the Negroes who have been involved in these areas, moreover, have been middle-class Negroes and college students, and they have had the active support and participation of whites with the same kinds of backgrounds in their activities (again, the voter registration drive presents an entirely different picture).

9. Over half of the Negroes twenty-four years of age in the United States are school dropouts, as contrasted to about one-fourth of all whites—a figure itself alarming. One-fourth of all teenage youths in the labor market (and some no longer actively seek work) are without jobs. While Negro family income has improved, it remains only slightly more than half that of white families.

If those involved in such acitivities were of middle-class status, the immediate rewards of such activities were, equally, of interest primarily to that group. Only a small proportion of American Negroes in the North or South have sufficient financial resources to exploit new housing opportunities. Even fewer, perhaps, can afford to patronize the luxury hotels and fine restaurants which have sometimes been the focus of the struggle over facilities. While many Negroes want better educational facilities for their children, many are essentially indifferent as to whether this takes place under conditions of token integration. They are more concerned with the quality of education than with its setting. Lower-class Negroes, moreover, are generally less likely to find themselves in the position of being embarrassed by denial of other kinds of public facilities such as libraries, parks and golf courses, simply because like lower-class white Americans, they do not ordinarily make use of them. Activities of the postwar years, in other words, have frequently been those of middle-class Negroes *for* middle-class Negroes. This is not to deny that those participating in such activities have had broader concerns over abstract principles of equal justice. It is merely to note that the goals of the movement have not been such, until most recently, as to inspire the participation of the less privileged sectors of the minority community.

Lower-class Negro concerns, and events of 1964 again can serve as evidence, have been with the more mundane matters of economic subsistence and decent living conditions, even within the ghetto, and of everyday relations with law enforcement agencies. In the South these questions have been inextricably tied to the problem of the franchise. It is in the context of the right to vote that the genuine racial violence of last summer occurred, as in the slaying of the three young civil rights workers in Philadelphia, Mississippi (and more recently, death over Selma). In the North, even with the franchise, Negroes have still found themselves to be economically an underclass and to receive different treatment from the police.

The question which has been raised in this second theme, then, is over the redefinition of goals.

Two sets of facts, examined simultaneously, explain the urban disturbances of last summer. The first is, as suggested immediately above, dissensus over goals sought by Negro leadership and by sectors of the community which were involved in the rioting. This dissensus, moreover, has occurred in a period characterized by a growing prosperity for some Negroes, and an increasingly high standard of living in which the Negro underclass has not shared. Concurrent with these increasingly marked disparities the lower-class Negroes, who have been generally apathetic and who have not participated in organized activity, have seen that the minority does have power, however that power may have been utilized. What they have not seen is that much of that power has been generated through disciplined activity. Moreover, while they share a vague sense of pride because Negroes have been successful in reaching goals in spite of the resistance of whites, they are not in sympathy with many of the goals that have been defined by the Negro leadership, a group itself representative of many of the values of a class system which has brought *them* no satisfactions. The rioting was a result, then, of deep-seated frustration, a sense of potential power and a lack of organization and direction.

The Negro rioting in the summer of 1964 was aimless and unorganized. There were few mobs. Rather there were clusters of atomistic individuals and small groups. While there was property damage and looting, the looting was hardly systematic and goal-directed. The highly sporadic nature of the disturbances makes untenable any explanation which seeks for evidence of a sinister Communist conspiracy. It is doubtless true that extremists of all hues tried to profit from the disturbances, but to give the extremists credit for their inception is to vastly overrate their power and to grossly misperceive the amount of organization in the disturbances.

There are almost twenty million Negroes in the United States. Taking all of the Northern urban disturbances together, it is doubtful whether there were ten thousand active participants. There were much larger numbers of spectators, some of whom doubtlessly were at least partially in sympathy, although many others were concerned about the effects of such activity on the larger course of the civil rights movement. It is true, moreover, that many of the active participants were active only in the sense of a kind of cathartic expression of the carnival, and that they had no ideological motives in mind, either consciously or unconsciously. The magnitude of the disturbances has been much exaggerated.

Even if it is true, however, that press reports have been exaggerated, the riots were symptomatic of a basic problem in American society, perhaps even more basic than that of race relations. Michael Harrington (1964) in his report on poverty in America, *The Other America,* estimated that some forty million Americans are permanently underprivileged, hungry and without prospects. If middle-class Negroes continue to be increasingly successful in the pursuit of *their* goals, estrangement by class, already marked, can be expected to grow within the Negro minority. If this is the case, we must expect a gradual shift from social definitions by race to social definitions which emphasize class membership. The extremes of wealth and poverty are being reduced in neither the white nor the Negro communities. Years to come may reveal some interesting changes in group alignments.

It can be safely said that the middle-class leadership of neither the white nor the Negro community espouses social violence as a mode of resolving interracial conflicts. Leaders and middle-class people of both groups, generally, are too self-consciously concerned over America's world image to let this be the case. In addition, Negro middle-class leaders share the common values of the middle-class, including patterns of socialization which emphasize the control of aggression. There will be occasional outbursts of racial violence in which both groups are involved, but the great discipline of the Negro middle classes in events of the last decade suggests that violence will be a consequence of police activity or inactivity rather than a consequence of policy decisions by the "respectable middle classes."

Events of last summer were dramatic. With all the excitement, however, the "racial blood-bath" which had been predicted, whether with relish or dismay, never materialized. There were isolated cases of murder, and these can be expected to continue in the years immediately ahead. There has been continual harassment of electoral registration workers—it would have been a surprise if this had not occurred. There have been racially defined incidents in cities in the North and South, and these can be expected to continue for some years. But the important fact is that the disturbances which occurred last summer were not confrontations of whites and Negroes with large-scale violence in mind, as has been the case in the major riots of the twentieth century in Chicago, Detroit, East St. Louis and so on. The disturbances which occurred were, rather, frustrated uprisings of a *minority within a minority*. This again, perhaps, we must expect to continue unless major changes occur in the larger economic and social structure of American society.

.   .   .   .

POSTSCRIPT (May, 1968)

The article reprinted above was written only slightly more than three years ago for presentation to a symposium whose participants were charged to look at and "explain" all the new varieties of violence which were appearing on the American scene. It is clear that in some particulars I may have been an accurate reporter but a poor prognosticator. This is most clear in the observation that the violence in 1964 was not in the mainstream of the civil rights struggle and in the comment that participants represented the most totally dispossessed members of the (then) Negro (now black), community. I have suggested elsewhere (Grimshaw, 1968a, reprinted in Chapter 11, pp. 385–396 of this volume) that while a "class" as contrasted to a "race" interpretation of disorders of the Sixties may be correct in some ways, it is even more startlingly incorrect in others. The re-redefinition of social conflict in this country along lines of color I have suggested (*Ibid.*) reflects, in substantial part, the failures of the dominant majority and its government to respond realistically and with adequate magnitude to the demands of the minority that the majority suppress its racism and structurally rearrange the society so as to provide both legal and real equality to all citizens. The events of the summers since 1964 and, more recently, the assassination of Dr. Martin Luther King have underlined the necessity for continuing and close observation of the changing meaning of social violence in this country. The growth of new militance on university campuses and the emergence of new leadership cadres of increasing intransigeance will, I am sure, necessitate continuing revision of scholarly interpretation. In retrospect, however, I believe that the 1965 paper was correct as a current interpretation.

Morris Janowitz

Social Control of Escalated Riots *

In the building of institutions to reduce and eliminate race rioting in urban centers of the United States, two "sociological" assumptions supply a point of departure. There is a considerable body of evidence to support these assumptions, but it is best to consider them as assumptions.

1. Social tensions generated by discrimination, prejudice and poverty offer essential but only partial explanations of Negro mass rioting in the urban centers of the United States. Allen Grimshaw, one of the most careful students of race riots, concluded in 1962 that "there is no direct relation between the level of social tension and the eruption of social violence" (Grimshaw, 1962b, p. 18. See also Williams, 1965).

Because of the complex meaning of the term "no direct relation" it is not necessary to accept all that this proposition implies. It is enough to re-emphasize the obvious fact that in the United States, social tension exists where riots break out, and to accept his alternative formulation that "in every case where major rioting has occurred, the social structure of the community has been characterized by weak patterns of external control" (Grimshaw 1963b, p. 288).

2. Among elements that account for the outbreak of mass rioting are both (a) the organizational weaknesses and professional limitations of law enforcement agencies and (b) a moral and social climate that encourages violence. Of particular importance is the widespread availability of weapons and the impact of the mass media, both in its imagery of violence and in its specific treatment of riots and law enforcement agencies. In the language of the sociologist, a key element in the outbreak of riots is a weakness in the system of social control.

* This article has been abridged and edited by Morris Janowitz for inclusion in this volume.

Race riots are an expression of the position of the Negro in American society, for the history of the Negro has been markedly different from that of the other immigrant and minority groups. Institution-building aimed at political, social and economic reform is at the heart of short- and long-range programs designed to alter the status of the Negro. One cannot overlook the fact that militant action by Negro groups, and even the occurrence of riots have dramatized the plight of Negroes and have focused public attention on the necessity for reform. Arbitrary and mechanical demands for law and order have been voiced by particular leadership groups as a device for inhibiting social change and political reform. If public policy is concerned merely with police action, both the short term and long term consequences are certain to be self-defeating. Yet there is a core problem in the handling of urban violence, for continued massive violence would hardly serve the objectives of the Negro community and would disrupt the growth of programs required for social change.

Therefore, my basic point of view is that in addition to institution-building aimed at social and economic reform, social control of rioting requires independent efforts in the de-escalation of violence; domestic disarmament, if you will. In strengthening social control, a fusion of two elements is involved. First, the law enforcement agencies and the mass media need to develop policies which articulate with the realities of new forms of urban violence that have emerged in recent years. Second, this is not merely a technical problem in the management of violence. It is essential to recognize that political and moral considerations are overriding. Thus, for example, the concept of the constabulary is an effort to base the practices of law enforcement agencies on fundamental political and moral commitments. The constabulary function as applied to urban violence emphasizes a fully alert force committed to a minimum resort to force and concerned with the development and maintenance of conditions for viable democratic political institutions.[1] The constabulary approach implies a continuing review of the division of responsibility between local and federal authorities, as well as of the social prestige and professional self-concept of the police. While the elimination of race riots is at the center of the constabulary concept, we are dealing with a wide range of issues of social control, especially, the legitimacy of law enforcement agencies in the United States.

THE ANATOMY OF RACIAL VIOLENCE

Racial violence has a history as old as the nation itself. The institution of slavery was rooted in ready resort to violence. . . . During World War I and its aftermath, however, the "modern" form of the race riot

1. For a discussion of the constabulary concept at the level of the federal armed forces in international affairs, see Janowitz, 1960, pp. 417–440.

developed in Northern and border cities where the Negro was attempting to alter his position of subordination. These outbreaks had two predisposing elements. First, relatively large numbers of new migrants—both Negro and white—were living in segregated enclaves in urban centers under conditions in which older patterns of accommodation were not effective. The riots were linked to a phase in the growth and transformation of American cities. Second, the police and law enforcement agencies had a limited capacity for dealing with the outbreak of mass violence. The historical record indicates that they did not anticipate such happenings.

The riots of this period could be called "communal" riots or "contested area" riots. They involved an ecological warfare because they were a direct struggle between white and Negro areas . . . The whites generally invaded Negro areas where the residents were predominantly newcomers. The restoration of law and order involved the police in separating the two groups and in protecting the enclaves of Negroes from whites. . . .

During World War II, the pattern of rioting underwent a transformation which has taken full form with outbreaks in Watts in 1965 and in Newark and Detroit in 1967. For lack of a better term there has been a metamorphosis from "communal" riots to "commodity" riots. The Detroit riot of 1943 conformed to the communal or contested area pattern. It involved concentrations of recently arrived Negro migrants, and the precipitating incident occurred in a contested area, Belle Isle. The violence spread rapidly and produced clashes between Negroes and whites. However, the Harlem riots of 1943 contained features of the new type of rioting. The Negro population was composed of a higher concentration of long-term residents in the community. Most important, it was a riot which started within the Negro community, not at the periphery. It did not involve a confrontation between white and Negro civilians. It was an outburst against property and retail establishments, plus looting—therefore the notion of the commodity riot in the Negro community. These establishments were mainly owned by outside white proprietors. The deaths and casualties resulted mainly from the use of force against the Negro population by police and national guard units. Some direct and active participation by white civilians may take place in such a riot, as was the case in Detroit in 1967, but this is a minor element.

The style of intervention by the law enforcement officers has deeply influenced the anatomy of race riots in the United States. The ability of the local police to seal off contested areas has reduced the prospect of communal riots. Since the riots of World War I, there has been a gradual increase in the capacity of local police to prevent riots at the periphery of the Negro community, but not without conspicuous exceptions. The use of radio communications and motorized local police forces have been the essential ingredients of control. Most Northern cities have witnessed a steady and gradual expansion of the Negro residential areas, accompanied by bitter resentment and continuous minor outbreaks of violence including bombings. But the police almost daily contain these tensions, which could explode into communal riots if there were defects in their performance. But the capacity of local enforcement agencies to deal with "border" incidents has not been matched with a capacity for controlling the resort to violence within the Negro community.

The stark reality of the new type commodity riot is in the use of weaponry. It is truly an escalated riot. In the old fashioned communal riot, the police were armed with pistols and an occasional rifle. The national guard or federal units carried rifles tipped with bayonets, plus limited amounts of heavy infantry weapons. The bulk of the fighting by civilians was with brickbats of a variety of types plus a sprinkling of small arms. The central fact about the commodity riots is the wide dispersal of small arms and rifles among the rioters. These firearms are partially the result of individual stockpiling. There are no adequate statistics on the percentage of such weapons which were in the hands of participants before the riot started, but a significant stock of weapons appears to be accumulated during the actual rioting. Important sources of supplies have come from looting of sporting goods stores, general merchandise establishments and pawn shops. (It is incredible that in the United States, local law does not require that guns, while on sale, should be rendered inoperative or at least kept in a secure vault.)

When I speak of escalated riots, I am referring to the development of these weapons and the sniper fire they create. Available documentation indicates that such firing usually involves single individuals and occasionally groups of two or three persons. There is little evidence of forethought by rioters in the deployment of weapons as to location or mutual fire support. Supporting fire by such snipers could render them much more destructive. In isolated cases, there is evidence of limited coordination and planning of firepower. But these cases are of minor importance in accounting for the firepower involved or its destructiveness. The impact of the sniper fire derives from its interplay with arson activities. Sniper fire immobilizes fire fighting equipment, which permits widespread destruction by fire which, in turn, contributes to more rioting and sniper fire. The spread of fire is frequently facilitated by various incendiary bombs of a homemade nature. These fire bombs have been used as antivehicle bombs, but generally with little effectiveness.

. . . The new type of rioting is likely to be set off by an incident involving the police in the ghetto, which is defined as police brutality, where some actual violation of accepted police practice has taken place. The very first phase is generally nasty and brutish, while the police are being stoned, crowds collect and tension mounts. The second stage is reached with the breaking of glass windows. Local social control breaks down and the population recognizes that a temporary opportunity for looting is available. The atmosphere changes quickly, and this is when positive enthusiasm is released. But all too briefly. If the crowds are not dispersed and order restored, the third stage of the riot is the transformation wrought by sniper fire, widespread destruction and the countermeasures created by police and uniformed soldiers.

There can be no doubt that the countermeasures employed deeply influence the course of rioting—even in prolonging the period of reestablishing law and order. One is, of course, struck by the great variation in local response to escalated rioting and in the skill and professionalism of the forces in their counter efforts.

. . . Differences in police strategy are partly the result of conscious policy, since law enforcement officials have a past record to draw on, and since they are continuously alerted to the possibility of riots. Thus, for example, there are wide differences in response patterns to early manifestations of disorder by local police. In Detroit, Ray Girardin, former police reporter who became Police Commissioner, explicitly acknowledged that he followed a loose policy in the early phase of the Detroit rioting, assuming that local civilian Negro leadership would contain the disorder. He cited his previous experience when this approach worked effectively. In his theories and riot behavior, he made frequent recourse to "sociological" terms.

By contrast, the operational code of the police in New York City under Commissioner Howard Leary and in Chicago has been to intervene with that amount of force judged to be appropriate for the early stages of the confrontation. The objective is to prevent the spread of contagion. No special steps are taken to prevent routine police performance from developing into incidents which might provoke tension. But if an incident becomes the focal point for tension and the collection of a crowd, the police respond early and in depth in order to prevent the second stage from actually expanding. Numerous police are sent to the scene or kept in reserve nearby. The police seek to operate by their sheer presence, not to provoke further counteraction. They seek to prevent the breaking of windows and the starting of looting which would set the stage for an escalated riot. If actual rioting is threatening, one element is the early mobilization of local national guard units and their ready reserve deployment in inner city garrisons. In part, this is designed to reduce the time required for their deployment on city streets and in part as a containment policy which enables the local police to commit their reserves and feel that they have a supporting force available.

Once a commodity riot enters the second phase of widespread looting and especially during the third phase of extensive scattered sniper fire, effective countermeasures are difficult and require highly trained and specialized units. It is, in some respects, a type of military situation, but the notion of an insurrection has little meaning, for snipers have no intention or capability for holding territory, nor are they part of a scheme to do so even temporarily. The sniper fire exposes police officers and national guard units without battle experience (or without simulated battlefield training experience) to fire fight with which they are not accustomed. The amount of firepower is not very high, although personal risk is clearly present. The basic problem is the scattered source of fire which envelops the law enforcement units. It is this envelopment fire, especially from behind, which has led to the use of the term guerrilla tactics, but the guerrilla concept is also not relevant since guerrillas are part of an organization, proceed with a plan, prepare paths of withdrawal and develop sanctuaries.

The police feel surrounded and, in the absence of effective command and control, they often respond with indiscriminate and uncontrolled fire. The immediate result is that they expose numerous civilians to danger. Such fire does not eliminate snipers, which can only be eliminated by carefully directed fire and counter-sniper procedures. In fact, the initial counterfire can actually mobilize new rioters into the fire fight.

In a major riot, law enforcement officers are exposed to an environment which most have not previously experienced. Their behavior is conditioned by the sheer feeling of the unreality of the rioting situation and the physical disruption which takes place. One response, elimination of street lights by rifle fire, turns an advantage to the snipers and contributes to the sense of unreality. In effect, for prompt control of snipers, special teams of police and national guardsmen are required, using highly exact fire or semiautomatic weapons and trained to respond directly to the source of sniper fire and avoid general displays of fire power. At night, they require support by massed beacon lights to illuminate the area rather than to plunge it into darkness.

Some police forces had organized, by the summer of 1967, special antisniper teams, but such police resources are limited and there is considerable variation in planning and training from one police department to another.

Likewise, the recent summers of 1964 through 1967 demonstrate wide variations in the capacity of national guard units to respond to and assist local police. On the whole, national guard units have received little specific training in riot control and the contents of such training would not appear particularly germane to contemporary problems. The level of effectiveness derives from their military preparedness in general. The performance of national guard units in Newark and in Detroit has been judged by expert observers as deficient. By contrast, the behavior of the national guard units in Maryland and in Wisconsin (Milwaukee) has been reported as much more in accordance with the requirements of the constabulary function. The basic question is fire control and an effective communications network. By contrast, federal troops used in Detroit were highly professional units with extensive training who clearly displayed a higher degree of unit control and were less prone to employ unnecessary fire. The superiority of the federal troops reflects past experience and indicates that more effective military training per se (even without additional civil disorder training), and more effective officers, produces more appropriate responses.

A central index to national guard effectiveness is the failure to integrate units. Because of its fraternal spirit, the national guard has been able to resist federal directives and Negroes account for less than two percent of its personnel. Units in Detroit and Newark were not integrated, while Chicago based units that were employed during the summer disturbances of 1965 were integrated and had Negro officers. Charles Moskos, Northwestern University sociologist who witnessed these events, has reported that integration clearly contributed to the local populations' acceptance of these units and their legitimacy.

NEXT STAGE: POLITICAL VIOLENCE

There is reason to believe that the mechanisms for preventing and controlling escalated rioting can be improved in the United States. A number of concrete proposals for strengthening social control by police and military units are described below, some of which were partially being implemented by local authorities after the Newark and Detroit experiences. Many measures will require federal intervention and federal assistance.

There is also reason to believe that the socioeconomic position of the Negro in American society will continue to improve, especially as federal programs of assistance become more effective. . . . However, expected changes in the socioeconomic position of the Negro during the period from 1967 to 1968 or from 1967 to 1970, and even from 1967 to 1972, do not lead to an estimate that social tensions will decline so drastically that problems of social control will become minor. In fact, in our open society, it is necessary to realize that the present commodity riots bear a parallel to the outbursts of militancy in the trade union movement in the 1930's which displayed their vigor not during the depth of the depression, but during 1936 and 1937, a period of halting but increasing prosperity. . . .

Thus the likelihood of destruction on the level of Newark and Detroit declines, although the escalated riot remains a possibility in any area of heavy Negro population concentration. Likewise, as Negro enclaves develop in suburban areas, forms of communal riots between Negroes and whites become a reality in these areas for the first time. As the increased capacity of law enforcement officers to contain and repress communal rioting was accompanied by a transformation of the patterns of violence, so the increased ability of the police and military formations to repress escalated riots foretells a new transformation in urban racial violence. The signs are clear. In the process of conflict and adjustment, not only do law enforcement institutions change their tactics but elements in the Negro population learn to modify their behavior.

Escalated rioting and the rioting of commodity looting appears to be giving way to more specific, more premeditated and more regularized uses of force. It is as if the rioters learned the lesson emphasized in the mass media, that mass destruction achieves no tangible benefits. New outbursts appear to have more of a goal; a diffuse goal at times, at other times a very specific one. It is almost appropriate to describe these outbursts as political violence or political terror. It is not inaccurate to describe this shift as one from expressive outburst to a more instrumental use of violence.

The participants are likely to be persons who have taken part in previous outbursts. There is an element of organization at least to the extent that activists are concerned with personal survival and avoidance of the police. There is an element of organization to the extent that the target seems to be selected, and the patterns repeated for a specific purpose. The local school is a particular target. The form of violence can be the harassment of a group of white schoolteachers active in union work, an assault on teacher picket lines during a strike, or a small scale outburst at the neighborhood schoolyard with sniper fire against the police, which involves a mimeographed appeal and members of a youth gang. Housing projects, especially integrated housing projects, are repeatedly subject to rifle fire and fire bombing. Negro policemen are harassed. These incidents are created for the purpose of developing solidarity in local gangs and in paramilitary groups. The object seems to be to establish a vague political presence. Conspiratorial overtones are involved and the assaults spill over against social agencies and local political leaders. The line between random outbursts and these forms of political violence or political terror is difficult to draw. However, these outbursts often take place with the explicit appeal of "Black Power." Traditional youth gang activities in the Negro community develop more of a conscious political orientation and their leaders openly speak of organized force leading to political action.

It is almost as if one were dealing with a form of "defiance" politics. As these activities increase and become institutionalized, they supply a new power base in the Negro community. In the past, the rackets and the periphery of the political party organizations made use of violence to extract a financial toll from slum communities. These groups confined violent outbursts to the maintenance of the flow of economic privilege. Practitioners of political violence and political terror are now more open in advocating violence and opposition to the larger society. It represents an effort to achieve goals much broader and vaguer than those of the racketeer. There are crude ideological overtones and especially a desire to carry violence into the white community.

It will be very difficult to contain such disruptions. The toll is small at a given point and therefore does not produce a violent public reaction. The tactics and organizational plans are more secret and only surveillance and covert penetration supplies an effective technique of management. The emerging forms are those of a combination of a conspiratorial and predatory gang and a paramilitary unit. . . .

TOWARD THE CONSTABULARY FUNCTION

Any analysis of the steps that need to be taken to cope with contemporary forms of urban racial violence must take into account the historical fact that the American law enforcement system, deeply influenced by British institutions, did not develop a middle level of a national police force for the control of civil disorder. Moreover, the United States relied on a decentralized and locally controlled police, even more decentralized than the British system. A popular government did not require, at least in theory, a national police force, such as the gendarmerie in France and Italy, to enforce the authority of the central government over the opposition of the local population.

In reality the United States has had extensive civil disorder throughout its history, and the country had to find its equivalent to a national police force. The state militia has mainly served this purpose. This issue was of pressing importance before the Civil War in the southern states, where local police forces were backed up by the state militia in order to maintain slavery. After the Civil War, the organizing efforts of the labor unions and radical political groups supplied the focal point of unrest and armed intervention. The state guards assumed this task with increasing reliance on federal troops. The mass rioting in Northern and border states after the period of World War I broadened the tasks of national guard and federal troops.

The reliance on national guard units as the equivalent of a national police force was generally an unfortunate necessity although, as mentioned above, variation in the level of performance was and continues to be tremendous. State militia units and later national guard units were organized to be mobilized both for domestic and for national defense purposes, but in effect, the federal military function was seen as the overriding one. Their training and operational code fitted this objective. Thus, the national guard fell between the horns of a dilemma. As a defense arm, it has been criticized for its recruitment practices and level of military readiness. On the other hand, it did not develop an effective police outlook and an acceptable tradition in this regard. The result has been that in both labor disputes and in race riots, federal troops have performed with high levels of effectiveness, not because of their specialized training for the task, but because of generally higher organizational effectiveness.

The adaptation of local police forces, national guard units, and federal armed forces to the control of urban violence must articulate with the basic format of federalism on which American political institutions rest. In my view, on the basis of technical and organizational considerations, this country requires a metropolitan-regional police force system which would relate to actual urban population concentration. . . . But the notion of a metropolitan-regional police system is completely incompatible with the realities and advantages of the existing federal system. Law enforcement will continue to be organized on a municipal, county, state and federal level, and an appropriate division of labor between these elements is required.

. . . In the Detroit difficulties, federal troops were not deployed on the basis of the request of state and local authorities alone, but only after the presidential representative had personally inspected the "battle front" and certified to the need for federal troops. Realistically, the office of the President is struggling to avoid premature commitment of federal troops whenever local authorities feel under pressure; but the credibility of swift federal intervention must be maintained as an essential element of riot control. If federal forces are to be committed only after a federal representative certifies to their need, it becomes essential that there be a procedure for making this possible without delay. Delay not only is unwise from the point of view of the mechanics of riot control, but also creates bitterness and recriminations which could only weaken political consensus. Therefore, it seems essential that the federal government have a representative in each major metropolitan center who can serve as a federal listening post. This function could be assigned to an existing federal officer such as the federal marshal. . . .

The national guard has been under pressure to integrate its forces but with few positive results. By contrast United States army commanders have recognized that a racial balance involves positive personnel recruitment policies, training and educational programs plus equality of opportunity. While federal forces moved toward increased integration, the national guard resisted. In fact, it operated as a haven for those who wished to avoid integration; informally, it excluded Negroes. Thus, the essential question is whether the Department of the Army possesses sufficient power in setting standards to achieve meaningful integration.

Perhaps new legislation is required, but the crux of the issue rests in the application of existing powers of the federal government over national guard units. It is clear that where integration of the Negro into the national guard has taken place, it has been the result of state and local political leadership. Integration has been achieved in metropolitan centers where mayors and governors have sought to exercise supervision over the practice of their national guard, rather than to let existing mechanisms of command exert organizational inertia.

In seeking to improve training, the new issue in control of escalated riots is preparation for the elimination of sniper and gun fire. Training in counter-sniper fire is required for all national guard and federal troop units and for specialized units of the local police. The better general training these personnel have, the stronger their group cohesion and the more effective their command structure, the less likely they are to engage in discriminate fire fights. Specifically, they need realistic training in sharpshooting and precision firing. Wherever possible, they need experience under simulated conditions. Improved police practice to deal with escalated riots requires the deployment of senior officers in the field, especially men with long experience and mature judgment.

. . . Under the constabulary concept the bayonet would be eliminated. The bayonet in the American military is a strange example of the power of tradition. The United States armed forces have placed greater emphasis on the bayonet than have most major powers . . . In fact, the bayonet is a symbolic effort to maintain the distinctiveness of the military from civilian occupations and professions.[2] In any case, the bayonet is completely useless as an instrument of riot control and the management of civil disorder. As a device for separating hostile groups or controlling mobs, it has some of the impact of a police dog, in that it produces countereffects that are not desired. . . .

Instead, riot control forces require helmets, water hose equipment, batons, wicker shields, and the like. They must opt for a minimum use of force if they are to achieve their goals effectively and quickly. If the riot involves gunfire, trained counter-sniper tactics are required, as described above, not display of the ceremonial bayonet. In each case the emphasis is on a selective response and a concern with the minimum application of force. The response of some police departments to engage in widespread arming of their personnel with rifles or to plan to procure armored personnel vehicles does not appear to be appropriate.

The constabulary approach of riot control also requires extensive and ever widening gun control and widespread disarmament programs. Local city ordinances can immediately eliminate the dangers of the acquisition of guns by looting; this can be accomplished by the requirement that all types of guns be rendered inoperative while being stored for sale. Local and state ordinances are required to develop effective gun control but, fundamentally, comprehensive federal legislation is needed. Four years after the assassination of President John F. Kennedy, no such legislation has been passed, and prospects for this action appear to be increasing only gradually. The symbolic and moral significance of any type of gun control legislation should not be overlooked. It might well be possible to take the first steps by concentrating on heavy automatic weapons and making their possession illegal.

The likelihood of effective gun control legislation would probably increase if clearer recognition were given to the need to develop alternative institutions for dealing with the desires of the public to engage in

---

2. If such symbolism is needed, the small sheathed dagger of the Swiss army is more compatible with the political and moral purposes of a professional army in a democratic society.

hunting and various types of target practice. Public shooting galleries for target shooters could be established in urban areas, where owners could store their rifles and pistols. . . .

The main outlines of adapting police and law enforcement agencies to the requirements of escalated riots are, therefore, beginning to be recognized. Yet the question remains whether these professional developments are adequate to meet emerging requirements of urban racial violence. There can be no doubt that they will contribute to some degree to containment of political violence and selected terror, especially as they contribute to the general effectiveness of the police. But police forces, like military formations, constantly run the risk of preparing to wage the last battle over again. Conspiratorial violence requires surveillance, both overt and covert. Such control requires counterintelligence procedures; the more secret and cohesive the group, the greater the problems of intelligence penetration. There is considerable hope on the basis of experience to date that many of these paramilitary groups will break into factions and their operational code become quickly known to law enforcement agencies. If not, the task will become extremely difficult; it bodes ill when it is necessary to rely on covert operators. The control of secret operations is at best difficult; for the United States, it is more difficult (Blackstock, 1964). The task becomes even more complex and troublesome when these surveillance agencies develop the conception, as they often do, that to collect information is not enough. They begin to believe that they must act as active agents of control, particularly in spreading distrust within these organizations. The task becomes endless if the operators play a game without an end or develop an interest in maintaining the groups whom they are supposed to be monitoring.

THE IMPORT OF THE MASS MEDIA

. . . The mass media both reflect the values of the larger society and at the same time are agents of change and devices for molding tastes and values. It is a complex task to discern their impact since they are at the same time both cause and effect. Controversies about the mass media focus particularly on the issue of their contribution to crime and delinquency and to an atmosphere of lawlessness. Among social scientists, it is generally agreed that consequences of the mass media are secondary as compared with the influence of family, technology, and the organizational structures of modern society. . . .

Two separate but closely linked issues require attention. First, what are the consequences of the mass media with its high component of violence on popular attitudes toward authority and on conditioning and acceptance of violence in social relations? Second, what have been the specific consequences of the manner in which the mass media have handled escalated rioting since the period of Watts? . . .

In my judgment, the cumulative evidence collected by social scientists over the last thirty years has pointed to a discernible, but limited, negative impact of the media on social values and on personal controls required to inhibit disposition into aggressive actions. Other students of the same data have concluded that their impact is so small as to not warrant intervention. In part, the research methodology limited more definitive results. . . .

In a democratic society, the content of mass media must be determined by self regulation. But there is reason to believe that the United States could be a more effectively integrated society if popular features on violence and crime were drastically reduced. In achieving such an objective, government agencies, especially those charged with regulating radio and television, have a positive and facilitating role to play. . . . A long-range objective is to make effective and positive use of the mass media to strengthen democratic values.

. . . It is also necessary to assess the coverage of the riots themselves by television and the impact of this coverage on social control. While there are no adequate statistical studies, it appears that the contemporary coverage of racial violence conforms to the crime wave pattern. The national crisis produced by escalated riots warranted massive coverage according to existing standards of mass media performance. However, the result had a secondary effect of bringing into the scope of coverage violent events which would not have been reported under "normal circumstances." Likewise, the media have been criticized for imbalance in coverage and for not adequately reporting successful accomplishments in police and law enforcement agencies.

. . . Knowledge of the riot would spread in any case, but immediate extensive and detailed coverage both speeds up the process and gives it a special reality. On balance, I would argue that these images serve to reinforce predispositions to participate and even legitimate participation. To generate mass media coverage, especially television coverage, becomes an element in the motivation of the rioters. The sheer ability of the rioters to command mass media attention is an ingredient in developing legitimacy. . . .

The riots and their presentation in the mass media have had a profound, if difficult to determine, impact on public opinion toward the civil rights movement. Within the Negro community, there is no reason to believe that the riots and their aftermath have produced a widespread radicalization of opinion and mass basis for support of extremist or Black Power leadership, even though these events have given a sense of accomplishment to such leaders and their immediate followers. National opinion polls are perhaps not a completely adequate instrument for measuring political sentiment, but on national polls the overwhelming bulk of the Negro population reject the leaders and the strategy of direct violence.[3] . . .

Since the end of World War II, the mass media have been helping to modify the imagery of the Negro and thereby weaken the prejudiced symbolism. The advances of the Negro in economic, social and political life have supplied a basis by which the mass media could project a more realistic and more favorable picture of the Negro. The reasoned and moral arguments in defense of racial equality by Negro and white leaders supply the basis for extensive editorial commentary in the mass media. Mass media images of the Negro were enhanced by the role of Negro troops in the Korean conflict and by the increasing presentation of the Negro as policemen. Regardless of Negro leadership opinion on the war in South Vietnam, the Negro soldier's role has served to modify in a positive direction the image of the Negro in both white and Negro communities. The early phase of the civil rights movement with its emphasis on orderly and controlled demonstrations served also to alter the symbolism of the Negro from that of a weak powerless figure. The climax of this phase of change, as presented by the mass media, was the dramatic events of the march on Washington led by Martin Luther King. As an event in the mass media, it was unique. The national media were focused on a predominantly Negro assemblage moving in an orderly and powerful fashion. In a real sense, it was a symbolic incorporation of the Negro into American society because of the heavy emphasis on religion and the setting in the nation's Capital. . . .

Only when the mass media operate with standards of performance which reflect the satisfactory content of interracial contacts, can they be said to be filling their social responsibility. At the moment, in the guise of reporting the news, they present a most distorted image of social reality. In particular they are searching for evidence of conspiratorial action, rather than explaining the dynamics of rioting. Moreover, the mass media need to develop techniques of reporting which disseminate the essential news, but yet do not serve to weaken patterns of social control or to legitimate resort to violence.

Effective social control involves a delicate balance of a wide range of institutions; the family, the school, religious organizations, and voluntary associations. The goal of social control in a political democracy is to enhance the personal competence and personal control of the individual. Racial equality, if it is to be more than mechanical compliance, must make use of personal controls and individual decisions. This analysis has focused on the police and the mass media. It is in error to think of them as institutions whose inherent operations weaken personal controls. Their effective management can directly contribute to strengthening

3. Compare, however, the attitudinal materials reported in "Black Response to Contemporary Urban Violence: A Brief Note on the Sociology of Poll Interpretation," pp. 317-319 in this volume.

such controls or to easing the conditions for effective contributions by other institutions.

Allen D. Grimshaw

Government and Social Violence: The Complexity of Guilt

Conflict is both a continuing theme of the world's great literature and drama and a source of grave concern for heads of states. As a social process and as an individual psychological problem it is everywhere present in human affairs. But scholarly study of violence and force (the most extreme mode of conflict resolution) has not been proportionate to the importance of violence in the affairs of men. It is not surprising that, in the nuclear years since World War II, students of society have become increasingly concerned with the nature of social conflict, particularly in international relations. Yet even today sociologists, whose disciplinary interests should lead them to a major concern with conflict, have largely neglected its systematic study. Sociologists can always defend objective research, and hence could defend study of conflict and violence as social processes. Nonetheless, they have generally shied away from this area. They have particularly avoided assessments of relative guilt and responsibility as between conflicting parties, lest they lose their "scientific" standing by taking sides or showing welfare concerns. Unfortunately, moral issues do not evaporate in the face of aloof detachment.

This paper has dual objects: first, to consider government relations with internal groups and the effects of governmental actions on the occurrence or non-occurrence of social violence, and second, to comment on issues of guilt and responsibility resulting from the action, or lack of action, of governments.

Violence is social when it is directed against an individual or his property solely or primarily because of his membership in a social category. While this definition could include other assaults upon human dignity such as slavery and the dehumanizing practices of segregation, analysis in this article will be restricted to physical violence. Negro-white riots in the United States, inter-tribal violence in new African states, French-

Muslim warfare in Algeria, and Hindu-Muslim communal rioting in India are all examples of social violence, as are cases where individual members of categories are assaulted because of their group identification. Obviously, not all violence is social violence: armed robbery, and wanton vandalism are cases in point.

As we shall see, an effective and impartial government can control most violence between groups in its population. A government which is partisan, corrupt, or ineffective (and if it is any of these it is likely to become the others as well) may be either unable or unwilling to prevent overt conflict. Studies of social violence have documented the conclusion that heightened social tension is not automatically accompanied by social violence. Violence does not always occur when tension is high; violence has occurred when tension was not apparent. The explanation for this seeming anomaly can be found in the part played by agencies of external constraint: usually the government, with its monopoly of legal force.

Governments have rarely made the use of violence a conscious policy for resolution of social conflicts. Social violence usually results, rather, from reactions by a dominant group to real or perceived assaults on the *status quo*. That violence does not always occur when the *status quo* is threatened is likely to find its ultimate explanation in the role played by the state.

There are four positions available to governments in their relations to conflicting groups.[1] The first position is that in which the state itself, or its agencies, directly attacks members of a social category. In a second pattern, the government, while not actually participating in violence, gives, or appears to give, its tacit approval to the violence. Approval is sometimes made more material by provision of arms or by assuring favored treatment in the judicial process. A third position taken by government is non-partisan in that the state either ignores the conflict or takes impartial steps to stop it. A final relationship is that in which the state itself becomes the object of violence. This last situation, of course, frequently creates a relation of the first type, thereby raising a problem regarding initial responsibility.

I

It would be impossible to catalog the inumerable cases of direct government action against internal groups. The shots fired at Sharpesville in the South African Union in 1956 were, perhaps, heard round the world. But the repressive actions of a white South African government, directed against Indians and colored Africans alike, are only a very recent contemporary example of massive state activity against a local populace. World Jewry, victim of systematic massacre in medieval England and

1. This kind of distinction is implicit in much of the literature on social conflict and social violence. The formulation which follows first appeared in Lambert, 1951.

Europe, the pogroms of Czarist Russia, and of concerted assaults by the Nazis in Germany and in countries brought under its rule represents thousands of years of oppression. Such experiences by religious or ethnic groups are, unfortunately, hardly unusual. The slaughter of Armenian Christians in 1921, which earned the Ottomans the title of "Terrible Turks," stands out only because of its scope and intensity in the twentieth century—a relatively moderate one for large-scale slaughter until the advent of the Nazis. More recently, Menderes' mass murder of Greeks in Turkey in 1956 finally resulted in a trial in which additional evidence of government-inspired slaying of Turkish students culminated in his own sentence and execution. While the United States has seen little direct government violence against the populace in this century, the depredations of state, county and municipal officials on migrant groups in California are not completely forgotten. This activity, however, hardly compares with that of the Governor of Missouri who, a little over one hundred years ago, ordered his state militia to drive the Mormons from the State—or to exterminate them. Nor, for that matter, does it compare with the political purges in the Soviet Union which occurred in the Thirties.

In all of these cases, and in numerous others which might be cited, the direct responsibility of the state involved is clear. However, assessment is not always so simple. It requires answers to specific questions, answers which are frequently not available. Many factors are involved in government decisions to follow repression as a policy. To understand, even partially, the activities of states using this policy it is necessary to assess relationships among: (1) the domestic strength of the government, (2) the strength of the state in its external affairs, (3) the strength of the attacked group, and (4) the past history of discrimination and violence. Thus, governments which are internally insecure because of economic or other difficulties may seek scapegoats and find a convenient "traitor" group as in the case of Jews in Germany. Such states may seek to label some domestic minority responsible for their failures in dealing with other nations (for instance minorities considered to be a legacy of imperial domination).

The fact that social violence is frequently a reaction to a real or perceived threat to the *status quo* helps in illuminating some of the social processes involved in direct government action, but raises further questions on the subject of guilt. (As used here guilt includes a failure to act positively for victims of attacks by others.) Legal attribution of guilt requires the demonstration of *mens rea*. In dealing with government actions which seem to be policy decisions, we are frequently confronted with what seem to be manufactured threats to the *status quo*, but completely reliable proof is seldom available.

Perhaps even more basic to problems of guilt is the question, "Who is the government?" That is, does the government action rest on the massive support of all the populace who are not members of the assaulted social category? Is its action viewed with indifference or with apathy? Is the action perhaps even unknown? Is it opposed by other groups in the population? Answers to these questions might illuminate different varieties of individual and collective guilt. We would hardly hold an individual responsible for his government's activities against a group in the event he was genuinely ignorant of those activities. Similarly, it is known that there were some Germans in the Third Reich who actively opposed the anti-Semitic policies of the government and who actively aided Jews. These individuals share in no collective guilt, though references have frequently been made to the "guilt of the German people." Can we even hold responsible those who actively participated in the institutionalized slaughter of Jews, but who were young children when the Nazis came to power and who grew up in a world in which Jews were defined as subhuman and fit only for extermination? Philosophers and humanists can argue problems of ultimate guilt and responsibility. Most social scientists, with their disciplinary emphases on the importance of childhood socialization, are reluctant to assign full responsibility to the individual when he engages in socially approved behavior. Cultural determinisms and assessments of individual moral guilt are not easily compatible.[2]

A recapitulation of the free will determinism argument is not one of the purposes of this paper. For purposes of analysis it will be assumed that men and societies have some freedom of behavior and can therefore be held responsible. Guilt, as the term is used here, involves a knowing violation of written or informal law to the detriment of some well-defined collectivity. Failure to act, in this interpretation, can be as blameworthy as direct assault. From such a perspective it can be seen that governments other than those directly involved in assault on an internal minority can be guilty. At the very least, there are questions about the guilt of individuals in other governments who are aware of the plight of oppressed minorities but fail to take any action and in some instances even refuse to make diplomatic protests. Governments have refused to admit immigrants who are members of a victimized minority in the oppressor country. They have failed to apply economic sanctions to governments persecuting minorities. They have rebuffed representatives of the affected minorities when they have appeared in the councils of world organizations.

Hitler's oppression of the Jews was not a well-kept secret. If we assert that the leadership of all governments must share some responsibility for activity directed against oppressed minorities, wherever it occurs, we must similarly examine the possible guilt of rank-and-file nationals of all nations. It will be admitted that the possibilities of citizens for taking

2. At least one social scientist who read this noted strong disagreement with this conclusion and asserted, "you *must* assume some free will." His own work, like that of most social scientists, shows little evidence of "free will" assumptions. There is an interesting ambivalence between the public determinism and objectivity and the private voluntarism and emotion of social scientists. This seems particularly marked in assessments of moral and ethical issues.

effective action are more limited than those of their leaders. However, individual citizens well aware of the activities of another government against its own populace seldom protest the inaction of their own government or engage in any type of relief activity. Many Americans, for example, ignored or tacitly, even actively, approved the activities of the German government against the Jewish population of Germany. Educated Americans have not been unaware of exchanges of atrocities in Algeria, of British treatment of interned Jews in Cyprus, of patterns of Portuguese brutality in Angola, of the treatment of the native population in the South African Union, and of a host of other instances of institutionalized brutality. With few exceptions, one apparently being the massive support given by English citizens to British government policies against the slave trade, individual citizens seem to have been fairly indifferent to the problems of oppressed groups in other nations. One may ask if they are less guilty because they are not citizens of the oppressive government. Guilt, as the term has been used here, includes failure to act. These individuals may be less guilty but they are not guiltless.

Finally, it has sometimes happened that governments have been captured by parties to social conflict. In our own country it happened in the labor strife of the late nineteenth and early twentieth centuries. The history of the coal and iron police in Pennsylvania is well documented as is the labor violence in western mining districts in which state governments were apparently dominated by friends of the miners. The Federal government itself took direct action against labor in the widespread industrial violence of 1877.

II

Governments need not take direct action against social groups in order to be found culpable. Mark Twain, an outraged and unusually articulate observer of the American scene, expressed the belief that lynchings would not occur if a few martial personalities stood up to mobs. He may have been right; evidence indicates that when government officials have taken strong stands, social violence has been prevented. But he perhaps failed to take into consideration the fact that in many cases of lynching in this country, and of anti-minority violence around the world, governments have frequently given tacit and even active support to the mob.

E. J. Hobsbawm (1963), in his interesting volume, *Primitive Rebels,* gives examples of cases where members of social categories have incorrectly believed that the government wanted them to attack another group. Such was the case, for example, in Poltava in 1902, when the rural peasantry believed that a general had come from Petersburg with a manifesto (written in gold), with orders from the Tsar to attack and plunder agrarian estates. That the stories were not true is irrelevant, thus bearing out the sociological principle that "If men define situations as real, they are real in the consequences."

Needless to say, it is true that governments sometimes have looked with approval upon mob action. The history of our own country is replete with instances. A goodly share, though not all, of the inter-ethnic violence in the United States has had the tacit approval of governmental authorities on some level—local, state, or federal. This is true not only of white-Negro violence (in cases ranging from the New Orleans "massacre" immediately after the Civil War and other violence in the South, to urban violence in the North in the twentieth century) but also of violence directed against American Indians, Chinese, Japanese, and Mexicans. Tacit approval of management violence against labor characterized government throughout the long period of organizational strife starting in the middle of the last century and lasting into the decade of the Thirties—appearing again, some claim, in the Koehler strike in Wisconsin in the 1950's. A more popular focus of government approved violence in recent years was the Communist Party and its alleged fellow travelers. It was claimed that during the Poughkeepsie riots against Paul Robeson police even rerouted automobiles so that they would have to pass by the "anti-Communist" mob.

A question in these cases may be not so much, "Who is the government?" as "Which government?" The Federal government of the United States has not given any indication of approval of violence directed against the Negro minority during most of the years of this century. Some state and many municipal governments, or at least elected officials of those governments, have been less clear in defining their position. In the Little Rock crisis of the Fifties a situation occurred in which the local and Federal governments were determined to keep order but high elected officials of the state government apparently were willing to approve, perhaps even encourage, violence against Negros.

What seem to have been cases of middle-level governmental approval and even collusion of social violence occurred in the riotous periods surrounding Indian Independence in 1947. While the tangled skein of crimination and recrimination may never be completely unraveled, there seems to be evidence that while the new national governments of India and Pakistan were decrying violence, and even while Gandhi was fasting, high officials in the government of, for example, East and West Bengal were not only looking the other way, but even encouraging violence against religious minorities within their states. Both religious fanaticism and attempted political aggrandizement were manifest in early stages, while genuine outrage and a desire for revenge later may have become increasingly important. In a novel of unusual introspective honesty, Khushwant Singh (1956) has shown how government officials on the district level in the Punjab, originally concerned with maintaining the peace, were driven to a point where they considered that intervention to prevent communal violence would not only be politically disastrous, but would also deprive them of an economical and politically feasible solution to an otherwise almost insurmountable domestic problem. They did not, Singh seems to say, overtly encourage the violence, but neither did they take steps to counter the violence. Instead they released known homicidal thieves in a village where minority members had been protected from outsiders, and where agitators were attempting to stir up communal slaughter.

The question can be raised whether failure to prevent violence against a substantially weaker minority by a stronger one is much different from actual participation. Governments have sometimes claimed an inability to control the group attacking a victimized minority. When this happens questions can be raised about the possibility of multiple dimensions of corruptness, ineffectiveness and partisanship. If a government is honestly unable to control a dominant group in its population, it is ineffective. If it lies in saying it cannot control the attacking group it is corrupt, or partisan, or both. If it actually encourages violence it is, perhaps, both corrupt and partisan. It *may* be that the difference between dishonest claims of inability to control and the actual encouragement of violence reflects only differences in the actual strength of the government, of the attacking and attacked groups, rather than any measure of degree of corruptness.

The case of Negro-white relations in the American South and of Hindu-Muslim communal violence in the Indian sub-continent amply illustrate the complexity of problems involved in assessments of guilt and responsibility. The question, who is the government, may be more integral and important in these instances even than in cases of direct government assault. In both these cases it can be suggested that governments were dominated by members of the attacking group. This need not, however, always be the case when governments tacitly support an attacking group. Students of ancient history claim that the Romans and Byzantines sometimes incited one subject group against another. More recent and better-documented cases are harder to find. Furthermore, even in the Negro-white and Hindu-Muslim cases there were large numbers of individuals both in and out of the government who sought actively to prevent or ameliorate the patterns of social violence.

III

There are probably very few cases in which *every* member of a government is genuinely non-partisan in cases of social violence. Certainly all cases of social violence produce problems of government responsibility. Nevertheless, governments occasionally have maintained an essentially neutral position in cases of internal social violence.

Governments have shown their neutrality in two ways. First, they have

sometimes intervened with force to quell social conflict or social violence
by direct action against both or all groups. They have separated belligerent groups through quarantine or barred zones or have themselves
applied sanctions not involving force. Success in such action is dependent
on several factors. Control is possible only if the government can effectively muster its forces. However, sheer superiority in armed force is not
in itself sufficient if any party suspects the motives or neutrality of the
government. In some cases of urban racial violence in the United States,
prompt, effective and non-biased intervention has exemplified this
variety of neutrality.

Governments have also followed policies of non-intervention. One
variety of non-intervention reflects, allegedly, a government policy of
tertius gaudens—"divide and rule." Both Hindu and Muslim spokesmen
have accused the British of pursuing such a policy during the period of
communal violence preceding Independence. The British, of course,
claim they took a position from which they exercised unbiased and
direct action against any disturbers of peace.

A second policy of non-intervention by government represents the
view, "a plague on both your houses." This is, perhaps, a variation of a
policy of divide-and-rule, in which governments have occasionally seen
neither gain nor loss as resultant from violence and have been essentially
indifferent. The government of the United States, for example, did not
intervene in struggles among Indian tribes so long as the violence did
not upset the equilibrium of the larger pattern of Indian-white relations
or spread to direct assault on the government.

A final variety of non-intervention results from a belief by the government that it is powerless to cope with the situation. This was, in the
United States, the case in a few famous American feuds and in the
western "range wars." It may also provide a partial explanation for the
apparent inability of some metropolitan police forces to deal with widespread juvenile disturbances.

Whether or not a government takes a strong stand in cases of internal
violence, there are problems of responsibility. Is it not, perhaps, the
responsibility of government to prevent situations conducive to social
violence among internal factions? The claim can be made that it is a
function of good government to prevent any group within its borders
from either gaining a permanently dominant position or being relegated
to permanent minority status. Institutionalized inequality between social
groups or categories will inevitably produce situations in which real or
imagined assaults on the system by the subordinated group will occur.
Until there is a much closer approximation to full equality in race relations in this country we can expect that some whites will continue to
perceive Negroes as "getting out of their place," and to respond, occasionally, with violence. How much responsibility does government have
for rectifying such a situation? Events of the last decade have shown that
had our federal government long ago taken a firmer stance and more

positive action, the present pattern of American race relations would be far more amicable.

Cases where governments fail to intervene in social violence are patently different from those in which direct action is taken to control social violence. Indeed, insofar as a government pursues a policy of *tertius gaudens,* the situation is hardly distinguishable from that where it tacitly approves assault or discrimination by one group against another. In the latter instance (as in cases of direct action against minorities), government and citizen alike must bear the same burden of collective guilt and individual responsibility.

IV

Assaults upon governments take a variety of forms including rebellion, insurrection, revolt and revolution. More spectacular cases of historical interest include: the slave revolt of Spartacus; slave rebellions and insurrections in Brazil and in the United States; anti-colonial revolutions; the Russian and French revolutions; the Taiping rebellion in China; and, to show variety, Shays' Whiskey rebellion. In the twentieth century we have witnessed the cataclysmic eruption of the Warsaw ghetto, uprisings in Hungary, Poland and East Germany, the successful overthrow of the government in Cuba, and recent tragic events in Algeria. These, and countless other instances, are of interest both because they have precipitated direct government action against minorities and because of the complex problems of responsibility which they present.

In every case where a government is directly attacked by subjects, citizens or dependents, the claim is made that it is corrupt, oppressive, traitorous, or that is has some combination of equivalently unpleasant attributes. To say that the assailants may have equally unpleasant characteristics and suspect motives does not resolve questions of ultimate responsibility. While such resolutions cannot be essayed here, some subsidiary questions may be raised. The sociological premise that perceptions of a situation are more meaningful than the realities has the same cogency here as in the case mentioned above, where Russian peasants believed that they had been ordered by the Tsar himself to attack agrarian estates. If large sectors of a population believe that a governing power is corrupt or oppressive and engage in assault, its actual purity becomes irrelevant. Their perceptions may, of course, be manipulated by unscrupulous outsiders. The situation may also, of course, be one in which the government is clearly ineffective, but not necessarily corrupt or oppressive. In any event, questions of responsibility for social violence can be difficult to unravel. If a government has been falsely portrayed, is attacked, and responds to the assault, does it, in responding, somehow have a different variety of responsibility than in the case where it itself initiates violence?

From our current historical perspective it seems to be agreed that slave revolts in Haiti and San Domingo were directed against corrupt and brutal master classes who controlled the government. More recently, western observers are similarly in agreement that the ill-fated Hungarian uprising was directed against a corrupt and partisan state; but the Communists hardly agree. In any event, where there are cases of corrupt and oppressive governments and where there are rebellions or uprisings, some questions of responsibility remain. Should United States citizens, for example, have made it their business to be aware of the treatment of American Indians which led to Indian uprisings and to late nineteenth century Indian wars? What are the responsibilities of governments to intervene in what are claimed to be internal affairs of other sovereign powers: in the case of Hungary? in the case of Portuguese Angola? What are the responsibilities of citizens of other countries? What responsibilities do we have as citizens to support, or to urge our government to support, the claims of Africans in Angola? What responsibility must we bear for the incitement by non-official groups of the Hungarian people? What responsibility does our government have for actions of those citizen groups?

V

Social violence internal to national states can result from disturbances of the *status quo*. Such disturbances may result from changing value systems, from rising levels of aspiration, from political alienation, or from changes actually generated outside of the polity. Whether or not disruption of the polity, and of relations among internal groups, will result in social violence is dependent in large part upon the strength and stance of the government of the state. When that government is strong, and when subjects or citizens believe the government to be non-partisan, overt social violence is not likely to occur. When the government is weak, corrupt, or oppressive, social violence is much more likely to occur.

A fourfold classification of the location of government power relative to social categories involved in violence is heuristically useful in organizing and understanding material on internal disturbances. That lines of demarcation are not always clear does not destroy the usefulness of this mode of analysis; it only underlines the necessity for caution in generalization. Scrutiny of cases of internal social violence from such a perspective raises interesting questions of guilt and responsibility. It can tentatively be concluded, for example, that strong partisan governments which engage in or encourage violence against a minority may be morally condemned while weak non-partisan governments which are unable to prevent violence are guilty only of being weak—though the source of weakness may have meaning in a final assessment of responsibility.

One conclusion seems clear. Responsibility for social violence or massive discrimination does not stop at national boundaries. Eichmann and Verwoerd may be identified as culprits, but the fact of their identification does not conceal the secondary fact that while they were engaging in activities against minorities, others outside of their national boundaries were clearly aware of those actions. When other governments or individuals studiously ignore what is going on, they must share some responsibility. We too are guilty, though this fact cannot serve to excuse either Germans of the Third Reich or white South Africans of the 1960's.

The reader may ask, "What is the value of attempts to assess responsibility for internal violence? What, if anything, has or can be done to punish the guilty or to correct situations which exist even today?" The legality of the Nuremberg trials has been questioned and it has been said that the only thing that kept American and British leaders from being tried as war criminals was the fact that they were on the winning side. It is certainly true that the violence done to humanity by the Nazis could not be undone, and it is probably also true that such trials and subsequent convictions will not deter any future war criminals. But it is probably also true that the war crimes trials and the trial of Eichmann did have the salutary effect of awakening the moral conscience of persons previously apathetic or indifferent. People in the world today seem increasingly aware of events elsewhere and increasingly willing to understand the meaning of those events. Collective action is now more likely to occur than was previously the case, as can be seen in recent happenings within the British Commonwealth as well as in broader United Nations participation in the Congo and elsewhere.

BIBLIOGRAPHY

ADAMS, JAMES T.
    1928. Our Lawless Heritage. *Atlantic Monthly*, 142:732-740.
AKERS, ELMER R. and VERNON FOX
    1944. The Detroit Rioters and Looters Committed to Prison. *Journal of Criminal Law, Criminology and Police Science*, 11:4:27-31.
ALROY, GIL C.
    1967. The Peasantry in the Cuban Revolution. *Review of Politics*, 29:87-99.
ANGLE, PAUL M.
    1952. *Bloody Williamson*. New York: Knopf.
ANONYMOUS
    1906. The Atlanta Massacre. *The Independent*, 71:3018:799-800.
    1908. The So-Called Race Riot at Springfield, Illinois. *Charities and the Commons*, September 19. Pp. 709-711.
    1919a. Racial Tension and Race Riots. *The Outlook*, 122:533.
    1919b. Order in Chicago. Editorial, *New York Times*, July 31, 68:22,468.
    1919c. Lynching in Omaha. *New York Times*, September 30, 68:22,529.
    1919d. Nine Killed in Fight with Arkansas Posse. *New York Times*, October 2, 68:22,531.
    1919e. Plotters Behind the Plots. Editorial, *New York Times*, October 8, 68:22,537.
    1921. Mob Fury and Race Hatred as a National Danger. *The Literary Digest*, 69:12.
    1946. Trial and Terror. *Newsweek*, November 4, 28:33.
APTHEKER, HERBERT
    1943. *American Negro Slave Revolts*. New York: International Publishers.
BANTON, MICHAEL
    1959. *White and Coloured: The Behaviour of British People Towards Coloured Immigrants*. London: Jonathan Cape.
BEARDWOOD, ROGER
    1968. A Fortune Study of the New Negro Mood, *Fortune*, 77:1:146-151 and 230-232.

BEDAU, HUGO A.
    1958. Survey of the Debate on Capital Punishment in Canada, England and the United States, 1948-1958. *The Prison Journal*, 38:2:35-45.

BLACKSTOCK, PAUL
    1964. *The Strategy of Subversion*. Chicago: Quadrangle Books.

BLALOCK, HUBERT M., JR.
    1967. *Causal Inferences in Nonexperimental Research*. Chapel Hill, North Carolina: University of North Carolina Press.

BLAUNER, ROBERT
    1966. Whitewash over Watts. *Trans-Action*, 3:3:3-9, 54.

BLOCH, JOSEF
    1922. *Israel und die Volker nach judischer Lahr*. Berlin: Benjamin Harz.

BLOOMBAUM, MILTON
    1968. The Conditions Underlying Race Riots as Portrayed by Multidimensional Scalogram Analysis: A Reanalysis of Lieberson and Silverman's Data. *American Sociological Review*, 33:1:76-91.

BLUMER, HERBERT
    1951. Collective Behavior. In Alfred McClung Lee (Ed.), *New Outline of the Principles of Sociology*. New York: Barnes and Noble, pp. 165-222.

BONTEMPS, ARNA and JACK CONROY
    1945. *They Seek a City*. Garden City, New York: Doubleday. Co.

BRAMSON, LEON
    1961. *The Political Context of Sociology*. Princeton, New Jersey: Princeton University Press.

BRESSLER, MARVIN B.
    1960. The Myers Case: An Instance of Successful Racial Invasion. *Social Problems*, 8:126-142.

BRINK, WILLIAM and LOUIS HARRIS
    1967. *Black and White*. New York: Simon and Schuster.

BRITT, STEUART H.
    1941. *Social Psychology of Modern Life*. New York: Holt, Rinehart, and Winston.

BROWN, LEE
    1944. *Why Race Riots?*, Public Affairs Pamphlet No. 87. New York: Public Affairs Committee, Inc.

BROWN, ROGER W.
    1954. Mass Phenomena. In Gardner Lindzey (Ed.), *Handbook of Social Psychology*, Vol II, *Special Fields and Applications*. Cambridge, Massachusetts: Addison-Wesley.

BROYARD, ANATOLE
    1950. Portrait of the Inauthentic Negro, *Commentary*, 10:1:56.

BUREAU OF CENSUS
    1944. (see U.S. Department of Commerce, Bureau of the Census, 1944)

BUREAU OF CRIMINAL STATISTICS
    1966. Watts Riots Arrests (see California Department of Criminal Justice)

CALIFORNIA ADVISORY COMMITTEE TO THE U.S. COMMISSION ON CIVIL RIGHTS
    1966. An Analysis of the McCone Commission Report. January.

CALIFORNIA DEPARTMENT OF CRIMINAL JUSTICE, BUREAU OF CRIMINAL STATISTICS
    1966. Watts Riots Arrests: Los Angeles, August, 1965.
CAMPBELL, ANGUS and HOWARD SCHUMAN
    1968. Racial Attitudes in Fifteen American Cities. National Advisory
        Commission on Civil Disorders, *Supplemental Studies.*
CANTRIL, HADLEY
    1941. *The Psychology of Social Movements.* New York: John Wiley.
CAPLAN, NATHAN S. and JEFFREY M. PAIGE
    1968. Data on Newark and Detroit Negro Residents. In National Ad-
        visory Commission on Civil Disorders, *Report of the National
        Advisory Commission on Civil Disorders.* Washington, D.C.: U.S.
        Government Printing Office. Pp. 171-178, fn. 111-143.
CARLSON, JOHN
    1943. *Under Cover.* New York: E. P. Dutton and Company.

———

    1946. *The Plotters.* New York: E. P. Dutton and Company.
CHICAGO COMMISSION ON HUMAN RELATIONS
    n.d. *The Trumbull Park Homes Disturbances: A Chronological Re-
        port, August 4, 1953, to June 30, 1955.*
CHICAGO COMMISSION ON RACE RELATIONS
    1922. *The Negro in Chicago.* Chicago: The University of Chicago Press.
CLARK, KENNETH B.
    1944. Group Violence: A Preliminary Study of the Attitudinal Pattern
        of its Acceptance and Rejection: A Study of the 1943 Harlem
        Riot. *Journal of Social Psychology,* 19:319-337.

———

    1965. *Dark Ghetto.* New York: Harper and Row.
CLARK, KENNETH B. and JAMES BARKER
    1945. The Zoot Effect in Personality: A Race Riot Participant. *Jour-
        nal of Abnormal and Social Psychology,* 40:143-148.
CLARKE, JOHN HENRIK (Ed.)
    1968. *William Styron's Nat Turner: Ten Black Writers Respond.*
        Boston, Massachusetts: Beacon Press.
CLINARD, MARSHALL B.
    1957. *Sociology of Deviant Behavior.* New York: Holt, Rinehart and
        Winston.
COHN, WERNER
    1955. Jehovah's Witnesses as a Proletarian Movement. *The American
        Scholar,* 24:3:284-288.
COLEMAN, JAMES S.
    1956. Social Cleavage and Religious Conflict. *Journal of Social Issues,*
        12:3:53.

———

    1957. *Community Conflict.* New York: Free Press.
COLLINS, SYDNEY
    1957. *Coloured Minorities in Britain.* London: Lutterworth Press.
COMMUNITY STUDIES, INC.
    n.d. *An Attitude Survey of Negro Infiltration into a White Residential
        Area, Kansas City, Missouri.* Unpublished report of survey done
        for the Kansas City, Missouri, Commission on Human Relations.

CONOT, ROBERT
  1967. *Rivers of Blood, Years of Darkness.* New York: Bantam Books.
COX, OLIVER C.
  1948. *Caste, Class and Race: A Study in Social Dynamics.* Garden City,
    New York: Doubleday.
DAHLKE, H. OTTO
  1952. Race and Minority Riots—A Study in the Typology of Violence.
    Social Forces, 30:4:419-425.
DAVITT, MICHAEL
  1903. *Within the Pale.* New York: A. S. Barnes & Company.
DEUTSCH, MORTON and MARY E. COLLINS
  1951. *Inter-racial Housing: A Psychological Evaluation of a Social Ex-
    periment.* Minneapolis, Minnesota: University of Minnesota Press.
DOLLARD, JOHN, LEONARD W. DOOB, NEAL E. MILLER, ORVAL H. MOWRER, and
ROBERT R. SEARS
  1939. *Frustration and Aggression.* New Haven, Connecticut: Yale Uni-
    versity Press.
DUNCAN, OTIS D. and BEVERLY DUNCAN
  1957. *The Negro Population of Chicago: A Study of Residential Suc-
    cession.* Chicago: University of Chicago Press.
DURKHEIM, EMILE
  1933. *The Division of Labor in Society.* New York: Free Press. Trans-
    lated from the French by George Simpson.
EDWARDS, GEORGE
  1965. Order and Civil Liberties: A Complex Role for the Police. *Michi-
    gan Law Review,* 64:47-62.
ELLISON, RALPH
  1952. *Invisible Man.* New York: Random House.
ERSKINE, HAZEL
  1968. The Polls: Demonstrations and Race Riots. *Public Opinion
    Quarterly,* 31:4:655-677.
FANON, FRANZ
  1963. *The Wretched of the Earth.* New York: Grove Press.
FEDERAL BUREAU OF PRISONS
  1954. *National Prisoner Statistics: Prisoners in State and Federal In-
    stitutions, 1950.* Leavenworth, Kansas: U. S. Penitentiary.
FISHER, LLOYD H.
  1947. The Problem of Violence: Observations on Race Conflict in Los
    Angeles. Chicago: American Council on Race Relations.
FOGELSON, ROBERT M.
  1967. White on Black: A Critique of the McCone Commission Report
    on the Los Angeles Riots. *Political Science Quarterly,* 82:337-367.
FOGELSON, ROBERT M. and ROBERT B. HILL
  1968. Who Riots? A Study of Participation in the 1967 Riots. In Na-
    tional Advisory Commision on Civil Disorders, *Supplemental
    Studies.* Washington, D.C.; Superintendent of Documents. Pp. 221-
    248.
FRAZIER, E. FRANKLIN
  1953. Theoretical Structure of Sociology and Sociological Research.
    British Journal of Sociology, 4:4:293-311.

1957. *The Negro in the United States.* New York: Macmillan.

FREUD, SIGMUND
1933. *A New Series of Introductory Lectures on Psychoanalysis.* Trans. by W. J. H. Sprott. New York: Norton.

FROMM, ERICH
1962. "Alienation under Capitalism." In Eric and Mary Josephson (Eds.), *Man Alone.* New York: Dell Publishing Company. Pp. 56-73.

GARDINER, E. FRANK
1919. "Vice and Politics as Factors in Chicago Riots." *New York Times,* 68:22, 471, August 3.

GARFINKEL, HERBERT
1959. *When Negroes March.* Glencoe, Illinois. The Free Press.

GLASS, RUTH
1960. *Newcomers: The West Indian in London.* Allen & Unwin for Centre for Urban Studies.

GORE, PEARL M. and JULIAN B. ROTTER
1963. "A Personality Correlate of Social Action," *Journal of Personality,* 37:58-64.

GOVERNOR'S COMMISSION ON THE LOS ANGELES RIOTS
1965. *Violence in the City—An End or a Beginning? A Report by the Governor's Commission of the Los Angeles Riots.* Los Angeles: State of California. (Also known as the McCone Commission Report.)

GOVERNOR'S SELECT COMMISSION ON CIVIL DISORDER, STATE OF NEW JERSEY
1968. *Report for Action.*

GREER, SCOTT
1959. *Last Man In: Racial Access to Union Power.* Glencoe, Illinois: The Free Press.

GREMLEY, WILLIAM
1952. Social Control in Cicero, *British Journal of Sociology,* 3:4:322-338.

GRIER, GEORGE and EUNICE GRIER
1960. *Privately Developed Interracial Housing: An Analysis of Experience,* Berkeley: University of California Press.

GRIMSHAW, ALLEN D.
1959a. "Lawlessness and Violence in America and their Special Manifestations in Changing Negro-White Relationships," *Journal of Negro History,* 44:1:52-72.

1959b. *A Study in Social Violence: Urban Race Riots in the United States.* Unpubilshed Ph. D. dissertation. University of Pennsylvania, Philadelphia.

1959c. The Harlem Disturbance of 1935 and 1943: Deviant Cases? In Allen D. Grimshaw, *A Study in Social Violence: Urban Race Riots in the United States.* Pp. 374-379. Unpublished Ph.D. dissertation. University of Pennsylvania, Philadelphia, Pennsylvania.

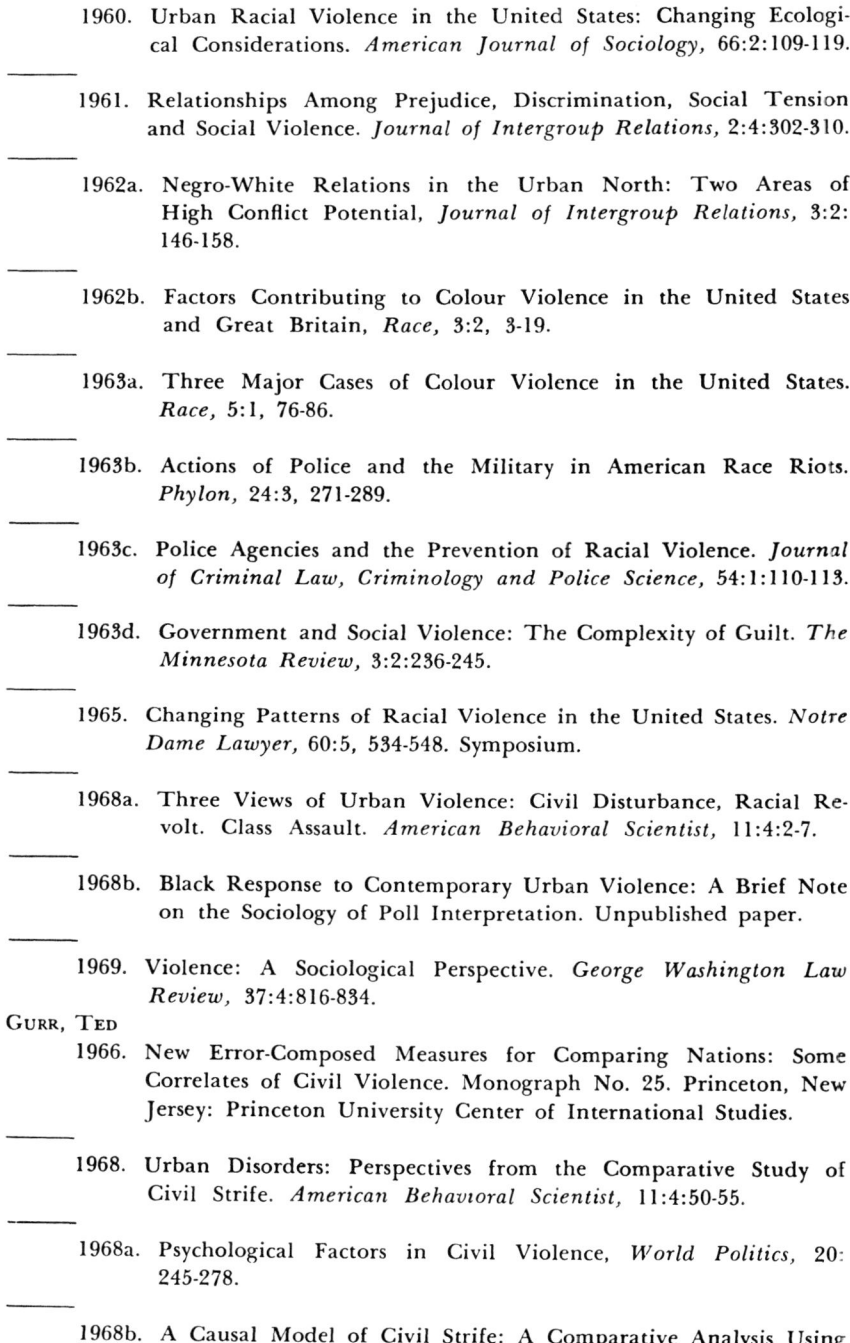

1960.   Urban Racial Violence in the United States: Changing Ecological Considerations. *American Journal of Sociology*, 66:2:109-119.

1961.   Relationships Among Prejudice, Discrimination, Social Tension and Social Violence. *Journal of Intergroup Relations*, 2:4:302-310.

1962a. Negro-White Relations in the Urban North: Two Areas of High Conflict Potential, *Journal of Intergroup Relations*, 3:2: 146-158.

1962b. Factors Contributing to Colour Violence in the United States and Great Britain, *Race*, 3:2, 3-19.

1963a. Three Major Cases of Colour Violence in the United States. *Race*, 5:1, 76-86.

1963b. Actions of Police and the Military in American Race Riots. *Phylon*, 24:3, 271-289.

1963c. Police Agencies and the Prevention of Racial Violence. *Journal of Criminal Law, Criminology and Police Science*, 54:1:110-113.

1963d. Government and Social Violence: The Complexity of Guilt. *The Minnesota Review*, 3:2:236-245.

1965.   Changing Patterns of Racial Violence in the United States. *Notre Dame Lawyer*, 60:5, 534-548. Symposium.

1968a. Three Views of Urban Violence: Civil Disturbance, Racial Revolt. Class Assault. *American Behavioral Scientist*, 11:4:2-7.

1968b. Black Response to Contemporary Urban Violence: A Brief Note on the Sociology of Poll Interpretation. Unpublished paper.

1969.   Violence: A Sociological Perspective. *George Washington Law Review*, 37:4:816-834.

GURR, TED

1966.   New Error-Composed Measures for Comparing Nations: Some Correlates of Civil Violence. Monograph No. 25. Princeton, New Jersey: Princeton University Center of International Studies.

1968.   Urban Disorders: Perspectives from the Comparative Study of Civil Strife. *American Behavioral Scientist*, 11:4:50-55.

1968a. Psychological Factors in Civil Violence, *World Politics*, 20: 245-278.

1968b. A Causal Model of Civil Strife: A Comparative Analysis Using New Indices, *American Political Science Review*, 62:1104-1124.

GURR, TED and CHARLES RUTTENBERG
  1967. *The Conditions of Civil Violence: First Tests of a Causal Model.*
    Research Monograph No. 28. Princeton, New Jersey: Princeton
    University Center of International Studies.
GUZMAN, JESSIE PARKHURST (Ed.)
  1952. Lynching, *1952 Negro Yearbook: A Review of Events Affecting
    Negro Life.* New York: William H. Wise.
——— (Director)
  1964. Routine Violence in the South—1963. *A Tuskegee Institute
    Report.* Tuskegee, Alabama: Tuskegee Institute, March 12, pp.
    36-41.
HARRINGTON, FRED H.
  1942. The Fort Jackson Mutiny, *Journal of Negro History,* 27:420-
    431.
HARRINGTON, MICHAEL
  1964. *The Other America: Poverty in the United States.* New York:
    Macmillan.
HARTZ, LOUIS
  1955. *The Liberal Tradition in America.* New York: Harcourt, Brace,
    and World.
HERSEY, JOHN
  1968. *The Algiers Motel Incident.* New York: Knopf.
HILL, HERBERT (Ed.)
  n.d. *The Revolt of the Powerless: Negroes in the Cities.* New York:
    Random House. Forthcoming.
HILLER, ERNEST T.
  1947. *Social Relations and Structures.* New York: Harper Brothers.
HOBSBAWM, ERIC J.
  1963. *Primitive Rebels.* New York: Praeger.
HORTON, JOHN E., and WAYNE E. THOMPSON
  1962. Powerlessness and Political Negativism: A Study of Defeated
    Local Referendums, *American Journal of Sociology,* 67:485-493.
HOVLAND, CARL I., and ROBERT R. SEARS
  1940. Minor Studies in Aggression: VI Correlation of Lynchings with
    Economic Indices, *Journal of Psychology,* 9:301-310.
JACK, HOMER A.
  1949. Chicago's Violent Armistice. *Nation,* 169:571-572.
JANOWITZ, MORRIS
  1960. *The Professional Soldier: A Social and Political Portrait.* New
    York: Free Press.
———
  1968. *Social Control of Escalated Riots.* Published by the University of
    Chicago Center for Policy Study. Chicago: University of Chicago
    Press.
JEFFRIES, EDWARD A.
  1943. Report. *Journal of the Common Council of the City of Detroit*
    1826-1829.
JOHNSON, BEN, JOHN E. RAKER, M. D. FOSTER, and HENRY ALLEN COOPER
  1918. United States Congress, House of Representatives, Select Com-
    mittee on the New Orleans Riots, *Report, House of Representa-*

tives. 65th Congress, Second Session, House Document 1231, Vol. 114, 7444. Washington, D. C.

JOHNSON, CHARLES S.
1943. *Patterns of Negro Segregation.* New York and London: Harper Brothers.

KEPHART, WILLIAM M.
1954. Negro Visibility. *American Sociological Review,* 19:462-467.

KERNER REPORT
1968. (see National Advisory Commission on Civil Disorders)

KERR, CLARK, and ABRAHAM SIEGEL
1954. The Interindustry Propensity to Strike—An International Comparison. In Arthur Kornhauser, Robert Dubin, Arthur M. Ross (Eds.), *Industrial Conflict.* New York: McGraw-Hill Book Company, pp. 189-212.

KILLIAN, LEWIS M., and CHARLES M. GRIGG
1961. Rank Orders of Discrimination of Negroes and Whites in a Southern City, *Social Forces,* 39:235-239.

KORNHAUSER, WILLIAM
1959. *The Politics of Mass Society,* New York: Free Press.

KRAMER, BERNARD M.
1950. *Residential Contact as a Determinant of Attitudes Toward Negroes.* Unpublished Ph. D. dissertation, Harvard University, Cambridge, Mass.

KULISCHER, ROBERT M.
1943. *Jewish Migrations: Past Experiences and Post-War Prospects.* New York: Research Institute on Peace and Post-War Problems, American Jewish Committee. (Jews and the Post-War World: Pamphlet series, No. 4)

LADER, LAWRENCE
1959. New York's Bloodiest Week. *American Heritage,* 10:4:48-49.

LAMBERT, RICHARD D.
1950. Unpublished report presented before Seminar on Social Tensions, United Nations Education, Social and Cultural Organization. New Delhi.

1951. *Hindu-Muslim Riots.* Unpublished Ph. D. dissertation, University of Pennsylvania.

LANG, KURT, and GLADYS E. LANG
1961. *Collective Dynamics.* New York: Thomas Y. Crowell.

LAWRENCE, CHARLES R., JR.
1947. Race Riots in the United States 1942-1946. In Jessie Parkhurst Guzman (Ed.), *Negro Year Book, 1941-46.* Tuskegee, Alabama. Department of Records and Research. Pp. 232-257.

LEE, ALFRED M., and NORMAN D. HUMPHREY
1943. *Race Riot.* New York: Dryden Press.

LIEBERSON, STANLEY and ARNOLD R. SILVERMAN
1965. The Precipitants and Underlying Conditions of Race Riots. *American Sociological Review,* 30:6:887-898.

LIPSET, SEYMOUR M.
   1960. *Political Man: The Social Bases of Politics.* New York: Doubleday.
   and Company.
LOFTON, WILLISTON H.
   1949. Northern Labor and the Negro During the Civil War. *Journal
   of Negro History,* 34:251-273.
LOHMAN, JOSEPH D.
   1947. *The Police and Minority Groups.* Chicago: Chicago Park District.
LONG, HERMAN H. and CHARLES S. JOHNSON
   1947. *People vs. Property.* Nashville, Tennessee: Fisk University Press.
LORENZ, KONRAD
   1966. *On Aggression.* New York: Harcourt, Brace and World.
MAN, ALBON P.
   1951. Labor Competition and the New York Draft Riots of 1863.
   Journal of Negro History, 36:4:375-405.
MANGUM, CHARLES S.
   1940. *The Legal Status of the Negro.* Chapel Hill, North Carolina:
   University of North Carolina Press.
MARSHALL, THURGOOD
   1943. The Gestapo in Detroit. *Crisis,* 50:8:232-233.
MARTIN, JOHN B.
   1949. Incident at Fernwood. *Harper's Magazine,* 199:86-98.
MARX, GARY T.
   1967. *Protest and Prejudice: A Study of Beliefs in the Black Community.*
   New York: Harper and Row.
MASOTTI, LOUIS H., and DON R. BOWEN (Eds.)
   1968. *Riots, Riots and Rebellion: Civil Violence in the Urban Community.* Beverly Hills, California: Sage Publications, Inc., 1968.
MAYER, ALBERT
   n.d. *Russell Woods: Change Without Conflict. Mimeo.* This study was
   one of thirty special studies done for the Commission on Race
   and Housing, an independent private citizen's group, under the
   direction of Davis McEntire. All of these studies are available in
   the library of the University of California at Berkeley.
MAYOR'S COMMISSION ON CONDITIONS IN HARLEM
   1936. The Complete Harlem Riot Report. *The New York Amsterdam
   News,* July 18.
McCONE, *et al.*
   1965. McCone Commission Report (see Governor's Commission on the
   Los Angeles Riots)
McWILLIAMS, CAREY
   1944. Race Discrimination and the Law. *Science and Society,* 9:1-22.
MEDALIA, NAHUM Z., and OTTO N. LARSEN
   1958. Diffusion and Belief in a Collective Delusion: The Seattle
   Windshield Pitting Epidemic. *American Sociological Review,* 23:
   180-186.
MEIER, NORMAN C., G. H. MENNINGA, and H. J. STOLZ
   1941. An Experimental Approach to the Study of Mob Behavior,
   Journal of Abnormal and Social Psychology, 36:506-524.

MERTON, ROBERT K.
  1948. Discrimination and the American Creed. In R. M. MacIver (Ed.), *Discrimination and the National Welfare*, New York: Institute for Religious and Social Studies, Jewish Theological Seminary; distributed by Harper.

MEYER, PHILIP
  1967. *The People Beyond 12th Street: A Survey of Attitudes of Detroit Negroes after the Riot of 1967*. Detroit, Michigan, sponsored by the Detroit Urban League and Co-ordinated by the Detroit Free Press.

MING, WILLIAM K.
  1948. Racial Restrictions and the Fourteenth Amendment: The Restrictive Covenant Cases. *University of Chicago Law Review*, 16: 203, 216-224.

MINTZ, ALEXANDER
  1946. A Re-examination of Correlations between Lynchings and Economic Indices. *Journal of Abnormal and Social Psychology*, 41: 154-160.

MURPHY, RAYMOND J., and JAMES M. WATSON
  1967. *The Structure of Discontent: The Relationship between Social Structure, Grievance, and Support for the Los Angeles Riot*. Los Angeles: University of California Institute of Government and Public Affairs.

  ———

  1969. Ghetto Social Structure and Riot Support: The Role of White Contact, Social Distance and Discrimination. Prepared especially for this volume by the authors. It is based on R. J. Murphy and J. M. Watson (1967).

MURRAY, FLORENCE (ed.)
  1944. *Negro Handbook*. New Rochelle, New York: Progressive Press.

MYERS, ROBERT C.
  1948. Anti-Communist Mob Action. *Public Opinion Quarterly*, 12:57-67.

MYRDAL, GUNNAR
  1944. *An American Dilemma*. New York: Harper and Brothers.

  ———

  1948. Social Trends in America and Strategic Approaches to the Negro Problem. *Phylon*, 9:196-208.

NATIONAL ADVISORY COMMISSION ON CIVIL DISORDERS
  1968. *Report of the National Advisory Commission on Civil Disorders*. Washington, D.C.: Government Printing Office. (Also known as the Kerner Report.)

  ———

  1968. *Supplementary Studies for the National Advisory Commission on Civil Disorders*. Washington, D.C.: Government Printing Office.

NEAL, ARTHUR G., and MELVIN SEEMAN
  1964. Organizations and Powerlessness: A Test of the Mediation Hypothesis, *American Sociological Review*, 29:216-226.

NOEL, DONALD L., and ALPHONSO PINKNEY
>   1964. Correlates of Prejudice: Some Racial Differences and Similarities. *American Journal of Sociology*, 69:6:609-622.

OBERGSHALL, ANTHONY
>   1968. The Los Angeles Riot of August 1967. *Social Problems*, 15:3: 322-341.

ORLANSKY, HAROLD
>   1943. Harlem Riot: A Study in Mass Frustration. New York: Social Analysis Report No. 1.

PAIGE, JEFFREY M.
>   1968. *Collective Violence and the Culture of Subordination: A Study of Participants in the July, 1967, Riots in Newark, New Jersey, and Detroit, Michigan*, Unpublished Ph.D. dissertation, University of Michigan, Ann Arbor, Michigan.

PETERS, W.
>   1950. Race War in Chicago. *New Republic*, 122:2:10-12.

POUND, ROSCOE
>   1922. *Criminal Justice in the American City—A Summary*. Cleveland, Ohio: Cleveland Foundation.

RANSFORD, H. EDWARD
>   1966. *Negro Participation in Civil Rights Activity and Violence*. Unpublished Ph. D. dissertation, University of California, Los Angeles.

———
>   1969. Isolation, Powerlessness and Violence: A Study of Attitudes and Participation in the Watts Riot. *American Journal of Sociology*, 73:5:581-591.

RAPER, ARTHUR F.
>   1933. *The Tragedy of Lynching*. Chapel Hill, North Carolina: University of North Carolina Press.

REPORT OF THE MAYOR'S COMMISSION ON CONDITIONS IN HARLEM
>   1936. *New York Amsterdam News*. July 18, 1936.

REPORT OF THE SELECT COMMITTEE ON THE NEW ORLEANS RIOTS
>   1867. (See U. S. Congress, House of Representatives, Select Committee on the New Orleans Riots)

RICHMOND, ANTHONY H.
>   1954. *Colour Prejudice in Britain: A Study of West Indian Workers in Liverpool, 1941-1951*. London: Routledge & Kegan Paul.

———
>   1961. *The Colour Problem*. Harmandsworth, Middlesex: Pelican Books.

ROSS, MALCOM H.
>   1948. *All Manner of Men*. New York: Reynal and Hitchcock.

ROTTER, JULIAN B.
>   1966. Generalized Expectancies for Internal vs. External Control of Reinforcements. *Psychological Monographs*, 80:1:1-28.

RUDE, GEORGE
>   1959. *The Crowd in the French Revolution*. New York: Oxford University Press.

———
>   1964. *The Crowd in History: A Study of Popular Disturbances in France and England, 1730-1948*. New York: John Wiley & Sons.

RUDWICK, ELLIOTT M.
  1964. *Race Riot at East St. Louis, July 2, 1917.* Carbondale, Illinois:
    Southern Illinois University Press.
RUSHTON, H. J., W. E. DOWLING, O. OLANDER and J. H. WITHERSPOON
  n.d. *Committee to Investigate the Riot Occurring in Detroit on June
    21, 1943. Factual Report.* Detroit, Michigan (mimeo).
RUSTIN, BAYARD
  1966. The Watts "Manifesto" and the McCone Report. *Commentary,*
    41:29-35.
R. W.
  1946. Tennessee Trial. *Crisis,* 53:329-330.
SARTRE, JEAN PAUL
  1948. *Anti-Semite and Jew.* New York: Schocken Books.
SCHERMER, GEORGE
  1949. *The Fairgrounds Park Incident: A Study of the Factors which
    Resulted in the Outbreak of Violence at the Fairgrounds Park
    Swimming Pool on June 21, 1949. An Account of What Happened,
    and Recommendations for Corrective Action.* St. Louis, Missouri,
    (mimeo, conducted for the St. Louis Council on Human Relations).
SCHULER, EDGAR A.
  1944. The Houston Race Riot, 1917. *Journal of Negro History,* 29:
    300-338.
SCHULER, EDGAR A., and CHARLES G. GOMILLION
  n.d. The Pattern of Military Race Riots. Unpublished study.
SCOBLE, HARRY M.
  1966. The McCone Commission and Social Science. Unpublished paper
    written for the U. S. Office of Economic Opportunity.
SEAGLE, WILLIAM
  1934. Riot: Legal Aspects. *Encyclopedia of Social Science,* 13:388-392.
SEARLES, RUTH, and J. ALLEN WILLIAMS, JR.
  1962. Negro College Students' Participation in Sit-ins. *Social Forces,*
    40:215-220.
SEARS, DAVID O.
  1966. Riot Activity and Evaluation: An Overview of the Negro Sur-
    vey. Unpublished paper written for the U.S. Office of Economic
    Opportunity.
SEARS, DAVID O., and TOMMY M. TOMLINSON
  1968. Riot Ideology in Los Angeles: A Study of Negro Attitudes. Un-
    published manuscript.
SEARS, ROBERT R., and PAULINE S. SEARS
  1940. Minor Studies of Aggression: V. Strength of Frustration-Reaction
    as a Function of Strength of Drive. *Journal of Psychology,* 9:297-
    300.
SEEMAN, MELVIN
  1959. On the Meaning of Alienation. *American Sociological Review,*
    24:783-791.
SELIGMAN, HERBERT J.
  1919. Race War? *New Republic,* 20:48-50.

SELLIN, THORSTEN (Ed.)
> 1952. "Murder and the Penalty of Death." *Annals of the American Academy of Political and Social Science,* 284.

SHULGIN
> 1949. History of Western Civilization. In *Source Book for History,* Vol. 2. Brooklyn, New York: Brooklyn College, Department of History.

SILBERMAN, CHARLES E.
> 1964. *Crisis in Black and White.* New York: Random House.

SILVER, ALLAN A.
> 1968. Official Interpretations of Racial Riots. In *Urban Riots: Violence and Social Change, Proceedings of the Academy of Political Science,* 29:1.

SIMMEL, GEORG
> 1955. *Conflict and the Web of Group-Affiliations.* New York: Free Press. Translated by Kurt H. Wolff.

SIMPSON, GEORGE E., and JOHN M. YINGER
> 1953. *Racial and Cultural Minorities: An Analysis of Prejudice and Discriminations.* New York: Harper and Row.

SINGH, KHUSHWANT
> 1956. *Mano Majra.* New York: Grove Press.

SKINNER, GEORGE W.
> 1957. *Chinese Society in Thailand: An Analytical History.* Ithaca, New York: Cornell University Press.

SKOLNICK, JEROME
> 1969. *The Politics of Protest: The Skolnick Report to the National Commission on the Causes and Prevention of Violence.* New York: Ballantine.

SMELSER, NEIL J.
> 1963. *Theory of Collective Behavior.* New York: Free Press.

SOCIAL SCIENCE RESEARCH COUNCIL
> 1947. *The Reduction of Intergroup Tensions,* Bulletin 57, New York.

SOUTHERN COMMISSION ON THE STUDY OF LYNCHING
> n.d. *Lynchings and what they mean.* Atlanta, Georgia: Southern Commission on the Study of Lynching.

SPIEGEL, JOHN P.
> 1967. The Social and Psychological Dynamics of Militant Negro Activism: A Preliminary Report. Paper presented at the winter meeting of the American Academy of Psychoanalysis, New York, December 2, 1967.

> 1968a. Hostility, Aggression and Violence. Prepared for the Lowell Lecture Series sponsored by the Lowell Institute in cooperation with Tufts-New England Medical Center Boston, Massachusetts: March 12, 1968.

> 1968b. The Functions of the Scenario in Collective Violence. Paper presented for panel discussion on *Violence in the Streets and Everywhere: The Growing Menace* at the annual meeting of the

American Psychiatric Association, Boston, Massachusetts, May 14, 1968.

1968c. Psychosocial Factors in Riot—Old and New. Presented at the May 15, 1968, annual meeting of the American Psychiatric Association, Boston, Massachusetts.

STAHLIN, KARL
1939. *Geschichte Russlands.* Königsberg, Ost-Europa Verlag.

STERBA, RICHARD
1947. Some Psychological Factors in Negro Race Hatred and in Anti-Negro Riots. In Geza Roheim (Ed.), *Psychoanalysis and the Social Sciences,* Vol. I. New York: International Universities Press. Pp. 411-426.

STYRON, WILLIAM
1967. *The Confessions of Nat Turner.* New York: Random House.

TAEUBER, CONRAD B., and IRENE TAEUBER
1958. *The Changing Population of the United States.* New York: Wiley.

TAYLOR, GRAHAM
1919. Chicago in the Nation's Race Strife. *The Survey,* 42:695-697.

THOMAS, DOROTHY S.
1925. *Social Aspects of the Business Cycle.* New York. Dutton.

THOMPSON, WAYNE E., and JOHN E. HORTON
1960. Political Alienation as a Force in Political Action. *Social Forces.* 38:190-195.

TOMLINSON, T. M.
1968. The Development of a Riot Ideology among Urban Negroes. *American Behavioral Scientist,* 11:4:27-31.

TURNER, RALPH H., and LEWIS M. KILLIAN
1957. *Collective Behavior.* Englewood Cliffs, New Jersey: Prentice-Hall.

TURNER, RALPH H., and SAMUEL J. SURACE
1956. Zoot-Suiters and Mexicans: Symbols in Crowd Behavior. *American Journal of Sociology,* 62:14-20.

TUSKEGEE INSTITUTE
1964. Routine Violence in the South—1963. *A Tuskegee Institute Report* (Jessie Parkhurst Guzman, Director). Tuskegee, Alabama: Tuskegee Institute. Pp. 36-41.

TWAIN, MARK
1946. *The Portable Mark Twain.* (Bernard DeVoto, ed.). New York: Viking.

UCLA INSTITUTE OF GOVERNMENT AND PUBLIC AFFAIRS
1966. *The Los Angeles Riot Study.* Los Angeles: UCLA Institute of Government and Public Affairs.

UNDERWOOD, KENNETH M.
1957. *Protestant and Catholic,* Boston, Massachusetts: Beacon Press.

UNITED STATES BUREAU OF THE CENSUS
1963. (See United States Department of Commerce, Bureau of the Census, 1963.)

UNITED STATES CONGRESS, HOUSE OF REPRESENTATIVES, SELECT COMMITTEE ON THE NEW ORLEANS RIOTS
1867. Report of the Select Committee on the New Orleans Riots. *The*

Reports of the House of Representatives (made during the second session of Congress, 1866-67). Washington, D.C.: U.S. Government Printing Office. (The members of this committee were Thomas Eliot, Samuel Shellabarger, and Benjamin Bayer.)

UNITED STATES CONGRESS, HOUSE OF REPRESENTATIVES, SPECIAL COMMITTEE AUTHORIZED BY CONGRESS TO INVESTIGATE THE EAST ST. LOUIS RIOTS

1918. *Report, House of Representatives.* 65th Congress, Second Session, House Doc. 1231, Vol. 114, 7444. Washington, D.C.: U.S. Government Printing Office. (The members of this committee were Ben Johnson, M. D. Foster, John E. Raker, and H. A. Cooper.)

UNITED STATES DEPARTMENT OF COMMERCE, BUREAU OF THE CENSUS

1920. *1920 Census of the United States, Vol. III, Population: Composition and Characteristics of Population by States.* Washington, D.C.: U.S. Government Printing Office.

1944. Series CA-3. June.

UNITED STATES DEPARTMENT OF LABOR, MANPOWER ADMINISTRATION

1968. *The Detroit Riot.* Washington, D.C.: U.S. Government Printing Office.

———

1965. (See the Governor's Commission on the Los Angeles Riots.)

VITTACHI, TARZIE

1958. *Emergency '58: The Story of the Ceylon Race Riots,* London, Andre Deutsch.

WALKER, DANIEL

1968. *Rights in Conflict: The Violent Confrontation of Demonstrators and Police in the Parks and Streets of Chicago During the Week of the Democratic National Convention of 1968* (report submitted to the National Commission on the Causes and Prevention of Violence), New York: Bantam.

WALLING, WILLIAM ENGLISH

1908. The Race War in the North. *The Independent,* 65:529-534.

WASKOW, ARTHUR, I.

1966. *From Race Riot to Sit-In: 1919 and the 1960's.* Garden City, New York: Doubleday.

WEAVER, MAURICE and Z. ALEXANDER LOOBY

1946. What Happened at Columbia? *Crisis,* 53:110-111.

WEAVER, ROBERT C.

1944. Race Restrictive Housing Covenants. *Journal of Land and Public Utility Economics,* 20:3:183.

———

1948. *The Negro Ghetto.* New York: Harcourt, Brace and Company.

WEDGE, BRYANT

1967. Student Participation in Revolutionary Violence: Brazil, 1964, and Dominican Republic, 1965. Paper read at the 1967 Annual Meeting of the American Political Science Association, Chicago, Sept. 5-9.

WEISBERG, BERNARD

1951. Racial Violence and Civil Rights Law Enforcement, *University of Chicago Law Review,* 18:769-783.

WERSTEIN, IRVING
   1957. *July, 1863*. New York. Ace Books.
WEST, REBECCA
   1948. Heil Hamm. *New Yorker*, August 7, p. 24, August 14.
WESTLEY, WILLIAM A.
   1955. *The Formation, Nature, and Control of Crowds*. Canadian Defence
   Research Board.
WHITE, WALTER F.
   1919. Chicago and its Eight Reasons. *Crisis*, 18:293-297.
WHITE, WALTER F. and THURGOOD MARSHALL
   1943. *What Caused the Detroit Riot?* New York: National Association
   for the Advancement of Colored People.
WICKENDEN, JAMES
   1958. *Colour in Britain*. London: Oxford University Press for the Institute of Race Relations.
WILLIAMS, ROBIN M., JR.
   1947. *The Reduction of Intergroup Tensions*. New York: Social Science
   Research Council.

   _____

   1956. Religion, Value-Orientations, and Intergroup Conflict. *Journal
   of Social Issues*, 12:3:12-20.

   _____

   1965. Social Change and Social Conflict, Race Relations in the United
   States, 1944-1964. *Sociological Inquiry*, 35:1:8-25.
WILLIAMS, ROBIN M., JR., *et al.*
   1964. *Strangers Next Door: Ethnic Relations in American Communities*.
   Englewood Cliffs, New Jersey: Prentice-Hall.
WILNER, DANIEL M., ROSABELLE P. WALKEY and STUART W. COOK
   1955. *Human Relations in Interracial Housing: A Study of the Contact
   Hypothesis*, Minneapolis, Minnesota: University of Minnesota
   Press.
WILSON, JAMES Q.
   1960. *Negro Politics*. New York: Free Press.
WISH, HARVEY
   1937. American Slave Insurrections before 1861. *Journal of Negro His-
   tory*, 22:299-320.
WOOD, MARGARET MARY
   1960. *Paths of Loneliness*, New York: Columbia University Press.
WOODWARD, C. VANN
   1957. *The Strange Career of Jim Crow*. New York: Oxford University
   Press.
WORK, MONROE (Ed.)
   1921. *Negro Year Book 1921-1922*. Tuskegee Institute, Alabama: Negro
   Yearbook Publishing Company.

   _____

   1931. Negro Yearbook, 1931-1932. Tuskegee Institute, Alabama: Negro
   Yearbook Publishing Company.
WORKS, ERNEST
   1961. The Prejudice-Interaction Hypothesis from the Point of View of

the Negro Minority Group. *American Journal of Sociology,* 67: 47-52.

ZAWODNY, JANUSZ K.

1961. Guerrilla Warfare and Subversion as a Means of Political Change. Paper given at the 1961 Annual Meeting of the American Political Science Association, St. Louis, Missouri, September 6-9, 1961.

ZIONISTICHFN HILFSFOND IN LONDON VON DER ZUR ERFORSACHUNGDEN POGROME EINGESETZTEN KOMMISSION

1910. *Die Judenpogrome in Russland.* Koln and Leipzig. Judischer Verlag.

INDEX

NOTE: It was originally planned that this index would be comprehensive and organized analytically. It soon became evident, however, that an index so constructed would be logistically unmanageable, excessively lengthy, and of marginal usefulness in locating topics of interest to the user. There are, for example, references to police and other agencies of external control on almost one page out of four—and many pages on which literally dozens of concepts, places, and persons are mentioned. The final format and contents of the index represent a compromise between comprehensiveness and our assessments of what wanted items would be most difficult to locate. Thus, we are assuming that theoretical topics can be located through the table of contents, while places, persons, and events need to be tagged since there are fewer clues about their location in the titles of chapters or of individual selections. Most major events and personages referred to in the text are listed, as are all authors and some particularly salient topics. The decisions about inclusion or exclusion of categories were mine; the difficult and frequently tedious work of locating pages and completing and verifying identifications was done by Kathleen George. We both hope that the index will be useful.—A. D. G.